Fodor's

WALT DISNEY WORLD

Welcome to Walt Disney World

Walt Disney World and Orlando offer a complete, sun-wrapped vacation package. Theme parks have coaster thrills, water-slide spills, magical worlds, and faraway galaxies. Hotels accommodate families seeking quality bonding time and couples seeking romance. Restaurants in and outside the parks satisfy all tastes. Thriving nightlife and arts scenes, superb shopping ops, and beaches (Gulf Coast or Atlantic) are on hand, too. Note that this book was updated during the COVID-19 pandemic. As you plan, confirm that places are still open, and let us know when we need to make updates at editors@fodors.com.

TOP REASONS TO GO

★ **Walt Disney World:** Quite simply, the magic of the Disney parks touches all who visit.

★ **Universal Orlando:** Islands of Adventure and Universal Studios are high-energy fun.

★ **Resorts:** Elaborately themed resorts offer visitors fun and memorable experiences.

★ **International Drive:** Bustling strip with attractions like Fun Spot and Aquatica.

★ **Downtown Orlando:** Top restaurants, theater, and music create a thriving scene.

★ **LEGOLAND Florida:** A unique family-friendly theme park with fun rides, shows, and attractions.

Contents

MAPS

Fodor's Features

Chapter 1

EXPERIENCE ORLANDO AND THE PARKS

25 ULTIMATE EXPERIENCES

Walt Disney World and Orlando offer terrific experiences that should be on every traveler's list. Here are Fodor's top picks for a memorable trip.

1 Visit the Galaxy's Edge

Walt Disney World's otherworldly land is devoted to a Star Wars galaxy far, far away and features two of the park's most impressive and technologically advanced rides. *(Ch. 5)*

2 Ride the Tower of Terror

This classic takes you on a stomach-flipping elevator ride into the Twilight Zone. The best part? It's different every single time you ride it. *(Ch. 5)*

3 Channel your Inner Child

Dedicated to your favorite building blocks, the sprawling LEGOLAND theme park, 45 minutes from Orlando, is a great non-Disney option if you have younger kids. *(Ch. 11)*

4 Let It Go

After touring Arendelle on the Frozen Ever After ride, you can feast on Scandinavian fare and stock up on Viking gear at EPCOT's Norway pavilion. *(Ch. 4)*

5 Find Prehistoric Thrills

The new (in 2021) high-altitude (150 feet), high-speed (70 mph) VelociCoaster at Universal's Islands of Adventure is a real scream. *(Ch. 9)*

6 Experience Pandora

This popular land in Animal Kingdom includes Avatar Flight of Passage in addition to the otherworldly beauty of Pandora's bioluminescent flora and fauna. *(Ch. 6)*

7 Visit Winter Park

This historic gem is a great place to spend some quality family time, shop on fashionable Park Avenue, and take a scenic boat ride across the town lake. *(Ch. 11)*

8 Ride Jurassic Park

At Universal Islands of Adventure, you can ride on a river past dinosaurs both gentle and scary, ending your journey with an 85-foot plunge. You will get wet. *(Ch. 9)*

9 Party at CityWalk

Like Disney Springs, Universal's outdoor mall is full of restaurants and entertainment, but the experience feels more Las Vegas than Orlando. *(Ch. 9)*

10 Kayak the Wekiwa River

Wekiwa Springs State Park, an hour from Orlando, gives you a break from the go-go-go vibe in all the parks, with plenty of space to enjoy a quiet river adventure. *(Ch. 11)*

11 Stroll Down a Garden Path

If theme parks aren't your thing, you can relax in more than 50 acres of lush greenery at the Harry P. Leu Gardens, which offer flora and fauna from all over the world. *(Ch. 10)*

12 Get Spooked

No matter the time of year, the Haunted Mansion is a classic that can't be missed. It's more fun than spooky and definitely good for the whole family. *(Ch. 3)*

13 Stay at a Disney Resort

Staying at a Disney-owned resort gives you perks such as free transportation, early access to reservations, and extra time at the parks. *(Ch. 3, 4, 6, 7)*

14 Soar Over the World

Soarin' lets you travel around the world on a simulated hang-glider, offering 180-degree panoramas and other special effects. You'll feel like you're really flying. *(Ch. 4)*

15 Ride the Waves

Cool your heels (and the rest of you) at water parks like Disney's Blizzard Beach and Typhoon Lagoon, Universal's Volcano Bay, and SeaWorld's Aquatica. *(Ch. 5, 7, 9, 10)*

16 "Park It" Downtown

In Downtown's verdant, 43-acre Lake Eola Park, ducks and swans (and swan-shape paddleboats) bob on the water, and a landmark fountain features a light-and-music show on summer evenings. *(Ch. 10)*

17 Be Their Guest

It's worth booking a prix-fixe breakfast, lunch, or dinner at Be Our Guest, the Magic Kingdom's most popular restaurant. Be sure to try the "grey stuff"—it's delicious! *(Ch. 3)*

18 Frolic at Disney Springs

Disney's dining and shopping megacomplex is a fitting way to end your day with a meal, a movie, or a stroll. *(Ch. 7)*

19 Explore Everest

Journey to the summit of the world's highest peak at Animal Kingdom's exciting thrill ride, which moves both backward and forward. *(Ch. 6)*

20 Dine (or Drink) Around the World

With dozens of dining options, many of them in the World Showcase, EPCOT allows you to eat a wide variety of cuisines, from American to Mexican to Moroccan. *(Ch. 4)*

21 Toy Story Land

Explore Andy's backyard and ride Slinky Dog Dash or the Alien Flying Saucers as you enjoy Pixar's movieland. *(Ch. 5)*

22 Meet the Characters

One of the best parts of going to Disney? Meeting beloved characters—from Minnie and Mickey to your favorite princess. *(Ch. 3, 4, 5, 6)*

23 Putt Putt Your Way to Victory

If you're looking to hit the links, Orlando has you covered—from Walt Disney World to Universal Orlando to I-Drive—with more than a dozen courses. *(Ch. 12)*

24 Ride the Mega Coasters

Universal Orlando is home to two of the country's biggest and most exciting roller coasters: The Incredible Hulk Coaster and the Hollywood Rip Ride Rockit. *(Ch. 9)*

25 Get the Harry Potter Experience

Harry is the biggest draw at Universal Orlando Resort, whether you're going to Hogsmeade at Islands of Adventure or Diagon Alley at Universal Studios. *(Ch. 9)*

What's New in Orlando and the Parks

Prior to 1971, Orlando was a quiet town whose main industry was citrus. There was a new interstate highway and a nature park where you could see alligators, but that was about it. But then came Walt Disney World. The boom in tourism meant the city needed a more modern airport and new hotels. That, of course, meant Orlando would need more workers, which meant more housing and successively more theme parks, malls, as well as arts, culture, and industry to keep things going.

Change is a constant in Orlando, and the city you see in the 2020s will continue to grow and be transformed. Indeed, when the pandemic descended, and workers realized they didn't necessarily have to report to an office, Central Florida saw a massive influx of newcomers who were keen to work from home in a more temperate climate. To keep pace with this growth, a modern, new-in-2022 terminal at Florida's busiest airport, Orlando International, increases its capacity by 10 million more travelers each year.

And there are always new shows, events, and attractions at the theme parks as creative teams at Disney and Universal try to out-tech and out-dazzle each other.

PANDEMIC PRESSURES

The COVID-19 pandemic put the theme parks, attractions, restaurants, and many hotels in Orlando under lockdown during the spring of 2020. Even with the availability of vaccines in 2021, the enduring pandemic demanded changes and modifications to area tourism.

For example, to better manage visitation and crowds, Disney created its Park Pass System requiring not only tickets but also reservations for visits to Magic Kingdom, EPCOT, Hollywood Studios, and Animal Kingdom. To the dismay of many, the system is likely to continue through at least 2023.

The pandemic also led the theme parks to put previously announced developments on hold. Many of the changes that insiders have been awaiting will likely be delayed into 2023 and beyond.

WALT DISNEY WORLD

When Universal was creating its Wizarding Worlds, Disney responded with the world of Pandora. As Universal continues to enhance all things Potter, with new attractions like Hagrid's Magical Creatures Motorbike Adventure, Disney counters by applying its distinctive creativity to Marvel, Star Wars, and Disney film–theme experiences.

One example of Disney drawing inspiration from its movies is the Magic Kingdom's new-in-2022 TRON Lightcycle Power Run, which nods to the 1982 Disney cult classic *Tron*. Like its Shanghai Disneyland counterpart, this attraction lets guests straddle a mock-up motorcycle for a high-speed ride into the heart of an adrenaline-fueled video game.

Other exciting developments in the offing include the premiere of the highly anticipated, highly themed Star Wars: Galactic Starcruiser resort hotel; the opening of the Guardians of the Galaxy: Cosmic Rewind coaster at Wonders of Xandar (formerly the Universe of Energy) in EPCOT's World Discovery area; and the launch of the *Disney Wish,* Disney Cruise Line's newest vessel. As more vaccinations go into more arms and the restrictions of 2020 and 2021 recede, Disney will no doubt accelerate the pace of expansion.

UNIVERSAL ORLANDO

Universal Orlando completed several large-scale projects and announced several others. At Islands of Adventure in mid-2021, the VelociCoaster ride debuted, with guests happily lining up to be strapped in, hoisted 150 feet in the air, and then sped through twists and turns at speeds of up to 70 mph.

Although Universal's most ambitious development—a fourth theme park called Epic Universe—was delayed by the pandemic, construction resumed in 2021. When the park does open, it will fill 750 acres with new attractions, shops, entertainment, and restaurants.

SEAWORLD

Although it has a vibe that's decidedly different from that of its high-paced, deep-pocketed counterparts, SeaWorld has found a way forward by creating a popular water park (Aquatica), as well as an all-inclusive tropical retreat (Discovery Cove) where guests can swim with dolphins. The original park has been developing thrill rides, too, with attractions such as the new-in-2022 Ice Breaker, a steel roller coaster that reaches a height of 93 feet and speeds of up to 52 mph.

ELSEWHERE IN ORLANDO

Roughly midway between SeaWorld and Universal Orlando, ICON Park is noticeable due to the towering presence of The Wheel, which, at 400 feet, makes the list of the Top Ten of the World's Tallest Ferris Wheels. It's the centerpiece of a complex that is also home to Madame Tussauds Orlando, SEA LIFE Orlando Aquarium, Museum of Illusions, the Pearl Express Train for kids, and America's tallest swing ride—the 450-foot Orlando StarFlyer.

Anticipated ICON Park thrill-ride additions include the Orlando Slingshot, which will rocket passengers 450 feet straight up, and the Orlando Gyro Drop Tower, which will drop passengers into a free fall of up to 75 mph. Note that unlike the major theme parks, this park charges for each attraction—a practice that can result in considerable sticker shock with each purchase.

Several miles west of Walt Disney World, near the junction of Highway 192 and the Highway 429 toll road, music legend Jimmy Buffett lent his name and vision to the highly themed, 175-room Margaritaville Orlando Resort. Next door, the 14-acre Island H2O Live! water park is now open between March and November and features waterslides, a lazy river, and live entertainment.

Surprisingly, what feels *new* to visitors may well be familiar to locals. With the pandemic throwing kinks into even the best-laid plans, travelers have "discovered" classics elsewhere in the region like Seminole-Lake Gliderport, where they can climb into a silent sailplane for rides and lessons high above the untrammeled countryside; Wilotree Park, which offers high-flying experiences in tandem with a skilled hang glider pilot; and Revolution Adventures, which has a fleet of rentable ATVS, quads, four-wheelers, and buggies, as well as an eight-wheeled amphibious vehicle that can traverse land, lakes, and ponds.

Other recently rediscovered regional classics include airboat rides on area waterways; wandering charming Florida communities like Winter Garden, Winter Park, and Mount Dora; lounging on Atlantic beaches; and finding still more space at nearby Kennedy Space Center.

In short, sometimes everything old is new again.

WHAT'S WHERE

1 Magic Kingdom Park and Resort Area. The centerpiece of Walt Disney World's most popular park is Cinderella Castle. Nearby are several of Walt Disney World's premier hotels.

2 EPCOT Park and Resort Area. EPCOT is made up of four distinct worlds: World Discovery, World Nature, World Celebration, and World Showcase, which celebrates the cuisine and cultures of Canada, the United Kingdom, France, Japan, Morocco, America, Italy, Germany, China, Norway, and Mexico.

3 Disney's Hollywood Studios Park. Paying tribute to the movies, especially Disney movies, this park offers stunt shows, thrill rides, characters, and plenty of *Star Wars*.

4 Disney's Animal Kingdom Park and Resort Area. This park is far more than just a zoo thanks to Disney's trademark blend of details, designs, thrills, and laughs at imaginative attractions like Expedition Everest, It's Tough to Be a Bug, and Pandora—The World of Avatar.

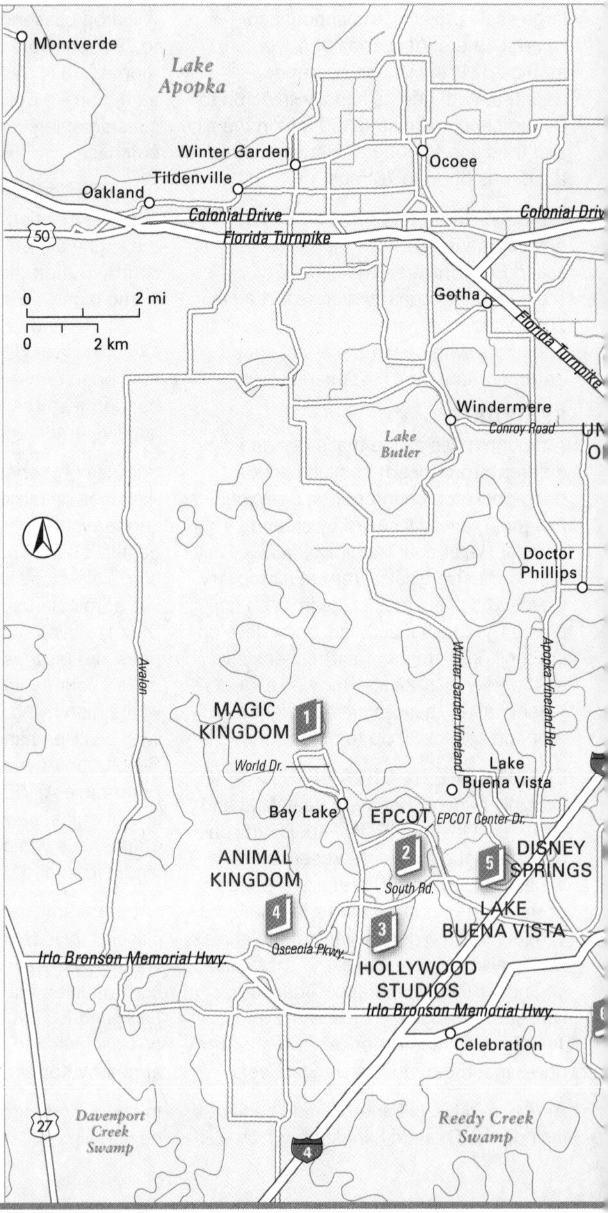

5 Disney Springs and Resort Area. Both resort guests and locals head for Disney's popular shopping, dining, and nightlife area to eat, bowl, go to the movies, and just hang out.

6 Kissimmee, Lake Buena Vista, and Celebration. Immediately adjacent to Walt Disney World are two communities, Lake Buena Vista and Disney's planned community of Celebration. Nearby Kissimmee retains a small-town feel.

7 Universal Orlando. Though it already has two theme parks (Universal Studios and Islands of Adventure), a water theme park (Volcano Bay), and several resort hotels, Universal is expanding to offer even more attractions.

8 Orlando. The sleepy citrus town was completely transformed by Walt Disney World, but its busy downtown district and 1920s-era residential districts give visitors plenty of reasons to go beyond the theme parks.

9 Excursions from Orlando. In the vicinity are several worthy trips: Winter Park, Maitland, Wekiwa Springs, Sanford, Mount Dora, LEGOLAND, and Bok Tower Garden.

Ways to Save Money in Orlando

TRAVEL OFF SEASON

The off-season in Orlando, times when the parks are less crowded, is becoming shorter each year. That being said, those who can travel in January, February, May, and September will still see significant savings over those visiting at other times of the year.

CONSIDER FAMILY SUITES

Many properties in Orlando, which has more hotel rooms than any other American city except for Las Vegas, offer family suites that can sleep five or six people and can include an extra bathroom or a kitchenette where you can make meals.

SPLIT MEALS

Disney caters to hefty eaters, with most entrées big enough for an adult and a child to share, so consider splitting meals. There's no upcharge if you ask for an extra plate—especially at counter-service locations—and you can always fill up later, outside the theme parks (buffets are affordable and popular with kids).

BRING YOUR OWN BREAKFAST

Even those staying in a room without a kitchenette will find it easy to bring their own breakfast to the parks. Packing breakfast bars and a couple of bottles of apple juice is a hands-down easy way for a family of four to save up to $75 a day on a vacation. Pair that with the in-room coffeemaker for adults, and you're ready to start the day. Ambitious travelers can even make sandwiches and snacks to bring into the park.

RIDESHARE TO THE PARKS

Visitors staying at hotels outside Disney property face the dilemma of how to get to the parks affordably. Although most hotels offer shuttles, these are usually slow and inconvenient. Instead of paying for a costly rental car and the exorbitant parking fees of the theme parks, plan to Uber or Lyft around Orlando. Most trips will actually cost less than the fee for a single day's parking.

CHECK OUT DINING PLANS

If you have big eaters in your group and have booked a Disney Vacation Package or are staying at a Disney-owned-and-operated property and have bought tickets to the parks, look into one of the four, prepaid Disney Dining Plans. These can save money, though selecting the one that's best for you requires thought to ensure that it includes what you want or need—and no more.

Free Locations to Visit

FLY INTO SANFORD
Flying into Orlando? Instead of heading to the overwhelming Orlando International Airport, check out flights into Orlando Sanford Airport (SFB) north of the attractions. Though it is farther from Disney World and Universal and about an hour from most hotels, flights to it can be significantly cheaper, and toll roads make the drive easy.

EAT OFF-SITE
When you can, dine at restaurants just beyond Disney's property boundary, something that's especially easy to do if you're staying at an off-site hotel. Although it isn't worth interrupting a theme-park visit to head outside Walt Disney World for a meal, you can eat off-site on your first night in town, on a day off, or on the way back to your hotel.

DEVISE A SOUVENIR STRATEGY
Impulse purchases can add up, so consider giving kids a "per-park" allowance and insisting you have the final say on how they spend it. Note, too, that off-site souvenir stores often have bargains on T-shirts, towels, and myriad other theme-park and Orlando souvenirs.

LOOK INTO FREE ACTIVITIES
If you have an extra day, look around Orlando for free alternatives to the theme parks. Disney Springs and Universal's CityWalk are free to enter, though both have tempting wares to buy. Disney's BoardWalk Inn has an active boardwalk, often with street performers, midway games, and music. Though not free, the mini-golf courses that line International Drive are much cheaper than the theme-park options. And families often find that a day at the hotel swimming pool is just as entertaining as a day in a park.

Best Orlando Thrill Rides

THE INCREDIBLE HULK COASTER
Roller coaster enthusiasts regularly list this as not only the smoothest roller coaster in Orlando, but also one of the most intense. Impossible to miss from the gates of Islands of Adventure, the Incredible Hulk Coaster is so extreme that you are required to empty your pockets before riding.

MAKO
Mako launched at SeaWorld in 2016 as the tallest, fastest, and longest roller coaster in Orlando. Some of the turns are sharp enough to make you feel like you've gotten some airtime.

HARRY POTTER AND THE FORBIDDEN JOURNEY
On the main attraction in Universal Studios' Hogsmeade, a "flying bench" takes you around Hogwarts. Screens and technology make this nontraditional thrill ride intense.

HOLLYWOOD RIP RIDE ROCKIT!
Hollywood Rip Ride Rockit! is Universal Studios' most intense ride. You begin with a completely vertical takeoff at a 90-degree angle. And you get to choose your own soundtrack for the experience.

HARRY POTTER AND THE ESCAPE FROM GRINGOTT'S
The signature ride in Diagon Alley at Universal Studios is an indoor coaster that is more atmospherically thrilling than traditional attractions: 3-D projections with original *Harry Potter* cast members make the effects seem more real.

MANTA
This flying roller coaster at SeaWorld simulates the feeling of—you guessed it—a manta in the water. You'll board Manta sitting upright and then be lowered down onto your stomach before departure, with safety bars, a vest harness, and flaps on your feet keeping you in place.

STAR WARS: RISE OF THE RESISTANCE
At Disney's Hollywood Studios, Star Wars: Galaxy's Edge—the most immersive area in any of the Orlando theme parks—this multipart attraction drops you right into the action of a Star Wars film. You don't board a roller coaster, but this ride is a wild one.

Expedition Everest

ROCK 'N' ROLLER COASTER STARRING AEROSMITH
At Hollywood Studios, Disney's only roller coaster with inversions features the sounds of the classic band Aerosmith. The takeoff is intense, as you travel directly into two inversions, but the ride itself is smooth, and most older kids can handle it. Plus, the soundtrack is fun.

EXPEDITION EVEREST
Located deep in Disney's Animal Kingdom, this coaster tries to take you up Mount Everest but is run off its rails by a ferocious yeti. Hands-down the most exciting part of Expedition Everest is when you find the yeti has torn up your track. This forces the car to careen backward in a circle so tight and so dark that those in the front will feel like they're being flipped upside-down.

ICE BREAKER
SeaWorld takes things to the next level with its thrill ride: the Ice Breaker. Your car will undergo four different launches, as you travel forward and backward along the track. The final reverse launch is the steepest in all of Florida. You'll fall back 93 feet at a 100-degree angle. This is the culmination of SeaWorld's quest to become known for its roller coasters, so expect sharp thrills and long lines here.

Best Non-Theme Park Restaurants in Orlando

Café Tu Tu Tango

SOCO
At this restaurant in the trendy Thornton Park neighborhood near Downtown, the menu is inspired by those found in diners across the South. Playful dishes might include lobster-mashed potatoes with meat loaf or chicken-fried cauliflower steak. Be sure to order some buttermilk biscuits on the side—and to save room for a Moon Pie.

CAFÉ TU TU TANGO
Designed to look like a Parisian artist's loft, this lively International Drive restaurant features a tapas-style menu that takes you on a culinary trip around the world, with dishes such as guava-glazed barbecue pork ribs, hazelnut-lemongrass fish, and spiced alligator bites. The drinks list and the weekend entertainment line-ups are also eclectic and worldly.

HAWKERS
The adventurous Asian street food menu at this Central Orlando restaurant, developed by four Florida friends, includes *roti canai*, a flaky bread with a chicken-curry dip; curry *laksa*, a noodle soup with exotic flavors; and crispy Korean wings.

The Ravenous Pig

SEITO SUSHI AND NEW JAPANESE
Traditional or contemporary ramen bowls featuring hand-pulled noodles, exquisitely crafted sushi, and Wagyu steak tartare epitomize the modern Japanese cuisine at this Central Orlando restaurant. The bar is intriguing, too, offering Japanese cask whiskey and exclusive brands of sake.

COLUMBIA RESTAURANT
You can't go wrong with any of the paellas on offer at this the Celebration branch of a well-established, family-owned chain that originated in Tampa.

LUKE'S KITCHEN & BAR
Head to Maitland for acclaimed chef Braden McGlamery's innovative American cuisine, on the kitchen side of things, and craft cocktails that might incorporate house-made tinctures on the bar side of things. Sunday brunch here is a must.

PRIMO
South Orlando's upscale JW Marriott Orlando Grande Lakes is home to this restaurant helmed by chef Melissa Kelly whose Italian creations often incorporate produce grown in the hotel's organic garden. Seafood and chicken are also sourced locally, the pasta is made on site, and the pizza is primo—just like everything else.

KNIFE & SPOON
At this elegant-casual steak house in the Ritz-Carlton in South Orlando, two-time *Top Chef* contestant John Tesar focuses on prime (and pricey), house-aged steaks and premium (and equally pricey) seafood.

DEEP BLU SEAFOOD GRILLE
The raw bar is super fresh and the crab mac 'n' cheese is divine at this sophisticated, critically acclaimed restaurant in Lake Buena Vista's Wyndham Grand Orlando Resort Bonnet Creek.

THE RAVENOUS PIG
This popular Winter Park gastropub has been making waves in the Orlando food scene since its 2007 opening, and owners James and Julie Petrakis have launched spin-offs such as the Cask & Larder at Orlando International Airport and the Polite Pig at Disney Springs.

Best Hotels in Orlando

ROSEN SHINGLE CREEK
Shingle Creek is equidistant to the Orange County Convention Center and Orlando International Airport, but more than placement sets this resort apart. The tropical setting merges with the Florida landscape and the rolling greens of the championship golf course.

DISNEY'S ANIMAL KINGDOM LODGE
No one matches Disney's ability to dazzle, and that's exactly what this resort hotel does best, from the soaring lobby and the signature restaurants to the wildlife-inspired pool area and the animals grazing in the savanna just outside your window.

HILTON ORLANDO BUENA VISTA PALACE
Although this family-friendly resort, a short walk from Disney Springs, isn't owned by Disney, as a partner hotel it offers special perks such as Disney stores, character breakfasts, free park shuttles, and early admission to Disney parks.

DISNEY'S CONTEMPORARY RESORT
This treasured classic is the closest resort hotel to the Magic Kingdom, resting between natural Bay Lake and the man-made Seven Seas Lagoon. Its timeless A-frame design is still sleek and stylish, as is the iconic visual of monorails slipping through the hotel via the Grand Canyon concourse. Guests love dining at the rooftop California Grill.

HYATT REGENCY GRAND CYPRESS
There's a lot that goes into a 1,500-acre resort, including nearly 800 rooms and suites; five dining establishments; a private lake; a tennis and racquet club; an 800,000-gallon lagoon-style pool with caves, waterfalls, and slides; a Marilyn Monroe–themed spa; and an award-winning, 18-hole golf course with Jack Nicklaus–designed holes.

GRAND BOHEMIAN
In the heart of Downtown Orlando, at the epicenter of class and elegance, the Grand Bohemian has a style that is naturally appealing to overnight and day guests, who have made dining at The Boheme restaurant or having drinks at the famed Bösendorfer Lounge a pre- and postshow ritual when attending performances at the adjacent Dr. Phillips Center for the Performing Arts.

Disney's Contemporary Resort

RITZ-CARLTON ORLANDO
This 582-room resort inspired by the grand palazzos of Italy promises elegance in every way, from the meticulously groomed Greg Norman–designed golf course to the array of personalized indulgences found in its 40,000 square-foot spa and salon. Culinary extravagances can be discovered in nearly a dozen dining establishments. From check-in to departure, the total experience affirms Ritz as the synonym for luxury.

UNIVERSAL'S HARD ROCK HOTEL
The "Hotel California" style of this premier Universal Orlando resort puts guests in a musical state of mind, and that feeling is enhanced by an eye-popping collection of memorabilia, as well as by a sun-sparkled free-form pool that seems inspired by a rock 'n' roll fantasy. It's a short walk from CityWalk and the Universal theme parks, where flashing your room key gets you front-of-line access at any attraction.

DISNEY'S POLYNESIAN RESORT
With a tranquil setting on the shores of the Seven Seas Lagoon, one of Disney's original resort hotels is beloved by guests who long to escape to a South Pacific wonderland.

GAYLORD PALMS RESORT
This Kissimmee resort pays tribute to the Everglades in the flora and vegetation found in a soaring glass atrium; to St. Augustine with its cobblestone streets; and to Key West through vibrant, tropical colors that create a thoroughly comfortable feeling of Florida. Adding to all this is a pool with waterpark features, a full-service spa, and a high level of hospitality.

Best Theme Park Foods in Orlando

EARL GREY AND LAVENDER ICE CREAM
In Universal Studios' Wizarding World of Harry Potter: Diagon Alley brave the lines at Florean Fortescue's Ice-Cream Parlour. The tempting list of frosty treats includes the unusual and very tasty Earl Grey and lavender ice cream (yes, it's better than butterbeer).

TIRAMISU
Look for this classic dessert at Mama Melrose's Ristorante Italiano in Disney's Hollywood Studios. It might be hard to find room after feasting on delicious entrées like chicken parmigiana or shrimp in a four-cheese sauce, but you can always split an order of tiramisu at the end—or make a reservation just for dessert.

PINEAPPLE DOLE WHIP
There are many great theme-park foods, but only a few are as good the Pineapple Dole Whip Float at Aloha Isle in the Magic Kingdom. Fresh pineapple juice is topped with either vanilla or pineapple-flavored ice cream to make this much sought-after treat. Use Disney's mobile app to order ahead and skip the lines.

CASEY'S CORN DOG NUGGETS
A twist on the traditional corn dog, these little bites thrill kids and adults alike. Since Casey's Corner at the Magic Kingdom is always popular for lunch, plan on grabbing a pick-me-up snack to chow down while watching the afternoon parade. For a sharper bite, add jalapeños and chili-lime seasoning.

PLOUGHMAN'S PLATTER

The Ploughman's Platter is one of the best things on the menu at the Leaky Cauldron in Universal Studios' Wizarding World of Harry Potter: Diagon Alley. This meal is made to serve two, and includes Scotch eggs, apple beet salad, two large pieces of bread, three English cheeses, tomatoes, and salad.

BUTTERBEER

How can anyone miss Harry Potter's favorite drink? In the Wizarding World of Harry Potter, you'll find butterbeer available at every cart and restaurant you turn to. This butterscotch-esque sweet treat is also available as an ice cream flavor!

BAKLAVA

You cannot beat the pistachio baklava found in the Morocco pavilion at EPCOT's World Showcase. Grab some as part of an assortment of treats at the quick-service Oasis Sweets & Sips on the World Showcase Lagoon.

Braised lamb shank

PEANUT BUTTER AND JELLY MILK SHAKE

This is a specialty at 50's Prime Time Café in Echo Lake at Disney's Hollywood Studios; if you can't get reservations, though, the milk shake is also offered at the neighboring Tune-In Lounge.

CARCIOFI PIZZA

Via Napoli Ristorante e Pizzeria in the Italy pavilion at EPCOT offers hand-tossed pizzas. The best is the family-sized carciofi, a white pizza with artichoke, fontina, mozzarella, and truffle oil.

BRAISED LAMB SHANK

One of the best dishes at Tiffins in Discovery Island at Disney's Animal Kingdom is the braised lamb shank. It's served with couscous, piquillo peppers, *kottu* (a stew of eggplant and chickpeas), and pan-roasted vegetables.

POTATO AND ONION WEB

A long-time Universal Studios favorite is Finnegan's Bar and Grill. Wise diners start with the potato and onion web, a beer-battered mixture of thinly sliced potatoes and onions that will satisfy the entire table.

Best Theme Park Souvenirs

EMBROIDERED MICKEY MOUSE EARS
The gold standard of Orlando souvenirs, these iconic chapeaux first appeared in the 1950s on the *Mickey Mouse Club* and continue to be a favorite for guests from around the world. The ubiquitous black beanie with the half-dome ears wouldn't be complete without your name.

PLUSH MICKEY OR MINNIE MOUSE
Nearly every character appearing in a Disney film is stamped, printed, stuffed, or otherwise memorialized in nearly every form and on nearly every surface. But of hundreds of characters, none rivals the stature of Mickey and Minnie, whose plush doppelgangers are a comforting and cuddly memento of your Orlando visit (and they pack well, too).

GOOFY BASEBALL CAP
The age-old question "Is Goofy a dog?" doesn't detract from his popularity with Disney guests. The combination of his big feet, baggy pants, turtleneck sweater, tall hat, and exclamations of "Oh, gawrsh!" have placed him among Disney's Fab Five with Mickey, Minnie, Donald, and Pluto. A Goofy cap captures his unique personality with dangling ears hanging on the sides and Goofy eyes peering down the length of his outstretched nose.

BANSHEE
Animal Kingdom is filled with hundreds of unusual and eye-catching sights. One head-turner is the colorful banshee that's often perched on the shoulders of park guests. Found at the shop at Pandora's–Avatar Flight of Passage, the multihued mechanical minidragons flap their wings, crane their necks, make sounds, and turn their heads (with a little bit of magic from you).

DROID
When you enter the Droid Depot at Galaxy's Edge in Disney's Hollywood Studios and see a line of parts and pieces speeding along a conveyor belt, it's easy to cast costs aside and get busy building your personalized BB or R unit. With hundreds of possible combinations, it's easy to get creative. Made using blueprints, your assembled, personality-rich droid will be ready to roll via remote control. These souvenirs are pricey, but for aficionados, it's a price worth paying.

HARRY POTTER WAND
As if by magic there happens to be several Orlando locations where Harry Potter fans can buy wands worthy of a wizard, including two branches of Ollivander's. Whether you're at Islands of Adventure or Universal Studios, you'll have access to multiple styles of wonderfully packaged wands either straightforward or, for a slight upcharge, "interactive." The latter version comes with a map and instructional chart that reveals how, with precise movements and the right incantation, you can cast a spell to animate objects throughout Hogsmeade and Diagon Alley.

Banshee

THING 1 (OR THING 2) T-SHIRT

Although it might be reaching the point where it's an old joke, couples (or kids or families) wearing Dr. Seuss–inspired Thing 1 and Thing 2 T-shirts is still a pretty funny joke. Visible at a hundred yards, the bright red shirt with the cartoonish lettering within a white circle is always good for a smile. More folks in the family? Things 3 and 4 are also available, as are Thing 1 and Thing 2 onesies.

GATORLAND T-SHIRT

One of Florida's original tourist attractions, Kissimmee's Gatorland has been a popular destination since opening in 1949. Its appealing kitsch factor (you enter through the gaping mouth of a concrete alligator) has no doubt contributed to its longevity. An impressive souvenir shop featuring all things alligator includes T-shirts in a variety of fonts, colors, and styles. Those featuring "1949" and/or the legend "Alligator Capital of the World," are perennial favorites.

FACE PAINTING

It's rare for a child to leave a theme park unchanged in some way. The most visible sign are kids whose faces are primed and painted with a specialty design or the likeness of their favorite Universal or Disney characters. Relatively inexpensive (and easy to wash off), the colors can get a free touch-up until you leave the park.

PLUSH ORCA

Orcas are iconic at SeaWorld. Of course, getting a life-size orca doll through airport security is an impossibility, but you can invest in the next best thing: a 12-inch super-soft plush toy or a pair of equally soft orca slippers. Either way, you'll have a touchingly tangible black-and-white snapshot of your vacation.

PICTURE WITH WALT AND MICKEY

Although no one changed the entertainment world more than Walt Disney, he was too gracious to accept all the credit. Instead, Walt maintained "It all started with a mouse. ..." Today the pair are inseparable in show business and in the statue *Partners*, which stands in the hub of the Magic Kingdom in front of Cinderella Castle. At one of Orlando's most popular photo ops, guests from around the world line up for a souvenir picture with Walt and Mickey.

Orlando Weddings and Honeymoons

Thanks to the diversity of botanical garden backdrops and fantastical theme park settings, Orlando is a popular destination for showers, weddings, and honeymoons. Starry-eyed young couples and, more and more, older couples who are marrying for the second time or are renewing their vows in the wedding-vacation-reunion of a lifetime travel from across America and around the world to mark their memorable moment here.

More than anyone else, Disney has created a cottage industry from weddings. Just visit its website (🌐 *www.disneyweddings.com)*, and you can begin designing the nuptials of your dreams, picking and choosing from hundreds of locations and enhancements until your imagination (or bank account) runs dry.

One bride made an entrance in Cinderella's glass coach; her groom rode in on a white horse. A thrill-seeking couple took the free-fall plunge on the Tower of Terror at Disney's Hollywood Studios. Two couples, on separate occasions, tied the knot in the middle of their Walt Disney World Marathon run, exchanging vows in front of Cinderella Castle at the Magic Kingdom. Moonlight on the Ritz-Carlton lawn set the scene for another couple's romantic vow exchange, and a rooftop Orlando wedding wowed yet another couple's guests with a 360-degree view of the downtown skyline and scenic Lake Eola Park.

PREWEDDING EVENTS

Showers and bachelor and bachelorette parties are easy to arrange in a city where there's so much to do—provided you have a lot of money to spend. At Disney, the Mad Hatter can show up for a bridesmaids' tea event at the Grand Floridian. Grooms who stay at Portofino Bay like to party at Universal CityWalk because no driving is required—a ferry will shuttle them back to the hotel.

For rehearsal dinners (or wedding receptions or honeymoons), Disney pulls out the stops to stage events ranging from an after-hours reception in one of the theme parks to an internationally themed affair at one of the World Showcase countries in EPCOT.

WEDDINGS

You can opt for a traditional ceremony at Disney's Wedding Pavilion on the Seven Seas Lagoon by the Grand Floridian Resort & Spa. Designed with the charming features of a Victorian summerhouse, the pavilion is an airy room with a view of Cinderella Castle just across the lagoon. Alternatively you can plan an informal beachside vow exchange at a lakeside Disney resort; a garden or gazebo ceremony; an over-the-top, Cinderella-style wedding; or a Broadway-theme blowout.

Downtown Orlando and historic Winter Park are popular wedding destinations as well. Elegant, yet affordable, lakefront ceremonies at Orlando's Lake Eola or Winter Park's Kraft Azalea Gardens on Lake Maitland are popular, with a variety of waterfront pavilions and gardens available in picturesque city and county parks and botanical gardens.

Other top wedding spots are downtown's Orange County Regional History Center; the Mennello Museum of American Art in the city's Loch Haven area; and Casa Feliz, a historic Spanish home–museum in Winter Park.

Another factor that makes Orlando the perfect choice for a wedding is the city's wealth of entertainment and resort hotels. Theme-park musicians and other performers often hire out for receptions at reasonable prices, and there's a lot of diversity, from zydeco and salsa bands to groups that specialize in swing music. Resort hotels like the Four Seasons, the Ritz-Carlton, Waldorf Astoria, and Portofino Bay at Universal feature romantic backdrops for the ceremony plus smaller ballrooms ideal for receptions. The hotels can also support activities ranging from spa parties to golf outings for those in the wedding party.

HONEYMOONS

Central Florida resorts cater to honeymooners with special packages. Honeymoon suites with whirlpools and other amenities create the backdrop for romance that's enhanced with extras like champagne and chocolate-covered strawberries. Resort pools with cabanas, beaches, waterfalls, swaying palms, and poolside margarita delivery make the subtropical setting seem as exotic as a tropical island.

Disney's Fairy Tale Honeymoons division helps you customize a vacation package and even offers a Honeymoon Registry if your guests wish to contribute to your postwedding getaway rather than give a traditional gift. There are package deals to be had at Walt Disney World resorts and at Disney's Vero Beach Resort. Some couples make their wedding dreams or vow renewals come true at sea, where the honeymoon follows immediately.

PLANNING TIPS

If you're dreaming about a Central Florida wedding, keep these tips from the experts in mind:

- If your budget can handle the expense, hire a reputable planner long before the big date. Though you'll pay a fee for your planner, he or she will be an advocate with barter power when dealing with vendors.

- For a destination wedding, build in plenty of time to book travel arrangements and accommodations for all who plan to attend.

- If your budget is tight, plan your Orlando wedding between Monday and Thursday during nonpeak season for the lowest hotel rates.

- Split the wedding-planning tasks with your partner. If the groom is focused more on the reception's music, food, and beverages, the bride can focus on, say, wedding flowers and photography.

- Let your wedding planner arrange romantic escapes from your guests, especially if you plan to wed and honeymoon in Orlando. If everyone's staying at the Gaylord Palms Resort or the Hard Rock Hotel, have your wedding planner book you a spa package at the Waldorf Astoria or Ritz-Carlton.

- Start your research by visiting two of Orlando's most popular wedding-planner websites: Visit Orlando (🌐 *www.visitorlando.com/plan/weddings*) features an overview of area wedding locations (theme parks, hotels, botanical gardens) and additional insights, and you'll find the extraordinary range (and prices) at Disney's Fairy Tale Weddings & Honeymoons (🌐 *www.disneyweddings.com*).

Disney Cruises

When Disney first went to sea in 1998, some assumed the *Disney Magic* would be its only vessel. But the *Disney Wonder* debuted the following year, and Disney's level of style, class, characters, and theming proved so popular that Disney Cruise Line (DCL) leaped to the top of passenger favorites. As a result, two more ships joined the fleet: the *Disney Dream* in 2011 and the *Disney Fantasy* in 2014. Three additional ships—starting with the *Disney Wish*—are now scheduled to head out to sea.

Disney Cruise Line. A winner of *Travel + Leisure's* World's Best Awards and Cruise Critic's Cruiser's Choice, Disney Cruise Line is a bucket-list pick for families with kids of all ages. Children can interact with Disney, Marvel, and Star Wars characters; join a pirate-themed deck party under fireworks; or sit back and watch their favorite films come to life during Broadway-worthy shows. ☎ *800/951–3532* 🌐 *disneycruise.disney.go.com.*

FOR GUESTS WITH DISABILITIES

Accessible staterooms for people with disabilities have ramps, handrails, fold-down shower seats, and handheld showerheads. Special communications kits are available with phone alerts, amplifiers, and text typewriters. Assisted-listening systems are offered in the ships' main theaters, and sign-language interpretation is offered for live performances on specified cruise dates.

ADULT ACTIVITIES

Poolside games, wine tastings, and behind-the-scenes seminars are among the adults-only diversions. Each ship's spa is a don't-miss for those who need some pampering—book early! In addition to shows and shore excursions, all the ships have an assortment of bars, lounges, dance clubs, piano bars, Irish pubs, sports bars, and nightclubs. You're sure to find a place that's perfect—whatever your mood.

For a romantic dinner, the intimate, adults-only **Palo** (all vessels) offers sweeping ocean views. Expect a fantastic wine list and dishes such as grilled salmon with creamy risotto and grilled filet mignon with a port-wine reduction and Gorgonzola cheese sauce. Reserve early for this hot ticket. The champagne brunch is another great Palo dining event.

The decor in the *Dream*'s and *Fantasy*'s exclusive, 80-seat restaurant, **Remy,** is a nod to the movie *Ratatouille,* and, of course, the cuisine is French inspired. The eight or nine tasting dishes served each night might include Kurobata pork tenderloin and belly with corn ragout and wild turbot with lemon, capers, and spinach. Wine pairings are amazing; so are the pastries. Remy also has a champagne brunch. Book as far ahead of your trip as possible.

CHILDREN'S ACTIVITIES

More than a few prospective passengers have passed on DCL, assuming the decks would be cluttered with kids. On the contrary—on all the ships, there's nearly an entire deck reserved for kids and you might enjoy a complete voyage without ever noticing them. Making it better for parents—and even better for the kids—are activity centers divided by age groups, for kids 10 and younger, for "tweens" 11–14, and for older teens ages 14–17.

Counselors keep them focused with a wide-ranging assortment of activities including playrooms, rope bridges, scavenger hunts, science experiments, sports challenges, karaoke games, video games, trivia contests, and evening dance parties. While you're having fun with other adults, kids are literally having a ball on their own level. To help stay in touch, an onboard mobile phone service keeps you connected with activities counselors.

RESTAURANTS

Dining is one of the most anticipated experiences aboard the Disney ships, and the **Animator's Palate** is a favorite. Scenes featuring Disney characters change from black-and-white to Technicolor as the meal progresses on the *Magic* and *Wonder*; on the *Dream* and *Fantasy*, diners are surrounded by an artist's studio where famous film scenes line the walls and fiber-optic "brush pillars" paint oversize ceiling "palettes" in vibrant colors. Dining is slightly more formal at **Lumiere's,** on the *Magic,* where beef tenderloin, lamb shank, and other entrées are served French style in a classic ocean-liner-style dining room.

At **Triton's,** on the *Wonder,* seafood, roast duck, pasta, and other selections are served in an elegant, art deco, under-the-sea-theme dining room. The *Dream*'s **Royal Palace** and the *Fantasy*'s **Royal Court** are inspired by Disney's princess films, with menus that might include crowned rack of lamb, beef Wellington, and other regal dishes. At the Caribbean-theme **Parrot Cay** restaurant (*Wonder*) and the Rio de Janeiro–theme **Carioca's** (*Magic*), the mood is casual and festive. On the *Fantasy* and *Dream,* **Enchanted Garden** is the whimsical, more informal rotation restaurant. Character breakfasts are offered one morning on most seven-nights-or-longer sailings.

Three restaurants are exclusive to the new *Disney Wish.* **Arendelle: A Frozen Dining Adventure** features Nordic cuisine and performers who turn every meal into a royal engagement party for Anna and Kristoff. **World of Marvel** diners participate in an Avengers mission while enjoying dishes inspired by Marvel locales (New York City, Wakanda, Sokovia). In a nod to the year that Walt and brother Roy formed the Walt Disney Company, the elegant **1923** has decor honoring the golden age of animation with drawings and movie props. The menu honors the wine and sophisticated cuisine of Napa Valley.

AFTER-DARK ENTERTAINMENT

Few can out-do Disney entertainment, and the **on-deck performances** and **character greetings**—featuring Disney, Star Wars, *and* Marvel characters—are spectacular. **Lavish stage shows** and variety acts entertain families nightly. These over-the-top theatricals have Broadway-quality sets and staging and are often musicals based on Disney blockbusters such as *Frozen, Tangled, The Little Mermaid, Aladdin,* or *Beauty and the Beast.* Whatever is playing, prepare to be dazzled. Each ship also has a **cinema** screening classic Disney films, and both films and shows might have digital 3-D enhancements.

Everyone, it seems, is in the mood for the **Pirate Night event**, when swashbuckling servers dish up Caribbean and Bahamian treats, cups of grog, and (on seven-night cruises) a pirate bandanna for every dinner guest. After dinner, you head off to a deck party where Captain Hook, Mr. Smee, and others appear for some high-spirited action, dancing, and fireworks.

CASTAWAY CAY

Disney's private Bahamian island, Castaway Cay, is paradise found. When the ship docks, you go ashore into a land of white-sand beaches, towering palms, swaying hammocks, and abundant food.

A MAN, A MOUSE, A LEGACY

By Jennie Hess

Walt Disney once said, "I only hope that we never lose sight of one thing—that it was all started by a mouse." His legendary mouse, Mickey, took the world by storm in 1928 in the theatrical debut of the animated short film *Steamboat Willie*. Today Walt is Mickey

There's a tale still told (and disputed) that Walt imagined Mickey while on a train from New York to California, after a disastrous meeting where he lost the rights to a character called Oswald the Lucky Rabbit. Walt's friend and colleague, gifted Dutch cartoonist Ub Iwerks, first drew Mickey, but it was Walt who gave him a voice and personality.

He planned to name the mouse Mortimer, but his wife, Lilian, insisted the name didn't fit the cheerful little rodent.

The man behind the mouse, Walter Elias Disney, was born December 5, 1901, in Chicago. His early Midwestern years were spent nurturing his love of drawing. After driving an ambulance for the Red Cross in France during World War I, Walt returned to the States and worked for an ad company, where he met Ub.

Though Mickey appeared in the silent short *Plane Crazy* in May of 1928, the amiable mouse didn't really take a bow until the November debut of *Steamboat Willie*. Walt's use of synchronized sound made all the difference. By 1937, Walt and company had released their first animated feature-length film, *Snow White and the Seven Dwarfs*.

The many films that followed formed the creative and financial bedrock for a legacy of one theme park after another. But perhaps the greatest legacy of Walt and his mouse is that they both make memories for generation upon generation.

TIMELINE

Hollywood studio opens	*Steamboat Willie* released	1930	*Snow White* wins special Oscar

Shirley Temple presents Disney with one big and seven dwarf-size Oscars for *Snow White*, 1939; right: Snow White; *Steamboat Willie* poster, 1928

1920s–30s

A Mouse Is Born

Walt and his brother, Roy, establish a Hollywood studio in 1923. Animated shorts *Plane Crazy* and *Steamboat Willie*, starring both Mickey and Minnie, are released in 1928. Thereafter, Walt and his artists create dozens of Mickey shorts like 1930's *The Chain Gang*, when an orange pup named Pluto first appears.

Two years later, good-natured Goofy debuts as an audience extra in *Mickey's Revue*. His spasmodic laugh earns him a series of his own animated short films. Hot-tempered Donald Duck and his loyal girlfriend, Daisy, follow.

In 1937, America's first full-length animated feature, *Snow White and the Seven Dwarfs*, becomes the highest-grossing feature of its time. *Gone with the Wind* doesn't blow by that record until 1939, the same year that Disney's groundbreaking feature earns a special Academy Award: one full-size Oscar and seven dwarf Oscars presented by Shirley Temple.

■ **Visit:** Walt Disney: One Man's Dream at Disney's Hollywood Studios

Goofy

1940s–50s

Characters Come to Life

Fans of all ages flock to see successive hits, from *Pinocchio* and *Fantasia* (both 1940) to *Dumbo* (1941) and *Bambi* (1942). Though *Fantasia* is panned by some, it earns Academy Awards kudos for innovating in the area of visualized music—specifically, animation set to music by composers such as Bach, Tchaikovsky, and Beethoven and recorded under the direction of conductor Leopold Stokowski.

During World War II, the Disney studio springs to patriotic action with a series of military training and propaganda films. After the war, the animation

First Disney theme park opens in California

1950 1960 1970

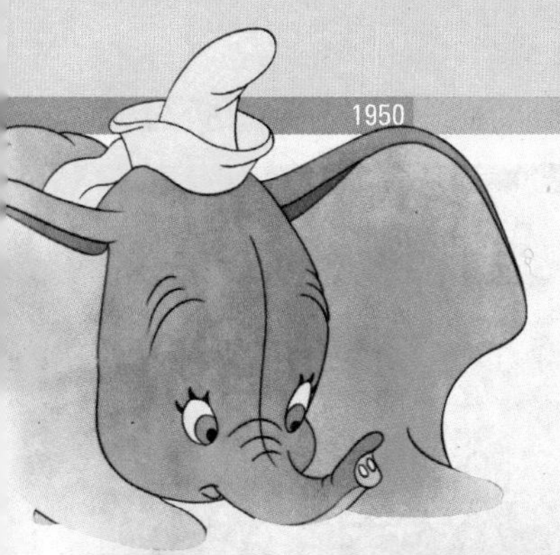

Left: Dumbo and Lady and the Tramp; right: entrance to Sleeping Beauty's Enchanted Castle, Disneyland, late 1960s

wizards cast a spell over the country with *Cinderella* (1950), *Alice in Wonderland* (1951), *Peter Pan* (1953), *Lady and the Tramp* (1955), *Sleeping Beauty* (1959), and others.

Walt's love for nature leads him to produce 13 True-Life Adventure films, eight of which win Oscars. Walt also brings his first live-action adventure film, *Treasure Island*, to the screen. He and his brother, Roy, begin dreaming up a new adventure altogether—Disneyland.

The first Disney theme park opens on July 17, 1955, in Anaheim, California. Many attractions and rides have Disney film themes. Drawing on his lifelong train infatuation, Walt encircles the park with the Disneyland Railroad.

- **Visit:** Cinderella Castle
- **Ride:** Prince Charming Regal Carrousel, Peter Pan's Flight, Dumbo the Flying Elephant, and Walt Disney World Railroad
- **See:** Mickey's PhilharMagic, all at Magic Kingdom

Cinderella Castle today

1960s–70s

A Magical New Frontier

In the early 1960s, Walt purchases 27,500 Orlando acres—an area twice the size of Manhattan. Sadly, he dies (December 1966) before Walt Disney World opens.

On October 1, 1971, the Magic Kingdom gates swing open, and a sleek monorail glides to the Contemporary and the Polynesian resort hotels. In November, a 640-acre western-style camping resort, Fort Wilderness, opens.

- **Visit:** Magic Kingdom
- **Ride:** The Monorail

Tokyo Disneyland opens

Disneyland Paris opens

1990

2000

Above: Disneyland Paris; Mickey hat; right: EPCOT's iconic Spaceship Earth

1980s–90s

A Worldlier Walt

Prior to his death, Walt begins work on what he hopes will be an ideal city. He names the project Experimental Prototype Community of Tomorrow. After the Magic Kingdom opens, Disney executives use some of Walt's ideas to create EPCOT Center. What opens in 1982 is the second Florida theme park—celebrating the world's cultures, the past, and the future—rather than an experimental community.

The 1980s are banner years for Disney Parks and Resorts. In 1983, the company's first international park—Tokyo Disneyland—opens. In 1989, Florida's third park, Disney-MGM Studios (later Disney's Hollywood Studios) premiers with celebrity fanfare. Not far from it, a new nightlife district, Pleasure Island, pumps up the volume, and Typhoon Lagoon crashes onto the scene with 6-foot waves and thrill-slide appeal.

The decade that follows is no less ambitious. In 1992, Euro Disney Resort (now Disneyland Paris) becomes the Mouse's second international destination; the first Disney cruise ships are launched from Port Canaveral, Florida; and the fourth Florida park, Disney's Animal Kingdom, earns raves for its authentic habitats. The icing on the Magic Kingdom's 20th anniversary cake? The animation studio is once again making big-screen hits with *Beauty and the Beast* (1991), *Aladdin* (1992), and *The Lion King* (1994)

■ **Visit:** Spaceship Earth at EPCOT; Beauty and the Beast—Live on Stage at the Studios; Kilimanjaro Safaris at Animal Kingdom; Typhoon Lagoon

Aladdin

Hong Kong Disneyland opens

Disney Dream cruise ship makes its maiden voyage

2010

2020

Finding Nemo's, Dory and Nemo

New Millennium

To Infinity and Beyond!

The new millennium sends the Mouse into overdrive. Hong Kong Disneyland opens (2005), as do several World attractions, among them one with a *Toy Story* theme and two with a *Nemo* theme. Disney World also adds to its accommodations, bringing the total to 30,000 rooms, 3,200 Disney Vacation Club villas, and 800 campsites. New eateries like the Trattoria al Forno at Disney's Boardwalk open, as do luxurious on-Disney property resorts including Four Seasons Resort Orlando.

Looking ahead, it seems as if pixie dust will permeate the World for years to come.

The Magic Kingdom's Fantasyland is complete with everyone's newest favorite ride, the Seven Dwarfs Mine Train family coaster. Disney Cruise Line now sails with five ships, including the newest, the *Disney Wish.* The multimillion-dollar makeover of Downtown Disney to Disney Springs has brought new shops, restaurants, and entertainment, and parking. In 2017, Pandora–The World of Avatar opened to acclaim. A new Toy Story Land opened in 2018, and Star Wars: Galaxy Edge opened in 2019.

Toy Story's Buzz Lightyear

FINDING MICKEY

A Hidden Mickey at EPCOT

Hidden Mickeys began as an inside joke among Disney Imagineers, the creative folks behind the theme parks. When finishing an attraction, they'd slip a Mickey into the motif to see who might notice. You can get a list of Hidden Mickeys at any Guest Relations location, at www.allears.net, or at www.disneyinsidertips.com. Here are just a few to get you started, though:

Big Thunder Mountain Railroad (Magic Kingdom). As your train nears the station, look to your right for three rusty gears on the ground.

DINOSAUR (Animal Kingdom). Stare at the bark of the painted tree in the far left background of the wall mural at the entrance.

Haunted Mansion (Magic Kingdom). As you move through the ballroom, notice the Mouse-eared place setting on the table.

Spaceship Earth (EPCOT). Mickey smiles down from a constellation behind the loading area.

Twilight Zone Tower of Terror (Hollywood Studios). In the boiler room, look for a water stain on the wall after the queue splits.

Did You Know?

The Orlando area is filled with waterways, including Kissimmee's Shingle Creek, a popular destination for kayaking along the calm waters right in the heart of town. Airboat rides are another popular boating activity if you are looking for something a little less "active."

Chapter 2

TRAVEL SMART

Updated by
Gary McKechnie

★ STATE CAPITAL
Tallahassee

POPULATION
307,000 (Orlando)

LANGUAGE
English

$ CURRENCY
U.S. dollar

AREA CODE
321, 407

EMERGENCIES
911

DRIVING
On the right side

ELECTRICITY
120–240 v/60 cycles; plugs have two or three rectangular prongs

TIME
Eastern Standard Time (same as New York); 3 hours ahead of Los Angeles

WEB RESOURCES
www.visitflorida.com
www.visitorlando.com

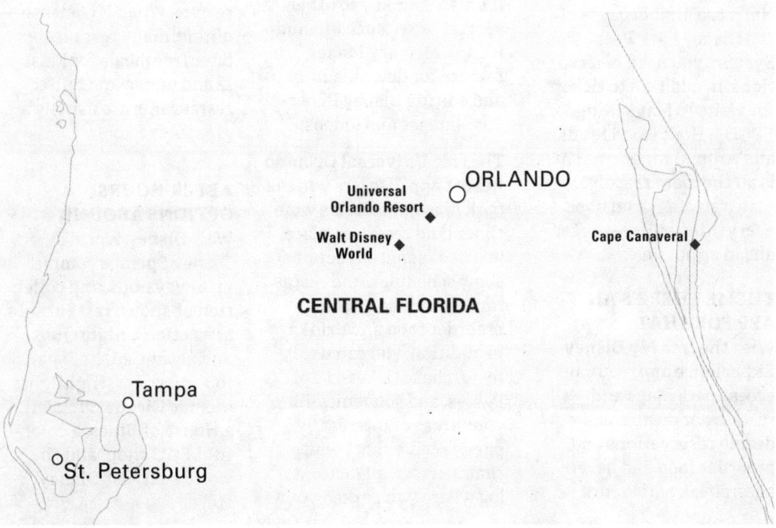

Know Before You Go

Although planning a Walt Disney World and Orlando vacation is easy enough, here are some tips to make it even easier.

YOU NEED A THEME PARK STRATEGY

Orlando has seven of the world's Top 10 theme parks: Walt Disney World's Magic Kingdom, EPCOT, Hollywood Studios, and Animal Kingdom; Universal Orlando's Universal Studios and Islands of Adventure; and SeaWorld. Visiting them all on one vacation would be difficult, so you need a plan. A good first-time trip might include seeing, say, Magic Kingdom, Universal Studios, and SeaWorld, plus two other parks of your choice. To squeeze in more, you can purchase a Disney or Universal pass that lets you embark on a one-day, two-park tour.

Note, too, that because of the Disney Park Pass System, you need reservations, in addition to tickets, for visits to Magic Kingdom, EPCOT, Hollywood Studios, and Animal Kingdom. This is all the more reason to plan a strategy and book everything online—as far ahead as possible.

THEME THERE'S AN APP FOR THAT

With the free **My Disney Experience app,** you can access park maps and restaurant menus; make dining reservations and preorder food and beverages; check park hours, show schedules, and ride wait times; and use the Genie function to create park itineraries. Add-on features are also available, though fees and/or conditions may apply.

Available for purchase individually or with the purchase of the Genie+ app upgrade, Lightning Lanes (which replaces Disney's Fastpass system) can fast-track you into the next available arrival window at select attractions.

The MagicMobile feature, like Disney's MagicBands or Cards, lets you use a smartphone to unlock your Disney resort guest room. It's also your key to other special experiences, including the Memory Maker feature for downloading and editing Disney PhotoPass images and videos.

The free **Universal Orlando Resort app** also lets you see park maps; check ride wait times (and reserve a place in line at some attractions), show schedules, and restaurant menus/hours; and preorder food and drinks. In addition, you can use it to purchase tickets, Express Passes, and souvenirs; filter your areas of interest by park; receive short-wait-time alerts at attractions; log where you parked your car; and find restrooms (though you could just ask a staffer).

BUYING PARK TICKETS ONLINE SAVES MONEY

Most Orlando theme park tickets cost well over $100 per day—and rates increase with alarming frequency. Buying tickets in advance can reduce some of the sting. Online prices are a few dollars less and buying ahead locks in your price even if rates go up. It also gives you time to decide exactly which ticket package is best for you—something that's nearly impossible to do at a ticket kiosk with other anxious visitors in line behind you.

THERE'S AFFORDABLE FAMILY FUN

Near the main theme-park attractions are affordable family activities like miniature golf, water parks, and dinner shows. Letting kids splash around in the hotel pool gives parents a much-needed physical and fiscal respite. When it comes to dining, many restaurants offer free meals for kids 12 and under, and buffet restaurants are usually a great value, too.

AFTER-HOURS OPTIONS ABOUND

Walt Disney World's Disney Springs complex is an always-buzzing collection of shops, restaurants, attractions, nightclubs, and activities that span four districts. Highlights include Cirque du Soleil, a House of Blues, a colorful LEGO shop, and the world's largest Disney store.

At Universal Studios, CityWalk has iconic restaurants and nightclubs, including the world's largest Hard Rock Café. On nearby International Drive are dinner shows, movie theaters, theme and hotel restaurants, comedy clubs, a towering Ferris wheel, and shopping and entertainment complexes that are popular with visitors, many of whom are taking breaks from conferences at the nearby Orange County Convention Center.

DOWNTOWN HAS ITS CHARMS

Long before the theme parks, Downtown Orlando had a theme based on the "City Beautiful" movement of the 1920s. This is sill reflected in the moss-draped Spanish oaks, the charming neighborhoods that mix Arts and Crafts bungalows with Spanish-Mediterranean mansions, and the pristine lakes, including Lake Eola, the city's centerpiece and the picturesque subject of postcards and photographs.

Downtown also has the added attractions of the Amway Center (with the NBA's Orlando Magic and touring concerts), the Dr. Phillips Center for the Performing Arts (with A-list performers and stage shows), Orange Avenue (with nightclubs and restaurants), and the Thornton Park district (with a bohemian urban vibe).

THERE'S PLENTY TO SEE BEYOND ORLANDO

Within 30 minutes of the theme parks, you'll find airboat rides into natural Florida; Wekiwa Springs State Park and its cool and crystal-clear pool and river; and small, authentically Old Florida towns like Mount Dora, Winter Garden, and Winter Park. An hour from Orlando is Cocoa Beach, the self-titled "Small Wave Capital of the World" and home to Ron Jon's, the world's largest surf shop (open 24 hours for your shopping and surfing convenience).

For some, the beach is reason enough to drive over to the coast, but there's another even more spectacular reason. At Kennedy Space Center, you can relive the glory days of the Mercury, Gemini, and Apollo missions in the Visitor Complex; look forward to the exciting new missions of SpaceX, Blue Origins, and the United Launch Alliance; and see the actual space shuttle *Atlantis*.

DRIVE TIMES ARE A FACTOR

When Walt Disney World opened in 1971 it attracted millions of happy guests, as well as thousands of new residents, park employees among them. Today, all these motorists take to Orlando's roads, and although the city continues to expand its network of highways, it never seems to get ahead of the curve when it comes to traffic. Before heading out, know where you're going and be ready to deal with stop-and-go drivers, road construction, and toll plazas.

If you're spending most of your time at the theme parks or are staying nearby them, consider skipping the rental car and calling a taxi, Lyft, or Uber for those rare times you need transportation. If you're staying at a theme park resort hotel, free transportation is provided to the parks and entertainment complexes, which saves you from paying exorbitant parking fees and having to reach the entrance from a parking lot far, far away.

THEME PARK RESORTS HAVE PERKS

The inevitable sticker shock that comes from theme park hotel rates—even at those billed as "value lodging"—is offset by staying at a property that fully evokes New Orleans, Saratoga Springs, Miami Beach, a South Seas Island, a pop culture cartoon, or anything else a designer can imagine. What's more, perks at these properties can include early admission to the theme parks; paying for tickets, meals, and merchandise via a theme-park app; and free transportation to and from resort entertainment complexes.

Getting Here and Around

Air

All the major and most discount airlines fly into Orlando International Airport (MCO, the initials referencing its original name as McCoy Air Force Base), which is among America's top 12 busiest airports. About 30 minutes north of town, Orlando-Sanford Airport (SFB) is a far smaller but far more manageable option.

AIRLINES

Major U.S. airlines (including Alaskan, American, Delta, Frontier, JetBlue, Silver, Southwest, Spirit, Sun Country, and United), and several international airlines (including British Airways, Aer Lingus, Air Canada, Air Transat, Icelandair, and WestJet) fly in and out of MCO, with more than 50 million passengers arriving and departing each year. Not only is this a busy airport with 850 daily flights that travel to 150 domestic and international destinations, but it's also a full-service one, with more than 120 dining options; an in-terminal hotel; a fleet of taxis, shuttles, and buses; and every rental car company you've heard of (and many you haven't). To accommodate the city's growing popularity, the airport has a new terminal whose 2021 opening date was pushed to 2022, owing to delays caused by the pandemic.

FLYING TIME

You can fly nonstop to Orlando from most major cities in the United States and from several international cities. It's 60 minutes from Miami; 90 minutes from Atlanta; less than three hours from Washington, D.C., Dallas, Chicago, Detroit, and New York City; roughly four hours from from Denver; and roughly five hours from Los Angeles, San Francisco, and Seattle. Internationally, a nonstop flight from London takes just under 10 hours.

DRIVING FROM THE AIRPORT

The Beachline Expressway, aka State Road 528, is the toll road that leads west from the airport to area attractions or east to the Space Coast, which encompasses the Kennedy Space Center, Cocoa, Cocoa Beach, Titusville, and Melbourne. South of the airport, an access road leads to the southern perimeter of SR 417, which is the nearly completed beltway around Orlando, while SR 436 heads due north to take you closer to downtown Orlando and the suburbs of Winter Park, Maitland, and Altamonte Springs. If you need to pay cash for tolls, make sure you follow the signs and stay in the correct lane, or you'll be surprised to receive a bill for the tolls you skipped.

TAXIS AND SHUTTLES

Disney's Magical Express, which not only shuttled Disney resort guests from the airport to their hotel but also retrieved their luggage from baggage claim and delivered it to their rooms, changed course in 2022. It stopped. The free service, once considered part of the Disney magic, was replaced by a fee-based service through Mears Connect.

The new system's one-way standard option requires guests to check in at the airport's Mears Connect desk before boarding dedicated buses for the various Disney World resort hotels. Fares are $16 per adult and $13.50 per child (ages 3–9). The round-trip express service option costs $250 for up to four passengers, adults or children. Your ride will be a small vehicle, a van, or a bus that might be shared with others. And your luggage? That's now up to you. Finally, if you're tagging a Disney Cruise onto your vacation, call ☎ *800/951–3532* to arrange bus transportation to and from Port Canaveral. The $39 service is available on embarkation and disembarkation days only.

The Mears Transportation Group also offers shuttle and charter services to other Orlando-area destinations; you can book in advance or at the airport on arrival. Many non-Disney hotels offer free airport shuttles. If yours doesn't, taxis from the airport to the Disney area run $60–$73 (excluding tolls and tip) and are available as you exit baggage claim. Below are approximate fares from the airport to popular tourist destinations.

Airport to:	By Shuttle (per person)	By Taxi/Car
Magic Kingdom	30–45 mins; $37 round-trip (RT); $23 one-way (OW)	35 mins; approx. $73 (taxi fare for up to 7 people, excluding tolls and tip)
Disney Springs	30–45 mins; $39 RT; $25 OW	25–30 mins; approx. $60
Animal Kingdom/ Hollywood Studios	30–45 mins; $35 RT; $23 OW	35 mins; approx. $74
Universal Orlando	30–40 mins; $35 RT; $23 OW	20 mins; approx. $57
Kissimmee	30–45 mins; $39 RT; $25 OW	30 mins; approx. $55
I-Drive (midway)	30–40 mins; $35 RT; $23 OW	20 mins; approx. $36
Downtown Orlando	30 mins; $35 RT; $23 OW	20 mins; approx. $34

Car

Whether or not you need a rental car depends on how much time you plan to spend in Orlando and how you plan to spend it. If you're staying for a few days at a Disney or Universal resort hotel to visit the theme parks, just catch a lift from the airport, and travel to the parks and entertainment complexes using the resorts' complimentary buses or boats. If you're staying off property but want to avoid rental car expenses, use taxis or ride share services. These will drop you fairly close to park entrances, and you won't have to pay for parking, which can cost around $25 per day—and much more for spots close to the entrance.

If you're staying a little longer and plan to explore the surrounding areas or you're staying in a condo or other rental, then you should probably rent a car. Just be prepared to pay for valet parking at hotels and to deal with highway traffic that is often stop-and-go, especially on Interstate 4 in the 10-mile stretch between Walt Disney World and Universal Orlando. Also note that Orlando, like Los Angeles, spills out in all directions, which can make reaching neighboring communities an epic journey.

SUNPASS

To save time and money (around 25%) while on the road, you have a few options. One is purchasing a SunPass (*sunpass.com*) for your vehicle at a local drugstore, supermarket, or welcome center. It costs between $5 and $15, provides a discount on most tolls, and lets you sail through collection booths. You also can use SunPass to pay for parking at Orlando, Tampa, Palm Beach, Miami, and Fort Lauderdale airports. In addition, SunPass now interfaces with North Carolina's Quick Pass and Georgia's Peach Pass.

Getting Here and Around

Rental car companies will offer a SunPass transponder to use during your stay, but more than a few travelers have been dismayed by the $5 daily fee and the fact that discounts were not applied to the tolls. An alternative is the Orlando Visitor Toll Pass (🌐 *visitortollpass.com*) transponder tag, which is good on all Florida toll roads. Download the app, create an account with your credit card, reserve a tag to retrieve from the kiosk on Level 1 of Terminal A at the Orlando airport, and hang it on the mirror of your rental car. Before flying home, remember to return the tag to the marked box at the airport, or you'll be charged $10.

ORLANDO DRIVING ROUTES

Beachline Expressway: Toll road from the airport to I-Drive and Disney ($2.25). Also good for Universal, SeaWorld, and Space Coast.

Interstate 4: Main east–west highway between Tampa and Daytona; it follows a north–south track through Orlando, making for a little confusion. **■TIP→ Think "north" when I–4 signs say east (toward Daytona, say) and "south" when they say west (toward Tampa).**

Key exits:

–Exit 64B: Magic Kingdom/U.S. 192; *heavy* peak-season traffic near this exit

–Exit 65: Animal Kingdom, ESPN Wide World of Sports

–Exit 67: EPCOT/Disney Springs, Typhoon Lagoon, Universal; less-congested exit

–Exit 68: Disney Springs, Typhoon Lagoon

–Exits 71 and 72: SeaWorld

–Exits 72, 74A, and 75A: I-Drive

–Exits 74B and 75A: Universal Orlando Resort

Magic Kingdom to:	By Shuttle	By Taxi/Car
Disney Springs	N/A (use Disney transportation)	10–15 mins; approx. $18
Animal Kingdom/ Hollywood Studios	N/A (use Disney transportation)	15 mins; approx. $24
Universal Orlando	25 mins; $22 RT	25 mins; approx. $44
Kissimmee	N/A	25–30 mins; approx. $35
I-Drive (midway)	N/A	30 mins; approx. $44
Downtown Orlando	N/A	40 mins; approx. $64

Semoran Boulevard: One of the main roads north to Orlando and Winter Park from the airport, Semoran Boulevard (aka SR 436) is heavily traveled but moves well and has plenty of restaurants and gas stations.

Spacecoast Parkway or Irlo Bronson Memorial Highway (U.S. 192): Runs east–west to Kissimmee. Continues east to the coast at Melbourne. Crosses I–4 at Exits 64A and 64B.

ROAD SERVICE

Walt Disney World's **Car Care Center** near the Magic Kingdom provides emergency services, including free towing on Disney property, even for non-AAA members. It's open daily, but hours vary. In a pinch, dial 511.

Universal CityWalk to:	By Shuttle	By Taxi/Car
Magic Kingdom	N/A	25 mins; approx. $40
Disney Springs	N/A	20 mins; approx. $28
Animal Kingdom/ Hollywood Studios	N/A	30 mins; approx. $45
Kissimmee	30 mins; $37 RT; $23 OW	25 mins; approx. $36
I-Drive (midway)	25 mins; $18 RT; $10 OW	5–10 mins; approx. $10
Downtown Orlando	N/A	10 mins; approx. $31

CAR RENTALS

Rates vary seasonally and can begin as low as $30 a day or $149 a week for an economy car (excluding 6.5% rental-car tax). **■TIP→ If you're returning a car to MCO, definitely fill up several miles from MCO. Some stations near the airport rip off unsuspecting travelers by doubling the price of a gallon.**

Cruise

For some families, a definite plus to an Orlando vacation is taking a cruise before or after their theme-park visits. Less than an hour from the attractions, Port Canaveral is the "berth-place" of five cruise lines—Carnival, Disney, MSC, Norwegian, and Royal Caribbean—whose range of excursions can take you to the eastern or western Caribbean or, with more time, to Mexico's Yucatàn peninsula, the Panama Canal, or South America. If you're traveling a distance to reach Florida (or if you're simply a fan of cruising), it might be worth adding days at sea to your vacation.

If you book a voyage with Disney Cruise Line, you can prearrange ground transportation from MCO or Walt Disney World. Other shuttle services between Orlando and the coast are Port Canaveral Shuttle and GoPort, each charging $16 one-way or $32 round-trip. Each will whisk you directly from MCO to the port in a little more than an hour, though when you book a private shuttle service, you will usually have to wait for the shuttle to fill before it departs.

Public Transportation

It is possible to get by using public transportation and perhaps a taxi or ride share or two on a visit to Orlando, though it's harder if you're staying off-site and are visiting Walt Disney World. Even then, however, some hotels provide free or reasonably priced shuttles to the parks.

The **I-RIDE Trolley** serves most attractions in the I-Drive area. It won't get you to Disney, but it does have a stop about ½ mile from Universal. A one-way trip is $2, but an all-day pass costs just $5, $7 for three days, and $9 for five days. This super-convenient option can take you as far south as the Orlando Vineland Premium Outlets south of SeaWorld (and to SeaWorld itself) and as far north as the Florida Turnpike and the Orlando International Premium Outlets with multiple stops in between.

The **LYNX** bus system provides service in Orlando, but it's geared toward the needs of commuters, not tourists. Similarly, **Sunrail** provides quick and convenient commuter train service on weekdays all the way from Kissimmee to Winter Park, but it doesn't run on weekends and probaby won't meet the needs of most travelers.

Getting Here and Around

Taxi

Taxis are widely available at the airport, at hotels, and even at theme parks. If you are at a Walt Disney World Resort hotel, the concierge can call a cab for you. At most other Orlando hotels, they're usually available at taxi stands; if not, they can be called for and will arrive quickly. Note that taxi fares can be high due to distances and traffic; a ride share is usually less expensive.

RIDE SHARES

Both Uber and Lyft ride-share services operate in Orlando and Walt Disney World, and you can save significantly by using them instead of taxis. They are also allowed to do pick-ups and drop-offs in designated areas near baggage claim at MCO. Most of the larger hotels (especially those at the theme parks) also have designated pick-up/drop-off areas. Getting between CityWalk and Universal Orlando Resort hotels is easy, but waits can be lengthy for the free bus that runs between the resort's hotels. A ride share may be your best bet to get from your hotel to, say, a restaurant at another hotel.

Essentials

Admission to the Parks

At **Walt Disney World,** for the Magic Kingdom, EPCOT, Hollywood Studios, or Animal Kingdom, the price of a standard, single-day, single-park ticket—purchased online in advance—for adults (i.e., ages 10 and up) starts at $109 per person, excluding a 6.5% Florida sales tax. **TIP→ Note that you also need reservations to visit Disney's four main theme parks, and it's best to make them as soon as you purchase your tickets.**

For Disney's Blizzard Beach or Typhoon Lagoon water park, a standard, single-day, single-park ticket (purchased online in advance and for ages 10 and up) starts at $64 per person, if you book with block-out dates, or $69 without them. Again, this excludes a 6.5% Florida sales tax.

Per-day ticket prices are higher during peak seasons and for tickets purchased at the entrance. Discounts apply for children under 10, for buying multiday single-park tickets, for buying an annual pass, and for being a resident of Florida.

To help you save a bit of money and maximize your time, Disney also offers ticket add-ons. The Disney Park Hopper Pass entitles you to visit more than one theme park per day's use. Choices include the Magic Kingdom, EPCOT, Hollywood Studios, or Animal Kingdom. Prices start at $174 per adult for a one-day Park Hopper; multiday options are available.

With the Disney Park Hopper Plus Pass you can visit a choice of entertainment and recreation venues (e.g., Blizzard Beach, Typhoon Lagoon, Disney's Oak Trail golf course, miniature golf courses, and the Wide World of Sports Complex any time after 2 pm). You get one visit for each day of your ticket. Prices start at $194 per adult for a one-day Park Hopper Plus; multiday options are available.

At **Universal Orlando,** the price of a ticket, purchased online in advance, to either Universal Studios (the Hollywood/show-biz park) or Islands of Adventure (the park of multiple lands of fantasy and fiction) starts at $109 per adult (ages 10 and up) per day, excluding tax. A one-day admission to the aquatic theme park, Volcano Bay, starts at $80 per adult per day. Universal's one-day, two-park ticket starts at $164.

As at Disney, all ticket prices can be higher on different days or in different seasons. They're always more expensive when purchased at the gate, and they're always slightly lower for visitors under age 10.

Health and Safety

Recent health scares such as Zika, the West Nile virus, and coronavirus (COVID-19) can spark more than a little anxiety in travelers. For the latest updates on health issues being monitored by Florida health officials, visit the website of the Florida Department of Health (🌐 *www.floridahealth.gov*) and search for "current hazards."

Stepped-up policing against thieves preying on tourists in rental cars has helped address what was once a serious issue in Florida. Still, be wary when driving in unfamiliar neighborhoods and leaving the airport. Don't leave valuables unattended while you walk the beach or go for a dip. And never leave handbags, cameras, and so on, visible in your vehicle. Try to use ATMs only during the day or in brightly lighted, well-traveled locales. Even better, just use your debit card when picking up snacks, souvenirs, or sundries at a Walgreens or CVS and then ask for cash

Essentials

back from your purchase. It's much safer, and you won't have to pay a bank's ATM service fee.

If you're visiting Florida during the June through November hurricane season and a storm is imminent, be sure to follow safety orders and evacuation instructions—which most often consist of heading inland, which, often, is Orlando.

COVID-19

Although COVID-19 brought travel to a virtual standstill throughout much of 2020 and 2021, vaccinations have made travel possible and safer. Remaining requirements and restrictions—including those for unvaccinated travelers—can, however, vary from one place (or even business) to the next. Check out the websites of the CDC and the U.S. Department of State, both of which have destination-specific, COVID-19 guidance. Also, in case travel is curtailed abruptly again, consider buying trip insurance. Just be sure to read the fine print: not all travel-insurance policies cover pandemic-related cancellations.

Hotels

Prior to the pandemic, more than 75 million visitors came the Orlando area each year, making it the most popular tourism destination on the planet. The numbers dropped to half that in 2020 and only increased slightly in 2021. What didn't change is that the area still offers tens of thousands of lodging choices, from tents to deluxe villas, so there is no lack of variety in price or amenities. Actually, narrowing down the possibilities is part of the fun.

More upscale hotels are opening to meet the demand for more luxurious surroundings, such as high-quality linens, tasteful and refined decor, organic toiletries, and ergonomic chairs and work desks. Many hotels have also adopted recycling, water conservation, and other environmentally conscious practices.

Resorts on and off Disney properties combine function with fantasy, as befits visitor expectations. Characters in costume perform for the kids, and pools are pirates' caves with waterfalls. The Gaylord Palms has gone so far as to re-create Florida landmarks under a gargantuan glass roof, so that you can experience more of the state than anticipated.

International Drive's expanding attractions, including the Wheel at ICON Park (a 400-foot tall Ferris—or "observation"— wheel), Madame Tussauds, and a widening array of eateries draw savvy conventioneers who often bring their families along for the fun.

Lodging comes in such a wide range of prices, themes, color schemes, brands, and guest-room amenities, that you will have no problem finding something that fits. Best of all, the sheer number and variety of hotel rooms means you can still find relative bargains throughout the Orlando area, even on Disney property, by researching your trip well, calling the lodgings directly, negotiating packages and prices, and shopping wisely.

Throughout this guide, hotel reviews have been shortened. For full reviews, visit Fodors.com.

AMENITIES AND FACILITIES

All hotels and resorts in Central Florida have air-conditioning, and most have rooms with coffeemakers (except Disney resorts), cable or satellite TV, mini-refrigerators, irons, and ironing boards. Properties in the moderate and expensive price ranges often provide bathrobes and hair dryers. High-speed wireless access (Wi-Fi) is common even at budget properties, but some hotels still charge a daily fee for Internet service. If being connected is important, it's best to ask. Most hotels, even the budget ones, have a pool, and many have fitness facilities and business centers.

If a particular amenity is important to you, ask for it; many hotels will provide extras upon request. ■ **TIP→ To avoid a disconcerting surprise on your final hotel bill, inquire about resort fees. These can be in excess of $20 a night, and, sadly, most Orlando hotels now charge them.** Regardless, always review your bill at checkout; if a charge seems unreasonable, this is the time to have it remedied.

A note to those traveling with pets: check on the hotel's pet policies. Some properties require substantial cleaning fees. A big note to smokers: most of the hotels and resorts in Central Florida are entirely smoke-free, meaning even smoking outdoors on hotel property is frowned upon or prohibited. And don't try to sneak a smoke in your room—you'll pay a fee for the hotelier to clear you room of residual smoke.

APARTMENT AND HOUSE RENTALS

The state's allure for snowbirds (Northerners "flocking" to Florida in winter) has caused a boom in private home and condo rentals, which can be better options, particularly families who want some extra space and cooking facilities. In some destinations, home and condo rentals are more readily available than hotels. In addition, a surplus of Airbnbs provides travelers with additional options while providing hoteliers and innkeepers with competition that doesn't play by the same rules.

Although you can check out rental websites like VRBO and Airbnb, finding a great rental agency can help you weed out the risky options. Look for offices that specialize in the area you want to visit, and have a personal conversation with a representative as soon as possible. Be honest about your budget and expectations. For example, ask the rental agent whether or not it's OK for the living room couch to pull double-duty as a bed.

Although websites listing rentals directly from homeowners are growing in popularity, there's a higher chance of coming across Pinocchios advertising "gourmet" kitchens that have one or two nice gadgets but fixtures or appliances from 1982. To protect yourself, talk extensively with owners in advance, see if there's a system in place for accountability should something go wrong, and make sure there's a 24-hour phone number for emergencies.

PARKING

Driving at Walt Disney World can be a challenge, as the property is vast, and you are dealing with fellow drivers who are unfamiliar with the area. But each park entrance is clearly marked, and once through the tollbooth you benefit from a mastery of the "queuing experience" as you are guided through the sprawling, open-air lots to a specific spot and told to remember the location by the signs on light posts. It's easier to take a picture of the signs closest to your car before boarding a tram to reach the park entrance. At Universal, you can also use the snapshot technique to capture your parking area in the multilevel garage.

Note that, depending on the hotel, Disney charges all overnight guests with cars a nightly parking charge of $15 to $25—though resort guests are then allowed to drive to and park at the Disney theme parks for no additional cost. If your hotel provides a shuttle, or if you arrive via public transportation, you can avoid the hassle of driving and parking altogether, which isn't a bad idea considering you'll have to pay $26 just to park a far distance from the entrance.

ROOM RATES

In the Orlando area there's an inverse relationship between temperature and room rates. The hot and humid weather in late summer and fall brings lower prices and possibly hurricanes. (One note about hurricane season—it officially begins in June, but a hurricane in Florida before August is rare.) Conversely, the balmy days of late February, March, and April attract lots of spring break visitors, and hotel owners charge accordingly. Rates are often low from early January to mid-February, from late April to mid-June, and from mid-August to the third week in November.

Always call several places—availability and special deals can drive room rates at a $$$$ hotel down into the $$ range—and don't forget to ask whether you're eligible for a discount, perhaps AAA, AARP, or military. You can always save by preparing a few meals in a room, suite, or villa with a kitchenette or kitchen. Websites will often offer a better room rate; so compare the prices offered online and through the hotel's local or toll-free number (if one is available). Always ask about special packages or corporate rates. Don't be shy. Polite assertiveness can save you money.

If you've booked a Disney Vacation Package or are staying at a Disney-owned-and-operated hotel and have tickets to the parks, you can add a Disney Dining Plan (🌐 *disneyworld.disney.go.com/dining/plans*) to your tab.

Throughout this guide, the hotel prices provided are the lowest cost of a standard double room in high season.

What It Costs

$	$$	$$$	$$$$
FOR TWO PEOPLE			
under $175	$175–$249	$250–$350	over $350

WHERE SHOULD WE STAY?

When it comes to Orlando lodging, no matter who you are and where you decide to stay, you should book months in advance (at least six months for hotels at Disney). This is particularly important for travel when rates are lowest, specifically early January to mid-February, late April to mid-June, and mid-August to the third week in November.

Your choices include resorts on Disney property (most owned and operated by Disney), those on Universal property, and those not in or affiliated with either park. Each type of property merits consideration.

HOTELS ON DISNEY AND UNIVERSAL PROPERTY

If you're interested solely in attractions at Disney or Universal, in-park hotels are best. For starters, they offer such convenient transportation options that you probably won't need a rental car—a huge cost savings.

Walt Disney World's massive campus is tied together by a dizzying array of complimentary monorails, buses, ferries, and water taxis. All get you anywhere on the property you want to go. Universal provides complimentary shuttles and water taxis between its two theme parks, the Volcano Bay water park, and its six on-site hotels, with shuttle buses ferrying guests staying at its two Endless Summer off-site hotels to the parks.

Where Should We Stay?

	Vibe	Pros	Cons
Disney	Thousands of rooms at every price; convenient to Disney parks.	Perks like early park entry and free transportation within the WDW complex.	Without a rental car, you likely won't leave Disney. On-site buses, although free, can take a big bite of time out of your entertainment day.
Universal	On-site hotels offer luxury, convenience, and value. There are less expensive options just outside the gates.	Central to Disney, Universal, SeaWorld, malls, and I–4; free water taxis to parks from on-site hotels.	Most on-site hotels are pricey; expect heavy rush-hour traffic during drives to and from other parks.
I-Drive	A hotel, convention center, and activities bonanza. A trolley runs from one end to the other.	Outlet malls provide bargains; world-class restaurants; The Wheel at ICON park lifts visitors up for a bird's-eye view; many hotels offer free park shuttles.	Transportation can be pricey, in cash and in time, as traffic is often heavy. After a rise in car burglaries and tourist-related crimes, security was increased.
Kissimmee	Mom-and-pop motels and upscale choices, restaurants, and places to buy saltwater taffy.	Just outside Disney, very close to Magic Kingdom. The town has Old Florida charm, and the lodgings offer low prices.	Some of the older motels here are a little seedy. Petty crime in which tourists are victims is rare—but not unheard of.
Lake Buena Vista	Many hotel and restaurant chains here. Adjacent to WDW, which is where almost every guest in your hotel is headed.	Really close to WDW; plenty of dining and shopping options; easy access to I–4.	Heavy peak-hour traffic. As in all neighborhoods near Disney, a gallon of gas will cost 10%–15% more than elsewhere.
Central Orlando	Parts of town have the modern high-rises you'd expect. Other areas have oak tree–lined brick streets winding among small, cypress-ringed lakes.	Locally owned restaurants, trendy hotels, vibrant nightlife, and some quaint B&Bs. City buses serve the parks. There's good access to I–4.	You'll need to rent a car. And you will be part of the traffic headed to WDW. Expect the 25-mile drive to take at least 45 minutes.
Orlando International Airport	Mostly business and flight-crew hotels and car-rental outlets.	Great if you have an early flight or just want to shop in a mall. There's even a Hyatt on-site.	Watching planes, buses, taxis, and cars arrive and depart is all the entertainment you'll get.

Babysitting in Orlando

If you're staying in a room, suite, or condo and need to rent baby equipment, such as a stroller, bassinet, high chair, or even wheelchairs and scooters, call **K&M Rentals** (☎ *407/363–7388* ⊕ *www.km-rentals.com*) located near the attractions.

If you want to plan an adults-only evening, consider the **Kid's Nite Out** (☎ *407/828–0920 or 888/632–2365* ⊕ *kidsniteout.com*) program, which works with hotels throughout Orlando. It provides in-room babysitting for children ages 6 weeks to 12 years. Fees start at $25 an hour for one child, and increase by $3 for each additional child. There's a four-hour minimum, plus a transportation fee of $12 for the sitter to travel to your hotel room. The service also rents baby equipment, such as strollers and jogging carriages, and will babysit your pet, too.

When you make a reservation, you must provide a credit-card number. There's a 24-hour cancellation policy; if you cancel with less than 24 hours' notice, your credit card is charged the four-hour minimum fee ($72 for one child, higher rates for multiple children booked). The service recommends booking from two weeks to 90 days in advance.

Staying at a resort on Disney property, or at a Disney Good Neighbor hotel, brings a variety of benefits that other hotels don't offer—some designed to save money, some designed to save time. Among the perks: early park entry; extended park hours; and, if a round of golf is on the itinerary, guests receive reduced rates when playing at three Disney courses, along with priority tee times and complimentary transportation to and from the course.

HOTELS OFF THEME-PARK PROPERTY

If you plan to visit several parks or go sightseeing elsewhere in Central Florida, consider off-site hotels. Those closest to Disney are clustered in a few areas: along I-Drive, in the U.S. 192 area and Kissimmee, and in the Disney Springs–Lake Buena Vista Area just off I–4 at Exit 68. I-Drive hotels such as the Holiday Inn and Suites and the Hyatt Place Orlando/Universal are closest to Universal. Nearly every hotel in these areas provides frequent (sometimes free) transportation to and from Disney or even Universal. In addition, there are some noteworthy and money-saving, if far-flung, options in greater Orlando. One suburban caveat: I–4 in Orlando experiences typical freeway gridlock during morning (7–9) and afternoon (4–6) rush hours, with the latter often continuing into the early evening as guests head out of the theme parks and locals head into the entertainment complexes of Disney and Universal.

■ TIP→ Anyone can visit Disney hotels. To save money and still have on-site resort experiences, stay at a moderately priced hotel off-site and then visit the animals at the Animal Kingdom Lodge, say, or rent a boat at the Grand Floridian.

CONSIDERATIONS FOR DIFFERENT TYPES OF TRAVELERS

Whether you stay on theme-park property or off, prioritize your needs. A great spa is wonderful, but if you're running around with three young kids, will you actually use it? Do you want luxury or rustic simplicity? A splurge or a supersaver?

In addition, weigh what you get for the money. Sure, you might spend more on a room at a Disney or Universal resort than at an off-site property. But if staying at a cheaper off-site hotel means renting a car or spending a lot of money and time on cab rides, you might not ultimately be saving that much. Conversely, if you're planning to split your time between, say, Disney, Universal, and SeaWorld, you probably won't make full use of all the Disney or Universal perks and might be better off shopping for a good-value, centrally located, off-site hotel with free theme-park shuttle service.

Finally, if you're traveling with children, be sure to mention their ages when you make reservations. Sometimes hotels have special features, such as rooms with bunk beds, just for families. Such things aren't necessarily offered up front, so be sure to ask.

■ TIP→ **Regardless of whether you stay at a hotel near the theme parks or at an on-site resort, it can take between 20 minutes and an hour to get to and from park entrances.**

FAMILIES WITH YOUNG KIDS

If this is a Disney trip, stick with Disney hotels or Hotel Plaza Boulevard properties: the transportation system makes it simple to scoot back for a nap or some downtime at the pool.

Many Disney properties are designed to appeal to kids, some with great children's facilities and supervised programs. There's the Cub's Den at Disney's Wilderness Lodge, Lilo's Playhouse at the Polynesian Village Resort, the Sandcastle Club at the Beach Club Resort, Simba's Cubhouse at Disney's Animal Kingdom Lodge, and Camp Dolphin at the Dolphin Hotel. What's more, most of these clubs are open from late afternoon until midnight, so parents can slip out for a romantic meal while the kids play games, do art projects, and enjoy a snack or dinner.

■ TIP→ **Surprise kids with a wake-up call from Mickey while staying at a Disney resort.**

If you do stay off-site, book a hotel geared to small children. The Holiday Inn Resort Orlando—Waterpark, in Lake Buena Vista, offers brightly colored suites with bunk beds. The resort has a huge waterpark, and tons of kids' activities, including 4-D movies and an arcade.

East of International Drive, the connected JW Marriott and Ritz-Carlton Orlando, Grande Lakes resorts have rooms with adjoining kids' suites, complete with miniature furniture and toys. The Ritz also has a Kids Club with an engaging play area and daily scheduled activities.

Wherever you stay, inquire about child equipment. Most hotels—and certainly all owned by Disney—have amenities such as cribs. (Some hotels require you to reserve cribs in advance. Ask whether there will be an additional charge, and make sure the crib meets current child-safety standards.)

FAMILIES WITH TWEENS

With tweens, you don't really need a hotel that's super close to a theme park, so your selection is greater. Even properties that seem adult-oriented have offerings that tweens love. The "lazy-river" pools at hotels including the Omni Orlando Resort at ChampionsGate and the JW Marriott, for instance, are generally big hits.

Essentials

Disney and Universal Resort Perks

Disney Perks

Extra Magic Hours. You get special early and late-night admission to certain Disney parks on specified days. Restrictions apply, though, so check ahead so you can plan your early- and late-visit strategies.

Free Theme-Park Parking. Parking at hotels is no longer free if you're a Disney hotel guest, but you do not have to pay the parking fee if you drive to and park in the theme-park lots.

Charging Privileges. You can charge most meals and purchases throughout Disney to your hotel room, using your MagicBands or Cards or the MagicMobile feature on the My Disney Experience app.

Package Delivery. Anything you purchase at Disney—at a park, a hotel, or in Disney Springs—can be delivered to the gift shop of your Disney hotel for free.

Priority Reservations. Using MagicBands or Cards or the My Disney Experience app, Disney hotel guests get priority reservations at Disney restaurants and Disney golf courses (for choice tee times) up to 30 days in advance.

Guaranteed Entry. Disney theme parks sometimes reach capacity, but on-site guests can always enter.

Universal Perks

Head-of-the-Line Access. When staying at one of Universal's premium resort hotels (Hard Rock Hotel, Loews Royal Pacific, and Loews Portofino Bay) your room key is your special pass that lets you go directly to the head of the line at most Universal Orlando attractions. You don't need to use this for a specific time slot; it's always good. Another perk for all guests staying at any Universal hotel is early admission (usually an hour) to select parks.

Priority Seating. Many of Universal's restaurants offer priority seating to those staying at on-site hotels.

Charging Privileges. You can charge most meals and purchases throughout Universal to your hotel room.

Delivery Services. If you buy something in the theme parks, you can have it sent directly to your room, so you don't have to carry it around.

Many hotels also have supervised camp-style programs, with trained counselors and fun, active, outdoorsy things to do. These are great for arrival and departure days, when you probably don't want to schlep to a park, but you also don't want to hear the dreaded "I'm so bored."

Standouts are at the Ritz-Carlton's Ritz Kids program, and in-room camping and the Camp Hyatt program at the Hyatt Regency Grand Cypress, near Disney Springs. The latter is a top-class resort with sprawling grounds that abut Walt Disney World property, so it's perfect for families who want to be near the Mouse but prefer to take a break from Disney each night.

FAMILIES WITH TEENS

A great hotel pool is a major boon for teens, who might not want to spend all their time in the theme parks. Stormalong Bay, the pool complex shared by the Yacht Club and Beach Club, has it all: a lazy river, waterslide, sandy-bottom pool, and elevated tanning deck. This location is also surrounded by the shops, restaurants, and leisure activities of Disney's BoardWalk, a great place for teens to explore on their own.

Teens are usually partial to Universal's thrills, so the 1950s beach-party theme Cabana Bay Beach Resort on Universal property is also an excellent choice. It has a swimming pool with a sandy beach and volleyball court; "dive-in" movies on select nights; and even a bowling alley. The rock-and-roll-theme Hard Rock Hotel is also a great (although expensive) Universal option, with underwater speakers piping rock music into the pool.

■ TIP→ If at all possible, book more than one room. As they say, the family that sleeps together .. hates each other in the morning.

Teens are used to having their own space; crabby moods stemming from cramped conditions can put a damper on the vacation. When booking, request connecting rooms—with a door linking your room to that of your teen—as opposed to adjoining rooms, which means only that your rooms are next to each other.

If booking more than one room is too pricey, look into accommodations at all-suites hotels or family suites at off-site hotels. These larger quarters are often reasonably priced and might include a kitchenette, which, on longer stays, can defray the expense of dining out. Just be sure to check on the hotel's definition of *suite*. Sometimes it's merely an L-shape room with a sitting area (i.e., there's no door separating you from your teen). The key question is, "Do your suites have two separate rooms with a door in between?"

SINGLES OR GROUPS OF FRIENDS

If you're traveling solo, you'll never feel lonely at a theme-park hotel. Consider one in Disney's BoardWalk area—perhaps the BoardWalk Inn and Villas, Disney's Yacht Club, or Disney's Beach Club. From here, you're just steps from shopping, dining, and nightlife. Similarly, Universal hotels like the elegant Loews Portofino Bay Hotel are just a blink away from the shopping and the hopping nightlife of CityWalk. Plus, Portofino has a spa.

If theme parks aren't your only interest, you can get your wow factor by staying at a hotel like the Gaylord Palms Resort. Its interior is like a Hollywood spectacular movie—about Florida. Just walking around in the 4-acre atrium is an adventure, with indoor gardens evoking the Everglades and old St. Augustine. There's also a lot to do on-site, including dining, shopping, swimming, indulging in spa treatments, or working out in the large fitness center.

For more adventurous solo travelers (or couples), yet another option is staying outside of the attractions area in a cabin or cottage at a fish camp. At these lake- or riverside Old Florida lodges, you'll be surrounded by the beauty and tranquility of nature and worlds away from the traffic, crowds, and congestion of the attractions areas.

COUPLES

Properties such as the Ritz-Carlton Orlando, Grande Lakes, or Four Seasons spell romance. Ultraluxurious rooms, restaurants, and spa programs, plus championship golf courses, make these resorts among the best in the Orlando area. Another romantic option is downtown's Grand Bohemian, with a rooftop pool, jazz in the Bösendorfer Lounge, and short-walk access to the Dr. Phillips Center for the Performing Arts and the Amway Center's NBA games and world-class concerts.

If you and your sweetie are Disneyphiles, Disney's five-star Grand Floridian absolutely drips with Victorian romance, and the Animal Kingdom Lodge offers the delights of sunsets over the savanna and giraffes and zebras munching leaves just below your balcony. The Port Orleans Resort–French Quarter, near Disney Springs, is a great, more affordable romantic choice.

LARGE GROUPS

All-suites properties are the logical choice. If you're coming mainly for the theme parks, stay on Disney or Universal grounds, as the many perks—especially those involving transportation—definitely make life easier. Some Disney properties with suites include the cabins at Fort Wilderness Resort, the Beach Club Villas, the BoardWalk Inn and Villas, the Bay Lake Tower at the Contemporary Resort, the bungalows at the Polynesian Village Resort, the cabins at Wilderness Lodge, and the villas at Animal Kingdom. At the Universal properties, Cabana Bay has 1,800 rooms, half of them suites. But rest assured, area hotel reps are very familiar with group travel and are happy to discuss options.

If you plan to spend time away from the parks or will be shuttling between Universal and Disney, consider reserving an apartment or condo. This works best for families who can handle communal living for an extended period.

If your family members tend to get in each other's hair, you're better off reserving a block of hotel rooms. Add a courtesy suite, and you have all the benefits of togetherness, plus a place to retreat to when you need it. Talk to a hotel agent to figure out how many people each room can accommodate comfortably and how many rooms you'll need.

RESERVATIONS

When booking by phone, expect a robot first, followed by a sometimes protracted wait before a real person—who will hopefully be polite and helpful.

Walt Disney Travel Co.

Packages can be arranged through the Walt Disney Travel Co., a service set up for U.K. and European travelers. Guests can find planning tools on the website that allow them to customize vacation itineraries based on interests as well as age, height restrictions, and medical needs. ✉ *3 Queen Caroline St.* ☎ *800/2006–0809 toll-free in U.K., 203/666–9911 paid call in U.K.* 🌐 *www.disneyholidays.com.*

WDW Reservations Office

You can book many accommodations—Disney-owned hotels and some non-Disney-owned hotels—through the WDW Reservations Office. The website allows you to compare prices at the various on-site resorts. People with disabilities can also use this number, as all the representatives have TTY capability and are knowledgeable about services available at resorts and parks for guests with special needs. The website is also a valuable source for such information. Go to Guest Services and search the word "disabilities." ☎ *407/939–4357* 🌐 *disneyworld.disney.go.com.*

Packing

In general, Florida has a temperate climate although first-time visitors are usually astounded by the humidity, which can make a summer day absolutely unbearable. For summer trips, consider packing a cooling towel to wrap around your neck—and perhaps adding cooling shirts that wick the moisture and heat from your body. Summer also has afternoon thunderstorms, which go along with Orlando's status as the lightning capital of the world and help explain why savvy travelers often pack a handful of inexpensive ponchos.

Bathing suits are a natural anytime of the year, but sweaters, fleeces, and jackets are usually needed only between December and February. If you forget apparel items, rest assured you can find them inside the parks; at souvenir shops near the attractions; and at Walmart, Walgreens, and CVS stores near the airport.

Finally, it's rare that a family will leave Orlando without a treasure chest of souvenirs and apparel. Assuming you arrived with luggage bursting at the seams, just head to a local thrift store where you'll find a surplus of used but fully functional suitcases to carry home your extra swag.

Passport

Non-American travelers always need a valid passport to visit Florida. Passengers on cruises that depart from and return to the same U.S. port aren't currently required to carry a passport, but it's always a good idea to bring one if your ship travels through Caribbean waters in the unlikely event that you must fly out of a Caribbean airport during your trip.

Restaurants

Orlando's dining scene was once epitomized by fast-food fare, but, in 1995, Disney's signature California Grill debuted, featuring farm-to-table cuisine and wonderful wines by the glass. Soon after, celebrity chefs started opening up shop, leading to an explosion of restaurants offering artisanal and locally sourced fare.

Orlando's culinary progress is also evident in the last place you might think: Disney's fast-food outlets. Every eatery on Disney property offers a tempting vegetarian option, and kiddie meals come with healthful sides and drinks unless you request otherwise. Chefs at Disney's table-service restaurants consult face-to-face with guests about food allergies.

Although some of the best restaurants are in Walt Disney World and Universal Orlando resort hotels and entertainment complexes, local treasures outside the parks abound. Around town, locals flock to gastropubs, where menus change regularly, and any number of dining establishments serving thoughtfully prepared, cutting-edge cuisine or the best steak.

Sand Lake Road is known by foodies as Restaurant Row for its eclectic collection of fashionable outlets for sushi and seafood, Italian and chops, Hawaiian fusion, and upscale Lebanese. Downtown Orlando, the Thornton Park neighborhood, and the city of Winter Park are prime locales for chow. Scattered throughout Central Florida, low-key ethnic restaurants specialize in the fare of Turkey, India, Peru, Thailand, Vietnam—you name it. Prices in these family-owned finds are usually delightfully low.

Throughout this guide, restaurant reviews have been shortened. For full reviews, visit Fodors.com. Restaurant prices cited are the average cost of a main course at dinner or, if dinner is not served, at lunch.

Essentials

CONSIDERATIONS FOR DIFFERENT TYPES OF TRAVELERS

FAMILIES WITH YOUNG KIDS

Except for the very formal Victoria & Albert's at Disney's Grand Floridian and the upscale Christini's on Sand Lake Road, most restaurants in and near the theme parks welcome children. Crayons, games, and kiddie menus are standard. If you're traveling with small children, they'll be over the moon if you book a character meal. At each of its four parks as well as at some of its resort hotels, Walt Disney World offers breakfast, lunch, and dinner with characters including Mickey, Donald, Goofy, Chip 'n' Dale, Cinderella, and other favorites who show up to sign autographs and pose for pics. Some dining events are buffets. Others are family-style or à la carte. All are fabulously entertaining.

Universal also offers a handful of character meals. Year-round there's the Despicable Me Character Breakfast at the Loews Royal Pacific Resort and the Marvel Character Dinner at Islands of Adventure's Cafe 4. During the winter holidays, the Grinch & Friends Character Breakfast is held at Islands of Adventure, and, in the fall, the Halloween Horror Nights Scareactor Dining Experience takes place at Universal Studios' Classic Monsters Cafe.

When possible, reserve your spot character meal spots far in advance. They are in high demand, especially at Walt Disney World. ■ **TIP→ If your young children are theme-park newbies, have your character meal near the end of a visit, so they'll be used to seeing the large and sometimes frightening figures.**

FAMILIES WITH TWEENS

Tweens who have outgrown character meals might be more impressed by highly themed restaurants like the 50's Prime Time Café in Disney's Hollywood Studios, a kitschy 1950s-theme space where "Mom," the waitress, might make parents finish their vegetables. At the Sci-Fi Dine-In Theater nearby, guests eat in top-down convertible cars that face a big screen airing 1950s and '60s sci-fi and monster trailers; there are even tasty vegetarian offerings.

Universal's Islands of Adventure also has theme eateries based on superheroes or other classic characters. The Three Broomsticks at Islands of Adventure and Leaky Cauldron at Universal Studios offer British pub food, and both are boons for Harry Potter fans.

FAMILIES WITH TEENS

CityWalk is filled with high-energy themed eateries that teens love. In fact, local high schoolers tend to congregate in the CityWalk common areas on weekend evenings. The lively Hard Rock Cafe is a consistent favorite.

At Disney's BoardWalk, the ESPN Club is a great choice for teen sports fans. Even its bathrooms are equipped with video monitors, so you don't have to miss a second of a great game.

COUPLES

Truly, you'd be hard-pressed to find more romantic restaurants than the ones on Disney property. Jiko, at the Animal Kingdom Lodge, pairs superb African-accented cuisine with an exceptional South African wine list and dramatic decor. If you really want to go all out, there's absolutely nothing like Victoria & Albert's in the Grand Floridian. Treat yourself to a gourmet, seven-course, prix-fixe meal to live harp music in one of only 26 restaurants in America to hold both the AAA Five Diamond and Forbes Travel Guide Five-Star Awards.

SINGLES OR GROUPS OF FRIENDS

Singles often dine at the bars of upscale-casual favorites, including Seasons 52, Prato, and downtown Orlando's Ceviche, a tapas restaurant. Groups enjoy the festive antics of International Drive's Taverna Opa Orlando, where visitors often find themselves dancing around the dining room, and the Cafe Tu Tu Tango, a tapas restaurant modeled after a Parisian artist's loft. Every piece of artwork that adorns the walls is for sale, including the pieces being created by visiting artists.

LARGE GROUPS

Restaurants in theme-park hotels, in nearby convention hotels, on Sand Lake Road, and on International Drive have private party rooms for large groups more often than not. For an alternative, consider dinner shows. The food is plentiful, and the entertainment keeps younger family members engaged. The concepts range from medieval jousting on horseback to pirates to comedic murder mysteries.

The luaus at Disney and Universal hotels are good for all ages, as is the wonderfully hokey Hoop-Dee-Doo Musical Revue at Disney's Fort Wilderness Resort. One of the longest-running shows in the world, it premiered at Pioneer Hall in June 1974 and is still one of the most popular shows at Disney.

RESERVATIONS

Reservations are strongly recommended throughout the theme parks. Indeed, you can make them for restaurants and character meals at both Universal and Disney at least 90 (and up to 180) days out. When booking, be sure to ask about the cancellation policy—at all table service Disney restaurants, for instance, you will be charged $10 per guest if you don't give 24 hours' notice.

For restaurant reservations within Walt Disney World, call (☎ *407/939–3463*) or book online. You can also get plenty of information on the Disney website, including the meals served, price ranges, and specialties at all Disney eateries. Menus for all restaurants are posted online and tend to be up to date. Call for Universal Orlando reservations (☎ *407/224–9255 theme parks and CityWalk or 407/503–3463 hotels*). You can also learn about the complex's 50-plus restaurants at the Universal website, 🌐 *www.universalorlando.com.*

In our reviews, reservations are mentioned only when they're essential or not accepted. Unless otherwise noted, the restaurants listed are open daily for lunch and dinner.

THEME-PARK MEAL PLANS

If you've booked a Disney Vacation Package or are staying at a Disney-owned-and-operated hotel and have purchased tickets to the parks, look into **Disney Dining Plans** (🌐 *disneyworld.disney.go.com/dining/plans*), which allow you to prepay for meals. Options include the Quick Service Dining Plan for meals at casual, counter-service locations; the Disney Dining Plan with meals at 50 table-service restaurants (reservations required); the Disney Dining Plan Plus, offering two meals a day at table-service and/or quick-service restaurants; and the comprehensive Disney Deluxe Dining Plan, which offers the most meals, letting you take "an epicurean journey from appetizers to desserts." Each plan generally includes nonalcoholic specialty beverages and, for guests 21 and older, beer, wine, and cocktails.

Disney Dining Plans are a good deal if you buy the one that best serves your needs. Moderate eaters can end up

Essentials

turning away appetizers and desserts to which they're entitled. Select your plan carefully, and use it wisely. You might be able to swap table-service meals you haven't used for, say, a Disney dinner show or an evening at a high-end restaurant like California Grill.

In 2021, Universal Studios Orlando suspended its dining plans indefinitely. These had featured options for sit-down or quick-service meals at Universal Studios and Islands of Adventure. Before visiting, be sure to check the status of the dining plans on the Universal website.

TIPPING AND TAXES

In most restaurants, tip the waiter 15%–20% of the food and beverage charges before tax. Tip at least $1 per drink at the bar and $2 for valet parking.

WHAT TO WEAR

Because tourism is king around Orlando, casual dress is the rule. Flip-flops and cutoffs are acceptable in just about all fast-food and mid-price restaurants. Although it's best to dress up for the ritzier restaurants, don't be shocked to find diners beside you in Levi's and polo shirts. Men need jackets only in the most exclusive establishments; however, such establishments are strict about enforcing dress code. If you plan to eat at a nicer place, check on dress codes so you aren't caught unprepared and turned away at the door.

What it Costs

$	$$	$$$	$$$$
AT DINNER			
under $15	$15–$21	$22–$30	over $30

Tipping Guides for Walt Disney World and Orlando

Bartender	$1–$5 per round of drinks, depending on the number of drinks
Bellhop	$1–$5 per bag, depending on the level of the hotel
Coat Check	$1–$2 per coat
Hotel Concierge	$5 or more, depending on the service
Hotel Doorstaff	$1–$5 for help with bags or hailing a cab
Hotel Maid	$2–$5 a day (in cash, preferably, and left daily since cleaning staff may be different each day you stay)
Hotel Room Service Waiter	$1–$2 per delivery, even if a service charge has been added
Porter at Airport or Train Station	$1 per bag
Restroom Attendants	$1 or small change
Skycap at Airport	$1–$3 per bag checked
Spa Personnel	15%–20% of the cost of your service
Taxi Driver	15%–20%
Tour Guide	10%–15% of the cost of the tour, per person
Valet Parking Attendant	$2–$5, each time your car is brought to you
Waiter	15%–20%, with 20% being the norm at high-end restaurants; nothing additional if a service charge is added to the bill

Tipping

Tip in Orlando as you would in any big U.S. city. Servers in high-end and tourist-related restaurants depend on these tips to live and expect at least 20%, as do bartenders. Bellhops, hotel doorstaff, and valet parking attendants are usually given tips each time you use their services ($1 to $5 depending on the service). Hotel maids are usually tipped $2 to $5 per night (left each morning).

Visa

For some international travelers, a tourism visa is required for traveling to Florida and the rest of the United States. To find out if you'll need a visa, visit the Department of State (🌐 *travel.state.gov*).

When to Go

Low Season: Orlando is the most visited place in the world, so you'll always have to deal with a lot of folks who, like you, wanted to come here on vacation. But you'll deal with a lot fewer of them if you visit in the slowest times of the year, which are traditionally mid-January through February (postholiday/pre-spring break; May (pre-summer vacation); October (kids back in school), and the weeks between Thanksgiving and December 20.

Shoulder Season: If you look at Orlando tourism like a Bell Curve, you'll find the attractions gearing up for, or winding down from, the peak seasons in early March, early May, early June, late August, and mid-December.

High Season: During spring break, summer vacation, and the holidays, plan on long waits for parking, dining, admission, and nearly every attraction. You can offset that by applying some of the tips listed earlier, such as downloaded park apps and reserving dining and attractions times.

Walt Disney World Great Itineraries

Walt Disney World can be overwhelming. Take a breath, relax, and consider one of these approaches.

If You Have One Day

If you just a single day to experience the essence of Disney, there's only one way to do it: visit the Magic Kingdom. Walt Disney's genius is on full display in this park adapted from his original at California's Disneyland, and you'll feel the pixie dust as soon as you step through the turnstiles.

Main Street, U.S.A. is a step into the past with horse-drawn streetcars rolling past, a barbershop quartet, and turn-of-the-20th-century buildings. Ahead, the draw is Cinderella Castle, the focal point of the park. On your left, Adventureland features two must-sees: the Jungle Cruise and its wisecracking skippers, and Pirates of the Caribbean, an entertaining ride that inspired the movie franchise.

Continue your clockwise walk and enter Frontierland where the standouts are the Big Thunder Mountain Railroad, a roller coaster mine train; Splash Mountain, a water flume ride that may be revamped to remove scenes from *Song of the South*; and the Country Bear Jamboree, the classic attraction featuring a band of rural bears. Liberty Square adjoins Frontierland with two more Disney classics: the spooky Haunted Mansion and the inspiring Hall of Presidents.

Fantasyland is next, highlighted by the Beast's Castle, Princess Fairytale Hall, and the Seven Dwarfs Mine Train, along with it's a small world, Dumbo the Flying Elephant, Under the Sea–Voyage of the Little Mermaid, and Prince Charming Regal Carousel.

Retro-futuristic Tomorrowland has favorites like the Speedway, Buzz Lightyear's Space Station Spin, Astro Orbiters, and Space Mountain. Be sure to check out the new TRON Lightcycle Power Run attraction, too. Your round-trip complete, consider taking time out to watch a parade or for a leisurely circle of the park aboard the authentic steam train.

If You Have Four Days

With four days, you can see each of Disney's theme parks. After visiting the Magic Kingdom on Day 1, you can slow down the pace at EPCOT—but be prepared for a lot of walking. The park's World Celebration, World Nature, and World Discovery areas open an hour earlier than the World Showcase, with its semicircle of nations.

Although all of EPCOT's worlds have their draws, among them the new Guardians of the Galaxy: Cosmic Rewind in World Discovery and the classic Soarin' Around the World virtual hang-gliding adventure in World Nature, what most visitors talk about is the World Showcase. If travel abroad is out of your budget, you can test-drive visits to exotic locations. At nearly every international pavilion—Canada, Great Britain, France, Morocco, Japan, United States, Italy, Germany, China, Norway, Mexico—there is usually entertainment (a movie, live show, street theater), a restaurant, an art gallery, and gift shops. That evening, stick around for the grand finale, namely HarmonioUS, the over-the-top fireworks and laser show that celebrates the music of Disney.

On Day 3, take in Disney's Hollywood Studios. Inspired by the movies (both Disney and not), the park ushers you in past a few Tinseltown landmarks and then sends you off to a galaxy far, far away—or to a small world in Andy's backyard. Must-sees include Muppet*Vision 3D; the Indiana Jones Epic Stunt Spectacular!; the mind-blowing Twilight Zone Tower of Terror; and the attractions of Star Wars: Galaxy's Edge, a new land that includes Millennium Falcon: Smuggler's Run and Star Wars: Rise of the Resistance. After dark, thousands flood into Hollywood for the evening's final show: Fantasmic!, a celebration of classic Disney films and characters accompanied by music, water effects, and fireworks.

Day 4 brings you to Disney's Animal Kingdom, consisting of two continents and a whole new world. Just off the Oasis (the junglelike area past the turnstiles), is Pandora–The World of Avatar, which turned the two-dimensional film blockbuster into a three-dimensional world with upside-down trees and a chance to fly on the back of a mountain banshee. In the center of the park, the Tree of Life conceals the must-see 4-D comedy film *It's Tough to Be a Bug!*, showing how insects affect our lives and featuring sensations that'll make you shiver—and laugh.

Farther inside the park, you'll enter Africa, where the popular Kilimanjaro Safaris offers a chance to see hippos, lions, giraffes, baboons, and more. Arrive early, though, as the wildlife is more active before the day gets too hot. Asia is also filled with photo ops—and one incredible coaster. Expedition Everest takes you high into the Himalayas in search of the fabled yeti. At the very peak of the mountain, a surprise twist finds the entire coaster racing backward through the hills. Nearby, the Kali River Rapids offers similar thrills but via a whitewater raft ride. It's easy to pack in a full day not only with rides and animal encounters but also with street performances and other shows.

If You Have Seven Days

Seven days will allow you to see a lot and incorporate some down time. After following the four-day itinerary, take a day to relax, perhaps lounging by the pool or heading out for some souvenir shopping. That evening, head to Disney Springs, take in a movie, go bowling at Splitsville, watch a live concert at the House of Blues, or catch the Cirque du Soleil show, Drawn from Life.

On Day 6, you can return to your favorite theme park, an especially good option if you purchased a multiple-day "all-parks" pass. Consider splitting up your time between two parks—perhaps Animal Kingdom for an early morning safari and EPCOT or the Magic Kingdom for the evening light show/fireworks display.

Start to wind things down on Day 7. Theme parks are still an option, but it's also a good time to review your wish list of souvenirs. That evening, make a reservation for dinner at the California Grill atop the Contemporary Resort (which is also a wonderful vantage point for the fireworks over the Magic Kingdom), or go all out and dine at Victoria & Albert's at the Grand Floridian—one of the rare AAA Five Diamond restaurants in Florida.

What a week! Thanks, Walt!

Orlando Great Itineraries

If you need a break from theme parks, you have people in your group who aren't interested in them, or you have extra time, it's easy to get out and explore Central Florida. There's plenty to do and see, particularly since Orlando is just an hour from the Atlantic Ocean and 90 minutes from the Gulf of Mexico.

If You Have One Day

Heading east from Orlando via SR 528 (the Beachline Expressway, a toll road), you can be at the Kennedy Space Center in about an hour. It's an easy drive, but you can also take an organized tour for about $100 per person. The exhibitions on American space travel and the pioneer astronauts who were launched into space from the Cape have enthralled visitors from around the world.

The IMAX 3-D films and Shuttle Launch Experience are highlights, as is the space shuttle *Atlantis,* which takes center stage at a namesake exhibit that's enhanced by movies, simulators, and hands-on experiments. A bus tour will take you to the Saturn V Center, where there's an actual Saturn V built for an Apollo mission that was never launched, as well as early spacesuit protoypes, the Apollo XIV capsule, and even a moon rock you can touch. With the right timing, you might even see an actual SpaceX or Delta rocket rising from the nearby launch pads.

On an overnight stay, you can lounge on the blissful beaches of Canaveral National Seashore, catch a wave like surfing legend (and local hero) Kelly Slater, or explore the adjacent 140,000-acre Merritt Island National Wildlife Refuge. There are also opportunities for horseback riding, hiking, bird-watching, and fishing. Cape Canaveral and Cocoa Beach make great bases if you want to explore the region further.

If it's Saturday, head out early so you can start a shopping spree at the Winter Park Farmers' Market, where there's free valet parking. Stalls sell locally sourced foods—including breakfast—and crafts. Regardless of the day, boutiques and galleries line the east side of Park Avenue, opposite an inviting oak-shaded park. An alfresco lunch will carry you through an afternoon of still more shopping. In the evening, head to Orlando's Sand Lake Road where you can choose from restaurants offering multicultural cuisines—from Italian and Mediterranean to Thai, Mexican, Indian, and Hawaiian fusion.

If You Have Four Days

Spend a day at Kennedy Space Center, but then explore Orlando itself. You can visit the Mennello Museum of Folk Art in Loch Haven Park, or, if you have kids, the Orlando Science Center, across the street. If it's a nice day, consider exploring the 50-acre Harry P. Leu Gardens, home to subtropical flora and a huge Floral Clock from Scotland. Arrive for one of the day's first guided tours (they start at 10) of the Leu House Museum.

Before returning to your hotel, a stroll around downtown's tranquil and beautiful Lake Eola Park brings views of the resident swans and waterbirds, along with the centerpiece fountain. Have a snack in the park's Relax Grill or at one of the many eateries in trendy Thornton Park. Afterward, there are many happy hours at the bars or clubs of Orange Avenue. The Dr. Phillips Center for the Performing Arts showcases A-list musicians, bands, and stage shows.

On your remaining three days, continue your exploration of the museums. The Orlando Museum of Art in Loch Haven Park has a stunning permanent collection of pre-Columbian artifacts. Downtown's Orange County Regional History Museum offers several floors of family-friendly local history. Winter Park's crowning jewel, the Charles Hosmer Morse Museum of American Art, houses the world's most complete collection of Tiffany windows, art glass, and ceramics.

If you need some time outdoors, take a picnic on Winter Park's historic scenic boat tour, which offers a pleasant two-hour voyage through lakes and canals, past luxurious homes and the campus of Rollins College, the Southeast's oldest hall of academe. Central Florida's subtropical ecosystem contains lush natural greenery and wildlife that can be observed at several nearby state and local parks. The Audubon Center for Birds of Prey in Maitland houses injured eagles, hawks, owls, vultures, and more who cannot return safely to the wild.

Just to the north is Wekiwa Springs State Park, where you can swim in crystal clear waters that power up from the Florida Aquifer, or rent a canoe to slip silently along the river, to glimpse alligators, turtles, herons, eagles, cranes, deer, and even bears. Blue Spring State Park, about 30 miles north near DeLand, is winter home to hundreds of manatees. A raised boardwalk meanders along the river to the springhead so you can observe manatees without disturbing them.

If You Have Seven Days

Expanding your range, one of Florida's most charming towns is Mount Dora, about 40 minutes northwest of Walt Disney World. The New England–style community rests on the shores of 4,500-acre Lake Dora and is centered on a historic shopping village filled with boutiques, gift shops, bakeries, bookstores, sidewalk cafés, and quiet parks. You could also spend a day shopping at one of Orlando's many outlet malls, explore the old-time Florida attraction Gatorland in nearby Kissimmee, drive out to Lake Wales to see beautiful Bok Tower Gardens, or head to Sanford along the St. John River, where you can visit the Central Florida Zoo & Botanical Gardens.

On the Calendar

If you've been to Orlando and its parks and enjoyed the top attractions at least once, consider a special trip around one of the many festivals and events. The year-end holiday season is particular festive.

Winter

Candlelight Processional. Each holiday season between Thanksgiving and New Year's, a succession of celebrity narrators visit Disney to retell the story of Christmas before a full orchestra and large choir comprised of guest singers from local schools and churches. Presented at EPCOT's American Gardens Theatre, the show is truly a spectacle with singalong carols and a stirring performance of the Hallelujah Chorus from Handel's *Messiah*. A Candlelight lunch or dinner package includes a meal at one of EPCOT's pavilions as well as VIP early-access seating. ✉ *World Showcase, America Gardens Theatre, EPCOT* ☎ *407/939–1929* 🌐 *disneyworld.disney.go.com/events-tours.*

Christmas in The Wizarding World of Harry Potter. Already steeped in magic, Universal's dual Wizarding Worlds, in winter they're further transformed with lights and festooned with Christmas ornaments. In Universal Studios' Diagon Alley, buskers sing holiday songs at King's Cross Station, and Celestina Warbeck and the Banshees change up their set with holiday favorites. At Islands of Adventure, Hogsmeade takes on even more the look of a traditional English village, with Hogwarts Castle lit for the season and each shop decorated in a garland. In the evening, the castle becomes a towering screen for The Magic of Christmas at Hogwarts, an elaborate projection show. ✉ *Islands of Adventure* ☎ *407/363–8000* 🌐 *www.universalorlando.com.*

Grinchmas Who-liday Spectacular. The holiday season takes a curmudgeonly turn at Seuss Landing during Grinchmas, an Islands of Adventure stage show based on the Dr. Seuss classic *How the Grinch Stole Christmas*. An original Mannheim Steamroller musical score backs up a half-dozen songs by an energetic and colorful cast including the Grinch and the Whos from Whoville. Stick around and this festive "Whobiliation" and the Grinch (as well as several Whos) will be out to say hello and pose for souvenir snapshots. ✉ *Islands of Adventure* ☎ *407/363–8000* 🌐 *www.universalorlando.com.*

Disney's Very Merriest After Hours Events. Visit the Magic Kingdom on select evenings in November and December, and you'll discover a variety of tis-the-season events. The park's twinkling lights, fantasy architecture, and grand Cinderella Castle are made even more festive with holiday parades, seasonal stage shows, fireworks, "snow" on Main Street, U.S.A., and platters of hot cocoa and cookies. It's the perfect setting for some wonderful photographs as well as lifelong memories. Check ahead to see what's happening and when and for details on special-event park admission. ✉ *Magic Kingdom* ☎ *407/939–1929* 🌐 *disneyworld.disney.go.com/events-tours.*

Universal's Holiday Parade featuring Macy's. When Macy's NYC location has finished with its Thanksgiving Day balloons, several of them are shipped to the Sunshine State to be displayed in a festive recreation of the iconic parade, joining other inflatables specifically designed for this popular holiday season event. Minions, Shrek, and other Universal film characters are part of a fun-filled parade that includes incredibly detailed floats adorned with elaborate lighting displays, sound systems, and animation. The grand finale, of course, is Santa Claus. ✉ *Universal Studios, International Drive* ☎ *407/363–8000* 🌐 *www.universalorlando.com.*

Walt Disney World Marathon. Walt Disney World Marathon Weekend attracts nearly 50,000 athletes from around the globe who compete in several races over several days in January. The most popular race of all is Sunday's 26.2-mile marathon, which takes runners through four theme parks and the ESPN Wide World of Sports Complex. Saturday is reserved for the 13.1-mile half marathon (through the Magic Kingdom and EPCOT). Goofy's Race and a Half is a two-day (weekends), 39.3-mile race through four theme parks. A 10K race on Friday and a 5K race on Thursday complete the calendar. Other running events include the Princess Half-Marathon Weekend in February, Star Wars Rival Run Weekend in April, and the Wine & Dine Half-Marathon Weekend in November. ✉ *Walt Disney World* ☎ *407/939–4786* 🌐 *www.rundisney.com.*

Spring

Mardi Gras at Universal Studios. One of the year's most popular events, Mardi Gras at Universal Studios is held on select evenings between February and April and brings the spirit of New Orleans to Orlando in a family-friendly festival. In addition to colorful floats, stilt walkers, New Orleans–style food and drinks, zydeco bands, and the distribution of nearly 2 million beads, there is a full calendar of concerts with past performers including The Roots, Diana Ross, REO Speedwagon, Kool & The Gang, the B-52s, and Kelly Clarkson. Best of all, all of it is free with park admission. ✉ *Universal Studios* ☎ *407/363–8000* 🌐 *www.universalorlando.com.*

Winter Park Sidewalk Art Festival. Far from the theme parks, this highly popular, low-key, community event captures the hearts of locals. Since 1960, the juried Winter Park Sidewalk Art Festival has found posh Park Avenue and oak-shaded Central Park filled with paintings, sculptures, and myriad works of art displayed by more than 225 artists and exhibitors. Held during the third week in March and consistently ranked among the nation's best arts festivals, it attracts an estimated 350,000 visitors and is enhanced by food vendors, art workshops for children and adults, and the upscale shops of peaceful Park Avenue. If you're in the neighborhood, this art festival is a must. ✉ *Park Ave. and Central Park, Winter Park* 🌐 *www.wpsaf.org.*

Summer

City of Kissimmee July 4th Celebration. Starting at 5 pm on the shores of Kissimmee's Lake Tohopekaliga (aka Lake Toho), the city makes the most of the Fourth of July and its Lakefront Park with live music by well-known artists, entertainment, food, and children's events and activities. Just after 9 pm, the sky explodes with thunderous and colorful fireworks that rattle this still slow-paced cattle community on the doorstep of Disney. ✉ *Kissimmee* 🌐 *www.experiencekissimmee.com.*

Fireworks at the Fountain. The focal point of downtown Orlando is the Rainbow Fountain at Lake Eola, a nod to the city's origins as "The City Beautiful." The fountain is so beloved by residents that it's used as part of Orlando's official logo. On all other nights of the year, the fountain is illuminated with a choreographed six-minute show set to music, with the colors and songs changing with the season. But on July 4, the main event is a free

On the Calendar

celebration that begins in the afternoon with games, food, and live entertainment. Encircling the picturesque lake is a 1-mile promenade that, just after 9 pm, gives everyone a perfect vantage point to watch fireworks burst high above Lake Eola Park. ✉ *Lake Eola Park, Downtown Orlando* 🌐 *www.orlando.gov/Events.*

Gay Days Orlando. In early June, Gay Days Orlando brings more than 150,000 members of the LGBTQ community to Orlando, primarily to visit theme parks—although Disney makes a point to say they don't "officially sponsor or promote" the event. Started in 1991 as a single day when participants wore red shoes as an identifier, it gathered steam and is now the largest such gathering in the world. The weeklong Gay Days celebration includes DJ and pool parties, music, and events at multiple theme parks, resort hotels, and locations throughout the metro area. ✉ *Orlando* ☎ *407/896–8431* 🌐 *www.gaydays.com.*

Fall

Epcot International Food & Wine Festival. A must for foodies, for six weeks (late September through mid-November) the EPCOT International Food & Wine Festival transforms the park into a food-and-wine wonderland with tasting seminars, culinary demonstrations, and a constant stream of celebrity chefs. Dine around the world at international marketplaces selling tasty bites, or splurge on wine schools and signature dinner events. Adding to the epicurean event is the Eat to the Beat concert series, featuring popular hit makers such as The Commodores, Pointer Sisters, Christopher Cross, and Squeeze. ✉ *World Showcase, EPCOT* ☎ *407/939–1929* 🌐 *disneyworld.disney.go.com/events-tours/epcot.*

Universal Orlando Halloween Horror Nights. This extremely popular event incorporates all the special effects and movie make-up skills you'd expect from one of the leaders in the horror genre. Each evening, Universal Studios opens about a dozen chill-inducing haunted houses as well as scare zones populated by characters from your worst nightmares. A new theme is introduced each year, but, at heart, this terror-rific event has a simple purpose: to attract teens and young adults who can't get enough of its heart-pounding horrors. Admission for this after-park-hours event is separate but less than the price of regular park admission. ✉ *Universal Studios* ☎ *407/224–7840* 🌐 *orlando.halloweenhorrornights.com.*

Disney After Hours Boo Bash. In contrast to Universal's super-intense Halloween Horror Nights, the parades held on select September and October evenings in the Magic Kingdom are only slightly spooky, featuring Minnie, Mickey, and others in Halloween costumes; classic Disney movie villains; or characters from Tim Burton's animated film, *The Nightmare Before Christmas.* Check ahead for schedules and special event admission details. ✉ *Magic Kingdom* ☎ *407/939–1929* 🌐 *disneyworld.disney.go.com/events-tours.*

Contacts

Air

AIRPORTS Orlando International Airport. (*MCO*). ✉ *1 Jeff Fuqua Blvd., Orlando* ☎ *407/825–2001* 🌐 *www.orlandoairports.net.* **Orlando Sanford International Airport.** ✉ *1200 Red Cleveland Blvd., Sanford* ☎ *407/585–4000* 🌐 *flysfb.com.*

AIRPORT TRANSFERS Disney Cruise Line. ☎ *800/951–3532* 🌐 *disneycruise.disney.go.com.* **Mears Transportation Group.** ✉ *Orlando* ☎ *407/423–5566* 🌐 *www.mearstransportation.com.*

Car

CAR RENTALS Avis. ☎ *800/352–7900* 🌐 *www.avis.com.* **Budget.** ☎ *800/214–6094* 🌐 *www.budget.com.* **Enterprise.** ☎ *800/736–8222* 🌐 *www.enterprise.com.* **Hertz.** ☎ *800/654–3131* 🌐 *www.hertz.com.*

ROAD SERVICE Car Care Center. ✉ *1000 W. Car Care Dr., Walt Disney World* ☎ *407/824–0976.*

Cruise

PORT CANAVERAL TRANSFERS GoPort. ☎ *321/735–8833* 🌐 *www.goport.com.* **Port Canaveral Shuttle.** ☎ *888/320–8497* 🌐 *www.portcanaveralquickshuttle.com.*

Public Transportation

I-RIDE Trolley. ✉ *Orlando* ☎ *407/248–9590* 🌐 *iridetrolley.com.* **LYNX.** ✉ *Orlando* ☎ *407/841–5969* 🌐 *www.golynx.com.* **Sunrail.** ✉ *Orlando* 🌐 *sunrail.com.*

Taxi

CONTACTS Star Taxi. ✉ *Orlando* ☎ *407/857–9999.* **Town & Country Transportation.** ✉ *Orlando* ☎ *407/828–3035.* **Yellow Cab.** ✉ *Orlando* ☎ *407/422–2222.*

Did You Know?

Mickey Mouse was the inspiration for the Disney ships' colors—black hull, white superstructure, yellow trim and lifeboats, and giant red funnels (a color scheme that took some conversation with the government agencies who had rules in place regarding lifeboat colors). The ships recall classic ocean liners of the 1930s, and when the captain hits the horn, it plays the first seven notes of "When You Wish Upon a Star."

DOING ORLANDO AND THE PARKS RIGHT

by Jennie Hess

Taumata Racer, Aquatica

You don't have to wish upon a star to make all your Orlando vacation dreams come true. Your trip will be memorable, whether you're traveling with small children, tweens, teens, or the whole gang of friends or family; whether you're on your honeymoon or flying solo.

Gather (or cyber-gather) all your travel companions together to create a wish list. Then, as you create your itinerary, consider everyone's needs and plan accordingly.

Got small children? Know their theme-park limits to prevent meltdowns, and factor in time away from crowded parks for a laid-back visit to smaller attractions. And, to avoid disappointments, don't wait to get to the parks to determine ride height restrictions.

Teens and tweens may want to head for some rides on their own. Determine theme-park meeting locations, and be sure everyone carries a cell phone in case they encounter longer ride lines and delays.

If some of your group are planning to hit the links and others want a spa day, don't wait until you're in town to reserve a tee time or a facial-mani-pedi package.

What follows are suggestions (and a few quick tips) on how you can do Orlando and the parks right—regardless of who's in your group. For still more inspiration, check out Experience Orlando and the Parks.

Shamu's Happy Harbor play area, SeaWorld

FAMILIES WITH SMALL KIDS

Things will go more smoothly if you stick to routines. It's easier than you think. During naptime, for instance, you can relax on a bench while your toddler snoozes in her stroller and the rest of the family heads for a park attraction. Finding sights for wee ones is easy in the parks and outside.

Magic Kingdom. This is the top Disney destination for families with tots. Fantasyland has a treasure trove of age-appropriate attractions. Tom Sawyer Island lets squirmy kids burn up some energy.

SeaWorld. Dolphins, whales, and other marine mammals mesmerize young children, and Shamu's Happy Harbor is a wet, wonderful play area.

Typhoon Lagoon. It sets an idyllic water-park scene for families with small children. Ketchakiddie Creek is a favorite splash zone.

Orlando Science Center. Exhibits—many of them interactive—at this center near downtown Orlando let kids experience science and the world around them.

Disney Springs. A kiddie carousel, splash fountains, a giant LEGO Store with a play area, Bibbidi Bobbidi Boutique (think princess makeovers) are among the attractions for kids.

Pirates of the Caribbean, Magic Kingdom

FAMILIES WITH TWEENS

You and your tweens will have more fun together if you involve them in pre-trip planning. Let each child scope out best bets on Orlando- and theme-park Web sites, then gather to compare notes and create a rough itinerary. Here are a few suggestions to jumpstart the research.

Magic Kingdom. Who ever really outgrows this classic? Tweens love rides ending in "mountain"—Space, Splash, and Big Thunder. The Haunted Mansion and Pirates of the Caribbean are both cool.

Islands of Adventure. This theme-park will be a hit with tweens who love thrill rides and/or superheroes like Spider-Man. For muggle fans of J.K. Rowling's books, the Wizarding World of Harry Potter is a must-see.

Disney's Animal Kingdom. The exotic animals and safari are highlights, but so are scream-inducing Expedition Everest, DINOSAUR, Kali River Rapids, and Avatar Flight of Passage.

Hollywood Studios. The addition of Toy Story Land has brought a new family coaster (Slinky Dog Dash) and Alien Swirling Saucer. Star Wars: Galaxy's Edge offers a true immersive experience.

Fun Spot America. Tweens love the go-kart racetrack best, but the carnival-style rides and arcades are a big draw, too.

WonderWorks. Tweens can "build" their own coaster, and then ride it; lie on a bed of nails; and pilot a simulated fighter jet.

Incredible Hulk Coaster, Islands of Adventure

FAMILIES WITH TEENS

Let teens make their own "gotta do" list and head out on their own. (Chances are at least some of the sights below will make it to every list.) Stay in touch by texting updates and meeting for meals.

Disney's Hollywood Studios. Teens rave about The Twilight Zone Tower of Terror and Rock 'n' Roller Coaster Starring Aerosmith. They will love Star Wars: Rise of the Resistence.

Islands of Adventure. Older kids are drawn to the action here—from the Amazing Adventures of Spider-Man to the Incredible Hulk Coaster.

Universal Studios. Teens love Hollywood Rip Ride Rockit, Revenge of the Mummy, and The Wizarding World of Harry Potter.

Blizzard Beach and Volcano Bay. Blizzard stands out for its wintry theme, mix of thrills, and laid-back "beach" scene. Volcano Bay has loud music and big-thrill slides.

Universal CityWalk. It gets high marks for trendy shopping, movie theaters, and concerts. The theatrics of Blue Man Group is a big teen draw around the corner.

Spa with Mom. Mother-daughter facials and pedicures make for a fun morning or afternoon at Orlando spas like the Buena Vista Palace or Disney's Grand Floridian.

Sleuths Mystery Dinner Show, Orlando

LARGE, MIXED GROUPS

Look into Disney's vacation-planning program, Grand Gatherings. Just remember that group members will be happier campers with some "me" time factored in. Here are some suggestions for shared and individual experiences.

Behind-the-Scenes Park Tours. Tours at SeaWorld, Magic Kingdom, EPCOT, and Animal Kingdom are great shared experiences. Note that the more people you have on the expensive but oh-so-cool VIP tour at Universal, the better value it is.

Dinner shows. Some area favorites are Medieval Times in Kissimmee, Sleuths Mystery Dinner Show on I-Drive, and Disney's Hoop-Dee-Doo Revue.

Discovery Cove. Book a "beach" day here to share the experience of swimming with the dolphins. Meals and snacks are included.

EPCOT. Everyone can fan out here to take in the attractions and rides like Frozen Ever After and Remy's Rattatouille Experience and then gather for dinner at a reserved table to share experiences.

Spa Visits and Golf Expeditions. These are perfect "breakaway" activities. And there are options for both at Disney and in the greater Orlando area.

Spring Training. In March, it's easy to arrange a group outing to a ballgame in one of several central Florida locations.

Dudley Do-Right's Ripsaw Falls, Islands of Adventure

COUPLES

Let us count the ways to be romantic in Orlando . . . there are too many to list here. Even if the kids are along for the trip, you can carve out time together by using a hotel's sitter service or by packing the children off to a resort kids' club.

Victoria & Albert's. Splurge on a dinner fit for royalty at the Grand Floridian's elegant eatery, central Florida's only AAA Five-Diamond restaurant. Reserve months ahead.

Spa Treatments for Two. Top spas for couples pampering include those in the Ritz-Carlton, Waldorf Astoria, Grand Floridian, Portofino Bay, Gaylord Palms, and Walt Disney World Dolphin, and the Four Seasons.

Wekiwa Springs State Park. Escape here for a picnic and/or to rent a canoe and share quiet time on the river.

Islands of Adventure and CityWalk. Plan a wild and crazy evening of roller-coaster thrills and then belly up to the bar for a cheeseburger in paradise at Jimmy Buffet's Margaritaville.

Lake Eola. Paddle a swan-shaped boat together at this lake in downtown Orlando. Then enjoy a romantic meal at a nearby Downtown or Thornton Park restaurant.

Disney's Boardwalk

SINGLES (OR GROUPS OF FRIENDS)

It's nice to have a traveling companion, but there's an advantage to visiting on your own—you can cover a lot more territory. Single but traveling with friends? You still may want to split up to sample from your own play list.

Animal Kingdom. Animal-loving singles can linger longer at this park to watch behaviors of many exotic creatures. Rough it on the excellent Wild Africa Trek for a fee.

Winter Park. On a day trip to this this town you can shop Park Avenue, take a scenic boat tour, and see the huge Tiffany collection at the Morse Museum of American Art.

Disney's Boardwalk. Let nostalgia take hold on a lakeside stroll. Or hop into a surrey or onto a bicycle built for two. Watch dueling pianos at Jellyrolls or a game at ESPN Club.

Run through the parks. Plan your visit in January and compete in the Walt Disney World Half- or Full Marathons—run both, and you'll go home with a Goofy medal as well as a Donald (half) and a Mickey (full)!

Tour new Worlds. Spend seven hours on Disney's Backstage Magic Tour of Magic Kingdom, EPCOT, and Hollywood Studios.

Chapter 3

THE MAGIC KINGDOM AND RESORT AREA

Updated by
Leigh Jenkins

Sights	Restaurants	Hotels	Shopping	Nightlife
★★★★★	★★★☆☆	★★★★★	★★★★☆	★★☆☆☆

PARK SNAPSHOT

TOP EXPERIENCES

■ **Buzz Lightyear's Space Ranger Spin.** A shoot-'em-up ride where space-ranger wannabes compete for the highest score (ages 7 and up).

■ **Dumbo the Flying Elephant.** The elephant ears get them every time, and the ride offers double the number of pachyderm vehicles as it did originally (ages 6 and under).

■ **Enchanted Tales with Belle.** Young girls and boys, and some parents, too, clamor to play characters from *Beauty and the Beast* in this well-done, interactive, story adventure (ages 6 and under).

■ **Seven Dwarfs Mine Train.** Train cars sway gently to and fro during the rollicking, musical ride through a mine full of glittery gems (ages 7 and up).

■ **Space Mountain.** The Magic Kingdom's scariest ride zips you along the tracks in near-total darkness except for the stars (ages 7 and up).

■ **Under the Sea: Journey of the Little Mermaid.** Wander past waterfalls and tide pools into the cave beneath Prince Eric's Castle for some interactive fun and a clamshell ride through Ariel's story (ages 6 and under).

GETTING HERE

If you're a Disney Resort guest, you can take a bus, monorail, or boat—depending on where you're staying—to the main gates of each park. However, getting to the entrance if you're not booked into a Disney Resort takes considerably more effort. Indeed, of the major Walt Disney World parks, the Magic Kingdom is the most difficult for off-site guests to reach. Those not staying at a Disney hotel must park in a distant lot, take a tram or walk to the Ticket and Transportation Center (TTC), and then take the monorail or a boat to the entrance. The whole process could easily take a half-hour.

PLANNING YOUR TIME

■ Given its popularity with both non-resort and resort guests, the Magic Kingdom is the busiest of Disney's four major theme parks. It's usually the most crowded in the early afternoon, which is the best time for on-site guests who arrived at the park early to take a break. You can come back after 6, when the crowds have thinned. Just be sure to return in time for the nightly fireworks display.

VIEWFINDER

■ As you exit the archway of Cinderella Castle, look left to discover a charming and often overlooked touch: Cinderella Fountain, a lovely brass casting of the castle's namesake, who's dressed in her peasant togs and surrounded by her beloved mice and bird friends. Note, too, that from the southern end of Liberty Square, you can head toward the park hub and stop at the Disney PhotoPass picture spot for one of the park's best, unobstructed ground-level views of Cinderella Castle. It's also a great place for a family photo.

Cinderella Castle is likely the first image that comes to anyone's mind when thinking of Disney—it's even part of The Walt Disney Company logo. Roy Disney understood the importance of the castle as a symbol, so when construction began on Walt Disney World in 1967, he ordered that the first building completed should be this landmark.

When Walt Disney World first opened in 1971, the Magic Kingdom and the hotels around the Seven Seas Lagoon were the entirety of Walt Disney World. And through every expansion—through every new park or new hotel—the Magic Kingdom still inspires guests and their imaginations. No trip to Disney would be complete without visiting the resort's most iconic and popular park. The hotels that make up the resort area—the Grand Floridian, the Polynesian Village, the Contemporary, Wilderness Lodge, and Fort Wilderness—are the most popular (and expensive) hotels in Walt Disney World.

The Magic Kingdom sits at the northernmost point in all of Walt Disney World. In front of the park's entrance is the Seven Seas Lagoon, on whose shores can be found the Grand Floridian, the Polynesian Village, and the Contemporary resorts. Around the edge of the lagoon runs the monorail, a highway in the sky that visits the Magic Kingdom, each of the three hotels, and the TTC (aka, the parking lot). Adjacent to the Seven Seas Lagoon is Bay Lake, where Wilderness Lodge and Fort Wilderness are located. Boats also travel from the five hotels to the Magic Kingdom.

Inside the Magic Kingdom, you will find a world of fantasy, just as Walt Disney imagined. Stepping onto Main Street, U.S.A. is like traveling back into the idyllic world of yesterday. Everything, from the steam trains to the pristine buildings waving American flags to the citizens roaming the streets, is designed to reflect middle America at the turn of the 20th century. At the end of Main Street stands Cinderella Castle. From here, you can enter the rest of the lands that make up the Magic Kingdom—Adventureland, Frontierland, Liberty Square, Fantasyland, and Tomorrowland. They surround Cinderella Castle like spokes of a wheel.

Adventureland is a mix of Caribbean and Southeast Asia, home to the world-famous Jungle Cruise and Pirates of the Caribbean. In Frontierland, you will encounter Splash Mountain and Big Thunder Mountain as you walk through the American West. Discover colonial America in Liberty Square, along with the spooky Haunted Mansion. Fantasyland, which now has three castles, is where you'll find princesses and storybook characters from famous Disney movies. Tomorrowland, with Space Mountain and Buzz Lightyear's Space Ranger Spin, is every space ace's dream.

These six distinct lands make up the Magic Kingdom, but they have changed and grown over the last 50 years. The most notable expansion was a complete redesign of Fantasyland in 2013. And although it's smaller than the rest of the Walt Disney World parks, the Magic Kingdom remains the most popular (and has the most Fastpass attractions). Throughout the day, numerous parades and shows also take place, all designed to entertain kids of all ages.

Whether you arrive at the Magic Kingdom via monorail, boat, or bus, it's hard to escape that surge of excitement or suppress the sure smile you'll have upon sighting the towers of Cinderella Castle or the spires of Space Mountain. So what if it's a cliché by now? There's magic beyond the turnstiles, and you aren't going to miss one memorable moment.

Planning

Most visitors have some idea of what they'd like to see and do during their day in the Magic Kingdom. Popular attractions like Space Mountain and Splash Mountain are on the list of any thrill seeker, and Fantasyland is a top destination for parents of small children and those who enjoy moderate thrills like the Seven Dwarfs Mine Train. Visitors who steer away from wilder rides are first in line at the Jungle Cruise or Pirates of the Caribbean in Adventureland.

It's great to have a strategy for seeing the park's attractions, grabbing a bite to eat, or scouring the shops for souvenir gold. But don't forget that Disney Imagineers—the creative pros behind every theme land and attraction—are famous for their attention to detail. Your experience will be richer if you take time to notice the extra touches—from the architecture to the music and the costumes. The same genius is evident even in the landscape, from the tropical setting of Adventureland to the red-stone slopes of Frontierland's Big Thunder Mountain Railroad.

■ TIP→ **Be sure to download the Disney Play app before you leave home. Since Wi-Fi is free in Walt Disney World, while in the parks, you'll be able to play games and answer trivia questions to collect different badges. This is a great way to make those long lines seem a bit shorter, but be careful—the app can easily drain your battery. Bring a charger or a back-up battery just in case.**

Wherever you go, watch for hidden Mickeys—silhouettes and abstract images of Mickey Mouse—tucked by Imagineers into every corner of the Kingdom. For instance, at the Haunted Mansion, look for him in the place settings in the banquet scene.

Much of the Magic Kingdom's pixie dust is spread by the people who work here, the costumed cast members who do their part to create fond memories for each guest who crosses their path. Maybe the grim ghoul who greets you solemnly at the Haunted Mansion will cause you to break down and giggle. Or the sunny shop assistant will help your child find the perfect sparkly shoes to match her princess dress. You get the feeling that everyone's in on the fun; actually, you wonder if they ever go home!

Getting Oriented

The park is laid out like a wheel, with Cinderella Castle as the "hub" and the lands acting as the spokes of the wheel. As you pass underneath the railroad tracks, symbolically leaving behind the world of reality and entering a world of fantasy, you'll immediately notice the charming buildings lining Town Square and Main Street, U.S.A., which runs due north and ends at the hub (also called Central Plaza), in front of Cinderella Castle. If you're lost or have questions, cast members are available at almost every turn to help you.

Park Amenities

Baby Care: The quiet baby-care center is next to the Crystal Palace between Main Street and Adventureland. Rocking chairs and low lighting make nursing comfortable, though it can get crowded. Toddler-size toilets are a hit with tots. There are also changing tables, formula, baby food, pacifiers, diapers, and children's pain relievers. Most park restrooms also have changing tables.

Cameras: The camera center at Town Square Theater (formerly Exposition Hall), opposite City Hall, sells batteries, digital memory cards, and film. If a Disney photographer took your picture in the park, you can buy digital copies here, or use the Memory Maker option ($169 in advance, $199 in park) to view and download all PhotoPass images. This area is a Mickey Mouse meet-and-greet spot and features a talking Mickey.

First Aid: The first-aid center, staffed by registered nurses, is beside the Crystal Palace. More than a dozen automated external defibrillators are across the park.

Guest Relations: To the left in Town Square as you face Main Street, City Hall houses Guest Relations (aka Guest Services), the Magic Kingdom's principal information center (☎ *407/824–4521*). Here you can search for misplaced belongings or companions, ask questions of staffers, and pick up a guide map and a *Times Guide* with schedules of events and character-greeting information.

■ TIP→ If you're trying for a last-minute lunch or dinner reservation, you might be able to book it at City Hall.

Lockers: Lockers ($10 to $15 per day, plus $5 deposit) are in an arcade under the Main Street railroad station. If you're park hopping, use your locker receipt to get a free locker at the next park; the fee is for the full day.

Lost People and Things: Instruct your kids to talk to anyone with a Disney name tag if they lose you. Lost children will be taken to Baby Care to be reunited with their family. City Hall also has a Lost and Found and a computerized message center, where you can leave notes for your companions in the Magic Kingdom and other parks.

Main Lost and Found

After a day, found items across Walt Disney World are taken to the Lost and Found office at Disney Springs. If you realize you've lost an item, either visit Guest Relations or use the My Disney Experience app to fill out a lost-and-found claim form. Within 48 hours, you will receive an email stating if your item has been found or not. ✉ *City Hall, Main Street, U.S.A., Magic Kingdom* ☎ *407/824–4245* 🌐 *www.disneyworld.com.*

Package Pick-Up: Have large purchases sent to Package Pick-Up at the Chamber of Commerce next to City Hall, so you won't have to carry them around. Allow three hours for the delivery. You also can have packages delivered to your Disney hotel if you are a resort guest.

Services for People with Disabilities: The Magic Kingdom gets decent marks from visitors with disabilities. Level entrances and ramps provide wheelchair access. Frontierland is the only area of the park, aside from Main Street, that has sidewalk curbs; there are ramps in several locations.

Pick up a *Guide for Guests with Disabilities* at Guest Relations, or download it from the Disney website. It gives mobility details and notes where you can use handheld-captioning, assisted-listening, video-captioning, and other devices (which are available for free but require a deposit). The guide also indicates which attractions have sign-language interpretation and when, which attractions don't permit service animals, and locations of designated "break" areas for animals.

Braille maps of the park can be found near Guest Relations locations. You can rent wheelchairs only at the park's entrance before passing under the train station for $12 daily, $10 a day for multiday rental. Electronic convenience vehicles (ECVs) are $50 per day plus a refundable $20 security deposit.

■ TIP→ Neither wheelchairs nor ECVs can be booked ahead, so arrive early to rent them—ECV availability is limited.

Stroller Rentals: The Stroller Shop is near the entrance on the east side of Main Street. Single strollers are $15 daily, $13 for multiday rental; doubles are $31 daily, $27 for multiday rental. Keep your receipt; Disney will replace a lost stroller or will not charge you again if you move from park to park.

Wait-time Updates: Make sure you have downloaded the My Disney Experience app on your smartphone to receive up-to-the-minute wait times around the park.

Park Tours

Book any park tours ahead of your visit by calling ☎ *407/939–8687.*

Family Magic Tour

SPECIAL-INTEREST TOURS | It's a two-hour "surprise" scavenger hunt in which your guide encourages you to find things that have disappeared. Disney officials don't want to reveal the tour's components—after all, it's the Family "Magic" Tour—but they will say that a special character-greeting session awaits you at the end of the adventure. Tours leave the Chamber of Commerce adjacent to City Hall in Town Square daily ($39 for adults and children 3 and up). ✉ *Main Street, U.S.A., Magic Kingdom* ☎ *407/939–8687.*

Keys to the Kingdom Tour

SPECIAL-INTEREST TOURS | The five-hour tour gives you a feel for the Magic Kingdom's layout and what goes on behind the scenes. The walking tour, which costs $99, includes lunch. Park admission must be purchased separately. No one younger than 16 is allowed. Tours leave from the Chamber of Commerce adjacent to City Hall in Town Square several times daily. Included are visits to "backstage" zones: the parade staging area, the wardrobe area, and other locations in the web of tunnels beneath the Magic Kingdom. ✉ *Main Street, U.S.A., Magic Kingdom* ☎ *407/939–8687.*

Magic Behind Our Steam Trains

SPECIAL-INTEREST TOURS | This tour, which gives you an inside look at the daily operation of the WDW railroad, became so popular that it was lengthened from two to three hours and is offered on six days. Tours begin at the front-entrance turnstile at 7:30 am Monday through Saturday. Visitors 10 years old and up may participate. The cost is $54 per person, plus park admission. ✉ *Main Street, U.S.A., Magic Kingdom* ☎ *407/939–8687.*

Magic Kingdom Guided Tours

SPECIAL-INTEREST TOURS | Several Disney-run Magic Kingdom guided tours are available. Ask about discounts when booking, and arrive 15 minutes ahead of time to check in. Park admission is required in addition to the tour fee unless otherwise noted. ✉ *Magic Kingdom* ☎ *407/939–8687.*

Walt Disney: Marceline to Magic Kingdom Tour

SPECIAL-INTEREST TOURS | Walt Disney spent much of his early childhood in Marceline, Missouri, and this insider's walking tour offers insight into the boy who became the man behind the Disney kingdom. It also offers a peek at the design and operation of attractions. Open to ages 12 and up, tours ($49) leave from the Main Street Chamber of Commerce, next to City Hall, daily at 8 am. ✉ *Main Street, U.S.A., Magic Kingdom* ☎ *407/939–8687.*

Visiting Tips

Use insect repellent. Take advantage of the Disney-provided repellent at locations throughout the park, especially in the warm months.

Take advantage of parades. Ride a star attraction during a parade, when lines ease considerably. (But be careful not to get stuck on the wrong side of the parade route when it starts, or you may never get across.)

Pick up a map. You'll find maps at City Hall, near the park's Town Square entrance. Also get a *Times Guide,* which lists showtimes, character-greeting times, and hours for attractions and restaurants. If you are using your smartphone to access maps and wait times, bring a charger or back-up battery; the app can be draining.

Book character meals early. Main Street, U.S.A.'s The Crystal Palace, A Buffet with Character has breakfast, lunch, and dinner with Winnie the Pooh, Tigger, and friends. All three meals at the Fairy Tale Dining experience in Cinderella Castle are extremely popular—so much so that you should reserve your spot six months out. The same advice goes for booking the full-service dinner at Be Our Guest Restaurant in the Beast's Castle in Fantasyland. All meals can be booked 180 days in advance of your visit.

Main Street, U.S.A.

With its pastel Victorian-style buildings, antique automobiles ahoohga-oohga-ing, sparkling sidewalks, and an atmosphere of what one writer has called "almost hysterical joy," Main Street is more than a mere conduit to the other enchantments of the Magic Kingdom. It's where the spell is first cast.

You emerge from beneath the Walt Disney World Railroad Station into a realization of one of the most tenacious American dreams. The perfect street in the perfect small town in a perfect moment of time is burnished to jewel-like quality, thanks to a four-fifths-scale reduction, nightly cleanings with high-pressure hoses, and constant repainting. And it's a very sunny world, thanks to an outpouring of welcoming entertainment: live bands, barbershop quartets, and background music from Disney films and American musicals played over loudspeakers. Horse-drawn trolleys and omnibuses with their horns tooting chug along the street. Vendors in Victorian costumes sell balloons and popcorn. And Cinderella's famous castle floats enchantingly in the distance where Main Street disappears.

Although attractions with a capital "A" are minimal on Main Street, there are plenty of inducements—namely, shops and eateries—to while away your time and part you from your money. The largest of these, the Emporium, is often the last stop for souvenir hunters at day's end. At the Main Street Bakery, you can find your favorite Starbucks latte and a sandwich or baked treats like cupcakes and brownies. The Harmony Barber Shop lets you step back in time for a haircut ($18 for children 9 and under, $19 for anyone older). Babies or tots get free Mickey Ears, a souvenir lock of hair, and a certificate if it's their first haircut ever, but you pay $25 for the experience. At the Town Square Theater, Mickey Mouse meets you for photos and autographs. While you're here, stock up on batteries and memory cards or disposable cameras.

Be sure to check out the proprietors' names above the shops: Roy O. Disney, etched above the Main Street Confectionery, is the name of Walt's brother. Dick Nunis, former chairman of Walt Disney Attractions, is honored above the bakery. At the Hall of Champions, Card Walker—the "Practitioner of Psychiatry and Justice of the Peace"—is a one-time executive-committee chairman. For more insight on such details, stop by City Hall, or take the Keys to the Kingdom tour.

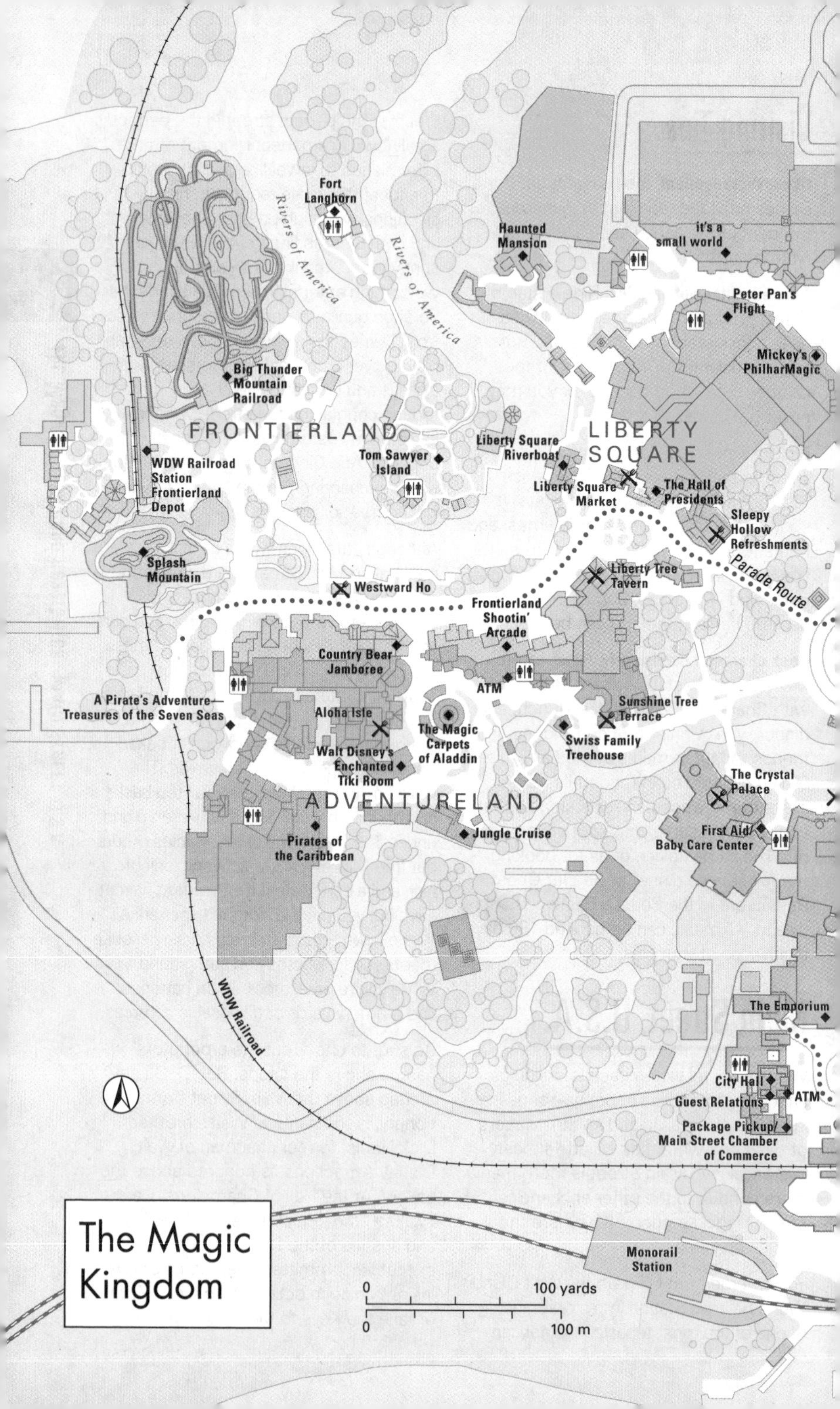

The Magic Kingdom

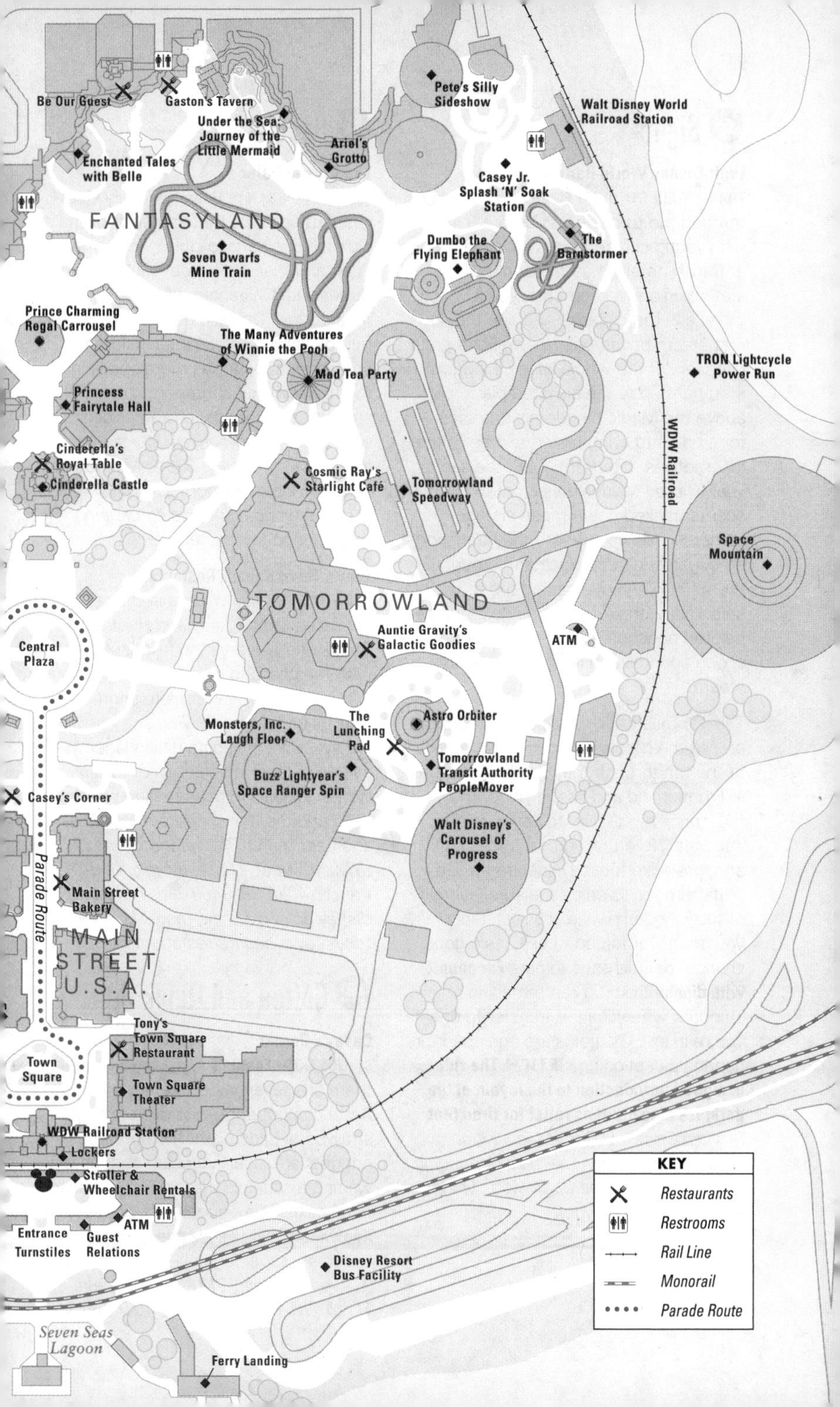
Be Our Guest
Gaston's Tavern
Under the Sea: Journey of the Little Mermaid
Ariel's Grotto
Pete's Silly Sideshow
Walt Disney World Railroad Station
Enchanted Tales with Belle
Casey Jr. Splash 'N' Soak Station
FANTASYLAND
Seven Dwarfs Mine Train
Dumbo the Flying Elephant
The Barnstormer
Prince Charming Regal Carrousel
The Many Adventures of Winnie the Pooh
Mad Tea Party
TRON Lightcycle Power Run
Princess Fairytale Hall
WDW Railroad
Cinderella's Royal Table
Cinderella Castle
Cosmic Ray's Starlight Café
Tomorrowland Speedway
Space Mountain
TOMORROWLAND
Central Plaza
Auntie Gravity's Galactic Goodies
ATM
The Lunching Pad
Astro Orbiter
Monsters, Inc. Laugh Floor
Buzz Lightyear's Space Ranger Spin
Tomorrowland Transit Authority PeopleMover
Casey's Corner
Walt Disney's Carousel of Progress
Parade Route
Main Street Bakery
MAIN STREET U.S.A.
Tony's Town Square Restaurant
Town Square
Town Square Theater
WDW Railroad Station
Lockers
Stroller & Wheelchair Rentals
ATM
Entrance Turnstiles
Guest Relations
Disney Resort Bus Facility
Seven Seas Lagoon
Ferry Landing
KEY
Restaurants
Restrooms
Rail Line
Monorail
Parade Route

Sights

Walt Disney World Railroad

TRAIN/TRAIN STATION | **FAMILY** | If you click through the turnstile just before 9 am with young children in tow, wait at the entrance before crossing beneath the station. In a few moments, you'll hear a whistle in the distance and see the day's first steam-driven train arrive. For a great overview of the whole Magic Kingdom, step right up to the elevated platform above the Magic Kingdom's entrance for a ride into living history. Some of the locomotives date from 1928, the same year Mickey Mouse was created. Disney scouts tracked down these vintage carriers in Mexico (where they transported sugarcane in the Yucatán), brought them back, and overhauled them. They're splendid, with striped awnings, brightly painted benches, authoritative "choo-choo" sounds, and hissing plumes of steam.

The 1½-mile track runs along the perimeter of the Magic Kingdom, with much of the trip through the woods, and stops in Frontierland and Fantasyland. The four trains run at five- to seven-minute intervals. Note that you can't load bulky strollers—like those Disney rents. Go midafternoon to enjoy a leisurely circuit of the Kingdom while you rest. Since you are never forced to exit, it's a good chance for little ones to nap. **For people with disabilities:** You can remain in a standard wheelchair or transfer to one if you're in an ECV. Trains are equipped for handheld-captioning. **■ TIP→ The ride is a good introduction to the layout of the park; it's also great as relief for tired feet.** ✉ *Main Street, U.S.A., Magic Kingdom* ☞ *Duration: 21 mins. or less depending where you disembark. Crowds: Moderate. Audience: All ages.*

Restaurants

The Crystal Palace

$$$$ | **AMERICAN** | **FAMILY** | A lovely Victorian setting is the perfect place for the old-fashioned and lovable Winnie the Pooh and friends to greet your kids via A Buffet with Character, offered here three meals a day. Upscale goodies are served for adults while a separate children's spread features foods more appealing to them. **Known for:** shrimp, meat-carving, and dessert stations; character dining with Disney favorites; all-you-can-eat buffet. [$] *Average main: $39* ✉ *Main Street, U.S.A., Magic Kingdom* ☎ *407/939–3463* 🌐 *disneyworld.disney.go.com/dining/magic-kingdom/crystal-palace.*

Tony's Town Square Restaurant

$$$ | **ITALIAN** | **FAMILY** | Inspired by the animated classic *Lady and the Tramp,* Tony's offers everything from spaghetti with meatballs to smoked pork belly with cremini mushrooms to shrimp scampi with linguini. Wine and beer are available, including Italian lagers and an extensive selection of Italian wines. **Known for:** hand-tossed pizza pie; Lady and the Tramp references; wine-and-beer menu. [$] *Average main: $27* ✉ *Main Street, U.S.A., Magic Kingdom* ☎ *407/939–3463* 🌐 *disneyworld.disney.go.com/dining/magic-kingdom/tonys-town-square-restaurant.*

Coffee and Quick Bites

Casey's Corner

$ | **HOT DOG** | **FAMILY** | At Casey's Corner there are seven ways to enjoy a classic American hot dog—one even features strawberry-bacon jam. The corn-dog nuggets are a perfect snack to grab while waiting for the parade, and try a pressed penny silk pie for a taste of yesterday. **Known for:** chili-cheese fries; plant-based sausage dogs; all-beef hot dogs. [$] *Average main: $12* ✉ *Main Street, U.S.A., Magic Kingdom* ☎ *407/939–3463* disneyworld.disney.go.com/dining/magic-kingdom/caseys-corner.

Main Street Bakery

$ | **AMERICAN** | Most people stop here on their way into the park—and end up waiting in their first long line of the day. Instead, return to the Main Street Bakery in the afternoon for a coffee and a delicious brownie. **Known for:** giant cinnamon rolls; Starbucks beverages; breakfast to go. *Average main: $6* *Main Street, U.S.A., Magic Kingdom* *407/939–3463* *disneyworld.disney.go.com/dining/magic-kingdom/main-street-bakery.*

Performing Arts

MAGIC KINGDOM SPECTACLES

★ Disney Festival of Fantasy Parade

FESTIVALS | Who'd want to miss a parade that delivers 12, entertainment-packed minutes of Disney characters and royalty, a Steampunk-inspired, fire-breathing dragon, elaborate towering floats, and handsome pairs of dancers twirling to some of Disney's best tunes? This daily 3 pm parade celebrates Walt's legacy with vignettes featuring the glamour, drama, and fun of classic films like *Sleeping Beauty, Beauty and the Beast,* and *Peter Pan* while also catering to fans of contemporary box-office hits like *Brave* and *Frozen.* The colorful pageant of nine floats features amazing costumes, inventive technology, a cast of nearly 100 gung-ho performers, and a score that invites singing along with familiar medleys.

From the 50-foot-long topiary garden float of Disney royal couples led by dancers in ball gowns with iridescent feathers to the 32-foot-tall Airship float finale with Mickey and Minnie, the parade energizes spectators as it rolls past. A Lost Boy from *Peter Pan* might grab your hand and kiss it. A stilt-walker might lean into your camera for a snapshot. You'll hear viewers gasp or shout when the towering 53-foot-long, green-eyed Maleficent Dragon, created with help from Tony Award–winning designer Michael Curry, rears its head and spews flames. **For people with disabilities:** There are viewing areas for guests in wheelchairs along the route; ask any cast member for guidance. A sign-language schedule is available at Guest Relations.

TIP→ The parade runs from Frontierland to Town Square. Check your guide map for the complete route. Find shade beneath a Frontierland porch at least an hour before showtime. If you've seen the parade, this is a good time to head for popular rides in Fantasyland or Tomorrowland while crowds gather along the route. *Magic Kingdom* *Duration: 12 mins. Crowds: Heavy. Audience: All ages.*

Mickey's Royal Friendship Faire

CONCERTS | **FAMILY** | The Cinderella Castle forecourt provides the perfect location for several daily performances of this celebration of friendship starring Mickey Mouse, Minnie Mouse, Donald Duck, Daisy Duck, Goofy, and their friends. In their 50th anniversary costumes, Mickey and pals interact with new Disney characters: Tiana and others from the Land of the Bewitching Bayous arrive, moving to a Dixieland beat, with Goofy; Donald brings a troupe of rowdy Vikings while Daisy's friends, Rapunzel and Flynn, encourage them to sing instead of carouse; the final newcomers are the popular *Frozen* characters Elsa, Anna, and Olaf the snowman. For the finale, everyone takes the stage for the new original song "Where the Magic Feels Like Home." **TIP→ If you want to sit (and don't mind an obstructed view) try to arrive 30 to 40 minutes before showtime to snag a seat on the bench. For an unobstructed view, you can stand on the pavement near the stage.** *Central Plaza, Magic Kingdom* *Duration: 20 mins. Crowds: Heavy. Audience: All ages.*

FIREWORKS AND NIGHTTIME SHOWS

Both in the theme parks and around the hotel-side waterways, Walt Disney World offers up a wealth of fabulous sound-and-light shows after the sun goes down. WDW is one of the Earth's largest single consumers of fireworks—perhaps even rivaling mainland China. Traditionally, sensational short shows have been held at the Magic Kingdom just before closing. Starting times might vary throughout the year, so just ask a Disney host or Guest Relations for the evening's schedule.

Fireworks are only part of the evening entertainment. Disney's latest technology creates projections on Cinderella Castle, making it seem as if the icon is actually moving. Scenes of Disney movies play, characters scamper around the towers, at one point the turrets turn into a rocket ship ready to blast off. These effects are so jaw-dropping that Disney had to expand the Central Plaza to accommodate more guests. For the best viewing, stand in front Cinderella Castle or on Main Street.

■ **TIP→ If you've seen the nighttime shows before, either exit before they begin, or take the time to ride Big Thunder Mountain or Fantasyland attractions while most crowds are in another section of the park. You can continue to ride up until the park closes, so if you don't want to leave early, consider staying deep within the park until closing time and then exiting after most of the crowds are gone. Disney won't kick you out!**

Beacons of Magic

SOUND/LIGHT SHOW | FAMILY | For its 50th Anniversary Celebration, Disney added the Beacons of Magic, a projection light show, at all four theme parks. At the Magic Kingdom, it features images dancing on Cinderella's Castle and usually happens at dusk (check your times guide). However, as this show is very short, lasting just one minute, only make your way over if it's convenient. ✉ *Central Plaza, Magic Kingdom.*

Disney Enchantment

SOUND/LIGHT SHOW | FAMILY | Crafted especially for the 50th Anniversary Celebration, Disney Enchantment is an all-new show that combines fireworks, lights, projections, and Tinker Bell's iconic flight. Everyone will be singing along to a medley of favorite Disney hits, including reimagined songs from *The Princess and the Frog, Moana*, and *Frozen 2*. For the best viewing, find a spot along Main Street at least 30 minutes before the show is scheduled to begin. ✉ *Main Street, U.S.A., Magic Kingdom* 🌐 *disneyworld.disney.go.com/entertainment/magic-kingdom/disney-enchantment.*

Shopping

Crystal Arts

GLASSWARE | This shop dazzles with Arribas Brothers–engraved crystal pieces like a sparkling Cinderella coach or an iconic glass slipper in one of many sizes (though none will fit your foot!). ■ **TIP→ Be sure to visit the glass studio and its 2,100°F furnaces in the back, where a glassblower explains the process while creating wineglasses and bowls. Fascinating!** ✉ *Main Street, U.S.A., Magic Kingdom* 🌐 *disneyworld.disney.go.com/shops/crystal-arts.*

The Emporium

SOUVENIRS | FAMILY | This 17,000-square-foot department store (strategically placed right before the exit) is one of the largest souvenir shops in any of the parks. You'll find thousands of Disney character products, from pins to plush toys. Princess items rock, the costume jewelry is reasonably priced, and there seem to be enough Mickey sweatshirts and T's to clothe everyone in the entire park. Ask cast members about deals or marked-down merchandise. Also available here are MagicBands, colorful wristbands that can be linked with your My Disney Experience app to enter the parks, buy food and merchandise, and even unlock your Disney resort room.

Main Street, U.S.A., Magic Kingdom *disneyworld.disney.go.com/shops/magic-kingdom/emporium.*

Uptown Jewelers

JEWELRY & WATCHES | This upscale boutique is a treasure chest of jewelry, figurines, art, and designer handbags and accessories. It's here you can buy Pandora's Disney Park Collection gems and charms and order canvases from a computerized kiosk. *Main Street, U.S.A., Magic Kingdom* *disneyworld.disney.go.com/shops/magic-kingdom/uptown-jewelers.*

Adventureland

From the scrubbed brick, manicured lawns, and meticulously pruned trees of the Central Plaza, an artfully dilapidated wooden bridge leads to the jungles of Adventureland. Here, South African cape honeysuckle droops, Brazilian bougainvillea drapes, Mexican flame vines cling, spider plants clone, and three varieties of palm trees sway. The bright, all-American, singalong tunes that fill the air along Main Street and Central Plaza are replaced by the recorded repetitions of trumpeting elephants, pounding drums, and squawking parrots. The architecture is a mishmash of the best of Thailand, the Middle East, the Caribbean, Africa, and Polynesia, arranged in an inspired disorder that recalls comic-book fantasies of far-off places.

Once contained within the Pirates of the Caribbean attraction, Captain Jack Sparrow and the crew of the Black Pearl are taking over more of Adventureland. You can get pirate and mermaid gear from Plaza del Sol Caribe Bazaar. At A Pirate's Adventure: Treasures of the Seven Seas, embark on an interactive quest with a pirate map and talisman to complete "raids" through Adventureland as you fight off pirate enemies along the way. Shiver me timbers—it's a pirate's life for ye!

Sights

Jungle Cruise

AMUSEMENT RIDE | FAMILY | Cruise through three continents and along four rivers: the Congo, the Nile, the Mekong, and the Amazon. The canopied launches are loaded, the safari-suited guides spin the helm, and the *Irrawady Irma* or *Mongala Millie* is off for another "perilous" journey. The guide's shtick is surprisingly funny in a wry and cornball way, provided he or she has mastered the art of enunciation. Along the way, you'll encounter Disney's famed Audio-Animatronics creatures of the African veld: bathing elephants, slinky pythons, an irritated rhinoceros, and a bunch of hyperactive hippos. Then there's Old Smiley, the crocodile, who's always waiting for a handout—or, as the guide quips, "a foot out."

The animals are early-generation and crude by Disney standards—anyone who's seen the real thing at the Animal Kingdom or even a good zoo won't be impressed. Unless you're an old-school Disney fan, the Jungle Cruise isn't really worth longer than a 45 minute wait. **For people with disabilities:** Several boats have lifts that allow wheelchair access. The ride is equipped for assisted-listening, and sign language is provided some days. **TIP→ Don't go after dark—you miss too much.** *Adventureland, Magic Kingdom* *Duration: 10 mins. Crowds: Heavy. Audience: All ages.*

The Magic Carpets of Aladdin

AMUSEMENT RIDE | FAMILY | Brightening the lush Adventureland landscape is this jewel-tone ride around a giant genie's bottle. You can control your own four-passenger, state-of-the-art carpet with a front-seat lever that moves it up and down and a rear-seat button that pitches it forward or backward. Part of the fun is dodging the right-on aim of a water-spewing "camel." The ride is short but a big hit with kids, who are also dazzled by the colorful gems implanted in the surrounding

Adventureland Adventure Number 1: Being shipwrecked with the Swiss Family Robinson and exploring their tree house.

pavement. Parents must ride with toddlers. **For people with disabilities:** There's ramp access for guests in wheelchairs. If you're in an ECV, you must transfer to a standard wheelchair. **■TIP→ Lines here are relatively short and move fairly quickly: visit when Pirates of the Caribbean or Jungle Cruise have long lines—they may have shortened by the time you're done with this ride.** ✉ *Adventureland, Magic Kingdom* ☞ *Duration: 3 mins. Crowds: Heavy. Audience: All ages.*

★ Pirates of the Caribbean

AMUSEMENT RIDE | FAMILY | This is one of the few rides in the world that inspired a film (*Haunted Mansion* with Eddie Murphy and *Jungle Cruise* with The Rock are the others) rather than the other way around. The gracious arched entrance soon gives way to a dusty dungeon, redolent of dampness and of a spooky, scary past. Lanterns flicker as your boat sails, and a ghostly voice intones, "Dead men tell no tales." Next, a deserted beach, strewn with shovels, a skeleton, and a disintegrating map indicating buried treasure prefaces this story of greed, lust, and destruction. You'll pass right through a water-mist screen featuring the maniacal mug of Davy Jones, complete with squirming tentacle beard and barnacle-encrusted hat. Emerging from a pitch-black tunnel after a mild, tummy-tickling drop, you're caught in the line of fire as a pirate ship cannon blasts away at a stone fortress. Look for Captain Barbossa, evil nemesis of Captain Jack Sparrow. Audio-Animatronics pirates hoist the Jolly Roger while brave soldiers scurry to defend the fort—to no avail.

The wild antics of the pirates—Captain Jack Sparrow pops up in several situations—result in a conflagration; the town goes up in flames, and all go to their just reward amid a catchy chorus of "A Pirate's Life for Me." **For people with disabilities:** Boarding requires transferring from a standard wheelchair to the ride vehicle; the very small flume drop may make the attraction inappropriate for those with limited upper-body strength or those wearing neck or back braces. The attraction is quipped for audio-description and handheld-captioning devices. ■ **TIP→ It's best to ride in the heat of the afternoon, and lines move steadily through the air-conditioned attraction.** ✉ *Adventureland, Magic Kingdom* ☞ *Duration: 12 mins. Crowds: Moderate. Audience: All but very young kids.*

Swiss Family Treehouse

AMUSEMENT RIDE | **FAMILY** | Inspired by the classic novel by Johann Wyss about the adventures of the Robinson family, who were shipwrecked en route to America, the tree house shows what you can do with a big faux tree and a lot of imagination. Disney detail abounds: the kitchen sink is a giant clamshell; the boys' room, strewn with clothing, has two hammocks instead of beds; and an ingenious system of rain barrels and bamboo pipes provides running water in every room. As you clamber around the narrow wooden steps and rope bridges that connect the rooms in this split-level dwelling, notice the Spanish moss. It's real, but the tree itself—some 90 feet in diameter, with more than 1,000 branches—was constructed by the props department. The 300,000 leaves are vinyl. Toddlers unsteady on their feet might have trouble with the stairs. **For people with disabilities:** With its 100 steps and lack of narration, this attraction gets low ratings among those with mobility and visual impairments. ■ **TIP→ If you're with children 4 to 12 who like to explore, plan to climb while you're already in Adventureland.** ✉ *Adventureland, Magic Kingdom* ☞ *Duration: Up to you. Crowds: Light to moderate. Audience: All ages.*

Walt Disney's Enchanted Tiki Room

AMUSEMENT RIDE | **FAMILY** | The latest version of Disney's first Audio-Animatronics attraction brings back the original show, Tropical Serenade. Winged hosts Jose, Fritz, Pierre, Michael, and the boys take you on a tour of the attraction while cracking lots of jokes. The original ditty "In the Tiki, Tiki, Tiki, Tiki, Tiki Room" is second only to "it's a small world" as the Disney song you most love to hate. Many people do hate this attraction, finding the talking birds obnoxious and the music too loud and peppy. But you can also hear old-timers singing along to "Let's All Sing Like the Birdies Sing," tweet, tweet tweet, tweet, tweet. Plus, it's a haven of cool in the summer heat. **For people with disabilities:** Accessible for those in standard wheelchairs; equipped for handheld-captioning, audio description, and assisted-listening devices. ■ **TIP→ Go when you need to sit down with air-conditioning.** ✉ *Adventureland, Magic Kingdom* ☞ *Duration: 12 mins. Crowds: Moderate. Audience: All ages.*

Coffee and Quick Bites

★ Aloha Isle

$ | **CARIBBEAN** | **FAMILY** | Few snacks are so popular as to have spawned their own merchandise, but the Pineapple Float at Aloha Isle has done just that. Dole pineapple ice cream on pineapple juice is one of the iconic treats offered at the Magic Kingdom, and it can only be found at Disney or at the Dole Plantation in Hawaii. **Known for:** pineapple and orange Bundt cakes; pineapple ice cream; famous Pineapple Floats. [$] *Average main: $6* ✉ *Adventureland, Magic Kingdom* ☎ *407/939–3463* 🌐 *disneyworld.disney.go.com/dining/magic-kingdom/aloha-isle.*

Sunshine Tree Terrace

$ | **ICE CREAM** | **FAMILY** | If you're looking for a pick-me-up after climbing the entire Swiss Family Treehouse, stop by the Sunshine Tree Terrace for a root beer float. Kids will enjoy fresh orange or strawberry ice cream just as much as vanilla or chocolate. **Known for:** fruit-flavored ice cream; ice cream floats; pot stickers. [$] *Average main: $6* ✉ *Adventureland, Magic Kingdom* ☎ *407/939–3463* 🌐 *disneyworld.disney.go.com/dining/magic-kingdom/sunshine-tree-terrace.*

Adventureland Adventure Number 2: Gliding through the muggy, steamy Caribbean world of pirates. Yo ho ho!

Shopping

Agrabah Bazaar

SOUVENIRS | FAMILY | A Hollywood-fantasized version of an open-air Arabian market, this wildly colorful shop is the retail equivalent of a maharaja's treasure. Shelves are replete with Aladdin wear and Jasmine costumes, maracas and other inexpensive percussion instruments, gold- and silver-plated bangles, collectible pins, sunglasses, housewares, plush toys, and snappy safari hats. ✉ *Adventureland, Magic Kingdom* 🌐 *disneyworld.disney.go.com/shops/magic-kingdom/agrabah-bazaar.*

Plaza del Sol Caribe Bazaar

SOUVENIRS | FAMILY | Just outside the Pirates of the Caribbean, you can stock up on pirate hats, swords, flintlocks, and hooks-for-hands. T-shirts, candy, and figurines are plentiful, but the ultimate scalawag topper is a Captain Jack Sparrow hat complete with braids. ✉ *Adventureland, Magic Kingdom* 🌐 *disneyworld.disney.go.com/shops/magic-kingdom/plaza-del-sol-caribe-bazaar.*

Frontierland

Frontierland recalls the American frontier and is planted with mesquite, twisted Peruvian pepper trees, slash pines, and cacti. The period evoked here is the latter half of the 19th century, and the West is being won by Disney cast members dressed in checked shirts, leather vests, cowboy hats, and brightly colored neckerchiefs. Banjo and fiddle music twangs from tree to tree, and every once in a while a line dance flash mob will erupt in front of the Country Bear Jamboree. (Beware of hovering seagulls that migrate to the parks during cooler months—they've been known to snatch snacks.)

The screams that drown out the string music aren't the result of a horse throwing a cowboy. They come from two of the Magic Kingdom's more thrilling rides: Splash Mountain, an elaborate flume ride, and Big Thunder Mountain Railroad, a roller coaster. The Walt Disney World Railroad tunnels past a colorful scene in Splash Mountain and drops you off between it and Thunder Mountain.

Sights

★ Big Thunder Mountain Railroad

AMUSEMENT RIDE | FAMILY | Set in gold-rush days, this thrilling roller coaster simulates a runaway train. It's a bumpy ride with several good drops (pregnant women and guests wearing back, neck, or leg braces should avoid this one). There are moments when you feel like you're going to fly right off the tracks. Overall, it's more fun than scary, and you'll see kids as young as 7 lining up to ride, though there is a 40-inch height requirement. The train rushes and rattles past 20 Audio-Animatronics figures—mostly critters—as well as $300,000 worth of genuine antique mining equipment, tumbleweeds, a derelict mining town, hot springs, and a flash flood.

The 197-foot mountain landscape is based on the windswept scenery of Arizona's Monument Valley, and, thanks to 650 tons of steel, 4,675 tons of concrete, and 16,000 gallons of paint, it replicates the area's gorges, tunnels, caverns, and dry river beds. **For people with disabilities:** You must be able to step into the ride vehicle and walk short distances. Service animals aren't permitted. **■ TIP→ To avoid long lines go first thing in the morning or during a parade. The ride is most exciting at night, when you can't anticipate the curves and the track's rattling really sounds as if something's about to give.** ✉ *Frontierland, Magic Kingdom* ☞ *Duration: 4 mins. Crowds: Absolutely. Audience: Not small kids.*

Country Bear Jamboree

PERFORMANCE VENUE | FAMILY | Wisecracking, cornpone, lovelorn Audio-Animatronics bears joke, sing, and play country music and 1950s rock and roll in this stage show. Even timid youngsters love them. The emcee, the massive but debonair Henry, leads the stellar cast of Grizzly Hall, which includes the robust Trixie, who laments love lost while perching on a swing suspended from the ceiling; Bubbles, Bunny, and Beulah, harmonizing on "All the Guys That Turn Me on Turn Me Down"; and Big Al, the off-key cult figure who has inspired his own shopping kiosk. **For people with disabilities:** Wheelchair accessible; reflective captioning provided; equipped for assisted-listening devices. If you lip-read, ask to sit up front. **■ TIP→ Visit during an afternoon parade or late in the day. Stand to the far left in the anteroom for the front rows and to the far right for the last row, where small kids can perch atop seats to see better.** ✉ *Frontierland, Magic Kingdom* ☞ *Duration: 17 mins. Crowds: Moderate. Audience: All ages.*

★ Splash Mountain

AMUSEMENT RIDE | FAMILY | One of the most popular thrill rides after Space Mountain, this log-flume water ride was based on animated sequences in Disney's 1946 film *Song of the South*. Here the Audio-Animatronics creations of Brer Rabbit, Brer Bear, Brer Fox, and a menagerie of other Brer beasts frolic in bright, cartoonlike settings. Settle into the eight-person, hollowed-out logs, and the fun begins.

As the boat carries you up the mountain, Brer Rabbit's silhouette hops merrily ahead to the tune of the ride's theme song, "Time to Be Moving Along." Every time some critter makes a grab for the bunny, your log boat drops out of reach. But Brer Fox has been studying his book *How to Catch a Rabbit*, and our lop-eared friend looks as if he's destined for the pot. Things don't look so good for the flumers, either. You get one heart-stopping pause at the top of the mountain—just long enough to grab the safety bar—and then the boat plummets about five stories at a 45-degree angle into a large, wet briar patch. It's enough to reach speeds of 40 mph—and makes you feel weightless. Clench your teeth and smile:

Coasting down Splash Mountain in Frontierland will put some zip in your doo-dah and some water on your clothes.

as you begin to drop, a flashbulb pops. Another photographic memento for sale as you "Zip-a-Dee-Doo-Dah" your way to the next ride.

You might get wet, so plan accordingly. If you need to use Baby Swap, you can take the young ones to a play area in a cave under the attraction; riders must be at least 40 inches tall. Do not ride if you're pregnant or have heart, back, or neck problems. **For people with disabilities:** You must be able to step into the ride vehicle and walk short distances. Service animals aren't permitted. ■ **TIP→ Disney has announced plans to re-theme this attraction around the hit movie "The Princess and the Frog." Although this process could take years, the same track will most likely be used, so check to see if this attraction will be open during your visit.** ✉ *Frontierland, Magic Kingdom* ☞ *Duration: 11 mins. Crowds: Yes! Audience: Not small kids.*

Tom Sawyer Island

OTHER ATTRACTION | **FAMILY** | Tom Sawyer Island is a playground of hills, trees, rocks, and shrubs. Most attractions are on the main island, where your raft docks. The Mystery Mine is like a secret passageway to exploration. Children love Injun Joe's Cave, where there are lots of columns and crevices from which to jump out and startle siblings. As you explore the shoreline on the dirt paths, watch out for the barrel bridge—the whole contraption bounces at every step.

On the other island is Fort Langhorn, a log fortress from which you can fire air guns with great booms and cracks at the passing *Liberty Belle* riverboat. **For people with disabilities:** With its stairs, bridges, inclines, and narrow caves, this attraction isn't negotiable by those using a wheelchair. ■ **TIP→ Get away from the crowds here. Watch toddlers closely, as it's easy to lose track of them.** ✉ *Frontierland, Magic Kingdom* ☞ *Duration: Up to you. Crowds: Light. Audience: Kids and tweens.*

Coffee and Quick Bites

Westward Ho

$ | **AMERICAN** | **FAMILY** | This cart is ready for hungry trailblazers. Stop here to enjoy jalapeño poppers, corn-dog nuggets, and a bear claw, complete with a fresh-off-the-trail frozen lemonade. **Known for:** hearty breakfast sandwiches; bacon on a skewer; frozen slushies. *Average main: $6 ✉ Frontierland, Magic Kingdom ☎ 407/939–3463 🌐 disneyworld.disney.go.com/dining/magic-kingdom/westward-ho.*

Shopping

Big Al's

TOYS | **FAMILY** | This merchandise cart across the walkway from the Country Bear Jamboree has Davy Crockett coonskin caps, cowboy hats like Woody wears in *Toy Story,* personalized sheriff's badges, and other gear that draws oohs and aahs from aspiring cowboys and cowgirls. *✉ Frontierland, Magic Kingdom 🌐 disneyworld.disney.go.com/shops/magic-kingdom/big-als.*

Liberty Square

The rough-and-tumble West gently folds into Colonial America as Liberty Square picks up where Frontierland leaves off. The weathered siding gives way to solid brick and neat clapboard. The mesquite and cactus are replaced by stately oaks and masses of azaleas. The theme is Colonial history, which is portrayed here as solid Yankee. The buildings, topped with weather vanes and exuding prosperity, are pure New England.

A replica of the Liberty Bell, crack and all, seems an appropriate prop to separate Liberty Square from Frontierland. There's even a Liberty Tree, a more than 150-year-old live oak, transported here from elsewhere on Disney property. Just as the Sons of Liberty hung lanterns on trees as a signal of solidarity after the Boston Tea Party, the Liberty Tree's branches are decorated with 13 lanterns representing the 13 original colonies. Around the square are tree-shaded tables for an alfresco lunch and plenty of carts and fast-food eateries to supply the goods.

Did You Know?

It's hard to keep the Haunted Mansion's 200-odd trunks, chairs, harps, dress forms, statues, rugs, and knickknacks appropriately dusty. Disney buys its dust in five-pound bags and scatters it with a gadget resembling a fertilizer spreader. Word is, enough dust has been dumped since the park's 1971 opening to completely bury the mansion. Where does it all go? Perhaps the voice is right in saying that something will follow you home.

Sights

The Hall of Presidents

PERFORMANCE VENUE | **FAMILY** | With the latest in Disney Audio-Animatronics (this attraction introduced the technology in 1971 and underwent a total high-tech transformation in 2017), this show, housed in a redbrick building inspired by Philadelphia's Independence Hall, tells a moving story of "The Idea of a President." Producers reshot the accompanying film in high-definition video and added more than 130 images culled from the National Archives, Library of Congress, and other collections. A digital soundtrack, LED lighting, and a dramatic narration further enhance the experience. The film covers more than two centuries of U.S. history and emphasizes what it means to lead the nation. Both George Washington and Abraham Lincoln grab a bit of the spotlight, the latter by delivering his famous Gettysburg Address.

Liberty Square's Haunted Mansion by day—pretty scary or just pretty? You decide.

The best part of the show is a roll call of all 45 U.S. presidents. (Fun fact: Joe Biden is officially the 46th president because Grover Cleveland is counted twice due to his having served nonconsecutive terms.) The current president always recites the oath of office. Each chief executive responds with a nod or a wave, and both George Washington and Abraham Lincoln rise from their seats. The robots nod and whisper to each other as the roll call proceeds. Anyone interested in presidential artifacts will enjoy the wait in the lobby area, where First Ladies' dresses, presidential portraits, and even George Washington's dental instruments are on display. **For people with disabilities:** The attraction is wheelchair accessible; enter through a door on the right. Reflective captioning available; equipped for assisted-listening devices. **■TIP→ Visit in the afternoon when a chance to rest will be welcomed.** ✉ *Liberty Square, Magic Kingdom* ☞ *Duration: 22 mins. Crowds: Moderate to heavy. Audience: Not small kids.*

★ Haunted Mansion

AMUSEMENT RIDE | FAMILY | The special effects here are a howl. You're greeted at the creaking iron gates of this Gothic mansion by a lugubrious attendant, who has one of the few jobs at Disney for which smiling is frowned upon, and ushered into a spooky picture gallery. A disembodied voice echoes from the walls: "Welcome, foolish mortals, to the Haunted Mansion. I am your ghost host." An audio system with 30-plus surround-sound speakers ups the ghost-host fright factor. A scream shivers down, the room begins to "stretch," and you're off into one of Disney's classic attractions. Don't rush out of this room when other visitors depart; linger for some ghoulish bonus whispers. Note that as the Haunted Mansion is basically a slow-moving ride in a cocoonlike "doom buggy," it's really scary only for younger children, and that's mostly because of the darkness. If, however, the stretch room proves too scary, see a cast member to exit instead of riding.

Watch the ghostly ballroom dancers, Madame Leota's talking head in the crystal ball, and ghostly footprints that move along a staircase. In the "bride in the attic" scene, keep an eye on the portraits. Just when you think the Imagineers have exhausted their bag of ectoplasmic tricks, you discover that your doom buggy has gained an extra passenger. This is a high-capacity, fast-loading ride, and lines usually move steadily. **For people with disabilities:** Those in wheelchairs must transfer to the doom buggies and take one or more steps; however, if you can walk up to 200 feet, you'll enjoy the preshow as well as the ride's sensations and eerie sounds. Equipped for handheld-captioning and audio-description devices. **■TIP→ When you reach a fork in the queue before entering the mansion, go left through the cemetery for interactive graveyard fun. The Musical Crypt and Secret Library help you forget you're in line. Nighttime adds an extra fright factor.** ✉ *Liberty Square, Magic Kingdom* ☞ *Duration: 8 mins. Crowds: Heavy. Audience: Not small kids.*

Liberty Square Riverboat

AMUSEMENT RIDE | FAMILY | An old-fashioned steamboat, the *Liberty Belle* is authentic, from its calliope whistle and the gingerbread trim on its three decks to the boilers that produce the steam that drives the big rear paddle wheel. The boat misses authenticity on only one count: there's no mustachioed captain needed to guide it during the ride around the Rivers of America. That task is performed by an underwater rail. The 1½-mile cruise is slow and not exactly thrilling, but there are lovely views of Tom Sawyer Island and surrounding attractions. Children like exploring the boat, and lines move quickly. **For people with disabilities:** Wheelchair accessible; enter through exit on right or left. **■TIP→ Come when you need a break from the crowds. Check the Times Guide—the riverboat is open only seasonally.** ✉ *Liberty Square, Magic Kingdom* ☞ *Duration: 15 mins. Crowds: Light to moderate. Audience: All ages.*

Restaurants

★ Liberty Tree Tavern

$$$$ | AMERICAN | FAMILY | Now serving beer and wine, this formerly dry tavern holds a prime spot on the parade route, so you can have a good meal while you wait. Each of the six dining rooms commemorates a historical U.S. figure, such as Betsy Ross or Benjamin Franklin. **Known for:** Samuel Adams Boston Lager and wine; Patriot's Platter of roast turkey, sliced pot roast, and carved pork roast; multiroom, authentic-looking Colonial decor. [$] *Average main: $39* ✉ *Liberty Square, Magic Kingdom* ☎ *407/939–3463* 🌐 *disneyworld.disney.go.com/dining/magic-kingdom/liberty-tree-tavern.*

Coffee and Quick Bites

Liberty Square Market

$ | AMERICAN | FAMILY | The Liberty Square Market is filled with all sorts of fruits, trail mixes, yogurts, and cheese. Those looking for a heftier option can pick up a turkey leg to enjoy with their orange. **■TIP→ This place is located perfectly along the parade route: grab a spot in the shade, and send one adult over to pick up a few items while you wait. Known for:** healthful snacks; great for grab-and-go items; location on the parade route. [$] *Average main: $3* ✉ *Liberty Square, Magic Kingdom* ☎ *407/939–3463* 🌐 *disneyworld.disney.go.com/dining/magic-kingdom/liberty-square-market.*

Sleepy Hollow Refreshments

$ | AMERICAN | FAMILY | What food does the Headless Horseman like the most? It must be waffles, because Sleepy Hollow Refreshments has waffles a plenty. **Known for:** hidden gem; plenty of seating; rarely crowded, even at lunch time. [$] *Average main: $11* ✉ *Liberty Square, Magic Kingdom* ☎ *407/939–3463* 🌐 *disneyworld.disney.go.com/dining/magic-kingdom/sleepy-hollow.*

Shopping

Memento Mori

SOUVENIRS | FAMILY | If you can't get enough of the Haunted Mansion, visit this themed shop along the crosswalk between Liberty Square and Fantasyland. Here you'll find not only Haunted Mansion clothing and art prints, but also ghosts in a jar, mugs, and even Haunted Mansion–themed salt and pepper shakers. ✉ *Liberty Square, Magic Kingdom* 🌐 *disneyworld.disney.go.com/shops/magic-kingdom/memento-mori.*

Ye Olde Christmas Shoppe

SOUVENIRS | FAMILY | You might think you've wandered into the North Pole at this quaint store, which sells character-themed stockings and ornaments, Mickey wedding top hats and Minnie bridal veils, plus art, housewares, and collectibles. ✉ *Liberty Square, Magic Kingdom* 🌐 *disneyworld.disney.go.com/shops/magic-kingdom/ye-olde-christmas-shoppe.*

Fantasyland

Walt Disney called this "a timeless land of enchantment," and Fantasyland does conjure pixie dust. Perhaps that's because the fanciful gingerbread houses, gleaming gold turrets, and, of course, the rides are based on Disney-animated movies. What's more, although many of the rides here could ostensibly be classified as those for children, they're packed with enough delightful detail to engage adults, too. Perhaps this is one reason why Fantasyland is always the most heavily trafficked area in the park, with rides and shows that are almost always crowded.

Another reason might be that, in 2012, Fantasyland underwent an expansion—the largest in park history—to increase the number of attractions and experiences. Dumbo the Flying Elephant doubled in size, flying above circus-themed grounds that also include the Great Goofini coaster, starring Goofy as stuntman. A circus-theme Casey Jr. Splash 'N' Soak Station provides water-play respite for kids. Ariel of *The Little Mermaid* invites you to her own state-of-the-art attraction, Under the Sea: Journey of the Little Mermaid. Disney princesses welcome you for a photo op in the glittering Princess Fairytale Hall. You can be part of the show when you join Belle, Lumiere, and Madame Wardrobe of *Beauty and the Beast* at the Enchanted Tales with Belle attraction for a story performance. Meanwhile, Beast might be brooding in his castle, where the Be Our Guest dining room beckons lunch and dinner guests. The musical Seven Dwarfs Mine Train family coaster completes the expansion.

You can enter Fantasyland on foot from Liberty Square and Tomorrowland, or you can arrive via the Walt Disney World Railroad, which has a station here. The classic introduction, however, is wandering through Cinderella Castle.

Sights

Ariel's Grotto

OTHER ATTRACTION | FAMILY | Every mermaid princess should have a giant seashell throne, and that's where Ariel fans can meet the fashionably finned, redheaded beauty. Built into the rock work of Prince Eric's castle, the grotto provides shade for those waiting in the queue and a more secluded experience for families who want to photograph or record the royal meet-up. ✉ *Fantasyland, Magic Kingdom* ☞ *Duration: About 2 mins. Crowds: Yes. Audience: Young kids.*

The Barnstormer

AMUSEMENT RIDE | FAMILY | This coaster stars the Great Goofini, stunt master—a perfect fit for Fantasyland's Storybook Circus area. The twisting, turning roller coaster "flight" takes you high above the circus fun. It's perfect for young children's first thrill ride if they are 35 inches or

Did You Know?

The quintessential Disney icon, Cinderella Castle, was inspired by the palace built by the mad Bavarian king Ludwig II at Neuschwanstein. At 189 feet, it's 100 feet taller than Disneyland's Sleeping Beauty Castle.

taller. Circus props and theme posters tell Goofini's tale with references to some of the short films of Goofy's heyday. **For people with disabilities:** You must be able to walk a few steps from your wheelchair to board the ride. Service animals are not permitted. ✉ *Fantasyland, Magic Kingdom* ☞ *Duration: 1 min. Crowds: Heavy. Audience: All but smallest kids. Height requirement: 35 inches.*

Casey Jr. Splash 'N' Soak Station

WATER PARK | FAMILY | The Casey Jr. circus train has just pulled into town, and train cars full of faux circus animals are taking a break in this circus-theme play area across from Dumbo the Flying Elephant. The critters might not be real, but they sure do put out a lot of water as children run hooting and squealing past spitting camels, spraying elephants, and other water hazards. **For people with disabilities:** Wheelchair accessible. **■TIP→ While the kids cool off and burn energy, parents can take a break and grab a hot dog or soft pretzel from nearby carts. Pack towels and fresh clothing for cooler days.** ✉ *Fantasyland, Magic Kingdom* ☞ *Duration: As long as you like. Crowds: Moderate to heavy. Audience: Young kids.*

Cinderella Castle

NOTABLE BUILDING | FAMILY | Although similar to Disneyland's Sleeping Beauty Castle, at 189 feet this iconic structure is more than 100 feet taller, and, with its elongated towers and lacy fretwork, it's more graceful. Don't miss the elaborate mosaics on the walls of the archway as you rush toward Fantasyland from the Hub. The five panels, measuring some 15 feet high and 10 feet wide were created from a million bits of multicolored Italian glass, silver, and 14-karat gold by mosaicist Hanns-Joachim Scharff. The mosaics tell the story of the little cinder girl as she goes from pumpkin to prince to happily ever after.

The fantasy castle has absolutely real foundations, made of solid steel beams, fiberglass, and 500 gallons of paint. Instead of dungeons, there are service tunnels for the Magic Kingdom's less-than-magical quotidian operations, such as Makeup and Costuming. These are the same tunnels that honeycomb beneath much of the park.

Within the castle's archway is the Bibbidi Bobbidi Boutique, where the "royal treatment" transforms little girls age three and older into princesses or divas. Hair and makeup are by a Fairy Godmother-in-training. The valiant Knight Package offers a heroic makeover that includes hairstyle, sword, and shield. If you have reservations to dine at Cinderella's Royal Table, you enter the castle by way of an ascending spiral staircase. You are attended by costumed waiters and joined by Cinderella and other princesses in one of Disney's most popular character-dining experiences. **For people with disabilities:** For those with limited mobility, elevator access to the dining experience is provided. **■TIP→ Call or book online 180 days ahead, if possible, to reserve the character breakfast, lunch, or dinner at Cinderella's Royal Table.** ✉ *Fantasyland, Magic Kingdom.*

Dumbo the Flying Elephant

AMUSEMENT RIDE | FAMILY | Based on the movie about the gigantic-eared baby elephant who learns he can fly, the ride consists of flying pachyderms, each packing a couple of kids and a parent. A joystick controls your Dumbo's up-and-down movement. A popular feature for parents and children: the Big Top "play while you wait" indoor area chock full of climbing equipment for kids of most ages. As you enter the colorful circus tent, a Disney "ringmaster" hands you a pager that buzzes when it's your turn to join the ride queue. Parents can supervise tots in a small circus ring of play equipment while older kids burn up energy on multilevel climbers like the Thrilling Tower of Flames. Adults enjoy the bench seating. **For people with disabilities:** If using a wheelchair, prepare to transfer

See Lumiere chat with Belle at Enchanted Tales with Belle in Fantasyland.

to a ride vehicle. ■ **TIP→ This is a great place to visit in the afternoon when kids may need to run around and parents may need to sit down. Let the kids enjoy the play area before riding.** ✉ *Fantasyland, Magic Kingdom* ☞ *Duration: 2 mins. Crowds: Heavy. Audience: Young kids.*

★ Enchanted Tales with Belle

PERFORMANCE VENUE | FAMILY | Stroll the path through an artfully planted woodland and meadow to a rustic French cabin complete with waterwheel, where Belle's father, Maurice, tinkers with his inventions. The small homestead oozes Belle's provincial life, with a giant pot hanging in the fireplace and books stacked on a simple wooden chair. Inside her father's workshop, amid blueprints and tools, a giant gold-framed mirror hangs. A costumed cast member welcomes your group to the workshop (*Bonjour!*) and implores everyone to chant, "Take me back to the day Belle and Beast fell in love!" *Voilà!* The mirror becomes an animated screen straight from the Disney film *Beauty and the Beast* before transforming into a portal that leads to an elegant room of Beast's Castle.

Inside, an Audio-Animatronic Madame Armoire encourages you to grab props and play character roles from the "tale as old as time." Then it's on to the library, where a spot-on Audio-Animatronic Lumiere holds court from the mantle. Grab a cushy bench as a coiffed actress playing Belle joins you to perform a scene from the enchanted tale. You'll dance around the room to "Be Our Guest," and you might shed a tear as the interactive story unfolds. This live performance gets to the heart of Disney storytelling, and every participant poses for photos with Belle before a very happy ending. **For people with disabilities:** Wheelchair accessible; equipped for handheld captioning and assisted listening. ■ **TIP→ This is a slow-moving line that is mostly outside, so visit here first thing in the morning.** ✉ *Fantasyland, Magic Kingdom* ☞ *Duration: 15 mins. Crowds: Yes. Audience: All ages; perfect for families.*

it's a small world

AMUSEMENT RIDE | FAMILY | Visiting Walt Disney World and not stopping for this tribute to terminal cuteness—why, the idea is practically un-American. The attraction is essentially a boat ride through different bright-color lands, each representing a continent, complete with landmarks. First created for the 1964–65 New York World's Fair, the original ride opened in Disneyland with the same peppy theme song of international brotherhood and friendship written by the Sherman Brothers (of Mary Poppins fame). You'll float by 450 dolls created by Disney legend Mary Blair—Dutch babies in clogs, Spanish flamenco dancers, sari-wrapped Indians waving temple bells, Swiss yodelers, Japanese kite fliers, Middle East snake charmers, and young French cancan dancers, to name just a few—all singing the earworm song together. Take enchanted tots through again if the line is short. **For people with disabilities:** You can board with your standard wheelchair through the designated entrance; if you use a scooter, transfer to one of the attraction's standard chairs available at the ride entrance. Equipped for handheld-captioning and audio-description devices. ✉ *Fantasyland, Magic Kingdom* ☞ *Duration: 11 mins. Crowds: Heavy. Audience: All ages.*

Mad Tea Party

AMUSEMENT RIDE | FAMILY | This whirling carnival staple is for the vertigo addict looking for a fix. The Disney version is based on its own 1951 film *Alice in Wonderland*, in which the Mad Hatter hosts a tea party for his un-birthday. You hop into oversize, pastel-color teacups and whirl around a giant platter. Add your own spin to the teacup's orbit with the help of the steering wheel in the center. Check out the soused mouse that pops out of the teapot centerpiece. **For people with disabilities:** If using a wheelchair, enter through the exit on right, then transfer to a ride vehicle. ✉ *Fantasyland, Magic Kingdom* ☞ *Duration: 2 mins. Crowds: Moderate. Audience: Small kids.*

★ The Many Adventures of Winnie the Pooh

AMUSEMENT RIDE | FAMILY | The famous honey lover and his exploits in the Hundred Acre Wood are the theme for this ride. You can read posted passages from A. A. Milne's stories as you wait in line. Once you board your "Hunny Pot," Pooh and his friends wish you a "happy windsday." Pooh flies through the air, held aloft by his balloon, in his perennial search for "hunny," and you bounce along with Tigger, ride with the Heffalumps and Woozles, and experience a cloudburst. This ride replaced Mr. Toad's Wild Ride; look for the painting of Mr. Toad handing the deed to Owl. **For people with disabilities:** If using a scooter, see a cast member about transferring to a standard wheelchair for the ride. Equipped for handheld-captioning and audio-description devices. ✉ *Fantasyland, Magic Kingdom* ☞ *Duration: 3 mins. Crowds: Heavy. Audience: Small kids.*

Mickey's PhilharMagic

PERFORMANCE VENUE | FAMILY | Mickey Mouse might be the headliner here, but it's Donald Duck's misadventures—reminiscent of Mickey's as the sorcerer's apprentice in *Fantasia*—that set the comic pace in this 3-D animated film. As you settle into your seat, the on-screen action takes you behind the curtains at a grand concert hall where Donald and Mickey prepare for a performance. But when Donald misuses Mickey's sorcerer's hat, he finds himself on a whirlwind journey that includes a magic carpet ride and an electrifying dip under the sea. And you go along for the ride. On the way, you meet Ariel, Simba, Aladdin, Jasmine, Peter Pan, Tinker Bell, and others.

The film startles with its special-effects technology—you'll smell a fresh-baked apple pie, feel the rush of air as champagne corks pop, and get lost in the action on the 150-foot-wide screen. The 3-D film marks the first time that classic

Disney characters appear in a computer-generated animation attraction. Some of the effects can startle small children, and some of the darker scenes are a bit muddy through the recycled 3-D glasses. **For people with disabilities:** There's a special viewing area for guests in wheelchairs. Reflective captioning is provided; equipped for assisted-listening and audio-description devices. ✉ *Fantasyland, Magic Kingdom* ☞ *Duration: 12 mins. Crowds: Heavy. Audience: All ages.*

Peter Pan's Flight

AMUSEMENT RIDE | FAMILY | This sweet indoor ride was inspired by Sir James M. Barrie's 1904 novel about the boy who wouldn't grow up, which Disney animated in 1953. Aboard two-person magic sailing ships with brightly striped sails, you soar into the skies above London en route to Neverland. Along the way you can see Wendy, Michael, and John get sprinkled with pixie dust while Nana barks below, wave to the Lost Boys, spot the evil Captain Hook, and cheer for the ticktocking, clock-swallowing crocodile who breakfasted on Hook's hand.

Children—especially preschoolers—love this ride. Adults enjoy the dreamy views of London by moonlight. The downsides are the ride's brevity and its low-tech look. **For people with disabilities:** You must transfer from your wheelchair to the ride vehicle. Service animals aren't permitted. Equipped for handheld-captioning and audio-description devices. ✉ *Fantasyland, Magic Kingdom* ☞ *Duration: 2½ mins. Crowds: Heavy. Audience: Small kids.*

Pete's Silly Sideshow

PERFORMANCE VENUE | FAMILY | No other Disney character meet-and-greet location is quite as much fun as Pete's Silly Sideshow, named after the Mickey Mouse archenemy created in 1925. But you won't meet Strongman Pete under this big top, although he does make a poster appearance. Instead, you'll grip and grin with Goofy, Minnie Mouse, Donald Duck, and his sweetheart, Daisy. Each character poses for photos and signs autographs against a sideshow backdrop: the Great Goofini, "Broken Bone Record Holder," in his stunt garb; the Astounding Donaldo dressed as a snake charmer; Minnie Magnifique, pretty in pink feathers, and her "pirouetting Parisian poodles," and Madame Daisy Fortuna with crystal ball as "seer of all fate and destinies." Two queues move guests along fairly quickly, and elaborate themed backdrops offer extra-fun photo ops. ✉ *Fantasyland, Magic Kingdom* ☞ *Duration: About 1–2 mins. per character meet and greet. Crowds: Yes, but double queue makes wait shorter. Audience: Young kids.*

Prince Charming Regal Carrousel

AMUSEMENT RIDE | FAMILY | This ride is great for families and for romantics, young and old. Seventy-two of the 90 dashing wooden steeds date from the original carousel built in 1917 by the Philadelphia Toboggan Company; additional mounts were made of fiberglass. All are meticulously painted, and each one is completely different. One wears a collar of bright yellow roses; another, a quiver of Native American arrows. For a bit of extra magic, look for the horse with a golden ribbon in its tail: this is Cinderella's horse. Eighteen panels beneath the wooden canopy depict scenes from Disney's 1950 film *Cinderella*. As the ride spins, the mirrors sparkle, the fairy lights glitter, and the band organ plays favorite Disney movie tunes. **For people with disabilities:** If using a wheelchair, or if you have a service animal, check with a host for boarding information. ✉ *Fantasyland, Magic Kingdom* ☞ *Duration: 2 mins. Crowds: Moderate to heavy. Audience: Families.*

★ Seven Dwarfs Mine Train

AMUSEMENT RIDE | FAMILY | Quick! Can you name all Seven Dwarfs in seven seconds? Sleepy, Doc, Grumpy, Bashful, Sneezy, Happy, and Dopey. Snow White's hardworking pals display impressive

Audio-Animatronics flair as they mine a mountain full of glittering gems and "heigh-ho" their way into theme-park fans' hearts at the Seven Dwarfs Mine Train. Set amid a steep Enchanted Forest landscaped with red poppies, cedars, and birch trees, the attraction is a visual feast of LED-illuminated gems, playful woodland creatures, and beloved characters from Walt Disney's 1937 animated film classic, *Snow White and the Seven Dwarfs.* A rough-hewn entrance to the mine leads to a covered queue designed to keep you occupied as you wend your way toward the train load area. Fun interactive diversions include animated "floating" gems that you can catch and match in a touch-screen jewel-washing trough.

The musical family coaster serves up thrills, but no stomach-churning plunges, with cars that twist, climb, drop rapidly, and rock gently when slowing down for you to enjoy the artfully crafted scene of the dwarfs at work in the mine. As the train rounds its final curve, you'll see Snow White dancing with her diminutive pals in the storybook cottage as the Wicked Queen, disguised as an old hag, lurks outside. The ride is not appropriate if you're pregnant or have heart, back, or neck problems, and although it's billed as a family coaster, there's a 38-inch height requirement. **For people with disabilities:** You must transfer from wheelchair to ride vehicle. **TIP→ This is one of the two Magic Kingdom attractions that uses the individual Lightning Lane instead of Genie+. Upon entering the park, you'll use the My Disney Experience app to purchase a time slot to return and ride without waiting in line. With young kids and an outdoor line, the purchase could be well-worth it on a crowded day.** ✉ *Fantasyland, Magic Kingdom ☞ Duration: 2½ mins. Crowds: Heavy. Audience: All ages.*

Under the Sea: Journey of the Little Mermaid

AMUSEMENT RIDE | FAMILY | The shipwreck theme, craggy grotto rock work, waterfalls, lagoons, and magical landscape of this attraction draw you into Ariel's world long before you board a giant clamshell for a journey under the sea. While you enjoy standing in a shaded queue, you'll see starfish embedded in rocks, a sandy beach, palm trees, sea-grape plants, and other authentic seaside touches. Once inside the cavern beneath Prince Eric's Castle, you can join in an interactive game that plays out around every corner and stars Scuttle the seagull and his animated crab pals.

Through a cave portal, you enter the castle's stone hallways, where you hop aboard a clamshell ride vehicle and, thanks to cold air and light effects, feel the sensation of descending under the sea. You then float past animated and Audio-Animatronic scenes from *The Little Mermaid* film, including a Broadway-style "Under the Sea" number with Sebastian conducting the undersea orchestra. There are fish conga lines and ominous scenes starring villainess Ursula, but, of course, a fairy-tale ending is in store featuring the Menken-Ashman show-stopper "Kiss the Girl." Most children love this ride, but some tots are afraid in the dark Ursula scene. **For people with disabilities:** Guests in scooters must transfer to a standard wheelchair to ride; equipped for handheld captioning and audio description. ✉ *Fantasyland, Magic Kingdom ☞ Duration: 7 mins. Crowds: Absolutely! Audience: All ages.*

Restaurants

★ Be Our Guest

$$$$ | FRENCH | FAMILY | This massive restaurant offers a *Beauty and the Beast* theme, French flair, and the Magic Kingdom's first wine and beer served with a prix-fixe menu for lunch and dinner. Seating is in one of three theme rooms: the Grand Ballroom, whose ceiling sports cherubs with the faces of Imagineers' children; the tattered West Wing, with a slashed painting that changes from prince to beast during faux storms; and the Castle Gallery. **Known for:** character appearances; herb-salted pork tenderloin; dessert platter. *Average main: $62* ✉ *Fantasyland, Magic Kingdom* ✣ *North end of Fantasyland* ☎ *407/939–3463* 🌐 *disneyworld.disney.go.com/dining/magic-kingdom/be-our-guest-restaurant.*

Cinderella's Royal Table

$$$$ | AMERICAN | FAMILY | Cinderella and other Disney princesses appear at this eatery in the castle's old mead hall, offering prix-fixe Fairyland dining as only Disney can supply. The Fairytale Breakfast offers all-you-can-eat options such as beef tenderloin and eggs and caramel apple–stuffed French toast; the Fairytale Lunch and Dinner, prix-fixe table-service meals, include entrées like chickpea panisse or grilled beef tenderloin. **Known for:** distinctive medieval castle decor; breakfasts from oatmeal to shrimp and grits; character appearances and autograph signings. *Average main: $62* ✉ *Fantasyland, Magic Kingdom* ☎ *407/939–3463* 🌐 *disneyworld.disney.go.com/dining/magic-kingdom/cinderella-royal-table.*

Coffee and Quick Bites

Gaston's Tavern

$ | AMERICAN | FAMILY | If you're looking for a snack to satisfy even the most villainous of appetites, come to Gaston's Tavern. While you won't find his four dozen eggs on the menu, the warm cinnamon roll is big enough for an entire family to split, and the gluten-friendly peanut butter mousse is surprisingly good. **Known for:** LeFou's brew; giant cinnamon rolls; turkey legs. *Average main: $7* ✉ *Fantasyland, Magic Kingdom* ☎ *407/939–463* 🌐 *disneyworld.disney.go.com/dining/magic-kingdom/gastons-tavern.*

Tomorrowland

The "future that never was" spins boldly into view as you enter Tomorrowland, where Disney Imagineers paint the landscape with whirling spaceships, flashy neon lights, and gleaming robots. This is the future as envisioned by sci-fi writers and moviemakers in the 1920s and '30s, when space flight, laser beams, and home computers were fiction, not fact. Retro Jetsonesque styling lends the area lasting chic.

TIP→ Though Tomorrowland Transit Authority (TTA) PeopleMover isn't a big-ticket ride, it's a great way to check out the landscape from above as it zooms in and out of Space Mountain and curves around the entire land, and there's usually no big line.

Magic Kingdom's newest attraction is the TRON Lightcycle/Run thrill ride. Based on the popular attraction of the same name in Shanghai Disneyland, it lets you race lightcycles along an intense track behind Space Mountain.

Sights

Astro Orbiter

AMUSEMENT RIDE | FAMILY | This gleaming superstructure of revolving planets has come to symbolize Tomorrowland as much as Dumbo represents Fantasyland. Passenger vehicles, on arms projecting from a central column, sail past whirling planets, and you control your car's altitude but not its velocity. The line is directly across from the entrance to the TTA PeopleMover. **For people with disabilities:** You must be able to walk several steps and transfer to the vehicle. **TIP→ The line moves slowly; skip this attraction on your first visit if time is limited.** ✉ *Tomorrowland, Magic Kingdom* ☞ *Duration: 2 mins. Crowds: Moderate to heavy. Audience: All ages.*

In Tomorrowland, interplanetary travel is within your reach on the Astro Orbiter.

★ Buzz Lightyear's Space Ranger Spin

AMUSEMENT RIDE | FAMILY | Based on the wildly popular *Toy Story*, this ride gives you a toy's perspective as it pits you and Buzz Lightyear against the evil Emperor Zurg. You're seated in a fast-moving, two-passenger Star Cruiser vehicle with infrared laser guns and a centrally located lever for spinning your ship to get a good vantage point. Throughout the ride, you shoot at targets to help macho space toy, Buzz, defeat the emperor and save the universe. You have to hit the targets marked with a "Z" to score, and the rider with the most points wins. To infinity and beyond! **For people with disabilities:** To board you must transfer to a standard wheelchair. Equipped for audio-description and handheld-captioning devices. **■ TIP→ Go first thing in the morning or during a parade. If you're with kids, time the wait and—if it's only 15 or 20 minutes—ride twice so they can have a practice run.** ✉ *Tomorrowland, Magic Kingdom* ☞ *Duration: 5 mins. Crowds: Heavy. Audience: All ages—truly.*

Monsters, Inc. Laugh Floor

PERFORMANCE VENUE | FAMILY | The joke's on everyone at this interactive attraction starring Mike Wazowski, the one-eyed hero from Disney-Pixar's hit *Monsters, Inc.* In the 400-seat theater, you can interact with an animated Mike and his sidekicks in the real-time, unscripted way that the character Crush from *Finding Nemo* performs at EPCOT in Turtle Talk with Crush at The Seas with Nemo & Friends. Here, the premise is that Mike realizes laughter can be harnessed as a power source, and Mike's new comedy club is expected to generate power for the future. The more the audience yuks it up, the greater the power produced. You can text-message jokes from cell phones to the show's producer; they might even be used in the show. **For people with disabilities:** Wheelchair accessible. Sign language is available some days. Equipped for assisted-listening and video-captioning devices. ✉ *Tomorrowland, Magic Kingdom* ☞ *Duration: 15 mins. Crowds: Heavy. Audience: All ages.*

★ Space Mountain

AMUSEMENT RIDE | FAMILY | The needlelike spires and gleaming, white, concrete cone of this 180-foot-high attraction are almost as much a Magic Kingdom landmark as Cinderella Castle. Inside is one of the world's most imaginative roller coasters, one that had a real astronaut, Gordon Cooper, for a creative consultant. Although there are no loop-the-loops or high-speed curves, the thrills are many as you take a trip into the depths of outer space—in the dark.

You can pass the wait time playing one of the many games on the Disney Play app. As you walk to the loading area, you'll pass whirling planets and hear the screams and shrieks of the riders, pumping you up for your own launch. Once you blast off, the ride lasts only two minutes and 38 seconds, with a top speed of 28 mph, but the devious twists and invisible drops in the dark make it seem twice as long. You can hear the screams from other cars, but you don't know where they are, adding an additional fright factor.

Stow personal belongings securely, and note that this ride isn't appropriate for pregnant women or guests wearing back, neck, or leg braces. **For people with disabilities:** You must be able to step into the ride vehicle and walk short distances. Guests in wheelchairs should see a cast member for boarding options. Service animals aren't permitted. **■ TIP→ The wait can be long. Come early, late, or during a parade. This is one of the two Magic Kingdom attractions that uses the individual the Lightning Lane (offered seasonally), but, as the line is in indoors amid air-conditioning, purchasing it is only worth it when the wait is more than two hours.** ✉ *Tomorrowland, Magic Kingdom* ☞ *Duration: 2½ mins. Crowds: You bet! Audience: Not young kids. Height requirement: 44 inches.*

Tomorrowland Speedway

AMUSEMENT RIDE | FAMILY | This is one of those rides that incites instant addiction in children and immediate regret in their parents. The reasons for the former are evident: the children drive brightly colored Mark VII model cars that swerve around the four 2,260-foot tracks with much *vroom-vroom-vrooming*. Like real sports cars, the vehicles are equipped with rack-and-pinion steering and disc brakes; unlike the real thing, these run on a track. But the track is so twisty that it's hard to keep the car on a straight course. Expect to spend a lot of time waiting your turn on the track and returning your vehicle after your lap. All this for a ride that achieves a top speed of 7 mph. **For people with disabilities:** To drive the cars, you must be able to steer, press the gas pedal, and transfer into the low car seat. **■ TIP→ Skip this on a first-time visit unless it'll break your child's heart.** ✉ *Tomorrowland, Magic Kingdom* ☞ *Duration: 5 mins. Crowds: Moderate. Audience: Young kids and tweens. Height requirements: With an adult must be at least 32 inches; those who wish to drive must reach 54 inches.*

Tomorrowland Transit Authority PeopleMover

AMUSEMENT RIDE | FAMILY | A reincarnation of what Disney old-timers might remember as the WEDway PeopleMover, the TTA PeopleMover gives you a nice, leisurely ride with great views of Tomorrowland, circling the Astro Orbiter and gliding through the middle of Space Mountain. Disney's version of future mass transit is smooth and noiseless, thanks to an electromagnetic linear induction motor that has no moving parts, uses little power, and emits no pollutants. **For people with disabilities:** You must be able to walk several steps and step on and off a moving ramp to transfer to a ride vehicle. Equipped for handheld-captioning and audio-description devices. **■ TIP→ Hop aboard to view Tomorrowland, to preview Space Mountain, if you have young children, or if you need a relaxing ride; if there's no line, this is a great nap spot for toddlers.** ✉ *Tomorrowland, Magic Kingdom*

Magic Kingdom Kids Tour

The Magic Kingdom is alive with thrilling distractions for young children, so let them take the lead now and then. Toddlers might want to jump from their strollers and dance along to the barbershop quartet on Main Street, U.S.A. Children who love to explore will have a ball scrambling around Frontierland and hopping a raft to Tom Sawyer's playground.

Stop and Smell the Roses

Head down Main Street, U.S.A., and, if you're lucky, the park's **Dapper Dan's Barbershop Quartet** will be harmonizing sweet tunes and tossing out one-liners from a small alcove along the street (check the park's *Times Guide* or the My Disney Experience app for performances). Young children are thrilled with the music and colorful costumes of these talented singers.

As you continue on, veer right toward the rose garden for a scenic picture spot where you can snap one of the prettiest shots in the park: the kids by the garden amid Mickey and Minnie topiaries, with Cinderella Castle in the background.

Fantasyland is dead ahead, and, after you've soared on **Dumbo the Flying Elephant**, head straight to **Enchanted Tales with Belle**, where the kids get to participate. Search for gems while you wait on the **Seven Dwarfs Mine Train** family coaster. Then try to catch a character performance in front of **Cinderella Castle** or during one of the daily parades or street parties.

Put the Zip in Your Doo-Dah

With little ones in tow, when it's time for food, fast is best. **Cosmic Ray's Starlight Café** is a high-energy quick stop with multiple choices for the entire family. Kids can head straight to the dance floor where Audio-Animatronics entertainer Sonny Eclipse keeps the tunes coming. After refueling, board the **Walt Disney World Railroad** at Main Street, U.S.A., Fantasyland, or Frontierland. While in Frontierland, too-short-to-ride kids can burn energy in the cavelike play area beneath **Splash Mountain** while parents take turns riding. The short raft trip to **Tom Sawyer Island** is worth it for kids who like exploring. Not far from the Country Bear Jamboree, sure shots can take aim at Western-style targets in the often-missed **Frontierland Shootin' Arcade**—at about $1 per 35 shots, it's a blast for any aspiring sheriff.

Become the Character

Get the makeover of a lifetime ($74.95–$450 plus tax) at **Bibbidi Bobbidi Boutique**, in Cinderella Castle. Hair, nails, makeup—even a sprinkling of pixie dust—it's all here. Afterward, be sure to catch a character meet and greet (see *Times Guide* for schedule) so the little rascals get all the hugs, autographs, photos, and magical memories they desire.

Magic Kingdom Grown-Ups Tour

The kids are older, and they're interested in thrills not magic. Or there aren't any kids in tow, and this is your golden opportunity to enjoy me time. Seize the day! The Magic Kingdom is a whole new experience without young children. Maximize the big adventures, take time to dine and shop, and discover your own brand of magic along the way.

Classic Thrills

As you pass beneath the train station and into Town Square, you're entering the Happiest Place on Earth, and it's time to grab the golden ring. If thrill riding tops your list, power walk northwest from the park hub through Liberty Square to Frontierland, where you can ride **Splash Mountain**, then go next door to dry off on the bumpy, scenic, runaway train at **Big Thunder Mountain Railroad.** The next hot ticket on your must-ride list is the **Seven Dwarfs Mine Train** family coaster in Fantasyland.

For many, just seeing the Johnny Depp look-alike, Audio-Animatronics Captain Jack Sparrow is reason enough to ride **Pirates of the Caribbean** in Adventureland, a short stroll from Splash Mountain. Cut back through the park hub and straight to **Space Mountain** and **TRON Lightcycle Power Run** in Tomorrowland for your other big-deal thrills. While you wait, sip an iced cappuccino or smoothie from **Auntie Gravity's Galactic Goodies** and/or experience the interactive **Buzz Lightyear's Space Ranger Spin**, which is addictive for competitive types, who will probably want to ride more than once for a chance to raise their space ranger profile.

Play, Dine, Shop

Chill out afterward at **Tony's Town Square Restaurant**, a great, full-service, late-lunch spot where you can feast on pasta. Burn off the calories shopping on Main Street for a make-your-own Mouse Ears souvenir from **The Chapeau** or some character bling from **Uptown Jewelers.**

At **Crystal Arts**, you can buy a fluted glass bowl and then mosey to the rear of the glass shop to see an Arribas Brothers glassblower craft a piece using 2,100°F furnaces, a heated glass rod, and lots of talent. It takes about 20 minutes for the glassblower to shape a piece of glass and explain each step along the way.

Catch the Spirit(s)

You can skip the afternoon parade crowds and join 999 grim-grinning ghouls at the **Haunted Mansion** in Liberty Square. Afterward, stroll several paces to the **Hall of Presidents** and catch the patriotic spirit. Just around the corner in Fantasyland, don your goofy 3-D glasses for **Mickey's PhilharMagic**, starring the largest cast of Disney animated stars performing in a single show. Cap the evening with the **Disney Enchantment** fireworks, lasers, and projections display, featuring themes from more than a dozen Disney animated films. You'll be glad you stayed for the fairy-tale ending.

☞ *Duration: 10 mins. Crowds: Light. Audience: All ages.*

★ TRON Lightcycle Power Run
AMUSEMENT RIDE | **FAMILY** | First debuted in Shanghai Disneyland, the very popular TRON Lightcycle Power Run is the newest attraction at the Magic Kingdom. Based on the hit movie franchise, the coaster places riders on individual lightcycles (the motorcycles associated so strongly with TRON) that are situated two by two. Despite the lack of flips, this coaster gets high marks for being the fastest in Disney and for its accelerated launch. Your cycles will speed against an opposing team, shooting inside and out, as lights flash to make it feel as if you are in the TRON video game. Head here first or purchase a Lightning Lane pass if available. Note that this ride is not appropriate for pregnant women or guests wearing back, neck, or leg braces. **For people with disabilities:** You must be able to step into the ride vehicle and walk short distances. Guests in wheelchairs should see a cast member for boarding options. Service animals aren't permitted. ✉ *Tomorrowland, Magic Kingdom.*

Walt Disney's Carousel of Progress
PERFORMANCE VENUE | **FAMILY** | Originally seen at New York's 1964–65 World's Fair, this revolving theater traces the impact of technological progress on the daily lives of Americans from the turn of the 20th century into the near future. Representing each generation, an Audio-Animatronics family sings the praises of modern-day gadgets that technology has wrought. **For people with disabilities:** Wheelchair accessible; equipped for assisted-listening, handheld-captioning, audio-description, and video-captioning devices. **■ TIP→ Skip this on a first-time visit unless you adore nostalgia. Also, it might close early or entirely in low season.** ✉ *Tomorrowland, Magic Kingdom* ☞ *Duration: 20 mins. Crowds: Moderate. Audience: All ages.*

Coffee and Quick Bites

Auntie Gravity's Galactic Goodies
$ | **AMERICAN** | **FAMILY** | Looking for a snack on the go? Auntie Gravity's Galactic Goodies offers milkshakes, smoothies, and floats that are easy to eat while walking. **Known for:** brownie sundae; vanilla floats; plant-based strawberry smoothie. [$] *Average main: $6* ✉ *Tomorrowland, Magic Kingdom* ☎ *407/939–3463* 🌐 *disneyworld.disney.go.com/dining/magic-kingdom/auntie-gravitys-galactic-goodies.*

The Lunching Pad
$ | **HOT DOG** | **FAMILY** | Along with foot-long hot dogs, the Lunching Pad serves up tasty pretzels, stuffed with warm cream cheese. This is also a good spot for a blue-raspberry slushy or a midafternoon cup of coffee. **Known for:** Caribbean jerk-chicken strips; foot-long hot dogs; pretzels. [$] *Average main: $7* ✉ *Tomorrowland, Magic Kingdom* ☎ *407/939–3463* 🌐 *disneyworld.disney.go.com/dining/magic-kingdom/lunching-pad.*

Shopping

Mickey's Star Traders
SOUVENIRS | **FAMILY** | One of the largest shops in the Magic Kingdom, Star Traders trades on the purchase of all things Disney. Toys, pins, T-shirts featuring favorite characters like Mickey, Stitch, and Mike from *Monsters, Inc.* can be found here, as well as Goofy caps and oversize Mickey gloves. So much to see—so much to buy! ✉ *Tomorrowland, Magic Kingdom* 🌐 *disneyworld.disney.go.com/shops/magic-kingdom/star-traders.*

Magic Kingdom Resort Area

Despite being the oldest hotels on Disney property, the five properties in the Magic Kingdom Resort Area are some of the nicest, and all five have undergone refurbishment in the past 10 years. What's more, staying in this area makes everyone—from those who want a bar that's complete with a big band to families hoping to watch the fireworks while eating sushi—feel as if they're in the middle of all the action.

Those looking for a more upscale experience should consider the three hotels that are all connected to the Magic Kingdom by monorail: the Grand Floridian, the Polynesian Village Resort, and the Contemporary. Connected by boat are the Wilderness Lodge and the only camping location on Disney property, Fort Wilderness. Although these are not as pricey or upscale, they still offer easy transportation to the Magic Kingdom.

Adults looking for a nice night out will be thrilled with the many dining options at the Grand Floridian and the California Grill at the Contemporary. Big groups should look into the bungalows at the Polynesian Village Resort or the Boulder Ridge Villas at Fort Wilderness Lodge.

Restaurants

★ California Grill

$$$$ | **AMERICAN** | The view of the surrounding Disney parks from this 15th-floor restaurant—the World's signature dining establishment since 1995—is as stunning as the food, especially after dark, when you can watch the nightly Magic Kingdom fireworks from an outdoor viewing area. The space has stylish mid-century modern furnishings and chandeliers, and the exhibition kitchen is so well equipped that it has a cast-iron flat grill designed specifically for cooking fish. **Known for:** globally inspired, locally sourced dishes; stunning views of the parks and fireworks; great sushi. *Average main: $89 ✉ Disney's Contemporary Resort, 4600 N. World Dr., Magic Kingdom Resort Area ☎ 407/939–3463 🌐 disneyworld.disney.go.com/dining/contemporary-resort/california-grill ⏲ No lunch.*

★ Capa

$$$$ | **STEAKHOUSE** | The menu at this chic, modern dining room atop the luxury Four Seasons resort highlights the culinary culture of Spain, starting with authentic tapas and continuing with exceptional steaks, among them dry-aged strip and rib eye that are worth the price and worthy of the luxury setting. The ham croquettes with shishito pepper are especially creamy, and the Valor Chocolate confection is ultrarich, made with coffee ice cream, chocolate mousse, cardamom, and toffee crunch. **■ TIP→ The patio affords a unique view of every Disney fireworks display.** **Known for:** enviable view of Disney parks from the patio; superb steaks; grilled seafood, lobster, lamb, and a wide selection of caviars. *Average main: $80 ✉ Four Seasons Orlando, 10100 Dream Tree Blvd., Magic Kingdom Resort Area ☎ 407/313–7777 🌐 www.fourseasons.com/orlando/dining ⏲ No lunch.*

Chef Mickey's

$$$$ | **AMERICAN** | **FAMILY** | The fact that the Disney monorail zooms overhead right through the Contemporary Resort, and that Mickey, Minnie, or Goofy hangs around for breakfast and dinner, would be enough to make it popular, but the food here is surprisingly good. Chef Mickey's is shiny and bright, offering a breakfast buffet and brunch that includes French toast, scrambled tofu hash, and even a create-your-own waffle station. **Known for:** specialty cocktails for the grown-ups; character meals and Storybook Moments; family-fare buffet and lots of it. *Average main: $55 ✉ Disney's*

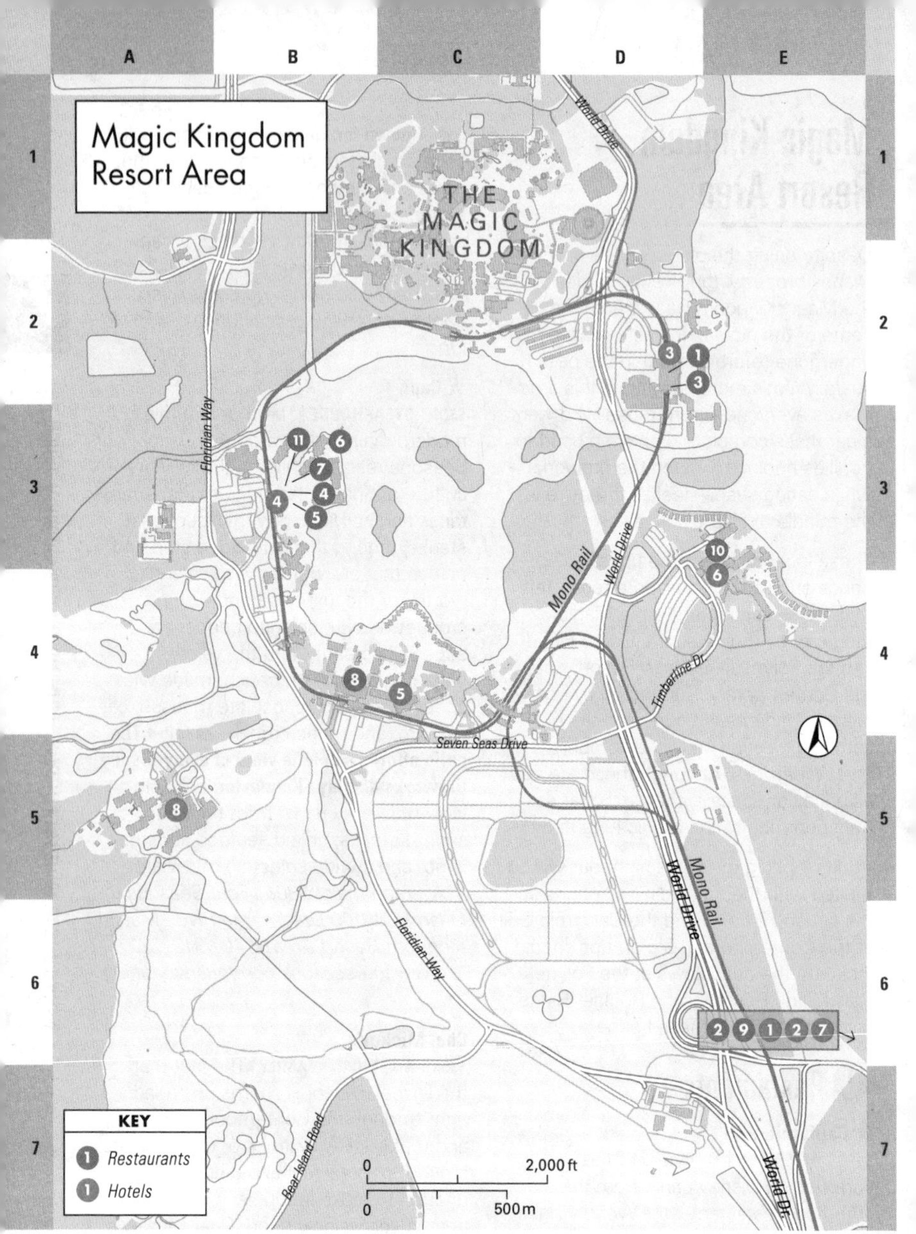

Restaurants

1 California Grill D2
2 Capa E6
3 Chef Mickey's D2
4 Cítricos B3
5 Garden View Tea Room B3
6 Narcoossee's B3
7 1900 Park Fare B3
8 'Ohana B4
9 Ravello E6
10 Story Book Dining at Artist Point with Snow White E3
11 Victoria & Albert's B3

Hotels

1 The Cabins at Disney's Fort Wilderness Resort E6
2 The Campsites at Disney's Fort Wilderness Resort E6
3 Disney's Contemporary Resort D2
4 Disney's Grand Floridian Resort & Spa B3
5 Disney's Polynesian Village Resort C4
6 Disney's Wilderness Lodge E4
7 Four Seasons Orlando at Walt Disney World Resort E6
8 Shades of Green A5

Contemporary Resort, 4600 N. World Dr., Magic Kingdom Resort Area ☎ *407/939–3463* 🌐 *disneyworld.disney.go.com/dining/contemporary-resort/chef-mickeys* ⊙ *No lunch.*

Citricos

$$$$ | **ECLECTIC** | With an ambitious menu that's fundamentally American—with influences of Tuscan, Provençal, and Spanish-Mediterranean cuisine—this Grand Floridian restaurant is one of the resort's best dollar-to-dining options. Standout entrées include Florida Cobia with mashed fingerling potatoes and local mushrooms, house-made rigatoni, and roulade of chicken with a corn cake. **Known for:** casually elegant atmosphere; excellent first-course choices; oak-grilled meats. [$] *Average main: $47* ✉ *Disney's Grand Floridian Resort & Spa, 4401 Floridian Way, Magic Kingdom Resort Area* ☎ *407/939–3463* 🌐 *disneyworld.disney.go.com/dining/grand-floridian-resort-and-spa/citricos* ⊙ *No lunch.*

Garden View Tea Room

$$$$ | **BRITISH** | **FAMILY** | Disney's Perfectly Princess Tea Party is afternoon tea at its grandest as children ages 3 to 9 enjoy the royal treatment. Dressing up is encouraged, and an early 9 am meal, featuring tea and sandwiches, is served on china plates (apple juice, peanut butter, and ham-and-cheese sandwiches for the kids; cheeses and finger sandwiches for adults). **Known for:** house-made scones, sandwiches, and sweets; highly elegant tea for young princesses and princes and refined adults; character appearances. [$] *Average main: $150* ✉ *Disney's Grand Floridian Resort & Spa, 4401 Floridian Way, Magic Kingdom Resort Area* ☎ *407/939–3463* 🌐 *disneyworld.disney.go.com/dining/grand-floridian-resort-and-spa/perfectly-princess-tea-party.*

Narcoossee's

$$$$ | **SEAFOOD** | The dining room, with Victorian-style columns, high ceilings, and hardwood floors, is not only a great place seafood and steaks, but also to gaze out at the nightly fireworks over the Seven Seas Lagoon (an announcement is made when fireworks commence, and music is piped in). The menu changes regularly, but typical choices are wild Alaskan halibut and the surf-and-turf centerpiece—a butter-poached lobster tail and a tender, grilled filet mignon. **Known for:** black Angus steaks; intimate and well-stocked bar; seafood flown in daily. [$] *Average main: $54* ✉ *Disney's Grand Floridian Resort & Spa, 4401 Floridian Way, Magic Kingdom Resort Area* ☎ *407/939–3463* 🌐 *disneyworld.disney.go.com/dining/grand-floridian-resort-and-spa/narcoossees* ⊙ *No lunch.*

1900 Park Fare

$$$$ | **AMERICAN** | Disney characters delight guests throughout the day at this sprawling, though dainty, lobby restaurant. Mary Poppins and friends join guests during the Supercalifragilistic Breakfast, posing for pics while cheerful tunes are played on an antique organ called Big Bertha, and the buffet features omelets made to order. **Known for:** Wonderland Tea Party; Florida strawberry soup; character dining buffets throughout the day. [$] *Average main: $45* ✉ *Disney's Grand Floridian Resort & Spa, 4401 Floridian Way, Magic Kingdom Resort Area* ☎ *407/939–3463* 🌐 *disneyworld.disney.go.com/dining/grand-floridian-resort-and-spa/1900-park-fare* ⊙ *No lunch.*

'Ohana

$$$$ | **SOUTH PACIFIC** | **FAMILY** | This Polynesian-themed restaurant offers two thoroughly entertaining, though incredibly different, experiences. Early in the day, the Best Friends Breakfast with Lilo & Stitch is destination-worthy; by night you'll find a Hawaiian-theme dinner. **Known for:** full bar for adults; storytelling, shows, and games between courses; chicken, seafood, and steak skillet. [$] *Average main: $54* ✉ *Disney's Polynesian Village Resort, 1600 Seven Seas Dr., Magic Kingdom Resort Area* ☎ *407/939–3463* 🌐 *disneyworld.*

disney.go.com/dining/polynesian-resort/ohana ⏲ *No lunch.*

Ravello

$$$$ | **ITALIAN** | **FAMILY** | Under the leadership of Neapolitan chef Fabrizio Schenardi, Ravello is a chic, modern Italian restaurant after dark. Hand-tossed pizzas emerge from the oven—perhaps finished with house-made ricotta, arugula, and truffle oil. **Known for:** Disney character breakfast; superbly executed cuisine of Naples; grilled lamb chops. Ⓢ *Average main: $32* ✉ *Four Seasons Orlando, 10100 Dream Tree Blvd., Magic Kingdom Resort Area* ☎ *407/313–6161* 🌐 *www.fourseasons.com/orlando* ⏲ *No lunch.*

Story Book Dining at Artist Point with Snow White

$$$$ | **AMERICAN** | **FAMILY** | This family-style restaurant deep inside the Wilderness Lodge offers character dining with Snow White and Dopey. The prix-fixe menu includes a shared appetizer, a single entrée per person, and then a shared dessert. **Known for:** shrimp cocktail; slow-braised pork shank; butter-poached sustainable fish. Ⓢ *Average main: $60* ✉ *Disney's Wilderness Lodge, 901 Timberline Dr., Magic Kingdom Resort Area* ☎ *407/939–3463* 🌐 *disneyworld.disney.go.com/dining/wilderness-lodge-resort/artist-point* ⏲ *No lunch.*

★ **Victoria & Albert's**

$$$$ | **AMERICAN** | A well-polished service team anticipates your every need, providing a truly sophisticated dining experience, one in which children under 10 aren't on the guest list. There's nothing quick about sitting down for dinner in the 7- and 10-course main dining room, the 10-course intimate Queen Victoria's Room, or the over-the-top Chef's Table in the restaurant's kitchen. **Known for:** exclusives like Osetra caviar and Miyazaki beef; highest-priced restaurant at WDW; enormous and expensive wine list. Ⓢ *Average main: $200* ✉ *Disney's Grand Floridian Resort & Spa, 4401 Floridian Way, Magic Kingdom Resort Area* ☎ *407/939–3862* 🌐 *disneyworld.disney.go.com/dining/grand-floridian-resort-and-spa/victoria-and-alberts* ⏲ *No lunch* 👔 *Jacket required.*

Hotels

The Cabins at Disney's Fort Wilderness Resort

$$$$ | **RESORT** | **FAMILY** | The cabins in this 750-acre resort campground just a boat ride away from the Magic Kingdom don't exactly constitute roughing it, as they are compact, air-conditioned log homes that accommodate four grown-ups and two youngsters. **Pros:** nightly, family-oriented entertainment; lots of traditional campground activities; you can save money by cooking, but you don't have to, as there is a three-meals-a-day restaurant. **Cons:** it's a long hike to many entertainment and dining sites; pricey for what is really just a mobile home encased in logs; shuttle to parks is free but slow. Ⓢ *Rooms from: $435* ✉ *4510 N. Fort Wilderness Trail, Magic Kingdom Resort Area* ☎ *407/824–2900* 🌐 *disneyworld.disney.go.com/resorts/cabins-at-fort-wilderness-resort* 🛏 *421 cabins* 🍽 *No Meals.*

★ **The Campsites at Disney's Fort Wilderness Resort**

$ | **RESORT** | **FAMILY** | One of the cheapest ways to stay on WDW property is in your own tent or RV, which can be set up in one of four different areas, from bargain-priced tent sites with water and electricity to deluxe RV sites equipped with electric, cable TV, Internet access, water and sewage hookups, outdoor charcoal grills, and picnic tables. **Pros:** wide choice of recreation and entertainment options; Disney's most economical lodging; pets allowed. **Cons:** the mosquitoes can be irritating; shuttle rides to Disney parks take a long time; amount of walking to reach the store, restaurants, and so on, can be a bit much. Ⓢ *Rooms from: $128* ✉ *4510 N. Fort Wilderness Trail, Magic Kingdom Resort Area* ☎ *407/939–6244, 407/824–2742*

The Grand Floridian is one of Walt Disney World's original hotels and also one of its most luxurious and expensive.

disneyworld.disney.go.com/resorts/campsites-at-fort-wilderness-resort *799 campsites* *No Meals.*

Disney's Contemporary Resort
$$$$ | **RESORT** | **FAMILY** | You're paying for location at this sleek, modern, luxury resort next to the Magic Kingdom that, despite having opened in 1971, still lives up to its name; park hopping is a breeze, as the monorail runs through the lobby. **TIP→ Dinner reservations at the rooftop California Grill come with 15th-floor views of Magic Kingdom fireworks.** **Known for:** health and wellness suites; monorail access; Chef Mickey's, the epicenter of character-meal world. **Pros:** health and wellness suites; monorail access; Chef Mickey's, the epicenter of character-meal world. **Cons:** lobby eateries can be crowded and noisy; fee for self-parking; the mix of conventioneers and vacationers can make for chaos in the lobby. *Rooms from: $534* *4600 N. World Dr., Magic Kingdom Resort Area* *407/824–1000* *disneyworld.disney.go.com/resorts/contemporary-resort* *1028 rooms* *No Meals.*

★ Disney's Grand Floridian Resort & Spa
$$$$ | **RESORT** | **FAMILY** | So close to the Magic Kingdom you can see the colors change on the Cinderella Castle, this red-roofed, Victorian-style resort emulates the look of the great railroad resorts of the past with beautifully appointed rooms, rambling verandas, delicate, white-painted woodwork, and brick chimneys. **Pros:** if you're a couple with no kids, this is definitely the most romantic on-property hotel; one monorail stop from the Magic Kingdom; Victoria & Albert's offers an evening-long experience in fine dining. **Cons:** vacationing couples might be more comfortable than families with young children; draws a large convention clientele; pricey. *Rooms from: $708* *4401 Floridian Way, Magic Kingdom Resort Area* *407/824–3000* *disneyworld.disney.go.com/resorts/grand-floridian-resort-and-spa* *867 rooms* *No Meals.*

Disney's Polynesian Village Resort
$$$$ | **RESORT** | **FAMILY** | This South Pacific–theme resort lies directly across the lagoon from the Magic Kingdom; is on the monorail and water taxi routes; and has lots of kids activities, making it a good family choice. **Pros:** kids' activities; on the monorail line; great atmosphere. **Cons:** Magic Kingdom ferry noise affects some bungalows; lots of loud children; pricey. *Rooms from: $703* ✉ *1600 Seven Seas Dr., Magic Kingdom Resort Area* ☎ *407/824–2000* 🌐 *disneyworld.disney.go.com/en_CA/resorts/polynesian-resort* *844 rooms* *No Meals.*

Disney's Wilderness Lodge
$$$$ | **RESORT** | **FAMILY** | The architects designed this luxury resort to mimic the majestic, turn-of-the-20th-century lodges of the American West. **Pros:** feels secluded but near Magic Kingdom; boarding point for romantic cruises or free water taxi to Magic Kingdom; good dining options. **Cons:** noise from the Whispering Canyon Cafe can be annoying; no monorail access; no direct bus to Magic Kingdom. *Rooms from: $508* ✉ *901 Timberline Dr., Magic Kingdom Resort Area* ☎ *407/824–3200* 🌐 *disneyworld.disney.go.com/resorts/wilderness-lodge-resort* *716 rooms* *No Meals.*

Four Seasons Orlando at Walt Disney World Resort
$$$$ | **RESORT** | **FAMILY** | The award-winning Four Seasons presides majestically over Disney's exclusive Golden Oak community, and its luxurious amenities and dedication to service are clear from the moment you step into the marble, flower-bedecked lobby and head for your room. **Pros:** no resort fee; free transportation to Disney parks; lots of on-site kids' entertainment and an exclusive golf course. **Cons:** remote from Disney parks; a long way from Universal or SeaWorld; pricey, but then, it is the Four Seasons. *Rooms from: $769* ✉ *10100 Dream Tree Blvd., Magic Kingdom Resort Area* ☎ *407/313–7777* 🌐 *www.fourseasons.com/orlando* *444 rooms* *No Meals.*

Shades of Green
$ | **HOTEL** | **FAMILY** | Operated by the U.S. Armed Forces Recreation Center, this resort is open only to active-duty and retired personnel from the armed forces, reserves, and National Guard; their families; and others connected with the military. **Pros:** Army–Air Force Exchange store discounts for people with military IDs; large standard rooms; monorail a short walk away. **Cons:** very crowded during holidays; no MagicBands or Cards; prices vary based on rank. *Rooms from: $115* ✉ *1905 W. Magnolia Palm Dr., Magic Kingdom Resort Area* ☎ *407/824–3600, 888/593–2242* 🌐 *www.shadesofgreen.org* *597 rooms* *No Meals.*

Activities

SPAS

Senses—A Disney Spa at Disney's Grand Floridian Resort
SPAS | All the senses—sound, sight, smell, touch, and taste—are engaged when you enter this Disney-designed-and-owned spa at the Grand Floridian Resort. Soothing fruit-based elixirs start the journey toward serenity, while soft lighting, gentle music, and the aroma of lavender encourage you to shed your stress. Separate and secluded men's and women's relaxation areas make it easy to further unwind as you wait. Massage tables are heated, as are the lounge chairs in the restful wet room (spend some time looking for the hidden Mickey on the wall). Swimsuits are required in all wet relaxation areas. Treatments include facials, scrubs, and many massages. A whimsical Mad Hatter chair offers little ones a special place for a pedicure. Prices do not include the 20% gratuity. ✉ *Grand Floridian Resort, 4401 Floridian Way, Magic Kingdom Resort Area* ☎ *407/824–3000* 🌐 *disneyworld.disney.go.com/spas/grand-floridian-resort-and-spa/senses-spa* ☞ *Parking: complimentary self-parking.*

Chapter 4

EPCOT AND RESORT AREA

4

Updated by Leigh Jenkins

Sights ★★★★★ | Restaurants ★★★★★ | Hotels ★★★★☆ | Shopping ★★★★★ | Nightlife ★★★☆☆

EPCOT INTERNATIONAL FOOD AND WINE FESTIVAL

A wine-and-cheese tasting at the EPCOT International Food and Wine Festival.

For an ever-increasing number of autumn weeks, EPCOT hosts the EPCOT International Food and Wine Festival, attracting folks more interested in a fine phyllo than a photo op with Cinderella.

The festival is essentially a compendium of food- and beverage-related offerings, some free with the price of EPCOT admission, others costing anywhere from $3.75 for a piece of cake to several hundred dollars for extravagant wine dinners. Mixology or cheese seminars compete with cookbook signings by famous chefs, and tapas-size portions of foods served from about 30 international theme stalls encircle the World Lagoon. Throughout the event, guest chefs host brunches, lunches, and wine-pairing dinners—casual, posh, or festive—at EPCOT and in hotels. The headliners change annually but might include names like chef Masaharu Morimoto or Rick Bayless. The festival's food and beverage lineup changes every year, too, so for more information and to make reservations (during festival season only, generally midsummer through early November) call ☎ *407/939–3378* or visit 🌐 *www.disneyworld.com/foodandwine.*

GARDEN OF EATING

EPCOT has expanded the offerings at its annual Flower & Garden Festival, which runs between early March and early July. The springtime celebration of all things green and floral features more than a dozen outdoor kitchens whose dishes are inspired by produce and fresh foods from around the world, and are served throughout the World Showcase—with paired beverages, of course.

SHOPPING FOR A SNACK

The heart of the Food and Wine Festival—and the most approachable event for hungry tourists on a budget—takes place around EPCOT's World Showcase. Ordinarily a miniature world of 11 pavilions themed around one country apiece, the area takes on new life when as many as 36 "international marketplaces" take up residence.

Most of the marketplaces offer a taste of one country—from Brazil to South Korea—and several appetizer-size food items and beverages, nearly all for $3.25 to $10 apiece. Although indisputably popular creations like the cheddar soup ladled out endlessly at Canada are perennials, most of the offerings change from year to year. Attendees might taste Brazilian crispy pork belly with black beans (paired with Xingu Black beer), Beijing roasted duck bao with hoisin sauce (with vodka "Kung Fu Punch"), or chicken with red-eye gravy and griddled corn cakes (with a Florida Orange Groves mango wine).

A few marketplaces feature items instead of locales. The Desserts and Champagne booth, for instance, pours a bounty of bubbly and serves special sweets. The craft beer marketplace puts out several regional brews along with complementary snacks like spicy pimento cheese with crackers. And the all-American Craft Beers market often specializes in fare U.S. citizens can be proud of, such as the Zesty Cheeseburger Handwich and Cigar City Brewing's Invasion Pale Ale from Tampa.

Lines get long, especially on weekends, when locals pour in for their regular fix of foreign fare, so consider timing your tour during the day or on a weekday evening, when most spots have shorter waits. And keep an eye on the budget: those little dishes can add up quickly.

The festival has up to 36 international marketplaces.

FESTIVAL OF THE SENSES

Several evenings throughout the festival, food and wine enthusiasts clad in cocktail attire saunter into the gala called Party for the Senses. Billed as a "grand tasting," the upscale bash starts booking in July and sells out within days. In a dramatically decorated, high-ceiling room, 10 to 15 chefs from around the country host as many as 50 food stations, serving a hearty appetizer-size portion of one passionately prepared dish. Some are Disney chefs eager to show their talents, and others are known nationally. Big names such as François Payard, Allen Susser, and Walter Staib have participated. Reserved seating is now offered, a welcome change from the "stand and carry" model. Live entertainment such as acrobats and vocalists gives attendees something to watch while taking a break between bites. Seats in the Wine View Lounge include early entrance and private transport.

PARK SNAPSHOT

TOP EXPERIENCES

■ **Frozen Ever After.** *Frozen* fans line up in droves to hop in a longboat and join Elsa and Anna in this chilly adventure based on the film.

■ **Guardians of the Galaxy: Cosmic Rewind.** Head out on an otherworldly adventure at Disney's newest attraction.

■ **Remy's Ratatouille Adventure.** This attraction uses 4-D technology to make you feel like you're really scurrying around the kitchens of Paris.

■ **Soarin' Around the World.** Everyone's hands-down favorite: feel the breeze as you hang glide over spectacular global scenery.

■ **Test Track.** Design your concept car, then rev up to 60 mph on a hairpin turn in this wild ride on a Chevrolet proving ground.

GETTING HERE

Disney's monorail and buses drop you off at the main entrance in front of World Celebration. But if you're staying at one of the EPCOT resorts (the BoardWalk, Yacht Club, Beach Club, Dolphin, or Swan), you can take a boat to the International Gateway entrance. The Disney Skyline, a large gondola system, also brings guests of the Caribbean Beach, Pop Century, Riviera Resort, and Art of Animation resorts to this back entrance.

PLANNING YOUR TIME

EPCOT is vast and generally requires two days to do it justice, one for World Celebration, World Discovery, and World Nature and another full day for World Showcase. Because World Showcase doesn't usually open until 11, make sure you ride any other top rides early in the day so you'll be prepared for the second rope drop, when you should head straight to Norway for Frozen Ever After or France for Remy's Ratatouille Adventure. (These rides sometimes open early.) It's easier to get a reservation for lunch at one of the better restaurants. If you want to have dinner in the park, eat during the fireworks.

VIEWFINDER

■ Jutting out amid gondolas and striped poles in World Showcase is Italy Isola, where you can take one great selfie with Spaceship Earth across the lagoon before pivoting to take another with the stunning Italian Pavilion in the background. A small fountain here is great for setting up group shots, and two bridges can give an elevated view.

PAUSE HERE

■ Tucked behind a tea shop in the United Kingdom Pavilion of World Showcase is a beautiful English garden, complete with a hedge maze, a bandstand, and a select number of benches and doorsteps. Kids can explore the maze while adults relax in this relatively calm and hidden spot. Check the *Times Guide* to see when the British Revolution is playing at the bandstand—it's a great show, but the area fills up quickly during their set.

Walt Disney said that EPCOT would "take its cue from the new ideas and new technologies that are now emerging from the creative centers of American industry."

He wrote that EPCOT—never completed, always improving—"will never cease to be a living blueprint of the future, a showcase to the world for the ingenuity of American free enterprise." That statement has never been more true than now, as so much in EPCOT is undergoing big changes. Several attractions have closed, and Disney officials have restructured the park and added new and often more kid-friendly attractions.

The permanent settlement that Disney envisioned wasn't to be. EPCOT opened in 1982—16 years after his death—as a showcase, ostensibly, for the concepts that would be incorporated into the real-life EPCOTs of the future. (Disney's vision *has* taken an altered shape in the self-contained city of Celebration, an urban-planner's dream opened in 1996 on Disney property near Kissimmee.)

EPCOT theme park is divided into four sections to highlight different aspects of the world we live in. World Celebration, the entrance to the park, pays tribute to the idea of joining together to celebrate all the nations of the Earth. World Showcase, where microcosms of 11 countries from four continents feature shops, restaurants, attractions, and live entertainment, highlights the cultures that make our world different. World Nature is dedicated to Mother Nature, encompassing the Land and Sea pavilions. Finally, World Discovery looks out to the stars—both real and imaginary—with new technology and space exploration. All four sections have new attractions, dining, and decorations.

For years, EPCOT was considered the more staid park, a place geared toward adults. But after its 10th anniversary, EPCOT began to evolve into a livelier, more child-friendly park, with such wow attractions as Test Track, Mission: SPACE, and Soarin'.

There's something for everyone here. The World Showcase appeals to younger children with the Kidcot Fun Stop craft stations and the Norway pavilion's Frozen Ever After ride. Soarin', in The Land pavilion, is a family favorite. And the Seas with Nemo & Friends—with one of the world's largest saltwater aquariums and a Nemo-theme ride—is a must-see for all. Adrenaline junkie? Don't miss Test Track presented by Chevrolet, where you can design your own custom concept car and then put it through its high-speed paces.

Wear comfortable shoes—there's *a lot* of territory to cover here. Arrive early, and try to stay all day, squeezing in extras like Bruce's Shark World and a relaxing meal. If you enter through International Gateway before 11 am, cast members will direct you to World Nature, as World Showcase opens just before lunch, or you can indulge in a latte and éclair at the France bakery, the sole quick-service eatery open early in World Showcase.

Planning

Getting Oriented

EPCOT has just experienced a massive transformation in time for Walt Disney World's 50th anniversary. The park is now divided into four sections, including the beloved World Showcase, as well as the new World Celebration, World Nature, and World Discovery areas in what was (and some might still refer to as) Future World. Of course, amid the park's classic offerings, you can expect to find plenty of new, innovative, and thrilling attractions.

At the entrance is the recently created World Celebration area, home to Spaceship Earth, a new festival space, and Dreamers Point, which will honor Walt Disney's vision for EPCOT. This area also has everything you need for your day at EPCOT, including stroller and wheelchair rentals, maps, and Guest Relations (aka Guest Services).

To the east, World Nature features favorites such as Soarin' and The Seas with Nemo & Friends. In The Land pavilion the *Awesome Planet* film complements Soarin' and Living with the Land. Soon to be added is the Journey of Water, a *Moana*-themed exploration trail; updates to the Imagination pavilion are also in the works.

In the west is World Discovery, which, with the help of Test Track and Mission: SPACE, focuses on science and technology. It's also the location of one of the newest attractions: Guardians of the Galaxy: Cosmic Rewind. The Space 2020 restaurant, beside Mission: SPACE, provides guests with celestial views. The PLAY! pavilion is full of interactive games based off the latest Disney Channel hits.

World Showcase pavilions are on the promenade encircling the World Showcase Lagoon. Each houses architectural examples of a country, with shops, restaurants, and friendly international staffers; some have films or displays. Live entertainment is scheduled at several pavilions, and ride options now include Remy's Ratatouille Adventure in France and Frozen Ever After in Norway.

Park Amenities

Baby Care: The baby-care center at Odyssey Center in World Discovery has rocking chairs and low lighting. The center sells formula, baby food, pacifiers, and disposable diapers. Changing tables are available here, as well as in all women's and some men's restrooms.

Cameras: Disposable cameras and memory cards are widely available, and you can use the Disney PhotoPass Service to gather memories throughout the park. Other photo services are available at the Imagination! pavilion.

First Aid: Staffed by registered nurses, first aid is in the Odyssey Center. More than a dozen automated external defibrillators are located across the park.

Guest Relations: The three locations where you can pick up schedules and maps are to the right of the ticket windows at the park entrance, to the left of Spaceship Earth inside World Celebration, and to the left before entering at the International Gateway. Guest Relations will also assist with dining reservations, ticket upgrades, and services for guests with disabilities.

Lockers: Lockers ($10 to $15 depending on size, with $5 refundable deposit) are at the International Gateway and to the west of Spaceship Earth. Coin-operated lockers also are at the bus information center by the bus parking lot.

Lost People and Things: Instruct children to speak to someone with a Disney name tag if you become separated. If you have lost an item, check the park's Guest Relations office.

EPCOT Lost and Found

Located in the Guest Relations lobby east of Spaceship Earth. ✉ *World Celebration, EPCOT* ☎ *407/560–7500.*

Main Lost and Found Office

After one day, all articles are sent to the main lost and found office at Disney Springs and can be retrieved between 9 am and 7 pm daily. ✉ *Disney Springs, Disney Springs* ☎ *407/824–4245.*

Package Pick-Up: Ask shop clerks to forward large purchases to Package Pick-Up at the Gift Stop in the Entrance Plaza and at the World Traveler at International Gateway. Allow three hours for delivery. You also can have packages sent to your Disney hotel.

Services for People with Disabilities: Accessibility standards are high. Many attractions and most restaurants and shops are fully wheelchair accessible. There are large Braille park maps at Guest Relations in World Celebration and International Gateway as well as to the left of the walkway from World Celebration to the World Showcase Plaza.

At Guest Relations, there's a schedule for sign-language presentations at some of the park attractions; you can also pick up special devices for hearing- and sight-impaired visitors.

At World Showcase most people stroll around the promenade, but there are also Friendship boats, which require visitors using oversize wheelchairs or scooters to transfer to Disney chairs.

You can rent wheelchairs at the gift stop outside the main entrance, at the Stroller & Wheelchair Rental Shop to the left of Spaceship Earth, or at the International Gateway. A limited number of electronic convenience vehicles (ECVs) are available only at the Stroller & Wheelchair Rental.

Wheelchairs are $12 daily, $10 for multiday rental. ECVs are $50 per day plus a refundable $20 security deposit. Arrive early, because neither conveyance can be reserved. Several Orlando-area companies also rent and deliver ECVs.

Stroller Rentals: You can rent strollers on the east side of the World Celebration and at the International Gateway. Singles are $15 daily, $13 for multiday rental; doubles cost $31 daily, $27 for multiple days. Even preschoolers will be glad for a stroller in this large park.

Park Tours

Backstage Magic

GUIDED TOURS | This tour begins at EPCOT and continues to the Magic Kingdom, Disney's Animal Kingdom, and several behind-the-scenes areas, including costuming and central shops, where most of the Disney magic is made. Tours depart at 9 am on weekdays. The cost for the seven-hour tour (12 and older only) includes lunch at Tiffins in Disney's Animal Kingdom and bus transportation but does not include park admission, which isn't required for the tour itself. Those using wheelchairs or ECVs must inform Disney at the time of booking. ✉ *EPCOT* ☎ *407/939–8687* 🌐 *disneyworld.disney.go.com/events-tours/backstage-magic* 🎟 *$275.*

Dolphins in Depth

GUIDED TOURS | During this three-hour experience ($199), guides escort you from EPCOT Guest Relations outside the main park entrance and backstage to the Caribbean Coral Reef. This 5.7-million-gallon, man-made saltwater aquarium is home to The Seas with Nemo & Friends at EPCOT, as well as several bottle-nosed dolphins. You must bring your own bathing suits to wade into the water to meet, but not swim with, the dolphins. Children must be 13 years or older, and neither park admission nor a diving certificate is required. ✉ *EPCOT* ☎ *407/939–8687* 🌐 *disneyworld.disney.go.com/events-tours/epcot/dolphins-in-depth* 🎟 *$199.*

EPCOT Seas Adventures—Aqua Tour

SPECIAL-INTEREST TOURS | For this tour (no park admission required or included) you wear a flotation device and snorkel gear, and you remain on the water's surface. Anyone age 8 and older can join the tour (those under 12 must be with a parent or legal guardian). Tours are limited to 12 guests, meet Tuesday through Saturday, and run about 2½ hours, with 30 minutes in the water. ✉ *EPCOT* 🌐 *disneyworld.disney.go.com/events-tours/epcot/epcot-seas-aqua-tour* 🎫 *$145.*

EPCOT Seas Adventures—DiveQuest

SPECIAL-INTEREST TOURS | The three-hour DiveQuest (park admission not required or included) experience begins with a guide collecting you at Guest Relations outside the entrance. You spend 40 minutes in the 5.7-million-gallon saltwater aquarium under the supervision of a master diver. Family and friends with EPCOT admission can view your dive through the huge windows that line the aquarium. The tour takes place Tuesday through Saturday in the afternoon. Guests ages 10 and up must have open-water adult scuba certification; children 10 to 12 must dive with a parent or legal guardian. Diving equipment is supplied. ✉ *EPCOT* ☎ *407/939–8687* 🌐 *disneyworld.disney.go.com/events-tours/epcot/epcot-divequest* 🎫 *$179.*

Gardens of the World Tour

SPECIAL-INTEREST TOURS | Plant lovers of all levels will enjoy this three-hour tour (not including park admission) with a Disney Horticulturist to see the World Showcase's wide range of exotic plantings and to learn about the role landscaping plays in Disney parks and resorts. Tours run on select days during the EPCOT International Flower and Garden Festival in the spring or during the EPCOT International Food and Wine Festival in the fall. For ages 12 and up. ✉ *EPCOT* ☎ *407/939–8687* 🌐 *disneyworld.disney.go.com/events-tours/gardens-of-the-world* 🎫 *$85.*

EPCOT by Boat

EPCOT is a big place at 305 acres, and while the most efficient way to get around is to walk, you can save some time by boating across the lagoon. The 65-foot water taxis known as Friendship Boats depart every 12 minutes from four World Showcase Plaza docks spaced around the lagoon. The boat closer to Mexico zips to a dock by the Germany pavilion; the one closer to Canada heads to Morocco.

UnDISCOVERed Future World

GUIDED TOURS | This tour (plus park admission) leaves at 8:30 am Monday, Tuesday, Friday, and Saturday from a meeting spot between Fountain View and Club Cool. The four-hour behind-the-scenes walk for guests 16 and older covers pavilions in the area formerly known as Future World, as well as some backstage areas, including the EPCOT wardrobe department. ✉ *EPCOT* ☎ *407/939–8687* 🌐 *disneyworld.disney.go.com/events-tours/epcot/undiscovered-future-world* 🎫 *$69.*

Visiting Tips

Take your time. EPCOT is so vast and varied that you really need two days to explore. With just one day, you'll have to be highly selective.

Shop in the World Showcase. While shopping is thin on the ground in the rest of the park, the country-specific shops in the World Showcase have unique items from around the globe.

Go early in the week. Magic Kingdom tends to be busiest early in the week, making it the perfect time to visit EPCOT.

Plan for the special events. If you like a good festival, visit during the International Flower and Garden Festival (early March through early July) or the International Food and Wine Festival (September through mid-November).

Ride the popular rides early. Once through the turnstiles at either the main World Celebration entrance or the back World Showcase entrance, make a beeline for the popular Guardians of the Galaxy: Cosmic Rewind and Test Track (for fast-paced thrills) or Remy's Ratatouille Adventure, Frozen Ever After, and Soarin' (for family fun).

World Celebration

World Celebration's centerpiece is the iconic Spaceship Earth geosphere and, beyond it, a plaza anchored by a pavilion for live events. Three stories high, this architectural masterpiece adds some much needed space for EPCOT's many festivals. And fans of Walt Disney will be thrilled with Dreamers Point, containing a statue and story fountain celebrating Walt Disney and his vision for the future.

Also in World Celebration are Guest Relations, wheelchair and stroller rental, and lockers. If you haven't already done so, you can purchase Memory Maker at the Camera Center ($199 in the park, $169 in advance). It gives you access to all Disney PhotoPass photos of your group shot by Disney photographers, which you can view here in person or through the My Disney Experience app.

Sights

Balanced like a giant golf ball waiting for some celestial being to tee off, the multifaceted, silver geosphere of Spaceship Earth is to EPCOT what Cinderella Castle is to the Magic Kingdom. As much a landmark as an icon, it can be seen on a clear day from an airplane flying down either coast of Florida. It's also the sight of the Beacons of Magic light show, added to all four theme parks for the 50th Anniversary Celebration. If you're only going to catch one of these shows, make it the EPCOT one.

Spaceship Earth

AMUSEMENT RIDE | **FAMILY** | Inside the giant geosphere you are transported past tableaux that explore human progress and the continuing search for better forms of communication. The journey begins in the darkest tunnels of time, proceeds through history, and ends poised on the edge of the future. Revered author Ray Bradbury helped design the iconic ball and wrote the original story. Ten-time Emmy winner Bruce Broughton composed the musical score.

Audio-Animatronics figures present Cro-Magnon man daubing mystic paintings on cave walls, Egyptian scribes scratching hieroglyphics on papyrus, Roman centurions building roads, Islamic scholars mapping the heavens, and 11th- and 12th-century Benedictine monks hand-copying manuscripts. As you move into the Renaissance, there's Michelangelo and Gutenberg, and, in rapid succession, the telegraph, radio, television, and computer come into being. A family views the moon landing on TV, and soon the personal computer is born.

This ride has been updated multiple times over the years, always trying to incorporate the newest ideas for the future. The current Spaceship Earth emphasizes storytelling as what connects humanity, culminating in guests exiting at Dreamers Point, which honors Walt Disney who had his own gift for storytelling. **For people with disabilities:** You must be able to transfer to a standard wheelchair, then walk four steps to the ride vehicle. Guests with service animals should check with an attraction host for boarding information. The ride is equipped for handheld-captioning and audio-description devices available at Guest Relations **■TIP→ Lines are longest in the morning and shortest just before closing.** ✉ *World Celebration, EPCOT* ☞ *Duration: 15 mins. Crowds: Moderate. Audience: All ages.*

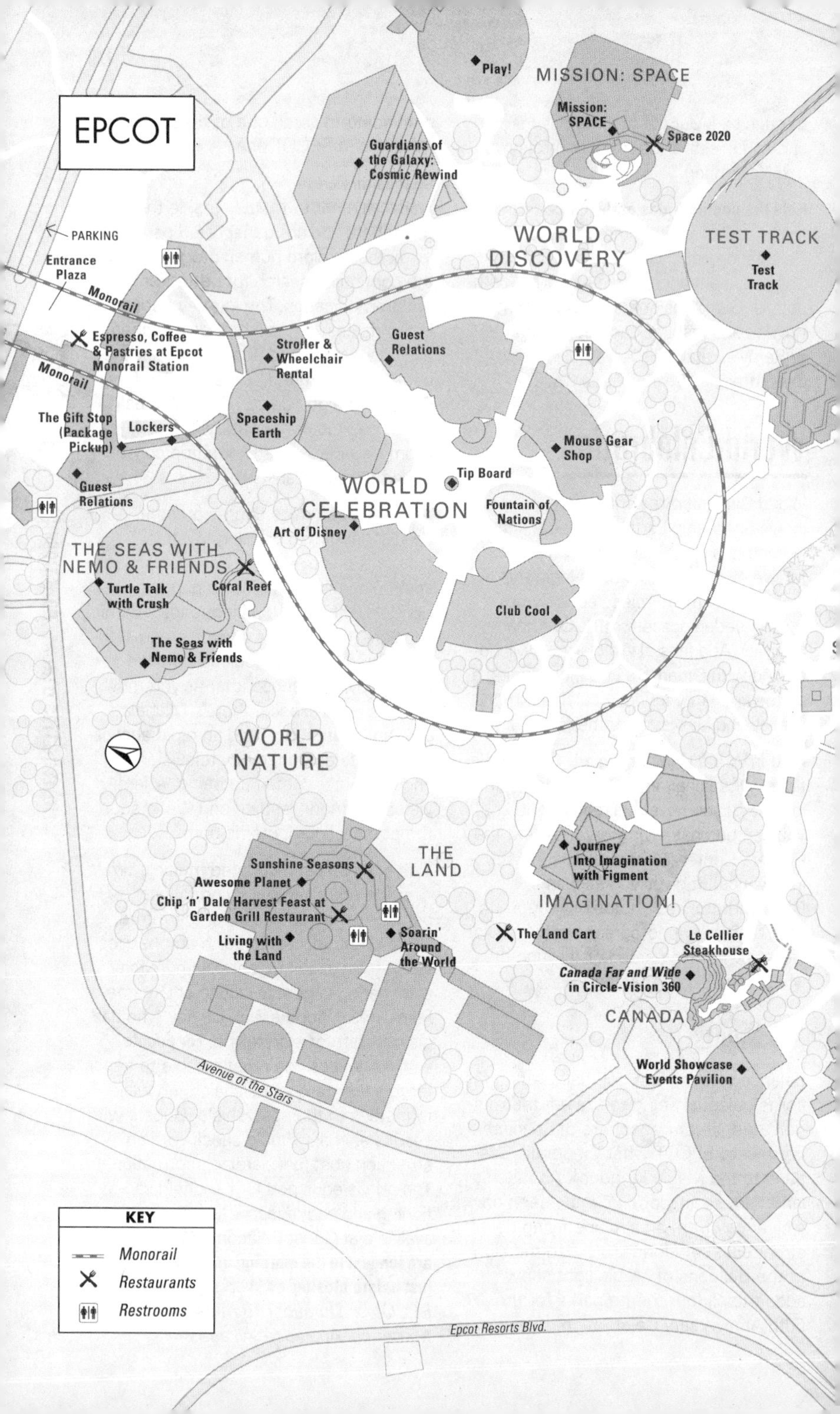
EPCOT
Play!
MISSION: SPACE
Mission: SPACE
Space 2020
Guardians of the Galaxy: Cosmic Rewind
PARKING
Entrance Plaza
Monorail
WORLD DISCOVERY
TEST TRACK
Test Track
Espresso, Coffee & Pastries at Epcot Monorail Station
Stroller & Wheelchair Rental
Guest Relations
Monorail
The Gift Stop (Package Pickup)
Lockers
Spaceship Earth
Mouse Gear Shop
Tip Board
Guest Relations
WORLD CELEBRATION
Fountain of Nations
Art of Disney
THE SEAS WITH NEMO & FRIENDS
Coral Reef
Turtle Talk with Crush
Club Cool
The Seas with Nemo & Friends
WORLD NATURE
THE LAND
Sunshine Seasons
Awesome Planet
Chip 'n' Dale Harvest Feast at Garden Grill Restaurant
Living with the Land
Soarin' Around the World
Journey Into Imagination with Figment
IMAGINATION!
The Land Cart
Le Cellier Steakhouse
Canada Far and Wide in Circle-Vision 360
CANADA
World Showcase Events Pavilion
Avenue of the Stars
KEY
Monorail
Restaurants
Restrooms
Epcot Resorts Blvd.

Avenue of the Stars
Avenue of the Stars
MEXICO
Frozen Ever After
NORWAY
CHINA
Gran Fiesta Tour Starring The Three Caballeros
Lotus Blossom Cafe
Wondrous China
Kringla Bakeri Og Kafe
Choza de Margarita
San Angel Inn Restaurante
Refreshment Outpost
La Cava del Tequila
Akershus Royal Banquet Hall
First Aid & Baby Care
La Cantina de San Angel
La Hacienda de San Angel
GERMANY
Biergarten Restaurant
Sommerfest
Boat Launch
Boat Launch
WORLD SHOWCASE PLAZA
ITALY
Tutto Gusto
Tutto Italia Ristorante
Via Napoli Ristorante e Pizzeria
World Showcase Lagoon
Ice Cream Cart
Boat Launch
WORLD SHOWCASE
ATM
America Gardens Theatre
Regal Eagle Smokehouse
The American Adventure
AMERICAN ADVENTURE
Kabuki Cafe
Rose & Crown Dining Room
Tokyo Dining and Teppan Edo
Katsura Grill
Yorkshire County Fish Shop
JAPAN
UNITED KINGDOM
Takumi-Tei
Spice Road Table
Boat Launch
INTERNATIONAL GATEWAY
FRANCE
MOROCCO
Stroller & Wheelchair Rental
Chefs de France
Restaurant Marrakesh
Monsieur Paul
Beauty and the Beast Sing-Along/ Impressions de France
L'Artisan des Glaces
Lockers
Les Halles Boulangerie & Pâtisserie
0
400 yards
0
400 m
Skyliner EPCOT
Friendship Launch
La Crêperie de Paris
Remy's Ratatouille Adventure

World Nature

To your right after passing under Spaceship Earth is World Nature, formerly known as Future World East. Here you'll find The Land pavilion, with the crowd favorite Soarin' Around the World, and The Seas with Nemo & Friends, a 5.7-million-gallon aquarium. The new Journey of Water exploration trail will let children follow "living water," just like Moana. Throughout this section of the park, guests will be in awe of nature's beauty.

Sights

Awesome Planet

OTHER ATTRACTION | FAMILY | This 11-minute film focuses on how we can work together to keep our awesome planet liveable in the future. The entire film is a real-estate pitch about how lucky we are to live on our planet, narrated by the ultimate real estate agent, Ty Burrell. For the first half, you're shown how Earth came to take form and the different biomes around the globe. The second half talks about how we are facing unprecedented changes to our planet and what can be done about it. There is breathtaking imagery from around the globe mixed in with this worthwhile message. ✉ *World Nature, EPCOT* ☞ *Duration: 11 mins. Crowds: Light. Audience: All ages.*

Journey into Imagination with Figment

AMUSEMENT RIDE | FAMILY | Figment, a fun-loving dragon, takes you on a sensory adventure designed to engage your imagination through sound, illusion, gravity, dimension, and color. After the ride you can check out ImageWorks, where several interactive displays allow you to further stretch your imagination. Although this ride is geared to smaller kids, there are a few bangs and a brief period of darkness. Though Disney hasn't announced anything, there is constant speculation that this attraction is going to be updated or closed during the EPCOT renovations. **For people with disabilities:** ride and ImageWorks are wheelchair accessible. Equipped for handheld-captioning and audio-description devices. ✉ *World Nature, EPCOT* ☞ *Duration: 8 mins. Crowds: Light. Audience: Small kids.*

Living with the Land

AMUSEMENT RIDE | FAMILY | A canopied boat cruises through three artificial biomes—rain forest, desert, and prairie—and into an experimental live greenhouse that demonstrates how food might be sourced in the future, not only on the planet but also in outer space. Shrimp, tilapia, eels, catfish, and alligators are raised in controlled aquacells, and tomatoes, peppers, squash, and other fruits and vegetables thrive in the Desert Farm area via drip irrigation that delivers just the right amount of water and nutrients to their roots. Gardeners are usually interested in the section on integrated pest management, which relies on "good" insects like ladybugs to control more harmful predators.

See Mickey Mouse–shape fruits and vegetables (there might be pumpkins, cucumbers, or watermelons) nurtured with the help of molds created by the science team; scientists also have grown a "tomato tree"—the first of its kind in the United States—that has yielded thousands of tomatoes from a single vine. Many of the growing areas are actual experiments-in-progress, in which Disney and the U.S. Department of Agriculture have joined forces to produce, say, a sweeter pineapple or a faster-growing pepper. The plants and fish that grow in the greenhouse are regularly harvested for use in The Land's restaurants. **For people with disabilities:** Those using an oversize wheelchair or ECV must transfer to a standard wheelchair. Equipped for handheld-captioning and audio-description devices. **TIP→ If your party finds Living with the Land interesting, check out Behind the Seeds, an hour-long tour providing a more detailed look at the greenhouse.**

Offered every 45-minutes, this tour is $29 per person ages 3 and up. A sign-up desk is beside the ride's exit. ✉ *World Nature, EPCOT ☞ Duration: 14 mins. Crowds: Moderate. Audience: All ages.*

The Seas with Nemo & Friends

AMUSEMENT RIDE | FAMILY | Hop into a "clamobile" and ride under the sea to look for Nemo, who has wandered off from Mr. Ray's class field trip. This ride adds clever fun to the aquarium attraction—an astonishing animation-projection effect makes it appear as if Nemo and his pals are swimming among the marine life of the actual Seas aquarium. As your ride progresses, Dory, Nemo's spacey sidekick, helps Bruce, Squirt, and other pals find him. After the ride, walk around the tank to Bruce's Shark World for some fun photo ops and shark facts, discover how dolphins communicate, and visit an endangered Florida manatee rehabilitation center. **For people with disabilities:** Guests in standard wheelchairs can wheel onto an accessible "clamshell" vehicle; those in ECVs must transfer to a standard wheelchair or the ride vehicle. Equipped for audio-description and handheld-captioning devices. **■TIP→ Though lines can be long, they move quickly.** ✉ *World Nature, EPCOT ☞ Duration: Up to you. Crowds: Moderate to heavy. Audience: All ages.*

★ Soarin' Around the World

AMUSEMENT RIDE | FAMILY | If you've ever wondered what it's like to fly, or at least hang glide, this attraction is your chance to enjoy the sensation without actually taking the plunge. It uses motion-based technology to literally lift you in your seat 40 feet into the air within a giant projection-screen dome. As you soar above the wonders of the world—from the sharp peaks of the Alps and the Great Wall of China to Sydney Harbor in Australia and the spires of Neuschwanstein Castle in Bavaria—you feel the wind and dodge the spray of leaping whales. The flight is so mild (and the view so thrilling) that even very timid children love it. **For people with disabilities:** Those with mobility impairments must transfer from their wheelchairs to the ride system. Equipped for video-captioning devices. Service animals aren't permitted on the ride. **■TIP→ Long lines mean this should be one of your first stops upon entering the park, or you can wait until just before fireworks to try for a shorter line.** ✉ *World Nature, EPCOT ☞ Duration: 5 mins. Crowds: Heavy. Audience: All ages. Height requirement: 40 inches.*

Turtle Talk with Crush

PERFORMANCE VENUE | FAMILY | Head for the Sea Base area to line up for this real-time animated show starring Crush, the ancient sea turtle from *Finding Nemo*. Crush chats and jokes with kids so convincingly that young children, eyes wide as sand dollars, have walked up and touched the screen where Crush "swims." It's in a small theater, and there's often a wait, but it's a hit with young children as well as their parents. **For people with disabilities:** The theater is wheelchair accessible, and assisted-listening devices can be used. **■TIP→ Check the Times Guide for show schedule; arrive about 20 minutes early during busy times to guarantee a seat.** ✉ *World Nature, EPCOT ☞ Duration: 15 mins. Crowds: Moderate to heavy. Audience: Small kids, but great for all ages.*

Restaurants

Chip 'n' Dale Harvest Feast at Garden Grill Restaurant

$$$$ | AMERICAN | FAMILY | Family-style dinner fare is served here as the restaurant revolves, giving you an ever-changing backstage view of the Living with the Land boat ride. Offering quantity over quality, the restaurant serves all-you-can-eat meals with visits from Chip 'n' Dale, Pluto, and occasionally Mickey. **Known for:** family-style servings with beer and wine available; character dining; unusual revolving restaurant within The Land pavilion. [$] *Average main: $55* ✉ *World Nature, EPCOT* ☎ *407/939–3463* 🌐 *disneyworld.disney.go.com/dining/epcot/garden-grill-restaurant.*

Coral Reef

$$$ | **SEAFOOD** | **FAMILY** | With stunning views of the 5.7-million-gallon aquarium, dining at Coral Reef is as entertaining as it is delicious. As you watch marine life—and sometimes scuba divers—swim by, enjoy dishes from a seasonal menu that's heavy on seafood offerings. **Known for:** Baileys almond and Jack Daniel's mousse; lobster bisque; scenic aquarium views. [$] *Average main: $30* ✉ *World Nature, EPCOT* ☎ *407/939–3463* 🌐 *disneyworld.disney.go.com/dining/epcot/coral-reef-restaurant.*

Coffee and Quick Bites

The Land Cart

$ | **AMERICAN** | **FAMILY** | If you're looking for a break from greasy vacation food, stop by The Land Cart for a fruit and cheese tray or a veggie and hummus tray. It's a short walk to benches where you can eat overlooking the upside-down water fountain by Journey in Imagination. **Known for:** fresh fruits and veggies; easy walk-up; pretty views. [$] *Average main: $7* ✉ *World Nature, EPCOT* ☎ *407/939–3463* 🌐 *disneyworld.disney.go.com/dining/epcot/the-land-cart.*

Sunshine Seasons

$ | **AMERICAN** | **FAMILY** | This market-style restaurant is great for a substantial meal or just a quick, healthy bite. Made using food sourced primarily on site, dishes might include stir-fried chicken or shrimp, vegetable korma, or oak-grilled salmon. **Known for:** local veggies, fruits, and fish; grilled salmon; quick, cafeteria-style service. [$] *Average main: $12* ✉ *World Nature, EPCOT* ☎ *407/939–3463* 🌐 *disneyworld.disney.go.com/dining/epcot/sunshine-seasons.*

World Discovery

World Discovery is to the left of World Celebration, which was formerly called Future World West. Sleek lines and an out-of-this-world atmosphere help tell the stories of science, technology, and space. The main rides have long been Test Track and Mission: SPACE. But this is also home to the much-anticipated, new-in-2022 coaster, Guardians of the Galaxy: Cosmic Rewind, which rotates 360 degrees and includes a reverse launch. In addition, an entire showcase pavilion dedicated to the planet Xandar, from the first Guardians of the Galaxy movie, immerses guests in a different world. Developments in this area of the park are ongoing, so check for updates before you travel.

Sights

★ Guardians of the Galaxy: Cosmic Rewind

AMUSEMENT RIDE | **FAMILY** | The peace-loving planet Xandar, from Marvel's Guardians of the Galaxy franchise, has opened as the first other-world exhibit at EPCOT. However, Rocket and his pals find the presentation "boring," so that's when you're off on a totally new (in summer 2022) adventure created especially for EPCOT. This attraction, which uses Audio-Animatronics and screens to tell the story, features the first reverse launch of any Disney ride. Like the movies, the direction for it was done by James Gunn. Expect it to have a height requirement of between 40 and 44 inches. There are no flips, and the harnesses are lap only, with guests sitting two-by-two, which can make nervous kids feel more relaxed. **For people with disabilities:** check with Guest Relations about boarding requirements. **■ TIP→ Expect massive crowds, which might mean that this attraction will become one of EPCOT's few that offer individual Lightning Lanes.** ✉ *World Discovery, EPCOT.*

★ Mission: SPACE

AMUSEMENT RIDE | FAMILY | It took five years for Disney Imagineers, with the help of 25 experts from NASA, to design Mission: SPACE, the first ride ever to take people "straight up" in a simulated rocket launch. The story transports you and co-riders to the year 2036 and the International Space Training Center, where you are about to embark on your first launch. Before you board the four-person rocket capsule, you're assigned to a position: commander, navigator, pilot, or engineer. And at this point, you're warned several times about the intensity of the ride and the risks for people with health concerns. After many guests became sick after riding, Disney created an "orange" and a "green" mission. The Orange mission heads to Mars and has a height requirement of 44 inches. A spinning motion creates the feeling of a rocket launch and weightlessness (the effect is also cumulative, so stick with one go-round unless you have a particularly hardy constitution). The Green mission on Earth, with a height requirement of 40 inches, is still plenty bumpy, but doesn't use spinning to create special effects. Pregnant women and anyone with heart, back, neck, balance, blood-pressure, or motion-sickness problems shouldn't ride either version.

For those who can handle the intense spinning, the sensation of liftoff is a turbulent, heart-pounding experience that flattens you against your seat. Once you break into outer space, you'll even feel weightless. After landing, you exit your capsule into the Advanced Training Lab, where you can play some very entertaining space-related games. **For people with disabilities:** This ride requires a transfer from wheelchair to seat. Service animals aren't permitted to board. Video-captioning devices can be used on the ride; assisted-listening devices can be used in the postshow Training Lab. ■ **TIP→ Both lines move swiftly, and people rarely ride this more than once, so if you see long wait times, give it an hour and try again. Don't ride on a full stomach.** ✉ *World Discovery, EPCOT* ☞ *Duration: 4 mins. Crowds: You bet! Audience: Not small kids. Height requirement: 40 inches.*

★ Test Track

AMUSEMENT RIDE | FAMILY | The white-knuckle finale of this fan favorite is as thrilling as ever. Create a custom concept vehicle at an interactive design station, and then buckle up in a six-person SimCar to put the design through its paces in a neon-splashed, futuristic setting that surrounds the attraction's original hills and mountain switchbacks. Everyone can create their own designs and see how they compare to everyone else's—first in their car and then at the end of the ride.

The High-Speed Test is last: your vehicle bursts through an opening in the Test Track building to negotiate a steeply banked loop at a speed of nearly 60 mph. At the special effects–laden postshow, you can see how your custom car performed and create your own car commercial. The speeds and some jarring effects can be unsettling, so this ride isn't suitable for pregnant women or guests wearing back, neck, or leg braces. **For people with disabilities:** Visitors in wheelchairs are provided a special area in which to practice transferring into the ride vehicle before actually boarding. One TV monitor in the preshow area is closed-captioned. Service animals aren't permitted onboard. ■ **TIP→ This ride won't function on wet tracks, so don't head here after a downpour. Also note that the Single Rider queue has been eliminated here.** ✉ *World Discovery, EPCOT* ☞ *Duration: 5 mins. Crowds: Heavy. Audience: Not small kids. Height requirement: 40 inches.*

Did You Know?

Disney's original conception for the EPCOT Center—as sort of a futuristic master-planned community—didn't quite pan out in the park but instead took form in the town of Celebration, near Kissimmee.

Restaurants

Space 2020

$$$$ | **MODERN AMERICAN** | At what is, literally, an out-of-this-world restaurant, you board a special elevator to travel 220 miles above the planet to a dining room with panoramas of Earth through viewports that use real-time, above-the-clouds imagery. The prix-fixe menu ($55 at lunch and $79 for dinner) includes a lift-off (read: appetizer) and a star (main) course. **Known for:** one of the newest restaurants at Disney; real-time views from space; unique craft beer. *Average main: $79* *World Discovery, EPCOT* *407/939–3463* *disneyworld.disney.go.com/dining/epcot/space-220.*

World Showcase

Nowhere but at EPCOT can you explore nearly a dozen countries in one day. As you stroll the 1.3 miles around the 40-acre World Showcase Lagoon, you circumnavigate the globe-according-to-Disney by experiencing native food, entertainment, culture, and arts and crafts at pavilions representing countries in Europe, Asia, North Africa, and the Americas. Pavilion employees are from the countries they represent—Disney hires them as part of its international college program.

By far the most popular attraction among youngsters is the Frozen Ever After ride in the Norway pavilion, and Remy's Ratatouille Adventure will have you scurrying around the kitchens of France. You'll see solid film attractions, as well as several art exhibitions, at the Canada, China, and France pavilions, and you can try your foreign language skills with the staff. Each pavilion also has a designated Kidcot Fun Stop, open daily from 11 or noon until about 8 or 9, where youngsters can try a cultural crafts project. Live entertainment is an integral part of the experience, and you'll enjoy watching the incredibly talented Jeweled Dragon Acrobats in China and the Matsuriza Taiko drummers in Japan or laughing along with Sergio, the mime and juggler in the Italy courtyard.

Water Play

Preschoolers love to play in the interactive fountains in front of Mission: SPACE and in the walkways between World Celebration and the World Showcase. Bring swimsuits and a towel!

Dining is another favorite pastime at EPCOT, and the World Showcase offers tempting, authentic dishes from the various cultures. Drinking is another draw, and there are plenty of theme bars and international drinks on hand to try.

For People with Disabilities: Attractions at Mexico, American Adventure, France, China, and Canada are all wheelchair accessible, as are the plaza areas where shows are presented. Mexico's Gran Fiesta Tour boat ride is also wheelchair accessible; personal-translator units amplify soundtracks. Most of the live entertainment around the World Showcase features strong aural and visual elements.

Canada

"Oh, it's just our Canadian outdoors," said a typically modest native guide upon being asked about the model for the striking rocky chasm and tumbling waterfall that represent just one of the pavilion's high points. The beautiful formal gardens do have an antecedent: Butchart Gardens, in Victoria, British Columbia. And so does the Hôtel du Canada, a French Gothic mansion with spires, turrets, and a mansard roof; anyone who's ever stayed at Québec's Château Frontenac or Ottawa's Château Laurier will recognize the imposing style favored by architects of Canadian railroad hotels.

Did You Know?

Totem poles, like the one at the Canada pavilion, tell stories—sometimes legends, other times histories of clans or important figures. It was once thought that the higher the figure on the pole, the more important it was (hence the phrase "the low man on the totem pole"), but this isn't necessarily so.

EPCOT Kids Tour

A trip to Italy is on hold, but Mom knows she can find a taste of Venice in the World Showcase. Dad, the *Popular Mechanics* devotee, can't wait to check out Test Track. Each can have a great day—in his or her own way.

Strategize

Devise a plan before pushing through the EPCOT turnstiles. Everyone will probably want to take off at **Soarin' Around the World** in The Land for the one-ride-fits-all thrill of simulated hang gliding (there are even special safety restraints for little ones). If your kids are too small for the height restrictions at **Test Track**, let Dad ride solo while Mom takes the kids on **Spaceship Earth.** Meet back up at the **Imagination!** pavilion to ride along with Figment, the purple dragon, or head back to **The Land** for a Sunshine Seasons treat. Don't miss an under-the-sea ride at the **Seas with Nemo & Friends** before meeting the coolest dude of all at **Turtle Talk with Crush.**

Get Your World Showcase Passports

On the way into the World Showcase, let the kids get their own passports, complete with stickers, at any merchandise location. As you visit each country, they can get their passports stamped—not only a fun lesson in geography but a great keepsake. Before you cross the border, stop and let young kids play in the dancing fountains if they're operating—it'll be one of their happiest memories. Bring a towel and a change of clothing, and you'll be happy, too.

For the Little Ones (and Mom)

Younger children can be creative at **Kidcot Fun Stops,** where a Disney cast member gets them started on a craft activity, such as coloring a Carnivale-style mask on a stick. At each of 11 Fun Stops, the kids can add something to the mask, such as a Viking ship at Norway after the **Frozen Ever After** ride. Children love Mexico because they can ride the boats at **Gran Fiesta Tour starring the Three Caballeros.** Now it's your turn, Mom. Italy is right around the corner, and the kids can watch a juggler or comedy troupe in the courtyard while you sip some wine at Tutto Gusto Wine Cellar or go shopping.

Live Performances

The Beatles, the Rolling Stones, Elton John, and more: hear top hits by iconic British musicians when the tribute band British Revolution amps up the fun outside the United Kingdom showcase five days each week. Grab a bench or dance to favorite tunes. Young children are thrilled to explore hedge mazes that surround the gazebo stage.

Live entertainment is one of EPCOT's strong suits—best shows for younger kids are the **Jeweled Dragon Acrobats** at China, **Mariachi Cobre** musicians at Mexico, **Sergio the clown and juggler** at Italy, and the **JAMMitors percussion group** at World Celebration (check the daily *Times Guide*).

EPCOT Grown-Ups Tour

Hang glide over a mountain, blast off into space, then journey to Mexico for a tequila flight and a "moonlit" dinner. Even if the adventures are faux fun, there's so much to soak up here that you'll want to return later to catch up on whatever you missed.

A Ticket to Ride

If you're aiming for high adventure, head straight for **Soarin' Around the World**, and hightail it over to **Test Track** right after. The new **Guardians of the Galaxy: Cosmic Rewind** should also be one of your top stops. Look for more interactive challenges in the Advanced Training Lab at the end of your **Mission: SPACE** ride and in the **Spaceship Earth** postride show.

World Travel

You can be in Canada one minute and England the next, once you cross into the World Showcase. Authentic replicas of famous landmarks like Venice's Piazza San Marco or Norway's 13th-century stave church will grab you. Once inside, you can practice your Italian, French, Spanish—Norwegian, even—with representatives of those countries.

You can also eat your way around the globe from a biergarten in Germany to a French bistro, and beyond. The margherita pizza delivers the flavor of Italy at Via Napoli. Enjoy a glass of Prosecco as you watch passersby in the courtyard, or buy a wine-tasting pass for two tastes at each wine shop in Italy, Germany, and France. You'll find silk (or washable poly) kimonos in Japan's Mitsukoshi store, hefty beer steins at Die Weihnachts Ecke in Germany, and belly-dancing garb and finger cymbals in Morocco. If you truly have your heart set on being able to eat your way across the world, visit during fall's Food and Wine Festival, when more than 30 booths offer tasty treats from around the globe.

Applause and a Toast

Too many people miss the great daily live acts around the park, so take time to check your *Times Guide* and choose a performance or two. Top acts include the **Voices of Liberty** at the American Adventure, a **traditional Berber music and dance troupe** at Morocco, and the **British Revolution** rock-and-roll cover band as well as a **Celtic folk music ensemble** at United Kingdom. The park's comedy troupes are a hoot, and the **Matsuriza drummers** at Japan are mesmerizing.

Before you venture to the edge of the lagoon for the fireworks-filled closing show, check out one of EPCOT's great watering holes. **La Cava del Tequila** in Mexico serves more than 200 varieties. It also offers tequila flights and specialty margaritas in unexpected flavors like jalapeño and cucumber. The **Rose & Crown pub** in the United Kingdom is EPCOT's most boisterous spot, where the pianist takes requests, and it's standing-room-only at the bar. Finally, grab a spot at the **Spice Road Table** in Morocco, and order a beer or wine flight and some tapas for lagoonside fireworks viewing. Cheers! *Salud! Prosit!* Be sure to take a bus or taxi back to your resort.

Like the size of the Rocky Mountains, the scale of the structures seems immense; unlike the real thing, it's managed with a trick called forced perspective, which exaggerates the smallness of the distant parts to make the entire thing look gigantic.

You can browse shops that sell maple syrup; Canadian sports jerseys; and plush huggable bears, beavers, and huskies. Le Cellier Steakhouse is a great place for a relaxing lunch or dinner; due to its increasing popularity, make reservations far ahead.

Sights

Canada Far and Wide in Circle-Vision 360
PERFORMANCE VENUE | **FAMILY** | Disney has updated and expanded this attraction, which uses 12 surrounding screens to give guests a 360-degree view of Canada's majestic landscape. The narrators break the nation down province by province, sharing knowledge, along with the breathtaking views, about this majestic country. There a couple downsides here: it's a standing-only theater, strollers aren't permitted, and toddlers and small children can't see unless they're held aloft. **For people with disabilities:** Wheelchair and ECV accessible; reflective captioning and equipped for assisted-listening and audio-description devices. ✉ *World Showcase, Canada Pavilion, EPCOT* ☞ *Duration: 14 mins. Crowds: Moderate to heavy. Audience: All ages.*

Restaurants

Le Cellier Steakhouse
$$$$ | **CANADIAN** | This popular eatery with stone arches and dark woods transports you to a cozy, well-heeled, Canadian-château setting and offers a good selection of wines and Canadian beer to complement such signature dishes as Prince Edward Island mussels, cheddar cheese soup, and AAA Canadian tenderloin. Lighter fare includes steamed Asian dumplings and red snapper; if you're itching to try yet another Canadian specialty, order one of the poutine dishes as a side. **Known for:** exceptional service; indulgent Canadian filet mignon; signature poutine. [$] *Average main: $55* ✉ *World Showcase, Canada Pavilion, EPCOT* ☎ *407/939–3463* 🌐 *disneyworld.disney.go.com/dining/epcot/le-cellier-steakhouse.*

Get a Passport

A World Showcase Passport ($13) is a wonderful way to keep a kid interested in this more adult area of EPCOT. The passports, available at vendor carts, come with stickers and a badge, and children can have them stamped at each pavilion. The World Showcase is also a great place to look for unusual gifts—you might pick up a Oaxacan wood carving in Mexico, a tea set in China, or a kimonoed doll in Japan.

Shopping

Northwest Mercantile
SOUVENIRS | **FAMILY** | Along with an abundance of hockey-related merchandise and maple syrup, the shop offers a number of Canadian-centric items not otherwise available in the United States. You'll find plenty of teddy bears (and far more moose) on the shelves, as well as mugs and clothing celebrating Canadian brews. ✉ *World Showcase, Canada Pavilion, EPCOT.*

United Kingdom

The United Kingdom rambles between the elegant mansions lining a London square to the bustling, half-timber shops of a village High Street to thatched-roof cottages from the countryside. (The thatch is made of plastic broom bristles due to local fire regulations.) Of course, there's a pair of iconic red phone booths. And EPCOT is anticipated to expand this nation with a Mary Poppins–inspired experience that's still in the planning stages.

Around 17 Cherry Tree Lane, you wander through shops selling tea, Welsh handicrafts, Scottish tweed, and English lavender fragrance by Taylor of London. There's a store with Beatles T-shirts, CDs, and memorabilia. At the Historic Research Center you can research your family name and purchase printed, hand-painted, or embroidered versions of your family coat of arms.

Tucked in the back are a lovely, though easy-to-miss, garden and park with benches—relax and kick back to the tunes of the British Revolution, a band known for its on-target Beatles and other Brit-band performances. Kids love to run through the hedge maze as their parents travel back in time to "Yesterday." Check the *Times Guide*, and arrive 30 minutes early for a bench or 15 minutes early for a curb. Restrooms are near the red phone booths.

Restaurants

Rose & Crown Dining Room

$$$ | **BRITISH** | **FAMILY** | If you're an Anglophile and you love a beer so thick you could stand a spoon up in your mug, head here—not only to soak up the suds but also to enjoy the British street culture and feast on the best fish-and-chips in town. Other traditional English fare includes Scotch eggs, bubble and squeak (fried potatoes and cabbage), shepherd's pie, and, at times, bangers-and-mash (sausage over mashed potatoes); vegetarians can always find an adapted item, such as a savory hot pot. **Known for:** great views of HarmonioUS from the outdoor terrace; wide selection of beers and ciders from the pub; Angus beef burger with beer cheese sauce. *Average main: $24* ✉ *World Showcase, United Kingdom Pavilion, EPCOT* ☎ *407/939–3463* 🌐 *disneyworld.disney.go.com/dining/epcot/rose-and-crown-dining-room.*

Coffee and Quick Bites

If you're in a hurry, grab some takeout fish-and-chips from **Yorkshire County Fish Shop** and then nab a lagoon-side table.

Nightlife

Rose & Crown Pub

PUBS | Patrons of this rollicking pub enjoy singing along with the piano or just listening to a jazzy version of last year's hits. On busy nights, people stand four- to six deep at the bar. The fish-and-chips are first-rate; think about pairing them with one of the many unique "pub blends." Grab a pint, and let the fun begin! ✉ *World Showcase, United Kingdom Pavilion, EPCOT* 🌐 *disneyworld.disney.go.com/dining/epcot/rose-and-crown-pub.*

Performing Arts

HarmonioUS

SOUND/LIGHT SHOW | **FAMILY** | The largest fireworks show ever created for a Disney park (a replacement for the long-lived and well-loved IllumiNations) is a spectacular ending to the day. Large barges combine LED panels, fountains, lights, lasers, and fireworks to create a display accompanied by the most inspiring music Disney has to offer. While this show can be viewed anywhere around the World Showcase Lagoon, arrive an hour before showtime at either World Showcase Plaza or by the International Gateway if you want to exit swiftly. Or take the other extreme: find a seat deep in the park, and meander out slowly after the show. Want a guaranteed seat? Book a reservation at the Rose & Crown, La Cantina de San Angel, or Spice Road Table to eat while you view the fireworks. ✉ *World Showcase, World Showcase Lagoon, EPCOT* 🌐 *disneyworld.disney.go.com/entertainment/epcot/harmonious.*

Shopping

In the cobblestone village at the United Kingdom, an English pub sits on one side and a collection of British, Irish, and Scottish shops beckons you on the other. The Toy Soldier carries popular British toys and memorabilia known by all Brits; the Sportsman Shoppe has books and team apparel from various U.K. football (aka soccer) teams; and the Tea Caddy sells Twinings tea, teacups, teapots, and British sweets.

The Crown & Crest

SOUVENIRS | This shop carries the widest range of items in the U.K. pavilion, from woolen sweaters from Scotland to Beatles-theme gifts and memorabilia. ✉ *World Showcase, United Kingdom Pavilion, EPCOT* 🌐 *disneyworld.disney.go.com/shops/epcot/the-crown-and-crest.*

Historic Research Center

OTHER SPECIALTY STORE | The focus at this U.K. outpost in the Crown & Crest is tracking down your family name and coat of arms. Take home a printout of both for about $70. Drop the bigger bucks for a framed, embroidered, or hand-painted version. ✉ *World Showcase, United Kingdom Pavilion, EPCOT.*

France

You don't need the scaled-down model of the Eiffel Tower to tell you that you've arrived in France, specifically Paris. There's the poignant accordion music wafting out of concealed speakers, the trim sycamores pruned in the French style to develop signature knots at the end of each branch, and the delicious aromas surrounding Les Halles Boulangerie & Pâtisserie bakeshop. This is the Paris of dreams, a Paris of the years just before World War I, when solid mansard-roof mansions were crowned with iron filigree, when the least brick was drenched in romanticism. Other dreams have arrived in this pavilion, namely Remy's Ratatouille Adventure and a Beauty and the Beast Sing-Along show.

Here's a replica of the original Les Halles—the iron-and-glass barrel-roof market that no longer exists in the City of Light; there's an arching footbridge; and all around, of course, are shops. You can inspect Parisian Impressionist artwork at Galerie des Halles; sample perfume at the Guerlain shop; and acquire a Julia Child cookbook or bottle of Pouilly-Fuisse at Les Vins de France. If you plan to dine at Les Chefs de France, make a reservation for a late lunch or dinner; the second-floor Monsieur Paul (dinner only) is a gourmet treat.

Sights

Beauty and the Beast Sing-Along

PERFORMANCE VENUE | **FAMILY** | As its name implies, little ones love singing along with beloved classics from *Beauty and the Beast* at this show, which plays in the same theater as Impressions de France. The traditional story has a twist, however. As Mrs. Potts narrates, you realize that LeFou, best known as Gaston's sidekick, was actually working behind the scenes to help Belle and the Beast fall in love. Although this 15-minute film is particularly good for younger kids, everyone will appreciate the chance to sit down and enjoy a cute story line. ✉ *World Showcase, France Pavilion, EPCOT* ☞ *Duration: 15 mins. Crowds: Moderate. Audience: All ages.*

Impressions de France

PERFORMANCE VENUE | The intimate Palais du Cinema, inspired by the royal theater at Fontainebleau, screens this homage to the glories of the country. Shown on five screens spanning 200 degrees, in an air-conditioned, sit-down theater, the film takes you to vineyards at harvest time, Paris on Bastille Day, the Alps, Versailles, Normandy's Mont-Saint-Michel, and the stunning châteaux of the Loire Valley. The music sweeps you away with familiar segments from Offenbach, Debussy, and Saint-Saëns, all woven together by longtime Disney musician Buddy Baker. **For people with disabilities:** Wheelchair- and ECV-accessible; reflective captioning and equipped for assisted-listening and audio-description devices. **■ TIP→ The Beauty and the Beast Sing-Along has proved so popular, that Impressions de France is now only shown at select times in the evening. Check the Times Guide.** ✉ *World Showcase, France Pavilion, EPCOT* ☞ *Duration: 20 mins. Crowds: Moderate. Audience: All ages.*

Remy's Ratatouille Adventure

AMUSEMENT RIDE | FAMILY | It's Remy's big night, and he's cooking to impress the food critic Anton Ego. To succeed, he needs the help of all his rat friends, including you! On this ride, the four-person cars, which are shaped like rats, begin by meandering through the oversized rooftops of Paris. Gusteau quickly takes you to his restaurant so you can assist Remy and Linguini with the cooking, all the while trying to avoid the gaze of Skinner, the head chef who has a terror of rats. Combined 3-D screens along with a giant kitchen create a 4-D effect so real it feels like you're really scurrying around. The trackless ride system furthers the notion of independence; often you and your fellow rats will hide in different places and then meet back up to help Remy. **For people with disabilities:** Wheelchairs can be loaded onto certain ride cars in a lane to the side of the boarding area. Those in ECVs will need to transfer to a standard wheelchair to use this feature or will need to walk to a wider car if they would prefer. **■ TIP→ Remy's is one of the two EPCOT attractions that has the Individual Lightning Lane selection, meaning you can pay extra to skip the line. Prices vary depending on the time of year, but if you're visiting late in the day or during the summer, the cost can be worth it.** ✉ *World Showcase, France Pavilion, EPCOT* ☞ *Duration: 5 mins. Crowds: Heavy. Audience: All ages.*

Restaurants

Chefs de France

$$$ | FRENCH | This plush, bustling brasserie remains true to the spirit and the vision of Paul Bocuse, Gaston Lenôtre, and Roger Vergé, three of France's most famous chefs (Bocuse's son, Jerome, continues to run the restaurant). Classic escargots, a good starter, are prepared in a casserole with garlic butter; you might follow up with salmon marinated in white wine and lemon and served in a champagne sauce or grilled beef tenderloin with green peppercorn sauce; naturally, ratatouille is available, as is the occasional three-course, prix-fixe meal. **Known for:** French charcuterie plate; sophisticated, classic French cuisine; beef bourguignon. *$ Average main: $30* ✉ *World Showcase, France Pavilion, EPCOT* ☎ *407/939–3463* 🌐 *disneyworld.disney.go.com/dining/epcot/chefs-de-france.*

★ **Monsieur Paul**

$$$$ | FRENCH | A mere staircase away from EPCOT's busy World Showcase, Monsieur Paul is a subdued, sophisticated (and not very kid-friendly) French restaurant. Make a reservation here if you are looking for an expensive, polished, and delightful diversion from the theme park's bustle. **Known for:** an extensive wine list; the service is so good you'll think you're at a Michelin-starred restaurant; magret de canard (roasted duck breast). *$ Average main: $42* ✉ *World Showcase, France Pavilion, EPCOT* ☎ *407/939–3463* 🌐 *disneyworld.disney.go.com/dining/epcot/monsieur-paul.*

Coffee and Quick Bites

It might be true in the real world, so it's true in the World Showcase: the best food is in France. It's worth it to brave the lines at **Les Halles Boulangerie & Pâtisserie,** a large, Parisian-style, counter-service café. Have wine with a cheese plate, quiche, or sandwich on crusty French bread. Or go for a creamy café au lait and a napoleon.

L'Artisan des Glaces ice cream and sorbet shop is praiseworthy for its ultracreamy treats that include an ice cream "martini" with Grand Marnier and flavor-customized ice-cream sandwiches made with brioche or macaron. **La Crêperie de Paris**, open for breakfast, lunch, and dinner, offers delicious fresh made crepes along with a Parisian soup of the day. ■ **TIP→ Looking to taste the best wines around? EPCOT's Wine Walk includes tastings in France, Italy, and Germany. For $32, you receive two plastic wine glasses and tastings in all three countries.**

Shopping

La Signature

PERFUME | Follow your nose for a sniff and a spritz of high-end French perfumes. Guerlain fragrances, cosmetics, and skincare products like the Orchidée Impériale eye cream (most recently selling for a whopping $200 apiece) draw fans from around the globe. ✉ *World Showcase, France Pavilion, EPCOT* 🌐 *disneyworld.disney.go.com/shops/epcot/la-signature.*

Morocco

Walk through the Bab Boujouloud Gate and be transported to this strikingly beautiful North African country. The gate's pointed arches are ornamented with wood carvings and encrusted with mosaics made of 9 tons of handmade, hand-cut tiles; 19 native artisans were sent to EPCOT to install them and to create the dusty stucco walls that seem to have withstood centuries of sandstorms. Look closely and you'll see that every tile has a small crack or other imperfection, and no tile depicts a living creature—in deference to the Islamic belief that only Allah creates perfection and life.

Koutoubia Minaret, a replica of the prayer tower in Marrakesh, acts as Morocco's landmark. Winding alleyways—each corner bursting with carpets, brasses, leatherwork, and other wares—lead to a tiled fountain and lush gardens. A highlight is Restaurant Marrakesh. Enjoy couscous and roast lamb while a traditional belly dancer performs.

Tangierine Café offers great, shareable snacks, such as hummus dips and grilled kebabs. Its fresh blood-orange juice is a real treat, too. Spice Road Table is the ideal lagoon-side spot for tapas and the best sangria in Orlando. All eateries are open for lunch and dinner. Restrooms on the France side of the pavilion offer quick access.

Restaurants

Restaurant Marrakesh

$$$ | MOROCCAN | FAMILY | At Restaurant Marrakesh, the Moroccan experience consists of both delicious food and a show, making it a great restaurant for kids—though everyone will enjoy watching the belly dancers and listening to the Moroccan band. The best appetizers are the beef brewat rolls, which combine savory beef with cinnamon and powdered sugar; entrées include exotic fare like different tangines, couscous, and kebabs, as well as more familiar dishes such as salmon and short ribs. **Known for:** beef couscous m'rouzia; authentic entertainment; bastilla, a crispy pastry. $ *Average main: $28* ✉ *World Showcase, Morocco Pavilion, EPCOT* ☎ *407/939–3463* 🌐 *disneyworld.disney.go.com/dining/epcot/restaurant-marrakesh.*

Spice Road Table

$$$ | MOROCCAN | FAMILY | To accommodate the clamor for more fireworks dining, this restaurant was built along World Showcase Lagoon, and it's a great place to catch a meal and watch HarmonioUS at 9 pm. Here you'll find the cuisine to be more Moroccan-American, so amid the rice-stuffed grape leaves and the tiropitakia, you'll find house-made hummus fries and spicy fried calamari. **Known for:** fireworks viewing; Moroccan beers; hummus fries. $ *Average main: $27* ✉ *World*

Nineteen native artisans were brought in to install the handcrafted-tile mosaics and other authentic details on Morocco's magnificent Bab Boujouloud Gate.

Showcase, Morocco Pavilion, EPCOT ☎ *407/939–3463* 🌐 *disneyworld.disney.go.com/dining/epcot/spice-road-table.*

Shopping

Tangier Traders

MARKET | FAMILY | Morocco's open-air market is a maze of shops selling straw bags and colorful carpets. It's also a great place to pick up something really different, like a Moroccan fez or belly-dancing gear, including a bright scarf, finger cymbals, and a CD with all the music you need to wow your audience. ✉ *World Showcase, Morocco Pavilion, EPCOT.*

Japan

A brilliant vermilion torii gate, based on Hiroshima Bay's much-photographed Itsukushima Shrine, frames the World Showcase Lagoon and stands as an emblem of Disney's serene version of Japan.

Disney horticulturists deserve a hand for authenticity: 90% of the plants they used are native to Japan. Rocks, pebbled streams, pools, and pruned trees and shrubs complete the meticulous picture. At sunset, or during a rainy dusk, the twisted branches of the corkscrew willows frame a perfect Japanese view of the winged pagoda that is the heart of the pavilion. Based on the 8th-century Horyuji Temple in Nara, the brilliant blue pagoda has five levels, symbolizing the five elements of Buddhist belief—earth, water, fire, wind, and sky.

The peace is occasionally interrupted by performances on drums and gongs. Mitsukoshi, an immense retail firm known as Japan's Sears Roebuck, carries everything from T-shirts to kimonos—as well as rows of Japanese dolls. For lunch and dinner, you'll be entertained by the culinary feats of chefs at Teppan Edo (which carries on the chop-toss-applaud antics of the original Teppanyaki Dining Room).

Tokyo Dining focuses on traditional presentation in its dishes, which include sushi. At the pavilion's rear is a sake tasting bar that you'll miss if you don't look for it. The newest addition is Takumi-Tei, which offers excellent service and food of superb quality on a high-end (and high-priced) omakase menu or an equally expensive à la carte menu.

Restaurants

★ Takumi-Tei

$$$$ | JAPANESE | Hidden in the back of the Japan Pavilion, intimate Takumi-Tei is split into five rooms inspired by different things: water, wood, earth, stone, and washi paper. Here you can to enjoy handcrafted sushi, A5 Wagyu beef, or *kamo* (marinated duck). **Known for:** omakase tasting menu with a tea ceremony; nine-course Chef's Table in the Water Room experience (reservations required); not very kid friendly. *$ Average main: $85 ✉ World Showcase, Japan Pavilion, EPCOT ☎ 407/939–3463 🌐 disneyworld.disney.go.com/dining/epcot/takumi-tei-restaurant.*

Tokyo Dining and Teppan Edo

$$$ | JAPANESE | FAMILY | Above the Mitsukoshi department store are sister restaurants Teppan Edo, a teppanyaki steak house where chefs do performance cooking at 20 grills, and Tokyo Dining, for sushi and pre-plated meals. Teppan Edo standouts include filet mignon and Tori chicken breast (it also has a small sushi selection and a kids' menu with Teppan-style chicken or shrimp with rice and veggies), whereas the more stylish Tokyo Dining offers tempura dishes; assorted sushi rolls; and grilled fish, chicken, or steak served with teriyaki or other sauces—plus "sukiyaki beef rice." Both restaurants have something great to watch: Teppan Edo has the performing chefs; Tokyo Dining has a great view of the Japan pavilion. **Known for:** family-fun teppanyaki meals; amazingly fresh sushi; attentive and knowledgeable service. *$ Average main: $30 ✉ World Showcase, Japan Pavilion, EPCOT ☎ 407/939–3463 🌐 disneyworld.disney.go.com/dining/epcot/teppan-edo.*

Photo Tip

You'll get a great shot of Spaceship Earth across the lagoon by framing it in the torii gate at the entrance to the Japan pavilion.

Coffee and Quick Bites

Tucked behind the pagoda is **Katsura Grill,** serving hand-rolled sushi or teriyaki plates if you're looking for a full meal. If you just want a quick drink, stop by **Kabuki Cafe** to try *kakigōri* (Japanese shaved ice) or a Japanese beer.

Shopping

Mitsukoshi Department Store

TOYS | FAMILY | Hello Kitty, one of Japan's most popular toys, is on hand here, as are the Transformers and Godzilla. Dress up with a washable poly kimono or a more luxurious silk version, or check out the shimmering pearl jewelry. Other popular items include animé art, chopsticks, and Kit Kat bars in assorted flavors. You'll be tempted to take home some sweets after watching a Japanese Candy Art demonstration just outside the store (see *Times Guide* for demo schedule). *✉ World Showcase, Japan Pavilion, EPCOT 🌐 disneyworld.disney.go.com/en_CA/shops/epcot/mitsukoshi-department-store.*

American Adventure

In a Disney version of Philadelphia's Independence Hall, the Imagineers prove that their kind of fantasy can beat reality hands down. The 110,000 bricks, made by hand from soft, pink Georgia clay, sheathe the familiar structure, which acts as a beacon for those across EPCOT's lagoon. The pavilion includes a barbecue restaurant, a shop, lovely rose gardens, and an outdoor theater. Restrooms are tucked away along the far left side of the restaurant; there's also a roomier restroom accommodation by the gift shop.

Sights

America Gardens Theatre

PERFORMANCE VENUE | FAMILY | On the edge of the lagoon, directly opposite Disney's magnificent bit of colonial imagery, is this open-air, partially tree-shaded venue for concerts and shows. Most performances are hot tickets with themes tied to EPCOT events, such as Garden Rocks concerts with pop legends during the March through July EPCOT International Flower and Garden Festival and Eat to the Beat concerts during the late September through mid-November EPCOT International Food and Wine Festival. Check the festival schedules before your trip, and plan to visit EPCOT on an evening with a musical guest you'll enjoy.

This is also the setting for the annual yuletide Candlelight Processional—a not-to-be-missed event if you're visiting during the holidays. The Candlelight Dinner Package (available through Disney's dining reservations hotline) includes lunch or dinner in a select World Showcase restaurant and preferred seating for the moving performance. Roomy restrooms are behind the Kidcot Fun Stop. ■ **TIP→ Arrive more than an hour ahead of time for holiday and celebrity performances, though the first show is always the least crowded.** ✉ *World Showcase, American Adventure Pavilion, EPCOT* ☞ *Duration: Performances vary. Crowds: Vary. Audience: Varies.*

★ The American Adventure

PERFORMANCE VENUE | FAMILY | The pavilion's key attraction is this 100-yard dash through history, and you'll be primed for the lesson after reaching the main entry hall and hearing the stirring a cappella Voices of Liberty. Inside the theater, the main event begins to the accompaniment of "The Golden Dream," performed by the Philadelphia Orchestra. This show combines evocative sets, a rear-projection screen (72 feet wide), enormous movable stages, and 35 Audio-Animatronics players.

Beginning with the arrival of the Pilgrims at Plymouth Rock and their grueling first winter, Benjamin Franklin and a wry, pipe-smoking Mark Twain narrate the episodes, both praiseworthy and shameful, that have shaped the American spirit. Each speech and scene seems polished like a little jewel. You feel the cold at Valley Forge. You're moved by Nez Percé Chief Joseph's forced abdication of ancestral lands, by Frederick Douglass's reminder of the miseries of slavery, and by women's rights campaigner Susan B. Anthony's speech. You laugh with Will Rogers's aphorisms and learn about the pain of the Great Depression through an affecting radio broadcast by Franklin Delano Roosevelt. **For people with disabilities:** Wheelchair- and ECV-accessible; reflective captioning and equipped for assisted-listening and audio-description devices. ■ **TIP→ Check your Times Guide, and arrive 10 minutes before the Voices of Liberty are slated to perform, then head inside to enjoy the a cappella tunes.** ✉ *World Showcase, American Adventure Pavilion, EPCOT* ☞ *Duration: 30 mins. Crowds: Heavy. Audience: All ages.*

Restaurants

Regal Eagle Smokehouse

$ | **BARBECUE** | **FAMILY** | This all-American smokehouse offers barbecue from Texas, Kansas, Memphis, and the Carolinas. Although some aficionados might find it sacrilegious, consider having everyone in your party order a different type of barbecue and then decide which region should reign supreme. **Known for:** s'more brownie; gluten-free, egg-free, and shellfish-free friendly; American beers. *Average main: $14 World Showcase, American Adventure Pavilion, EPCOT 407/939–3463 disneyworld.disney.go.com/dining/epcot/regal-eagle-smokehouse.*

Italy

Architectural reproductions of Venice's Piazza San Marco and the Doge's Palace are accurate right down to the gold leaf on the ringlets of the angel perched 100 feet atop the Campanile; the seawall stained with age and complete with barbershop-stripe poles to which two gondolas are tethered; and the Romanesque columns, Byzantine mosaics, Gothic arches, and stone walls that have all been carefully antiqued. Mediterranean plants such as grapevines, kumquat, and olive trees add verisimilitude. Shops sell Venetian beads and glasswork, leather purses, perfumes, olive oils, pastas, and Perugina cookies and chocolate kisses.

At Tutto Italia Ristorante, the offerings—wines, handmade mozzarella, and fresh bread among them—are from several regions of Italy. Limited outdoor dining beneath umbrellas is lovely. The hot ticket is on the edge of the piazza: Via Napoli is a casual, 300-seat pizzeria with wood-burning ovens and an airy, noisy dining room. Chefs use Caputo flour, San Marzano tomatoes, and handmade mozzarella to craft some of the best margherita pizza outside Naples! The Tutto Gusto Wine Cellar is a cool escape for a glass of Prosecco and a small plate.

Sergio, a clown–juggler, brings crowds to the piazza several times each day. This is also a great spot for viewing HarmonioUS.

Restaurants

Tutto Italia Ristorante

$$$ | **ITALIAN** | It's sometimes difficult to shake off the illusion that this is a restaurant in Venice or Rome; the service and food are that good. Offerings include penne alla vodka, grilled salmon in herb butter sauce, and traditional spaghetti or fettuccine. **Known for:** adjacent 200-option wine cellar with a limited food menu; generous antipasto platters and handmade pastas; casual but attentive service. *Average main: $28 Reservations Essential World Showcase, Italy Pavilion, EPCOT 407/939–3463 disneyworld.disney.go.com/dining/epcot/tutto-italia-ristorante.*

Via Napoli Ristorante e Pizzeria

$$$ | **PIZZA** | **FAMILY** | Loud, mad, bustling, and chaotic, this casual, family-friendly restaurant features authentic, thin-crust, Neapolitan-style pizzas cooked in massive ovens named after Italian volcanoes. Toppings include an array of cheeses, spicy Italian sausage, truffle oil, artichokes, prosciutto—even melon. **Known for:** generous kid portions; pizzas from wood-fired ovens; spaghetti with veal meatballs. *Average main: $30 World Showcase, Italy Pavilion, EPCOT 407/939–3463 disneyworld.disney.go.com/dining/epcot/via-napoli.*

Nightlife

Tutto Gusto

WINE BARS | This cool and cozy wine cellar adjoining Tutto Italia is an ideal place to escape the crowds. You can order from among 200 varieties of wine; switch things up with a cold beer; and complement either with a small-plate selection of meats, cheeses, calamari, and desserts. Entrées include gnocchi and pan-seared salmon in herb sauce. A small flight of desserts is the perfect way to end the meal. Wine flights from around Italy are also offered (ask your server for their favorite). This is the only sit-down restaurant in Walt Disney World that does not take reservations, so if you show up and are willing to wait around 20 or 30 minutes, you can usually get a table. A kids menu offers mozzarella sticks and spaghetti, though smaller kids might not be thrilled with the adult ambience or food. ✉ *World Showcase, Italy Pavilion, EPCOT* 🌐 *disneyworld.disney.go.com/dining/epcot/tutto-gusto-wine-cellar.*

Shopping

Il Bel Cristallo

HANDBAGS | Just like an elegant boutique in Milan, this shop sells chic Italian totes, designer handbags, clothing, collectibles, and fragrances by Fendi, Prada, and Bulgari. You'll also find porcelain, crystal, and Murano glass. ✉ *World Showcase, Italy Pavilion, EPCOT* 🌐 *disneyworld.disney.go.com/shops/epcot/il-bel-cristallo.*

Tutto Gusto Wine Cellar

WINE/SPIRITS | This café and wine bar is an exclusive seller of some of Italy's unique wines. ✉ *World Showcase, Italy Pavilion, EPCOT* 🌐 *disneyworld.disney.go.com/dining/epcot/tutto-gusto-wine-cellar.*

Germany

Germany, a make-believe village that distills the best folk architecture from all over that country, is so jovial that you practically expect the Seven Dwarfs to come "heigh-ho-ing" out to meet you. If you time it right, you will spot Snow White as she poses for photos and signs autographs. The fairy tale continues as a specially designed glockenspiel on the clock tower chimes on the hour. You'll also hear musical toots and tweets from cuckoo clocks, folk tunes from the spinning dolls sold at Der Teddybär, and the satisfied sighs of hungry visitors chowing down on hearty German cooking.

The Biergarten's wonderful buffet serves several sausage varieties, as well as sauerkraut, spaetzle, roasted potatoes, rotisserie chicken, and German breads—all accompanied by yodelers, dancers, and other lederhosen-clad musicians who perform a year-round Oktoberfest show.

There are shops aplenty, including Die Weihnachts Ecke (the Christmas Corner), which sells nutcrackers and other Christmas ornaments. It's hard to resist watching the miniature trains that choo-choo along a garden track dotted with tiny villages. Restrooms are just steps away.

Restaurants

Biergarten Restaurant

$$$$ | **GERMAN** | **FAMILY** | Oktoberfest runs 365 days a year at this restaurant, where cheerful crowds and an oompah band set the stage for a buffet of German specialties. The menu and level of frivolity are the same at lunch and dinner. **Known for:** buffet-style servings, including dessert bar; bratwurst, sausages, and other German specialties; lively oompah band music. 💲 *Average main: $47* ✍ *Reservations Essential* ✉ *World Showcase, Germany Pavilion, EPCOT* ☎ *407/939–3463* 🌐 *disneyworld.disney.go.com/dining/epcot/biergarten-restaurant.*

Coffee and Quick Bites

Refreshment Outpost
$ | **AMERICAN** | **FAMILY** | At the Refreshment Outpost, set on its own between Germany and China, kids love to test their drumming skills on the large authentic drums that invite players to improvise their own African folklore performances. Village Traders sells African handicrafts and—you guessed it—souvenirs relating to *The Lion King*. Buy a hot dog or ice cream float, and enjoy the break at a table by the lagoon. **Known for:** ice cream floats; Africa theme; short lines. *Average main: $8* ✉ *World Showcase, EPCOT* ☎ *497/939–3463* 🌐 *disneyworld.disney.go.com/dining/epcot/africa-outpost.*

Sommerfest
$ | **GERMAN** | **FAMILY** | If you're just looking for a bratwurst and a cold beer, pop by the Sommerfest counter at the entrance of the Biergarten restaurant. There's not much seating, so you might have to eat on the run. **Known for:** beer flights; bratwurst; sauerkraut. *Average main: $14* ✉ *World Showcase, Germany Pavilion, EPCOT* ☎ *407/939–3463* 🌐 *disneyworld.disney.go.com/dining/epcot/sommerfest.*

Shopping

Der Teddybär
TOYS | **FAMILY** | Although you can buy wines and beer steins in the Germany pavilion, they don't provide the warm, fuzzy feelings that the teddy bears on display here do. Bears (or "bärs") share the boutique with Rapunzel and Snow White snow globes and plush toys, Minnie dolls and figurines, and German confections. ✉ *World Showcase, Germany Pavilion, EPCOT* 🌐 *disneyworld.disney.go.com/shops/epcot/der-teddybar-toyshop.*

China

A shimmering, red-and-gold, three-tier replica of Beijing's Temple of Heaven towers over a serene Chinese garden, an art gallery displaying treasures from the People's Republic, a spacious emporium devoted to Chinese goods, and two restaurants. The gardens—planted with a native Chinese tallow tree, water lilies, bamboo, and a 100-year-old weeping mulberry tree—are tranquil. Inside, learn more about the Disneyland resort in Shanghai.

Piped-in traditional Chinese music flows gently over the peaceful hush of the gardens, which come alive with applause and cheers when the remarkable Jeweled Dragon Acrobats tumble into a roped-off area for their breathtaking act. At China's popular Nine Dragons Restaurant, try the chicken dumplings or the peppery shrimp with spinach noodles; there are also several chicken and stir-fry favorites.

Sights

Wondrous China
PERFORMANCE VENUE | **FAMILY** | The Temple of Heaven houses another of EPCOT's upgrades: the *Wondrous China* film. Now presented on a seamless 360-degree screen in digital format, this film highlights China's iconic images, both old and new. However, be prepared to stand and possibly hold children: strollers aren't permitted, and there are no seats. **For people with disabilities:** Wheelchair- and ECV-accessible; reflective captioning and equipped for assisted-listening and audio-description devices. **■TIP→ Come anytime, and, before the show, visit the Tomb Warriors gallery, where you can see replicas of the terra-cotta soldiers unearthed in 1974 by farmers in Xi'an, China.** ✉ *World Showcase, China Pavilion, EPCOT* ☞ *Duration: 14 mins. Crowds: Moderate. Audience: All Ages.*

Coffee and Quick Bites

Lotus Blossom Café

$$ | **CHINESE** | The open-air Lotus Blossom Café offers authentic pot stickers and egg rolls, as well as entrées such as orange chicken with steamed rice, chicken fried rice, and a Mongolian combo. The Joy of Tea cart along the promenade serves hot and cold tea, plus trendy bubble milk tea, beer, and cocktails. **Known for:** caramel-ginger ice cream; pot stickers; Chinese beer. *Average main: $15 ✉ World Showcase, China Pavilion, EPCOT ☎ 407/939–3463 🌐 disneyworld.disney.go.com/dining/epcot/lotus-blossom-cafe.*

Shopping

House of Good Fortune

SOUVENIRS | **FAMILY** | China's sprawling bazaar has a huge selection of tea sets ranging in style from traditional to contemporary, intricately embroidered robes, and fragranced candles that are sure to align your chi. Butterfly hair combs are beautiful, but the hottest items are little Buddha statues, available for less than $10. ✉ *World Showcase, China Pavilion, EPCOT* 🌐 *disneyworld.disney.go.com/shops/epcot.*

Norway

Although most visitors to the Norway pavilion are on their way to the Frozen Ever After ride, there's plenty to look at while waiting in line. Among the rough-hewn timbers and sharply pitched roofs—softened and brightened by bloom-stuffed window boxes and figured shutters—are lots of smiling young Norwegians, all eager to speak English and show off their country.

The pavilion complex contains a 14th-century, fortresslike castle that mimics Oslo's Akershus; cobbled streets; rocky waterfalls; and a stave church modeled after one built in 1250, with wood dragons glaring from the eaves. The church houses an exhibit called Gods and Vikings, which uses vintage artifacts to tell the legends of Odin, Thor, Loki, and Freya. It all puts you in the mood for the pavilion's shops, which sell *Frozen* souvenirs, spears, shields, and other Viking necessities perfect for next Halloween.

At Akershus Royal Banquet Hall, Princess Storybook Dining is a big deal. Visit the Norwegian *koldtbord* (buffet) for smoked salmon, fruit, and pastries, followed by a family-style hot breakfast of eggs, meats, and other treats served at the table. For lunch and dinner, you'll find traditional treats like chilled shrimp, salads, meats, and cheeses. Hot entrées served à la carte might include oven-roasted chicken breast, stuffed pasta, or the traditional Scandinavian meatball dish called *kjottkake*. Family-style dessert is a treat with three of the chef's sweet specialties.

■ TIP→ The restaurant is the only one in the park where you can dine with Disney princesses, who might include Aurora, Belle, or Snow White. Book here as early as possible. If you haven't made a reservation, it's worth checking at Guest Relations for seats left by cancellations.

Sights

★ Frozen Ever After

AMUSEMENT RIDE | **FAMILY** | In Norway's dandy boat-ride homage to the popular *Frozen* film, you pile into a 16-passenger, dragon-headed longboat for a dark-ride voyage around Arendelle. The familiar form of Olaf welcomes you as you enter the frozen willow forest and head to Queen Elsa's ice palace, meeting up with Anna and many familiar *Frozen* characters along the way and hearing the popular songs from the film. The animated figures are amazing, featuring Disney's first all-electric Audio-Animatronics, allowing much more fluid and graceful movement and utilizing projection-mapped faces,

Frozen Ever After has become a favorite ride at EPCOT.

which make the figures look exactly like their animated counterparts. For fans who miss the Maelstrom ride, which this attraction replaced, keep a sharp eye open for Easter eggs that remain, particularly in the castle finale. **For people with disabilities:** You must step down into and up out of a boat to ride. Equipped with reflective captioning and for assisted-listening, audio-description, or hand-held-captioning devices. ■ **TIP→ With the individual Lightning Lane selection (available seasonally), you can pay to skip this particular line. If you have young kids who can't handle a wait of an hour more, either make this purchase at 7 am before visiting, or come here first thing in the morning.** ✉ *World Showcase, Norway Pavilion, EPCOT ☞ Duration: 10 mins. Crowds: Moderate to heavy. Audience: All ages.*

Restaurants

Akershus Royal Banquet Hall

$$$$ | **SCANDINAVIAN** | **FAMILY** | This restaurant has character buffets at all three meals, with an array of Disney princesses, including Ariel, Belle, Jasmine, Snow White, Aurora, Mary Poppins, and even an occasional cameo appearance by Cinderella. The breakfast menu is American, but lunch and dinner find an ever-changing assortment of Norwegian specialties, which might be foreign to children. **Known for:** character dining with the princesses; an expansive buffet of Nordic specialties; Scandinavian appeal. *[$] Average main: $62 ✍ Reservations Essential ✉ World Showcase, Norway Pavilion, EPCOT ☎ 407/939–3463 🌐 disneyworld.disney.go.com/dining/epcot/akershus-royal-banquet-hall.*

Coffee and Quick Bites

Kringla Bakeri Og Kafe

$ | NORWEGIAN | FAMILY | Here you can order Norwegian treats such as *kringla,* a pretzel-shaped pastry with toppings; *lefse,* a soft flatbread with cinnamon, sugar, and butter; or a troll horn, a puff pastry filled with orange-marmalade cream. Wash it all down with a Nordic draft beer or a Viking coffee—hot or Elsa style (aka frozen). **Known for:** coffee; draft beer; Norwegian sweet treats. *Average main: $14* ✉ *World Showcase, Norway Pavilion, EPCOT* ☎ *407/939–3463* 🌐 *disneyworld.disney.go.com/dining/epcot/kringla-bakeri-og-kafe.*

Shopping

Puffin's Roost

TOYS | FAMILY | Viking wannabes go crazy for the soft toy spears and shields. The plush seals are sweet for tots, and you can find Norwegian pewter, leather goods, and colorful woolen sweaters and knit caps, along with a wide variety of character goods from the hit movie *Frozen.*The shop's larger-than-life troll is always ready for a selfie. ✉ *World Showcase, Norway Pavilion, EPCOT* 🌐 *disneyworld.disney.go.com/shops/epcot/puffins-roost.*

Mexico

Housed in a spectacular Mesoamerican pyramid surrounded by dense tropical plantings and brilliant blossoms, Mexico welcomes you onto a "moonlit" plaza that contains the Gran Fiesta Tour boat ride; an exhibit of pre-Columbian art; a very popular restaurant; and, of course, shopping kiosks where you can unload many, many pesos.

Modeled on the market in the town of Taxco, Plaza de los Amigos is well named: there are lots of friendly people—the women dressed in peasant blouses and bright skirts, the men in white shirts and dashing sashes—all eager to sell you trinkets from a cluster of canopied carts. The perimeter is rimmed with stores that have tile roofs, wrought-iron balconies, and flower-filled window boxes. What to buy? Sombreros, baskets, pottery, jewelry, and maracas.

One of the pavilion's key attractions is the San Angel Inn, featuring traditional Mexican cuisine and wine and beer, and overlooking the faux-moonlit waterway traversed by Gran Fiesta Tour boats. The pavilion's La Cava del Tequila bar serves up tequila flights, exotic blended margaritas, and light snacks like guacamole with corn chips. The casual, outdoor La Cantina de San Angel is a 150-seat quick-service eatery adjacent to La Hacienda de San Angel, a 250-seat table-service restaurant with a waterside view. You won't want to miss trying Mexican treats like the *queso fundido,* melted cheese with poblano peppers, chorizo, and tortillas, or the *alambre de res,* a seared tenderloin with poblano and bell peppers.

Sights

Gran Fiesta Tour Starring the Three Caballeros

AMUSEMENT RIDE | FAMILY | In this attraction—which shines with the polish of enhanced facades, sound system, and boat-ride props—Donald teams with old pals José Carioca (the parrot) and Panchito (the Mexican charro rooster) from the 1944 Disney film *The Three Caballeros.* The Gran Fiesta Tour film sweeps you along for an animated jaunt as the caballeros are reunited for a grand performance in Mexico City. Donald manages to disappear for his own tour of the country, leaving José and Panchito to search for their missing comrade. **For people with disabilities:** The boat is accessible to guests using wheelchairs, but those using ECVs or oversize chairs must transfer to a Disney model. Equipped for handheld-captioning and

The Temple of Quetzalcoatl (ket-zal-co-WAH-tal) at Teotihuacán (tay-o-tee-wah-CON), just outside Mexico City, is the model for the pyramid at the Mexico pavilion.

audio-description devices. ■ **TIP→ It's worth a visit if lines aren't long, especially if you have small children, who usually enjoy the novelty of a boat ride.** ✉ *World Showcase, Mexico Pavilion, EPCOT* ☞ *Duration: 9 mins. Crowds: Moderate. Audience: All ages.*

Restaurants

La Hacienda de San Angel

$$$ | **MEXICAN** | Open only for dinner, this restaurant combines authentic Mexican entrées with a perfect location to view the fireworks. The *alambre de res* (flank steak with bacon in poblano and bell peppers) is delicious, while the chile relleno is an excellent vegetarian dish. **Known for:** fireworks viewing; Mexican sorbets; premium margaritas. $ *Average main: $29* ✉ *World Showcase, Mexico Pavilion, EPCOT* ☎ *407/939–3463* 🌐 *disneyworld.disney.go.com/dining/epcot/hacienda-de-san-angel.*

San Angel Inn Restaurante

$$$ | **MEXICAN** | **FAMILY** | Set at a Mexican market in perpetual twilight, this restaurant gets high marks from guests for its food and atmosphere. Everyone enjoys sharing the guacamole or queso fundido, and the *camarones a la diabla* (pepper and garlic-sautéed shrimp over poblano rice and crispy Brussels sprouts) are especially good. **Known for:** fish tacos; darkened atmosphere; many healthy eating options. $ *Average main: $28* ✉ *World Showcase, Mexico Pavilion, EPCOT* ☎ *407/939–3463* 🌐 *disneyworld.disney.go.com/dining/epcot/san-angel-inn-restaurante.*

Coffee and Quick Bites

The line for **Choza de Margarita** can seem longer than any other in EPCOT, and for good reason. With eight different margaritas, this is the first stop for a drink during your lap around the World Showcase, and with options like spicy blackberry or "mango loco," you'll want to line up, too. If you just want a side of guacamole, stop by **La Cantina de San Angel** for a snack or to split an order of empanadas con queso.

Nightlife

La Cava del Tequila
BARS | This intimate bar serves more than 200 tequilas along with Mexican beers, wines, top-shelf cocktails, and a colorful array of margaritas. Try a tequila flight while snacking on tapas, chips, guacamole, and queso. ✉ *World Showcase, Mexico Pavilion, EPCOT* 🌐 *disneyworld.disney.go.com/dining/epcot/cava-del-tequila.*

Shopping

Plaza de Los Amigos
MARKET | **FAMILY** | As you enter the Mexico pavilion and descend the staircase, stop in the village square to browse the hand-painted wood carvings crafted by Zapotec Indians of Oaxaca in southern Mexico. Vendor carts offer silver jewelry, leather goods, sombreros, piñatas, pottery, home decor, and more. Don't miss indoor shops such as La Princesa de Cristal, which sells sparkling jewelry, etched glass, and Disney figurines cast in crystal, and La Tienda Encantada with fine jewelry, leather goods, and colorful accessories. Outside on the promenade is El Ranchito del Norte, a bazaar well stocked with similar items. ✉ *World Showcase, Mexico Pavilion, EPCOT* 🌐 *disneyworld.disney.go.com/shops/epcot/plaza-de-los-amigos.*

EPCOT Resort Area

If you're looking for the best on-site Disney location, this is it. Disney's BoardWalk Inn & Villas, Disney's Yacht and Beach Club resorts, and the Swan and Dolphin resorts surround Crescent Lake. Although the area is walkable, boats stop at all three resorts and provide access to Hollywood Studios and EPCOT. Also in this area are the Pop Century, Riviera Resort, Caribbean Beach, and Art of Animation—all great for families on a budget.

Disney's BoardWalk Inn & Villas is fronted by a ¼-mile, lakeside promenade with architecture and signage recalling turn-of-the-20th-century, Atlantic seaboard esplanades. It's a charming place for dining, meandering, or watching EPCOT fireworks. Boats chug across Crescent Lake toward Hollywood Studios or EPCOT, lights outline the buildings, and guests pedal bicycle surreys along the waterfront. You'll also find midway games, magicians, the ESPN sports bar, a piano bar, and the only dance club on Disney property. The action here, for better or worse, never stops.

Across Crescent Lake, the twin Yacht and Beach Club hotels pair a more relaxed atmosphere with an excellent location. The highlight is Stormalong Bay, a 3-acre water area with a sand-bottom pool, lazy river, towering waterslide, and three hot tubs. A large beach, the site of volleyball matches, movies, and campfires, sits along the Beach Club, and an array of watercraft is offered outside the Yacht Club. Don't be fooled by the simplicity of Beaches and Cream, the old-time soda shop, or the character breakfast at Cape May Cafe. Also here is Yachtman Steakhouse, one of the best restaurants on Disney property. A bonus of the Yacht and Beach—as well as the Swan and Dolphin—is that you can easily get to the entertainment at the BoardWalk and then retreat to quieter rooms at night.

Though not owned by Disney, the Swan and Dolphin are large convention hotels perfect for adults who want to take breaks from the parks. Restaurants such as Todd English's bluezoo offer upscale dining in a calm setting. With a sushi bar, a sports bar, and poolside cabanas, it is easy to forget that both Hollywood Studios and EPCOT are only a stone's throw away. And, if you're looking for a

Flying Fish is one of the original restaurants along Disney's Boardwalk. Opened in 1996, it was refurbished and reopened in 2016 with a new upscale seafood menu.

supreme spa experience, you can check into the Mandara Spa.

Caribbean Beach and the Riviera Resort are moderately priced yet still offer plenty of activities. Highlights include elaborate pools and the Disney Skyliner, a gondola that travels to EPCOT and Hollywood Studios. The Riviera also has upscale suites as well as Tower Studio rooms, which, though tight, are designed for two guests, have a kitchenette, and offer elegance on a budget.

In the far corner of Disney's property are the Art of Animation and Pop Century, which are connected by Hourglass Lake and emphasize value. The Art of Animation carries Disney all the way into its rooms, with themed shower curtains and other little touches. It also has reasonably priced family suites that can sleep six and have two bathrooms and a kitchenette. Pop Century, a traditional hotel, often hosts cheerleading and sports teams competing at Walt Disney World. Though farther out, these resorts are also served by the Disney Skyliner.

Restaurants

Big River Grille & Brewing Works

$$ | AMERICAN | FAMILY | Strange but good brews—Rocket Red Ale, Southern Flyer Light Lager, Steamboat Pale Ale, Gadzooks Pilsner—abound at this microbrewery, where you can sip your suds inside amid giant stainless-steel tanks or outside on a lake-view patio. The menu emphasizes meat and fish, with baby back ribs dry-rubbed and topped with honey chipotle barbecue sauce, elaborate hamburgers, or blackened fish tacos. **Known for:** ribs, steaks, and fish; massive burgers; Disney's only microbrewery. *Average main: $19 ✉ Disney's BoardWalk, 2101 EPCOT Resorts Blvd., EPCOT Resort Area ☎ 407/560–0253 🌐 www.bigrivergrille.com.*

Cape May Cafe

$$$$ | SEAFOOD | FAMILY | With the feel of a New England seafood house—the type your grandma might enjoy—this bustling spot in the Beach Club Resort features popular buffet meals. For breakfast,

A
B
C
D
E
F
1
2
3
4
5
6
7
8
9
World Drive
Epcot Resorts Boulevard
Mono Rail
EPCOT
World Showcase
Lagoon
Epcot
Station
Crescent
Lake
Disney Skyliner
Turn
Station
East Buena Vista Drive
Victory Way
Hollywood
Studios
Station
DISNEY'S
HOLLYWOOD
STUDIOS
Pop Century-
Art of Animation
Station
Osceola Parkway
Century Drive
KEY
Restaurants
Hotels

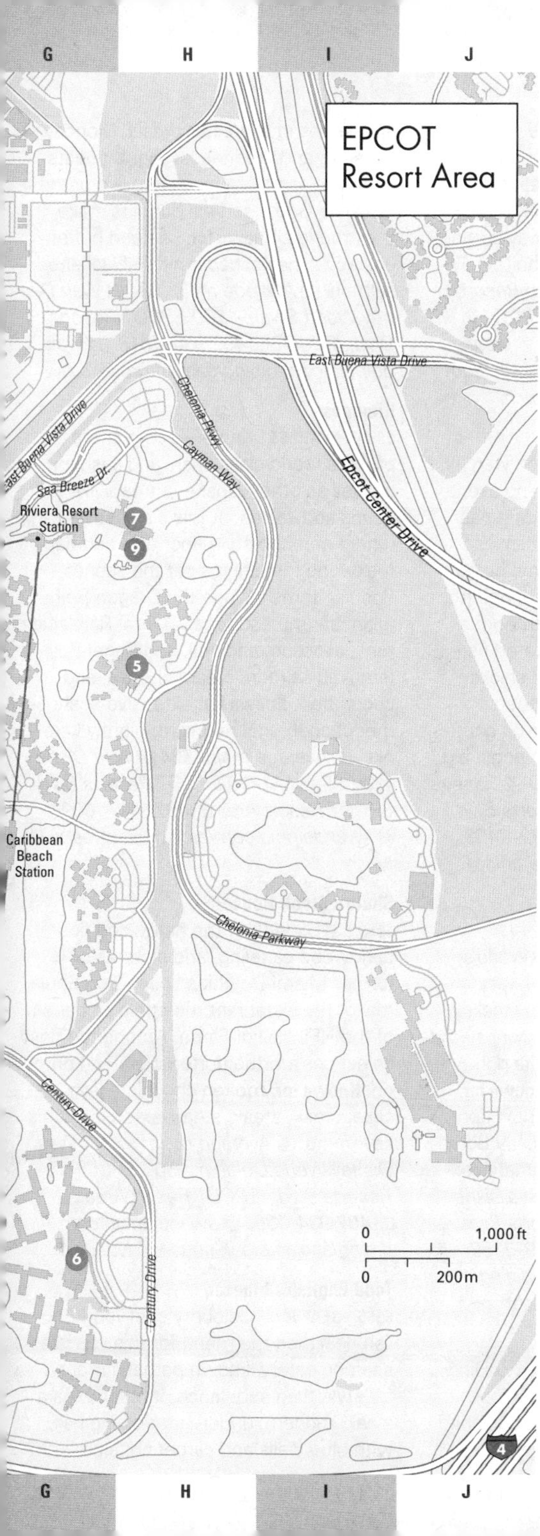

Restaurants

1 Big River Grille & Brewing Works **C3**
2 Cape May Cafe..................... **C2**
3 ESPN Club **D3**
4 Flying Fish **D3**
5 Garden Grove **C3**
6 Kimonos............................ **C3**
7 Shula's Steak House **B3**
8 Todd English's bluezoo **B3**
9 Topolino's Terrace – Flavors of the Riviera............. **H4**
10 Trattoria al Forno.................. **D3**
11 Yachtsman Steakhouse........... **C2**

Hotels

1 Disney's Art of Animation Resort............................... **F8**
2 Disney's Beach Club Resort...... **D2**
3 Disney's Beach Club Villas **D2**
4 Disney's BoardWalk Inn & Villas **D3**
5 Disney's Caribbean Beach Resort...................... **H4**
6 Disney's Pop Century Resort **G8**
7 Disney's Riviera Resort........... **H3**
8 Disney's Yacht Club Resort **C2**
9 Walt Disney World Dolphin....... **B3**
10 Walt Disney World Swan.......... **C3**

Minnie and other cast classics visit tables while families help themselves to American classics from waffles to sausage links from the buffet. **Known for:** casual atmosphere in an out-of-the-way setting; character breakfast; seafood boil. *Average main: $52 Beach Club Resort, 1800 EPCOT Resorts Blvd., EPCOT Resort Area 407/939–3463 disneyworld.disney.go.com/dining/beach-club-resort/cape-may-cafe No lunch.*

ESPN Club

$$ | AMERICAN | Not only can you watch every possible televised sporting event on a big-screen TV (the restaurant has about 100 monitors), but you can also periodically see ESPN programs being taped in the club itself. Food ranges from half-pound burgers, made with Angus chuck, to Guinness beer–battered fish-and-chips and buttermilk fried chicken. **Known for:** wine and regional beers; gigantic space that still fills up on game days; pub food: nachos, onion rings, big burgers. *Average main: $19 Disney's BoardWalk, 2101 EPCOT Resorts Blvd., EPCOT Resort Area 407/939–3463 disneyworld.disney.go.com/dining/boardwalk/espn-club.*

★ Flying Fish

$$$$ | SEAFOOD | One of Disney World's finest restaurants has a menu heavy on seasonal seafood as well as steaks. Options include oak-grilled salmon, swordfish and exotic fare like Kurabuta pork belly and Hokkaido scallops. **Known for:** AbracadaBAR cocktail lounge next door; sophisticated dining on the Disney BoardWalk; fresh daily local and international seafood. *Average main: $48 Disney's BoardWalk, 2101 EPCOT Resorts Blvd., EPCOT Resort Area 407/939–2359 disneyworld.disney.go.com/dining/boardwalk/flying-fish No lunch.*

Garden Grove

$$$$ | AMERICAN | FAMILY | With twinkling lights draped on its oversize, 25-foot, signature tree, this restaurant, designed to evoke New York's Central Park, specializes in character meals. Monday, Tuesday, and Wednesday night, guests dine on classic American fare like prime rib while Goofy and his buddies make their rounds. **Known for:** seafood buffet; character meals; cedar plank–blackened salmon. *Average main: $34 Walt Disney World Swan, 1200 EPCOT Resorts Blvd., EPCOT 407/934–1618 swandolphin.com/dining/garden-grove.*

Kimonos

$$$ | JAPANESE | Knife-wielding chefs prepare world-class sushi and sashimi, as well as other Japanese treats like soups and salads, at this sleek sushi bar, where bamboo-style floor tiles and dark teakwood furnishings set the scene. Popular items include the Dragon Roll (giant shrimp and tuna), Banzai Roll (spicy tuna, avocado, and eel), and Bagel Roll (smoked salmon, cream cheese, and cucumber). **Known for:** extensive sushi menu; open until midnight; nightly karaoke. *Average main: $24 Walt Disney World Swan, 1200 EPCOT Resorts Blvd., EPCOT Resort Area 407/934–1609 swandolphin.com/dining/kimonos No lunch.*

Shula's Steak House

$$$$ | STEAKHOUSE | The hardwood floors, dark-wood paneling, and pictures of former Miami Dolphins coach Don Shula make this restaurant resemble an annex of the NFL Hall of Fame. Among the best selections are the porterhouse and prime rib. **Known for:** molten chocolate lava cake; steak, steak, steak; extensive whiskey menu. *Average main: $79 Walt Disney World Dolphin, 1500 EPCOT Resorts Blvd., EPCOT Resort Area 407/934–1362 swandolphin.com/dining/shulas-steak-house No lunch.*

Todd English's bluezoo

$$$$ | SEAFOOD | Celebrity chef Todd English designed the menu for this upscale seafood eatery, known perhaps more for style than substance. It resembles a sleek, modern, underwater dining hall, with blue walls and carpeting, aluminum

The Disney Skyliner opened in September 2019, connecting EPCOT, Hollywood Studios, and several EPCOT Resort Area hotels.

fish along the wall behind the bar, and bubblelike lighting fixtures. **Known for:** two hours of complimentary child care while dining; variety of seafood; celebrity chef dining. *Average main: $44 Walt Disney World Dolphin Hotel, 1500 EPCOT Resorts Blvd., EPCOT Resort Area 407/934–1111 swandolphin.com/dining/todd-englishs-bluezoo No lunch.*

Topolino's Terrace–Flavors of the Riviera

$$$$ | ITALIAN | FAMILY | Featuring fantastic views of the resort and EPCOT, this pricey restaurant on the 10th floor of the Riviera Resort is one the best on Disney property. In the evening, try rigatoni, linguine, and other handcrafted pastas or the traditional bouillabaisse or tomahawk veal chop; at breakfast, enjoy a family-style character meal. **Known for:** King salmon; character breakfast; handcrafted pasta. *Average main: $50 Disney's Riviera Resort, 1080 Esplanade Ave., EPCOT Resort Area 407/828–7030 disneyworld.disney.go.com/dining/riviera-resort/topolinos-terrace.*

Trattoria al Forno

$$$ | ITALIAN | FAMILY | This restaurant melds old and new, with the cozy decor of a traditional Italian home and a menu of Italian-American dishes refreshed for today's tastes. Share a pizza topped with prosciutto, salami, sausage, and capicola, or indulge in wood-fired swordfish salmoriglio. **Known for:** house-made gelato and other desserts; large portions; roasted fish. *Average main: $27 Disney's BoardWalk, 2101 EPCOT Resorts Blvd., EPCOT Resort Area 407/939–3463 disneyworld.disney.go.com/dining/boardwalk/trattoria-al-forno No lunch.*

Yachtsman Steakhouse

$$$$ | STEAKHOUSE | The chefs at this New England–themed steak house are proud of their high-quality, aged beef, which is hand-cut on site and can be seen mellowing in a glass-enclosed butcher shop near the entryway. Although not easy on the wallet, dishes such as the 12-ounce New York strip with peppercorn-brandy sauce and truffle mac and cheese are quite tasty. **Known for:** beef carpaccio;

Disney's Pop Century Resort, in the EPCOT Resort Area, is one of the hotels on a Disney Skyliner route.

house-made truffle fries; an ambitious assortment of steaks. *Average main: $50* ✉ *Yacht Club Resort, 1700 EPCOT Resorts Blvd., EPCOT Resort Area* ☎ *407/939–3463* 🌐 *disneyworld.disney.go.com/dining/yacht-club-resort/yachtsman-steakhouse* ⏲ *No lunch.*

Hotels

Disney's Art of Animation Resort
$$ | **RESORT** | **FAMILY** | This colorful, three-story resort is a kid's version of paradise: each of its four wings features images from *Finding Nemo, Cars, The Lion King,* or *The Little Mermaid,* and linens and carpeting match the theme. **Pros:** images that kids adore; splash pad at the pool; reasonably priced family suites. **Cons:** only on-site dining options are quick-service; standard rooms fill up fast; can be crowded. *Rooms from: $195* ✉ *1850 Animation Way, EPCOT Resort Area* ☎ *407/938–7000* 🌐 *www.disneyworld.disney.go.com/resorts* *1984 rooms* *No Meals.*

★ **Disney's Beach Club Resort**
$$$$ | **RESORT** | **FAMILY** | Volleyball, bonfires, and movie nights are among the many activities offered at this resort on the Crescent Lake beach. **Pros:** beautiful gardens; many activities, including those at Stormalong Bay water park; closest to the International Gateway for EPCOT. **Cons:** fewer food options than other large hotels; not near Magic Kingdom; pricey. *Rooms from: $750* ✉ *1800 EPCOT Resorts Blvd., EPCOT Resort Area* ☎ *407/934–8000* 🌐 *disneyworld.disney.go.com/en_CA/resorts/beach-club-resort* *576 rooms* *No Meals.*

Disney's Beach Club Villas
$$$$ | **RESORT** | **FAMILY** | Each villa in this pale-turquoise-and-white waterfront property next to the Yacht and Beach Club Resort has a separate living room, kitchen, and one or two bedrooms. **Pros:** en suite kitchens let you save money on meals; short walk or boat ride to the BoardWalk, EPCOT, and Hollywood Studios; access to Stormalong Bay water park. **Cons:** pricey; not close to Magic Kingdom

or Animal Kingdom; boat traffic can be noisy. *Rooms from: $950* *1800 EPCOT Resorts Blvd., EPCOT Resort Area* *407/934–8000* *disneyworld.disney.go.com/en_CA/resorts/beach-club-resort* *576 units* *No Meals.*

Disney's BoardWalk Inn & Villas

$$$$ | RESORT | Evoking Atlantic City in its heyday, this red-and-white hotel has a lobby filled with potted palms overlooking a classic waterfront promenade. **Pros:** adjacent to EPCOT and Hollywood Studios; casual, upscale atmosphere; lots of activities just outside the door. **Cons:** noise can intrude if you have a BoardWalk room; long bus ride to Magic Kingdom; pricey. *Rooms from: $619* *2101 EPCOT Resorts Blvd., EPCOT Resort Area* *407/939–5100* *disneyworld.disney.go.com/en_CA/resorts/boardwalk-inn* *372 rooms* *No Meals.*

Disney's Caribbean Beach Resort

$$$ | RESORT | FAMILY | Consisting of five palm-studded island "villages," this charming resort with a 42-acre lake and white sand beaches is labeled with names straight from Pirates of the Caribbean. **Pros:** moderate price; abundant outdoor activities and a summer-camp feel; convenient to EPCOT, Hollywood Studios, and Disney Springs. **Cons:** long walks from rooms to the beach or restaurants; can't swim in the waters off the beach; you don't truly feel swept away to a tropical island. *Rooms from: $259* *900 Cayman Way, EPCOT Resort Area* *407/934–3400* *disneyworld.disney.go.com/en_CA/resorts/caribbean-beach-resort* *1536 rooms* *No Meals.*

Disney's Pop Century Resort

$ | RESORT | FAMILY | Giant jukeboxes, 65-foot-tall bowling pins, an oversize Big Wheel and Rubik's Cube, and other pop-culture memorabilia dot the grounds of this value resort. **Pros:** proximity to EPCOT, ESPN Wide World of Sports, and Disney's Hollywood Studios; great room rates; access to Disney Skyliner. **Cons:** lots of small kids around; small rooms; having close to 3,000 rooms means big crowds at the front desk and in the food court. *Rooms from: $153* *1050 Century Dr., EPCOT Resort Area* *407/938–4000, 407/934–4639* *disneyworld.disney.go.com/en_CA/resorts/pop-century-resort* *2880 rooms* *No Meals.*

Disney's Riviera Resort

$$$$ | RESORT | FAMILY | Designed to evoke a resort along the European Riviera, Disney's newest hotel offers options for every budget in its array of room choices—from Tower Studios (small rooms designed for only two guests but with a kitchenette) to grand, three-bedroom villas. **Pros:** lush gardens with bocci and chess boards; newly built; large range of room options. **Cons:** small pool; far from Magic Kingdom; expensive for smaller rooms. *Rooms from: $356* *1080 Esplanade Ave., Lake Buena Vista* *407/828–7030* *disneyworld.disney.go.com/en_CA/resorts/riviera-resort* *300 rooms* *No Meals.*

Disney's Yacht Club Resort

$$$$ | RESORT | FAMILY | Recalling a New England Yacht Club, this property offers Crescent Lake boating options, a sweet gazebo that's often used for weddings, and one of Disney's best steak houses. **Pros:** short walk to activities at Boardwalk Resort; many rooms sleep five; access to Stormalong Bay. **Cons:** small quick-service location can mean long lines at breakfast; large, winding hallways can mean a hike to your room; pricey. *Rooms from: $750* *1700 EPCOT Resorts Blvd., EPCOT Resort Area* *407/934–7000* *disneyworld.disney.go.com/en_CA/resorts/yacht-club-resort* *656 units* *No Meals.*

Walt Disney World Dolphin

$$$$ | RESORT | A pair of 56-foot-tall sea creatures bookends this 25-story glass pyramid, a luxe resort designed, like the adjoining Swan (which is also on Disney property but not a Disney-owned resort), by world-renowned architect Michael Graves and set close enough to the parks that you can escape the midday heat for a dip in the pool. **Pros:** new Swan Reserve annex with rooms and amenities geared to convention guests; character meals and free (boat or bus) transport to BoardWalk and Disney parks; access to all facilities at the Swan. **Cons:** no charging to room key at parks; a daily resort fee; daily self-parking fee. *Rooms from: $635 1500 EPCOT Resorts Blvd., EPCOT Resort Area 407/934–4000, 800/227–1500 swandolphin.com 1858 rooms No Meals.*

Walt Disney World Swan

$$$ | **RESORT** | This luxurious hotel, like its sister hotel the Dolphin, is not owned by Disney but still receives many of the same Disney perks, including Extra Magic Hours but excluding the ability to charge park purchases to your room. **Pros:** refurbished in 2019; boat service to EPCOT and Hollywood Studios; adult-oriented. **Cons:** self-parking fee; daily resort fee; no charging to room key at the parks. *Rooms from: $320 1200 EPCOT Resorts Blvd., Lake Buena Vista 407/934–4000, 888/828–8850 swan-dolphin.com 758 rooms No Meals.*

Nightlife

Atlantic Dance Hall

DANCE CLUBS | This popular, high-energy dance club plays music from the '80s onward and has a huge screen showing videos requested by the crowd. The parquet dance floor is set off by furnishings of deep blue, maroon, and gold, and the ceiling glows with stars and twinkling lights. Signature cocktails are in demand, and you can sip a cognac or choose from a selection of popular beers. *Disney's BoardWalk, 2101 EPCOT Resorts Blvd., EPCOT Resort Area 407/939–2444 disneyworld.disney.go.com/entertainment/boardwalk/atlantic-dance-hall.*

Big River Grille & Brewing Works

BREWPUBS | **FAMILY** | The BoardWalk's only brewpub serves craft brews and upscale American pub grub like barbecued ribs or blackened salmon in an intimate indoor dining area and on a waterfront patio. House brews on tap might include Southern Flyer Light Lager, Rocket Red Ale, and the seasonal Sweet Magnolia American Brown Ale. *Disney's BoardWalk, 2101 EPCOT Resorts Blvd., EPCOT Resort Area 407/560–0253 disneyworld.disney.go.com/dining/boardwalk/big-river-grille-and-brewing-works.*

ESPN Club

BARS | The sports motif here is carried into every nook and cranny—the main dining area looks like an arena, with a basketball-court hardwood floor and a giant scoreboard that projects the day's big game. More than 100 TVs throughout the 13,000-square-foot hall (even in the restrooms) carry satellite feeds of games from around the world. While you watch, you can munch on wings, nachos, and linebacker-size burgers. *Disney's BoardWalk, 2101 EPCOT Resorts Blvd., EPCOT Resort Area 407/939–1177 disneyworld.disney.go.com/dining/boardwalk/espn-club.*

Jellyrolls

PIANO BARS | Musicians double as comedians and emcees as they play dueling grand pianos nonstop. Their speed and intricacy is impressive, as is the depth of their playlists. The steady stream of conventions at Disney makes this the place to catch CEOs doing the conga to Barry Manilow's "Copacabana," and young Disney cast members checking in after they clock out. There's a nightly cover charge. *Disney's BoardWalk, 2101 EPCOT Resorts Blvd., EPCOT Resort Area 407/560–8770 disneyworld.disney.go.com/entertainment/boardwalk/jellyrolls Guests must be 21 and over.*

Chapter 5

DISNEY'S HOLLYWOOD STUDIOS

WITH BLIZZARD BEACH

Updated by
Leigh Jenkins

Sights	Restaurants	Hotels	Shopping	Nightlife
★★★★★	★★★★☆	★★★☆☆	★★★★☆	★★☆☆☆

CHARACTER MEALS

Character meals are larger-than-life experiences that might be the high point of your child's visit to Walt Disney World or Universal. Mickey, Minnie, and others come alive and welcome your kids as if they were old friends.

These meals, ranging from Alice in Wonderland–theme tea parties to Mickey Mouse–led parades (and everything in between) are unique, one-on-one opportunities during which characters pose for pictures and engage with the little ones. Kids adore hugging or getting an autograph from their favorites; even tots who may be shy at first will usually warm up to their most-loved character. Always confirm that characters will be present when booking your meals: this is one of the offerings that changes the most often.

TOP PICKS FOR BREAKFAST

WALT DISNEY WORLD

Chef Mickey's Family Feast, Disney's Contemporary Resort. This breakfast combines space-age Disney styling with Mickey Mouse, Donald, and the gang, plus the ever-popular Mickey-shaped waffles.

'Ohana's Best Friends Breakfast with Lilo & Stitch, Disney's Polynesian Resort. The intergalactic Stitch and his human friend, Lilo, join your family in a tropical setting for this very popular breakfast. Every 30 minutes, Mickey and Pluto join in while kids parade around the restaurant with maracas and wide grins.

Topolino's Terrace–Flavors of the Riviera, Disney's Riviera Resort. Mickey, Minnie, Donald, and Daisy are dressed with European elegance as you dine on the top floor of Disney's newest hotel. Entrées such as sour cream waffles, quiche Gruyère, and wild mushroom scrambles elevate this meal above other character dining.

UNIVERSAL

Despicable Me Character Breakfast, Loews Royal Pacific Resort. Every Saturday morning Gru, his three girls, and the lovable minions rotate around Royal Pacific's Tahitian Room while you dine on pancakes, bacon, and scrambled eggs.

TOP PICKS FOR LUNCH

WALT DISNEY WORLD

The Crystal Palace Character Meal, Magic Kingdom. A lovely Victorian setting is the perfect place for the old-fashioned and lovable Winnie the Pooh and friends to greet your kids. This is the only meal at which you'll find characters from the Hundred Acre Wood.

Minnie's Seasonal Dine at Hollywood & Vine, Disney's Hollywood Studios. Minnie Mouse hosts four different seasonal parties at the Hollywood & Vine restaurant, ranging from a silver screen party celebrating Hollywood to a beach-theme party in the summer. The buffet is a changing menu of carving meats, seafood offerings, and vegetable creations.

My Disney Girl's Perfectly Princess Tea Party, Disney's Grand Floridian Resort. Children ages 3 to 11 enjoy the princess experience here. Dressing up is encouraged, and lunch, featuring tea and sandwiches, is served on china plates. Princess Aurora (Sleeping Beauty herself) will make an appearance. Little ones receive a special Disney Girl Princess doll, jewelry, a ribbon tiara, and a photo scrapbook page.

TOP PICKS FOR DINNER

WALT DISNEY WORLD

Cinderella's Happily Ever After Dinner, Disney's Grand Floridian Resort. A dinner buffet of worldly cuisine is complete with Cinderella, Prince Charming, and their family (including the wicked steps) making the rounds.

Princess Storybook Dining at Akershus Royal Banquet Hall, EPCOT. Belle, Snow White, the *Little Mermaid*'s Ariel, and other princesses could appear at this medieval Norwegian castle-inspired restaurant.

Tusker House Restaurant, Disney's Animal Kingdom. With selections such as peri peri salmon, spit-roasted chicken, and African side dishes, this is some of the best food at any character meal; Minnie, Daisy, and Donald mingle in their safari gear.

UNIVERSAL

Halloween Horror Nights Scareactor Dining Experience, Universal Studios. During Halloween Horror Nights in the fall, a character experience unlike any other is available at Classic Monster Cafe. Character actors from the haunted park will visit your table in an experience so intense it's not recommended for anyone under age 13.

Marvel Character Dinner, Islands of Adventure. On Thursday through Sunday nights Captain America, Spider-Man, Wolverine, Storm, and Rogue can be found at Cafe 4, where you can enjoy specialty pizzas and pasta.

PARK SNAPSHOT

TOP EXPERIENCES

■ **Beauty and the Beast—Live on Stage!** Memorable music, talented performers, dancing kitchen objects, and a fairy-tale ending make this a must-see show (ages 7 and under).

■ **Disney Junior Dance Party!** The preschool crowd can't get enough of the characters here from Disney Junior shows like *Vampirina, Mickey and the Roadster Racers, Doc McStuffins,* and *The Lion Guard* (ages 7 and under).

■ **For the First Time in Forever: A "Frozen" Sing-Along Celebration.** Every audience member can "Let It Go" and sing along to the popular tunes from Disney's blockbuster film *Frozen* (ages 7 and under).

■ **Slinky Dog Dash.** In the spirit of the Seven Dwarfs Mine Train, this new family coaster offers some speed and thrills but no real scares (ages 8 and up).

■ **Star Wars: Rise of the Resistance.** Try to avoid the First Order while helping Rey, Finn, and Poe on a resistance mission (ages 8 and up).

■ **Toy Story Mania!** 3-D glasses? Check. Spring-action shooter? Check. Ride and shoot your way through the midway with Buzz, Woody, and others (ages 8 and up).

PLANNING YOUR TIME

Because of Star Wars: Galaxy's Edge, Hollywood Studios is incredibly crowded. To ride Rise of the Resistance, be on the My Disney Experience app at 7 am and purchase the Individual Lightning Lane Pass or prepare to wait in Disney's longest line. Younger kids and parents should go to Toy Story Land. The other hot ticket and Lightning Lane Pass attraction is Mickey and Minnie's Runaway Railway.

Make dinner reservations well in advance for 50's Prime Time Café, where you'll dine in the setting of a classic '50s sitcom. For an upscale dinner, consider the Hollywood Brown Derby. And be sure to catch Fantasmic!, by either reserving a dining package or showing up 30 minutes before show time.

GETTING HERE

■ Most guests staying at a Disney resort hotel will take a Disney bus to the entrance of Hollywood Studios. If you're at BoardWalk, Yacht and Beach Club, or Swan and Dolphin, a ferry leaves about every 15 minutes for the park. Guests at Pop Century, Art of Animation, Caribbean Beach, and Riviera Resort can take advantage of the Disney Skyliner gondola. Parking for those not staying in a Disney resort is $25 per day. If you're at a hotel near the Magic Kingdom, consider driving; the parking lot is compact, and driving will save you a long bus ride.

VIEWFINDER

■ Nothing says Star Wars more than the iconic *Millennium Falcon* that was flown throughout the movies. In the back of Galaxy's Edge, you'll find a life-size replica of the famous ship, ready for a family photo. Grab a shot from the outside, but keep your camera ready as you wind around in the line for Millennium Falcon: Smuggler's Run—there are plenty of great details, and opportunities for more great photos, along the edges as well.

The first thing you notice when you pass through the Hollywood Studios turnstiles is the laid-back California attitude. Palm-lined Hollywood Boulevard oozes old-time glamour.

The second thing you notice is that nostalgia for the past glories of Hollywood film is giving way to nostalgia for its depiction of the future and toward a more Disney-centric vision of the movies. As interest in Star Wars has grown, the newest land—called Star Wars: Galaxy's Edge—has transformed the park in many ways.

Rather than offering a visit to a working movie studio, as the park's original concept called for, Disney is looking to immerse you in the world of beloved movies. In addition, the popularity of the Toy Story film series brought another big change. Toy Story Land, which opened in 2018, takes visitors into Andy's backyard, and brings Woody, Buzz, and a host of familiar characters to life. One of the newest attractions, Mickey and Minnie's Runaway Railway, sits inside Grauman's Chinese Theatre, taking the spot once occupied by the Great Movie Ride.

When the park opened in May 1989, its name was Disney–MGM Studios. Disney changed the name in 2008 to broaden its appeal. Another name change in the near future is not outside the realm of possibility. But no matter the name, the inspiration springs from the same place: America's love affair with the movies.

Although the park was built with real film and television production in mind, that has mostly halted. There are still attractions that showcase how filmmakers practice their craft, so if you're wowed by action-film stunts, you can learn the tricks of the trade at the Indiana Jones Epic Stunt Spectacular!, then you can take a close look at the legend himself, at Walt Disney Presents, where sketches, artwork, and early animation join previews of what's coming next. But the focus has shifted toward transporting you directly into the action through such big-hit attractions as Toy Story Mania!; the 3-D, Star Wars–themed simulator ride, Star Tours—The Adventures Continue; The Twilight Zone Tower of Terror; and Rock 'n' Roller Coaster starring Aerosmith.

Just a couple miles down Buena Vista Drive is Blizzard Beach, one of Disney's two water parks. Geared more toward teens, this ski-themed park has lots of thrill rides such as Downhill Double Dipper and Summit Plummet, a 12-story, free-fall waterslide. If you're visiting when the weather is warm, allow a whole day for this park.

Planning

Getting Oriented

The entire park is 135 acres, but it has fewer than 20 attractions (compared with Magic Kingdom's 40-plus). It's small enough to cover in a day and even repeat a favorite ride or two.

Hollywood Boulevard is the main artery to the heart of the park and is where you find the glistening replica of Grauman's

Chinese Theatre. Encircling it are Sunset Boulevard, the Animation Courtyard, Toy Story Land, Pixar Place, Commissary Lane, Grand Avenue, Star Wars: Galaxy's Edge, and Echo Lake.

If you're staying at one of the EPCOT resorts (BoardWalk, Yacht or Beach Club, Swan, or Dolphin), getting to the Entrance Plaza on a motor launch is part of the fun. Disney resort buses also drop you at the entrance. Those staying at Pop Century, Art of Animation, Caribbean Beach, and the Riviera Resort can take the Disney Skyliner gondola to the parks. If you're staying off-property and driving, your $25 parking ticket will remain valid for parking at another Disney park later in the day—provided, of course, you have the stamina.

From Disney hotels, most buses labeled "Hollywood Studios" or "Animal Kingdom" share a stop with Blizzard Beach; just check with the driver before boarding. If you have a car, it's easier to drive yourself, and parking is free. Rather than visiting Blizzard Beach and another park on the same day, give this large water park its own day. Not only will kids want to experience the thrills over and over, but you'll actually take more steps—and stairs—here than elsewhere. Instead of tiring yourself out, pair a visit to Blizzard Beach with a character breakfast or dinner at one of the other parks, which open earlier and close later.

Park Amenities

Baby Care: The small baby-care center next to Guest Relations (aka Guest Services) has nursing and changing facilities. Formula, baby food, pacifiers, and disposable diapers are for sale next door at Movieland and at Oscar's Super Service. There are also diaper-changing areas in all women's and some men's restrooms.

Cameras: At the Darkroom (or next door at Cover Story) on Hollywood Boulevard, you can buy memory cards and disposable cameras. And if a Disney photographer takes your picture in the park, you can pick up a Disney PhotoPass from him or her that lets you see the pictures online. Memory Maker, digital copies of your photos, are $169 in advance and $199 in the parks, and you can purchase prints ($20.95 for an 8-by-10-inch photo; other sizes available).

First Aid: The station is in the Entrance Plaza adjoining Guest Relations.

Guest Relations: You'll find it just inside the turnstiles on the left side of the Entrance Plaza.

Lockers: You can rent lockers at the Crossroads of the World kiosk in the center of the Entrance Plaza. The cost is $10 to $15 with a $5 refundable key deposit. The lockers themselves are at Oscar's Super Service.

Lost People and Things: Instruct your kids to go to a Disney staffer with a name tag if they can't find you. If you lose them, ask any cast member for assistance; logbooks of lost children's names are kept at Guest Relations, which also has a computerized message center where you can leave notes for companions.

Tip Board: Small tip boards are located at the end of Hollywood Boulevard, by BackLot Express, near Tower of Terror, and at the entrance to Toy Story Land. These are especially helpful keeping an eye on Rise of the Resistance.

Disney's Hollywood Studios Lost and Found
Report lost or found articles at Guest Relations. ✉ *Hollywood Boulevard, Disney's Hollywood Studios* ☎ *407/560–4666.*

Main Lost and Found Office
After one day, all articles are sent to the main lost and found office at Disney Springs and can be retrieved between 9 am and 7 pm daily. ✉ *Disney Springs, Disney Springs* ☎ *407/824–4245.*

Package Pick-Up: You can ask shop clerks to forward purchases to your hotel if you're staying on Disney property or to Package Pick-Up next to Oscar's Super Service in the Entrance Plaza, so you won't have to carry them around. Allow three hours for delivery.

Services for People with Disabilities: The Studios' restaurants, shops, theaters, and attractions are wheelchair accessible, although there are boarding restrictions on some rides. Some theater-type attractions, including Muppet*Vision 3D, have reflective captioning, and most other attractions are equipped for assisted-listening and video- or handheld-captioning devices. There are large Braille park maps near the Guest Relations lobby and near the Tip Board at Hollywood and Sunset. Note that restaurants don't have Braille menus.

You can pick up Braille guides ($25 same-day refundable deposit) and assisted-listening devices (also $25 deposit) and check on sign-language interpretation schedules at Guest Relations. Although interpreters appear only two days each week, you can request them (at least 14 days in advance) on other days by calling ☎ *407/560–2547 or TTY 407/827–5141.*

Oscar's Super Service, to the right in the Entrance Plaza, rents wheelchairs ($12 daily, $10 multiday) and electronic convenience vehicles (ECVs; $50 per day plus a refundable $20 security deposit). Reservations aren't an option so arrive early, especially to snag an ECV.

Stroller Rentals: Oscar's Super Service rents strollers. Single strollers are $15 daily, $13 for more than one day; doubles are $31 daily, $27 multiday.

Visiting Tips

Visit early in the week. That's when most other people are at Magic Kingdom and Animal Kingdom.

Arrive 30 minutes before opening. Those who haven't purchased an Individual Lightning Lane Pass to Rise of the Resistance should head there first.

Keep your eyes open. Hollywood Studios has more shows than any other park. Keep an eye on your *Times Guide* or app to ensure you arrive in plenty of time to get a seat.

Arrive early for Fantasmic! Be at the Fantasmic! amphitheater at least an hour before showtime if you didn't book the dinner or dessert package.

Grab a bite. Need a burst of energy? On-the-run hunger pangs? Try Fairfax Fare on Sunset. Hollywood Scoops ice cream next door is the place to be on a hot day.

Disney's Hollywood Studios

Hollywood Boulevard

With its palm trees, pastel buildings, and flashy neon, Hollywood Boulevard paints a rosy picture of midcentury Tinseltown. There's a sense of having walked right onto a movie set of old, with art deco storefronts and roving starlets and nefarious agents—actually costumed actors known as the Citizens of Hollywood. Throughout the park, characters from Disney movies new and old—from Mickey Mouse to Toy Story friends—pose for photos and sign autographs.

The new Mickey and Minnie's Runaway Railway is the centerpiece of Grauman's Chinese Theatre. **■ TIP→ Dinner or dessert packages that include the Fantasmic! after-dark show can be booked by phone or online, in person at a Disney hotel, or at the park's Guest Relations.**

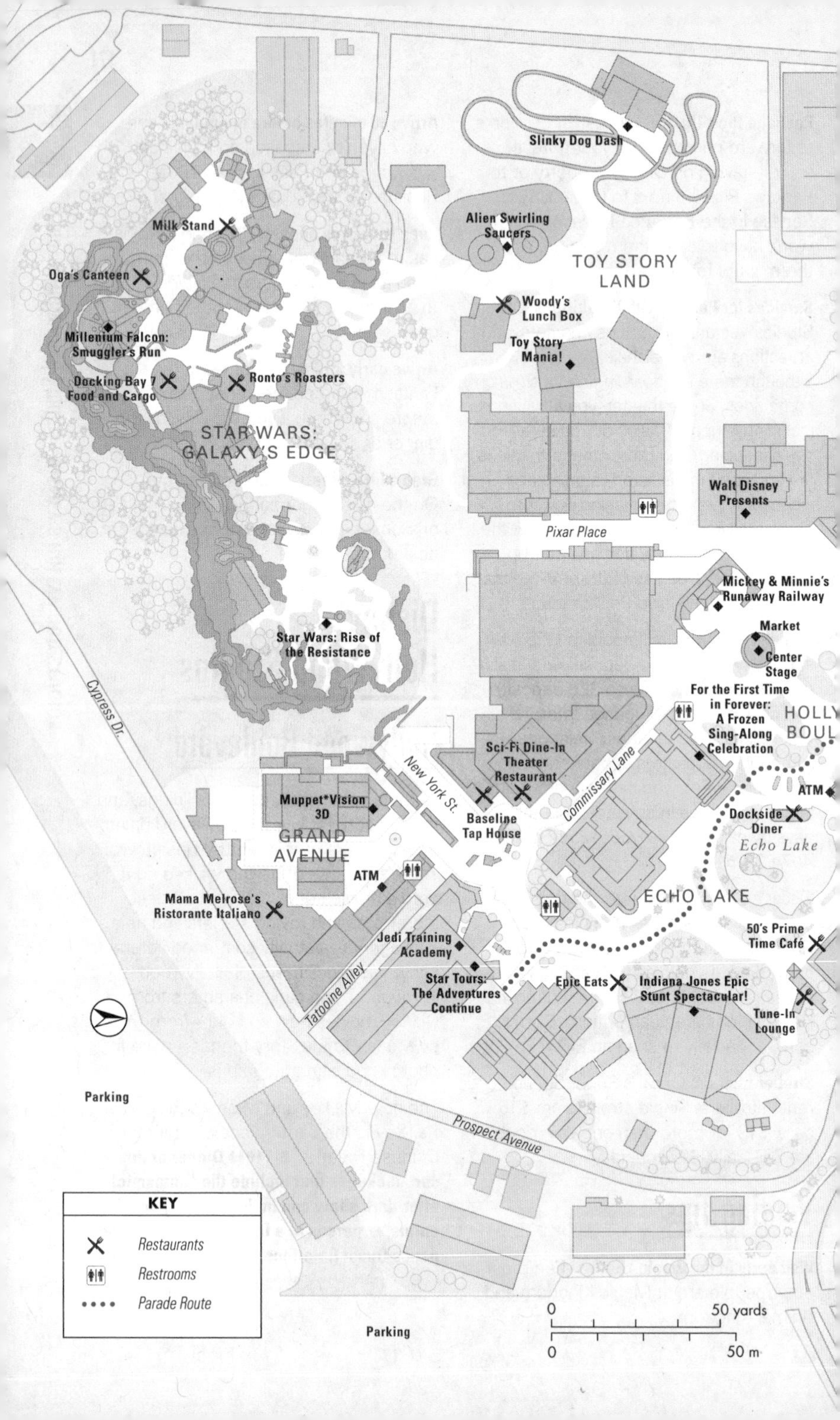

Slinky Dog Dash
Alien Swirling Saucers
TOY STORY LAND
Woody's Lunch Box
Toy Story Mania!
Milk Stand
Oga's Canteen
Millenium Falcon: Smuggler's Run
Docking Bay 7 Food and Cargo
Ronto's Roasters
STAR WARS: GALAXY'S EDGE
Walt Disney Presents
Pixar Place
Mickey & Minnie's Runaway Railway
Market
Center Stage
Star Wars: Rise of the Resistance
For the First Time in Forever: A Frozen Sing-Along Celebration
HOLLY BOUL
Cypress Dr.
Sci-Fi Dine-In Theater Restaurant
Commissary Lane
New York St.
ATM
Muppet*Vision 3D
Baseline Tap House
Dockside Diner
Echo Lake
GRAND AVENUE
ATM
Mama Melrose's Ristorante Italiano
ECHO LAKE
Jedi Training Academy
50's Prime Time Café
Tatooine Alley
Star Tours: The Adventures Continue
Epic Eats
Indiana Jones Epic Stunt Spectacular!
Tune-In Lounge
Parking
Prospect Avenue
KEY
Restaurants
Restrooms
Parade Route
0
50 yards
0
50 m
Parking

Disney's Hollywood Studios

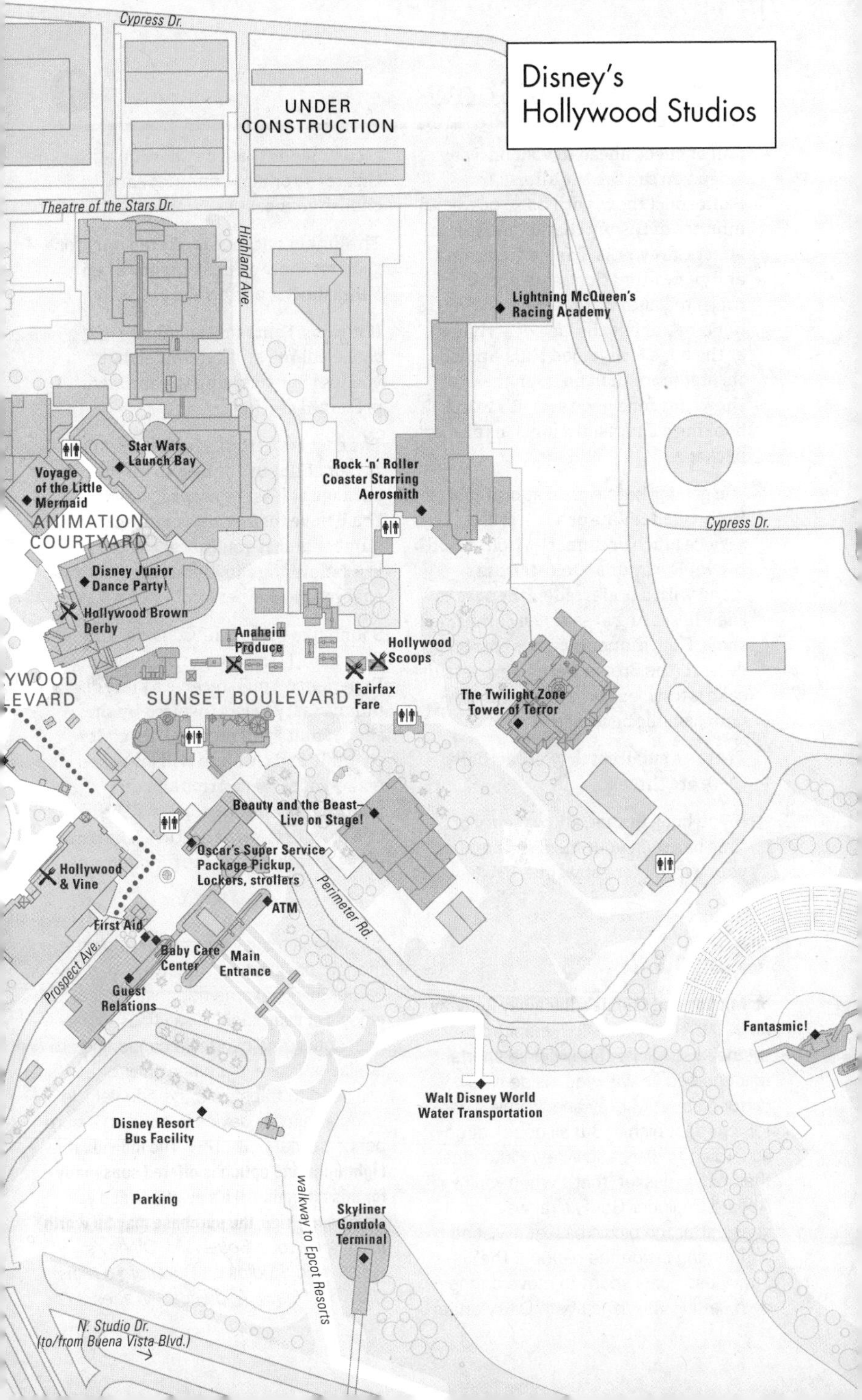

Dinner and a Show

Call or check ahead to visit on a day when you can see the after-dark Fantasmic! show, with its 30 powerful minutes of Disney characters, special effects, fireworks, flames, fountains, and even animation sequences projected onto water screens. If you're not crazy about the idea of arriving at the huge Hollywood Hills Amphitheater more than an hour ahead of showtime for a good seat, it's worth booking a Fantasmic! lunch or dinner package.

You get a prix-fixe meal at buffet-style Hollywood & Vine or a full table-service lunch or dinner at Hollywood Brown Derby or Mama Melrose's, along with a preferred-entry pass to the VIP seating area at the Fantasmic! show. Each dinner includes entrée, dessert (the Brown Derby's grapefruit cake is a sweet-tart wonder), and a nonalcoholic beverage.

There's a small catch (well, actually, there are three):

If you book dinner, allow plenty of time between your meal time and your arrival for showtime. (Disney recommends that you show up at the theater 30 or more minutes early to choose your seat.)

The dinner package is offered only for the first show on peak nights when Fantasmic! is performed twice.

If it rains, Fantasmic! might be canceled. You still get dinner, but you lose out on seeing the show with preferred seating.

The cost is $43 to $65 for adults, $18 to $41 for children. It's best to reserve the package at least 180 days in advance. You'll have to provide a credit-card number and, if you cancel 48 hours or less before the show, your card will be charged $10 per person.

Sound like too much? Consider the Fantasmic! Dessert and VIP Viewing Experience. You'll receive a plate of unique tasty treats inspired by the show, adults will receive a specialty cocktail, and children will love their make-your-own worms and dirt pudding. Then your party will be led to a private viewing section. The price is $39 for adults and $19 for children.

Sights

★ Mickey and Minnie's Runaway Railway
AMUSEMENT RIDE | **FAMILY** | Inspired by the newest Mickey and Minnie shorts, this ride begins with you inside a new cartoon about Mickey and Minnie's desire for a perfect picnic. But all does not go according to plan, and when Pluto steals their picnic basket, that's when you're off. Aboard Engineer Goofy's railway, you'll chase after the picnic basket, twisting and turning inside the cartoon. The "trackless" cars seem to move on their own, letting you dance with Daisy or get caught in a massive tornado. Don't fret, though: despite the "runaway" part of the name, this is a tame ride that any age can enjoy. **For people with disabilities:** Audio description and handheld captioning are available. Those in a wheelchair or ECV will need to transfer to the ride vehicle using a transfer device located on a number of the cars. **■ TIP→ The individual Lightning Lane option is offered seasonally for this attraction. If it's available and you have young kids, the purchase may be worth it.** ✉ *Hollywood Boulevard, Disney's Hollywood Studios* ☞ *Duration: 5 mins. Crowds: Heavy. Audience: All ages.*

Restaurants

Hollywood Brown Derby

$$$$ | AMERICAN | At this reproduction of the famous 1940s Hollywood favorite, the walls are lined with caricatures of old-time movie stars, and the specialty is a Cobb salad, which was invented by Brown Derby founder Robert Cobb and is still tossed table-side. While waiting for a table (it might take a while), or as an alternative, try the outdoor lounge, where you can order appetizers and drinks. **Known for:** grapefruit cake; old-Hollywood atmosphere; Cobb salad. *Average main: $40* ✉ *Hollywood Boulevard, Disney's Hollywood Studios* ☎ *407/939–3463* 🌐 *disneyworld.disney.go.com/dining/hollywood-studios/hollywood-brown-derby.*

Performing Arts

Star Wars: A Galactic Spectacular

SOUND/LIGHT SHOW | FAMILY | Combining imagery, lasers, and fireworks, this 14-minute show covers everyone's favorite Star Wars characters, from Darth Maul to Rey. Similar to the technology used on Cinderella Castle, images are projected onto Grauman's Chinese Theatre and the surrounding buildings, showing beloved characters and famous fight scenes. Note that this show is now only shown during certain times of the year; check ahead to see if it will be playing during your visit. ✉ *Hollywood Boulevard, Disney's Hollywood Studios* ☞ *Duration: 14 mins. Crowds: Moderate. Audience: Not small kids.*

Wonderful World of Animation

SOUND/LIGHT SHOW | FAMILY | This 12-minute nighttime projection show lights up the facade of the iconic Grauman's Chinese Theatre and begins with Mickey Mouse and his cartoon debut. Classic scenes from *Aladdin, The Little Mermaid,* and *The Incredibles* are projected across the entire theater, ending with, of course, Steamboat Willie and Mickey Mouse reminding you who started it all. ✉ *Hollywood Boulevard, Disney's Hollywood Studios.*

Shopping

Keystone Clothiers

MIXED CLOTHING | This shop pops with stylish clothing and accessories for adults. Disney characters are emblazoned on T-shirts and button-up-shirts, ties, and accessories, while handbags and totes sport classic Mickey Mouse artwork. Colorful scarves with hidden Mickeys and other designs are popular buys. ✉ *Hollywood Boulevard, Disney's Hollywood Studios* 🌐 *disneyworld.disney.go.com/shops/hollywood-studios/keystone-clothiers.*

Mickey's of Hollywood

TOYS | FAMILY | The largest store in Hollywood Studios is a miniversion of the Magic Kingdom's Emporium with toys, T-shirts, and doodads. Blue velvety *Sorcerer's Apprentice* hats have Mouse ears, as well as a moon and stars that light up. You'll also find Minnie Mouse and Donald Duck character key chains and lots of Disney-character-embossed tech accessories. ✉ *Hollywood Boulevard, Disney's Hollywood Studios* 🌐 *disneyworld.disney.go.com/shops/hollywood-studios/mickeys-of-hollywood.*

Sunset Boulevard

This avenue honors Hollywood with facades derived from the Carthay Circle Theatre, Fox Wilshire Theatre, and other City of Angels landmarks.

Sights

Beauty and the Beast—Live on Stage!

PERFORMANCE VENUE | FAMILY | This popular stage show takes place at the Theater of the Stars, a re-creation of the famed Hollywood Bowl. The actors playing a luminous Belle and delightfully vain Gaston sing passionately with a lively cast of characters and dancers. The enchanted prince (Beast) and household characters (Mrs. Potts, Chip, Lumière, and Cogsworth) deftly navigate the stage despite their bulky costumes. Even some set pieces sway along during the charming "Be Our Guest" number. There's high drama during the mob scene and a sweet ending when ballroom dancers in frothy pink and purple waltz along with the fairy-tale couple.

As you arrive or depart, check out handprints and footprints set in concrete of the TV personalities who've visited Disney's Hollywood Studios. **For people with disabilities:** Wheelchair and ECV accessible and equipped for hand-held-captioning, audio-description, and assisted-listening devices. Sign language twice a week. **■ TIP→ Arrive 30 minutes early on crowded days (which are rare) or if you want the "perfect" seat; otherwise show up 15 minutes before. Attend in the afternoon when you'll appreciate a chance to sit down.** ✉ *Sunset Boulevard, Disney's Hollywood Studios* ☞ *Duration: 30 mins. Crowds: Moderate. Audience: All ages.*

Lightning McQueen's Racing Academy

PERFORMANCE VENUE | FAMILY | If your little ones have always wanted to race with Lightning McQueen, then speed on over to Lightning McQueen's Racing Academy. A very convincing Audio-Animatronic car teaches the audience some of his tricks using a simulated track. Of course, the no-good Chick Hicks tries to out-race you, so, with the help of a wraparound screen, you'll get to watch Lightning race his long-time nemesis. This is a show, so while the Lightning McQueen figure is amazing, you will be sitting on a bench the whole time. **■ TIP→ This is a great place to take little ones while older kids ride the Tower of Terror or the nearby Rock 'n' Roller Coaster.** ✉ *Sunset Boulevard, Disney's Hollywood Studios* ☞ *Duration: 10 mins. Crowds: Moderate. Audience: Young kids.*

★ Rock 'n' Roller Coaster Starring Aerosmith

AMUSEMENT RIDE | FAMILY | Although this is an indoor roller coaster like Magic Kingdom's Space Mountain, the similarity ends there. With its high-speed launch (0 to 60 in 2.8 seconds), multiple inversions, and loud rock music, it generates delighted screams from coaster junkies, though it's smooth enough and short enough that even the coaster-phobic have been known to enjoy it. The vehicles look like limos, and the track resembles the neck of an electric guitar that's been twisted. Hard-driving rock tunes by Aerosmith blast from vehicle speakers to accentuate the flips and turns.

Pregnant women and guests with heart, back, or neck problems or motion sickness should skip this one. **For people with disabilities:** Guests using wheelchairs must transfer to a ride vehicle. Service animals aren't allowed. **■ TIP→ If you aren't heading to Star Wars first thing, take a right and do Rock 'n' Roller or Tower of Terror first. Lines are long in the afternoon but shorter in the morning, when everyone is at the newer rides.** ✉ *Sunset Boulevard, Disney's Hollywood Studios* ☞ *Duration: 1 min., 22 secs. Crowds: Huge. Audience: All but young kids. Height requirement: 48 inches.*

★ The Twilight Zone Tower of Terror

AMUSEMENT RIDE | FAMILY | After you enter the dimly lighted lobby of the deserted Hollywood Tower Hotel and then the dust-covered library, a lightning bolt zaps a TV to life. Rod Serling recounts the story of the hotel's demise and invites you to enter the Twilight Zone. On to the boiler room, where you board a giant elevator ride. The fifth dimension awaits, where you travel forward past scenes from the popular TV series. Suddenly, the creaking vehicle plunges into a terrifying, 130-foot free fall and then, before you can catch your breath, shoots quickly up, down, up, and down all over again. No use trying to guess how many stomach-churning ups and downs are in store—Disney's ride engineers have programmed random drop variations into the attraction for a different thrill every time.

Those who are pregnant or have heart, back, or neck problems shouldn't ride.

For people with disabilities: You must have full upper-body strength and be able to transfer to a ride seat. Equipped for video captioning. Service animals can't ride. ■ **TIP→ Come early or wait until evening, when crowds thin, and it's spookier.** ✉ *Sunset Boulevard, Disney's Hollywood Studios* ☞ *Duration: 10 mins. Crowds: You bet! Audience: All but young kids. Height requirement: 40 inches.*

Coffee and Quick Bites

Anaheim Produce

$ | **AMERICAN** | **FAMILY** | Assorted produce, tiny packs of oranges, and churros make this a great spot for an afternoon, pick-me-up snack. Featured craft beers, such as Kona's Longboard Island Lager or Schofferhofer Pink Grapefruit Hefeweizen can help calm you down after riding the Tower of Terror. **Known for:** fresh fruit; craft beers; frozen lemonade. $ *Average main: $5* ✉ *Sunset Boulevard, Disney's Hollywood Studios* ☎ *407/939–3463* 🌐 *disneyworld.disney.go.com/dining/hollywood-studios/anaheim-produce.*

Fairfax Fare

$ | **HOT DOG** | **FAMILY** | There's no such thing as a boring hot dog at this sunny location. The California BLTA Dog comes with lettuce, tomato, avocado, applewood bacon, ranch tortilla chips, and black pepper mayo, and the Pretzel Dog is covered in sauerkraut on pretzel bread. **Known for:** extreme hot dogs; blondies; Florida beers. $ *Average main: $11* ✉ *Sunset Boulevard, Disney's Hollywood Studios* ☎ *407/939–3463* 🌐 *disneyworld.disney.go.com/dining/hollywood-studios/fairfax-fare.*

Performing Arts

Fantasmic!

SOUND/LIGHT SHOW | **FAMILY** | The Studios' after-dark show wows huge audiences with its special effects and Disney characters. The omnipresent Mickey, in his sorcerer's apprentice costume, plays the embodiment of Good in the struggle against the forces of Evil, personified by Disney villains such as Cruella De Vil, Scar, and Maleficent. Animated clips of these famous baddies, alternating with clips of Disney sweethearts, are projected onto screens made of water—high-tech fountains surging high in the air. The epic battle plays out amid water effects and flames, explosions, and fireworks worthy of a Hollywood shoot-'em-up. All this, plus the villainous action, is why small kids may find this show frightening. If your little one is apprehensive, sit toward the back where the special effects aren't as intense.

Arrive early at the Hollywood Hills Amphitheater opposite the Twilight Zone Tower of Terror. Check ahead for information on show days and times. This show often runs twice nightly during peak season; fewer times during nonpeak periods. **For people with disabilities:** Wheelchair and ECV accessible. Equipped with reflective captioning and for assisted-listening, handheld-captioning, and audio-description devices. ■ **TIP→ Arrive at least an hour early and sit toward the rear, near the entrance/exit. Or consider the meal package, which includes a special block of seating for the show. If you sit in front rows, you will get wet.** ✉ *Sunset Boulevard, Disney's Hollywood Studios* ☞ *Duration: 30 mins. Crowds: Heavy. Audience: Not small kids.*

Shopping

Once Upon A Time

SOUVENIRS | **FAMILY** | It's the one shop you don't want to miss on Sunset Boulevard. Vintage-style T-shirts of Mickey, Pluto, Donald, and Grumpy are classy alternatives to standard-issue T's, and a white-sequined Mickey hat adds flair to any outfit. Women's fashion T's and costume bling draw lots of shoppers. Customized watches, like those sold at the Magic Kingdom's Uptown Jewelers, as well as purses and totes, are sold here, too. ✉ *Sunset Boulevard, Disney's*

Hollywood Studios 🌐 *disneyworld.disney.go.com/shops/hollywood-studios/once-upon-a-time.*

Tower Hotel Gifts

SOUVENIRS | FAMILY | After the screams and thrills of the Tower of Terror, what could be better than a mug from the hotel bar, the actual bell from the front desk, or a leather key fob from "your" room. In addition to leather handbags and bellboy hats, you can find some rather macabre takes on Disney characters that are exclusive to this shop. ✉ *Sunset Boulevard, Disney's Hollywood Studios* 🌐 *disneyworld.disney.go.com/shops/hollywood-studios/tower-shop.*

Animation Courtyard

As you exit Sunset Boulevard, veer right through the high-arched gateway to the Animation Courtyard. Straight ahead are Disney Junior Dance Party!, Star Wars Launch Bay, and Voyage of the Little Mermaid.

Sights

Disney Junior Dance Party!

PERFORMANCE VENUE | FAMILY | This is one of Walt Disney World's best shows for tots and preschoolers. DJ Deejay spins familiar Disney Junior tunes while Finn Fiesta acts as host for Doc McStuffins, Timon, and Vampirina. Throughout the show, kids are encouraged to sing and dance along as the characters cha-cha-cha their way through the fun. Special effects further inspire kids to participate. The entire event is capped off with Mickey appearing in his racing gear from *Mickey and the Roadster Racers.* **For people with disabilities:** Wheelchair and ECV accessible, equipped with preshow-area TV monitors with closed captioning, and equipped for assisted-listening, audio-description, and video- and handheld-captioning devices. ■ **TIP→ Come early, when your child is most alert and lines are shorter. Be prepared to sit on the carpet. Don't miss character meet and greets before or after the show.** ✉ *Animation Courtyard, Disney's Hollywood Studios* ☞ *Duration: 25 mins. Crowds: Moderate. Audience: Young kids.*

Star Wars Launch Bay

OTHER MUSEUM | FAMILY | This is the spot to check out costumes, concept art work, replica props, models, and artifacts from the Star Wars films on display in several galleries. A 10-minute film runs continuously in the Launch Bay Theater, documenting the creation of Star Wars through interviews with the directors, writers, and producers of this wildly popular film series. There's also an area where you can meet and have your photo taken with Star Wars characters. **For people with disabilities:** Guests can remain in wheelchairs and ECVs in specialty seating in the back of the theater. Handheld captioning, assistive listening, and audio description are available. ■ **TIP→ Disney Visa Cardholders can show their card ID for an exclusive Star Wars Magic Shot experience.** ✉ *Animation Courtyard, Disney's Hollywood Studios* ☞ *Duration: Up to you. Crowds: Moderate. Audience: All ages.*

Voyage of the Little Mermaid

PERFORMANCE VENUE | FAMILY | You join Ariel, Sebastian, and the underwater gang at this stage show, which condenses the movie into a presentation of the greatest hits. In an admirable effort at verisimilitude, a fine mist sprays the stage; if you're sitting in the front rows, expect to get spritzed. Although this show is suitable for all ages, smaller children might be frightened by the dark theater and the evil, larger-than-life Ursula. **For people with disabilities:** Wheelchair accessible, has reflective captioning and preshow-area TVs with closed captioning, and equipped for audio-description and assisted-listening devices. ■ **TIP→ Come while braver members of your party ride Rock 'n' Roller Coaster or Tower of Terror.**

Or wait until the stroller brigade's exodus later in the day. ⊠ *Animation Courtyard, Disney's Hollywood Studios* ☞ *Duration: 17 mins. Crowds: Moderate. Audience: All ages.*

Walt Disney Presents

OTHER MUSEUM | FAMILY | A self-guided tour through a treasure trove of Walt Disney memorabilia follows his life from early boyhood, through the founding of his first studio, to Disneyland, and then to Disney World. After viewing the unique artifacts, catch a 15-minute documentary about the life of Walt Disney. **For people with disabilities:** Wheelchair and ECV accessible. ■ **TIP→ Come in the afternoon, as this attraction is rarely busy.** ⊠ *Animation Courtyard, Disney's Hollywood Studios* ☞ *Duration: 15+ mins. Crowds: Light to moderate. Audience: Not young kids.*

Shopping

In Character

TOYS | FAMILY | Children love this open-air shop next to the Voyage of the Little Mermaid for the dolls, plush princess toys, and dress-up costumes. You can drop a small fortune on glass (plastic) slippers and a magical light-up wand—or splash out fully with the coveted Ariel mermaid costume gown. ⊠ *Animation Courtyard, Disney's Hollywood Studios* 🌐 *disneyworld.disney.go.com/shops/hollywood-studios/in-character-disneys-costume-shop.*

Toy Story Land

Pixar Place leads to one of the park's most popular attractions, Toy Story Mania!, as well as to Toy Story Land, where you enter Andy's backyard for adventures with Woody, Buzz, Slinky Dog, Rex, the Aliens, and many other beloved characters. The land has two other major attractions: a coaster called Slinky Dog Dash and a dizzying ride called Alien Swirling Saucers.

Sights

Alien Swirling Saucers

AMUSEMENT RIDE | FAMILY | Based on the toys Andy got from the Pizza Planet claw machine in the first *Toy Story* movie, this ride puts you on a rocket being driven by aliens in flying saucers, who are trying to have their rocket chosen by The Claw. Rather than just spinning, the cars swirl about in figure-eight formations, sending passengers back and forth within the car. Kids love the unexpected twist, making this a must-do for kids as young as 4. **For people with disabilities:** You must transfer from a wheelchair to ride. ⊠ *Toy Story Land, Disney's Hollywood Studios* ☞ *Duration: 2 mins. Crowds: Moderate. Audience: All ages.*

★ Slinky Dog Dash

AMUSEMENT RIDE | FAMILY | The centerpiece of Toy Story Land is meant to be a roller coaster built by Andy using his Mega Coaster Play Kit. The bright-red track surrounds a primary-color building-block city with towers featuring Toy Story icons such as Cowgirl Jessie and Rex the dinosaur. The coaster vehicles are Slinky Dogs, whose slinky springs surround the cars. Watch this ride a couple of times before boarding: it is faster than it looks! Kids who do well on Goofy's Barnstormer at the Magic Kingdom will love this longer coaster. **For people with disabilities:** You must transfer from a wheelchair to ride. ■ **TIP→ The line for this attraction gets surprisingly long; if you aren't heading straight to Galaxy's Edge, come here first.** ⊠ *Toy Story Land, Disney's Hollywood Studios* ☞ *Duration: 2 mins. Crowds: Heavy. Audience: All ages.*

★ Toy Story Mania!

AMUSEMENT RIDE | FAMILY | Great toys like Mr. Potato Head, Woody, and Buzz Lightyear from Disney's hit film franchise Toy Story never lose their relevance. The

Did You Know?

Toy Story Land's Toy Story Mania! combines the fun of a video game with 3-D technology interaction with favorite characters, like Mr. Potato Head. Man your spring-action shooter, and aim at playful targets along the colorful ride route. Scores are tallied at the end—will yours make you master of the midway?

action here involves these beloved characters and takes place inside the toy box of Andy, the boy whose toys come to life when he's not around. Step right up and grab a pair of 3-D glasses before boarding your jazzed-up carnival tram. Soon you're whirling onto the midway where you can use your spring-action shooter to launch darts at balloons, toss rings at aliens, and splatter eggs at barnyard targets.

You'll rack up points for targets hit and see your tally at ride's end. Try using a rat-a-tat shooting approach to increase your score. Don't let Rex's fear of failure slow you down—shoot for the stars, and earn a salute from the Green Army Men. **For people with disabilities:** Guests using ECVs must transfer to a standard wheelchair. Equipped for video-captioning and audio-description devices. Check with a host about boarding with a service animal. ■ **TIP→ It's so addictive that you might want to ride first thing and then return later in the day.** ✉ *Toy Story Land, Disney's Hollywood Studios* ☞ *Duration: 7 mins. Crowds: Heavy. Audience: All ages.*

Coffee and Quick Bites

Woody's Lunch Box

$ | **AMERICAN** | **FAMILY** | A lunch box meal never tasted so good! The turkey sandwich comes with tomato-basil soup, and the BBQ Brisket Melt has a deliciously tangy sauce, but the grilled three-cheese sandwich is so popular that Disney has actually shared the recipe on its website. **Known for:** BBQ Brisket Melt; grilled cheese and tomato soup; fresh-daily tarts. $ *Average main: $10* ✉ *Toy Story Land, Disney's Hollywood Studios* ☎ *407/939–3463* 🌐 *disneyworld.disney.go.com/dining/hollywood-studios/woodys-lunchbox.*

Grand Avenue

Formerly Streets of America, this area of the park has changed considerably in recent years, with many of the familiar facades fallen to Toy Story Land and Star Wars. But Miss Piggy, Kermit, and their Muppet pals are still entertaining fans at the theater on Grand Avenue.

Sights

Muppet*Vision 3D

PERFORMANCE VENUE | **FAMILY** | This combination 3-D movie and musical revue features appearances by all the Muppet characters, including Miss Piggy, in roles that include the Statue of Liberty. In the waiting area, movie posters advertise the world's most glamorous porker in *Star Chores* and *To Have and Have More*, as well as Kermit the Frog, who's "so mean, he's green" in an Arnold Schwarzenegger parody, *Kürmit the Amphibian*. Special effects are built into the theater's walls and ceilings, and the 3-D effects are coordinated with other sensory stimulation. Arrive early: the pre-show is as funny as the actual movie. **For people with disabilities:** Wheelchair accessible; has reflective captioning and preshow-area TVs with closed captioning; equipped for assisted-listening, video-captioning, and audio-description devices. ■ **TIP→ Continuous shows means a short wait here, so come in the afternoon. And don't worry—there are no bad seats.** ✉ *Grand Avenue, Disney's Hollywood Studios* ☞ *Duration: 25 mins. Crowds: Moderate to heavy. Audience: All ages.*

Restaurants

Baseline Tap House

$$$ | **AMERICAN** | This eatery (re)creates a downtown Los Angeles corner pub, serving California wines and craft beers. Charcuterie boards featuring California cheeses and Bavarian pretzels with fondue are snackable highlights. **Known for:** California beers, ciders, and wines; urban

Los Angeles feel; casual snacks. *$ Average main: $25 ✉ Grand Avenue, Disney's Hollywood Studios ☎ 407/939–3463 🌐 disneyworld.disney.go.com/dining/hollywood-studios/baseline-tap-house.*

Mama Melrose's Ristorante Italiano
$$$ | ITALIAN | FAMILY | To replace the energy you've no doubt depleted by miles of theme-park walking, load up on carbs at this casual restaurant that looks like a classic San Francisco Italian eatery. Good main courses include spaghetti with meatballs and sautéed shrimp in a four-cheese sauce with pasta and vegetables. **Known for:** tiramisu and traditional cannoli; old-fashioned Italian restaurant atmosphere; Fantasmic! dining package. *$ Average main: $25 ✉ Grand Avenue, Disney's Hollywood Studios ☎ 407/939–3463 🌐 disneyworld.disney.go.com/dining/hollywood-studios/mama-melrose-ristorante-italiano.*

Sci-Fi Dine-In Theater Restaurant
$$$ | AMERICAN | FAMILY | If you don't mind zombies leering at you while you eat, then head to this enclosed faux drive-in, where you can sit in a booth that looks like a candy-color, 1950s convertible while watching clips from classics like *Attack of the Fifty-Foot Woman* and *Teenagers from Outer Space.* The menu includes a variety of burgers, from barbecue to salmon, as well as pan-seared chicken pasta and oven-roasted turkey sandwiches. End with a hot-fudge sundae or warm glazed doughnut. **Known for:** wine, sangria, and fun cocktails; milk shakes; specialty chef burgers. *$ Average main: $25 ✉ Grand Avenue, Disney's Hollywood Studios ☎ 407/939–3463 🌐 disneyworld.disney.go.com/dining/hollywood-studios/sci-fi-dine-in-theater.*

Echo Lake

In the center of an idealized slice of Southern California is a cool, blue lake—an oasis fringed with trees, benches, and things like pink-and-aqua, chrome-trimmed restaurants with sassy waitresses and tableside black-and-white TVs. In addition to the shipshape Min & Bill's Dockside Diner, there's Tatooine Traders, where kids can build their own lightsabers and browse a trove of Star Wars–inspired goods. You'll also find two of the park's longest-running attractions, the Indiana Jones Epic Stunt Spectacular! and Star Tours—The Adventures Continue, where a 3-D attraction transformation jazzes up the galaxy.

Sights

For the First Time in Forever: A "Frozen" Sing-Along Celebration
PERFORMANCE VENUE | FAMILY | Ever since the Disney film *Frozen* hit the jackpot, Disney's theme parks have been mining the blockbuster with character meet and greets, entertainment vignettes, a ride, and this show, which packs the house up to 10 times a day. The comical emcees are two costumed "Royal Historians" of Arendelle, who pepper their *Frozen* story narration with witticisms. Animated segments of the film accompany the narration on a giant screen, and live actors portray Anna, Elsa, and Kristoff convincingly as they interact with the historians and audience. Song lyrics are displayed on two additional video screens, and everyone sings along to the film's playlist, especially the Academy Award–winning "Let It Go" and the sweetly melodic "Do You Want to Build a Snowman?" **For people with disabilities:** Wheelchair accessible. **■ TIP→ A large theater makes this is a great option for the afternoon.** *✉ Echo Lake, Disney's Hollywood Studios ☞ Duration: 30 mins. Crowds: Moderate. Audience: All ages.*

★ Indiana Jones Epic Stunt Spectacular!
PERFORMANCE VENUE | FAMILY | The rousing theme music from the Indiana Jones movies heralds action delivered by veteran stunt coordinator Glenn Randall, whose credits include *Raiders of the Lost Ark, E.T.,* and *Jewel of the*

Nile. Presented in a 2,200-seat amphitheater, the show starts with a series of near-death encounters in an ancient Maya temple. Indy slides down a rope from the ceiling, dodges spears, avoids getting chopped by booby-trapped idols, and snags a forbidden gemstone, setting off a gigantic boulder that threatens to flatten him.

Next comes the Cairo street scene, circa 1940, where lucky audience members are chosen to perform as extras. When the nasty Ninja-Nazi stuntmen come out, you start to think that it's probably better to remain seated. Eventually, Indy returns with his redoubtable girlfriend, Marian Ravenwood, portrayed by a Karen Allen look-alike. She's kidnapped and tossed into a truck while Indy fights his way free with bullwhip and gun, and bad guys tumble from every corner and cornice.

The actors do a commendable job of explaining their stunts, so you learn how cameras are camouflaged for trick shots. Only one stunt remains a secret: how do Indy and Marian escape the grand finale explosion? That's what keeps 'em coming back. Note, though, that there are continuous rumors about this show being updated or possibly dropped, in keeping with Disney's new "immersive" theme. **For people with disabilities:** Wheelchair accessible. Equipped for assisted-listening, audio-description, and handheld-captioning devices. There's sign language interpretation twice weekly. ■ **TIP→ Don't waste valuable early morning hours here; there's plenty of room in the afternoon. Come at night to see the idols' eyes glow.** ✉ *Echo Lake, Disney's Hollywood Studios* ☞ *Duration: 30 mins. Crowds: Moderate. Audience: All but very young kids.*

★ **Star Tours: The Adventures Continue**
AMUSEMENT RIDE | FAMILY | Star Wars fans, wield your lightsabers! This fan favorite multiplies the thrills with more than 50 ride scenarios powered up by Dolby 3-D video and motion-simulator technology. Here's the basic storyline: C-3PO and R2-D2, at the helm of a misappropriated spaceship, must navigate the galaxy with a rebel spy on board (it could be you!) while Imperial forces try to thwart the journey.

You'll encounter multiple thrills from the Star Wars universe including the lush Wookiee planet Kashyyyk and the underwater world of Naboo. Kef Bir, the water moon with a destroyed Death Star, has also been added to the lineup. One flight takes you to the climatic battle from *The Rise of Skywalker.* You might come face-to-menacing-mask with Kylo Ren or be recruited by Lando Calrissian. Other characters sprinkled throughout the different films include Admiral Ackbar, Chewbacca, and Boba Fett. Your 40-passenger Starspeeder 1000 rockets through space with enough high-speed twists, turns, and nosedives to guarantee that the Force is, indeed, with you.

Those who are pregnant or have heart, back, neck, or motion-sickness issues shouldn't ride. Children less than 40 inches tall may not ride. **For people with disabilities:** Guests using wheelchairs must transfer to a ride seat. Equipped for handheld-captioning and video-captioning devices. Service animals aren't allowed. ■ **TIP→ Lines swell when the Indiana Jones show lets out. If they're long, check back in an hour, they may have shrunk. For the wildest ride, sit in the back.** ✉ *Echo Lake, Disney's Hollywood Studios* ☞ *Duration: 6 mins. Crowds: Heavy. Audience: All but young kids.*

Restaurants

50's Prime Time Café
$$$ | AMERICAN | FAMILY | If you grew up in middle America in the 1950s—or you're just a fan of classic TV series like *I Love Lucy* and *The Donna Reed Show*—you'll appreciate the vintage atmosphere and diner-classic menu here. At tables with Formica tops, you can feast on

Hollywood Studios Kids Tour

Young children get a kick out of Hollywood Boulevard's wacky street performers and the park's energetic stage shows.

The minute you enter, get in line for **Toy Story Mania!** Everyone loves this busy ride—even young children who have to learn how to operate spring-action shooters to rack up midway points. If you can ride *and* return later in the day, you'll be your kids' hero. Next, head deeper into Toy Story Land for **Alien Swirling Saucers** or **Slinky Dog Dash** for the brave at heart.

Combine lunch with more playtime at the **Disney Junior Play n' Dine** at Hollywood & Vine family buffet, where characters from Disney Junior Dance Party! mix and mingle with the children. Don't forget the kids' autograph books!

See the Characters Come to Life

Shows and attractions based on Disney films and TV series really grab young children. Check your *Times Guide* for performances of **Beauty and the Beast: Live on Stage** and **Disney Junior Dance Party!** After tots and preschoolers have danced along at the Disney Junior show, they can meet the characters in the Animation Courtyard, then catch a Beauty and the Beast performance or watch Ariel "under the sea" in **Voyage of the Little Mermaid.**

Check other character greeting locations and times—the Green Army Men from Toy Story put the kids through their marching paces on Pixar Place, Mickey and Minnie Mouse wander along Commissary Lane, and The Incredibles pose for photos at the end of Pixar Place. Make time to catch Lightning McQueen at **Lightning McQueen's Racing Academy.** Then watch Kermit display his wry wit and Miss Piggy steal the show at **Muppet*Vision 3D.** It's not easy being green. ...

Grab the Spotlight

Jedi wannabes can suit up to clash with the dark side at **Jedi Training: Trials of the Temple**, which is scheduled throughout the day. As soon as you enter, head to the **50's Prime Time Café** so children ages 4–12 can sign up early for a chance to grab a lightsaber and let the Force be with them. During each 20-minute show, crowds gather and cheer the kids as they learn to "cut to the left shoulder, step back, and duck!" when clashing with a costumed Darth Vader. Needless to say, the dark side can't compete.

meat loaf, pot roast, or fried chicken accompanied by a malted milk shake, a root-beer float, or a bottle of wine or a cocktail from the Tune-In Lounge next door. **Known for:** golden-fried chicken, pot roast, and meat loaf sampler; shows clips of classic TV shows during dinner; "Mom" wanders around tables telling kids to eat their veggies. [$] *Average main: $22* ✉ *Echo Lake, Disney's Hollywood Studios* ☎ *407/939–3463* 🌐 *disneyworld.disney.go.com/dining/hollywood-studios/50s-prime-time-cafe.*

Hollywood & Vine

$$$$ | AMERICAN | FAMILY | Disney Channel stars come to life at this restaurant through its Disney Junior Play n' Dine breakfasts. Vampirina, along with friends of *Sofia the First* and *Doc McStuffins*, are among the cheerful characters marching around the room, singing

Hollywood Studios Grown-Ups Tour

At the Studios, the best of Disney animation—from Toy Story to *Beauty and the Beast*—is reborn in park attractions. The old small-screen favorite *The Twilight Zone* is taken to new heights, and Indiana Jones performs action-packed stunts to bring famous film moments to life.

Discover a New World

Head straight to **Rise of the Resistance** to sign-up with Rey, Finn, and the rest of the rebels. If you've purchased an Individual Lightning Lane for this, then go to **Millennium Falcon: Smuggler's Run** first and ride a time (or two!) to help Chewie earn the highest score.

After recovering with a drink at Oga's Cantina, a quick walk to Echo Lake lands you in Wookiee territory, where you can climb aboard the **Star Tours** flight simulator for a wild flight themed to the latest Star Wars movies; 3-D upgrades and more than 50 different ride scenarios increase the thrill factor. Leave plenty of time to take in the sights and sounds of Batuu!

Find Your Adrenaline Rush

Two words—thrills and chills—define the top two attractions for older kids and adults. In the afternoon, hike over to Sunset Boulevard, and grab the thrills at **Rock 'n' Roller Coaster Starring Aerosmith**, where multiple inversions, twists, and turns rock to the tune of "Dude (Looks Like a Lady)." Feel the chills at the **Twilight Zone Tower of Terror**, when something goes terribly wrong with your elevator car, and it veers off its eery course.

Tastes of the Past

Refuel at one of the park's many quick-service stands, let "Mom" serve you meat loaf and a peanut-butter-and-jelly shake at the **50's Prime Time Café**, or boost your image with a plush booth and a Cobb salad at the **Hollywood Brown Derby.**

Back at Echo Lake, the Tune-In Lounge is a great place to grab a mojito or margarita before heading to the nighttime extravaganza **Fantasmic!** That's a wrap.

and dancing to the delight of energetic fans. **Known for:** VIP dining package for Fantasmic! nighttime show; character meals; prix-fixe menu. *Average main: $55 Echo Lake, Disney's Hollywood Studios 407/939–3463 disneyworld.disney.go.com/dining/hollywood-studios/hollywood-and-vine.*

Coffee and Quick Bites

Dockside Diner

$$ | AMERICAN | FAMILY | While the smoked fish dip and shrimp salad roll here are delicious, it's the seaside brownie and milk shakes that you'll crave. In addition to vanilla and chocolate, shakes can be made with Baileys Irish Cream and Kahlúa Liqueur, while the Minute Maid Frozen Lemonade adds Tito's Handmade Vodka. **Known for:** spiked milk shakes; seafood rolls; sweet-and-sour margarita. *Average main: $15 Echo Lake, Disney's Hollywood Studios 407/939–3463 disneyworld.disney.go.com/dining/hollywood-studios/dockside-diner.*

Epic Eats

$ | ICE CREAM | FAMILY | The whole family will love sharing a funnel cake with strawberry or cookies 'n' cream topping. Root beer floats come traditionally or with Stoli Vanil Vodka. **Known for:** funnel cakes; root beer floats; ice cream. $ *Average main: $8* ✉ *Echo Lake, Disney's Hollywood Studios* ☎ *407/939–3463* 🌐 *disneyworld.disney.go.com/dining/hollywood-studios/epic-eats.*

Shopping

Indiana Jones Adventure Outpost
TOYS | **FAMILY** | Almost as popular as the pirate hats in the Magic Kingdom are the Indiana Jones felt fedoras sold at this outpost near the stunt amphitheater. Small kids can get a complete Indy play set with fedora, machete, pistol, and gems for about $20. You can also find crystal skulls, plush exotic animals, polished rocks, and *Raiders of the Lost Ark* action figures. ✉ *Echo Lake, Disney's Hollywood Studios* 🌐 *disneyworld.disney.go.com/shops/hollywood-studios.*

Tatooine Traders
TOYS | **FAMILY** | The Star Wars theme is strong in this desert dome shop outside the Star Tours ride. Guests of all ages can build their own single or double lightsabers complete with crystals, hilts, and blades. And what's a lightsaber without a droid to share it with? So build a droid as well. Collectible pins, books, action figures, art, clothing, and Vinylmation characters are also popular here. **TIP→ Don't feel up to the long line and price of building a lightsaber in Galaxy's Edge? The lightsabers here might not be as intricate, but they will still please younglings—and their parents' wallets.** ✉ *Echo Lake, Disney's Hollywood Studios* 🌐 *disneyworld.disney.go.com/shops/hollywood-studios/tatooine-traders.*

Star Wars: Galaxy's Edge

A gray, unmarked subway entrance leads to a setting with otherworldly slabs of concrete and rock formations. Emerging from the tunnel, you find you've entered Batuu, a special planet from the Star Wars universe, created just for the Disney theme parks. Everywhere you look, you'll see tiny details, from the droid prints in the concrete to signs written in Aurebesh, the language of Batuu (if you want to know what the signs say, there is a translator within the Disney Play app). Parked X-wings and droids provide atmosphere as you walk deeper and deeper into this fully immersive world.

The area's two rides, Millennium Falcon: Smuggler's Run and Star Wars: Rise of the Resistance, are both popular and spectacular attractions, but be sure to wander through the marketplace, look for Resistance paraphernalia "hidden" at stalls along the streets, visit Og's Cantina, and build your own droid at the Droid Depot. This land is so popular that even shops and restaurants can draw lines, so visit first thing in the morning.

Sights

★ **Millennium Falcon: Smuggler's Run**
AMUSEMENT RIDE | **FAMILY** | Star Wars fans will love being able to actually pilot the *Millennium Falcon* on a supply run. Hondo Ohnaka, who fans will recognize from *Star Wars: The Clone Wars,* has hired you to fetch "precious cargo" that will bring him big profits and help the Resistance by providing much-needed supplies. Chewie has offered use of the *Millennium Falcon,* but it will take a team of six to complete the mission. Groups are split into two pilots, who drive the Falcon; two gunners, who defend the Falcon; and two engineers, who rope in the cargo. The effects, first with the Audio-Animatronic Hondo Ohnaka and then with walking through the ship itself, are incredible. Be sure to take a picture at the legendary Dejarik (chess) table.

Once onboard, your crew must work together to retrieve the cargo and bring the Millennium Falcon back with minimal damage. At the end of your mission, Hondo tallies up how you did, minus repairs to the Falcon and his profit, of course. Most guests want to ride again to improve their score! **For people with disabilities:** Guests need to transfer to a standard wheelchair and then into the ride vehicle. Those wanting to be gunners or engineers can directly transfer; pilots will need to use a transfer wheelchair but will find the ride more secure once they are in place. Note that the many ramps throughout the line can be tough on standard-wheelchair users. **■TIP→ Visit this attraction first upon entering, and then plan to wait to ride again.** ✉ *Star Wars: Galaxy's Edge, Disney's Hollywood Studios* ☞ *Duration: 4½ mins. Crowds: Heavy. Audience: All ages.*

★ **Star Wars: Rise of the Resistance**

AMUSEMENT RIDE | **FAMILY** | The crowning jewel of Galaxy's Edge is more of an experience than a ride. You, along with other residents of Batuu, are led to a briefing room to join Rey and the rest of the Resistance off-planet. A holographic transmission, just like in the movies, appears before your group to explain that you'll be led by Lieutenant Bek to a rendezvous point with General Leia Organa. You'll then board a transport, walking outside past Poe Dameron's X-wing, all the while being rushed along by Resistance fighters. Aboard the transport, similar to a subway car, Lieutenant Bek flies you to outer space while Poe provides cover. But—surprise—the First Order is waiting for you! General Hux catches you in the tractor beam and pulls you into the hanger bay of his Star Destroyer.

Upon exiting, you'll be inside the hangar bay, with First Order officers barking commands while you file past impressive rows of stormtroopers. You're broken into groups and placed in containment cells, where first General Hux and then Kylo Ren show up to convince you to turn over the location of the rebel base you were heading to. When he's called away, you're rescued by the Resistance, led by Finn, and placed onto First Order Fleet Transports, each piloted by a reprogrammed droid. Kylo Ren isn't going to give up easily, though, and you're chased throughout the Star Destroyer, passing under AT-AT walkers, past turbo-laser cannons, and coming face to face with Kylo. Don't worry, you'll end up safely back on Batuu, but be prepared for a truly thrilling adventure.

This multipart experience is so popular that, within 30 minutes of the park opening, the lines swell enough so that there's a two-hour wait. If you are going to purchase an Individual Lightning Lane Pass for only one attraction, make it this one; to do so, be on the My Disney Experience app at exactly 7 am. Also note that though the ride itself is 18 minutes, the entire experience can be longer.
In addition, many of the effects can be jarring, and cast members acting as the First Order can be intense, so reassure younger riders that you're on a make-believe mission. **For people with disabilities:** Guests in an ECV or wheelchair must be able to transfer. **■TIP→ Purchase the individual Lightning Lane Pass, or be prepared to wait in galactically long lines.** ✉ *Star Wars: Galaxy's Edge, Disney's Hollywood Studios* ☞ *Duration: 18 mins. Crowds: Heavy. Audience: All ages. Height requirement: 40 inches.*

Restaurants

Docking Bay 7 Food and Cargo

$$ | **AMERICAN** | **FAMILY** | This hangar bay transformed into a quick-service-restaurant by Chef Strono "Cookie" Tuggs serves out-of-this world meals. Try the braised beef stir fry or the fried chicken tip yip with roasted vegetables. **Known for:** authentic Star Wars atmosphere; vegetarian hummus spread on pita; gluten-free options. 💲 *Average main: $16* ✉ *Star Wars: Galaxy's Edge, Disney's Hollywood Studios* ☎ *407/939–3463* 🌐 *disneyworld.disney.go.com/dining/hollywood-studios/docking-bay-7-food-and-cargo.*

Ronto's Roasters
$$ | **AMERICAN** | **FAMILY** | If you're looking for a quick meal in Galaxy's Edge, this is the place. Among the meats that have been "roasted over a pod racer engine," you'll find pork rinds, roasted pork, and vegetable wraps. **Known for:** quick meal; pork rinds; specialty beverages. *Average main: $15* ✉ *Star Wars: Galaxy's Edge, Disney's Hollywood Studios* ☎ *407/939–3463* 🌐 *disneyworld.disney.go.com/dining/hollywood-studios/ronto-roasters.*

Coffee and Quick Bites

Milk Stand
$ | **AMERICAN** | **FAMILY** | Stop by the Milk Stand to grab a glass of blue milk, Luke Skywalker's favorite drink (green milk is available, too—who knew?). Both drinks are made with coconut and rice milk mixed with different fruits. **Known for:** plant-based beverages; Star Wars collectibles; blue milk. *Average main: $8* ✉ *Star Wars: Galaxy's Edge, Disney's Hollywood Studios* ☎ *407/939–3463* 🌐 *disneyworld.disney.go.com/dining/hollywood-studios/milk-stand.*

★ Oga's Cantina
$$ | **AMERICAN** | No Star Wars land would be complete without a kooky bar. Here you'll find a variety of beers on tap along with Star Wars themed drinks such as the T-16 Skyhopper with vodka, melon liqueur, kiwi, and half and half; or the Dagobah Slug Slinger, made with tequila, curaçao, citrus, and ginger. **Known for:** cocktails and mocktails; meat-and-cheese plate; beer on tap and wine. *Average main: $18* ✉ *Star Wars: Galaxy's Edge, Disney's Hollywood Studios* ☎ *407/939–3463* 🌐 *disneyworld.disney.go.com/dining/hollywood-studios/ogas-cantina.*

Shopping

Black Spire Outfitters
MIXED CLOTHING | **FAMILY** | If you're visiting Galaxy's Edge to get in character, stop by Black Spire Outfitters for the perfect costume. It has everything from blaster belts to full Jedi robes. How "in character" you go is up to you. Many of the shirts are stylish on their own, and who doesn't need a good cloak when visiting the cliffs of Ahch-To? ✉ *Star Wars: Galaxy's Edge, Disney's Hollywood Studios* 🌐 *disneyworld.disney.go.com/shops/hollywood-studios/black-spire-outfitters.*

Droid Depot
TOYS | **FAMILY** | Here you can build your very own droid, on a miniature scale at least. Upon arriving, choose between a BB-series (like BB-8) or R-series (like R2-D2), then select your own color scheme and accessories. Once built, droids can communicate with one another using Bluetooth technology or be driven by their owners with a remote control. Note that droids aren't cheap (prices start at $99.99), and, without a reservation made on the My Disney Experience app, expect a wait just to enter the store. ✉ *Star Wars: Galaxy's Edge, Disney's Hollywood Studios* 🌐 *disneyworld.disney.go.com/shops/hollywood-studios/droid-depot.*

Savi's Workshop–Handbuilt Lightsabers
TOYS | **FAMILY** | If you're an aspiring Jedi, plan a trip to Savi's Workshop to build a lightsaber. More intense than just a toy from the store, this lightsaber allows its wielder to choose different themes and kyber crystals, creating a truly unique design. Reservations are highly recommended, and be prepared for sticker shock: prices start at $219.99. ✉ *Star Wars: Galaxy's Edge, Disney's Hollywood Studios* 🌐 *disneyworld.disney.go.com/shops/hollywood-studios/savis-workshop-handbuilt-lightsabers.*

Blizzard Beach's Toboggan Racers accommodates eight sliders at a time, who get to race 250 feet to the bottom of Mt. Gushmore.

Blizzard Beach

As its oxymoronic name implies, Blizzard Beach delivers the improbable—a seaside playground with an alpine theme. From its imposing ski-jump tower to its 1,200-foot series of rushing waterfalls, this water park offers cool fun even in the hot summertime. And where else can you wear your swimsuit on the slopes?

As with its older cousin, Typhoon Lagoon, Disney Imagineers have created a legend to explain the park's origin. The story goes that, after a freak winter storm dropped snow over the western side of Walt Disney World, entrepreneurs created Florida's first downhill ski resort. Saunalike temperatures soon returned. But, as the 66-acre resort's operators were ready to close up shop, they spotted a playful alligator sliding down the 120-foot-tall "liquid ice" slopes. The realization that the melting snow had created the world's tallest, fastest, and most exhilarating water-filled ski and toboggan runs gave birth to the ski resort–water park.

GETTING ORIENTED

The park is fairly easy to navigate. Once you enter and rent a locker, you cross a small bridge over Cross Country Creek before choosing a spot to park your towels and cooler. To the left is the Melt-Away Bay wave pool. Dead ahead you can see Mt. Gushmore, a chairlift to the top, and the park's many slopes and slides.

Older kids and devoted waterslide enthusiasts generally prefer Blizzard Beach to other water parks. If thrills are your game, come early and line up for Summit Plummet, Slush Gusher, and Downhill Double Dipper before wait times go from light to moderate (or heavy). Anytime is a good time for a dip in Melt-Away Bay or a tube trip around Cross Country Creek. Parents with young children should claim their spot early at Tike's Peak, to the park's right even before you cross the bridge.

You can take Disney bus transportation or drive to Blizzard Beach. There's no charge for parking. Once inside, your options are to walk, swim, or slide.

PARK AMENITIES

Dining: You can't bring oversize coolers, glass containers, or your own alcoholic beverages into the park. Picnicking is welcome, however, and there are several pleasant pavilions and other spots, most notably the terrace outside Lottawatta Lodge. This is also where you can reserve your own lodge umbrella ($40–$60 for a day), which includes chairs (two of them loungers), an umbrella and small table, and four beach towels. Arrive early enough, and you'll snag your ideal spot in the park for free. You can get burgers, hot dogs, and salads at Lottawatta Lodge or other eateries and food stands. You could go for the usual snacks—snowballs or ice cream. But a truly sublime nibble is the melt-in-your-mouth mini-doughnut from the Mini Donuts stand across from Lottawatta Lodge.

Dressing Rooms and Lockers: Dressing rooms, showers, and restrooms are in the village area, just inside the main entrance. There are other restrooms in Lottawatta Lodge, at the Ski Patrol Training Camp, and just past the Melt-Away Bay beach area. Lockers are near the entrance, next to Snowless Joe's Rentals, and near Tike's Peak (the children's area and the most convenient if you have little swim-skiers in tow). It costs $10 to rent a small locker and $15 for a large one; there's also a $5 deposit. Note that there are only small lockers at Tike's Peak. The towels for rent ($2) at Snowless Joe's are tiny. If you forgot yours, you're better off buying a proper one at the Beach Haus.

First Aid: The first-aid stand, overseen by a registered nurse, is in the village, between Lottawatta Lodge and the Beach Haus.

Guest Services: Disney staffers at the Guest Services window, to the left of the ticket booth as you enter the park, can answer questions. Get free life vests or rent towels and lockers at Snowless Joe's. Inner tubes, rafts, and slide mats are provided at the rides. Buy beach gear or rent towels or lockers at Beach Haus; purchase sunglasses at Shade Shack.

Lost People and Things: Instruct youngsters to let a lifeguard know if they get lost. The lost-children station is beneath a large beach umbrella near the front of the park. And don't worry about the kids—a Disney cast member will keep them busy with activities.

Private Patios: The park has 14 Polar Patios for groups of up to six people. For $325 a day in peak season (usually March through late August), and between $160 and $240 at other times of the year, you get plush loungers, chairs, a table with umbrella, refillable beverage mugs, an ice chest with two water bottles per person, a group locker, and an attendant who will take your orders for and deliver lunch and snacks (food costs extra). It's best to book a patio (☎ *407/939–8687*) far ahead, though, if you arrive early enough, there might be an open patio; check at the Shade Shack.

SERVICES FOR PEOPLE WITH DISABILITIES

Most of Blizzard Beach's paths are flat and level. Plan on transferring to a Water Chair, better known as a PVC chair. Available at Guest Services, this chair can be taken directly into the water at the wave pool, Meltaway Bay, and is allowed in special gondolas on the chair lift.

Team Boat Springs, Slush 'n' Gusher, Snow Stormers, Toboggan Racers, Runoff Rapids, and Cross Country Creek are all designed for transfer from the water chair into an inner tube. The rest of the slides are not wheelchair accessible.

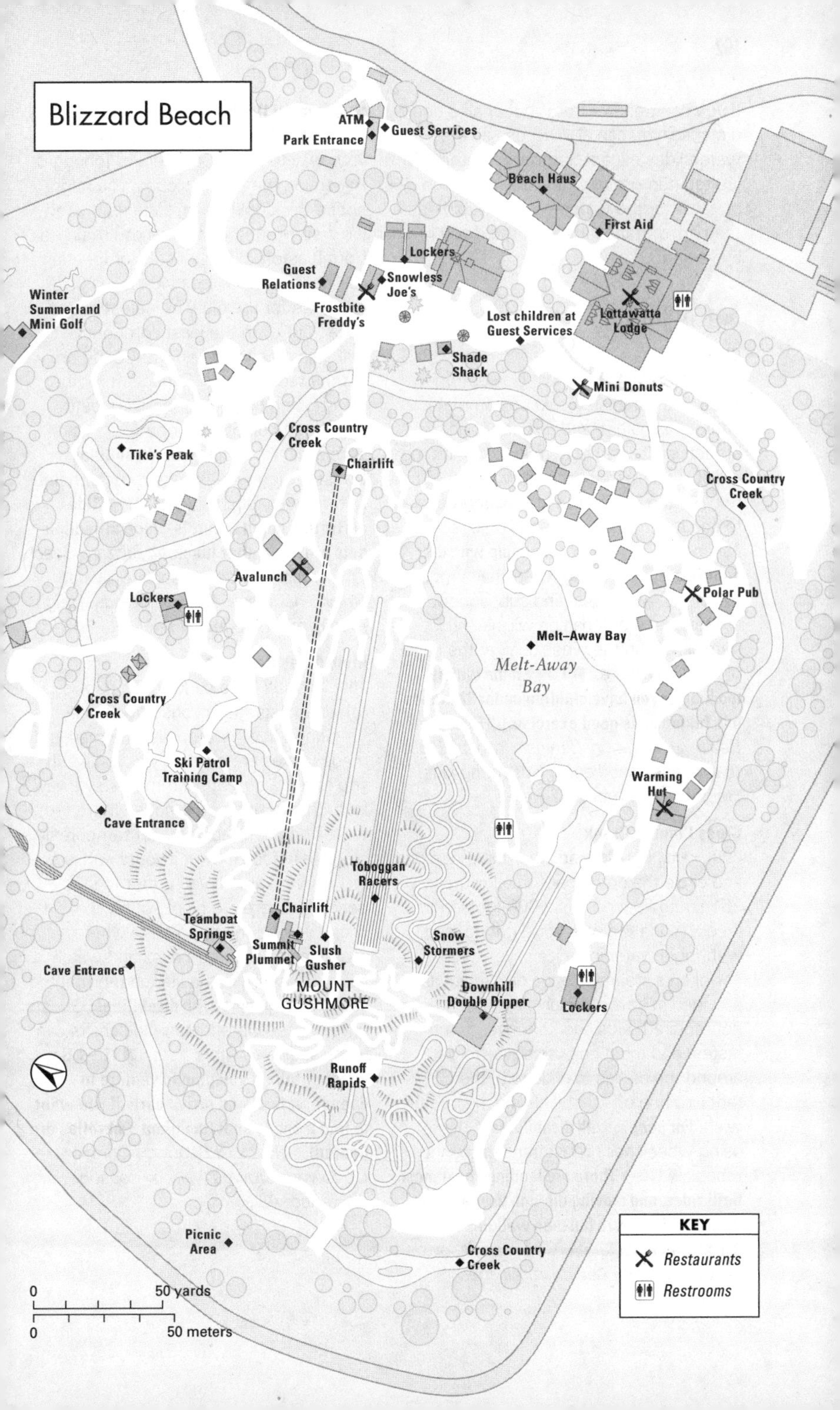
Blizzard Beach
ATM
Guest Services
Park Entrance
Beach Haus
First Aid
Lockers
Guest Relations
Snowless Joe's
Frostbite Freddy's
Winter Summerland Mini Golf
Lost children at Guest Services
Lottawatta Lodge
Shade Shack
Mini Donuts
Cross Country Creek
Tike's Peak
Chairlift
Cross Country Creek
Avalunch
Polar Pub
Lockers
Melt-Away Bay
Melt-Away Bay
Cross Country Creek
Ski Patrol Training Camp
Warming Hut
Cave Entrance
Toboggan Racers
Chairlift
Teamboat Springs
Summit Plummet
Slush Gusher
Snow Stormers
Cave Entrance
MOUNT GUSHMORE
Downhill Double Dipper
Lockers
Runoff Rapids
Picnic Area
Cross Country Creek
0
50 yards
0
50 meters
KEY
Restaurants
Restrooms

If you can transfer from your chair a short distance, you can also access all the waterslides except Summit Plummet. A limited number of wheelchairs—some suitable for the water—are available near the park entrance and are free if you leave an ID.

Sights

Chairlift

AMUSEMENT RIDE | FAMILY | No subtropical skiing paradise would be complete without a chairlift, and this one is an attractive alternative to trekking to the top of Mt. Gushmore over and over again. The two-minute ascent is a great opportunity to scout out other slides and enjoy the "ski beach" scenery. **For people with disabilities:** Guests using wheelchairs must transfer to a ride seat and subsequent attractions. A companion will have to meet you with the wheelchair at the base of Mt. Gushmore. ■ **TIP→ If the wait is too long or you have children under 32 inches tall, hiking up is good exercise.** ✉ *Blizzard Beach* ☞ *Duration: 2 mins. Crowds: Light to moderate. Audience: Not young kids. Height requirement: 32 inches.*

Cross Country Creek

POOL | FAMILY | Grab an inner tube, hop on, and circle the entire park on a leisurely 25-minute float on this 3,000-foot-long creek. Along the way, you'll get doused with frigid water in an ice cave—wonderful on a steamy Florida day. Tubes are provided at seven launch sites, but they're not required. Kids soon discover that the fastest and most enjoyable way to get around the park is to glide with the current and hop off at whichever landing they wish. **For people with disabilities:** Guests using wheelchairs must transfer to inner tubes. ■ **TIP→ There are landings near most thrill rides, and moving through the park this way is oodles more fun than walking.** ✉ *Blizzard Beach* ☞ *Duration: 25 mins. Crowds: Vary by season. Audience: All ages.*

★ Downhill Double Dipper

AMUSEMENT RIDE | FAMILY | If you're on your way to Snow Stormers or Toboggan Racers on the purple slopes, you might notice this cool-looking slide on the left. It's well worth the stop, as you're timed from blastoff to finish line! Competition can get heated as kids (48 inches or taller) vie for the glory of fastest speed slider, but even the least competitive will enjoy tearing down Mt. Gushmore in their racing tubes. Expectant mothers shouldn't ride, nor should guests with heart conditions or neck or back problems. **For people with disabilities:** Guests using wheelchairs must transfer to the tube-launch site. ■ **TIP→ Ride early; this popular purple-slope attraction gets crowded after lunch.** ✉ *Blizzard Beach* ☞ *Duration: Under 10 secs. Crowds: Heavy. Audience: Not young kids. Height requirement: 48 inches.*

Melt-Away Bay

POOL | FAMILY | The park's main pool is a 1-acre oasis that's constantly fed by "melting snow" waterfalls. The man-made waves are positively oceanlike. If you're not a strong swimmer, stay away from the far end of the pool, where the waves originate. You can get temporarily stuck in a pocket even if your head is still above water. If you prefer to stay beached, there are plenty of recliner chairs around the bay. This is where moms and dads often relax and watch their kids swim in the lifeguard-protected waters. **For people with disabilities:** Guests using water-appropriate wheelchairs can enjoy shallow waters here. ■ **TIP→ Get an inner tube if you plan to venture to deeper waters, and arrive early if you want to find a shady spot (the giant umbrellas are limited).** ✉ *Blizzard Beach* ☞ *Duration: Up to you. Crowds: Vary by season. Audience: All ages.*

Runoff Rapids

AMUSEMENT RIDE | FAMILY | It's easy to overlook this three-track flume ride hidden on the far red slope of Mt. Gushmore. Yet, if you have the courage to carry your tube all the way up to the top, you'll eventually come upon three twisting, turning, 600-foot-long flumes—even one that's in the dark (keep in mind the tunnel slide is for single riders only, while the open slides are for one- or two-passenger tubes). Once you're in, it's way more fun than scary. Still, guests who are pregnant or who have heart, neck, or back problems should skip it. **For people with disabilities:** Guests using wheelchairs must transfer to inner tubes. Your water chair will be sent to the bottom of the hill for you. **■TIP→ It's worth riding both an open slide and the tunnel slide, but remember that the tunnel slide is only for single riders.** ✉ *Blizzard Beach* ☞ *Duration: 35 secs. Crowds: Light to moderate. Audience: Not young kids.*

Ski Patrol Training Camp

OTHER ATTRACTION | FAMILY | Preteens might want to spend most of their time on the T-bar drop, Cool Runners slides, and Snow Falls downhill body slide. In addition, there's a chance to take on the Thin Ice Training Course, a wide-open area where kids can jump from one slippery mogul to the next. The moguls really look more like bobbing baby icebergs, and kids don't mind when they miss a berg and plop into the pool. **For people with disabilities:** Guests using water-appropriate wheelchairs can enjoy wading areas here. **■TIP→ The optimum time to come is early in the day or after a thunderstorm, when crowds thin out. That said, lines are often short at the zipline drop and the iceberg obstacle course.** ✉ *Blizzard Beach* ☞ *Duration: Up to you. Crowds: Light to moderate. Audience: Tweens.*

★ Slush Gusher

AMUSEMENT RIDE | FAMILY | This speed slide drops through a snow-banked mountain gully on a fast, hilly, green-slopes descent to the base of Mt. Gushmore. It isn't quite as intimidating as neighboring Summit Plummet, but it's a real thriller nonetheless. For guests who are pregnant or who have heart, back, or neck problems, this ride is not recommended. **For people with disabilities:** Guests using wheelchairs must transfer to the slide. **■TIP→ The earlier you ride, the better: on crowded days waits can last up to 90 minutes.** ✉ *Blizzard Beach* ☞ *Duration: 15 secs. Crowds: You bet! Audience: Not young kids. Height requirement: 48 inches.*

Snow Stormers

AMUSEMENT RIDE | FAMILY | No water park would be complete without a meandering waterslide, and Blizzard Beach has this one. Here three flumes, each 350 feet long, descend from the top of Mt. Gushmore along a switchback course of ski-type slalom gates on the purple slopes. Snow Stormers offers an exciting change of pace from the straight-down slides of the green slopes, and riders are in for a grand total of eight hairpin turns before finally splashing into the pool at the bottom. This ride isn't appropriate for guests who are pregnant or who have heart, neck, or back problems. **For people with disabilities:** Guests using wheelchairs must transfer to a toboggan-style slide mat with handles. **■TIP→ Hold on tight during this belly-down ride!** ✉ *Blizzard Beach* ☞ *Duration: 20 secs. Crowds: Moderate to heavy. Audience: All Ages.*

★ Summit Plummet

AMUSEMENT RIDE | FAMILY | This is Mt. Gushmore's big gun, one of the world's tallest, fastest, free-fall speed slides. From Summit Plummet's "ski jump" tower at the very top of the green slopes, it's a wild, 55-mph, 12-story plunge straight down and then into a tunnel before a white-water splash landing at the end of the 360-foot-long run. It looks almost like a straight vertical drop, and you can't help but feel like a movie stunt double as you take the plunge. If you're watching from the beach below, you can't hear the yells of the participants, but you can bet many of them are screaming their heads off. If you have heart, neck, or back problems or are pregnant, avoid this attraction—one of the most intense in all of Disney. **For people with disabilities:** This attraction requires walking up two flights of stairs and is not suited to those with mobility issues. **■ TIP→ Make this your first stop early in the day. Summer afternoon waits can be up to two hours.** ✉ *Blizzard Beach* ☞ *Duration: 10 crazy secs. Crowds: Absolutely. Audience: Not young kids. Height requirement: 48 inches.*

Teamboat Springs

AMUSEMENT RIDE | FAMILY | Six-passenger rafts zip along green slopes in one of the world's longest family whitewater raft rides. Since its original construction, it has doubled its speed of departure onto its twisting, 1,200-foot channel of rushing water, which ends with a refreshing waterfall dousing. This ride is a good place for kids too big for Tike's Peak to test more grown-up waters. Those who are pregnant or have heart, neck, or back problems should avoid this one. **For people with disabilities:** Guests using wheelchairs must transfer to the ride. **■ TIP→ This ride is great for the whole family: there aren't age or height requirements (beyond "no infants"), tubes seat four to six people, and lines move quickly.** ✉ *Blizzard Beach* ☞ *Duration: 1½ mins. Crowds: Moderate. Audience: Families.*

★ Tike's Peak

POOL | FAMILY | Disney never leaves the little ones out of the fun, and this junior-size version of Blizzard Beach, set slightly apart from the rest of the park, has scaled-down elements of Mt. Gushmore, with sand, slides (including one with tubes), faux snow drifts, and igloolike tunnels. Parents can find sun or shade beneath lean-tos. Lifeguards are on hand. **For people with disabilities:** Guests using water-appropriate wheelchairs can enjoy the wading areas. **■ TIP→ Stake out lounge chairs early, especially for a shady spot. If your tykes don't swim well, get them fitted with a free life vest, and pull your chair up to the water's edge.** ✉ *Blizzard Beach* ☞ *Duration: Up to you. Crowds: Vary by season. Audience: Small kids. Height requirement: Children must be shorter than 48 inches and accompanied by adults.*

Toboggan Racers

AMUSEMENT RIDE | FAMILY | Grab your mat, wait for the signal, and go! You and eight other racers whiz simultaneously down the watery trail on the purple slopes toward the finish line at the base of the mountain. The racing aspect and dips along the 250-foot-long slope make the ride fun, but it lacks the speed of single-rider green-slope rides like Slush Gusher. For a ride combining speed and friendly competition, check out the Downhill Double Dipper. Expectant mothers shouldn't ride, nor should guests with heart, neck, or back problems. **For people with disabilities:** Guests using wheelchairs must transfer to slide mats. **■ TIP→ It's more fun when you race family members or friends—up to eight people can ride at the same time.** ✉ *Blizzard Beach* ☞ *Duration: 10 secs. Crowds: Moderate to heavy. Audience: Not young kids.*

Restaurants

Lottawatta Lodge—a North American ski lodge with a Caribbean accent—is the park's main purveyor of fast food. To avoid long lines, order ahead using your My Disney Experience app. Open seasonally, the **Warming Hut** offers wraps, sandwiches, and ice cream. Specialty hot dogs and nachos are on the menu at **Avalunch. Frostbite Freddy's** and **Polar Pub,** on the main beach, sell frozen drinks.

Chapter 6

DISNEY'S ANIMAL KINGDOM AND RESORT AREA

Updated by
Leigh Jenkins

Sights	Restaurants	Hotels	Shopping	Nightlife
★★★★★	★★★☆☆	★★★★★	★★★★☆	★★☆☆☆

PARK SNAPSHOT

TOP EXPERIENCES

■ **Avatar: Flight of Passage.** It's simply one of the most exciting theme-park rides you'll experience.

■ **DINOSAUR!** Extremely lifelike giant dinosaurs jump out as your vehicle swoops and dips. We recommend it for fearless kids 8 and up.

■ **Expedition Everest.** This roller coaster is a spine-tingling trip into the snowy Himalayas to find the abominable snowman. It's best reserved for brave riders 7 and up.

■ **Festival of the Lion King.** Singers and dancers dressed in fantastic costumes representing many wild animals perform uplifting dance and acrobatics numbers and interact with children in the audience.

■ **Kilimanjaro Safaris.** You're guaranteed to see dozens of wild animals, including giraffes, gazelles, hippos, rhinos, zebras, and elephants, living in authentic, re-created African habitats. If you're lucky, the lions and cheetahs will be stirring, too.

■ **Tree of Life: It's Tough to Be a Bug!** This clever and very funny 3-D movie starring Flik from the Disney film *A Bug's Life* is full of surprises, including "shocking" special effects. Some young children are scared of the loud noises.

■ **Wild Africa Trek.** The price tag is hefty, but this behind-the-scenes wild-animal adventure is a memory maker.

PLANNING YOUR TIME

With the addition of Pandora–The World of Avatar, Animal Kingdom definitely earned its badge of honor, and now that the park closes late most nights, there are reasons to stay (or come back) after the sun goes down. Both The Tree of Life and Pandora, with its bioluminescent flora, really come alive at night. The Kilimanjaro Safari is also a completely different experience after sunset.

GETTING HERE

■ Animal Kingdom is the most isolated of the parks. In terms of Disney transportation, it's reachable only by buses, and, except for the Animal Kingdom Lodge and Villas, it's not really close to hotels. If you are staying at another Walt Disney World resort and have a car, it's worth driving, especially if you plan to remain at Animal Kingdom after dark.

VIEWFINDER

■ The bridge that connects Dinoland U.S.A. and Asia is the perfect place for a photo that captures just how impressive Expedition Everest is. If you want a landscape portrait of the mountain, try across the lagoon by Kali Cart, where there's an altar that replicates the mountain's peaks.

If you're thinking, "Oh, it's just another zoo, let's skip it," think again. Walt Disney World's fourth theme park pulls out all the stops, taking its inspiration from humankind's enduring love for animals and the environment. Your day will be packed with unique animal encounters, enchanting shows, and theme rides, one of them out of this world, that'll leave you breathless.

A large chunk of the park is devoted to animal habitats, especially the forest and savanna of Africa's Kilimanjaro Safaris. Towering acacia trees and tall grasses sweep across the land where antelopes, giraffes, and wildebeests roam. A lion kopje, warthog burrows, a zebra habitat, and an elephant watering hole provide ample space for inhabitants.

About 94 acres contain foliage like hibiscus and mulberry, perfect for antelope and many other species. The largest groups of Nile hippos and African elephants in North America live along the winding waterway that leads to the savanna. The generously landscaped Pangani Forest Exploration Trail provides roaming grounds for troops of gorillas and authentic habitats for meerkats, birds, fish, and other creatures.

Beyond the park's Africa territory, similar large spaces are set aside for the homes of Asian animals like tigers and giant fruit bats, as well as for creatures such as Galápagos tortoises and a giant anteater.

Disney Imagineers didn't forget to incorporate their trademark thrills, including the astonishing Avatar Flight of Passage in Pandora; the Kali River Rapids ride in Asia; the fast-paced DINOSAUR journey in DinoLand U.S.A.; and Expedition Everest, a "runaway" train ride on a faux rugged mountain complete with icy ledges, dark caves, and a yeti legend.

The latest land to open takes you totally off-planet to a world inspired by the film *Avatar.* Opened in 2017, Pandora–The World of Avatar is filled with breathtaking technology, astonishing alien beauty, and the park's biggest thrill attraction, Avatar Flight of Passage. The whole park is open at night allowing for the best views of the lighted alien landscape.

The only downside to the Animal Kingdom is that paths and spaces can get very crowded and hot in the warmest months. Arrive very early and see the animals first before the heat makes them (and you) woozy.

Be on the lookout for the flock of brightly colored macaws—scarlet, hyacinth, blue, and gold and more—that flies through the park periodically.

Planning

Getting Oriented

Animal Kingdom's hub is the Tree of Life, in the middle of Discovery Island and from which the park's lands, each with a distinct personality, radiate. To the southwest, lies Pandora–The World of Avatar, inspired by *Avatar*. Although its floating islands are spectacular at any time, the area is best viewed after dark, when the alien landscape lights up. North of the hub is Africa, where Kilimanjaro Safaris travel across extensive savanna.

In the northeast corner is Rafiki's Planet Watch with conservation activities. East of the hub is Asia, with thrills like Expedition Everest and Kali River Rapids. DinoLand U.S.A. brings *T. rex* and other prehistoric creatures to life in the park's southeast corner.

Although this is technically Disney's largest theme park, most of the land is reserved for the animals. Pedestrian areas are actually quite compact, with relatively narrow passageways. The only way to get around is on foot or in a wheelchair or electronic convenience vehicle (ECV). If you're staying on Disney property, you can take a Disney bus to the Entrance Plaza. If you drive, the $25 parking fee allows you to park at other Disney lots throughout the day.

Park Amenities

Baby Care: At Discovery Island, you can nurse babies in the quiet baby-care center, which is equipped with rocking chairs and low lighting. There are changing tables, which are also available in restrooms (including some men's restrooms), and you can buy disposable diapers, formula, baby food, and pacifiers.

Cameras: Film and digital memory cards are for sale at several shops throughout the park. If a Disney photographer takes your picture, sign up for a Disney PhotoPass—later, you can view and purchase the pictures online ($199 for full digital Memory Maker access) or at the park's photo center in the Oasis.

First Aid: The first-aid center, staffed by registered nurses, is in Discovery Island, and at least a dozen automated external defibrillators are in key park areas.

Mosquito Control: Disney offers complimentary insect repellent for guests throughout all its parks.

Guest Relations (aka Guest Services): This office will help with tickets at a window to the left just before you pass through the turnstile. Once you've entered, Guest Relations staffers in the Oasis can answer questions; provide park maps and schedules; and assist with dining reservations, ticket upgrades, and services for guests with disabilities.

Lockers: Lockers are in Guest Relations in the Oasis. Rental fees are $10 to $15 (depending on size) for a day plus a $5 key deposit. Lockers located immediately outside Kali River Rapids will help you keep bags and belongings from getting wet. Standard lockers are free for the first two hours; large lockers are $4.

Lost People and Things: Instruct your kids to speak to someone with a Disney name tag if you become separated. Lost children are taken to the baby-care center, where they can watch Disney movies, or to Guest Relations, whichever is closer. If you do lose your child, contact any cast member immediately, and Disney security personnel will be notified.

Animal Kingdom Lost and Found
To retrieve lost articles on the same day, visit or call Lost and Found, which is in the lobby of Guest Relations, just inside the park. ✉ *Oasis, Animal Kingdom* ☎ *407/938–2785.*

Main Lost and Found
If more than a day has passed since you've lost something, contact the Main Lost and Found office at Disney Springs. ✉ *Disney Springs* ☎ *407/824–4245.*

Package Pick-Up: You can have shop clerks forward purchases to Package Pick-Up near the Main Entrance in the Oasis, so that you won't have to carry them around all day. Allow three hours for the journey. If you're staying at a Disney hotel, you can also have packages delivered there.

Services for People with Disabilities:
Guests using wheelchairs will have ready access to restaurants, shops, and most attractions—including the Finding Nemo: The Musical theater in DinoLand U.S.A. and the Tree of Life theater showing It's Tough to Be a Bug! (Theaters also are accessible to ECVs.) Some monitor-equipped attractions have reflective-captioning boxes.

Scripts and story lines for all attractions are available, and you can book sign-language interpreters with notice of two or more weeks. Large Braille park maps are by Guest Relations and near the Tip Board at the entrance to Discovery Island. Guest Relations is also where you can borrow assisted-listening, handheld-captioning, and video-captioning devices with a refundable deposit. Service animals are allowed in most, but not all, areas of the park.

You can rent wheelchairs ($12 daily, $10 for multiple days) and ECVs ($50 per day plus a refundable $20 security deposit) at Garden Gate Gifts in the Oasis. You can't, however, reserve these items, so arrive early to get one—particularly if you want an ECV.

Stroller Rentals: Garden Gate Gifts in the Oasis rents strollers. Singles are $15 daily, $13 multiday; doubles run $31 daily, $27 multiday.

Park Tours

Caring for Giants
ECOTOURISM | FAMILY | During this 60-minute tour ($35), you'll learn about the African elephant herd that calls Animal Kingdom home. Animal specialists explain the daily care that the elephants receive, while an African cultural representative talks about conservation efforts Disney has started in Africa. For safety reasons, you view the elephants from 80 to 100 feet away and do not actually interact with them. Children must be 4 and over to participate; those under 18 must have adult supervision. Standard wheelchairs are allowed if Disney is notified in advance, but ECVs cannot be used on the tour. ✉ *Animal Kingdom* ☎ *407/939–8687* 🌐 *disneyworld.disney.go.com/events-tours/animal-kingdom/caring-for-giants.*

Up Close with Rhinos
ECOTOURISM | This 60-minute tour ($45) takes you behind the scenes to meet the white rhinoceroses that live at the Animal Kingdom. Disney's rhino handlers share their knowledge about rhinos and the extinction threat they face, while also demonstrating how the animals have been trained to cooperate with the handlers. If the rhinos are having a good day, you'll be allowed to pet them, but that's not guaranteed because these animals can be cantankerous. Children must be 4 and over to experience this tour, and it's only offered at certain times during the year. ✉ *Animal Kingdom* ☎ *407/939–8687* 🌐 *disneyworld.disney.go.com/events-tours/animal-kingdom/up-close-with-rhinos.*

★ Wild Africa Trek
ECOTOURISM | You will cover exciting ground on this three-hour, walking-riding adventure ($189 to $249 per person depending on season) into unexplored areas of the park. For a close-up view of the hippos, you'll wear a special vest with a harness that's tethered to a rail at

The Tree of Life is the iconic centerpiece of Disney's Animal Kingdom.

the edge of a bluff. The vest is also used to help you cross a rope bridge above a pool of Nile crocodiles. Your exclusive open-air safari vehicle makes multiple stops for leisurely viewing of giraffes, wildebeests, cheetahs, and other creatures of the savanna. Burning all those calories pays off when breakfast or lunch treats are served (think prosciutto, salmon, brie, and fresh fruit) at the open-air Boma Landing on the edge of the savanna. The tour is good for anyone age 8 and older who's fit. Included in the admission price is a CD-photo souvenir of your trek. A portion of the tour price is donated to the Disney Worldwide Conservation Fund. ✉ *Animal Kingdom* ☎ *407/939–8687* 🌐 *disneyworld.disney.go.com/en_CA/events-tours/animal-kingdom/wild-africa-trek.*

Visiting Tips

Try to visit during the week. Pedestrian areas are compact, and the park can feel uncomfortably packed on weekends.

Plan on a full day here. That way, while exploring Africa's Pangani Forest Exploration Trail, say, you can spend 10 minutes (rather than just two) watching vigilant meerkats stand sentry or tracking a mama gorilla as she cares for her youngster.

Arrive a half-hour before the park opens. This enables you to see the animals at their friskiest (first thing in the morning or at night are the best times for the safari ride) and get a jump on the crowds.

Eat here. Animal Kingdom has some of Disney World's best food, including Tiffins, which might be the best upscale restaurant anywhere in Walt Disney World.

Plan your meet-up. Good places to rendezvous include the outdoor Dawa Bar or Tamu Tamu Refreshments areas in Africa, in front of DinoLand U.S.A.'s Boneyard, or on one of the benches outside Expedition Everest in Asia.

The Oasis

This entrance makes you feel as if you've been plunked down in the middle of a rain forest. Cool mist, the aroma of flowers, playful animals, and colorful birds enliven a miniature landscape of streams and grottoes, waterfalls, and glades fringed with banana leaves and jacaranda. It's also where you can take care of essentials before entering. Here you'll find guide maps, stroller and wheelchair rentals, Guest Relations, and an ATM.

Discovery Island

The park's island hub, site of the Tree of Life, is encircled by Discovery River, which isn't an actual attraction but makes for attractive views: one from the bridge to Harambe and another between Asia and DinoLand U.S.A. The island's whimsical architecture, with wood carvings from Bali, lends charm and a touch of fantasy. The Discovery Island Trails that lead to the Tree of Life provide habitats for African crested porcupines, lemurs, Galápagos tortoises, and other creatures you won't want to miss.

You'll discover some great shops and good counter-service eateries here. Visitor services that aren't in the Oasis are here, on the border with Harambe, including the baby-care center and the first-aid center.

While walking through this area, watch for the awe-inspiring sight of a flock of multicolor macaws flying free over your head. Check with a cast member to see what time and where these majestic birds will be flying.

Sights

Tree of Life—It's Tough to be a Bug!
PERFORMANCE VENUE | **FAMILY** | A monument to all of Earth's creatures, the park's centerpiece is an imposing 14 stories high and 50 feet wide at its base. Its 100,000-plus leaves are several shades of green fabric, each carefully placed for a realistic effect. Carved into its thick trunk, gnarled roots, and soaring branches—some of which are supported by joints that allow them to sway in a strong wind—are nearly 350 intricate animal forms that include a baboon, a whale, a horse, the mighty lion, and even an ankylosaurus. At night, the tree is lit up by projections onto the vast trunk and leaves. Outside, paths tunnel underneath the roots as the fauna-encrusted trunk towers overhead.

The path leads you inside the tree trunk, where you get a bug's-eye view of life. The witty 3-D film adventure *It's Tough to Be a Bug!* is modeled on the animated film *A Bug's Life* from Disney-Pixar. Special effects spray you with "poison," zap you with a swatter, and even poke you with a stinger—all in good fun.

Although the show has something for all ages, it's very loud, and some effects frighten young children (during the hornet attack, have children lean forward to avoid a "sting"). **For people with disabilities:** Wheelchair accessible, but, to fully experience all the special effects, guests using wheelchairs should transfer to a seat. Equipped with reflective captioning and for audio-description and assisted-listening devices. If you have a service animal, check with a host before entering the theater. **TIP→ Short lines make this a good choice for the afternoon.** ✉ *Discovery Island, Animal Kingdom* ☞ *Duration: 20 mins. Crowds: Moderate to heavy. Audience: All but young kids.*

Restaurants

Flame Tree Barbecue
$ | **FAST FOOD** | **FAMILY** | This quick-service eatery is one of the park's relatively undiscovered gems; there's nothing fancy here, but you can dig into ribs, chicken, and pulled-pork sandwiches. Tables

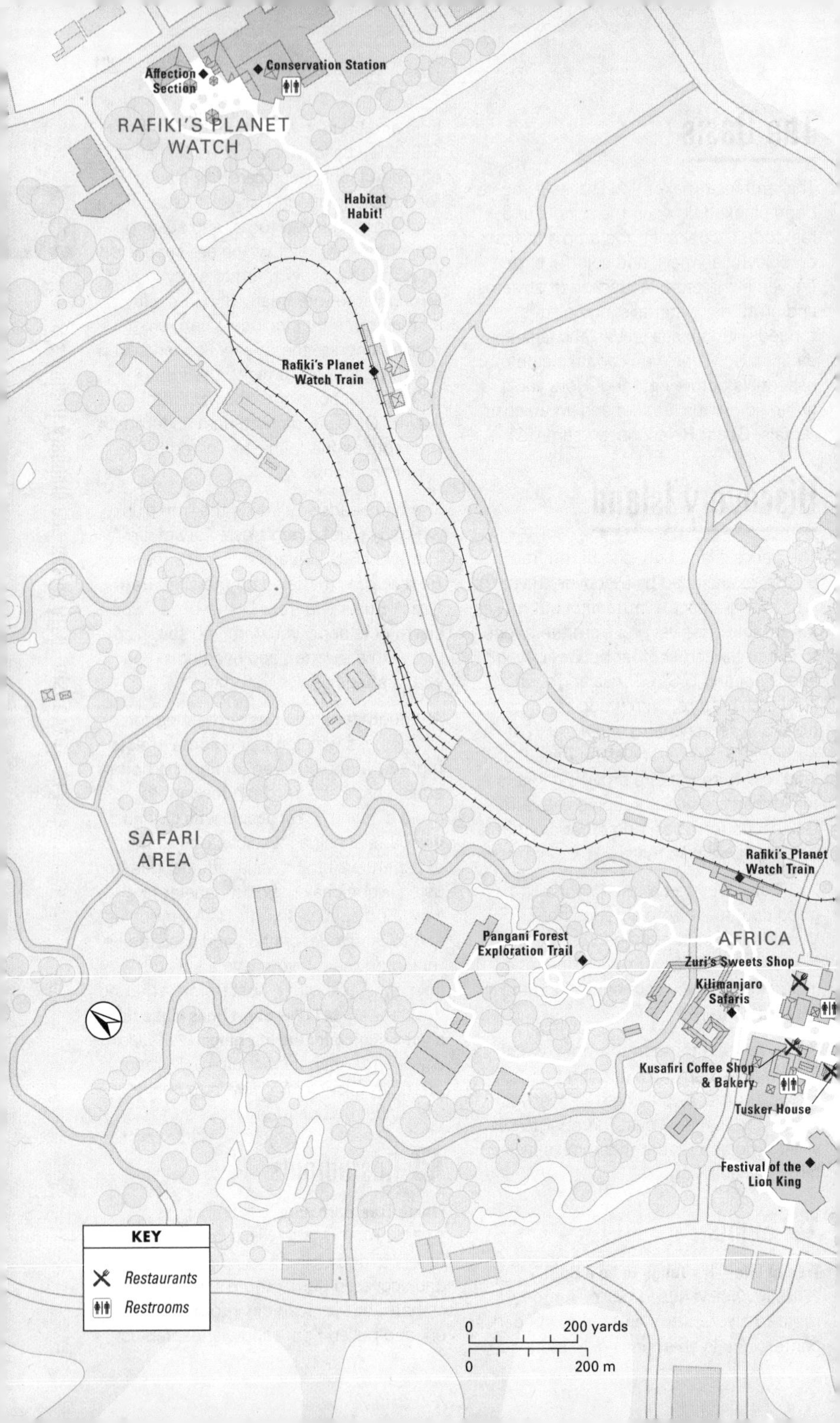
Affection Section
Conservation Station
RAFIKI'S PLANET WATCH
Habitat Habit!
Rafiki's Planet Watch Train
SAFARI AREA
Rafiki's Planet Watch Train
AFRICA
Pangani Forest Exploration Trail
Zuri's Sweets Shop
Kilimanjaro Safaris
Kusafiri Coffee Shop & Bakery
Tusker House
Festival of the Lion King
KEY
Restaurants
Restrooms
0
200 yards
0
200 m

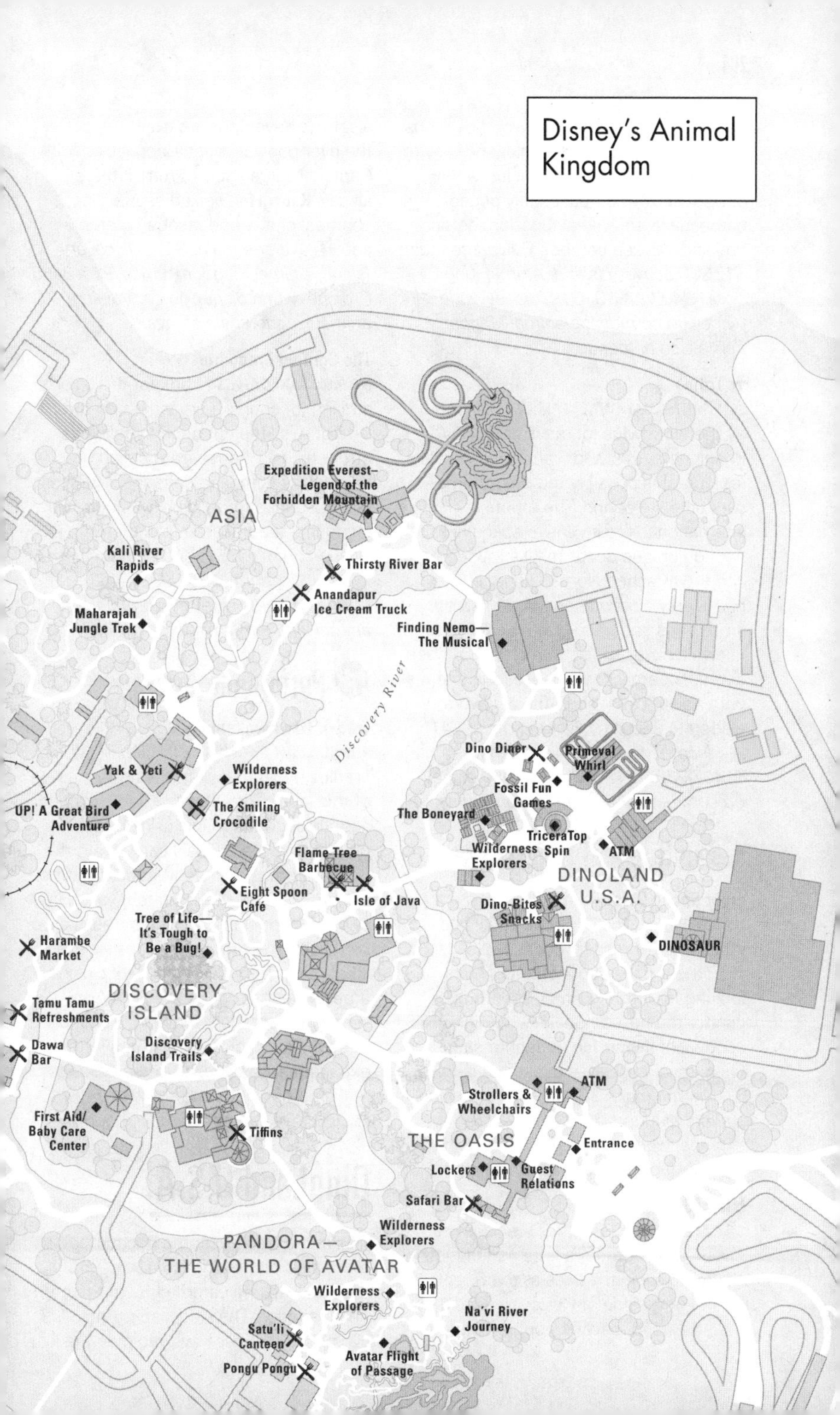

Disney's Animal Kingdom
Expedition Everest—Legend of the Forbidden Mountain
ASIA
Kali River Rapids
Thirsty River Bar
Anandapur Ice Cream Truck
Maharajah Jungle Trek
Finding Nemo—The Musical
Discovery River
Dino Diner
Primeval Whirl
Yak & Yeti
Wilderness Explorers
Fossil Fun Games
UP! A Great Bird Adventure
The Smiling Crocodile
The Boneyard
TriceraTop Spin
Flame Tree Barbecue
Wilderness Explorers
ATM
DINOLAND U.S.A.
Eight Spoon Café
Isle of Java
Dino-Bites Snacks
Tree of Life—It's Tough to Be a Bug!
Harambe Market
DINOSAUR
DISCOVERY ISLAND
Tamu Tamu Refreshments
Discovery Island Trails
Dawa Bar
ATM
Strollers & Wheelchairs
First Aid/Baby Care Center
Tiffins
THE OASIS
Entrance
Lockers
Guest Relations
Safari Bar
Wilderness Explorers
PANDORA—THE WORLD OF AVATAR
Wilderness Explorers
Na'vi River Journey
Satu'li Canteen
Avatar Flight of Passage
Pongu Pongu

beneath intricately carved wood pavilions make great spots for a picnic, and they're not usually crowded. **Known for:** variety of beer and wine; reasonably priced barbecue in an Animal Kingdom setting; ribs and chicken combo. *Average main: $12 Discovery Island, Animal Kingdom 407/939–3463 disneyworld.disney.go.com/dining/animal-kingdom/flame-tree-barbecue.*

★ Tiffins

$$$$ | INTERNATIONAL | FAMILY | Inspired by the worldwide journeys of Disney Imagineers, this wildly popular, upscale restaurant is possibly the best theme-park eatery—period. The menu is international, the inventive space has enough unique decor to fill a museum, and the attached Nomad Lounge (the park's only air-conditioned bar) serves small bites and hand-crafted cocktails. **Known for:** kids meals that aren't dumbed down; superbly cooked, seasonal menus with Asian, Latin, and African flavors; elaborate decor. *Average main: $41 Discovery Island, Animal Kingdom 407/939–1947 disneyworld.disney.go.com/dining/animal-kingdom/tiffins.*

Coffee and Quick Bites

Eight Spoon Café

$ | AMERICAN | FAMILY | Here you'll find small cups of mac 'n' cheese with or without pulled-pork on top. Those looking for a true culinary adventure can try the pulled-pork jelly doughnut sandwich. **Known for:** doughnut sandwich; mac 'n' cheese cups; fast service. *Average main: $7 Discovery Island, Animal Kingdom 407/939–3463 disneyworld.disney.go.com/dining/animal-kingdom/eight-spoon-cafe.*

Isle of Java

$ | CAFÉ | FAMILY | Be it for breakfast or a snack, stop here for a latte and blueberry muffin to avoid the lines at the Starbucks on the other side of Discovery Island. In the afternoon, several tropics-inspired alcoholic beverages are available, but the ever popular Island Cappuccino with Captain Morgan spiced rum is there all day. **Known for:** spiked cappuccino; pastries; cherry and raspberry lemonade. *Average main: $5 Discovery Island, Animal Kingdom 407/939–3463 disneyworld.disney.go.com/dining/animal-kingdom/isle-of-java.*

The Smiling Crocodile

$ | MEXICAN | FAMILY | Look for the colorful, smiling (of course!) crocodiles on the side of this little hut offering delicious street tacos. Choose from pulled pork, chicken, or corn, and combine it with an Island Sunrise for a quick snack. **Known for:** tacos; draft beer; mixed drinks. *Average main: $10 Discovery Island, Animal Kingdom 407/939–3463 disneyworld.disney.go.com/dining/animal-kingdom/smiling-crocodile.*

Performing Arts

Tree of Life Awakenings

SOUND/LIGHT SHOW | FAMILY | As night falls, fireflies begin to flicker among the leaves of this iconic tree. The tiny lights expand, and, through the magic of high-tech projections, the animals carved into the trunk—from dinosaurs to gorillas to tropical birds to a deer—begin to awaken in a swirl of color, until the whole tree is alive with light. The experience repeats every 10 minutes from dark until park closing time. Note that during the 50th Anniversary Celebration, the specialty show Beacons of Magic will alternate with this experience, so check a *Times Guide* to make sure you see the show you want. *Discovery Island, Animal Kingdom.*

DinoLand U.S.A.

This is the place to come encounter re-created prehistoric creatures—from the fear-inspiring carnotaurus to the gentle iguanodon. The landscaping includes live plants that have evolved over the last

65 million years. In collaboration with Chicago's Field Museum, Disney displays a complete, full-scale skeleton cast of Dino-Sue—also known as "Sue"—the 65-million-year-old *Tyrannosaurus rex* discovered near the Black Hills of South Dakota.

After admiring Sue, you can go on the thrilling DINOSAUR ride, play in the Boneyard, or take in the Finding Nemo: The Musical show at the Theater in the Wild. Kids will want to try the TriceraTop Spin and the Primeval Whirl family coaster, which has spinning "time machines." There's no need to dig for souvenirs at Chester and Hester's Dinosaur Treasures gift shop—all you need is your wallet.

Sights

★ The Boneyard

OTHER ATTRACTION | **FAMILY** | Youngsters can slide, dig, bounce, slither, and stomp around this archaeological dig site–playground, the finest play area in any of the four Disney parks. In addition to a huge sand pit where children can search for mammoth bones, there are twisting short and long slides, climbing nets, caves, a maze, and a jeep to climb on. Stomp on the dino footprints to make 'em roar. **For people with disabilities:** This fossil play maze is wheelchair accessible. **■ TIP→ Let the kids burn off energy here while older family members ride Expedition Everest or DINOSAUR. Also, this shaded play area is the perfect spot to let the kids run free late in the afternoon.** ✉ *DinoLand U.S.A., Animal Kingdom* ☞ *Duration: Up to you. Crowds: Moderate to heavy. Audience: Young kids.*

DINOSAUR

AMUSEMENT RIDE | **FAMILY** | This wild adventure through time puts you face-to-face with huge dinosaurs that move and breathe with uncanny realism. When a carload of guests rouses a cantankerous carnotaurus from his Cretaceous slumber, it's showtime. You travel back 65 million years on a fast-paced, twisting adventure and try to save the last living iguanodon as a massive asteroid hurtles toward Earth. Exciting Audio-Animatronics and special effects bring to life dinosaurs like the raptor, pterodactyl, styracosaurus, alioramus, and compsognather. Be prepared for a short but jolting drop toward the end of the ride.

Guests who are pregnant or have back, neck, or heart problems should avoid this very bumpy ride. The jostling and realistic carnivores might frighten young children. **For people with disabilities:** You must transfer from your wheelchair to board this ride. Equipped for video-captioning and assisted-listening devices. No service animals. **■ TIP→ This ride has been around since the park's opening day, so it's rarely as busy as Expedition Everest or Pandora. Come here in the afternoon, when the mostly indoor line will be appreciated.** ✉ *DinoLand U.S.A., Animal Kingdom* ☞ *Duration: Under 4 mins. Crowds: Heavy. Audience: All but young kids. Height requirement: 40 inches.*

★ Finding Nemo–The Musical

PERFORMANCE VENUE | **FAMILY** | Although favorite songs such as "Go With the Flow" and "Big Blue World" are guaranteed keepers, Disney has been busy "reimagining" this fan favorite, so check ahead on its status. Plans include modifying the story line, adding content, and developing the Theatre in the Wild where this show is held. **For people with disabilities:** Wheelchair accessible. Equipped with reflective captioning and for audio-description and assisted-listening devices. Check with Guest Relations for sign-language schedule. **■ TIP→ Arrive 30 to 40 minutes before showtime. Bring little kids here while older tweens and teens ride nearby Expedition Everest over in Asia.** ✉ *DinoLand U.S.A., Animal Kingdom* ☞ *Duration: 40 mins. Crowds: Heavy. Audience: All ages.*

On Asia's Expedition Everest, you'll chug, twist, turn, and plunge up, through, and down Mt. Everest on nearly a mile of track. Oh, yeah, and beware of the yeti!

Fossil Fun Games

AMUSEMENT PARK/CARNIVAL | FAMILY | A carnival-style midway in the center of DinoLand U.S.A. draws crowds with games like Whack a Packycephalosaur and the basketball-inspired Bronto-Score. The prehistoric fun comes at a price, however, and stone currency is not accepted. Prizes are mostly of the plush-character variety—you might win your sweetheart a stuffed Nala. **For people with disabilities:** Wheelchair accessible. **■ TIP→ It costs $5 a game. Buy vouchers at a stand amid the games or inside Chester and Hester's Dinosaur Treasures.** ✉ *DinoLand U.S.A., Animal Kingdom* ☞ *Duration: Up to you. Crowds: Light. Audience: All ages.*

Primeval Whirl

AMUSEMENT RIDE | FAMILY | In a free-spinning, four-passenger vehicle, you head on a brief journey back in time on this outdoor open-air coaster, twisting, turning, and even venturing into the jaws of a dinosaur "skeleton." Crazy cartoon dinosaurs in shades of turquoise, orange, yellow, and purple pop up along the track bearing signs that warn "The End Is Near." More signs alert you to incoming "Meteors!" and suggest that you "Head for the Hills!"—coaster hills, that is. Halfway through the ride, your car seems to spin out of control, and you take the next drop backward. The more weight in the vehicle, the more you spin.

Pregnant women or guests with back, neck, or heart problems should skip this one. **For people with disabilities:** Guests using wheelchairs must transfer to the ride vehicle. No service animals. **■ TIP→ This coaster is zippy. Kids might want to ride twice if the wait isn't long.** ✉ *DinoLand U.S.A., Animal Kingdom* ☞ *Duration: 2½ mins. Crowds: Heavy. Audience: All but young kids. Height requirement: 48 inches.*

TriceraTop Spin

AMUSEMENT RIDE | FAMILY | TriceraTop Spin is designed for playful little dinophiles who ought to get a kick out of whirling around this ride's giant spinning toy top and dodging incoming comets in their dino mobiles. "Pop!" goes the top, and out comes a grinning dinosaur as four passengers in each vehicle fly in a circle and maneuver up and down. **For people with disabilities:** Wheelchair accessible, but guests using ECVs must transfer to standard wheelchairs. **■ TIP→ Ride early, or take little ones while older kids are riding DINOSAUR or Primeval Whirl.** ✉ *DinoLand U.S.A., Animal Kingdom* ☞ *Duration: 2 mins. Crowds: Heavy. Audience: Young kids.*

Coffee and Quick Bites

Dino-Bite Snacks

$ | **ICE CREAM** | **FAMILY** | If things get too hot during your time in DinoLand U.S.A., stop by Dino-Bite Snacks for some ice cream or an old-fashioned ice cream sundae. **Known for:** old-fashioned ice cream; fresh-baked cookies; beer on draft. Ⓢ *Average main: $7* ✉ *DinoLand U.S.A., Animal Kingdom* ☎ *407/939–3463* 🌐 *disneyworld.disney.go.com/dining/animal-kingdom/dino-bite-snacks.*

Dino Diner

$ | **HOT DOG** | **FAMILY** | This adorable camper serves up old time favorites like hot dogs with chili, plus an unusual corn chip pie. **Known for:** cheese dogs; churros; snacks on the go. Ⓢ *Average main: $9* ✉ *DinoLand U.S.A., Animal Kingdom* ☎ *407/939–3463* 🌐 *disneyworld.disney.go.com/dining/animal-kingdom/dino-diner.*

Asia

Meant to resemble an Asian village, this land is full of remarkable rain-forest scenery and ruins. Groupings of trees grow from a crumbling shrine populated by roaming tigers, and massive towers—representing Thailand and Nepal—are the habitat for gibbons, whose hooting fills the air.

Sights

★ Expedition Everest—Legend of the Forbidden Mountain

AMUSEMENT RIDE | **FAMILY** | A fierce yeti guards the route to Mt. Everest. Of course, you're willing to risk running across the big guy in your roller-coaster quest to reach the summit. So, you board an "aging," seemingly innocuous, 34-passenger, steam-engine train into the mountains. You roll past bamboo forests, waterfalls, and glacier fields as you climb higher through snowcapped peaks. Suddenly, the train becomes a runaway, barreling forward then backward around icy ledges and through dark snowy caverns. Nearly a mile of twists and turns cut through the dark mountain, and, at one point, your train plunges a harrowing 80 feet. Will you find the yeti?

Buildings along the queue look like Himalayan mountain dwellings and teem with things like prayer flags, totems, and other artifacts from Tibet, Nepal, and the entire region. Because of the backwards portion of the ride, those wanting a wilder experience should ride up front.

Pregnant women or guests with back, neck, or heart problems shouldn't ride. **For people with disabilities:** You must transfer from your wheelchair to a ride vehicle; ask a cast member about the Transfer Practice Vehicle. No service animals. **■ TIP→ If you don't head straight to Pandora come here first. Individual Lightning Lane Pass is offered, but you only need it during the most crowded of days. Also, you can take little ones to nearby Finding Nemo—The Musical while older kids do this ride.** ✉ *Asia, Animal Kingdom* ☞ *Duration: 2½ mins. Crowds: Huge. Audience: All but young kids. Height requirement: 44 inches.*

Kali River Rapids

AMUSEMENT RIDE | **FAMILY** | Asia's thrilling water adventure ride mixes the fun of a rafting experience with a solemn message to save pristine lands and animal habitats that are threatened by development. Aboard a round raft that seats 12, you run the Chakranadi River. After passing through a huge bamboo tunnel filled with jasmine-scented mist, your raft climbs 40 feet upriver, lurches and spins through sharp twists and turns, and then approaches an immense waterfall, which curtains a giant carved tiger face. After traveling amid rain forests and temple ruins, you find yourself face-to-face with the denuded slope of a logged-out woodland burning out of control. There are many more thrills, but why spill the beans?

You will get wet—possibly even soaked. Unless you want to wring out your clothing in the nearest restroom afterward, bring a poncho. Better yet, bring a change of clothing in a plastic bag. Nearby lockers can keep bags dry while you ride. If you are pregnant or have heart, back, neck, or motion-sickness problems, sit this one out. **For people with disabilities:** Guests using wheelchairs must transfer to a ride raft. No service animals. ■ **TIP→ The line moves fast and is rarely one of the longest. Those who want to avoid soggy sneakers, bring a pair of flip-flops—you have to wear shoes while on board.** ✉ *Asia, Animal Kingdom* ☞ *Duration: 7 mins. Crowds: Heavy. Audience: All but young kids. Height requirement: 38 inches.*

Maharajah Jungle Trek

TRAIL | **FAMILY** | Along this trail, you get an up-close view of unusual animals, including giant fruit bats that hang to munch fruit from wires and fly very close to the open and glass-protected viewing areas and Bengal tigers in front of a maharajah's palace ruins. The tigers have their own view (with no accessibility, of course) of Asian deer and black buck, an antelope species. At the end of the trek, you walk through an aviary with a lotus pool. Disney animal experts are on hand to answer questions. **For people with disabilities:** Wheelchair accessible; equipped for audio-description devices. Guests with service animals should check with a host before entering the aviary. ■ **TIP→ Come anytime. Crowds stay fairly light, as people are constantly on the move.** ✉ *Asia, Animal Kingdom* ☞ *Duration: Up to you. Crowds: Light. Audience: All ages.*

UP! A Great Bird Adventure

PERFORMANCE VENUE | **FAMILY** | Check ahead on this presentation: it might be the more generic Feathered Friends in Flight!, which features birds but without characters from Disney's *Up*, or the version in which Russell and Doug from *Up* try to earn their Bird Badge from the wacky Wilderness Explorer troop leader. Fortunately, a bird expert is on hand to teach them about vultures, macaws, cranes, and even a singing parrot. Adults might groan at some of the corny jokes in the *Up* version, but everyone will be amazed as the birds soar right overhead. Those with questions, or who want a closer look at the birds, can walk down to the stage after the show. **For guests with disabilities:** Wheelchair- and ECV-accessible. ■ **TIP→ Guests who don't want birds directly overhead should sit in the elevated bleachers at the back.** ✉ *Asia, Animal Kingdom* ☞ *Duration: 25 mins. Crowds: Moderate. Audience: Kids.*

Restaurants

Yak & Yeti

$$$ | **ASIAN** | This two-story, 250-seat restaurant offers everything from noodles, curries, and wok dishes to Korean barbecue, with standout entrées that include seared miso salmon or roasted duck with plum barbecue sauce. The decor is pleasantly faux-Asian, with cracked plaster walls, wood carvings, and tile mosaic tabletops, and the adjacent bar is a great place to grab a drink while the kids are getting wet at Kali River Rapids. **Known for:** shareable appetizers; large menu with Indian, Japanese, Chinese, and Korean influences; welcoming lounge for escaping the weather. $ *Average main: $22* ✉ *Asia, Animal Kingdom* ☎ *407/939–3463* 🌐 *disneyworld.disney.go.com/dining/animal-kingdom/yak-and-yeti-restaurant.*

Coffee and Quick Bites

Anandapur Ice Cream Truck

$ | **ICE CREAM** | **FAMILY** | It's hard to miss this funky truck serving strawberry, lemon, vanilla, and chocolate ice cream in different twists. **Known for:** ice cream floats; fruit flavored sundae; easy access. $ *Average main: $5* ✉ *Asia, Animal Kingdom* ☎ *407/939–3463* 🌐 *disneyworld.disney.go.com/dining/animal-kingdom/anandapur-ice-cream-truck.*

Thirsty River Bar

$ | **AMERICAN** | If Expedition Everest isn't for you—or if you need something to help you relax before boarding or calm down after riding—head here for specialty margaritas and unusual beers such as the Funky Buddha Floridian Hefeweizen or Tiger Pale Lager. If you can get a seat at the bar, this is a great place to people watch for a bit. **Known for:** laid-back atmosphere; large beer selection; specialty cocktails. $ *Average main: $13* ✉ *Asia, Animal Kingdom* ☎ *407/939–3463* 🌐 *disneyworld.disney.go.com/dining/animal-kingdom/thirsty-river-bar.*

Pandora–The World of Avatar

As you cross the bridge from the hub into Pandora, you sense an immediate change: in landscape, in lighting fixtures, in tone. The details are important, and they leave no doubt you are entering another world. Disney Imagineers—along with *Avatar* film creator James Cameron and his Lightstorm Entertainment—worked for years to create the inventive, sometimes surreal, landscape of Pandora.

The experience is set far in the future, far beyond the war between the Na'vi and humans depicted in the film. Instead, Alpha Centauri Expeditions (ACE) are bringing humans back to the planet. The emphasis now is on cooperation between human and Na'vi to ensure the environment is protected. In the daytime, you'll be awe-struck by the gravity defying floating islands and the lush plants, both earthlike and unearthly, that envelop the land. At night, when the bioluminescence cranks up, you feel slightly off balance, as if you were truly on an alien world, seeing alien things for the first time. That feeling only grows with a trip along the Na'vi River or deeper into the jungle, where Avatar Flight of Passage puts you atop a banshee for a stomach-lurching journey.

But don't make the mistake of rushing to the thrill ride and missing all the beauty along the way. Be sure to stop by Satu'li Canteen, where you can refuel with a delicious and healthful bowl of grains or noodles topped with grilled meats and vegetables, or Pongu Pongu, where drinks have been known to glow in the dark.

Sights

★ **Avatar Flight of Passage**

AMUSEMENT RIDE | **FAMILY** | This stunning thrill ride puts you atop a dragonlike mountain banshee for the ride of your life. After a trek deep into the jungles of Pandora, you enter a room where scientists pair banshees with visitors. On instruction, you board a vehicle resembling a motorcycle that faces a blank wall. After hopping on, you don special 3-D goggles, the action begins, and you are one with your banshee. You feel it come to life beneath you, as Pandora comes to life before your eyes. The banshee's wing muscles pump as you hurtle down cliff faces and soar above the floating islands familiar from the film. The visuals are breathtaking, with dense

Pandora–The World of Avatar is the newest addition to Animal Kingdom.

jungles, seascapes, vast waterfalls, and alien plant life passing rapidly before your eyes. Even more astonishing, however, are the subtle smells and temperature changes that accompany different landscapes, immersing you totally in the experience. **For guests with disabilities:** Guests must transfer to a standard wheelchair and then on to ride vehicle. ■ **TIP→ Individual Lightning Lane Pass is best used here, especially during summer and holiday times.** ✉ *Pandora–The World of Avatar, Animal Kingdom* ☞ *Duration: 4½ mins. Crowds: Heavy. Audience: All but young kids. Height Requirement: 44 inches.*

★ Na'vi River Journey

AMUSEMENT RIDE | **FAMILY** | To enter this gentle river ride, you must first wander through the inventive landscape of Pandora, designed by Disney Imagineers to include many tropical and subtropical plants found in Florida, as well as creatively imagined alien plants, many of which light up at night. After entering the cavern and boarding a reed raft, you drift slowly past a bioluminescent rain forest with an even more diverse range of flora and fauna. The object of your quest is to find the Na'vi Shaman of Songs, the life force of Pandora, but you'll be so caught up in the stunning details of the landscape that you'll be surprised when the Audio-Animatronic Shaman shows up. **For guests with disabilities:** Guests must transfer from a wheelchair or ECV. ✉ *Pandora–The World of Avatar, Animal Kingdom* ☞ *Duration: 4½ mins. Crowds: Heavy. Audience: Young kids, adults, fans of Avatar.*

Restaurants

★ Satu'li Canteen

$ | **INTERNATIONAL** | **FAMILY** | Situated in the heart of Pandora, Satu'li walks a line between fast-casual and fine dining with counter service and surprisingly sophisticated, internationally inspired dishes. The menu features grain bowls with fresh-cooked ingredients and kids meals that are actually nutritious. **Known for:** phone-app ordering eliminates waiting;

grain bowls; fresh cooked, high-quality chicken, beef, and tofu. $ *Average main: $14* ✉ *Pandora–The World of Avatar, Animal Kingdom* ☎ *407/939–1947* 🌐 *disneyworld.disney.go.com/dining/animal-kingdom/satuli-canteen.*

Coffee and Quick Bites

Pongu Pongu

$ | AMERICAN | FAMILY | Na'vi-inspired treats, such as pineapple cream cheese spring rolls and giant pretzels, can be found here. But what kids will love is the Night Blossom, a limeade topped with passionfruit boba. **Known for:** breakfast; specialty mocktail; draft beers. $ *Average main: $4* ✉ *Pandora–The World of Avatar, Animal Kingdom* ☎ *407/939–3463* 🌐 *disneyworld.disney.go.com/dining/animal-kingdom/pongu-pongu.*

Africa

The largest of the lands is an area of forests and grasslands, predominantly an enclave for wildlife from the continent. Harambe, on the northern bank of Discovery River, is Africa's starting point. Inspired by several East African villages, this Disney town has so much detail that it's mind-boggling to try to soak it all up. Signs on the apparently peeling stucco walls are faded, as if bleached by the sun, and everything has a hot, dusty look. For souvenirs with Disney and African themes, browse through the Mombasa Marketplace and Ziwani Traders.

Sights

★ Festival of the Lion King

PERFORMANCE VENUE | FAMILY | If you think you've seen enough *Lion King* to last a lifetime, you're wrong—unless you've seen this show. Disney presents a delightful celebration of song, dance, and acrobatics that uses huge moving stages and floats. The show's singers are first-rate; lithe dancers wearing exotic animal-theme costumes portray creatures in the wild. Timon, Pumba, and other *Lion King* stars have key roles. The show is presented in the Harambe Theater in the park's Africa area. **For people with disabilities:** Wheelchair- and ECV-accessible; equipped for assisted-listening and handheld-captioning devices; sign-language interpretation is sometimes offered. **■ TIP→ If you aren't using Lightning Lane, arrive 30–40 minutes before showtime. If you have a child who might want to go on stage, try to sit up front to increase his or her chance of being chosen.** ✉ *Africa, Animal Kingdom* ☞ *Duration: 30 mins. Crowds: Moderate to heavy. Audience: All ages.*

★ Kilimanjaro Safaris

ZOO | FAMILY | A giant Imagineered baobab tree is the starting point for exploring this animal sanctuary. Although re-creating an African safari in the United States isn't a new idea, with this one, great pains were taken to create an authentic environment, allowing you to observe rhinos, hippos, antelopes, wildebeests, giraffes, zebras, cheetahs, elephants, lions, and the like as if you were seeing them in the wild. Illustrated game-spotting guides are available above the seats in the open-air safari vehicles that lurch and bump over some 110 acres of savanna, forest, rivers, and rocky hills. You'll see most of the Harambe Reserve's 34 species of animals—sometimes so close you feel that you could reach out and touch them. It's easy to suspend disbelief here because the landscape and habitats are so effectively modeled and replenished by Disney horticulturists.

Keep an eye out for animal babies here and on the post-safari Pangani Forest Exploration Trail; the park's breeding programs have been extremely successful, with new additions including elephants, rhinos, okapi, giraffes, and several gorillas. It's a completely different experience at night, and the animals are often much

Animal Kingdom Kids Tour

Animals fascinate young children, but when their attention wanes, you'll find plenty of other diversions: stage shows, fun-filled rides, and one very imaginative playground.

It's a Creatures Great and Small World

Upon entering, stop at the Wilderness Explorer kiosk to the right and sign kids up to earn their Wilderness Explorer badges. Badge stations around the park will help teach kids about wildlife, conservation, and culture. When you're traveling with young children, there's no better way to kick off a visit to this park than with a ride aboard **Kilimanjaro Safaris.** Your kids will enjoy seeing live hippos, rhinos, crocodiles, giraffes, gazelles, wildebeests, zebras, and elephants roaming their natural habitats. Hang on to toddlers, though—it's a bumpy ride!

When you disembark, go straight to **Pangani Forest Exploration Trail,** where kids can see gorillas and the real meerkats behind the animated character Timon from *The Lion King.* Children flock to the glass-walled habitat where tiny hairless mole rats scurry through tunnels.

Turn the kids loose on the **Maharajah Jungle Trek** in the park's Asia area to see giant fruit bats, Eld's deer, and Bengal tigers. Aviaries on both Pangani and Maharajah walks offer bird-spotting guides, so your family can find and compare different species.

Ride, Play, See a Show, Meet a Mouse

If the kids meet height requirements (38 inches) and are ready for some adventure, head for **Kali River Rapids**—an exciting family raft ride. Steer smaller children toward DinoLand U.S.A., where they'll be happy whirling around **TriceraTop Spin** and exploring the **Boneyard** play maze with its cool slides and its climbing and sandy fossil-dig areas.

Break for lunch at **Flame Tree Barbecue,** and then head around the corner to **Finding Nemo: The Musical,** where kids love the character puppets and lively, Broadway-style music. Toddlers may use this stop to nap in your arms.

Afterward, visit one of the park's character meet-and-greet areas, where you might find Mickey or Chip 'n' Dale. Back in Africa, you can take in **Festival of the Lion King,** where several children get to join "animal" dancers for one show number. Or take a break at **UP! A Great Bird Adventure** to marvel at the high-flying birds.

Board a Train, Save the Planet

Try to find time to board the Wildlife Express Train to **Rafiki's Planet Watch,** where the kids can see cotton-top tamarins and learn about taking care of the world's animals. You might be able to take part in a critter encounter with a Disney animal-care specialist at Conservation Station. The Affection Section petting yard is a comfortable place to meet domesticated animals from around the world.

Wrap up your day in **Pandora,** where the kids will marvel at the alien plant-life on the gentle Na'vi River Journey. Dinner at Satu'li Canteen offers a healthy but kid-pleasing bowl of roasted meats or grains, and a drink that might glow in the dark.

Animal Kingdom Grown-Ups Tour

Thrill rides, a hilarious 3-D film, and two Broadway-style shows can fill a memorable day.

Adventure Seekers Wanted

The park's most popular thrill ride is **Avatar Flight of Passage** in Pandora, which puts you aboard a mountain banshee for a heart-stopping 3-D experience that takes you soaring above floating islands and plummeting down cliffs.

Next, make a beeline for Asia and **Expedition Everest.** If there's a wait for the attraction's high-speed train ride, the queue snakes through authentic rammed-earth and stacked-stone buildings of a Himalayan village. While in Asia, pile into a **Kali River Rapids** raft for a whitewater ride on the park's Chakranadi River (bring a poncho or flip-flops to try to keep your shoes dry).

Time-travel back to DinoLand U.S.A. for a **DINOSAUR** journey through a primeval forest and white-knuckle encounters with carnivorous creatures like the razor-toothed carnotaurus and other menacing creatures of prehistoric doom.

If it's a cool day, the park's animals should be active, so head to Africa. Your **Kilimanjaro Safaris** open-air journey is a bumpy 20-minute quest to sight exotic animals, and you won't be disappointed. Adventurous guests with dollars to spare should sign up for the park's **Wild Africa Trek**, one of Disney's most thrilling guided tours.

Eat, Shop, Laugh

Animal Kingdom has some of the best food at Walt Disney World. **Tusker House Restaurant**, in Africa, offers a colorful buffet of vegetables and carved meats enhanced with African-inspired chutneys, hummus, spiced tandoori tofu, and couscous salad.

At **Tiffins**, on Discovery Island at the bridge to Pandora, the cuisine (it deserves the term) is inspired by adventure travel, and the globetrotting menu is served with style. It might very well be the best restaurant in all of Walt Disney World.

Burn the calories during a shopping excursion in **Mombasa Marketplace**, where you can buy a bottle of South African wine or pick up hand-painted dishes from Zimbabwe. Onward to Discovery Island for a stroll along Discovery Island Trails into the **Tree of Life show It's Tough to Be a Bug!** Expect to laugh a lot.

Discover Animal Attraction

Along the **Pangani Forest Exploration Trail**, you can view families of mountain gorillas through a glassed-in area or from a bridge. It's inspiring to see these magnificent primates move among the rocks and lush greenery.

Although you feel safe from Bengal tigers on the **Maharajah Jungle Trek**, several raised viewing spots offer clear views with no glass or fence to mar your photos. Backdrops like the Maharajah palace ruins create scenic props.

If you can squeeze in only one live show, make it **Festival of the Lion King.**

A silverback gorilla at Gorilla Falls Exploration Trail

more lively and interesting, so this experience definitely deserves a revisit. If you have to choose, the nighttime experience is probably superior.

Parents should hang on tightly to their small tykes. The ride is very bumpy and should be avoided by expectant guests or those with heart, back, or neck problems. **For people with disabilities:** Wheelchair accessible, but ECV users must transfer to standard wheelchairs. Equipped for assisted-listening and video-captioning devices. Guests with service animals should check with a host for boarding information.

■ TIP→ During the hottest months, come first thing in the morning when animals are most active. Otherwise come at day's end when it cools down a bit or at night. For the best photo ops, ask to be seated in the very last row of seats (you might have to wait for the next vehicle) where you can pivot for an unobstructed view of the animals you just passed. ✉ *Africa, Animal Kingdom* ☞ *Duration: 18 mins. Crowds: Moderate to heavy. Audience: All ages.*

Pangani Forest Exploration Trail

TRAIL | **FAMILY** | Calling this a nature walk doesn't really do it justice. A path winds through dense foliage, alongside streams, and past waterfalls. En route there are viewing points where you can watch a beautiful rare okapi (a member of the giraffe family) munching the vegetation, a family and a separate bachelor group of lowland gorillas, hippos (which you usually can see underwater), comical meerkats (a kind of mongoose), exotic birds, and a bizarre colony of hairless mole rats. Disney animal experts are at many viewing points to answer questions. **For people with disabilities:** Wheelchair accessible and equipped for audio-description devices. Guests with service animals should check with a host before entering. **■ TIP→ Come just after you exit your safari vehicle on Kilimanjaro Safaris; avoid coming at the hottest time of day, when the gorillas like to nap.** ✉ *Africa, Animal Kingdom* ☞ *Duration: Up to You. Crowds: Moderate to heavy. Audience: All ages.*

Restaurants

★ Harambe Market
$ | **AFRICAN** | **FAMILY** | Carved into the walkway leading to the Wildlife Express train, this four-station food mart offers a selection of ribs or chicken bowls and salads. Everyone will want their own watermelon lemonade. **Known for:** short lines; shaded, family-size, outdoor-market seating; African-inspired chicken and ribs. *Average main: $12* *Africa, Animal Kingdom* *407/939–5277* *disneyworld.disney.go.com/dining/animal-kingdom/harambe-market.*

★ Tusker House
$$$$ | **AFRICAN** | **FAMILY** | This good-value restaurant offers all-buffet dining three meals a day, and a Donald's safari-theme character crew complements the African-esque decor and menu. In addition to standard kids fare, the menu has healthful dishes like curry chicken, *peri-peri* (African hot pepper) marinated salmon, strip loin rubbed with *berbere* (an African spice mix), and saffron-infused root vegetables. **Known for:** wide-ranging buffet choices; great food with reasonable prices; character appearances. *Average main: $54* *Reservations Essential* *Africa, Animal Kingdom* *407/939–3463* *disneyworld.disney.go.com/dining/animal-kingdom/tusker-house-restaurant.*

Coffee and Quick Bites

Kusafiri Coffee Shop & Bakery
$ | **AFRICAN** | **FAMILY** | On your way to Kilimanjaro Safaris in the morning, stop by this coffee shop to grab a colossal cinnamon roll or pistachio honey croissant to split while waiting in line. In the afternoon, the spiced potato hand pies are an unusual choice, and everyone will enjoy the marinated chicken flatbread. **Known for:** selection of pastries; African coffee; African-inspired snacks. *Average main: $7* *Africa, Animal Kingdom* *407/939–3463* *disneyworld.disney.go.com/dining/animal-kingdom/kusafiri-coffee-shop-and-bakery.*

Tamu Tamu Refreshments
$ | **ICE CREAM** | **FAMILY** | If you liked the Dole Whip pineapple float in the Magic Kingdom, stop here for a twist. Try either the Scar's Lair, which uses sour apple syrup, or the Simba Sunset, which mixes in watermelon, strawberry, and coconut flavoring. **Known for:** Dole Whip pineapple ice cream; breakfast sandwiches and pastries; brownie sundae. *Average main: $5* *Africa, Animal Kingdom* *407/939–3463* *disneyworld.disney.go.com/dining/animal-kingdom/tamu-tamu-refreshments.*

Zuri's Sweets Shop
$ | **DESSERTS** | **FAMILY** | Within this shop, hidden in the back of the Africa section, you'll find enough to satisfy any sweet tooth. A constantly changing selection of candied apples, Mickey-theme cookies, and cupcakes can be found in abundance. **Known for:** candied apples; marshmallow treats; fudge. *Average main: $6* *Africa, Animal Kingdom* *407/939–3463* *disneyworld.disney.go.com/shops/animal-kingdom/zuris-sweet-shop.*

Rafiki's Planet Watch

While in Africa's Harambe section, board the 250-passenger rustic Wildlife Express steam train for a ride to a unique center of eco-awareness named for the wise baboon from *The Lion King*. Young children especially enjoy the chance to explore these three animal-friendly areas.

Sights

Affection Section
ZOO | **FAMILY** | In this petting zoo, children and adults can stroke and even borrow brushes to groom goats, sheep, donkeys, and other domesticated creatures.
For people with disabilities: Guests must transfer from ECVs to standard

Disney's Animal Kingdom Lodge

wheelchairs. No service animals are allowed in this area. ■ **TIP→ If you visit at the right time, you can see pigs demonstrate how they've learned to paint with their snouts.** ✉ *Rafiki's Planet Watch, Animal Kingdom* ☞ *Duration: Up to you. Crowds: Light to moderate. Audience: All ages, mostly children.*

Conservation Station

COLLEGE | **FAMILY** | This is a great place to meet some of the park's animal handlers and to gather round for a critter encounter. You'll learn about the park's veterinary care, ongoing research, and food preparation for hundreds of animal inhabitants. Interactive exhibits are simple fun for younger children and have messages about worldwide efforts to protect endangered species and their habitats. Here, you also can find out how to connect with conservation efforts in your own community. At The Animation Experience at Conservation Station, a Disney artist leads a class in drawing a famous (animal) Disney character. **For people with disabilities:** Guest may remain in wheelchairs or ECVs. ■ **TIP→ Begin a family conservation project here.** ✉ *Rafiki's Planet Watch, Animal Kingdom* ☞ *Duration: Up to you. Crowds: Light to moderate. Audience: All ages.*

Habitat Habit!

TRAIL | **FAMILY** | On this educational wildlife trail that focuses heavily on animal conservation efforts, you get a close-up look at the entertaining antics of cotton-top tamarins—small South American primates named for their flowing white manes—while you learn how to live with all of the Earth's animals. **For people with disabilities:** Wheelchair accessible. ■ **TIP→ Ask questions; the animal-care cast members enjoy telling you about these cute critters.** ✉ *Rafiki's Planet Watch, Animal Kingdom* ☞ *Duration: Up to you. Crowds: Light to moderate. Audience: All ages.*

Animal Kingdom Resort Area

The Animal Kingdom Resort Area has a good mix of hotels. Nearest to the park, the Animal Kingdom Lodge is an experience in and of itself, with some of the best restaurants on Disney property, great informational programs, and proximity to the savanna, where live animals roam in their own enclosure, so it's easy to hop from the pool to a viewing platform. Animal experts are on hand by day, and night-vision goggles are available in the evening. Coronado Springs offers beautiful rooms for an excellent price in a lively Mexican setting, complete with a Maya-themed waterslide.

On the other end of the spectrum are the three, no-frills, best-value-for-your-dollar All-Star Resorts. Here you'll find few amenities beyond a pool and a food court, but you can still take advantage of the Extra Magic Hours and free Disney bus service.

Restaurants

★ Boma–Flavors of Africa

$$$$ | AFRICAN | FAMILY | Boma takes Western-style ingredients and prepares them with an African twist. You walk through an African marketplace–style dining room to help yourself at counters piled high with flavor from an upscale buffet like no other. **Known for:** endless buffet with wonderful service that appeals to kids; superb food for both the timid and the adventurous; African flavors and dishes. *Average main: $49 Reservations Essential Animal Kingdom Lodge, 2901 Osceola Pkwy., Animal Kingdom Resort Area 407/939–3463 disneyworld.disney.go.com/dining/animal-kingdom-lodge/boma-flavors-of-africa No lunch.*

★ Jiko–The Cooking Place

$$$$ | AFRICAN | "Jiko" means "the cooking place" in Swahili, and this restaurant is certainly that, offering a menu that is more African-inspired than purely African, as well as a the largest selection of African wines in the country. The dining area surrounds two big, wood-burning ovens and a grill area where you can watch cooks in North African–style caps prepare your meal. **Known for:** Moroccan lamb; African cuisine with an American flair and Indonesian accents; sophisticated surroundings and decor. *Average main: $45 Reservations Essential Animal Kingdom Lodge, 2901 Osceola Pkwy., Animal Kingdom Resort Area 407/939–3463 disneyworld.disney.go.com/dining/animal-kingdom-lodge/jiko-the-cooking-place No lunch.*

★ Sanaa

$$$ | AFRICAN | FAMILY | Most of the flavors are from India, yet Sanaa is really a celebration of the Spice Islands—locales off the coast of Africa that, for centuries, enticed traders from the world's corners. Exotic yet approachable lunches and dinners make it a true find on the outer edges of the Disney empire; views of zebras and giraffes on the savanna right out the picture windows are another draw. **Known for:** African-inspired breakfast; surprising combinations of African and Indian flavors; Indian-style bread service. *Average main: $26 Animal Kingdom Villas–Kidani Village, 3701 W. Osceola Pkwy., Animal Kingdom Resort Area 407/989–3463 disneyworld.disney.go.com/dining/animal-kingdom-villas-kidani/sanaa.*

Hotels

Disney's All-Star Movies Resort

$ | RESORT | FAMILY | Scenes and characters from favorite Disney movies dot the grounds of this large, value-priced, family resort: *101 Dalmatians* of all sizes scamper along railings; Mickey, in his *Sorcerer's Apprentice* robes commands the waters at the *Fantasia* pool, and a larger-than-life Woody cavorts with his *Toy Story* pals. **Pros:** easy access to Animal Kingdom; lots to amuse the kids; room rates

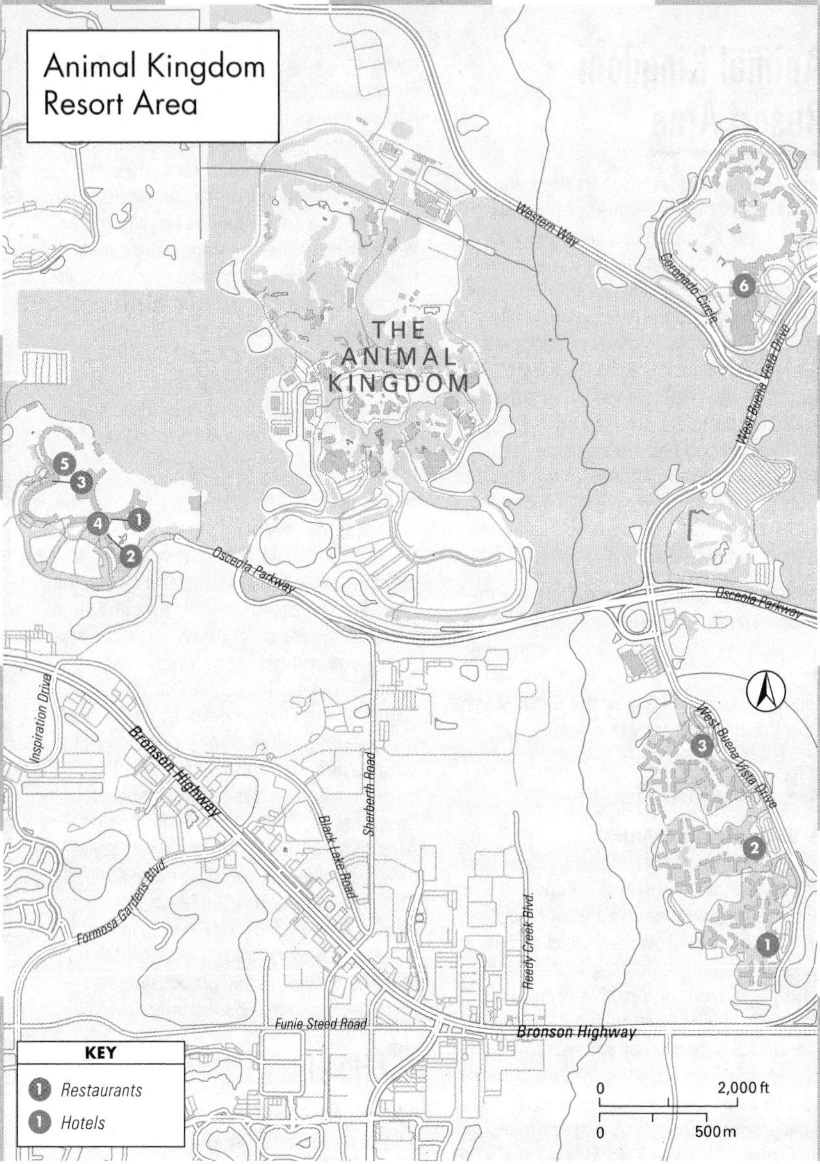

Restaurants

1 Boma—Flavors of Africa **A4**
2 Jiko—The Cooking Place...... **A4**
3 Sanaa **A3**

Hotels

1 Disney's All-Star Movies Resort............ **E6**
2 Disney's All-Star Music Resort............ **E6**
3 Disney's All-Star Sports Resort............ **E5**
4 Disney's Animal Kingdom Lodge **A4**
5 Disney's Animal Kingdom Villas–Kidani Village.... **A3**
6 Disney's Coronado Springs Resort **E2**

Did You Know?

The All-Star Sports, Music, and Movies Resorts are all thematically designed. Goofy is the pitcher in the baseball diamond–shaped pool at the Sports resort, a piano-shaped pool can be found at the Music resort, a huge Buzz Lightyear figure stands tall at the Movies resort.

among the lowest at Disney. **Cons:** dearth of device-charging outlets; rooms need refreshing; far from Magic Kingdom. *Rooms from: $138 ✉ 1901 W. Buena Vista Dr., Animal Kingdom Resort Area ☎ 407/939–7000 ⊕ disneyworld.disney.go.com/resorts/all-star-movies-resort 1920 rooms No Meals.*

Disney's All-Star Music Resort

$ | RESORT | FAMILY | Music rules in this colorful, value-priced, family-centric resort that resembles a Florida beach hotel of the 1950s. **Pros:** two heated pools; good value for family vacations; music theme is carried throughout. **Cons:** rooms and bathrooms are basic and small; long way to Magic Kingdom; suites have sleeper chair and sleeper ottoman. *Rooms from: $139 ✉ 1801 W. Buena Vista Dr., Animal Kingdom Resort Area ☎ 407/939–6000 ⊕ disneyworld.disney.go.com/resorts/all-star-music-resort 1704 rooms No Meals.*

Disney's All-Star Sports Resort

$ | RESORT | FAMILY | Stay here if you want the All-American, sports-mad, Disney-with-your-kids experience, or if you're a couple to whom all that pitter-pattering of little feet is a reasonable trade-off for a good deal on a room, albeit a small one. **Pros:** close to Disney's ESPN Wide World of Sports Complex; unbeatable price for a Disney property; kids love sports themes. **Cons:** farthest resort from Magic Kingdom means you'll spend time on the bus; vast distances between rooms and on-site amenities; no kids clubs or programs. *Rooms from: $139 ✉ 1701 W. Buena Vista Dr., Animal Kingdom Resort Area ☎ 407/939–5000 ⊕ disneyworld.disney.go.com/resorts/all-star-sports-resort 1704 rooms No Meals.*

★ Disney's Animal Kingdom Lodge

$$$$ | RESORT | FAMILY | Entering the vast atrium lobby of this African-inspired lodge is like entering a cathedral with a roof formed of thatch instead of stone; giraffes, zebras, and other wildlife roam just outside the windows of the resort, designed to resemble an African *kraal* (animal enclosure). **Pros:** breakfast buffet in Boma is a bargain; extraordinary on-site wildlife and cultural experiences; excellent restaurants. **Cons:** long corridors; concierge-level rooms have $100-plus surcharge; shuttle to parks other than Animal Kingdom can take more than an hour. *Rooms from: $436 ✉ 2901 Osceola Pkwy., Animal Kingdom Resort Area ☎ 407/938–3000 ⊕ disneyworld.disney.go.com/resorts/animal-kingdom-lodge 972 rooms No Meals.*

Disney's Animal Kingdom Villas–Kidani Village

$$$$ | RESORT | FAMILY | Most of the suites here accommodate five people, though there are smaller options, too. **Pros:** animal views from most rooms; biggest suites on Disney property; quieter hotel. **Cons:** lots of large families; no spa; farthest away of any luxury hotel. *Rooms from: $537 ✉ 3701 Osceola Pkwy., Animal Kingdom Resort Area ☎ 407/938–7400 ⊕ disneyworld.disney.go.com/resorts/animal-kingdom-villas-kidani 324 suites No Meals.*

Disney's Coronado Springs Resort

$$$ | RESORT | FAMILY | Popular with convention-goers and families, this colorful, Southwestern-style property has a lively food court, an elaborate swimming pool, and a moderate price for a Disney resort. **Pros:** wide range of dining choices; great pool with a play-area arcade for kids and a bar for adults; lots of outdoor activities. **Cons:** the lake is not for swimming; standard rooms are on the small side; some accommodations are a long trek from the restaurants. *Rooms from: $289 ✉ 1000 W. Buena Vista Dr., Animal Kingdom Resort Area ☎ 407/939–1000 ⊕ disneyworld.disney.go.com/resorts/coronado-springs-resort 2384 rooms No Meals.*

Chapter 7

DISNEY SPRINGS AND RESORT AREA

WITH TYPHOON LAGOON

Updated by
Gary McKechnie

Sights ★★☆☆☆ | Restaurants ★★★★★ | Hotels ★★★★★ | Shopping ★★★★★ | Nightlife ★★★★☆

NEIGHBORHOOD SNAPSHOT

TOP EXPERIENCES

■ **Being There:** Perhaps the most enjoyable aspect of Disney Springs is not a single store, club, or restaurant. It's soaking in the Springs' overall vibe (especially in the evening).

■ **Cirque du Soleil:** After an understandable delay, the newest Cirque show, Drawn to Life, premiered in late 2021. Created in partnership with Disney, the storyline follows a young girl whose animation comes alive, and it promises to draw guests to its surreal elegance for years to come.

■ **Dinner, then Launch:** Take a 25-minute waterfront tour in an Amphicar, a vehicle that drives on land and floats on water, which launches from beside the BOATHOUSE restaurant.

■ **Splitsville:** This retro bowling alley puts a new spin on knocking down pins. It's cool, hip, and hours of fun.

■ **Treat Yourself:** Disney Springs presents the resort's greatest concentration of upscale dining experiences. So set aside the fast food and quick-grab kiosks, and treat yourself to a memorable evening meal.

■ **World of Disney:** There will never be a shortage of Disney souvenirs, and this sprawling store (the world's largest purveyor of all things Disney) proves how many ways they can market their magic.

PLANNING YOUR TIME

Disney Springs offers two distinct experiences. By day, you can breeze through its four districts in about three hours, allowing roughly an hour for dining and two for shopping. At night, things really light up, so allow more time to navigate the throngs of other guests, watch street performers, and wait for an available table at a restaurant.

Head to Typhoon Lagoon early in the day to beat the crowds and stake your claim on the beach or beneath a palm tree.

GETTING HERE

■ You'll see Disney Springs from I-4. There are three big garages, as well as surface lots. Self-parking is free; valet parking costs $20. Disney resort guests can take a free shuttle from their hotel. Seasonal shuttles also run to Typhoon Lagoon, which is less than ½ mile from Disney Springs along Buena Vista Drive.

VIEWFINDER

■ Disney Springs is full of eye candy. Popular backdrops for selfies include the LEGO dragon, the Disney Springs water tower, the Aerophile hot air balloon, and the House of Blues water tower. A self-portrait taken while scooting through the water in an amphibious car will make for an interesting keepsake, too.

PAUSE HERE

■ Although the buzz and activity of Disney Springs are exciting, you might find that you need a break. On the West Side, step behind the House of Blues, and you'll find a pleasant promenade along the waterfront. In Town Center, a quiet dock juts out into the water just behind the welcome center. In the Marketplace, the performance-stage area offers plenty of seats and a bit of peace between shows.

East of EPCOT and close to I–4 along a large lake is a vast shopping, dining, and entertainment complex built to serve both locals and Disney guests.

The main draw of Disney Springs is its vast array of shops, restaurants, and entertainment options. In late 2021, Cirque du Soleil premiered Drawn to Life, which replaced its long-running show, La Nouba. There's also a multiplex cinema, a retro-hip bowling alley, live concerts, virtual-reality activities, and a level of evening energy unlike anywhere else at Disney.

Just a couple minutes west of Disney Springs is the Typhoon Lagoon water park. With waterslides, pools, and lazy rivers, it can be a refreshing place to spend a day before an evening of shopping, dining, and clubbing.

Disney Springs

Disney Springs has four areas: the Marketplace, West Side, The Landing, and Town Center. To anchor the development, Disney Imagineers created a beautiful network of clear, turquoise waterways that replicate the look of Florida's natural springs. Thousands gather here each evening for people-watching, leisurely strolls, shopping, dining, or simply to be part of the action. Several multistory garages offer free parking, which makes it easy to access, and conveniences include locker, stroller, and wheelchair rentals, as well as two Guest Relations (aka Guest Services) centers.

Marketplace

In the Marketplace, the easternmost Disney Springs area, you can meander along winding sidewalks and explore hidden alcoves. Children love to splash in fountains that spring from the pavement and ride the miniature train and old-time carousel. There are plenty of spots to grab a bite, sip a cappuccino, or enjoy an ice cream (at Ghirardelli's) along the lakefront.

Although the Marketplace offers little in the line of typical nightlife, there's hardly a better place for families to enjoy an evening stroll, indulge in a tasty treat at a courtyard café, and shop (or window-shop) for unique items. Toy stores entice with creation-stations and too many treasures to count. Here, you can also arrange for a princess-style makeover at the Bibbidi Bobbidi Boutique and peruse a dozen theme showrooms in the largest Disney store of all: The World of Disney.

Most Marketplace shops and eateries are open between 9:30 am and 11 pm or midnight. If you happen to run out of cash while you're shopping, you can apply for instant Disney credit at any register. How convenient.

Coffee and Quick Bites

The Marketplace has two table-service restaurants (**T-Rex Café** and the **Rainforest Café**), as well as several walk-up kiosks and counter-service options for casual, on-the-go sandwiches, snacks, and drinks. These include **AristoCrepes** (crepes with various fillings), **B.B. Wolf's Sausage Co.** (European-style sausages and sauces), **Dockside Margaritas** (plus brews), **Earl of Sandwich** (specialty sandwiches, soups, and salads), **Ghirardelli's Soda Fountain and Chocolate Shop** (sundaes, floats, malts, shakes, and … chocolate), **Joffrey's** (tropical smoothies), **Starbucks** (you know), and **Wetzel's Pretzels** (flavored pretzels, hot dogs).

Drumroll, please ...

Of more than 300 retail outlets at the Walt Disney World Resort, perhaps the best of all is the truly huge World of Disney store in the Marketplace section of Disney Springs. You could actually skip many of the stores in the theme parks, since you'll find just about everything you want right here. This store really *does* have something for everyone—from inexpensive princess pens to pricey Disney collectibles like an elegant Mickey timepiece or figurine.

Shopping

The Art of Disney

ART GALLERIES | **FAMILY** | For nearly a century, Disney has created distinct and iconic characters, theme parks, and films that have become fan favorites as well as the subjects of collectible works of art. In this intriguing gallery, a dazzling array of Disney images are captured in a variety of media, including sculptures, limited-edition Sericels, lithographs, framed prints, original paintings, and figurines. What's more, it doesn't necessarily cost a fortune to become a collector of Disneyana—just start with a collectible postcard. Check the calendar: Disney artists often come here to meet guests and sign their works. ✉ *The Marketplace, Disney Springs* 🌐 *www.disneysprings.com/shopping/the-art-of-disney.*

Disney's Pin Traders

SOUVENIRS | **FAMILY** | Many cast members and guests share (and wear) a common interest: pins that reflect favorite characters, special events, and all things Disney. Often affixed to lanyards, these pins are a curiously treasured part of Disney's subculture, with owners buying and swapping pins the way kids used to trade baseball cards. This Marketplace shop is one of the premier pin-trading destinations—and where you can also buy Mickey ears and MagicBands. ✉ *Marketplace, Disney Springs* 🌐 *www.disneysprings.com/shopping/disneys-pin-traders.*

The LEGO Store

TOYS | **FAMILY** | When you spy a LEGO sea serpent in the lagoon, you know you're in the right place for a LEGO shopping spree. Large, elaborate sculptures and piles of colorful bricks welcome children, who generally head straight to hands-on play tables and begin work on toy castles, cars, and pirate ships. At the Pick-A-Brick Wall, kids can create anything from a Star Wars spaceship to a miniature Sydney Opera House. Be sure to snap a photo with oversize character models like Woody and Buzz Lightyear. The discounted merchandise section is also worth a look. ✉ *Marketplace, Disney Springs* 🌐 *www.disneysprings.com/shopping/the-lego-store.*

Once Upon A Toy

TOYS | **FAMILY** | Classic board games and activity stations will keep you entertained in this well-stocked store. Theme toy rooms feature princess and fairy items or Star Wars stations, where you can create your own light saber. There are lots of games redesigned with Disney themes, like a Haunted Mansion version of the Game of Life. You can test-drive many of the toys, and at the Mr. Potato Head Creation Station, you can fill a box with assorted eyes, lips, noses—even Mickey ears—and make your own potato sculpture. ✉ *Marketplace, Disney Springs* 🌐 *www.disneysprings.com/shopping/once-upon-a-toy.*

Tren-D

MIXED CLOTHING | **FAMILY** | This Marketplace boutique has "hip" and "eclectic" written all over it (hence the name), with ever-changing merchandise that gives (primarily teenage) shoppers a chance to wear clothing imprinted with 1980s and '90s cartoon characters, fashions from the Disney Parks Forever Collection, and chic sundresses with subtle Mickey-ear designs that are perfect for an evening at the shops and clubs of Disney Springs. Designer items are from Billabong, Dooney & Bourke, Harveys (Original Seatbeltbags), and Roxy, with many featuring fairies and princesses. ✉ *Marketplace, Disney Springs* 🌐 *www.disneysprings.com/shopping/tren-d.*

★ World of Disney

TOYS | **FAMILY** | Beware of sensory overload at *the* world's largest Disney superstore—where approximately half a million items are featured in a dozen rooms that fill 50,000 square feet. Theme shopping areas like the princess room (hello, Cinderella dress or Ariel costume) help steer you to just the right toys, clothing, collectibles, candy, housewares, photo frames, books, dresses, cookware, and collectible Disney pins. The Bibbidi Bobbidi Boutique, similar to the one at the Magic Kingdom, finds skilled stylists applying make-up, costumes, glitter, and magic (it's best to reserve an appointment). ✉ *Marketplace, Disney Springs* 🌐 *www.disneysprings.com/shopping/world-of-disney.*

The Landing

Situated on a small island, this family-oriented Disney Springs district features nearly a dozen eateries, some run by celebrity chefs such as Masaharu Morimoto, Art Smith, and Rick Bayless. The restaurants all have indoor and patio dining, and some also offer entertainment. Raglan Road, for instance, has traditional Irish music and step-dance performances nightly and during weekend brunch.

A massive entertainment complex, The Edison, offers daytime dining and nighttime cabaret (and acrobats), while the adjoining Maria & Enzo's serves high-end Italian cuisine. The BOATHOUSE features attractive waterfront dining, with views of the water taxis delivering folks across the lake and the tiny, colorful boat-cars that tootle up and down the ramp. Paddlefish, a three-story eatery inspired by a Mississippi paddle steamer, serves seafood and has fabulous views. The Landing also has its share of cleverly appointed shops.

Restaurants

The BOATHOUSE

$$$$ | **SEAFOOD** | Who knows why the contemporary and upscale BOATHOUSE on the Disney Springs waterfront uses all CAPITALS in its name, but it does. Maybe it's just to draw attention to itself and its fresh seafood, raw bar, and premium steaks and chops. **Known for:** a good place to arrange "Amphicars" tours; fresh seafood; lobster bake for two with whole Maine lobster and clams. 💲 *Average main: $35* ✉ *The Landing, Disney Springs* ☎ *407/939–2628* 🌐 *www.disneysprings.com/dining/the-boathouse.*

Chef Art Smith's Homecomin'

$$$ | **AMERICAN** | **FAMILY** | Superstar chef Art Smith, recognized by foodies for having worked for Oprah and cooked for heads of state, incorporates ingredients from nearby farms, ranches, and

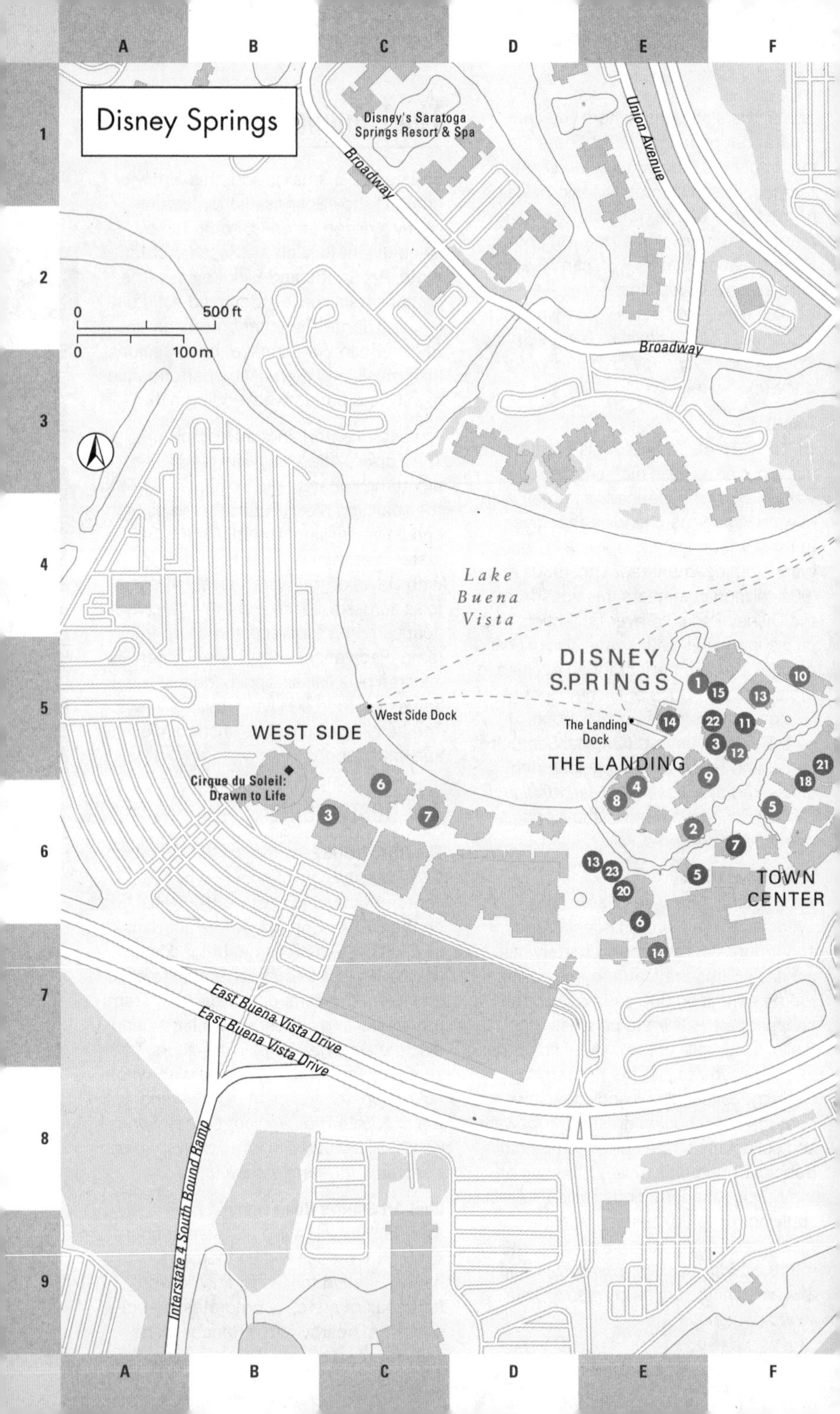

A
B
C
D
E
F
1
2
3
4
5
6
7
8
9
Disney Springs
Disney's Saratoga Springs Resort & Spa
Broadway
Union Avenue
0
500 ft
0
100 m
Broadway
Lake Buena Vista
DISNEY SPRINGS
West Side Dock
WEST SIDE
The Landing Dock
THE LANDING
Cirque du Soleil: Drawn to Life
TOWN CENTER
1
2
3
4
5
6
7
8
9
10
11
12
13
14
15
18
20
21
22
23
East Buena Vista Drive
East Buena Vista Drive
Interstate 4 South Bound Ramp

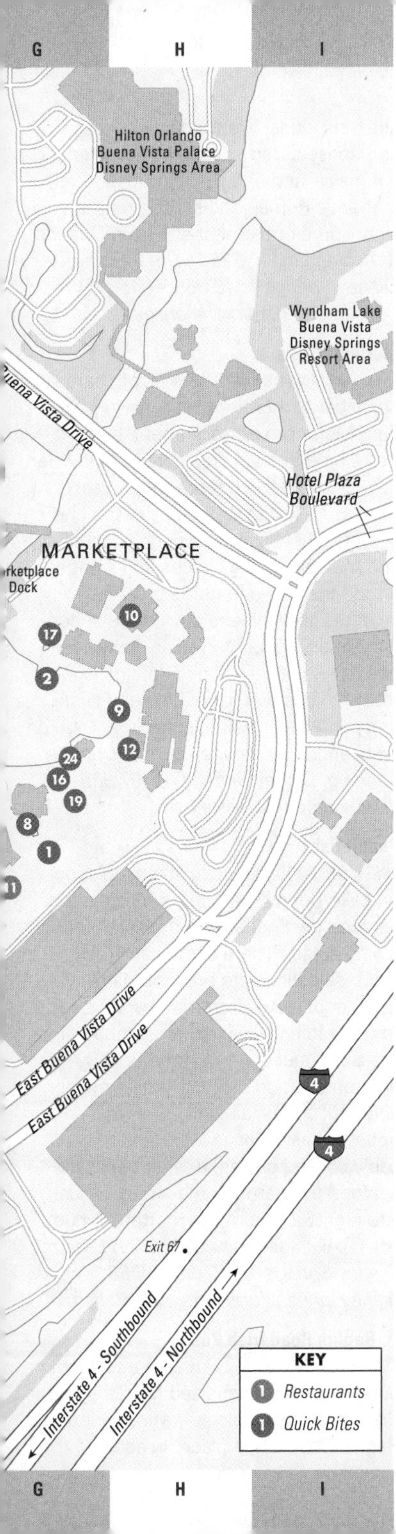

Restaurants

1. The BOATHOUSE **E5**
2. Chef Art Smith's Homecomin' **E6**
3. City Works Eatery and Pour House **C6**
4. The Edison **E6**
5. Frontera Cocina **F6**
6. House of Blues **C6**
7. Jaleo by José Andrés **C6**
8. Maria & Enzo's Ristorante **E6**
9. Morimoto Asia **F5**
10. Paddlefish **F5**
11. The Polite Pig **G6**
12. Raglan Road Irish Pub **F5**
13. Terralina Crafted Italian **F5**
14. Wolfgang Puck Bar & Grill **E7**

Quick Bites

1. Amorette's Patisserie .. **G6**
2. AristoCrepes **G4**
3. The Basket at Wine Bar George **F5**
4. B.B. Wolf's Sausage Co. **G5**
5. Blaze Pizza **E6**
6. Chicken Guy! **E6**
7. D-Luxe Burger **F6**
8. The Daily Poutine **G5**
9. Dockside Margaritas... **H5**
10. Earl of Sandwich **H4**
11. Erin McKenna's Bakery NYC **F5**
12. Ghirardelli's Soda Fountain and Chocolate Shop **H5**
13. Häagen-Dazs **E6**
14. Jock Lindsey's Hangar Bar **E5**
15. Joffrey's (coffees) **F5**
16. Joffrey's (tropical smoothies) **G5**
17. Rainforest Café **G4**
18. Sprinkles Disney Springs **F6**
19. Starbucks **G5**
20. Stargazers Bar **E6**
21. T-Rex Café **F5**
22. Vivoli il Gelato **F5**
23. YeSake Kiosk **E6**
24. Wetzel's Pretzels **G5**

fisheries in this tribute to down-home Southern cooking. Having been a part of Disney's College program (he started his career with a culinary internship here), he's returned to present dishes like his famous fried chicken, deviled eggs, shrimp and grits, pork chops, fried green tomatoes, mashed potatoes, and Southern slaw. **Known for:** signature cocktails and hummingbird cake; celebrity chef Art Smith's comfort food; fried chicken. *Average main: $28 ✉ The Landing, Disney Springs ☎ 407/939–5277 🌐 www.homecominkitchen.com.*

The Edison

$$$ | ECLECTIC | A massive brick structure that, according to Disney lore, was the original power plant for the town of Disney Springs, now houses The Edison, an entertainment arena of more than a half-dozen distinct and richly themed rooms where food and drink mingle with palm readers, aerialists, contortionists, and other sideshow acts. The steampunk decor includes a massive clock in the main lobby and a dramatic, working steam engine. **Known for:** intriguing industrial atmosphere in a "power plant" setting; sophisticated bar food like lamb balls and candied bacon; late-night club with entertainment. *Average main: $25 ✉ The Landing, Disney Springs ☎ 407/560–9288 🌐 www.theedisonfla.com Dance club dress code after 10 pm.*

★ Maria & Enzo's Ristorante

$$$ | ITALIAN | FAMILY | This complex of three restaurants is a haven of authentic Italian cuisine served up by two internationally known chefs (though the Disney "story" tells of an immigrant Italian couple who convert the Disney Springs Air Terminal into the eateries). Maria & Enzo's offers fine Italian cuisine in a sophisticated setting; neighboring Pizza Ponte has pizza by the slice, Italian pastries, and belly-filling sandwiches; Enzo's Hideaway, set in a former cast-access tunnel, serves classic dishes seldom seen in Florida, like fried artichokes and house-cured antipasti. **Known for:** whimsical and detail-rich atmospheres; authentic Roman and southern Italian cuisine; some of the best steaks in Orlando. *Average main: $25 ✉ The Landing, Disney Springs ☎ 407/560–8466 🌐 www.patinagroup.com/maria-enzos.*

Morimoto Asia

$$$$ | ASIAN FUSION | There is, of course, a sushi bar at this sleek, expansive Masaharu Morimoto establishment, and the Iron Chef himself takes control of it when he's in town (about four times a year), though it's fun to watch any of the chefs at work. There's also an open kitchen and multiple dining spaces and lounges where the menu features pan-Asian favorites like Chinese duck, Korean noodles, and Singaporean laksa. **Known for:** best views of the Disney Springs lagoon from the upstairs patio; high-end sushi and pan-Asian cuisine; open until 1 am on weekends. *Average main: $35 ✉ The Landing, Disney Springs ☎ 407/939–6686 🌐 www.morimotoasia.com.*

Paddlefish

$$$$ | SEAFOOD | Housed in a paddleboat on Lake Buena Vista, this sophisticated seafood destination has multiple outdoor dining areas, where same-day, fresh-catch selections are presented in any number of ways, from raw bar delicacies to the traditional Gulf-shore jambalaya or the Build-Your-Own Seafood Boil. There are non-seafood dishes like filet mignon and pork chops, as well as vegetarian options. **Known for:** raw bar and impeccably cooked dishes; freshest possible seafood from around the world; casual, late-night vibe from the rooftop lounge bar. *Average main: $34 ✉ The Landing, Disney Springs ☎ 407/939–2268 🌐 www.disneysprings.com/dining/paddlefish.*

★ Raglan Road Irish Pub

$$$ | IRISH | FAMILY | If an authentic Irish pub—actually transported from the Old Country plank by plank—is your thing, Raglan Road is the place. In addition to excellent fish-and-chips and shepherd's pie, the inventive chefs twist Irish cuisine to include dishes like Gulf shrimp and risotto with buffalo mozzarella and fresh peas. **Known for:** nightly, sometimes hourly, entertainment; first-rate dining and special chef-driven events; extensive beer and ale selections, including exclusive brews. *Average main: $25* *The Landing, Disney Springs* *407/938–0300* *www.raglanroad.com.*

Terralina Crafted Italian

$$$ | **ITALIAN** | Under the guidance of James Beard Award–winner and *Top Chef* master Tony Mantuano, Terralina brings back sophistication and southern Italian cuisine to Disney Springs. Meticulously planned to look like a resort in Italy's Lake District, Terralina's open design and wood-fired grills provide a stylish atmosphere and some of the best recipes Mantuano can create, including wood-fired, hand-tossed pizzas along with salads and sandwiches. **Known for:** stylish, Italian country atmosphere; antipasti tower starter; wood-fired pizzas, steaks, and seafood. *Average main: $30* *The Landing, Disney Springs* *407/934–8888* *www.terralinacrafteditalian.com.*

Coffee and Quick Bites

When on-the-go in The Landing, look for some along-the-way places like **The Basket at Wine Bar George** (small-plate meals and more than 100 wines), **Erin McKenna's Bakery NYC** (gluten-free and vegan pastries and desserts), **Jock Lindsey's Hangar Bar** (beers, cocktails, small plates), **Joffrey's** (coffees), and **Vivoli Il Gelato** (gelato, panini, and espresso).

Shopping

The Art of Shaving

OTHER SPECIALTY STORE | Sure, shaving is a daily task for many men, but there's something wonderfully indulgent about really doing it right. For that, the staff at this intriguing shop will help you select high-end shaving creams, brushes, gels, after-shaves, moisturizers, and razors. For added indulgence, drop by the Barber Spa for a hot towel shave, haircut, facial, scalp therapy, or any assortment of special treatments that "make handsome happen." *The Landing, Disney Springs* *www.disneysprings.com/shopping/the-art-of-shaving.*

Chapel Hats

HATS & GLOVES | Bride-and-groom ears are among the most recognizable fashion statements you'll see here, but they represent just a fraction of the inventory. Shelves are stacked with every shape and style: broad-brimmed sun hats, jaunty Panama hats, 1960s-style porkpie hats, brightly colored fascinators, Indiana Jones–inspired fedoras, and a few dozen others to top off your trip. *The Landing, Disney Springs* *www.disneysprings.com/shopping/chapel-hats.*

West Side

Disney's West Side was fairly quiet following the closure of Cirque du Soleil's long-running show, La Nouba, but when the troupe premiered its Drawn to Life show in late 2021, the district got a boost. Nightlife here is primarily anchored by this production and the happenings at the House of Blues. A short walk away, though, are the Disney Springs 24 movie multiplex as well as Splitsville Luxury lanes, a modern take on the classic American bowling alley, with 30 lanes on two floors, weekend DJs, and upscale eats like filet sliders and sushi at indoor and outdoor tables. Take a water taxi across the lagoon to the Marketplace, and you've got yourself a splendid evening.

Elsewhere in this entertainment-rich district, you can enjoy the Sunday morning Gospel Brunch at the House of Blues, which has its own gift shop; dine at such restaurants as Jaleo by José Andres or

City Works Eatery & Pour House; and marvel at aerial park views on a tethered flight aboard the classic Aéro30 helium balloon. Note that West Side shops open at 9:30 or 10:30 am and close between 11 pm and 2 am.

Restaurants

City Works Eatery and Pour House

$$ | **AMERICAN** | Nearly 100 beers as well as eight wines on tap provide reasons enough for Disney guests and a fair share of Disney cast members to frequent what's called the "ultimate sports bar." Paired with a global collection of rare, limited, and special brews are meals large enough to share; burgers big enough for one; and bar bites like flatbreads, nachos, and wings to whet your appetite. The 17 high-def televisions make watching live sporting events a natural in this active joint. **Known for:** discounted drinks and food during extended happy hours; extensive selection of beers on tap; over-the-top sports bar atmosphere. *Average main: $16* ✉ *West Side, Disney Springs* ☎ *407/801–3730* 🌐 *www.disneysprings.com/dining/city-works.*

House of Blues

$$ | **AMERICAN** | **FAMILY** | Be prepared for a soundtrack of music that's equal parts groovy, funky, and soulful as you dine on an eclectic menu that offers everything from ribs to shrimp and grits to a tasty chicken Caesar salad. Consider trying the Juicy Lucy, a bacon cheeseburger with jalapeño and chipotle mayo; the pulled-pork sandwiches and the cornbread are also delicious. **Known for:** loud background music at all times; high-end burgers and Southern fare; Sunday gospel brunch. *Average main: $21* ✉ *West Side, Disney Springs* ☎ *407/934–2583* 🌐 *www.houseofblues.com/orlando.*

Jaleo by José Andrés

$$ | **SPANISH** | Jaleo (pronounced huh-*lay*-oh) means "revelry," and in this contemporary and spacious setting, diners celebrate with authentic paellas cooked over a wood fire, as well as chef José Andrés's signature *gambas al ajillo* (shrimp sautéed with garlic and chili) or *croquetas de pollo* (Spanish chicken fritters). The extensive tapas options are perfect for taste-driving a variety of items: the Jaleo Experience prix-fixe includes traditional and modern tapas, or go Jose's Way, with a larger and more elaborate selection of the chef's favorite tapas and plates. **Known for:** contemporary, multilevel design; authentic Spanish entrées and tapas; fire-pit prepared paellas and steaks. *Average main: $18* ✉ *West Side, Disney Springs* ☎ *321/348–3211* 🌐 *www.disneysprings.com/dining/jaleo-by-jose-andres.*

Coffee and Quick Bites

In this area, a few simple dining and drinking options stand out: **Chicken Guy!** created by celebrity chef Guy Fieri and restaurateur Robert Earl (chicken sandwiches and chicken tenders with 20 types of sauces), **Häagen Dazs** (ice cream, shakes, and malts), **Stargazers Bar** (cocktails and mixed drinks), and **YeSake Kiosk** (a mix of Asian and Mexican counter service meals).

Nightlife

House of Blues

LIVE MUSIC | The restaurant serves up live blues performances and rib-sticking Mississippi Delta cooking all week long, and there's often a jam session on the front porch. The attached concert hall has showcased name performers such as David Byrne, Los Lobos, Steve Miller, and Willie Nelson, but check the calendar in advance since health considerations have reduced the numbers of concerts. Come hungry (and with an admission ticket) for the popular Sunday Gospel Brunch, where there's always a show and all-you-can-eat Southern food. ✉ *West Side,*

Disney Springs ☎ *407/934–2583* 🌐 *www.houseofblues.com/orlando.*

Performing Arts

Cirque du Soleil - Drawn to Life

CIRCUSES | **FAMILY** | After a nearly two-year, pandemic-prompted delay, this entirely new Cirque du Soleil experience—the first collaboration between Cirque and Disney Animation—replaced long-running La Nouba. It's designed to wow both young and old by bringing timeless Disney stories to life in fresh, unforgettable ways. The story follows Julie, a courageous and determined girl who discovers an unexpected gift left by her late father: an unfinished animation piece. Guided by a surprising pencil, she embarks on an inspiring quest sprinkled with her Disney childhood memories. During her journey, she learns to imagine new possibilities and animate the story of her future. ✉ *West Side, Disney Springs* ☎ *877/924–7783 Tickets* 🌐 *www.cirquedusoleil.com/drawn-to-life* 🎫 *From $85.*

Shopping

Pelé Soccer

SPORTING GOODS | **FAMILY** | Soccer (or football, as the rest of the world knows it) has certainly become more popular in the United States, especially during both the Men's and the Women's World Cups. Here, teams from around the world are represented in a colorful array of club jerseys, including those of superstar Pelé, from both his time in Brazil and his time with the New York Cosmos. If you don't find a jersey you like, create your own by choosing a design and adding your favorite player's name and number. Also featured are soccer gear and apparel for all ages and Pelé's own World Cup trophy (which makes for a wonderful photo op). ✉ *West Side, Disney Springs* 🌐 *www.disneysprings.com/shopping/pele-soccer.*

Town Center

Town Center is the shopping mecca of Disney Springs, with several blocks of shops featuring retailers like Anthropologie, Kate Spade, Pandora, Sephora, Superdry, Tommy Bahama, Vera Bradley, and Uniqlo. Central Florida's legendary Ron Jon Surf Shop is also here.

In between sprees, have a bite at The Polite Pig, a locally owned eatery that serves fast-casual farm-to-table fare. Or, if a Mexican snack is what you want, try Rick Bayless's Frontera Cocina to-go window.

Restaurants

Frontera Cocina

$$$$ | **MEXICAN** | **FAMILY** | Under the watchful eye of celebrity chef Rick Bayless, Frontera brings a sophisticated yet casual approach to classic Mexican food. Look for genuine dishes from Oaxaca and Mexico City like house-made guacamole and short-rib tacos, as well as exquisite pan-roasted Florida shrimp. **Known for:** fun and flavorful kids' meals; hand-crafted tortillas and guacamole; vegetarian options like zucchini enchiladas and mushroom tortas. 💲 *Average main: $31* ✉ *Town Center, Disney Springs* ☎ *407/560–0100* 🌐 *www.fronteracocina.com.*

The Polite Pig

$$ | **AMERICAN** | **FAMILY** | The James Beard Award–nominated chef-owners of the Ravenous Pig gastropub in nearby Winter Park opened this sit-down restaurant to give Disney visitors a taste of Orlando's finest. They do it by sourcing as many ingredients as possible from local farmers and purveyors, as well as by house-smoking the ribs, brisket, and chicken and offering special Southern sides like tomato-and-watermelon salad or smoked corn with lime butter. **Known for:** locally owned and operated by critcally acclaimed chefs; locally sourced ingredients; meats smoked on premises. *Average main: $18* *Town Center, Disney Springs* 407/938–7444 *www.politepig.com.*

Wolfgang Puck Bar & Grill

$$$$ | **AMERICAN** | **FAMILY** | Celebrity chef Wolfgang Puck's California-crafted eatery serves a mixture of dishes, from Mediterranean-influenced entrées and signature pizzas to seared Florida red snapper with mango and corn salsa to whole grilled fish, mesquite-grilled pork chops, flat-iron steaks, and filet mignon. Gooey desserts, crafted cocktails, and a gelato bar complete the cosmopolitan scene. **Known for:** world-famous pizza; name-brand dining in familiar surroundings; California ranch–style atmosphere. *Average main: $31* *Town Center, Disney Springs* 407/815–2100 *wolfgangpuck.com/dining/orlando-bar-grill.*

Coffee and Quick Bites

Although Town Center is the smallest of Disney Springs' four districts, you'll never go hungry. Aside from table service restaurants, there's **Amorette's Patisserie** (high-end pastries), **Blaze Pizza** (build-your-own pizza in just three minutes), **D-Luxe Burger** (classic, barbecue, veggie, and more), **The Daily Poutine** (Canadian snack of thick-cut fries smothered in cheese curds and gravy), **Sprinkles Disney Springs** (cookies, slow-churned ice cream, and handcrafted cupcakes).

Shopping

L'Occitane en Provence

COSMETICS | This fragrant, French-inspired apothecary has everything you need to pamper yourself, from all-natural lotions, gels, creams, and oils to toners and serums to cleansers, moisturizers, and exfoliating scrubs. Shaving and grooming items for men are also well represented. Stop by to sample products, mix your own essential oils, and even get a complimentary minifacial or hand massage. *Town Center, Disney Springs* *www.disneysprings.com/shopping/loccitane-en-provence.*

Orlando Harley-Davidson

OTHER SPECIALTY STORE | America's largest motorcycle manufacturer has been going strong since 1903, and its apparel has been popular for nearly as long. Harley enthusiasts of all ages can buy biker jackets, vests, T-shirts, patches, and other gear. Climb aboard an iconic hog for a photo op. *Town Center, Disney Springs* *www.disneysprings.com/shopping/orlando-harley-davidson.*

Disney Springs Resort Area

A half-century ago, as Walt Disney World was welcoming its first guests, this area was simply the Lake Buena Vista shopping village, with a handful of stores. As Disney World expanded, so did this district. Initially, there were only two hotels and a campground close to the Magic Kingdom, which was then Disney's only theme park. Over time, Lake Buena Vista saw the addition of hotel after hotel, and today, there are more than dozen in or near the area now known as Disney Springs. And that original handful of shops? Well, it's now a robust selection of stores, restaurants, and nightclubs—not to mention a golf course right around the corner.

The proximity to Walt Disney World naturally means that Disney Springs lodgings—a mix of hotels that are both Disney owned and not—tend to have higher room rates. If you can swing a stay here, though, you'll be in a good location, and, since the district's non-Disney hotels are on Disney property, they have some (but not all) of the privileges of official Walt Disney World Resort hotels.

Disney's sprawling Port Orleans Resort has two sections: the French Quarter and the more family-friendly Riverside, pictured here.

Restaurants

Boatwright's Dining Hall

$$$ | **CAJUN** | **FAMILY** | Located riverside at Disney's Port Orleans Resort, this very impressive, handcrafted dining hall looks like the interior of a wooden sailing ship, complete with an inverted hull on the ceiling and weathered shipbuilding tools. True to the N'awlins theme is a menu of tasty bayou dishes ranging from Louisiana étouffée to crawfish bisque to andouille-stuffed catfish. **Known for:** Charleston-style seafood grits; out of the way resort with a full bar; Cajun bayou catfish and jambalaya. *Average main: $30* *Disney's Port Orleans Resort–Riverside, Disney Springs Resort Area* *407/939–5277* *disneyworld.disney.go.com/dining/port-orleans-resort-riverside/boatwright-dining-hall* *No lunch.*

Hotels

In addition to the Walt Disney World hotels, several properties on Hotel Plaza Boulevard, which carry a Lake Buena Vista address but are still on Disney property, are designated as "official" Walt Disney World hotels and are within walking distance of Disney Springs. These include the B Resort & Spa, DoubleTree Suites by Hilton Orlando, Hilton Orlando Buena Vista Palace, Hilton Orlando Lake Buena Vista, Holiday Inn Orlando–Disney Springs Area, and Wyndham Lake Buena Vista.

Guests of these hotels get some, but not all, of the perks (e.g., free park shuttles and Extra Magic Hours) of Disney resort guests. For reviews of these hotels, see Kissimmee, Lake Buena Vista, and Celebration.

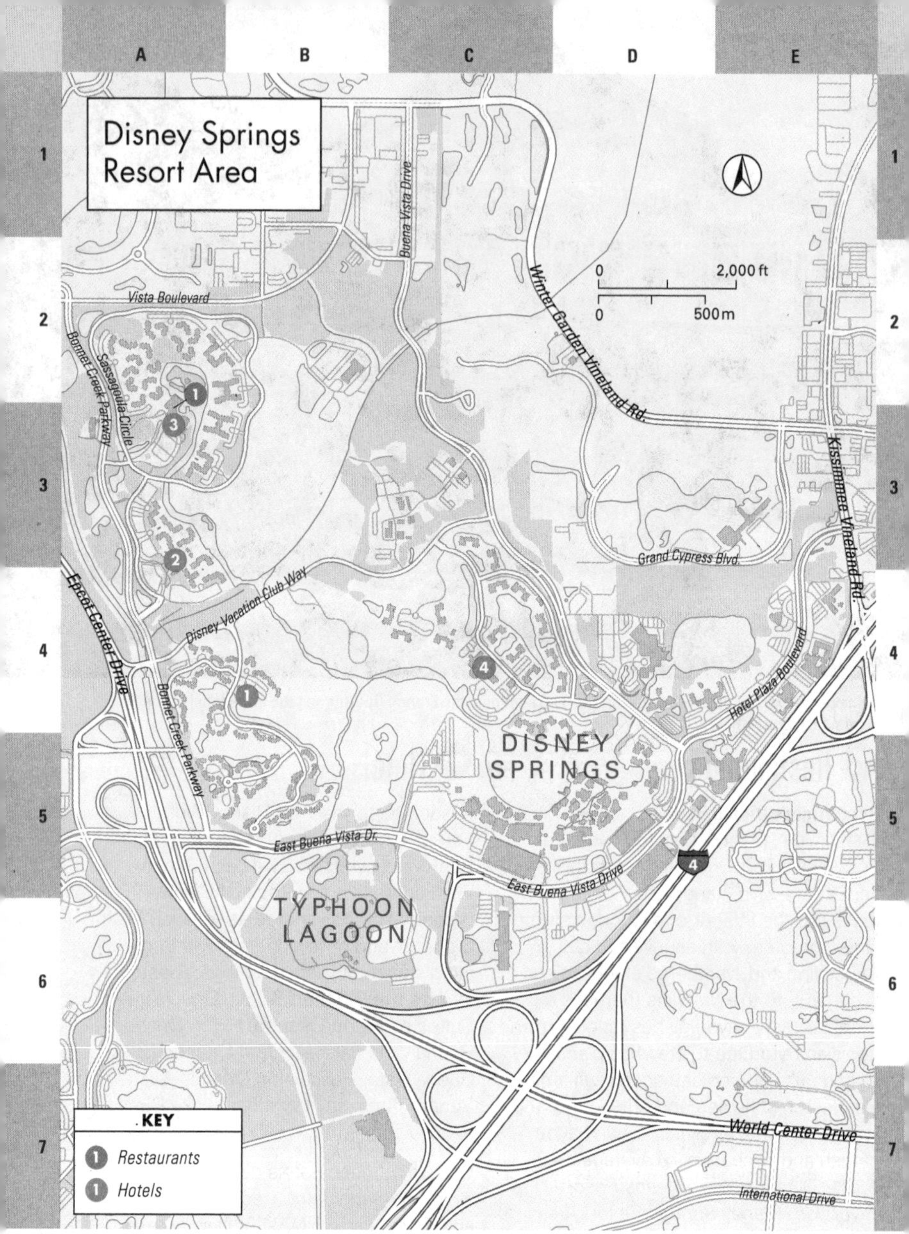

Restaurants ▼

1 Boatwright's Dining Hall.............. **A3**

Hotels ▼

1 Disney's Old Key West Resort.................... **B4**

2 Disney's Port Orleans Resort–French Quarter.......... **A3**

3 Disney's Port Orleans Resort–Riverside **A3**

4 Disney's Saratoga Springs Resort & Spa ... **C4**

Disney's Old Key West Resort
$$$$ | RESORT | FAMILY | Disney is nothing if not a master of theming, and this collection of home-style villas and studio units reflective of vintage Key West homes is a shining (and pricey) example. **Pros:** laundry facilities; quiet and romantic; full kitchens in villas. **Cons:** no elevators; bus service to parks can be frustrating; long walks between rooms and restaurants, recreation facilities, bus stops. *Rooms from: $445* ✉ *1510 N. Cove Rd., Disney Springs Resort Area* ☎ *407/827–7700* 🌐 *disneyworld.disney.go.com/resorts/old-key-west-resort* *761 units* *No Meals.*

Disney's Port Orleans Resort–French Quarter
$$$ | HOTEL | Cobblestone streets, gas lamps, wrought-iron balconies and fragrant magnolia blossoms create a Disneyfied (i.e., clean) version of the French Quarter. **Pros:** lots of recreation options, including elaborate pool, boat rentals, and carriage rides; authentic—or as authentic as Disney can make it—fun, New Orleans style; moderate price. **Cons:** food court is the only on-site dining option; shuttle service is slow; even though there are fewer kids here, public areas can still be noisy. *Rooms from: $276* ✉ *2201 Orleans Dr., Disney Springs Resort Area* ☎ *407/934–5000* 🌐 *disneyworld.disney.go.com/resorts/port-orleans-resort-french-quarter* *1008 rooms* *No Meals.*

Disney's Port Orleans Resort–Riverside
$$$ | RESORT | FAMILY | Considered a more family-friendly choice than its neighbor (the French Quarter resort), this lodging on the man-made Sassagoula River immerses you in a Creole setting—from the white-column mansions of Magnolia Bend to Alligator Bayou's backwoods cottages. **Pros:** lots of recreation options for kids; carriage rides through picturesque settings; river transportation to Disney Springs. **Cons:** the Old South vibe might not be everyone's cup of tea; no shortage of noisy youngsters; shuttle to parks can be slow. *Rooms from: $276* ✉ *1251 Riverside Dr., Disney Springs Resort Area* ☎ *407/934–6000* 🌐 *disneyworld.disney.go.com/resorts/port-orleans-resort-riverside* *2048 rooms* *No Meals.*

Disney's Saratoga Springs Resort & Spa
$$$$ | RESORT | FAMILY | This sprawling property takes its inspiration from 19th-century Gilded Age spa resorts in upstate New York, where hot springs and lakes ruled the landscape. **Pros:** abundance of rooms with whirlpool baths; water taxis whisk you to Disney Springs; kitchens can shave down the food bill. **Cons:** bus transportation can be slow and crowded; one bar-and-grill restaurant; it's a fair hike from some accommodations to the restaurant and other facilities. *Rooms from: $483* ✉ *1960 Broadway, Disney Springs Resort Area* ☎ *407/827–1100* 🌐 *disneyworld.disney.go.com/resorts/saratoga-springs-resort-and-spa* *1260 units* *No Meals.*

Activities

SPAS

★ Senses Spa at Disney's Saratoga Springs Resort
SPAS | This two-story, stone-and-wood spa is inspired by the legendary lodges at Adirondack mineral springs. Fruit-infused elixirs and the scent of frankincense soothe you as you enter either the separate men's or women's waiting room. Signature treatments include the Citrus Milk Experience, with a sugar scrub and milk bath; the Orange Blossom Fusion, combining a coconut-sugar scrub and citrus-oil massage; and the Sweet Treats Mani-Pedi for kids ages 4–12. Other amenities include a couples' treatment room and relaxation rooms (swimsuits required) with steam bath, pool, and heated, glass-tile-covered lounge chairs. ✉ *Disney's Saratoga*

Top Spas

If you need to shift your pace from "fast forward" to "pause," head directly to one of Orlando's resort spas. The area has enough standout pampering palaces to indulge every theme-park-weary parent, aching golfer, parched sunbather, and Disney princess.

Each spa is known for something special, whether it's the Balinese massage at the Mandara at Portofino Bay or Himalayan salt therapies at the Waldorf. Several spas draw on Florida's citrus-producing region to offer refreshing orange, grapefruit, and lime therapies. And you can go global with massage techniques from Japan, Thailand, Polynesia, and Sweden.

Families who want to stay together can even spa together at treatment centers specializing in youth facials, massages, and manicure/pedicure (aka: mani-pedi) packages. Disney's Senses Spas at Saratoga Springs and the Grand Floridian offer Sweet Treats Manicures and Pedicures.

Make your spa excursion special by planning enough time to use complimentary whirlpools, saunas, and steam rooms. Most spas offer free access to impressively equipped fitness centers and relaxation rooms stocked with herbal teas, fresh fruits, and other goodies. Book treatments early, and ask about gratuities—often 18% to 20%—which might or might not be included in your treatment or package.

Top Spas

Blue Harmony, Wyndham Grand Orlando Resort Bonnet Creek, Lake Buena Vista

Eforea Spa at Hilton Orlando, Destination Drive, Orlando

Mandara Spa, Portofino Bay Resort, Universal Orlando

Ritz-Carlton Spa, Grande Lakes Orlando, South Orlando

Senses Spa, Disney's Saratoga Springs Resort, Disney Springs Resort Area

Senses Spa, Grand Floridian Resort, Magic Kingdom Resort Area

Springs Resort, 1960 Broadway, Disney Springs Resort Area ☎ 407/939–7727 🌐 disneyworld.disney.go.com/spas/saratoga-springs-resort-and-spa/senses-spa-saratoga.

Typhoon Lagoon

According to Disney legend, Typhoon Lagoon was created when the lush Placid Palms Resort was struck by a cataclysmic storm. It left a different world in its wake: surfboard-sundered trees, once-upright palms imitating the Leaning Tower of Pisa, and a lagoon cut off from the sea, trapping thousands of tropical fish.

Nothing, however, topped the fate of *Miss Tilly,* a shrimp boat from Safen Sound, Florida, which was hurled high in the air and became impaled on Mount Mayday, a magical volcano that periodically tries to dislodge *Miss Tilly* with huge geysers.

Ordinary folks, the legend continues, would have been crushed by such devastation. But the resourceful residents of Placid Palms were made of heartier stuff—and from the wreckage they created 56-acre Typhoon Lagoon, the self-proclaimed "world's ultimate water park."

Speed down waterslides with names like Crush 'n' Gusher and Humunga Kowabunga, bump through rapids and falls at Mount Mayday, rubberneck as fellow human cannonballs are ejected from the Storm Slides.

On the mellower side of things, bob along in 5-foot waves in a surf pool the size of two football fields, float in inner tubes along the 2,100-foot Castaway Creek, or hunker down with a book in a hammock or lounge chair. Ketchakiddee Creek, for young children, replicates adult rides on a smaller scale. It's Disney's version of a day at the beach—complete with friendly lifeguards

GETTING ORIENTED

Most people agree that kids under 7 and older adults like Typhoon Lagoon (bigger kids and teens like Disney's other water park, Blizzard Beach), where the layout is very simple. The swimming lagoon is at the park's center, with waves originating on the Mount Mayday side and breaking on the beaches closest to the entrance. Any attraction requiring a gravitational plunge starts around the summit of Mount Mayday.

The cleverly named Miss Adventure Falls and Ketchakiddee Creek flank the lagoon, to Mount Mayday's right and left, respectively, as you enter. The Crush 'n' Gusher water coaster is due right of Singapore Sal's.

You can take Disney bus transportation or drive to Typhoon Lagoon. There's no parking charge. Once inside, your options are to walk, swim, slide, or sleep.

PARKS AMENITIES

Dining: Picnicking is permitted, but coolers too large for one person to carry are forbidden, as are glass containers and alcoholic beverages not bought in the park. Getaway Glen, Typhoon Tilly's, and NS pavilions across the park have picnic tables. You can always fork out $40 to $70 a day (excluding tax), depending on the season, for a reserved umbrella from Getaway Glen, which includes two loungers, two beach chairs, a drink table, and towels. Arrive early, though, and you can stake out a great spot for free. Park eateries and food stands have salads, burgers, pizza, and other treats, with a sweet emphasis on ice cream.

Dressing Rooms and Lockers: There are thatched-roof dressing rooms and lockers to the right on your way into the park. It costs $10 a day to rent a small locker and $15 for a large one; there's also a $5 deposit. There are restrooms in every nook and cranny. Most have showers and are much less crowded than the dressing rooms. If you forgot your towel, rent ($2) or buy one at Singapore Sal's.

First Aid: The small first-aid stand, run by a registered nurse, is on your left as you enter the park.

Guest Services: The staff at the Guest Services window outside the entrance turnstiles, to your left, can answer many questions. **■ TIP→ A chalkboard inside gives water temperature and surfing information.**

Lost People and Things: Ask about your misplaced people and things at the Guest Services window near the entrance turnstiles. Lost children are taken to an area by the Tip Board near the front of the park, where Disney cast members entertain them with games.

Private Patios: The park has a dozen premium, roped-off Beachcomber Shacks (patios, really) that groups of as many as six can rent. They generally offer shade and sun as well as plush loungers and other chairs, a table with an umbrella, and an ice chest with two bottles of water per guest (up to six). Each guest also gets two beach towels and a refillable soft-drink mug. The whole group gets a locker to share and an attendant to take and deliver food orders (cost of meals not included). The patios cost $225 to $340 per person, excluding tax. Reserve (☎ *407/939–7527* 🌐 *disneyworld.disney.*

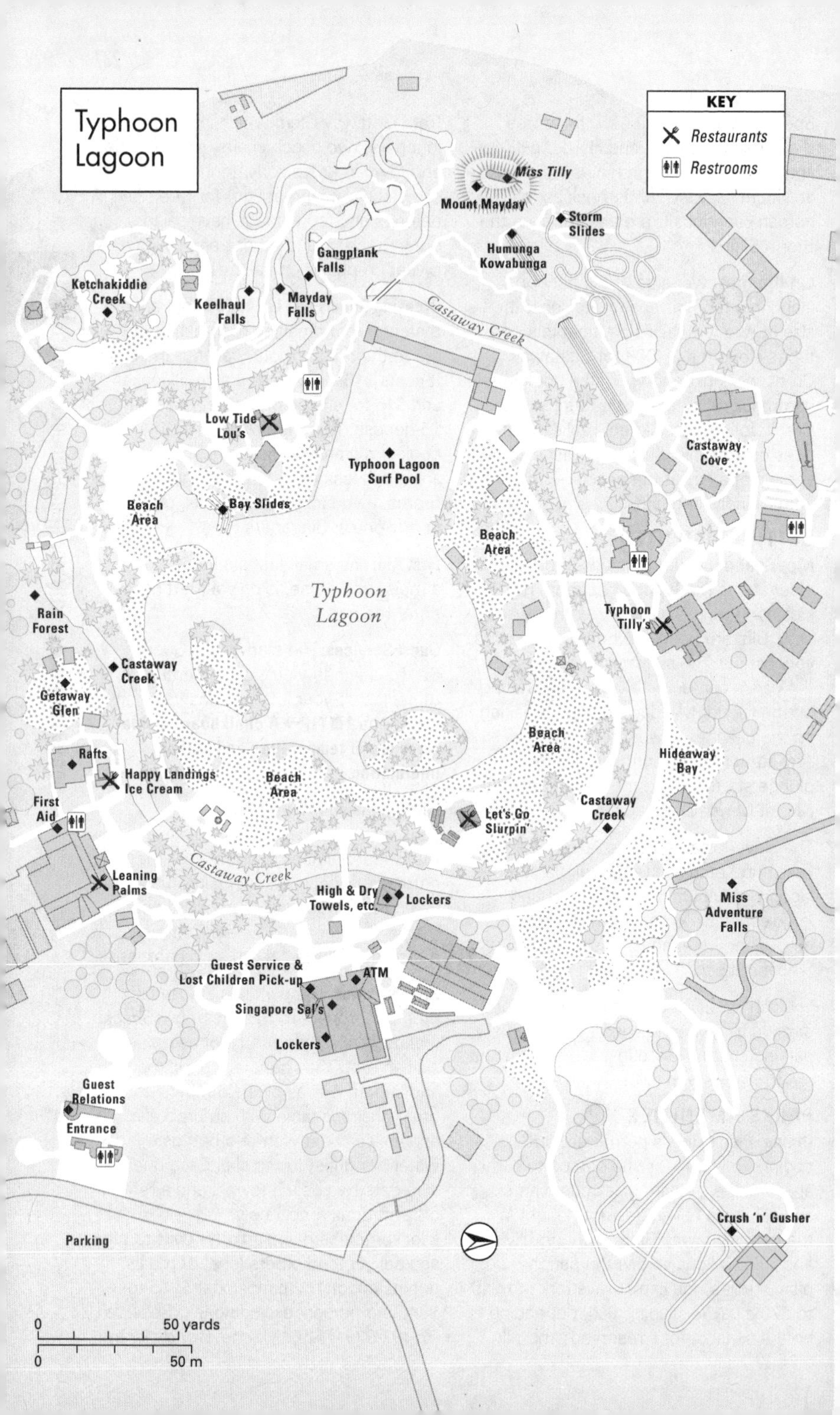

Typhoon Lagoon
KEY
Restaurants
Restrooms
Miss Tilly
Mount Mayday
Storm Slides
Humunga Kowabunga
Gangplank Falls
Ketchakiddie Creek
Keelhaul Falls
Mayday Falls
Castaway Creek
Low Tide Lou's
Typhoon Lagoon Surf Pool
Castaway Cove
Beach Area
Bay Slides
Beach Area
Typhoon Lagoon
Rain Forest
Typhoon Tilly's
Castaway Creek
Getaway Glen
Beach Area
Hideaway Bay
Rafts
Happy Landings Ice Cream
Beach Area
First Aid
Let's Go Slurpin'
Castaway Creek
Leaning Palms
Castaway Creek
High & Dry Towels, etc.
Lockers
Miss Adventure Falls
Guest Service & Lost Children Pick-up
ATM
Singapore Sal's
Lockers
Guest Relations
Entrance
Crush 'n' Gusher
Parking
0
50 yards
0
50 m

go.com/recreation/typhoon-lagoon/beach-comber-shacks) well in advance or arrive very early to book one at High 'N Dry. In summer, any patio that isn't prebooked sells out within a half hour of the park opening.

Services for People with Disabilities: The paths connecting the different areas are wheelchair accessible, but most of the waterslides are not. There is, however, an elevator that takes you to the loading zone of the Crush 'n' Gusher water coaster. If you transfer from your chair to a raft or inner tube, you can float in Typhoon Lagoon Surf Pool or Castaway Creek.

Wheelchairs are available at the entrance turnstile area and are free with ID. You can trade a land-based wheelchair for chairs that go into the water by asking a lifeguard.

Supplies: You can get inner tubes at Castaway Creek and inner tubes, rafts, or slide mats at the rides. Borrow life vests at **High 'N Dry**. Near the main entrance is **Singapore Sal's,** where you can pick up free life jackets, buy sundries, and rent (or buy) towels and lockers.

VISITING TIPS

Time things right. To make a whole day of it, avoid weekends, when the park is packed with both locals and visitors. In summer, come first thing in the morning, preferably 30 minutes before opening so you can park, buy tickets, rent towels, and snag inner tubes before the crowds descend.

Alternatively, visit late on summer afternoons, when park hours run later, or when the weather clears after a seasonal thundershower (rainstorms drive away crowds).

Afternoons are also good in cooler weather, as the water is a bit warmer. Note, though that, during the off-season between October and April, Typhoon Lagoon closes for routine maintenance and refurbishment. Check park calendars (🌐 *disneyworld.disney.go.com/destinations/water-parks*) for details.

Have the right gear. Plan to slather sunscreen on several times throughout the day. An inexpensive pair of water shoes will save tootsies from hot sand and walkways and from restroom floors.

Women and girls should wear one-piece swimsuits unless they want to find their tops somewhere around their ears at the bottom of the waterslide.

Sights

Bay Slides

AMUSEMENT RIDE | **FAMILY** | Kids scramble up several steps tucked between faux-rock formations, where a lifeguard sits to supervise their slide into Blustery Bay. The incline is small, but the thrill is great for young kids, who whoosh into the bay (sometimes into the arms of waiting parents). These two scaled-down versions of the Storm Slides are geared to kids shorter than 60 inches. **■ TIP→ Kids really burn up energy going up the steps and down the slides repeatedly. Parents should be prepared for their wanting to ride over and over again.** ✉ *Typhoon Lagoon* ☞ *Duration: Up to you. Crowds: Light to moderate. Audience: Small kids.*

Castaway Creek

AMUSEMENT RIDE | **FAMILY** | This circular, 15-foot-wide, 3-foot-deep, 2,000-foot-long waterway is supremely relaxing and satisfyingly soothing. Just snag an inner tube and float placidly along a clear creek that winds through the park and around the Surf Pool and beaches. You'll pass through a rain forest that showers you with spray, slide through caves and grottoes, float by overhanging trees and flowering bushes, and get drenched from the "broken pipes" at the Water Works. The current flows a gentle 2½ feet per second. Along the way are five landing areas where you can hop in and out. **For people with disabilities:** Guests using wheelchairs must transfer to an inner tube. **■ TIP→ A**

full circuit takes about 20 minutes, longer if you stop at one of the five lifeguard-manned launches. ✉ *Typhoon Lagoon* ☞ *Duration: Up to 20 mins. Crowds: Vary by season. Audience: All ages.*

★ Crush 'n' Gusher

AMUSEMENT RIDE | FAMILY | If flume rides, storm slides, and tube races aren't wild enough for you, get ready to defy gravity on Disney's multipassenger water coaster. Designed to propel you uphill and down along flumes, caverns, and spillways, this ride should satisfy the most enthusiastic daredevil. Keeping with park lore, Crush 'n' Gusher flows through what appears to be a rusted-out tropical fruit factory, weaving in and out of the wreckage and debris that once transported fruit through the plant's wash facilities. Three "fruit chutes" are aptly named Banana Blaster, Coconut Crusher, and Pineapple Plunger—one of which is designed for solo riders. Guests shouldn't ride if they are pregnant or have heart, back, or neck problems. **For people with disabilities:** An elevator takes guests using wheelchairs to the loading area; there's a short distance between this area and the ride. **■TIP→ Ride first thing in the morning before lines get too long. And don't forget to say cheese for the cameras!** ✉ *Typhoon Lagoon* ☞ *Duration: 1 min. Crowds: Moderate to heavy. Audience: Not small kids. Height requirement: 48 inches.*

Gangplank Falls

AMUSEMENT RIDE | FAMILY | Families who scale Mount Mayday have to haul their raft to the peak before the adventure begins. Upon takeoff, a 6½-foot-long inflated raft plunges down the slide with impressive speed, with things getting bumpy at times along the 300-foot river. It's a pleasant ride for families—not too scary for kids, and not too dull for adults. Those who are pregnant or have heart, back, or neck problems should sit this one out. **■TIP→ The inner tubes are heavy, so have at least two willing carriers. Also be prepared to ride with two to four riders (five if some are smaller kids).** ✉ *Typhoon Lagoon* ☞ *Duration: 1 min. Crowds: Vary by season. Audience: Not small kids.*

Humunga Kowabunga

AMUSEMENT RIDE | FAMILY | The basic question here is: do you want to get scared out of your wits in four seconds flat? Three side-by-side speed slides drop 214 feet downhill at a 60-degree angle in seconds. Oh yes, and then you go through a cave. In the dark. The average speed is 30 mph, but you can really fly if you lie flat on your back, cross your ankles, wrap your arms around your chest, and arch your back. A couple caveats: the ride lasts only a few seconds—too short for us—and lines are often too long to requeue for another plunge. Also, this ride isn't appropriate for guests who are pregnant or who have heart, back, or neck problems. **■TIP→ Race against your friends or family.** ✉ *Typhoon Lagoon* ☞ *Duration: 4 secs. Crowds: Heavy. Audience: Not small kids. Height requirement: 48 inches.*

Keelhaul Falls

AMUSEMENT RIDE | FAMILY | If you need to chill out after the high-velocity Humunga Kowabunga, venture up to Keelhaul Falls, a laid-back trip down the left side of Mount Mayday. Just kick back and relax as your blue tube cruises down the 400-foot slide and splashes into a pool. Although its winding path and scenic descent can be satisfying for guests of all ages, thrill seekers might be disappointed. Nevertheless, this ride isn't appropriate for guests who are pregnant or who have heart, back, or neck problems. **■TIP→ Ride before or after Mayday Falls.** ✉ *Typhoon Lagoon* ☞ *Duration: 1 min. Crowds: Vary by season. Audience: Not young kids.*

Grab an inner tube, and head for Castaway Creek, Typhoon Lagoon's lazy river.

Ketchakiddee Creek

OTHER ATTRACTION | FAMILY | Typhoon Lagoon's play area for young children has slides, mini rapids, faux sand castles, squirting whales and seals, bouncing barrels, waterfalls, sprinklers, and all the other ingredients of a splash fiesta. The bubbling sand ponds, where youngsters can sit in what seems like an enormous whirlpool bath, are favorites, as is the tiny-scale tube ride. Kids can have spray battles using small water cannons, and families can camp beneath lots of shady lean-tos when not in the water. **For people with disabilities:** Accessible for people using water-appropriate wheelchairs. **■ TIP→ Parents can take turns watching the kiddies here and riding the thrill slides.** ✉ *Typhoon Lagoon* ☞ *Duration: Up to you. Crowds: Light. Audience: Small kids. Height requirement: Adults must be accompanied by a child under 48 inches and vice versa.*

Mayday Falls

AMUSEMENT RIDE | FAMILY | This 460-foot slide in bright-yellow inner tubes is the longest and bumpiest of the three falls. It's a long trek up—even higher than that at Keelhaul—but the increased speed and longer descent are worth the climb since the watery route slips through caves, slides under bridges, and skims past thundering waterfalls before splash down. This ride isn't appropriate for guests who are pregnant or who have heart, back, or neck problems. **■ TIP→ While you're in the neighborhood, ride Keelhaul Falls, too.** ✉ *Typhoon Lagoon* ☞ *Duration: 1 min. Crowds: Vary by season. Audience: Not young kids.*

Mount Mayday

VIEWPOINT | FAMILY | What goes down can also go up—and up and up. Climbing Mount Mayday "[is] like climbing Mount Everest," one teenager moaned about a climb that seems a lot steeper than an 85-foot peak should be. Nevertheless, after you've passed hibiscus flowers, traversed a rope bridge, and trod across stepping-stones set in plunging waters you'll be near the summit where the view encompasses the entire park. Lovers of white-water rafting should head over to Mayday Falls, Keelhaul Falls, and Gangplank Falls, which utilize oversize inner tubes as they take guests plunging down the mountain's slope. ✉ *Typhoon Lagoon.*

★ Storm Slides

AMUSEMENT RIDE | Each of these three body slides is about 300 feet long and snakes in and out of rock formations, through caves and tunnels, and under waterfalls, but each has a slightly different view and offers a twist. The one in the middle has the longest tunnel; the others feature secrets you'll have to discover for yourself. Brace for splashdown on all three slides! Maximum speed is about 20 mph, and the trip takes about 30 seconds. These slides are not appropriate for guests who are pregnant or who have heart, back, or neck problems. **■TIP→ Try each of the three slides for different twists.** ✉ *Typhoon Lagoon ☞ Duration: 30 secs. Crowds: Moderate to heavy. Audience: Not young kids.*

★ Typhoon Lagoon Surf Pool

POOL | FAMILY | The heart of the park is this 2½-acre swimming area with almost 3 million gallons of clear, chlorinated water. It's scalloped by coves, bays, and inlets, all edged with beaches of white sand—that's spread over a base of white concrete, as bodysurfers discover when they try to slide onto the shore. Ouch! The waves are the draw. Twelve huge water-collection chambers hidden in Mount Mayday dump their load into trapdoors with a resounding whoosh to create 6-foot waves large enough for Typhoon Lagoon to host amateur and professional surfing championships.

A piercing double hoot from *Miss Tilly* (the boat that legend says was deposited on Mount Mayday's highest peak during a storm) signals the start and finish of the wave action. Ninety-minute periods generating bigger waves every 90 seconds are punctuated by 30-minute sessions of placid bobbing waves. Even during the big-wave periods, however, the waters in Blustery Bay and Whitecap Cove are protected.

On certain days, skilled surfers and novices alike can enter the park before it opens for private sessions (☎ *407/939–7529 for reservations*). Instruction and a soft-sided surfboard are included in the $199 cost, and the experience (ages 8 and older) lasts 2½–3 hours. **For people with disabilities:** Accessible for people using water-appropriate wheelchairs. **■TIP→ See the chalkboard at beach's edge for the day's wave schedule.** ✉ *Typhoon Lagoon ☞ Duration: Up to you. Crowds: Heavy. Audience: All ages.*

Coffee and Quick Bites

To your left as you enter the park, **Leaning Palms** has burgers, pizzas, turkey sandwiches, salads, beer, and, of course, ice cream and frozen yogurt. **Typhoon Tilly's,** on the right just past Miss Adventure Falls, is a walk-up kiosk where you can grab fried shrimp, fish baskets, and chicken wraps. It also serves sandwiches, salads, and snacks of all kinds and pours of mostly sugary, nonalcoholic grog—though you can grab a Davy Jones "lager." **Let's Go Slurpin'** is a beach shack on the edge of Typhoon Lagoon that dispenses frozen margaritas as well as wine and beer.

Other options include **Happy Landings Ice Cream,** between Getaway Glen and Leaning Palms, and near Bay Slides, **Low Tide Lou's,** which serves sandwich wraps, snacks, and booze.

Chapter 8

KISSIMMEE, LAKE BUENA VISTA, AND CELEBRATION

8

Updated by
Jennifer Greenhill-Taylor
and Joseph Reed Hayes

Sights	Restaurants	Hotels	Shopping	Nightlife
★★★☆☆	★★★☆☆	★★★★☆	★★★★☆	★★★☆☆

NEIGHBORHOOD SNAPSHOT

TOP EXPERIENCES

■ **Celebration:** Celebration, formerly a spark in Walt Disney's imagination, has become a place for fine dining, casual bike excursions, and relaxing in small town comfort.

■ **Downtown Kissimmee:** downtown Kissimmee is historical and quaintly modern, with an air of Old Florida and a buzz of approaching modernity.

■ **Entertainment:** Route 192 across the lower boundary of Disney has unique entertainment possibilities, like dinner shows at Capone's, Medieval Times, and Pirates Dinner Adventure.

■ **Fishing:** Kissimmee is one of the fishing capitals of America, with record-breaking catches recorded every year in a variety of massive lakes.

■ **Old Florida Attractions:** southern Orlando lets you experience Florida's past, with Gatorland, swamp airboat rides, and eco-tourism kayaking available.

■ **Proximity to Disney Springs:** the respite from Lake Buena Vista's hotel canyons, aside from Disney itself, is the shopping and dining extravaganza of Disney Springs.

GETTING HERE

Kissimmee is 18 miles south of Orlando, 10 miles southeast of Walt Disney World. Celebration is tucked along U.S. 192, the main east–west route to downtown Kissimmee. Lake Buena Vista is actually on the eastern edge of Disney property.

PLANNING YOUR TIME

The draw of these three communities, which abut Walt Disney World, are proximity without the high Disney prices. If you are looking for cheaper places to stay and eat but still want to be within easy reach of Disney's gates (and also the rest of Orlando), any of these areas can be good places to stay. And at night there are even entertainment and dining options to pull you away from the resorts.

VIEWFINDER

■ On the shore of Lake Tohopekaliga, near Kissimmee's downtown and its handy train station, is the charming, public Lakefront Park. For a restful photo session, grab picnic fixings from one of the nearby eateries, and relax in a shady pavilion overlooking the lake and its wetlands. Ample, redbrick, palm-lined paths lead around the shore to a little lighthouse. Have the camera to snap pictures of native fauna in the wild. Red-headed sandhill cranes are common sights, as are elegant white egrets and flocks of ibis. There are turtles and gators, too.

PAUSE HERE

■ Where better to take a break than a serene cathedral built to serve Central Florida's tourists? The vast Basilica of the National Shrine of Mary, Queen of the Universe (✉ *300 Vineland Ave., Lake Buena Vista*), lined with inspirational stained-glass windows, seats 2,000 and is open to all—just as it has been since 1993. A huge Schoenstein organ, installed in 2021, consists of 5,200 pipes, from giant 37-footers to tiny flutes. The grounds contain a Rosary Garden, several chapels (one with stunning blue windows), and a gift shop. Call ☎ *407/239–6600* for information on concerts and tours.

In an area of contrasts, you can vacation just outside Disney's doors in the still-pristine wilderness of Kissimmee, visit the new old small town community of Celebration, and stay in vast resorts or quirky boutique hotels in the manufactured neighborhood called Lake Buena Vista.

Kissimmee is a prime example of Old Florida retaining its charm. Here, you can relax along clear lakes that yield prize-winning fish, visit cattle ranches and rodeos, and ride in airboats along waterways that have changed little since the days of the Florida cowboys.

The SunRail commuter train has made downtown Kissimmee a recreation destination. As it's now just 30 minutes from Downtown Orlando, more people take advantage of the lunchtime and early dinner treats of Kissimmee's main street and the Lake Tohopekaliga waterfront.

There's no shortage of places to stay on the boulevards surrounding the Disney theme parks in an area that has long been called Lake Buena Vista (there really is such a lake, but it's not for recreation). Hotels that offer posh rooms and intimate dining compete with family- and pet-friendly resorts. Properties with names like Waldorf and Four Seasons are also home to some of the best restaurants in Orlando and some of the most extravagant spas anywhere in the country.

Celebration offers good dining, pleasant and bikeable surroundings, and a touch of small-town flair.

For entertainment, there's nothing like the unique dinner-and-a-show spots that line the east–west corridor between Celebration and Kissimmee. Shows here combine food with jousting (Medieval Times), gangsters (Capone's Dinner and Show), and magic (The Outta Control Magic Comedy Dinner Show).

Kissimmee

18 miles south of Orlando, 10 miles southeast of Walt Disney World (WDW).

Although Kissimmee is primarily known as the gateway to Disney (technically, the vast Disney property of theme parks and resorts lies in both Osceola and Orange counties), its non-WDW attractions just might tickle your fancy. They range from throwbacks to old-time Florida to dinner shows for you and 2,000 of your closest friends. Central Florida used to be prime cattle country, and the best sampling of what life was like then is during the Silver Spurs Rodeo in February and June.

With at least 100,000 acres of freshwater lakes, the Kissimmee area brings anglers and boaters to national fishing tournaments and speedboat races. A 50-mile series of lakes and canals, the

Sights

1 Gatorland... D2

2 Mortem Manor....... C3

3 Old Town USA.......... C3

Restaurants

1 Old Hickory Steakhouse. B3

Hotels

1 Gaylord Palms Resort and Convention Center....... B3

2 The Grove... A2

3 Omni Orlando Resort at Champions-Gate......... A4

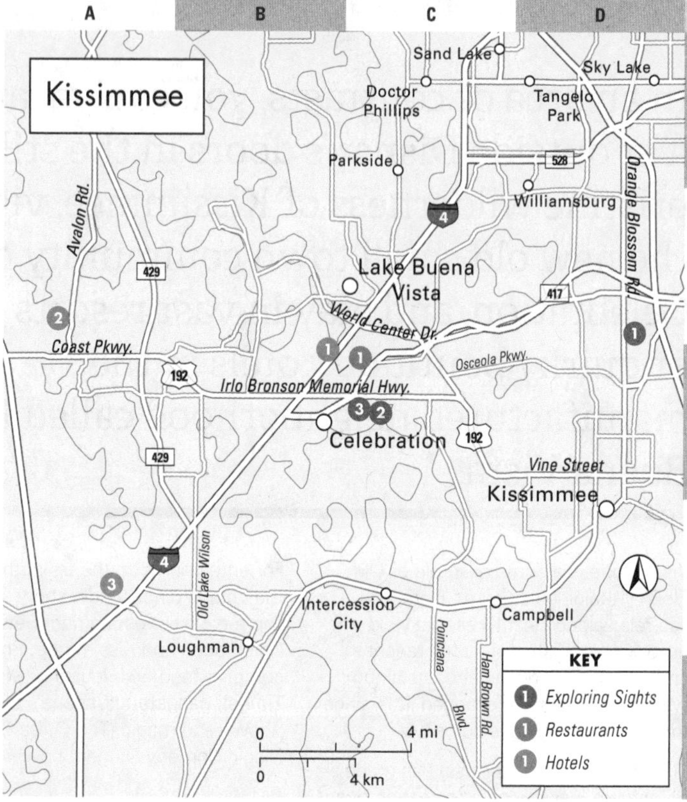

Kissimmee Waterway, connects Lake Tohopekaliga—a Native American name that some say means "Sleeping Tiger"—with Lake Okeechobee in South Florida, and, from there, to both the Atlantic Ocean and the Gulf of Mexico.

From Downtown Orlando it's easy to reach Kissimmee's main road, U.S. 192, from Interstate 4, via Exit 64. Osceola Parkway (Toll Road 522) heads directly from Disney property, and Florida's turnpike runs north–south through Kissimmee.

TOURS

Historic Downtown Kissimmee

SELF-GUIDED TOURS | **FAMILY** | Established well over a century ago, Kissimmee has a story rooted in the founding of the state. It was an important air base during World War II (even a POW camp), and, with ranches and a railroad hub, it was vital in the development of the Orlando cattle and orange industries. The community is easy to reach from Downtown Orlando via the SunRail commuter train, and it hosts special events throughout the year, from classic car shows to a farmers market. You can learn more on the self-guided audio tour or free map tour available at the Main Street Welcome Station or downloadable from the Experience Kissimmee website. ✉ *215 Celebration Pl., Kissimmee* ☎ *407/569–4800* 🌐 *www.experiencekissimmee.com/visitor-information.*

★ Kissimmee Swamp Tours

ECOTOURISM | **FAMILY** | The 60- or 90-minute cruises in high-powered airboats take you through the marshes and swamps of Lake Kissimmee—home to hundreds of species of birds and other critters. The 36,000-acre lake offers a view of (very)

Old Florida. ✉ *4500 Joe Overstreet Rd., Lake Kissimmee, Kenansville* ☎ *407/436–1059* 🌐 *www.kissimmeeswamptours.com* 🎫 *From $49.*

VISITOR INFORMATION

CONTACTS Experience Kissimmee. ✉ *215 Celebration Pl., Suite 200, Kissimmee* ☎ *407/569–4800* 🌐 *www.experiencekissimmee.com.*

Sights

Gatorland

ZOO | FAMILY | This campy, 110-acre attraction near the Orlando–Kissimmee border on U.S. 441 has endured since 1949, despite competition from the major parks. Indeed, over the years, Gatorland has managed to retain much of its original gator-rasslin' spirit, providing an entertaining glimpse into Florida's swamp life.

The Gator Gulley Splash Park has giant "egrets" spilling water from their beaks, dueling water guns mounted atop giant gators, and other water-park splash areas. There's also a small petting zoo and an aviary. A train ride is a high point, taking you through an alligator breeding marsh and a natural swamp setting where you can spot gators, birds, and turtles. A three-story observation tower overlooks the marsh, swamped with gator grunts, especially come sundown during mating season.

The Stompin' Gator Off-Road Adventure takes you straight into a gator swamp in a vehicle that is a cross between a pontoon boat and an off-road monster truck. This is a genuine experience, and you leave knowing the difference between a gator and a croc.

To see eager gators leap from the water to catch their food, come on cool days (summer heat just puts them to sleep) for the *Gator Jumparoo Show,* which is the most thrilling first thing in the morning, when these creatures are at their hungriest. There's also the *Gator Wrestlin' Show,* and although there's no doubt who's going to win the wrestling match, it's still fun to see the handlers take on those tough guys with the beady eyes. The park is also home to the largest community of rare albino alligators in the United States. In the educational *Upclose Encounters* show, the host handles a variety of snakes. If you are looking for even more excitement, the park offers Screamin' Gator and Gator Gauntlet ziplines (additional cost). ■**TIP→ Discount coupons are available online.** ✉ *14501 S. Orange Blossom Trail, Orlando* ✣ *Between Orlando and Kissimmee* ☎ *407/855–5496, 800/393–5297* 🌐 *www.gatorland.com* 🎫 *$30; $10 off-road tours. Free parking.*

Mortem Manor

AMUSEMENT RIDE | FAMILY | This year-round haunted attraction turns the haunted house on its head. The two-floor, actor- and animatronic-filled house frankly scares the heck out of visitors, with dark tableaux and unexpected frights. For those with unshakable stamina, the Last Ride "burial simulator" reduces the experience down to several sound-filled minutes in an actual coffin; it might be of questionable taste, but visitors seem to enjoy it. ✉ *5770 W. Irlo Bronson Memorial Hwy., Kissimmee* ☎ *407/507–0051* 🌐 *www.mortemmanor.com* 🎫 *$15; $5 Last Ride Simulator* ⊗ *Closed Mon. and Tues.*

Old Town USA

TOWN | FAMILY | Old Town is the heart of tourist Kissimmee, with carnival-type attractions and a 1950s theme. Highlights include magic shows in the Great Magic Hall, a haunted funeral parlor attraction, video game and shooting arcades, a laser-tag hall, go-karts and bumper cars, and regularly scheduled classic car shows. Shopping has become the realm of "As Seen on TV" stores and flea market staples, and dining takes the form of generic food courts and sports

Did You Know?

Old Town in Kissimmee—just one of many Orlando-area sights outside the theme parks—has several dozen shops, nine restaurants, 18 rides and attractions, and an events calendar that's filled with antique-car shows.

bars. ✉ *5770 W. Irlo Bronson Memorial Hwy., Kissimmee* ☎ *407/396–4888* 🌐 *www.myoldtownusa.com* 🎫 *Free.*

Restaurants

Kissimmee offers a huge number of dining choices, many of which are of the "burger barn" or dinner theater variety, but there are notable exceptions. Allow about 15 to 25 minutes to travel from WDW or about 35 minutes from International Drive.

Old Hickory Steakhouse

$$$$ | **STEAKHOUSE** | **FAMILY** | This upscale steak house in the Gaylord Palms resort is designed to look like rustic cabins in the Everglades. Beyond the playful facade is a polished, dinner-only restaurant with a classic menu of steaks and chops. **Known for:** consistently good service; particularly good steaks; free valet parking. $ *Average main: $47* ✉ *Gaylord Palms Resort, 6000 W. Osceola Pkwy., Kissimmee* ✥ *I–4 Exit 65* ☎ *407/586–1600* 🌐 *www.marriott.com* ⏲ *Closed Sun.–Thurs. No lunch.*

Hotels

Gaylord Palms Resort and Convention Center

$$$ | **RESORT** | **FAMILY** | Built in the style of a grand, turn-of-the-20th-century Florida resort, this huge building is meant to inspire awe, with an enormous glass-roofed atrium and re-creations of iconic Florida destinations such as the Everglades, Key West, and Old St. Augustine; there's also a water park and movie events. **Pros:** excellent on-site dining; you could have a great vacation without ever leaving the grounds; free shuttle to Disney. **Cons:** hotel is so big that you will get your steps in just walking within the building; distant from Universal or Downtown Orlando; $30 daily resort and parking fee. $ *Rooms from: $350* ✉ *6000 W. Osceola Pkwy., Orlando* ☎ *407/586–0000* 🌐 *www.marriott.com* *1406 rooms* 🍽 *No Meals.*

The Grove

$$$ | **RESORT** | **FAMILY** | A large, all-suites property near the back gate of Disney offers upscale, modern decor in the rooms and public areas, as well as a substantial water-park area with a surf simulator and waterslides. **Pros:** rural location but five-minute drive to busy dining/shopping district on Highway 192; all-suites accommodations suitable for families and groups; choice of on-site eateries and water park. **Cons:** 25-minute drive to Magic Kingdom; long walk from some suites to lobby and amenities; $45 resort fee; $19 parking. $ *Rooms from: $349* ✉ *14501 Grove Resort Ave., Kissimmee* ☎ *407/545–7500, 844/203–0209* 🌐 *www.groveresortorlando.com* *1,040 units* 🍽 *No Meals.*

Omni Orlando Resort at ChampionsGate

$$$ | **RESORT** | **FAMILY** | This huge, award-winning, Mediterranean-style resort, just 6 miles south of Disney and within a 45-minute drive of LEGOLAND, includes a 1,200-acre golf club with two courses, a David Leadbetter academy, and a multifield sports complex. **Pros:** several restaurants ranging from casual to upscale; excellent Mokara spa; huge water park with lazy river and wave pool. **Cons:** separate daily fee for parking; daily resort fee for Internet, Disney shuttles, and gym; remote location. $ *Rooms from: $314* ✉ *1500 Masters Blvd., South of Kissimmee, ChampionsGate* ☎ *407/390–6664, 800/843–6664* 🌐 *www.omnihotels.com* *720 units* 🍽 *No Meals.*

Nightlife

DINNER SHOWS

Capone's Dinner and Show

THEATER | **FAMILY** | This musical dramedy transports you to gangland Chicago of the 1930s, when mobsters and their molls were the height of underworld society. You'll meet "Al Capone" and learn that you can become a member of the "family," but you've got to help take

Go gator! After a visit to Kissimmee's authentic, rustic Gatorland, you'll truly know the difference between a gator and a croc (and you'll see both).

care of a rat in the organization. Flashy costumes and musical numbers are accompanied by a four-course American and Italian dinner that includes beer, wine, and cocktails, as well as nonalcoholic drinks for kids. Check the website for a 50% off coupon. ✉ *4740 W. Irlo Bronson Memorial Hwy., Kissimmee* ☎ *407/397–2378, 800/220–8428* 🌐 *www.alcapones.com* 🎫 *$75; online discounts.*

Medieval Times

THEATER | FAMILY | In a huge, ersatz-medieval manor you'll marvel at sword fights, jousting matches, and other exciting games. The two-hour tournament and four-course feast has more than a dozen charging horses and a cast of 75 knights, nobles, wizards, and maidens. Sound silly? It is. But it's also a true extravaganza. That the show takes precedence over the meat-and-potatoes (or vegetarian) fare is obvious: everyone sits facing forward at long, narrow banquet tables, stepped auditorium-style, above the tournament area. Kids love eating without forks; adults are swept away by the tremendous horse-riding artistry. Check the website and area attractions booklets for discounts. ✉ *4510 W. Vine St., Kissimmee* ☎ *407/396–2900, 888/935–6878* 🌐 *www.medievaltimes.com* 🎫 *From $65.*

Activities

RODEOS

Silver Spurs Rodeo

RODEO | FAMILY | A throwback to the days when cattle and horses ruled Central Orlando, Silver Spurs claims to be the largest rodeo east of the Mississippi. Started in 1944, the twice-yearly show brings contestants from across the country to compete in bull riding, saddle bronc riding, and barrel racing for $100,000 in prize money. Rodeos fill Kissimmee with cowboys during the second and third weekend in February and first weekend in June (the summer rodeo is free). ✉ *1875 Silver Spur La., Kissimmee* ☎ *321/697–3495* 🌐 *www.silverspursrodeo.com* 🎫 *$20.*

SPAS

Mokara Spa at Omni Orlando Resort at ChampionsGate

SPAS | Golf courses surround this resort, which might explain why its Mokara Spa offers special treatments to ease tension and soreness in stressed shoulders and backs. There are plenty of choices for the nongolfer in the group—customized massages, deep tissue, aromatherapy, reflexology, hot stones, salt stones, and a full-service salon for hair and nail treatments. Separate locker rooms, steam rooms, and relaxation rooms ensure privacy while you wait. Packages include the Mokara Classic, a 2½-hour treatment that consists of an 80-minute signature massage followed by a 50-minute facial for $285. A 20% gratuity is added to the bill, and parking is validated if you're a day-spa visitor. ✉ *Omni Orlando Resort at Championsgate, 1500 Masters Blvd., ChampionsGate* ☎ *407/390–6603* 🌐 *www.omnihotels.com.*

Relâche Spa & Salon at Gaylord Palms Resort

SPAS | The 20,000-square-foot spa is in the Everglades Atrium of this giant, Florida-theme resort, and you might feel like an explorer in a tropical wilderness as you make the trek toward tranquility. Soft pastels and generous chaise longues make the tearoom truly serene. Fresh fruit and beverages keep you hydrated while you wait, then it's on to serious relaxation. The spa offers a wide variety of massage therapies, skin care treatments, and tanning. A 20% gratuity is added onto the bill, and a day pass is available for a fee. ✉ *Gaylord Palms Resort, 6000 W. Osceola Pkwy., Kissimmee* ☎ *407/586–4772* 🌐 *www.marriott.com.*

Lake Buena Vista

Approximately 20 miles southwest of Downtown Orlando.

This small city northeast of Walt Disney World rings the Disney theme parks with additional lodging options, chain restaurants, and heavy traffic. On Hotel Plaza Boulevard, several hotels—within walking distance of Disney Springs and actually on Disney property—are designated as "official" Walt Disney World Hotels. Guests at these get a few of the perks of staying at Disney, including free park transportation and Extra Magic Hours, but that's about it. Similarly, two hotels in Bonnet Creek (the Hilton Orlando Bonnet Creek and Waldorf Astoria Orlando) are also designated as "official" hotels with similar park perks even though they're not on Disney property.

Restaurants

Lake Buena Vista, just to the east of Disney Springs, is essentially a collection of midscale hotels, convention hotels, and chain restaurants catering to off-site visitors to Disney World.

★ Bull & Bear

$$$$ | CONTEMPORARY | Everything about the restaurant is first rate, from the New York City trappings to the superb menu. Noteworthy dishes include a Caesar salad that's prepared table side, escargot and gnocchi, pan-seared sea bass with black Venus rice risotto, veal Oscar served with fresh lump crab, and crème brûlée flambé. **Known for:** Florida seafood; high-end service and award-winning kitchen; Wagyu beef and Colorado lamb. [$] *Average main: $47* ✉ *Waldorf Astoria Orlando, 14200 Bonnet Creek Resort Lane, Lake Buena Vista* ☎ *407/597–5413* 🌐 *bullandbearorlando.com* ⏲ *Closed Mon.* 👔 *No shorts, hats, flip-flops, or athletic clothing.*

Kissimmee's Lake Tohopekaliga (affectionately known as Lake Toho) is famous with fishers the world over. It's also great for wildlife spotting—an especially exhilarating experience when done from an airboat.

Covington Mill

$$ | **AMERICAN** | **FAMILY** | A polished space offering hearty buffet and à la carte breakfasts and light lunches, Covington Mill turns into a kidfest on Sunday morning. That's when Disney characters join the early risers, cheerfully signing autographs and posing for photographs. **Known for:** create your own omelet option; buffet breakfast free for hotel guests; Disney character Sunday. *Average main: $20 Hilton Orlando Lake Buena Vista, 1751 Hotel Plaza Blvd., Lake Buena Vista 407/827–4000 hiltonorlandolakebuenavistahotel.com No dinner.*

★ deep blu Seafood Grille

$$$$ | **SEAFOOD** | Seafood is everything at deep blu, a restaurant that has won every local award available, and with good reason. Grilled Florida prawns and Spanish octopus vie with the "deep blu" crab mac 'n' cheese (so worth it). **Known for:** super-fresh raw bar; award-winning seafood; blue crab mac 'n' cheese. *Average main: $40 Wyndham Grand Orlando Resort Bonnet Creek, 14651 Chelonia Parkway, Lake Buena Vista 407/390–2420 deepbluorlando.com Closed Mon.–Wed.*

★ La Luce

$$$ | **ITALIAN** | La Luce brings Italian cuisine with a farm-fresh, Napa Valley flair to this upscale Hilton at the edge of Walt Disney World. Pastas are made fresh, steaks are handled with care, and the very popular cocktail bar is second to none. **Known for:** craft cocktail bar; upscale and authentic Italian cuisine; house-made pasta and wood-oven pizza. *Average main: $30 Signia by Hilton Orlando Bonnet Creek, 14100 Bonnet Creek Resort La., Bonnet Creek, Lake Buena Vista 407/597–3600 www.laluceorlando.com Closed Tues. No lunch.*

LakeView Restaurant

$$$ | **AMERICAN** | **FAMILY** | Lake views keep this hotel restaurant bustling. And, yes: for now, LakeView is a breakfast-only restaurant. **Known for:** Mickey Mouse waffles; daily breakfast buffet; lakefront view. *Average main: $24 Wyndham*

Lake Buena Vista Resort, 1850 Hotel Plaza Blvd., Lake Buena Vista ☎ 407/828–4444 🌐 www.wyndhamlakebuenavista.com ⊗ No lunch or dinner.

Letterpress Cafe

$ | **AMERICAN** | **FAMILY** | Southern-style cooking is the highlight of the breakfast menu. High-end, Florida-sourced ingredients like Anson Mills grits and locally baked bread elevate the Letterpress Cafe above the ordinary hotel restaurant. **Known for:** Southern-style cooking; kettle soups; Belgian and buttermilk waffles. *[$] Average main: $13 ✉ Buena Vista Palace Hotel & Spa, 1900 E. Buena Vista Dr., Lake Buena Vista ☎ 866/397–6516 🌐 www.buenavistapalace.com ☞ Buffet breakfast only.*

The Venetian Chop House

$$$$ | **EUROPEAN** | This award-winning, fine-dining restaurant inside one of Lake Buena Vista's many convention hotels might have been designed as a place for execs on expense accounts to seal deals, but it has also become a haven for locals seeking an old-fashioned romantic retreat. The architecture alone—it looks like Renaissance Venice—is enough to lure you. **Known for:** black Angus beef; lobster bisque; romantic Italian decor. *[$] Average main: $40 ✉ Caribe Royale, 8101 World Center Dr., Lake Buena Vista ☎ 407/238–8060 🌐 www.cariberoyale.com ⊗ Closed Sun. and Mon. No lunch.*

Hotels

Several of the hotels on Hotel Plaza Boulevard within walking distance of Disney Springs are considered "official" hotels, so they have a few extra perks. Hotels just beyond the Disney Springs area tend to be less expensive than those right on Hotel Plaza Boulevard. If you're willing to take a 10-minute drive or shuttle ride, you might save as much as 35% off your room tab.

B Resort & Spa Disney Springs Resort Area

$$ | **RESORT** | **FAMILY** | Driving up Hotel Plaza Boulevard toward the Disney Springs complex, you'll come to this towering hotel whose chic and contemporary interior suggests it's designed solely for hip young couples, but families might be impressed by the offering as well. **Pros:** park shuttles, Extra Magic Hours; walk to Disney Springs; kids' activities. **Cons:** need a car to get to Universal or Downtown Orlando; daily parking fee $25; daily resort fee $32. *[$] Rooms from: $239 ✉ 1905 Hotel Plaza Blvd., Lake Buena Vista ☎ 407/828–2828 🌐 www.bhotelsandresorts.com/b-resort-and-spa 394 rooms 🍽 No Meals.*

Caribe Royale All-Suite Hotel & Convention Center

$$$ | **RESORT** | **FAMILY** | This big, pink, all-suites palace, on 53 tropical acres just 10 minutes from Disney, melds affordable prices with luxurious decor, business-traveler amenities, and family-friendly ingredients. **Pros:** scheduled shuttle to Disney; family-friendly; award-winning restaurant. **Cons:** daily $28 resort fee; $20 parking; no shuttle to Universal or SeaWorld; a hike to other shops and restaurants. *[$] Rooms from: $260 ✉ 8101 World Center Dr., Lake Buena Vista ☎ 407/238–8000, 800/823–8300 🌐 www.cariberoyale.com 1335 suites 🍽 No Meals.*

DoubleTree Suites by Hilton Orlando Disney Springs Area

$$ | **HOTEL** | **FAMILY** | Price and location make this all-suites, Hilton-owned hotel a good choice for families and business travelers, as there are amenities for both. **Pros:** access to Disney golf courses; within walking distance to Disney Springs; free Disney park shuttle, Extra Magic Hours. **Cons:** daily resort fee ($23) and parking fee ($22); inconvenient to Universal and Downtown Orlando; daily fee for Wi-Fi. *[$] Rooms from: $220 ✉ 2305 Hotel Plaza Blvd., Lake Buena Vista ☎ 407/934–1000, 800/222–8733 🌐 www.*

A
B
C
D
E
F
1
2
3
4
5
6
7
8
9
Lake Buena Vista and Celebration
Vista Boulevard
Epcot Center Drive
Disney Vacation Club Way
EPCOT
DISNEY SPRINGS
East Buena Vista Drive
Epcot Center Dr.
World Drive
DISNEY'S HOLLYWOOD STUDIOS
Chelonia Pkwy
Century Dr
Victory Way
Osceola Parkway
Bronson Highway
Southern Connector Extension (toll)
Celebration Ave.
CELEBRATION
417
4

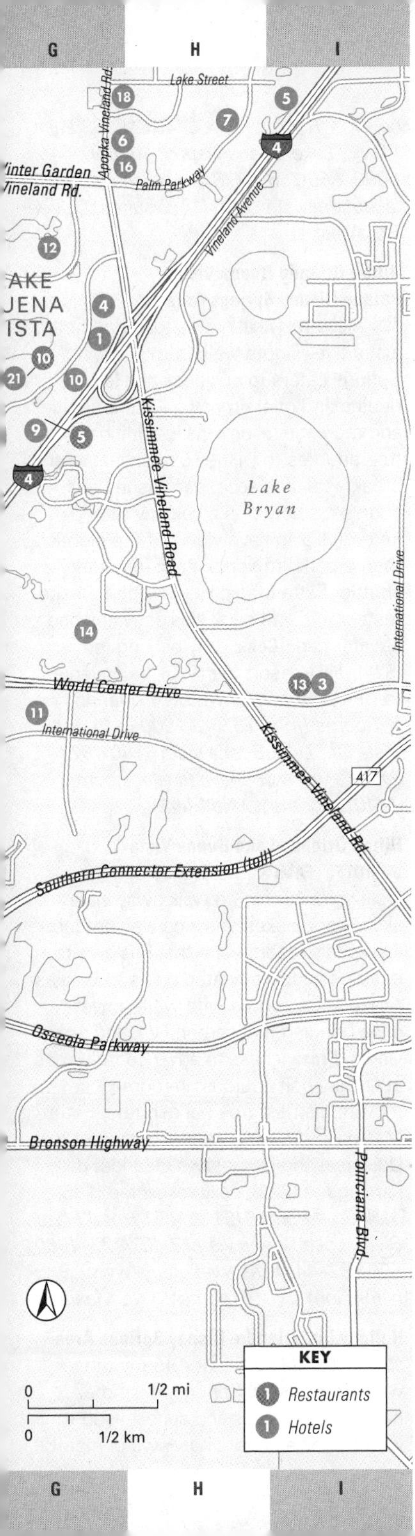

Restaurants ▼

1 Ari Celebration D9
2 Bull & Bear D5
3 Celebration Town Tavern D9
4 Columbia Restaurant D9
5 Covington Mill G3
6 deep blu Seafood Grille D4
7 Eleven Reunion Resort A9
8 La Luce D5
9 Lakeside Bar + Grill C9
10 LakeView Restaurant .. G2
11 Letterpress Cafe F2
12 360 American Bistro D8
13 The Venetian Chop House I4

Hotels ▼

1 B Resort & Spa Disney Springs Resort Area G2
2 Bohemian Hotel Celebration D9
3 Caribe Royale All-Suite Hotel & Convention Center I4
4 DoubleTree Suites by Hilton Orlando Disney Springs Area ... G2
5 Embassy Suites by Hilton Orlando Lake Buena Vista Resort I1
6 Fairfield Inn & Suites Orlando Lake Buena Vista H1
7 Hawthorn Suites by Wyndham Lake Buena Vista Orlando H1
8 Hilton Orlando Buena Vista Palace Disney Springs Area F2
9 Hilton Orlando Lake Buena Vista G3
10 Holiday Inn Orlando–Disney Springs Area ... G3
11 Holiday Inn Resorts Orlando Suites—Waterpark G5
12 Hyatt Regency Grand Cypress Resort G2
13 Meliá Orlando Suite Hotel at Celebration D8
14 Orlando World Center Marriott G4
15 Reunion Resort & Golf Club A9
16 Sheraton Lake Buena Vista Orlando Resort ... H1
17 Signia by Hilton Orlando Bonnet Creek D5
18 Sonesta ES Suites Lake Buena Vista G1
19 Waldorf Astoria Orlando D5
20 Wyndham Grand Orlando Resort, Bonnet Creek D4
21 Wyndham Lake Buena Vista Disney Springs Resort Area G2

doubletreeguestsuites.com *229 units* *No Meals.*

Embassy Suites by Hilton Orlando Lake Buena Vista Resort

$$$ | **HOTEL** | **FAMILY** | This Spanish-style all-suites hotel just off I–4 near Disney Springs offers a central location for park hoppers with a car and roomy accommodations with refrigerators and microwaves; there's also a heated pool with cabanas, a tennis court, and kids activities. **Pros:** free manager's cocktail reception; free shuttle to all Disney parks; free Wi-Fi. **Cons:** long walk to shops and restaurants; no shuttle to other parks; daily resort fee of $25 and $15 self-parking fee. *Rooms from: $269* *8100 Lake St., Lake Buena Vista* *407/239–1144, 800/257–8483, 800/362–2779* *www.embassysuites.com* *334 suites* *Free Breakfast.*

Fairfield Inn & Suites Orlando Lake Buena Vista

$$$ | **HOTEL** | **FAMILY** | Less than a mile from Disney Springs and within walking distance of a variety of restaurants and shops, this hotel has decent in-room amenities and an attractive budget price. **Pros:** free breakfast, free parking; refrigerators and microwaves in every room; free shuttle to Disney. **Cons:** no room service; small pool; no real on-site restaurant. *Rooms from: $250* *12191 S. Apopka Vineland Rd., Lake Buena Vista* *407/239–1115, 800/228–2800* *www.marriott.com* *170 rooms* *Free Breakfast.*

Hawthorn Suites by Wyndham Lake Buena Vista Orlando

$ | **RESORT** | **FAMILY** | A large, marble-columned lobby welcomes guests to this all-suites lodging less than a mile from Disney's door, and the amenities continue into the suites, most with a fully equipped kitchen, living room, and bedroom with multiple TVs. **Pros:** on public bus route; free breakfast and parking; free Wi-Fi. **Cons:** no free shuttles; no on-site restaurant; pool area can be noisy. *Rooms from: $149* *8303 Palm Pkwy., Lake Buena Vista* *407/597–5000, 866/756–3778* *www.hawthorn-lakebuenavista.com* *112 suites* *Free Breakfast.*

Hilton Orlando Buena Vista Palace Disney Springs Area

$$$ | **RESORT** | **FAMILY** | This towering hotel just a five-minute walk from Disney Springs caters to business and leisure guests and offers many on-site amenities and recreational options in addition to free shuttles to Disney parks, character breakfasts, and access to Disney golf courses; splurge on a balcony room, and you'll also have views of the nightly theme-park fireworks. **Pros:** free park shuttle, Extra Magic Hours; good on-site restaurants and bars; kids activities and a water park. **Cons:** daily parking fee ($24); daily resort fee ($35); inconvenient to Universal and Downtown Orlando. *Rooms from: $315* *1900 E. Buena Vista Dr., Lake Buena Vista* *407/827–2727* *www.buenavistapalace.com* *1012 rooms* *No Meals.*

Hilton Orlando Lake Buena Vista

$ | **HOTEL** | **FAMILY** | Its Disney Springs location (a 10-minute walk away via a skybridge) makes this a convenient family-friendly resort—one that has on-site eateries and two heated pools as well as relaxed, airy rooms with white duvet-style bedding, flat-screen TVs, and great views. **Pros:** access to advance tee times at Disney golf courses; in-room kids movies, games; free park shuttle, Extra Magic Hours. **Cons:** need a car to get to Universal and Downtown Orlando; daily parking fee ($24); daily resort fee ($35). *Rooms from: $151* *1751 Hotel Plaza Blvd., Lake Buena Vista* *407/827–4000, 800/782–4414 reservations* *www.hilton.com* *814 rooms* *No Meals.*

Holiday Inn Orlando–Disney Springs Area

$$ | **HOTEL** | **FAMILY** | Just a 15-minute walk from Disney Springs, this hotel has modern rooms and suites—some with balconies affording views of nightly

theme-park fireworks—that feature free Wi-Fi, flat-screen TVs, and mini-refrigerators. **Pros:** free park shuttle, Extra Magic Hours; free Wi-Fi, kids under 12 eat free; walking distance to Disney Springs. **Cons:** need a car to get to Orlando; daily resort fee ($35), parking fee ($20); no free shuttle to Universal or SeaWorld. *Rooms from: $239* ✉ *1805 Hotel Plaza Blvd., Lake Buena Vista* ☎ *407/828–8888, 888/465–4329* 🌐 *www.hiorlando.com* *323 rooms* *No Meals.*

Holiday Inn Resorts Orlando Suites—Waterpark

$ | RESORT | FAMILY | The six-story resort, formerly the Nickelodeon Hotel, is built around a colorful water park with slides, a splash bucket, and climbing zones. **Pros:** minigolf course and waterpark; kids eat breakfast and dinner free; theme-park shuttles included in resort fee. **Cons:** poolside rooms can be noisy; way too frenetic for folks without kids; daily resort fee ($49), parking fee ($15). *Rooms from: $132* ✉ *14500 Continental Gateway, Lake Buena Vista* ☎ *407/387–5437, 866/462–6425* 🌐 *www.ihg.com* *777 rooms* *Free Breakfast.*

★ Hyatt Regency Grand Cypress Resort

$$ | RESORT | FAMILY | Sitting amid 1,500 palm-filled acres just outside Disney's gate, this huge luxury resort has four golf courses, miles of trails, and a private lake with watercraft. **Pros:** shuttles to Disney Springs; elaborate spa; lots of recreation options, huge pool, golf courses, equestrian center, and good restaurants. **Cons:** lots of conventioneers; daily resort fee ($37) and parking fee ($25); need a car or taxi to get to Universal or Orlando. *Rooms from: $239* ✉ *1 Grand Cypress Blvd., Lake Buena Vista* ☎ *407/239–1234, 800/233–1234* 🌐 *www.hyatt.com* *779 rooms* *No Meals.*

Orlando World Center Marriott

$$ | RESORT | FAMILY | This luxury golf resort is one of Orlando's largest, catering to conventions and families (because of its proximity to Disney). **Pros:** Hawk's Landing Golf Course; full-service spa; wide variety of on-site eateries. **Cons:** nothing within walking distance; on-site restaurants have expense-account-size prices; daily resort fee ($30) and parking fee ($24). *Rooms from: $249* ✉ *8701 World Center Dr., Lake Buena Vista* ☎ *407/239–4200, 800/621–0638* 🌐 *www.marriottworldcenter.com* *2010 rooms* *No Meals.*

Sheraton Lake Buena Vista Orlando Resort

$ | RESORT | FAMILY | Conveniently situated near the the Disney Springs entrance to WDW, the hotel is a pool-centered oasis of cool; some guest rooms transform into family suites with a separate bedroom and bunk beds. **Pros:** waterslides for kids; Disney shuttles; on-site restaurants. **Cons:** on a busy commercial strip; daily resort fee ($24), parking fee ($22); relatively close to Disney Springs but a tad too far to walk in the summer heat (about 1 mile). *Rooms from: $166* ✉ *12205 S. Apopka Vineland Rd., Lake Buena Vista* ☎ *407/239–0444, 800/423–3297* 🌐 *www.marriott.com* *486 rooms* *No Meals.*

Signia by Hilton Orlando Bonnet Creek

$$$$ | RESORT | FAMILY | This hotel, surrounded by Walt Disney World, more than lives up to its next-door neighbor the Waldorf Astoria Orlando, with plenty of amenities, including a 3-acre lagoon pool with a lazy river, rooms with deluxe bedding and flat-screen TVs, family-friendly activities, a golf course, and transportation to Disney parks. **Pros:** next door to Waldorf and its amenities; serene setting, just moments from Disney by shuttle; access to Waldorf Astoria Golf Club. **Cons:** daily $45 resort fee; $29 daily parking fee; nothing within walking distance, so a car is helpful. *Rooms from: $400* ✉ *14100 Bonnet Creek Resort La., Bonnet Creek, Lake Buena Vista* ☎ *407/597–3600* 🌐 *www.hiltonbonnetcreek.com* *1009 rooms* *No Meals.*

Sonesta ES Suites Lake Buena Vista
$$ | **HOTEL** | **FAMILY** | Close to Disney, this pleasant all-suites hotel is the perfect home away from home for big families on small budgets; it's also only a few miles along Palm Parkway from SeaWorld, Universal, and even the airport, so the frenzy of I–4 can be avoided altogether. **Pros:** free Wi-Fi; fully equipped kitchens; free grab-and-go breakfast. **Cons:** pool and dining areas can be crowded; daily parking fee $15; no restaurant or shuttles. *Rooms from: $209* *8751 Suiteside Dr., Lake Buena Vista* *407/238–0777* *www.sonesta.com* *150 suites* *Free Breakfast.*

★ **Waldorf Astoria Orlando**
$$$$ | **RESORT** | Although it can't duplicate the famed original in New York City, this Waldorf echoes it with imagination and flair. **Pros:** great spa and Rees Jones–designed golf course; lavish and luxurious hotel; continuous transportation to Disney parks. **Cons:** $45 daily resort fee, $30 parking; if you can bear to leave your cabana, you'll need a car to see anything else in the area; pricey, but you knew that. *Rooms from: $663* *14200 Bonnet Creek Resort La., Bonnet Creek, Lake Buena Vista* *407/597–5500* *www.waldorfastoriaorlando.com* *328 rooms* *No Meals.*

Wyndham Grand Orlando Resort, Bonnet Creek
$$$ | **RESORT** | **FAMILY** | Despite being surrounded by Disney property, the lakeside locale of this family-friendly resort feels serene and remote, and generous accommodations, transportation to Disney parks, a full spa, access to Disney golf, five pools, and two lazy rivers offer diversions for everyone. **Pros:** pet friendly; practically in Mickey's lap; free shuttles to Disney parks. **Cons:** $27 parking fee; $35 daily resort fee; not convenient to Universal or Downtown Orlando. *Rooms from: $299* *14651 Chelonia Pkwy., Bonnet Creek, Lake Buena Vista* *407/390–2300* *www.wyndhamgrandorlando.com* *400 rooms* *No Meals.*

Wyndham Lake Buena Vista Disney Springs Resort Area
$$$ | **RESORT** | **FAMILY** | Any hotel within a skip and a hop of Disney Springs is a great draw, and one with a water-playground complex that can entice kids away from the Magic Kingdom during the midday heat is even better; deluxe bedding, large TVs, and Disney fireworks views are the icing on the cake. **Pros:** free shuttle to all Disney parks and attractions; good kids' programs; walk to Disney Springs. **Cons:** daily parking fee ($20); no shuttle to Universal and downtown Orlando; daily resort fee ($32). *Rooms from: $259* *1850 Hotel Plaza Blvd., Lake Buena Vista* *407/828–4444* *www.wyndhamlakebuenavista.com* *623 rooms* *No Meals.*

Activities

SPAS

★ **Blue Harmony**
SPAS | Infused with the colors of ocean and sky, this spa lives up to its name. Its signature treatment combines exfoliation with marine salt and oil, polishing with marine salt and lavender, and a massage based on Thai techniques. Body treatments use oil-infused seawater gels to add natural minerals to the skin, and they end with a cozy wrap and massage. Two of the eight treatment rooms are outdoors, and daily specials include the Marvelous Monday's complimentary enhancement and the Tuesday Two-fer, which combines massages and facials at a reduced rate. The serene relaxation lounge offers beverages and tea while you wait for your treatment. Bring the family, as the spa offers treatments for teens as well. *Wyndham Grand Orlando Resort Bonnet Creek, 14651 Chelonia Pkwy., Lake Buena Vista* *407/390–2442* *www.blueharmonyorlando.com.*

The Spa at Orlando World Center Marriott

SPAS | Finding the spa in this sprawling, multitower resort outside the entrance to Walt Disney World can be a challenge, but once you arrive, tranquility rules. Robes and slippers are provided in the locker rooms, but there are no private changing rooms, so, if you're modest, you must retreat to the bathroom or shower. The waiting room is co-ed. Steam rooms, a pool, and a fitness facility are available for use before or after a therapy in one of the 14 treatment rooms. The $135, hour-long, custom massage can include reflexology, deep tissue, prenatal, Swedish, stretching, and more. Gratuities are at your discretion. ✉ *Orlando World Center Marriott, 8701 World Center Dr., Lake Buena Vista* ☎ *407/238–8705* 🌐 *thespaatworldcenter.com.*

The Waldorf Astoria Spa

SPAS | In this spacious, 22-treatment-room spa, everything is designed for the hotel guest—not a coincidence, since they are the only ones privy to treatments. In your plush robe and slippers, you can flit from an experiential shower (it surrounds you with water, sound, and light) to a tea lounge. Try the Golden Body Treatment, a decadent, over-the-top process that incorporates gold-enriched creams to scrub and strengthen the skin for $185. The salon offers every service imaginable. A 20% service charge is added. ✉ *Waldorf Astoria Orlando, 14200 Bonnet Creek Resort La., Bonnet Creek, Lake Buena Vista* ☎ *407/597–5360* 🌐 *www.waldorfastoriaorlando.com* ☞ *Parking: valet only, complimentary with spa validation, but please tip.*

Celebration

3 miles southeast of WDW, 20 miles southwest of Downtown Orlando.

Walt Disney's original residential concept for EPCOT has emerged farther south with designer homes, beautiful lakeside diversions, and a small-town-feeling center. If you are acquainted with Seaside and some of the planned towns in Florida's Panhandle, this area will be familiar. There's also a hotel and several restaurants, so some guests visiting Walt Disney World base themselves here.

This community, where every blade of grass in every lawn seems perfect, is as picturesque as a movie set—although, to some critics, it would be one used in *The Stepford Wives*. But Celebration is a model of good American architecture and urban planning as well as a delightful place to spend a morning or afternoon.

Things appear nearly as faux as on Main Street, U.S.A., but as they unfold, you see signs of reality—and a pleasant one it is. Celebration is a real town, with its own hospital and school system. Houses and apartments spread out from the compact, restaurant-filled downtown area, which wraps around the edge of a lake. Sidewalks are built for strolling, restaurants have outdoor seating with lake views, and inviting shops beckon. After a walk around the lake, take youngsters over to the huge interactive fountain and have fun getting soaked.

The town has a year-round roster of special events and a noteworthy Sunday Farmers' Market. Starting the last Saturday in November and continuing through New Year's Eve, honest-to-goodness snow sprinkles softly down over Main Street every evening.

Celebration has a picture-perfect main street, and no wonder since it's a planned community designed by Disney.

Restaurants

The town's Market Street–area restaurants (predominately upscale) face a pastoral (though man-made) lake. To get here, take I–4 to Exit 64 (192) and follow the "Celebration" signs.

Ari Celebration

$$$ | **ASIAN FUSION** | **FAMILY** | This bright, modern restaurant serves fairly standard sushi rolls and an interesting range of hot dishes. Menu standouts include the bulgogi or shrimp bibimbap rice bowl. **Known for:** unusual roll combos; Japanese and Korean specialties; affordable lunch specials. *Average main: $22 671 Front St., Celebration 407/566–1889 www.arisushicelebration.com.*

Celebration Town Tavern

$$$ | **SEAFOOD** | **FAMILY** | Operated by a family with Boston roots, this New England–cuisine eatery has a double personality: the interior is a brass, glass, and dark-wood-paneling kind of place, while the outside patio has table seating plus the Paddy O' Bar. The food ranges from landlubber treats like baby back ribs, prime rib, and half-pound burgers (from $8) to exquisite seafood including Ipswich clams, lobster rolls, scrod, and 2-pound lobsters (all flown in from Boston), plus, on occasion, a salute to the Sunshine State with Florida stone crabs in season. **Known for:** steak scampi; 99-beer selection; fried Boston scrod. *Average main: $27 721 Front St., Celebration 407/566–2526 thecelebrationtowntavern.com Sunday brunch.*

★ Columbia Restaurant

$$$ | **LATIN AMERICAN** | **FAMILY** | Celebration's branch of this high-end, family-owned chain might be better than the original in Tampa, which has been operating for more than a century. For your main course, zero in on the paella—either *à la Valenciana* (with meat and seafood) or *campesina* ("farmer's" paella with beef, pork, chorizo, and chicken). **Known for:** paella à la Valenciana; oldest continuous restaurant chain in Florida; upscale Cuban cuisine. *Average main: $29 ✉ 649 Front St., Celebration ☎ 407/566–1505 🌐 columbiarestaurant.com.*

Eleven Reunion Resort

$$$ | **ECLECTIC** | Eleven, highly thought of in an area of town dominated by fast food and golf clubhouse eateries (including the ones at Reunion), features high-class small plates crafted around seafood from Maine and Florida, house-made charcuterie, and shareable dishes. The location high atop the resort affords panoramic views of still-forested Florida and, in the right weather, theme park fireworks 10 miles away. **Known for:** views of pristine Florida and theme park fireworks; well-crafted small plates and cocktails; Wagyu beef and New England mussels. *Average main: $25 ✉ 7593 Gathering Dr., Celebration ☎ 833/258–0472 🌐 www.reunionresort.com/dining ⏲ Closed Sun.–Wed. and Fri. (but check). No lunch.*

★ Lakeside Bar + Grill

$$$ | **ECLECTIC** | The menus at Kessler restaurants are always special. From waffles served with Grand Marnier syrup for breakfast to extravagant Saturday and Sunday brunch to tenderloin au poivre for dinner, the fare is sophisticated. **Known for:** generous servings for Bohemian brunch; sophisticated dinner creations; the famous Kessler calamari. *Average main: $24 ✉ Bohemian Hotel Celebration, 700 Bloom St., Celebration ☎ 407/566–6000 🌐 kesslercollection.com/lakeside-bar-grill.*

360 American Bistro

$$ | **AMERICAN** | **FAMILY** | A large and interesting selection of American dishes is served at breakfast and lunch, as well as, perhaps, an early dinner (as in before 6 pm). Offerings range from burgers and hand-tossed pizza to gator bites and frog legs. **Known for:** lobster Benedict breakfast; a quick bite before or after theme park visits; eclectic American menu. *Average main: $15 ✉ Meliá Orlando Celebration, 225 Celebration Place, Celebration ☎ 407/964–7676 🌐 melia.com/en/hotels/united-states/orlando ⏲ Closed weekends.*

Hotels

Celebration is immediately south of the Walt Disney World Resort, and although it's relatively close to the parks, the resorts in Lake Buena Vista, just east of Disney Springs, are closer to everything but Animal Kingdom.

Bohemian Hotel Celebration

$$$$ | **HOTEL** | **FAMILY** | Like everything in the Disney-created town of Celebration, this dog-friendly boutique hotel in the middle of the charming village borrows from the best of the 19th, 20th, and 21st centuries. **Pros:** transportation available to Celebration Golf and Fitness Center; Lakeside Bar & Grill has great high-end dining; rental bikes make touring the village a breeze. **Cons:** it's a long way to Universal; need a car (or ride share) to get anywhere other than Celebration; daily $16 fee for parking. *Rooms from: $389 ✉ 700 Bloom St., Celebration ☎ 407/566–6000, 888/249–4007 🌐 www.kesslercollection.com 115 rooms No Meals.*

Meliá Orlando Suite Hotel at Celebration

$$ | **HOTEL** | **FAMILY** | Much like a European boutique hotel, the Meliá Orlando is very human in scale and minimalist in decor; it also offers a bed-and-breakfast option and is only minutes from Disney. **Pros:** dog-friendly; shuttle to Celebration and Disney parks; spa privileges at Celebration Day Spa. **Cons:** need a car to visit Universal, SeaWorld, or Downtown Orlando; $20 daily resort fee; pool activities can be noisy. *Rooms from: $184 ✉ 225 Celebration Pl., Celebration ☎ 407/964–7000, 888/956–3542 🌐 www.melia.com 240 rooms No Meals.*

Reunion Resort & Golf Club

$$ | **RESORT** | **FAMILY** | Ten miles southwest of Disney and 45 minutes from LEGOLAND, this 2,300-acre resort with condo-style villas and estate-style houses contains three private golf courses—designed by Tom Watson, Arnold Palmer, and Jack Nicklaus—nine pools, a 5-acre water-park complex, a spa, and tennis courts. **Pros:** good on-site restaurants; shuttle to Disney; multiple pools and water park. **Cons:** need a car for Universal, SeaWorld, and Downtown Orlando; about a 10-mile drive to Disney parks; $35 daily resort fee, $25 parking. *Rooms from: $216 ✉ 7593 Gathering Dr., I–4 Exit 58, Reunion ☎ 407/396–3200, 866/880–8563 🌐 www.reunionresort.com 360 units No Meals.*

Chapter 9

UNIVERSAL ORLANDO

UNIVERSAL STUDIOS, ISLANDS OF ADVENTURE, VOLCANO BAY, CITYWALK

Updated by
Gary McKechnie

Sights	Restaurants	Hotels	Shopping	Nightlife
★★★★★	★★★★★	★★★★★	★★★★★	★★★★★

PARK SNAPSHOT

TOP EXPERIENCES

■ **CityWalk:** Strategically placed at the hub of both theme parks, this complex of shops, restaurants, nightclubs, and concert venues buzzes day and night (especially night).

■ **Hard Rock Live:** While it's not the most comfortable concert venue around (hard seats), Universal guests often arrive to find there's an A-list performer taking the stage that night.

■ **Harry Potter:** Not just one, but two lands based on J.K. Rowling's fantastical books and the characters she created have given Universal Orlando an enormous boost—and fans new worlds to explore.

■ Hollywood Rip, Ride Rockit: This weirdly beautiful structure begins with a vertical track that hoists you 170 feet straight up before plunging you into a series of wild twists, turns, loops, and rolls—all to a soundtrack of your choice.

■ **Incredible Hulk Coaster:** Although Universal loves to showcase its high-tech virtual-reality attractions, this super-fast and super-exciting roller coaster gets back to the basics.

PLANNING YOUR TIME

With two theme parks, a water park, and CityWalk, exploring this resort complex requires a strategy. On a first visit, prioritize Universal Studios. The original theme park, with such classic attractions as E.T.'s Adventure and more recent additions like The Bourne Stuntacular, merits a full day or two. If, however, time is short and Harry Potter is your main draw, then a one-day, two-park ticket will provide access to the Studios and Islands of Adventure—and both Harry Potter areas.

The parks are less crowded in February, May, and early October. Another dip in attendance happens between Thanksgiving and the days before Christmas.

GETTING HERE

■ Universal Orlando is midway between downtown Orlando and Walt Disney World, off I-4. From the interstate as well as bordering Kirkman Road, International Drive, and Sand Lake Road, well-marked signs point you toward two massive parking garages ($27) or, for an extra fee, valet parking, which puts you much closer to the park entrances.

■ It's even easier if you catch a ride here via taxi, Lyft, Uber, or a shuttle bus from your hotel since they can drop you off closer to the park entrance and without the parking premiums. Staying at a Universal resort hotel can also save you the parking fee and provides free transportation to the parks as well as (at some hotels) expedited admission into the attractions with the use of Universal Express.

VIEWFINDER

■ Given its theme, Volcano Bay is overflowing with photo ops that place you in the South Pacific. Stand on Waturi Beach, and use the towering volcano as a dramatic backdrop. Traveling with a friend or family? Have them ready to snap a shot as you plunge down a slide or float gently down the stream.

Universal Orlando's personality is revealed the moment you arrive in the theme parks, where music, cartoonish architecture, abundant eye candy, subtle and overt sound effects, whirling and whizzing rides, plus a throng of fellow travelers will follow you nearly everywhere (Hint: If you're a Universal resort hotel guest and crave some peace and quiet, set aside time to leave the park for a few hours of sanctuary in your room or by the pool).

At a breathless pace, there's a chance you *could* visit both Universal parks (Universal Studios and Islands of Adventure, aka IOA) in a single day, but to do that you'll have to invest in a Universal Express Pass to avoid spending lots of time waiting in lines at the premium attractions. It really is best to allow two days, or perhaps three; a day for each park plus a a day to either return to your favorite attractions or to visit Universal's Volcano Bay water park.

What are the main attractions? At Universal Studios, Revenge of the Mummy and The Simpsons are always popular; at IOA, the Incredible Hulk Coaster and the Amazing Adventures of Spider-Man are hits. At both parks, it's definitely the entire gamut of rides, shops, and restaurants in Harry Potter's Wizarding Worlds.

Universal Studios appeals primarily to those who like loud, fast, high-energy attractions—generally teens and adults. Covering 444 acres, it's a rambling montage of sets, shops, and soundstages housing theme attractions, as well as reproductions of New York, San Francisco, London, and the fictional town of Springfield.

When IOA first opened in 1999, it took attractions to a new level. Each section—from Marvel Super Hero Island to Toon Lagoon to Seuss Landing and the Lost Continent—was impressive enough to suggest that Universal had out-Disneyed Disney. And when the 20-acre Wizarding World of Harry Potter–Hogsmeade opened in 2010, IOA received well-deserved worldwide attention.

Universal Studios made another huge leap forward with the 2014 unveiling of a full-scale version of Diagon Alley, complete with Gringotts Bank and a magical train that departs for IOA from Platform 9¾. Knowing how Harry's cast a spell on generations of fans, Universal is always finding ways to expand the Potter magic with new angles, attractions, and shows so stay tuned.

In 2017, Universal completed a mammoth project that had earlier required them to buy Wet n' Wild, one of America's first and most innovative water parks, close it down, raze it, and then build the Endless Summer resort. Finding itself without a water park, Universal then got busy creating Volcano Bay, a richly detailed, South Pacific–style "aquatic theme park" just a short distance from Universal Studios and Islands of Adventure.

Planning

Admission

The per-person, per-day, single-park rate for either Universal Studios Florida or IOA changes throughout the year based on how busy the parks are. The least-expensive, one-day, one-park admission is $109 for an adult (i.e., ages 10 and up). Both multipark and multiday passes are available in an array of prices and combinations. Tickets for children under 10 are less expensive, and you save a bit of money (and avoid the painfully long lines at the ticket kiosks) if you order your tickets in advance online.

Contacts

Universal Orlando Resort: ☎ *407/363–8000* 🌐 *www.universalorlando.com.*

Universal (Loews Resorts) Room Reservations: ☎ *877/819–7884.*

Dining Plans

In 2021, Universal suspended its dining plans indefinitely. Because these plans do enable you to save some money by prepaying for in-park meals, it would be wise to check their status on the Universal Orlando website before visiting.

Express Passes

The Universal Express Pass takes you to the front of most lines and can save you a lot of time. The price for a standard one-park pass starts at around $80 in the off-season and climbs to around $140 during peak and holiday seasons. Keep in mind that the pass is for one use only at select attractions (new or unusually popular attractions may not honor it).

The more expensive "unlimited" pass, which takes you to the head of the line again and again and again, costs between $90 and $170 for a single park; a two-park unlimited pass surpasses $300 during the holidays. **■ TIP→ If you're a guest at one of Universal's premium hotels (Royal Pacific, Hard Rock, Portofino Bay), your room key serves as an unlimited Express Pass from the day you check in to the day you check out.**

For People with Disabilities

The *Studio Guide for Guests with Disabilities* (aka *Rider's Guide*) details attractions with special entrances and viewing areas, interpreters, Braille scripts, and assistance devices. In general, if you can transfer from your wheelchair unassisted or with the help of a friend, you can ride many attractions. Some rides have carts that accommodate manual wheelchairs, though not motorized wheelchairs or electronic convenience vehicles (ECVs).

Additional insights for guests with cognitive disabilities, prostheses, oxygen tanks/devices, and hearing/vision disabilities, as well as for those arriving with service animals, can be found on the Universal website (search for "accessibility").

Getting Here and Around

East on I–4 (from WDW and Tampa), exit at Universal Boulevard (75A); take a left into Universal Orlando, and follow the signs. Heading west on I–4 (from downtown or Daytona), exit at Universal Boulevard (74B), turn right, and follow Hollywood Way.

Both Universal Studios and IOA require a whole lot of serious walking. Use the parking area's moving walkways as much as possible. Arrive early at either park, and you might be able to complete a single lap that will get you to the main attractions.

At Volcano Bay, an early start is recommended for a few reasons, one of which is that you can pick a prime spot on the beach or arrange for a private cabana before the crowds arrive. Another is that, unless someone drops you off at the entrance, you'll have to park at the main parking structure and wait for a shuttle bus to transport you to the park. This, in turn, means that your arrival depends on the bus, as well as the number of guests waiting in line ahead of you.

Hours

Universal Studios and IOA are open 365 days a year, with opening/closing times that vary by the season (and, sometimes, by the week) but are typically from 9 am to 7 pm. Check online for the most accurate hours of each park and CityWalk. Note that some Universal resort hotel guests receive early admission.

Volcano Bay is generally open from 10 am to 5 pm during the winter and spring, with longer hours (say, 9 to 9) in summer. Note, too, that inclement weather can sometimes cause the park to close.

Parking

Universal's two garages total a whopping 3.4 million square feet. The Universal app has a feature that enables you to note your parking space. If you haven't downloaded the app, take a smartphone picture of your space.

The cost is a super steep $27 for cars and motorcycles (although it's free after 6 pm as a nod to guests arriving for the nightlife of CityWalk), $32 for RVs and buses, and $50 for "prime" parking, which puts you on a lower level closer to the entrance.

Although moving walkways get you partway, you could walk up to a ½ mile to reach the gates, which explains why some guests opt for valet parking ($27 for up to two hours, $75 for more than two hours), which literally puts them at the entrance to CityWalk and near the park turnstiles.

Universal Studios

Inspired by the California original and opened in Orlando in 1990 (when the city assumed it would become "Hollywood East"), Universal Studios was meant to celebrate the movies. Like the back-lot sets at a film studio, the park is a jumble of areas and attractions makes navigating a challenge, but the payoff is the opportunity to immerse yourself in this highly creative take on motion picture magic.

The first area past the entrance is Production Central, where large soundstages house attractions based on TV programs and films like *Shrek, Despicable Me,* and *The Transformers.* Because it's right near the entrance, it can be the park's most crowded area.

Past Production Central is New York. Nearly every studio has its own Big Apple sets, and Universal is no exception. A cleverly constructed collection of sparkling public buildings, well-worn neighborhoods, and back alleys is the next-best thing to Manhattan itself (but not even NYC has Revenge of the Mummy or a Jimmy Fallon virtual-reality ride).

Subtle changes in architecture and design tell you you're entering San Francisco, home of Fast & Furious: Supercharged. This is a nice area to pause for a bite, and you'll find places for burgers, pastries, and candy as well as table-service meals at the waterfront Lombard's Seafood Grille.

You'll next reach the land adored by wizards and muggles alike—the Wizarding World of Harry Potter: Diagon Alley. What the books describe and what filmmakers created, Universal has replicated in great detail, immersing you in this fantastic world.

Just ahead, World Expo features a single attraction—MEN IN BLACK: Alien Attack, a futuristic experience that's the polar opposite of neighboring Springfield: Home of the Simpsons, which is perhaps the park's most visually dynamic area. Its next door neighbor, Woody Woodpecker's KidZone, offers colorful attractions designed for the under-10 crowd, including toddlers, with diversions that include a junior-sized roller coaster, a mini–water park, and a chance to meet E.T.

Although the quiet parks, theme restaurants, and facades of flashy Rodeo Drive are truly appealing, Hollywood also has a few standout attractions, including Universal Orlando's Horror Make Up Show and the Bourne Stuntacular. By the time you've circled the park, you really will feel that Universal has put you in the movies.

GETTING ORIENTED

On a map, the park appears neatly divided into eight areas positioned around a huge lagoon. First, there's Production Central, which covers the entire left side of the Plaza of the Stars. This is followed by New York, with rides and street performances; San Francisco and its prime attraction, Fast & Furious: Supercharged; the streets of London that lead to the Wizarding World of Harry Potter: Diagon Alley; the futuristic World Expo; Homer and Bart's hometown of Springfield; Woody Woodpecker's KidZone; and, finally, Hollywood.

What's tricky is that—because it's designed like a series of movie sets with side streets, city blocks, and alleyways—it's a hodgepodge of disparate scenes so there's no straightforward way to tackle the park. You'll probably make some detours and do some backtracking.

PARK AMENITIES

Baby Care: There are diaper-changing stations in many of the men's and women's restrooms, and a nursing station offers comfort and privacy at the park's first-aid station near the entrance. Baby supplies (diapers, food, wipes, and so on) are available at larger stores; ask for them at the counter, though, as they're not displayed on shelves.

Photos: Just inside the main entrance, On Location was primarily a camera and film shop before cameras and film were condensed into smartphones. Nowadays, the shelves are stocked with gifts, sunglasses, hats, souvenirs, and drinks. Staffers here also assist guests with souvenir photos taken by Universal's squad of photographers.

First Aid: There are two first-aid centers—one just inside the turnstiles, to the right near the Studio Audience Center, and another around the corner from Louie's Italian Restaurant in New York.

Guest Services (aka Guest Relations): You can get strategic advice *before* visiting the park by calling Guest Services at ☎ *407/224–4233.*

Lockers: Daily rates for lockers near the park entrance are $12 for a small unit and $15 for a larger one. There are free lockers near the entrances of some high-speed attractions (such as MEN

Save the planet from interstellar invaders in World Expo's interactive MEN IN BLACK: Alien Attack. Zap aliens in city streets and compete with other guests to score points.

IN BLACK: Alien Attack and Revenge of the Mummy), where you can stash your stuff before your ride. Those lockers are available to you for up to 90 minutes.

Lost People and Things: If you plan to split up, be sure everyone knows where and when to reconnect. Staffers take lost children to Guest Services near the main entrance. This is also where you might find lost personal items.

Services for People with Disabilities: Universal has made it as easy as possible for guests with disabilities to enjoy the park. It starts when you arrive in the parking garage and extends to guide-books with icons indicating which shows feature sign-language interpreters. Other services include special viewing areas for people in wheelchairs, automatic doors, well-equipped restrooms, and walking areas for service animals. Be sure to pick up the *Studio Guide for Guests with Disabilities* (aka *Rider's Guide*), which is full of details on equipment and other services.

Guest Services (near the entrance just outside and inside the park) is the place to pick up assisted-listening and other devices, such as clickers that trigger closed-captioning. You can rent manual wheelchairs ($15 per day) at the parking garages and inside the main entrance. Because there are limited quantities of ECVs (available in the park for $65), reserve one in advance. A photo ID and a $50 deposit on a credit card are required for wheelchairs. ECVs with a sunshade canopy are $85 per day.

Accessibility information is posted at each attraction. Note that although ride lines can accommodate standard wheelchairs, often you'll be ushered into a waiting area while the rest of your party goes through the line. Many shows have seating to accommodate manual wheel-chairs, but, in general, you'll have to transfer from your chair to ride vehicles.

For hearing-impaired guests, captioning, assisted-listening, and/or ASL inter-preters are available at Despicable Me, Shrek, MEN IN BLACK: Alien Attack,

Transformers: The Ride 3-D, and Animal Actors.

Stroller Rentals: Just inside the main entrance, there are double strollers for $35 a day.

SHOPPING

Sprinkled throughout the park, amid its massive soundstages and busy streets, are kiosks, shops, and department stores. The largest concentration is near the park entrance, around Production Central and Hollywood. The Universal Studios Store—at the nexus of the two areas—offers one-stop shopping, with items from the Studios and some merchandise from IOA's most popular attractions. The busiest shops, though, are those in the Wizarding World of Harry Potter: Diagon Alley.

TOURS

VIP Tours

GUIDED TOURS | **FAMILY** | Universal has several VIP tours that are worthwhile if you're in a hurry, if crowds are heavy, if you're with a large group—and if you have the money to burn. The tours include extras like front-of-the-line access, plus breakfast and lunch. You can also arrange for priority restaurant seating, bilingual guides, gift bags, refreshments at check-in, wheelchairs, strollers, and valet parking. You must book these tours at least 48 hours in advance by phone or online. Prices cited here do not include sales tax or, more important, park admission. Also, tour prices vary by season, so consider these just estimated costs.

Nonexclusive one-day tours (i.e., you'll tour with other park guests) cost $189 per person for one park (five hours) and visit a minimum of eight major attractions. The cost goes up to $199 per person for a two-park, seven-hour tour. Then there are exclusive tours for your group only. If you're traveling with up to 10 people, consider splitting the cost of an eight-hour customized tour, which includes a sit-down breakfast, lunch, and dinner at the park of your choice. The private VIP tour starts at $3,099 plus tax for a group of five, plus an extra $350 for each additional person. ✉ *Orlando* ☎ *866/346–9350* 🌐 *www.universalorlando.com.*

VISITING TIPS

Buy tickets in advance. Tickets cost a bit less online and buying ahead gives you time (far more than you'd have at the entrance!) to consider the many options. Also, if you find the array of ticket options confusing, call Universal for advice before you spend a dime. Staffers can help you make an informed decision by explaining the various ticket packages.

Map out a route. Spend a few minutes studying the park layout, either on the Universal app or a map that you pick up in the entryway to CityWalk or by the park turnstiles. One tip: upon entering, avoid the temptation to go straight toward the towering soundstages and loop the park clockwise. Instead, head to the right—bypassing shops, restaurants, and some crowds to primary attractions like the Bourne Stuntacular, The Simpsons Ride, and MEN IN BLACK: Alien Attack.

Optimize your photo ops. Signs indicating photo spots also offer advice on how best to frame your shot.

Pick a rendezvous point. Good meeting spots include the Hello Kitty shop near the entrance; Mel's Drive-In, which is roughly in the center of the park at the top of the lagoon; or the purple triple-decker Knight Bus in the Wizarding World of Harry Potter.

Hollywood

This area to the right of the park entrance celebrates the Golden Age of Hollywood and is truly the quintessential tribute to the Silver Screen.

Sights

★ Bourne Stuntacular

PERFORMANCE VENUE | **FAMILY** | While it may be a hard claim to qualify, this certainly *appears* to be the most exciting indoor stunt show in America. Following an eight-minute preshow that fills you in on the backstory (an assassin trained in a secret government program has gone off-script and eluded his handlers), what ensues is an international chase that takes place with live actors and right before your eyes. Against a series of dazzling, always-in-motion film backdrops you follow Bourne around the world as he eludes his pursuers. From the Middle East to the middle of the desert to Washington, D.C. and other capitals, Bourne is running, racing cars, and riding motorcycles to stay alive. The widescreen images, the rapid pace, and the constant adrenaline will keep you on the edge of your seat throughout the solid 20-minute show. ■ **TIP→ This attraction accepts Universal Express Pass.** ✉ *Hollywood, Universal Studios* ☞ *Duration: 20 mins. Crowds: Moderate to Heavy. Audience: Not small kids.*

Universal Orlando's Horror Make-Up Show

PERFORMANCE VENUE | **FAMILY** | The show begins in an intriguingly creepy pre-show area where masks, props, and rubber skeletons from classic and contemporary horror films and tributes to great makeup artists like Lon Chaney, Rick Baker, and Jack Pierce make a great backdrop for a horrifying family photo. Inside the theater, your host brings out a special-effects expert who describes and shares some secrets about what goes into (and oozes out of) creepy movie effects (e.g., corn syrup and food coloring make for a dandy blood substitute).

Older children, in particular, eat up the blood-and-guts stories. But despite the potentially frightening topic, most audiences get a kick out of the show, because the subject is handled with an extraordinary amount of dead-on humor, including one-liners delivered with comedy-club timing. **For people with disabilities:** The theater is wheelchair accessible. Good scripts and good shtick mean that those with visual impairments can enjoy the show. ■ **TIP→ If busy, use Express Pass, or come in the afternoon or evening. Arrive about 15 minutes before showtime (doors close immediately after show starts).** ✉ *Hollywood, Universal Studios* ☞ *Duration: 25 mins. Crowds: Light. Audience: Not small kids.*

Restaurants

Mel's Drive-In

$ | **AMERICAN** | **FAMILY** | At the corner of Hollywood and Vine is a flashy 1950s-style eatery with a pink-and-white, 1956 Ford Crown Victoria parked out in front. Thanks to its location and look, this is one of the most popular choices in the park, so you might have to brave crowds for an extra-thick shake or an order of the decadent chili-cheese fries. **Known for:** frosty milk shakes and grilled burgers; drive-in styling; live entertainment. $ *Average main: $13* ✉ *Hollywood, Universal Studios* ☎ *407/363–8766* 🌐 *www.universalorlando.com.*

Coffee and Quick Bites

Food segments are an integral part of talk morning shows, and that sets the stage for the **TODAY Cafe**—modeled after the *Today* show's familiar Studio 1-A—across from the Universal Studios Store. Step into the set and grab a quick meal of baked goods, freshly prepared salads, healthy sandwiches, specialty coffees, beer, and wine.

In the heart of Hollywood, **Schwab's Pharmacy** is a re-creation of the legendary drugstore where—studio publicists claim—Lana Turner was discovered. What you'll discover is a place to order soda-fountain treats like milk shakes, sundaes, banana splits, and hand-dipped ice cream. The

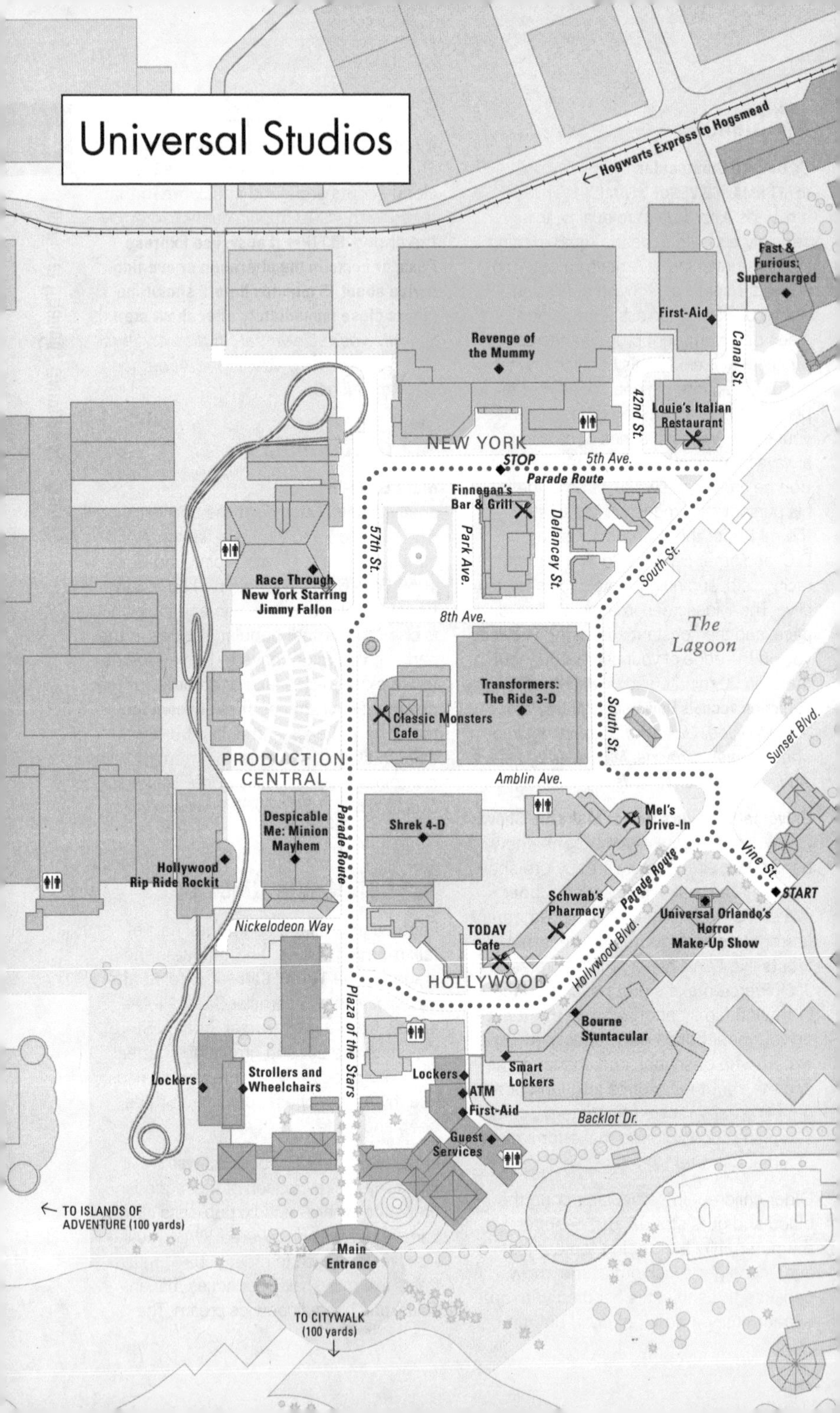
Universal Studios
← Hogwarts Express to Hogsmead
Fast & Furious: Supercharged
First-Aid
Canal St.
Revenge of the Mummy
42nd St.
Louie's Italian Restaurant
NEW YORK
STOP
5th Ave.
Parade Route
Finnegan's Bar & Grill
57th St.
Park Ave.
Delancey St.
South St.
Race Through New York Starring Jimmy Fallon
8th Ave.
The Lagoon
Transformers: The Ride 3-D
Classic Monsters Cafe
South St.
Sunset Blvd.
PRODUCTION CENTRAL
Amblin Ave.
Despicable Me: Minion Mayhem
Parade Route
Shrek 4-D
Mel's Drive-In
Hollywood Rip Ride Rockit
Vine St.
START
Schwab's Pharmacy
Parade Route
Universal Orlando's Horror Make-Up Show
Nickelodeon Way
TODAY Cafe
Hollywood Blvd.
HOLLYWOOD
Plaza of the Stars
Bourne Stuntacular
Smart Lockers
Lockers
Strollers and Wheelchairs
Lockers
ATM
First-Aid
Backlot Dr.
Guest Services
← TO ISLANDS OF ADVENTURE (100 yards)
Main Entrance
TO CITYWALK (100 yards)

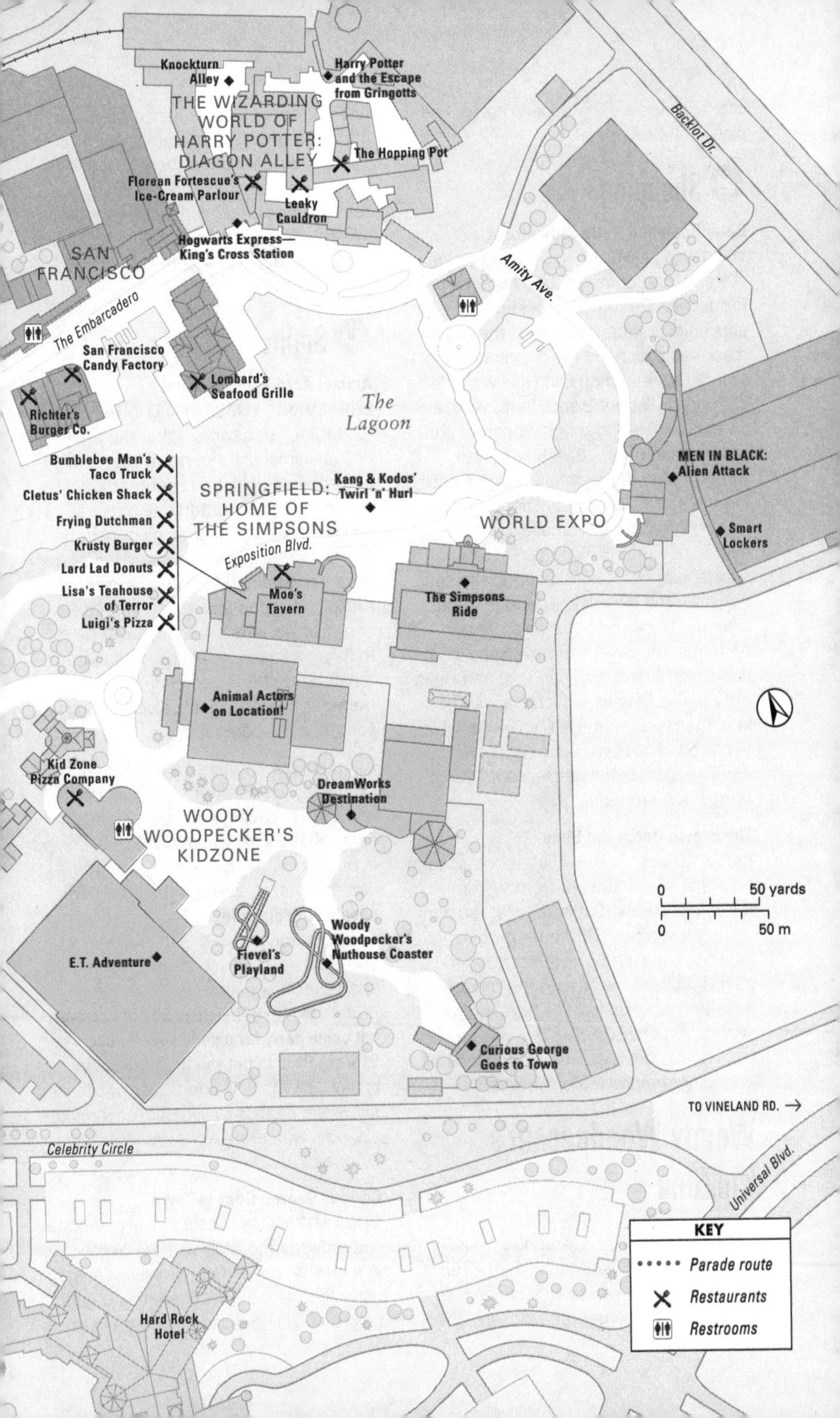

Knockturn Alley
Harry Potter and the Escape from Gringotts
THE WIZARDING WORLD OF HARRY POTTER: DIAGON ALLEY
The Hopping Pot
Florean Fortescue's Ice-Cream Parlour
Leaky Cauldron
Hogwarts Express—King's Cross Station
Backlot Dr.
SAN FRANCISCO
Amity Ave.
The Embarcadero
San Francisco Candy Factory
Lombard's Seafood Grille
Richter's Burger Co.
The Lagoon
Bumblebee Man's Taco Truck
Cletus' Chicken Shack
Frying Dutchman
Krusty Burger
Lard Lad Donuts
Lisa's Teahouse of Terror
Luigi's Pizza
SPRINGFIELD: HOME OF THE SIMPSONS
Kang & Kodos' Twirl 'n' Hurl
MEN IN BLACK: Alien Attack
WORLD EXPO
Smart Lockers
Exposition Blvd.
Moe's Tavern
The Simpsons Ride
Animal Actors on Location!
Kid Zone Pizza Company
DreamWorks Destination
WOODY WOODPECKER'S KIDZONE
0
50 yards
0
50 m
Woody Woodpecker's Nuthouse Coaster
Fievel's Playland
E.T. Adventure
Curious George Goes to Town
TO VINELAND RD. →
Celebrity Circle
Universal Blvd.
Hard Rock Hotel
KEY
Parade route
Restaurants
Restrooms

catch? Hours are limited, and it might be closed off-season.

Shopping

Betty Boop and Hello Kitty Stores

SOUVENIRS | FAMILY | These side-by-side stores at the corner of Hollywood and Production Central are packed with souvenirs celebrating two of the most marketable icons in the merchandising world. Representing Old Hollywood is cartoonish flapper Betty Boop, whose image is affixed to mugs, apparel, gifts, jewelry, and other collectibles. Walk through the rainbow archway connecting the stores to find similar souvenirs celebrating the internationally popular (and supercute) Hello Kitty. There's no shortage of choices, with specialty sections like the Hello Kitty Lounge (robes, slippers, toys, and other pajama-party items); the Sweet Yummy Shop's cupcakes, fudge, and candies; and Hello Kitty at the Movies, which places Kitty in some classic films. ✉ *Hollywood, Universal Studios* 🌐 *www.universalorlando.com/web/en/us/things-to-do/shopping/betty-boop-store-usf.*

The Brown Derby Hat Shop

HATS & GLOVES | FAMILY | Felt fedoras, bush hats that seem straight from wardrobe for *Jurassic Park,* Cat in the Hat red-and-white stovepipes, Duff beer mug hats, baseball caps, and colorful cartoon-inspired toppers are among the many novelty chapeaux for sale here. ✉ *Hollywood, Universal Studios* 🌐 *www.universalorlando.com/web/en/us/things-to-do/shopping/the-brown-derby-hat-shop.*

Woody Woodpecker's KidZone

Colorful rides, shows, and play areas cater to preschoolers in this pint-sized Promised Land, where kids can try out a roller coaster and get sprayed, splashed, and soaked in a water-park area. Surprisingly, this area is also a great place for parents, since it gives them a needed break after nearly circling the park. Just turn the kids loose and catch your breath. All shows and attractions except Curious George and Fievel accept Universal Express Pass.

Sights

Animal Actors on Location!

PERFORMANCE VENUE | FAMILY | The tricks (or, rather, "behaviors") that the arkful of live animal stars perform are mostly audience-participation segments, which makes this show entertaining for young and old alike. Birds, cats, pigs, parrots, otters, ducks, dogs, hawks, and a skunk have been trained to portray a range of thespian actions that are woven into a series of vignettes, from a clever parrot that has a knack for plucking cash from the outstretched hand of an audience member to a dog that is a convincing actor in a melodrama.

Although the line-up of animals and the scenes they perform might vary, the show's fast pacing and variety make it seem that you're watching several shows in one. Enjoy it! These are some of the cutest actors ever to hit the stage. **For people with disabilities:** The theater is equipped for assisted-listening devices and is wheelchair accessible. Some shows include a sign language interpreter. **■ TIP→ There's plenty of seating, but come early for a good seat, or use Express Pass to get you in ahead of the crowd.** ✉ *Woody Woodpecker's KidZone, Universal Studios* ☞ *Duration: 20 mins. Crowds: Moderate to heavy. Audience: All ages.*

Curious George Goes to Town

OTHER ATTRACTION | FAMILY | The celebrated simian visits the Man with the Yellow Hat in a no-line, no-waiting, small-scale water park. The main town square has brightly colored building facades, and the plaza is an interactive aqua playground that adults avoid but kids are drawn to like fish to water. Yes, there's water, water everywhere, especially atop the clock tower, which periodically dumps a mighty 500 gallons down a roof and straight onto a screaming herd of preschoolers. Kids love the levers, valves, pumps, and hoses that gush at the rate of 200 gallons per minute, letting them get sprayed, spritzed, splashed, and splattered.

At the head of the square, footprints lead to a dry play area, with a rope climb and a ball cage where youngsters can frolic among thousands of foam balls. You can get into the act, sit it out on nearby benches, or take a few minutes to buy souvenir towels to dry off your waterlogged kids. **For people with disabilities:** Most of this attraction is barrier-free. **■ TIP→ Crowds are heavy midmorning: come in late afternoon or early evening—especially in the summertime. Kids will get drenched; so stash a bathing suit or change of clothing in a nearby locker.** ✉ *Woody Woodpecker's KidZone, Universal Studios* ☞ *Duration: Up to you. Crowds: Moderate to heavy. Audience: Small kids.*

DreamWorks Destination

PERFORMANCE VENUE | FAMILY | Taking over the venue once occupied by Barney the Dinosaur, this character experience features many of the stars of DreamWorks' animated features. Anyone who's seen *Kung Fu Panda, Madagascar,* or *Trolls* will be thrilled when they enter the theater in the round, which is festively decorated and illuminated to give it a bright party atmosphere. Guests sit around an elevated stage where an emcee begins by welcoming larger-than-life characters who are joined by extremely energetic dancers performing to soundtrack songs. During the finale, guests can join in on a dance party and spend time taking pictures with their favorite characters. For adults: it's a treat for the kids. For kids: it may make them feel like adults would if they scored backstage passes to a McCartney concert. ✉ *Woody Woodpecker's KidZone, Universal Studios* ☞ *Duration: Three different character sets every 20 minutes. Crowds: Light to moderate. Audience: Small kids.*

E.T. Adventure

AMUSEMENT RIDE | FAMILY | This well-meaning, circa 1990, ride is looking (and even smelling) a little tired, although you might still get a kick out of the take on Steven Spielberg's *E.T.* Once Spielberg himself advises you that it's your mission to help E.T. return to his planet, you board a bicycle mounted on a movable platform and fly 3 million light years from Earth, past a squadron of policemen and FBI agents, to reach E.T.'s home. Here colorful characters climb on vines, play xylophones, and swing on branches in what looks like an alien Burning Man festival. Listen very closely for the payoff: having given your name to a host at the start of the ride, E.T. is supposed to bid you a personalized good-bye.

This ride isn't suitable for guests with heart, back, neck, or motion-sickness problems. **For people with disabilities:** Guests with mobility issues must be in a standard-size wheelchair or transfer to a ride vehicle. Service animals aren't permitted. There's some sudden tilting and accelerating, but those for whom these movements are a concern can ride in E.T.'s orbs (spaceships) instead of on the flying bicycles. **■ TIP→ Use Universal Express Pass, or come early.** ✉ *Woody Woodpecker's KidZone, Universal Studios* ☞ *Duration: 5 mins. Crowds: Moderate to heavy. Audience: All ages. Height requirement: 34 inches.*

Fievel's Playland

OTHER ATTRACTION | FAMILY | Based on the Spielberg animated film *An American Tail,* this playground features larger-than-life props and sets designed to make everyone feel mouse-size, with an ingenious collection of massive boots, cans, and other ordinary objects. Here you'll find tunnel slides, water play areas, and ball

Universal Studios Grown-Up Tour

The genius here is in the details, so take your time, and notice the secondhand items in the windows of New York shops, for instance, or the cable-car tracks running through San Francisco.

South Side

Upon entering, don't head straight into Production Central; instead, turn right—onto Rodeo Drive. In a few steps, you're in the heart of Hollywood, where the first attraction you'll pass is the **Bourne Stuntacular**, a live-action stunt show. If you're tempted to stop for a soda at Schwab's or a burger at Mel's, try to schedule your meal in time to catch **Universal Orlando's Horror Make-Up Show** just down the street. As you continue past the lovely Garden of Allah bungalows (that look as if they were actually moved from Tinseltown), you'll see the entrance to Woody Woodpecker's KidZone, which most adults will be happy to skip.

After this, it's Springfield: Home of the Simpsons. Although **The Simpsons Ride** is a thrill, so is the amazing pop art that sets the stage for it. The facade is decorated like a carnival, with games of chance bordering the towering face of Krusty the Clown. Watch for the kiosk that sells Squishees ("America's favorite icy goo"), and take your time along Fast Food Boulevard where you'll have plenty of food ops—and photo ops—including Lard Lad (of doughnut fame), Moe's Tavern, and Bumblebee Man's taco truck. Really.

North Side

The facade of this park's Wizarding World looks like a fashionable London district, but watch for the broken brick wall that masks the entrance to **Diagon Alley**, a complete re-creation of Harry Potter's world.

Cobblestone streets, redbrick buildings, and a waterfront inspired by Fisherman's Wharf create San Francisco, which is home to the full-throttled attraction, **Fast & Furious: Supercharged.**

With narrow alleys, fire escapes, a Chinese laundry, pawnshops, secondhand stores, offices, Italian restaurants, and an Irish pub, New York captures the character of nearly every borough. Round a corner, and you'll even see the Guggenheim Museum. It's an amazing assemblage, with clever signage, props, effects, and attractions like **Revenge of the Mummy** and **Race Through New York Starring Jimmy Fallon.**

Completing the circle, you'll arrive in Production Central, where several blocks of soundstages present attractions that bring movies and television to life.

crawls, as well as a gigantic net-climb equipped with tubes, ladders, and rope bridges. A harmonica slide plays music when you slide along the openings, and a 200-foot waterslide gives kids (and a parent if so desired) a chance to swoop down in Fievel's signature sardine can. It should keep the kids entertained for hours. The downside? You might have to build one of these for your backyard when you get home. **For people with disabilities:** Unfortunately, this attraction isn't fully accessible to people using wheelchairs, although an elevator can transport wheelchairs to the top of the waterslide. **■ TIP→ On hot days, come after supper to avoid waits for the waterslide. Kids will get drenched; stash a bathing suit or change**

of clothing in a nearby locker. ✉ *Woody Woodpecker's KidZone, Universal Studios* ☞ *Duration: Up to you. Crowds: Light to moderate. Audience: Small kids.*

Woody Woodpecker's Nuthouse Coaster
AMUSEMENT RIDE | FAMILY | Unlike the maniacal coasters that put you through zero-g rolls and inversions, this is a low-speed, mild-thrill version (top speed 22 mph) that makes it a safe bet for younger kids and action-phobic adults. It races (a relative term) through a structure that looks like a gadget-filled factory; the cars are shipping crates—some labeled "mixed nuts," others "salted nuts," and some tagged "certifiably nuts." Children generally love this low-level introduction to thrill rides (which is duplicated at Flight of the Hippogriff at the Wizarding World of Harry Potter). **For people with disabilities:** Guests using wheelchairs must transfer to a ride vehicle. **■ TIP→ Use Express Pass and/or come at park closing, when most little ones have gone home.** ✉ *Woody Woodpecker's KidZone, Universal Studios* ☞ *Duration: 1½ mins. Crowds: Moderate to heavy. Audience: Small kids. Height requirements: 36 inches.*

Coffee and Quick Bites

For pizza—by the slice or a whole pie—head to the quick-service **KidZone Pizza Company,** situated between E.T. Adventure and Animal Actors on Location!

Shopping

SpongeBob StorePants
SOUVENIRS | FAMILY | With its cartoonish nautical theme (pink jellyfish overhead, a pineapple home in the middle of the store), this silly shop will have you stocking up on weird, fascinating SpongeBob merchandise from mugs to shorts to swimwear. ✉ *Woody Woodpecker's KidZone, Universal Studios* 🌐 *www.universalorlando.com/web/en/us/things-to-do/shopping/spongebob-storepants.*

Springfield: Home of the Simpsons

One of television's longest-running shows inspired one of the park's most enjoyable lands. This strangely surreal yet familiar small town is filled with landmarks you'd recognize, from Moe's Tavern to the towering Lard Lad of doughnut fame. The two primary attractions—The Simpsons Ride and Kang & Kodos' Twirl 'n' Hurl—accept the fast-access Universal Express Pass.

Sights

Kang & Kodos' Twirl 'n' Hurl
AMUSEMENT RIDE | FAMILY | This ride is inspired by the intergalactic creatures that make an occasional appearance in Springfield. About a dozen flying saucers encircle a towering statue of Kang (or Kodos), the one-eyed, fang-toothed, octopus-tentacled alien. Once you've climbed into your saucer, the spinning ride takes flight and whirls you and your co-pilot around Kang (or Kodos). Kids who love the opportunity to take the controls raise and lower the craft in hopes of avoiding the jets of water shot from surrounding poles. It's a pleasing, fun, low-thrill ride. **■ TIP→ This attraction accepts Express Pass.** ✉ *Springfield: Home of the Simpsons, Universal Studios* ☞ *Duration: 3 mins. Crowds: Light to medium. Audience: Small kids and up.*

★ The Simpsons Ride
AMUSEMENT RIDE | FAMILY | As you enter this ride through Krusty the Clown's gaping mouth, and then receive a video greeting by citizens of Springfield, police chief Clancy Wiggum reminds you that if you must get sick, do it in your hat—and thus the tone is set for your arrival in one of television's most popular animated

One of the most popular areas of Universal Studios (after The Wizarding World of Harry Potter) is Springfield: Home of the Simpsons.

communities. The preshow explains that Krusty has expanded his empire to include a theme park, which his disgruntled former sidekick, Sideshow Bob, plans to sabotage. After a fairly tame start, your virtual car soars through virtual Springfield, plunging toward familiar businesses and buildings and narrowly escaping disaster as Sideshow Bob tears up the tracks and sends you racing through wild scenes in a variety of locations such as Disney, SeaWorld—and hell. Several times you're saved by the split-second timing of an unexpected hero.

If you have even a scintilla of motion sickness, this one will throw you for a colorful, cartoonish loop. Guests who are pregnant or who have heart, back, or neck problems shouldn't ride. **For people with disabilities:** Guests in wheelchairs must transfer to a ride vehicle. **■ TIP→ Use Express Pass.** ✉ *Springfield: Home of the Simpsons, Universal Studios* ☞ *Duration: 6 mins. Crowds: Heavy. Audience: Not small kids. Height requirement: 40 inches minimum; under 48 inches must ride with an adult.*

Coffee and Quick Bites

Near The Simpsons Ride, Fast Food Boulevard has several Springfield-inspired, quick-service eateries, including **Bumblebee Man's Taco Truck** (Mexican); **Cletus' Chicken Shack** (chicken sandwiches, platters); **Frying Dutchman** (fried seafood); **Krusty Burger** (hamburgers, hot dogs); **Lard Lad Donuts** (pastries, sweets); **Lisa's Teahouse of Terror** (salads, wraps, sandwiches); and **Luigi's Pizza** (pizza, sandwiches, salads).

Want a cold one? Drop by **Moe's Tavern** for a Duff's beer or a Flaming Moe.

Shopping

Kwik-E-Mart

SOUVENIRS | FAMILY | This re-creation of the animated convenience store from *The Simpsons* is one of the park's most popular shopping stops. You'll find

Kwik-E-Mart (Apu Nahasapeemapetilon, proprietor) caps and smocks, Duff Beer mugs, Lard Lad doughnuts, Marge-style blue bouffant wigs, and Homer T-shirts packaged in Duff Beer cans. ✉ *Springfield: Home of the Simpsons, Universal Studios* 🌐 *www.universalorlando.com/web/en/us/things-to-do/shopping/kwik-e-mart.*

World Expo

At the far end of the park is a futuristic set of buildings containing one of Universal Studios' most popular attractions, MEN IN BLACK: Alien Attack (which happens to be the only attraction in this land).

Sights

MEN IN BLACK: Alien Attack

AMUSEMENT RIDE | FAMILY | The preshow of "the world's first ride-through video game" provides the storyline: To earn membership in MIB, you must round up aliens that escaped when their shuttle crashed on Earth. On board your vehicle with a few others, you enter the backstreets of a city where aliens pop out from windows, trash cans, and doorways. Fire at them with that laser gun mounted to your futuristic car, and since there's no limit to the number of shots you can take, blast away. Even though the gun's red laser dot is just a pinpoint, an onboard scoreboard helps you keep track of what you've hit. Aliens fire back at you, and if they score a hit, it'll cause your car to spin out of control. Depending on the collective score, your ride will wrap up with one of 35 endings, ranging from a hero's welcome to a loser's farewell.

All in all, it's pretty exciting, though the spinning nature of the cars might cause dizziness. Use caution if you're prone to motion sickness, and don't ride if you have heart, back, or neck problems. **For people with disabilities:** Equipped for assisted-listening devices. Guests using wheelchairs must transfer to a ride vehicle. **■TIP→ In summer, waits can be up to an hour. Come first thing, or save time by using Express Pass.** ✉ *World Expo, Universal Studios* ☞ *Duration: 4½ mins. Crowds: Heavy. Audience: Not small kids. Height requirement: 42 inches to ride without an adult.*

The Wizarding World of Harry Potter: Diagon Alley

Don't think the facade of London row homes is all there is here: as in the Harry Potter movies, the good stuff remains hidden to mere mortals. When you spy an opening through a broken brick wall and step into Diagon Alley, the world changes as you see what an incredible blueprint J.K. Rowling created through her words. You can literally spend hours in this one district marveling at all Potter-centric shops and eateries.

When you're ready to head to the village of Hogsmeade, make sure you have a park-to-park pass before stepping aboard the wonderful, magical Hogwarts Express—now departing to IOA from Platform 9¾.

Sights

★ Harry Potter and the Escape from Gringotts

AMUSEMENT RIDE | FAMILY | How do you find Gringotts Bank? Look for the massive dragon atop the building and the statue of a Gringotts goblin standing on a towering stack of gold coins. The queue to the ride is an essential part of the attraction: you'll walk through the bank where a multitude of goblins work at their desks, diligently, wordlessly, and eerily. Soon you're in a ride vehicle and, after it departs the station, it's only a matter of moments before Bellatrix

Lestrange notices your presence and then does everything in her supernatural power to prevent you from traveling any farther. So, from here on out, your vehicle will come face to 3-D face with a towering security detail that destroys the tracks and sends you deeper into the bank's recesses.

Be warned that your first encounter with the one who shall not be named (aka Lord Voldemort) isn't your last. After he presents you with a fiery souvenir, he and Bellatrix return again—but they're no match for the scaly superhero who comes to your rescue. This ride's technology is a blend of virtual reality, 3-D effects, 4-D sensations, and gargantuan movie screens featuring scenes synchronized with the motion of your vehicle. **For people with disabilities:** Guests using wheelchairs must transfer to a ride vehicle. ■ **TIP→ Lines can be quite long, so use an Express Pass.** ✉ *The Wizarding World of Harry Potter: Diagon Alley, Universal Studios* ☞ *Duration: 5 mins. (ride) Crowds: Yes! Audience: Everyone but small kids. Height requirement: 42 inches.*

Hogwart's Express—King's Cross Station
AMUSEMENT RIDE | **FAMILY** | When Universal announced the Studios' Diagon Alley would connect to IOA's Hogsmeade via a train ride, many people assumed an open-air train ride through the park's backstage area. But many people aren't nearly as creative as the geniuses at Universal. To reach Hogsmeade, you walk through an exact re-creation of a London rail station, where a magical effect takes you to Platform 9¾. When the train arrives, settle into the compartment with other guests. Outside your window as you chuff away from the station, an owl follows you, music plays, and it feel as if you're traveling through the English countryside.

Adding to the magic, silhouettes of Harry, Ron, and Hermione appear in the corridor outside your window, with their narration adding to the drama of the trio's attempt to banish Dementors (and to corral a loose box of chocolate frogs). By the time Hagrid appears, and you arrive in Hogsmeade, you really feel as if ... you've arrived in Hogsmeade. ■ **TIP→ Express Pass is accepted here, but it might not save you a lot of time except near park closing, when the lines can be very long.** ✉ *The Wizarding World of Harry Potter: Diagon Alley, Universal Studios.*

Restaurants

Leaky Cauldron
$$ | **BRITISH** | **FAMILY** | British pub staples are fitting fare for Diagon Alley's signature restaurant. The drinks menu complements hearty meals like stews and cottage pies with kooky-sounding beverages from the Harry Potter books like Tongue-Tying Lemon Squash, Otter's Fizzy Orange Juice, and Fishy Green Ale. **Known for:** butterbeer, of course; quick-service, Potter-inspired meals; Ploughman's Platter of meats, cheeses, and salad. Ⓢ *Average main: $16* ✉ *The Wizarding World of Harry Potter: Diagon Alley, Universal Studios* ☎ *407/224–9716* 🌐 *www.universalorlando.com/web/en/us/things-to-do/dining/leaky-cauldron.*

Coffee and Quick Bites

Although the lines can be long, the ice cream at **Florean Fortescue's Ice-Cream Parlour** is worth the wait. In addition to the famous butterbeer flavor, there's clotted cream, Earl Grey and lavender (as good as, if not better than, butterbeer), sticky toffee pudding, and strawberry and peanut putter. You can also get butterbeer ice cream at **The Hopping Pot,** which also serves regular and frozen butterbeer (or, in colder weather, hot butterbeer).

A fire-breathing dragon is the centerpiece of The Wizarding World of Harry Potter: Diagon Alley.

Shopping

In this magical village, the cobblestone streets are lined with Harry Potter–themed shops. And more shops. Spend a few hours getting lost in Madame Malkin's for a cloak, Ollivanders for a wand, Weasleys' Wizard Wheezes for jokes and gags, and Quality Quidditch Supplies for a broom or an elusive Golden Snitch. Practitioners of the Dark Arts should venture down Knockturn Alley and step inside Borgin and Burkes for objects and oddities.

Borgin and Burkes
SOUVENIRS | **FAMILY** | Step through Knockturn Alley to enter this somewhat gloomy shop where the somewhat macabre items include Death Eater masks, skulls, pendants, rats (fake), snakes (same), wanted-poster replicas and picture frames, costume replicas, apparel, jewelry, collectibles, a variety of T-shirts (with an assortment of characters and graphics), and the famed Vanishing Cabinet. ✉ *The Wizarding World of Harry Potter: Diagon Alley, Universal Studios* 🌐 *www.universalorlando.com/web/en/us/things-to-do/shopping/borgin-and-burkes.*

Madam Malkin's Robes for All Occasions
MIXED CLOTHING | **FAMILY** | If you're wondering where some park guests found their Potter-themed apparel, there's a chance it came from here. In this shop "Where Well-Dressed Witches and Wizards Buy Their Wares" the couture is dazzling. For those who love to play dress-up, the choices include replicas of Hermione's Yule Ball gown and the full line of Hogwarts apparel—not just robes but also house scarves and sweaters, as well as anything else you can think of. ✉ *The Wizarding World of Harry Potter: Diagon Alley, Universal Studios* 🌐 *www.universalorlando.com/web/en/us/things-to-do/shopping/madam-malkins-robes-for-all-occasions.*

Ollivanders Wand Shop
SOUVENIRS | **FAMILY** | As you explore Diagon Alley, you might feel empty-handed when you notice other guests are carrying wands—some with the ability

to cast spells throughout the streets (through the magic of a laser pointer that triggers lights, fountains, signs, and other inanimate objects). Inside this cramped shop are thousands of wands waiting to choose their wizards—which they do with a little help from the wand keeper himself. Although it may take a few minutes before you're ushered inside, the interactive experience as a wand looks for its new owner is clever and fun. ✉ *The Wizarding World of Harry Potter: Diagon Alley, Universal Studios* 🌐 *www.universalorlando.com/web/en/us/things-to-do/shopping/ollivanders-diagon-alley.*

Quality Quidditch Supplies

SOUVENIRS | FAMILY | Like Star Trek fans learning to speak Klingon, Harry Potter fans have learned to appreciate Quidditch, and this richly themed shop is one of the world's leading suppliers of this fantasy sport's equipment. Fans of the game will be thrilled at the range of Quidditch sweaters, brooms, hats, pennants, Golden Snitches, Bludgers, Bludger bats, Quaffles, and more. ✉ *The Wizarding World of Harry Potter: Diagon Alley* 🌐 *www.universalorlando.com/web/en/us/things-to-do/shopping/quality-quidditch-supplies.*

Weasleys' Wizard Wheezes

SOUVENIRS | FAMILY | Practical jokes and novelties are a never-ending source of amusement—at least for the person who owns them. This is where you can stock up on cheap gags that'll keep you entertained (and others annoyed) for weeks. Highlights included Pygmy Puffs, U-No-Poo pills, Skiving Snackboxes, Puking Pastilles, Sneakoscopes, Bombtastic Bombs, Peruvian Instant Darkness Powder, Decoy Detonators, Extendable Ears, chattering teeth, and whoopee cushions. It's everything a kid (and some juvenile adults) could ever want. ✉ *The Wizarding World of Harry Potter: Diagon Alley, Universal Studios* 🌐 *www.universalorlando.com/web/en/us/things-to-do/shopping/weasleys-wizard-wheezes.*

San Francisco

Although this neighborhood is adjacent to and blends in with New York, changes in architecture and design indicate when you've crossed the continent to the wharves and warehouses of San Francisco's Embarcadero and Fisherman's Wharf districts.

Sights

Fast & Furious: Supercharged

AMUSEMENT RIDE | FAMILY | For fans of the film franchise, the chance to join the crew on a hair-raising car chase is the appeal of this virtual reality attraction. Two preshows lead to a ride vehicle that travels down the highway in a bumper-to-bumper, side-by-side, combination race and gunfight (including helicopter gunships) complete with adrenaline-inducing rocking-and-rolling movements.

To help distract you while waiting in line, more than a dozen cars from the film are displayed in the queue area. Knowing guests will have downloaded the Universal Orlando app, which includes a game that lets you test your Fast & Furious knowledge in trivia matches, receive messages from the crew, and take a quiz to reveal what kind of ride suits your personality. **For guests with disabilities:** Guests in wheelchairs must be able to transfer to the ride vehicle. **■ TIP→ Universal Express Pass is accepted.** ✉ *San Francisco, Universal Studios* ☞ *Crowds: Moderate. Audience: Not younger kids. Height requirement: 40 inches minimum; under 48 inches must ride with an adult.*

Restaurants

Lombard's Seafood Grille

$$ | SEAFOOD | FAMILY | Designed to resemble a Fisherman's Wharf warehouse from 19th-century San Francisco, Universal Studios' flagship full-service restaurant serves fresh fried fish, fried shrimp, and assorted other takes on seafood. You can also get a Boursin steak sandwich with fried onion strips, hamburgers, chicken sandwiches, and big salads. **Known for:** Lombard's lobster roll; Fisherman's Wharf decor; fresh-catch fish basket. [$] *Average main: $20* ✉ *San Francisco, Universal Studios* ☎ *407/224–6400* 🌐 *www.universalorlando.com/web/en/us/things-to-do/dining/lombards-seafood-grille.*

Coffee and Quick Bites

Richter's Burger Co. (across from Fast & Furious: Supercharged) lets you drop in and dress up your own burger or grilled-chicken sandwich. It's pretty quick, pretty convenient, and there are seats inside and out.

For a sugar rush that will keep you going until the park closes, head to **San Francisco Candy Factory,** which features an over-the-top selection of fresh fudge, caramel apples, gourmet cookies, and bulk candies of every confection.

New York

Universal has gone all out to re-create New York's skyscrapers, commercial districts, ethnic neighborhoods, and back alleys—right down to the cracked concrete. Within these structures are restaurants, arcades, gift shops, and key attractions. And although they're from Chicago, the Blues Brothers drive from the Second City to New York City in their Bluesmobile for free performances at 70 Delancey. Here you can use Universal Express Pass at Revenge of the Mummy and Race Through New York Starring Jimmy Fallon.

Sights

★ Race Through New York Starring Jimmy Fallon

AMUSEMENT RIDE | Walking through the queue area takes you through the history of *The Tonight Show,* with memorabilia honoring the hosts—Steve Allen, Jack Paar, Johnny Carson, Jay Leno, Conan O'Brien, Jimmy Fallon—who have all put their stamp on the most famous program in late night. Nostalgia paves the way to a rocketing road trip that begins after a serenade by the Ragtime Gals, a visit by Hashtag the Panda, and a preshow area where, for the first time anywhere (more than likely) safety instructions are offered in a freestyle rap performed by Tariq "Black Thought" Trotter of The Roots.

When the doors finally open, you'll find a seat before a towering screen that really comes to life when you fasten your seat belt, put on your 3-D glasses, and find yourself on the set of the show getting ready to race Jimmy through the halls of 30 Rock, down Broadway, through the streets of New York—and beyond. You follow in your own "car" beside Jimmy as you whip past taxis, pedestrians, and landmarks, before heading into space to land on the moon. Why not? **For people with disabilities:** Guests using wheelchairs must transfer to a ride vehicle. ■ **TIP→ Cut down on wait times by using Express Pass, or come early or late. Free lockers are available for loose items. Use them.** ✉ *New York, Universal Studios* ☞ *Duration: 7 mins. Crowds: Heavy. Audience: Not young kids (under 7). Height requirement: 40 inches.*

Revenge of the Mummy

AMUSEMENT RIDE | **FAMILY** | Action, adventure, and horror are in abundance in this spine-tingling thrill ride that combines roller-coaster technology, pyrotechnics, and some super-scary skeletal warriors. The entrance is set up like the tomb of a pharaoh, which means you'll walk through winding catacombs in the near-dark, passing Egyptian artifacts and archaeological scenes before reaching your vehicle. After boarding the multi-passenger coaster car and zipping into the heart of a haunted labyrinth, "dead" ahead, you're given the chance to sell your soul for safety and riches. Whether you take the deal or not, a guardian mummy thinks it's high time to send you hurtling through underground passageways, where you must escape a beetle-infested burial chamber, zip backward through fog, and then race full-tilt into the mummified mouth of Imhotep.

Take note: you feel the 1.5 g-forces when flying uphill, and much of the ride takes place in the dark, which adds to its unforgettable intensity. Needless to say, this isn't a good choice for expectant mothers or anyone with neck, back, or heart problems. **For people with disabilities:** Guests using wheelchairs must transfer to a ride vehicle. ■ **TIP→ Cut down on wait times by using Express Pass, or come early or late. By all means, use the available free lockers to stash loose items.** ✉ *New York, Universal Studios* ☞ *Duration: 3 mins. Crowds: Heavy. Audience: Not small kids. Height requirement: 48 inches.*

Restaurants

Finnegan's Bar & Grill

$$ | **IRISH** | **FAMILY** | This Irish pub would look just right in lower Manhattan during the Ellis Island era. The menu offers classic Irish comfort food like shepherd's pie, corned beef and cabbage, bangers and mash, and fish-and-chips, plus Guinness on tap and a five-beer sampler. **Known for:** good place for a quick, filling sandwich; live music; classic Irish comfort food like shepherd's pie and beef stew. *$ Average main: $20* ✉ *New York, Universal Studios* ☎ *407/363–8757* 🌐 *www.universalorlando.com/web/en/us/things-to-do/dining/finnegans-bar-grill.*

Coffee and Quick Bites

Head to **Louie's Italian Restaurant,** next to Revenge of the Mummy, for a slice, a sub, or some minestrone soup.

Production Central

Expect plenty of loud, flashy, rollicking rides that appeal to tweens, teens, and adults. Clear the turnstiles, and go straight. You can use the Universal Express Pass at all attractions.

Sights

Despicable Me: Minion Mayhem

AMUSEMENT RIDE | **FAMILY** | Even if you've never seen the hit animated films, it doesn't take long to fall for Gru, the Scourge of Humanity, in this wild virtual-reality chase through the movie. Two extremely funny (and cute) preshow rooms—Gru's living room and laboratory—set the stage for the 3-D ride. With help from his adopted daughters Margo, Edith, and Agnes (and ever-so-anxious minions), Gru reviews everyone to make sure they're ready to become minions. Next, sporting your "minion goggles" (aka 3-D glasses) you are transformed into minions for the rollicking ride, which is filled with close calls and colorful characters as you pursue the ever-elusive prize: the girls' gift for their dad on the one-year anniversary of their adoption. To celebrate, the ride exits into a minion disco (of course).

This attraction is not recommended for expectant mothers or anyone with motion sickness or back, neck, or heart problems. **For people with disabilities:** Closed-captioned devices are available; those in wheelchairs may remain in them. ■ **TIP→ Go for the stationary seats if you think you'll suffer from motion sickness. This ride accepts Express Pass.** ✉ *Production Central, Universal Studios* ☞ *Duration: 5 mins. Crowds: Heavy. Audience: All ages. Height requirement: 40 inches.*

★ Hollywood Rip Ride Rockit

AMUSEMENT RIDE | FAMILY | Looking like an endless strand of spaghetti, this ½-mile-plus coaster loops, twists, dives, and winds above and through Production Central. After you're locked into your seat, you'll select your personal soundtrack (choose from heavy metal, techno, country, rap, and pop) to accompany the video (starring you) that's shot as you scream your way along. And you will scream! It all starts as you're hauled nearly *17 stories straight up* and then dropped nearly *17 stories straight down* before being lifted again into a towering loop and released into what seems like a never-ending series of twists, curves, sideways slings, and snap rolls at speeds up to 65 mph.

By the time you return to the station, you might be woozy and a little spent—but you might spend a little more: the video with the soundtrack you selected is available for purchase. Off-season, the line never seems too bad. In season, consider using a Universal Express Pass. The ride isn't suitable for expectant mothers; anyone with neck, back, or heart problems; or people with a fear of heights. **For people with disabilities:** Closed-captioning is included, and guests using wheelchairs must transfer to a ride vehicle. **■TIP→ Come early or late, and be sure to stow loose items in the available lockers. This ride accepts Express Pass.** ✉ *Production Central, Universal Studios* ☞ *Duration: 2 mins. Crowds: You Bet! Audience: Not small kids. Height requirement: 51 inches minimum; 79 inches maximum.*

Shrek 4-D

AMUSEMENT RIDE | FAMILY | It's been years since the hit film premiered, but *Shrek* fans still line up for this animated 3-D saga. Mike Myers, Eddie Murphy, Cameron Diaz, and John Lithgow reprise their vocal roles as the swamp-dwelling ogre, Shrek; his faithful chatterbox companion, Donkey; Shrek's bride, Princess Fiona; and the vengeful Lord Farquaad (or rather his ghost). The preshow stars the Gingerbread Man, Magic Mirror, and the Three Little Pigs, and, although this intro is slightly entertaining, at about 15 minutes long, it's longer than the main attraction. Afterward, you're given OgreVision (aka 3-D) glasses through which to view Shrek as he attempts to rescue Fiona from Lord Farquaad.

The adventure includes a battle between fire-breathing dragons and a pretty scary plunge down a virtual 1,000-foot waterfall—all made more intense by special theater seats and surprising sensory effects (mainly blasts of air and sprinkles of water) that create the "4-D" part. The ride can be unsettling for those with motion sickness—but fun as all get-out for everyone else. **For people with disabilities:** Equipped for assisted-listening devices. Those using wheelchairs don't need to transfer to a ride seat. There are, however, eight seats that allow guests with disabilities to fully experience the sensory effects. **■TIP→ Despite a capacity for 300, you might wait up to an hour to reach the preshow. Come early or late in the day. This ride accepts Express Pass.** ✉ *Production Central, Universal Studios* ☞ *Duration: 12 mins. Crowds: Heavy. Audience: All ages.*

Transformers: The Ride 3-D

AMUSEMENT RIDE | FAMILY | Based on the toy-turned-film franchise that's generated billions of dollars, this high-intensity attraction has the ability to generate a lot of thrills and screams. You board your transport inside the stark industrial building that's the headquarters of NEST (Nonbiological Extraterrestrial Species Treaty). In a flash, you're in an illusory world where 60-foot screens, fast-paced action, and plenty of 3-D effects ratchet up the excitement in a battle to save the planet as the heroic Autobots (including Optimus Prime and Bumblebee) try to keep the Allspark from falling into the hands of the evil Decepticons (Confused? Ask your kids).

Did You Know?

On Production Central's Hollywood Rip Ride Rockit, you choose the coaster-ride soundtrack from several genres of music. After the whole experience, you can buy a video of your ride with the music you selected.

The attraction spins, twirls, splashes, and drops you. You'll also have some tremendously realistic intergalactic encounters that rock and roll you through the Transformers' world. Like the movies, this ride is very loud and very wild. Unlike the movies, this isn't suitable for expectant mothers; anyone with neck, back, or heart problems; or people with a fear of heights. **For people with disabilities:** Guests using wheelchairs must transfer to a ride vehicle. **TIP→ Come early or late, or use Express Pass.** ✉ *Production Central, Universal Studios* ☞ *Duration: 5 mins. Crowds: You bet! Audience: Not small kids. Height requirement: 40 inches.*

Coffee and Quick Bites

In the heart of Production Central, and resembling a mad scientist's lab, the quick-service **Classic Monsters Cafe** offers wood-fired pizzas, pastas, chef salads, four-cheese ravioli, and rotisserie chicken. Actual props and costumes from vintage Universal horror films provide great photo ops.

Shopping

Super Silly Stuff
SOUVENIRS | **FAMILY** | Talk about truth in advertising: this colorful gift shop tied to Despicable Me: Minion Mayhem is filled with what seems to be millions of cute minions (both one-eyed and two-eyed) on T-shirts and mugs and in the form of stuffed dolls. Gru fans can also find a black-and-gray scarf like the one worn by the supervillain. If you feel it's too hot in Florida for the actual scarf, buy a T-shirt with one silk-screened onto it. ✉ *Production Central, Universal Studios* 🌐 *www.universalorlando.com/web/en/us/things-to-do/shopping/super-silly-stuff.*

Universal Studios Store
SOUVENIRS | **FAMILY** | Like Disney's Emporium in the Magic Kingdom, this sizable store is the last retail outlet you see before exiting the park. Although it doesn't have all the merchandise sold in individual park gift shops, as the park's central shopping destination it does have *most* of it—and some of the best, including T-shirts, stuffed animals, hats, backpacks, gifts, mugs, and limited-edition Universal trading pins. A big plus is that even if you don't visit IOA, you'll find some of the popular merchandise that's sold primarily at the neighboring park. ✉ *Production Central, Universal Studios* 🌐 *www.universalorlando.com/web/en/us/things-to-do/shopping/universal-studios-store-citywalk.*

Islands of Adventure

IOA has gone all out to transport you from the real into the surreal. What's more, no one island here has much in common with any other, so a visit here is almost like a visit to half a dozen different parks.

The park's unique nature is first revealed at the Port of Entry, where a kaleidoscope of sights and a cacophony of sounds put you in the frame of mind for adventure. When you reach the central lagoon, your clockwise journey commences with Marvel Super Hero Island and its concentration of roller coasters and thrill rides, including the dazzling Amazing Adventures of Spider-Man. Although you'll get your recommended daily allowance of adrenaline on this one island alone, you've only just begun.

Stepping into Toon Lagoon is like stepping into the pages of a comic book, the exact opposite of the feeling you'll get at neighboring Skull Island. Here, though, the prehistoric battles set just the right the tone for the next island, Jurassic Park, where you'll come face-to-face with dozens of dinosaurs and the new-in-2021 VelociCoaster.

You then transition from the world of science fiction to the world of magic.

In the Wizarding World of Harry Potter: Hogsmeade, you can wander through the magnificently fictional, yet now very realistic, realm of the young wizard and his Hogwarts classmates and tutors. Beyond belief.

But that's not the end of it. In the Lost Continent, the mood is that of a Renaissance fair, where crafters work inside colorful tents. It's as pronounced an atmosphere as that of the final island: the topsy-turvy Seuss Landing, where a riot of colors and shapes and fantastic wildlife honor's the good doctor's vivid imagination.

GETTING ORIENTED

Getting your bearings at IOA is far easier than at its sister park, Universal Studios. Nevertheless, use the Universal app or a foldout print map (available just beyond the turnstiles) to acquaint yourself with the park's simple layout (it's a circle).

The Port of Entry area has park services and amenities, the Trading Company store, and a couple of eateries. Ahead, by the lagoon, boards are posted with up-to-the-minute ride and show information, including the length of lines at the major attractions. (Again, though, the Universal app also has such insights.) From here it's easy to navigate the park, as the theme islands are connected by walkways around the lagoon. When you've done the full circuit, you'll realize that there can be truth in advertising: this park really *is* an adventure.

PARK AMENITIES

Baby Care: There are diaper-changing stations in many of the men's and women's restrooms, as well as a nursing station for comfort and privacy at the first-aid station near the entrance. Baby supplies (diapers, food, wipes, and so on) are available at larger stores; ask for those items at the counter, though, as they aren't out on the shelves.

Cameras: Just inside the park, on your right after the turnstiles, is DeFoto's, which was a camera and film shop before cameras and film were condensed into smartphones. Nowadays the shelves are stocked with gifts, souvenirs, and drinks, and the staff helps guests with souvenir photos taken by Universal's squad of photographers.

First Aid: There are two health-services/first-aid centers: one at the front entrance inside Guest Services and another in the Lost Continent. Just look for the Red Cross symbol on the building across from Oasis Coolers (or ask a park host).

Lockers: There are $12-a-day lockers across from Guest Services at the entrance; for $15 a day you can rent a family-size model. You have unlimited access to both types throughout the day, although it's a hike back to retrieve things. Scattered strategically throughout the park—notably at the Incredible Hulk Coaster and Forbidden Journey—are so-called Smart Lockers that are free while you ride (usually up to 75 minutes). Fee lockers, which are available near other attractions like Jurassic Park River Adventure, cost a few dollars per hour and are useful for stashing backpacks and cameras while you're being drenched on a watery ride or going through the spin cycle on a twisty one.

Lost People and Things: If you've misplaced something, head to Guest Services in the Port of Entry. This is also where park staffers take lost children.

Services for People with Disabilities: IOA has made an all-out effort to ensure that the premises are accessible for people with disabilities. Most attractions and all restaurants are wheelchair accessible, and all employees attend workshops on how to meet the needs of guests with disabilities. You might occasionally spot staffers using wheelchairs, and many employees have had basic sign-language training. There's also a counter in Guest Services where you can pick up assisted-listening and other devices.

You can rent manual wheelchairs ($15 per day) and ECVs ($65 per day, $85 for a model with a sun canopy) at the Port of Entry to the left after you enter the turnstiles. A photo ID and a $50 deposit on a credit card are required. Because it's a long way between the parking garages and the park entrance, you might want to rent a push wheelchair at the garages and then upgrade to an ECV when you reach the entrance. Quantities of the latter are limited, so reserve in advance.

Even when the crowds are heavy, the park's avenues are wide enough to maneuver a wheelchair. Hosts and hostesses will direct you to a special attraction entrance or a special show seating area. Icons on guide maps indicate which shows include an interpreter.

Assisted-listening devices are available for Cat in the Hat, Spider-Man, Incredible Hulk, Doctor Doom, Jurassic Park, and Poseidon's Fury.

Stroller Rentals: You can rent double strollers for $35 per day at the Port of Entry to your left after the turnstiles.

SHOPPING

The merchandise varies in each section of the park. If you simply must have a Spider-Man T-shirt or Incredible Hulk coffee mug, for example, head to Marvel Super Hero Island, and, of course, for wizarding supplies, visit Hogsmeade Village in the Wizarding World of Harry Potter. (This is also where you'll find the train for the magical journey to Diagon Alley at Universal Studios; a two-park ticket is required, though.) Also keep in mind that the exit of each attraction often empties into a gift shop stocking attraction-related items.

The largest concentration of stores is the Trading Company near the gates at the Port of Entry. As at Universal Studios, this sprawling shop carries nearly every coveted collectible from nearly every park shop.

VISITING TIPS

Check in with your hosts. Just about any employee is a host, whether they're at a kiosk or attraction or turnstile. Ask them about their favorite experiences—and for suggestions for saving time. Since they work here, they often know best.

Get the best photos. Signs throughout the park indicate picture spots and show how best to frame your shot.

Allow for downtime. The crowds and noise of this park can wear anyone down. Explore little-used sidewalks and quiet alcoves, and you'll find sanctuaries to counter IOA's manic energy.

Split the difference. If the park's open late, a good strategy is to see part of it in the morning and then head off-site to a restaurant for lunch (your parking ticket is good all day) and to your hotel for a swim or a nap (or both). Return to the park in the cooler, less crowded evening.

Port of Entry

The Port of Entry plaza is a bazaar that brings together bits and pieces of architecture, landscaping, music, and wares from many lands—Dutch windmills, Indonesian pedicabs, African masks, restrooms marked "Loo's Landing," and Egyptian figurines that adorn a massive archway inscribed with the notice "The Adventure Begins."

If you haven't had breakfast, you can grab a quick bite at the Croissant Moon Bakery. Or return here later in the day for a bite and a brew at Confisco Grill and the adjacent Backwater Bar. The Trading Post emporium, where you can load up on souvenirs, is also in this area.

Restaurants

Confisco Grille

$$ | **AMERICAN** | **FAMILY** | In your hurry to reach the attractions, you could walk right past this full-service restaurant without noticing it, but if you want a good meal and sit-down service, don't pass by too quickly. The menu is American with international influences. **Known for:** Backwater Bar next door; Italian, Greek, Asian, and Mexican dishes; overlooked location means better chance of seating. *Average main: $17* *Port of Entry, Islands of Adventure* *407/224–4404* *www.universalorlando.com/web/en/us/things-to-do/dining/confisco-grille.*

Coffee and Quick Bites

Early in the day, grab a Sunrise Breakfast (served till 11 am) or a pastry at **Croissant Moon Bakery.** Later in the day, grab a sandwich—or another pastry.

Shopping

Islands of Adventure Trading Company

SOUVENIRS | **FAMILY** | The rambling emporium inside the entrance/exit of IOA is the largest store in the park. It's filled with a little something of everything from everywhere, even some items from the attractions of Universal Studios. Here you'll find Kong, Spider-Man, superheroes, and *puh-lenty* of Potter themes plastered on sandals, frames, mugs, cups, caps, and clothing. It's perhaps the park's best one-stop shopping experience. *Port of Entry, Islands of Adventure* *www.universalorlando.com/web/en/us/things-to-do/shopping/islands-of-adventure-trading-company.*

Marvel Super Hero Island

The facades on Stanley Boulevard (named for Marvel's famed editor and co-creator Stan Lee) put you smack in the middle of an alternatively pleasant and apocalyptic comic-book world—complete with heroes, villains, and cartoony colors and flourishes. Although the spiky, horrific towers of Doctor Doom's Fearfall and the vivid green of the Hulk's coaster are focal points, the Amazing Adventures of Spider-Man is the must-see attraction.

At various times, Doctor Doom, Spider-Man, and the Incredible Hulk are available for photos, and sidewalk artists are on hand to paint your face like your favorite hero (or villain). All rides here accept Universal Express Pass.

Sights

★ Amazing Adventures of Spider-Man

AMUSEMENT RIDE | **FAMILY** | One of Universal's most popular attractions, the experience combines moving vehicles, 3-D film with the highest-definition resolution available, simulator technology, and special effects. What does that mean? It means that after donning 3-D glasses, you drive through the streets of New York in a special car that will pitch and roll as you get swept into a weird, all-encompassing cartoon battle. How weird? When Spider-Man lands on your car, you experience the bump; when Electro runs overhead, you hear his steps. You feel the sizzle of electricity, the frigid spray of water from Hydro Man, and the heat from a flaming pumpkin tossed by the Hobgoblin. No matter how many times you visit, you cringe when Doc Ock breaks through a brick wall, raises your car to the top of a skyscraper, and then releases it for a 400-foot free fall. The bizarre angles and perspectives really do make you feel as if you're swinging from a web. *Do not miss this one.*

Youngsters accustomed to action TV shows should be fine, but timid kids won't. Also skip this ride if you're pregnant or have heart, back, or neck problems. **For people with disabilities:** Equipped for assisted-listening devices. Guests using wheelchairs must transfer to a ride vehicle. ■**TIP→ Use Express Pass or come early or at dusk to save on your wait time. Be sure to check out the wanted posters of Spider-Man villains on the walls.** ✉ *Marvel Super Hero Island, Islands of Adventure* ☞ *Duration: 4½ mins. Crowds: Absolutely. Audience: All but small kids. Height requirement: 40 inches minimum; under 48 inches must ride with an adult.*

Doctor Doom's Fearfall
AMUSEMENT RIDE | FAMILY | Although the 200-foot towers look really scary, the ride itself is just *kind* of scary (but still pretty cool). Several sets of four chairs wrap around the tower, and you and three fellow guests are seated and strapped in just out of the sight of other riders before the disembodied voice of Dr. Doom tells you the contraption is designed to extract fear he'll collect to use and rule the world. Without warning, all the chairs are rocketed to the peak, which jump-starts a surge of adrenaline as it rises, falls, rises, and falls again in a very brief, but quite thrilling, experience.

Often it's easy enough to have a second go, as you can actually step off and get right back into line again. Guests who are pregnant or have heart, back, neck, or motion-sickness problems should sit this one out. **For people with disabilities:** Guests using wheelchairs must transfer to a ride vehicle. ■**TIP→ Line moves fairly fast, though it's crowded early in the day; come late or use Express Pass.** ✉ *Marvel Super Hero Island, Islands of Adventure* ☞ *Duration: 1 min. Crowds: Light to moderate. Audience: All but small kids. Height requirement: 52 inches.*

Incredible Hulk Coaster
AMUSEMENT RIDE | FAMILY | Just seeing this attraction from the sidewalk is a thrill: its cars shoot out from a 150-foot catapult that propels them from 0 to 40 mph in less than *two seconds*. If this piques your interest, get in line, where the wait for the prized front-row seats is the longest. That said, every seat lets you experience flesh-pressing g-forces that match those of an F-16 fighter. When you're launched into the ride (and we mean *launched*), you're whipped into an upside-down, zero-g position more than 10 stories up before being zipped into a dive at some 60 mph. You then race along the track before spinning through seven rollovers and plunging into two deep, foggy, subterranean enclosures. Just when you think it's over—it's not. This coaster seems to keep rolling along well after you've exhausted your supply of screams and shrieks. Powerful.

The smooth track creates a smooth ride for the neon-trimmed train cars; this also makes the ride itself quieter—an aspect that seems to amplify the sound effects and screams. Pregnant women and people with neck, back, heart problems, or motion-sickness issues shouldn't ride. **For people with disabilities:** Guests using wheelchairs must transfer to a ride vehicle. ■**TIP→ Come here first (effects are best in the morning and up front). Use Express Pass. Loose articles are not permitted, so stow things in a convenient locker.** ✉ *Marvel Super Hero Island, Islands of Adventure* ☞ *Duration: 2¼ mins. Crowds: Yes! Audience: All but small kids. Height requirement: 54 inches.*

Storm Force Accelatron
AMUSEMENT RIDE | FAMILY | On this whirling ride, X-Men character Storm harnesses the weather to battle Magneto by having people like you board Power Orbs. Yes, the story line is that the containers convert human energy into electrical forces through the power of "cyclospin." Strip away the veneer, however, and what you've got seems like a faster version of Disney World's twirling teacups. Still, it's a high-adrenaline ride that's not for anyone who suffers from motion sickness. It's also not suitable for guests who are pregnant or who have heart, back, or neck problems. **For people with disabilities:** Guests using wheelchairs must transfer to a ride vehicle.

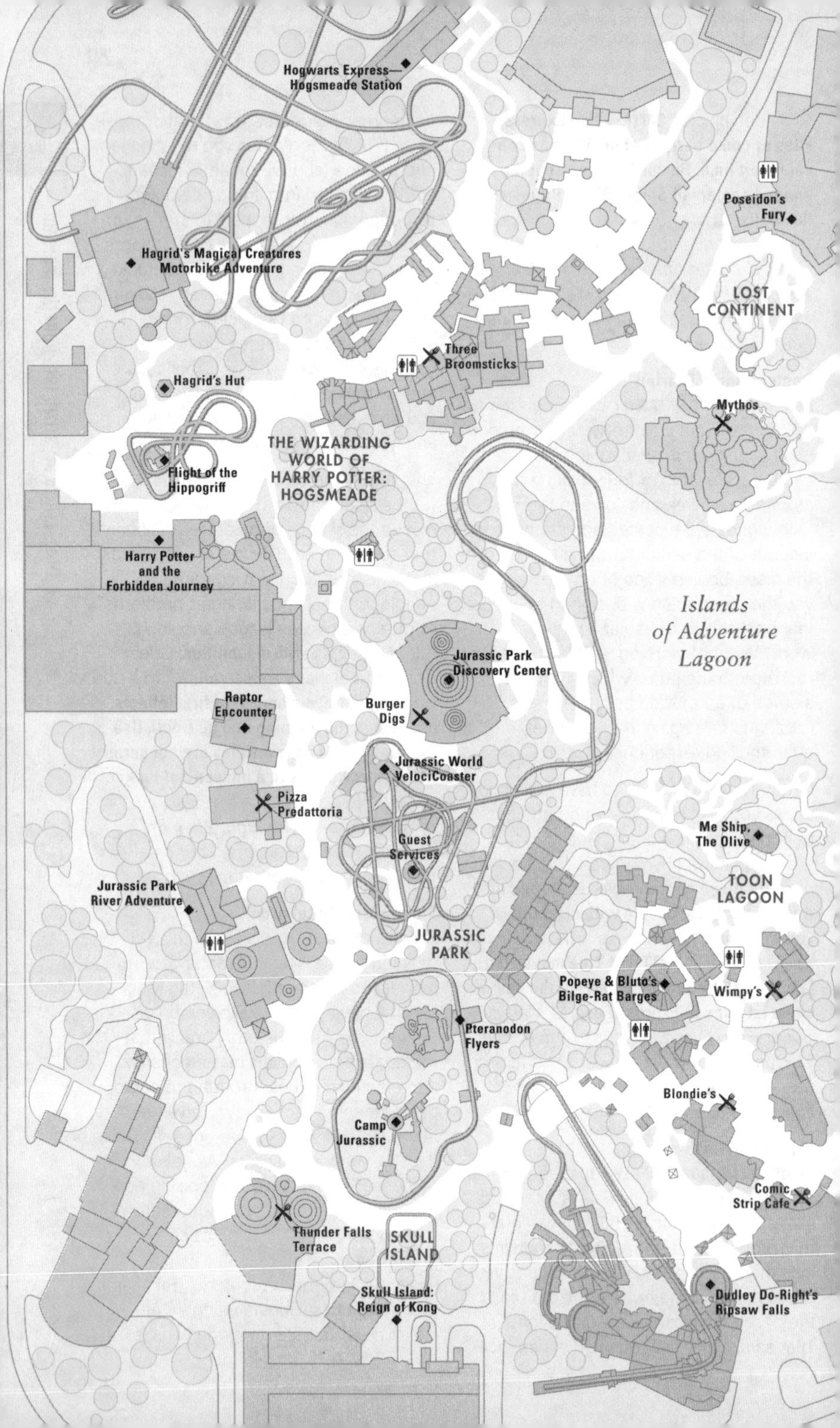
Hogwarts Express—
Hogsmeade Station
Poseidon's Fury
Hagrid's Magical Creatures Motorbike Adventure
LOST CONTINENT
Three Broomsticks
Hagrid's Hut
Mythos
THE WIZARDING WORLD OF HARRY POTTER: HOGSMEADE
Flight of the Hippogriff
Harry Potter and the Forbidden Journey
Islands of Adventure Lagoon
Jurassic Park Discovery Center
Raptor Encounter
Burger Digs
Jurassic World VelociCoaster
Pizza Predattoria
Me Ship, The Olive
Guest Services
TOON LAGOON
Jurassic Park River Adventure
JURASSIC PARK
Popeye & Bluto's Bilge-Rat Barges
Wimpy's
Pteranodon Flyers
Blondie's
Camp Jurassic
Comic Strip Cafe
Thunder Falls Terrace
SKULL ISLAND
Skull Island: Reign of Kong
Dudley Do-Right's Ripsaw Falls

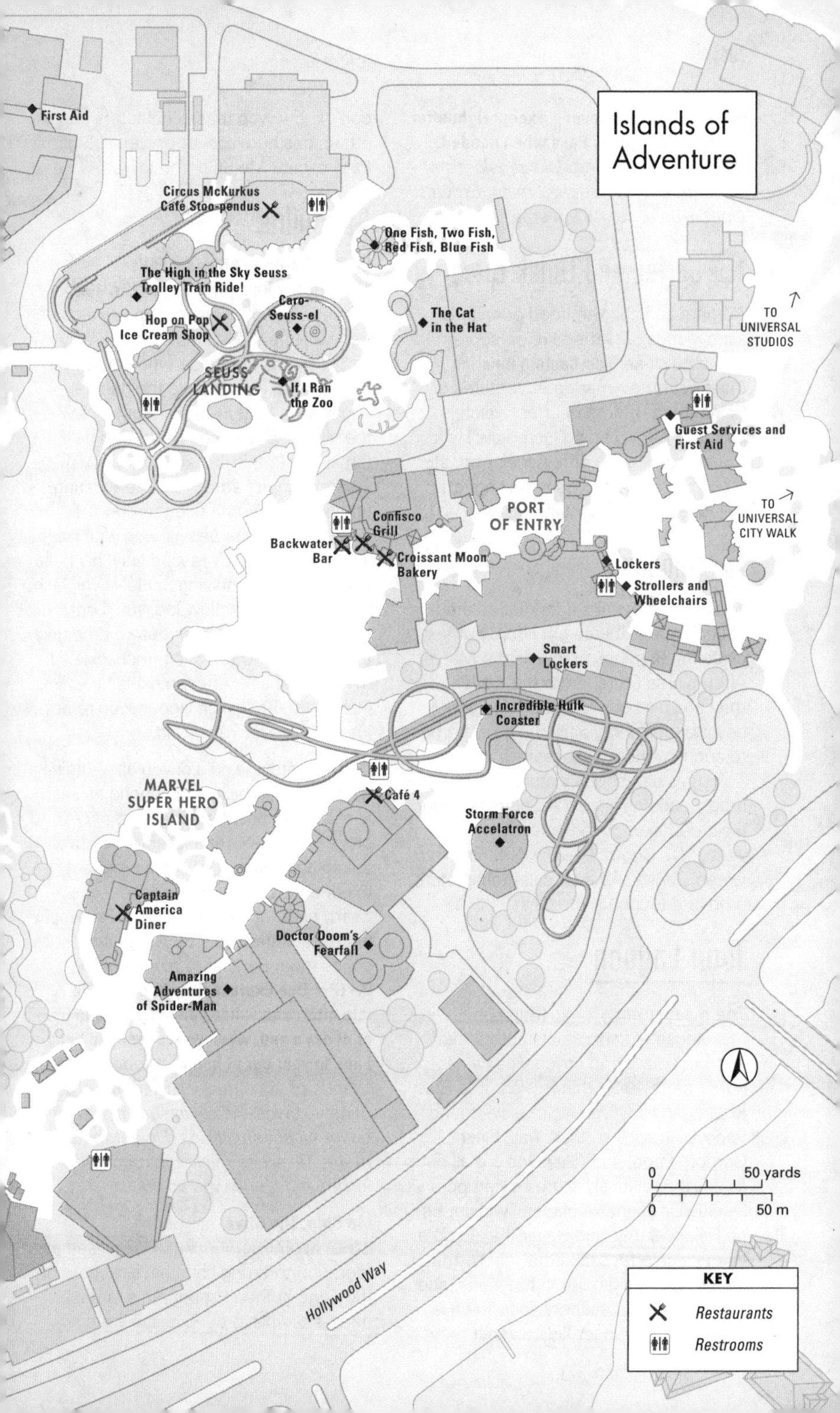
Islands of Adventure
First Aid
Circus McKurkus Café Stoo-pendus
One Fish, Two Fish, Red Fish, Blue Fish
The High in the Sky Seuss Trolley Train Ride!
Caro-Seuss-el
Hop on Pop Ice Cream Shop
The Cat in the Hat
SEUSS LANDING
If I Ran the Zoo
TO UNIVERSAL STUDIOS
Guest Services and First Aid
PORT OF ENTRY
Confisco Grill
Backwater Bar
Croissant Moon Bakery
TO UNIVERSAL CITY WALK
Lockers
Strollers and Wheelchairs
Smart Lockers
Incredible Hulk Coaster
MARVEL SUPER HERO ISLAND
Café 4
Storm Force Accelatron
Captain America Diner
Doctor Doom's Fearfall
Amazing Adventures of Spider-Man
Hollywood Way
0
50 yards
0
50 m
KEY
Restaurants
Restrooms

■ **TIP→ Ride whenever—except right after eating. Use Express Pass when needed.** ✉ *Marvel Super Hero Island, Islands of Adventure* ☞ *Duration: 2 mins. Crowds: Light. Audience: All but small kids.*

Coffee and Quick Bites

Burgers and chicken (fried or grilled in sandwiches or platters) reign supreme at the quick-service **Captain America Diner** near the Amazing Adventures of Spider-Man. Before or after (which is probably better) riding Incredible Hulk Coaster or Storm Force Accelatron, stop for pizza, a meatball sub, or spaghetti Bolognese at nearby **Café 4.**

Shopping

You'll find souvenirs attraction-related at each ride exit area gift shop, but the place for all things Marvel is the Marvel Alterniverse Store. From the X-Men to the Fanastic Four to Spider-Man and beyond, this shop is filled with superhero and film-theme souvenirs including T-shirts, sweatshirts, pictures, poster, mugs, and plush toys. A bonus is having a picture taken with Spider-Man, Wolverine, Dr. Doom, Captain America, the Green Goblin and their pals—characters drop in throughout the day.

Toon Lagoon

The main street, Comic Strip Lane, makes use of cartoon characters that are recognizable to anyone—anyone born before 1940, that is. Pert little Betty Boop, gangly Olive Oyl, muscle-bound Popeye, Krazy Kat, Mark Trail, Flash Gordon, Pogo, and Alley Oop are all here, as are the relatively more contemporary Dudley Do-Right, Rocky, Bullwinkle, Beetle Bailey, Cathy, and Hagar the Horrible. With its colorful backdrops, chirpy music, hidden alcoves, squirting fountains, and highly animated scenery, Toon Town is a natural for younger kids (even if they don't know who these characters are). All attractions here accept Universal Express Pass except Me Ship, The Olive.

Sights

Dudley Do-Right's Ripsaw Falls

AMUSEMENT RIDE | FAMILY | In the 1960s, Dudley Do-Right was recognized as the well-intentioned (but considerably dim) Canadian Mountie who somehow managed to always save the damsel and always "get his man" (that is, foil the villain). But you don't need to be familiar with this character to enjoy this "waterlogged" attraction. The twisting, up-and-down flume ride through the Canadian Rockies begins with your mission to help Dudley rescue Nell, his belle, from the evil, conniving Snidely Whiplash. Tucked inside a hollow log, you'll drift gently down the stream before dropping through the rooftop of a ramshackle dynamite shack. After an explosive dive into a 400,000-gallon lagoon, you're not just damp—you're soaked.

If the weather is cold or you absolutely must stay dry, pick up a poncho at Gasoline Alley, opposite the ride entrance, and store other items in a locker. This isn't suitable for guests who are pregnant, experience motion sickness, or have heart, back, or neck problems. **For people with disabilities:** Guests using wheelchairs must transfer to a ride vehicle. ■ **TIP→ Use Express Pass and come in late afternoon, when you're hot as can be, or at day's end, when you're ready to head back to your car or hotel.** ✉ *Toon Lagoon, Islands of Adventure* ☞ *Duration: 5½ mins. Crowds: Heavy in summer. Audience: All but small kids. Height requirement: 44 inches minimum; under 48 inches must ride with an adult.*

Me Ship, The Olive

OTHER ATTRACTION | FAMILY | Disguised as a teetering-tottering ship that's moored on the edge of Toon Lagoon, this fantastic, three-story playground has, from bow

to stern, dozens of climbing and other activities to keep kids busy. Toddlers enjoy crawling in Swee' Pea's Playpen, and with high-powered squirt guns, older children and their parents can take aim at unsuspecting riders twisting through the rapids over at Popeye & Bluto's Bilge-Rat Barges ride. The most excited participants are small kids, who can't get enough of the whistles, bells, tunnels, and ladders. Check out the view of the park from the top of the ship. **For people with disabilities:** The playground area is wheelchair accessible. ■ **TIP→ Come in the morning or around dinnertime.**
✉ *Toon Lagoon, Islands of Adventure*
☞ *Duration: Up to you. Crowds: Heavy. Audience: Small kids.*

Popeye & Bluto's Bilge-Rat Barges
AMUSEMENT RIDE | **FAMILY** | As with every ride at IOA, there's a story line here, but the real attraction is boarding the wide circular raft with 11 other passengers and then getting splashed, sprayed, or deluged as the watercraft bounces and bobs down and around the twisting stream. The degree of wetness varies, since the direction your raft spins might or might not place you beneath torrents of water flooding from a shoreline water tower or streaming from water guns fired with enthusiasm by guests at an adjacent play area. Pregnant women and guests with heart, back, neck, or motion-sickness problems should skip this one. **For people with disabilities:** Guests using wheelchairs must transfer to a ride vehicle. ■ **TIP→ Come first thing in the morning or an hour before closing. Use Express Pass, and stow your items in a locker if needed, since you will likely get completely soaked.**
✉ *Toon Lagoon, Islands of Adventure*
☞ *Duration: 5 mins. Crowds: Heavy. Audience: All but small kids. Height requirement: 42 inches minimum; under 48 inches must ride with an adult.*

Coffee and Quick Bites

Blondie's has the Dagwood—the jumbo club sandwich that's sold in sections as it's much too large for any one person to tackle—as well as turkey, roast beef, and tuna sandwiches; Nathan's hot dogs (Chicago, chili, Reuben, slaw); and cookies. Nearby **Wimpy's** serves hamburgers, cheeseburgers, salads, and ice cream.

At the **Comic Strip Cafe,** the setting is colorful, and the menu is varied with a selection of Asian noodle or rice dishes, Mexican *arepas* (cornmeal cakes with various fillings), and pizza.

Skull Island

If you've seen the 1933 classic *King Kong,* you might recall that it had incredible characters and, for its time, thrilling special effects. This incarnation re-creates the mood and settings of the original movie. Tucked in an area between Toon Lagoon and Jurassic Park, Skull Island has one truly singular attraction featuring an ongoing battle between King Kong and a host of oversize adversaries. Parents should note that this is the only attraction where there's a warning that the *preshow* area might be too intense for kids.

Sights

Skull Island: Reign of Kong
AMUSEMENT RIDE | **FAMILY** | As you wind along a path into the heart of a towering mountain, the mood grows more ominous. Navigating darkened corridors that are inhabited by "scare actors" (hence the warning that kids might find the preshow too intense), you pass a proliferation of skulls and then meet an old crone, who hints that something unsettling lies ahead—and you'll find that out when you and your fellow travelers enter a primeval world where things get very scary, very quickly.

To the eerie chants of "Kong! Kong! Kong!" your guided tram drives through a towering set of doors where the skeletal remains of a great ape greet you. Put on your 3-D glasses, and soon other amazing sights will appear—namely Peg, a steely nerved scientist whose exploits are the centerpiece of the attraction. Swarms of bats are followed by swarms of pteranodons that lift her up and away, and now it's up to you to come to her rescue. Although Peg works to save herself, she lands in the middle of swamp infested with scorpions and slimy snakelike creatures. As she blasts them with a machine gun, you feel the splash of their guts before the tram speeds to the next scene, where velociraptors try taking a bite out of your tram. Those agile, snapping dinosaurs are soon overshadowed by a *Tyrannosaurus rex,* who is soon overshadowed by your hero: King Kong.

With the action taking place on both sides of the tram, you're in the middle of a high-energy, over-the-top battle that's thrilling from start to finish. Hint: After riding it once, go back again and wait for a seat on the opposite side to catch scenes you may have missed (they're just as exciting). This ride might be too intense for preteens. Pregnant women and guests with heart, back, neck, or motion-sickness problems should also skip this one. **For people with disabilities:** Guests using wheelchairs must transfer to a ride vehicle. **■ TIP→ The preshow is part of the fun, so go even if the line is long—but if it's really long, use the Express Pass.** ✉ *Skull Island, Islands of Adventure* ☞ *Duration: 5 mins. Crowds: Often heavy. Audience: All but small kids. Height requirement: 36 inches.*

Jurassic Park

Pass through the towering gates of Jurassic Park, and the music becomes slightly ominous, the vegetation tropical and junglelike. All of this, plus the high-tension wires and warning signs, does a great job of re-creating the Jurassic Park of Steven Spielberg's blockbuster movie (and its sequels).

The half-fun, half-frightening Jurassic Park River Adventure (the only attraction here that uses Express Pass) was the standout attraction until mid-2021, when the high-speed, high-thrill, dino-themed Jurassic World VelociCoaster made its debut—and was so exciting it even drew fans from neighboring Hogsmeade.

Sights

Camp Jurassic

OTHER ATTRACTION | **FAMILY** | Remember when you were content with just a swing set and monkey bars? Well, such playground standards have been replaced by theme play areas like this. Though the prehistoric camp is primarily for kids, some adults join in, racing along footpaths through the forests, slithering down slides, clambering over swinging bridges and across streams, scrambling up net climbs and rock formations, and exploring mysterious caves full of faux lava. Watch for the dinosaur footprints: when you jump on them, a dinosaur roars somewhere (and different footprints have different roars). Also look out for the watery crossfire nearby—or join in the shooting yourself. **For people with disabilities:** Much of this attraction is wheelchair accessible (its upper levels probably aren't). **■ TIP→ Great anytime.** ✉ *Jurassic Park, Islands of Adventure* ☞ *Duration: Up to you. Crowds: Light to moderate. Audience: All ages.*

Jurassic Park Discovery Center

CHILDREN'S MUSEUM | **FAMILY** | Since it sits to the side of the walkway, this unassuming, museumlike attraction is often overlooked, but it's worth a visit if your kids love dinosaurs. In demonstration areas, a realistic raptor hatches, and you can see what you'd look (or sound) like

In the Jurassic Park Discovery Center, your kids might just learn something about dinosaurs that they didn't already know.

if you were a dino. In the Beasaur area ("Be-a-Saur"), you get a dinosaur's view of the world. There's also a dinosaur trivia game, as well as numerous hands-on exhibits. Burger Digs, the quick-service upstairs restaurant, is a nice place for an indoor air-conditioned break or a lagoon-view respite at a table out on the balcony. A wide promenade also affords lovely views of the entire park. **For people with disabilities:** The attraction is fully wheelchair accessible. ✉ *Jurassic Park, Islands of Adventure* ☞ *Duration: Up to you. Crowds: Light. Audience: All but small kids.*

Jurassic Park River Adventure

AMUSEMENT RIDE | FAMILY | Your excursion begins as a peaceful raft cruise on a mysterious river past friendly, vegetarian dinosaurs. Naturally, something has to go awry, and a wrong turn is all that it takes to float you into the Raptor Containment Area. Drifting into a research lab, you'll see that it's been overrun by spitting dinosaurs and razor-clawed raptors—and this is when things get plenty scary: straight ahead is a towering, roaring *T. rex,* ready to use its sharp claws and teeth the size of hams to guard the getaway route.

Just when you think you're about to become a Cretaceous period entrée, your raft slips down a tremendously steep, 85-foot plunge that will start you screaming. Smile! This is when the souvenir photos are shot. Thanks to high-capacity rafts, the line moves fairly quickly. The ride is not, however, suitable for guests who are pregnant or who have heart, back, or neck problems. **For people with disabilities:** Guests using wheelchairs must transfer to a ride vehicle; assisted-listening devices are available. **■ TIP→ Come early in the morning and/or use Express Pass.** ✉ *Jurassic Park, Islands of Adventure* ☞ *Duration: 6 mins. Crowds: Heavy. Audience: All but small kids. Height requirement: 42 inches.*

★ Jurassic World VelociCoaster

AMUSEMENT RIDE | FAMILY | Predatory velociraptors patiently await your arrival on this new-in-2021 roller coaster featuring extremely wild twists and turns. Sparking the adventure is a high-speed launch that accelerates the string of cars from 0–50 mph *in just 2 seconds.* What immediately follows is a 90-degree twist and then a series of rises, turns, and S-bends before yet another boost that increases the speed from 40 to 70 mph in 2.4 seconds. It's just enough acceleration to get you to the peak of the attraction, a 155-foot "top hat" that's essential for what follows, namely, a 140-foot drop at an 80-degree angle, followed by a rapid series of turns of varying degrees and culminating with the "Mosasaurus Roll"—a loop at 53 mph. What you experience on this adrenaline-filled attraction might just explain why dinosaurs are extinct. It probably goes without saying, but we'll say it anyway: women who are pregnant and anyone who has a heart, neck, or back condition should avoid this coaster. **For people with disabilities:** the attraction has a device that can help people using wheelchairs transfer to the ride (see an attendant). ✉ *Jurrasic Park, Islands of Adventure* ☞ *Duration: 2 mins. Crowds: Heavy. Audience: All but small kids. Height requirement: 51 inches.*

Pteranodon Flyers

AMUSEMENT RIDE | FAMILY | These prehistoric, bird–style gondolas are eye-catching and tempting. The catch is that this very slow, very low-capacity kids' ride can eat up a lot of your park time. Do it only if (1) your child asks, (2) you want a prehistoric-bird's-eye view of the Jurassic Park compound, or (3) you've been to the park a dozen times and this is the last ride to conquer. **For people with disabilities:** Guests using wheelchairs must transfer to a ride vehicle. **■ TIP→ Crowds are usually perpetual, and waits can be long. Skip this on your first visit.** ✉ *Jurassic Park, Islands of Adventure* ☞ *Duration: 2 mins. Crowds: Heavy. Audience: All ages. Height requirement: Between 36 and 56 inches tall; taller adults must ride with a child who meets these height requirements.*

Raptor Encounter

OTHER ATTRACTION | FAMILY | What ultimately amounts to a photo op (albeit a very intense one) begins with a guide offering the members of your group safety instructions prior to entering the paddock, where a life-size velociraptor resides. Once inside the paddock, the guide coaxes Blue (the dinosaur) into view, which sets the stage for souvenir photos. But with your back turned and a row of razor-sharp teeth directly behind you, the snapshots are usually framed with a look of fear. It can be a very interesting, and very intense, experience that easily frightens kids—and usually scares adults. If you can handle it, the souvenir picture might be worth the brief flash of fear. ✉ *Jurassic Park, Islands of Adventure.*

Coffee and Quick Bites

Thunder Falls Terrace is open for lunch and dinner. Beneath towering ceilings in a spacious setting, one side is entirely glass, which makes it a great place to view the plunge at the adjacent Jurassic Park River Adventure. On a nice day, consider sitting outdoors next to the thundering waterfall and dine on barbecue ribs, wraps, chicken, turkey legs, soup, and salads. If Thunder Falls is too crowded, a short distance away are **Burger Digs** and **Pizza Predattoria.**

Shopping

Dinostore

SOUVENIRS | FAMILY | Above a juvenile chorus of "I want this!" are adults counseling their kids on what they actually *need.* That can be a monumental task in this large store, which is packed with dino hats, shorts, necklaces, cards, mugs, squirt guns, figurines, and the clever *T. rex* T-shirt emblazoned with the helpful suggestion "Bite Me." Rest assured there are educational dino toys, too. ✉ *Jurassic Park, Islands of Adventure* 🌐 *www.universalorlando.com/web/en/us/things-to-do/shopping/Dinostore.*

The Wizarding World of Harry Potter: Hogsmeade

IOA fulfilled the fantasy of Harry Potter devotees when it unveiled Universal's biggest theme-park addition in its history. At the highly publicized premiere, even the actors from the Potter film franchise were amazed. Having performed their roles largely before a green screen, they had never seen anything like this. Neither have you.

The re-creations of mythical movie locales such as Hogwarts and Hogsmeade Village are the stars, with a handful of exquisitely themed candy shops, souvenir stores, and restaurants playing supporting roles. Expect to be impressed—and to wait in line unless you can use your Express Pass.

In the village, it feels as if you really are in Harry's world. Send a postcard or letter stamped with a novelty (but very real cancellation mark) at Owl Post before stopping at Ollivanders or other small shops and kiosks to select (or be selected by) a magic wand. Some wands are even interactive and come with a chart informing you how to trigger flowing water, turn on lights, start a sign swinging, and so on at spots throughout Hogsmeade.

Pick up practical jokes (shrunken heads, extendable ears, screaming yo-yos) at Zonko's; sample strange sweets at Honeydukes; and shop for Hogwarts school uniforms, robes, scarves, T-shirts, and broomsticks—including the legendary Nimbus 2000—at Dervish and Banges. If you have a two-park pass, board the Hogwarts Express for a delightful train journey to Diagon Alley at Universal Studios.

Savor your time here at the signature restaurant, Three Broomsticks, which serves traditional British fare as well as an assortment of kids' meals, and the Hog's Head Pub, where you can down a pint of butterbeer (tastes like cream soda, butterscotch, and shortbread cookies) or pumpkin juice (pumpkin, apple cider, and spices).

Sights

Flight of the Hippogriff
AMUSEMENT RIDE | FAMILY | This kid-friendly coaster is a simple way to introduce your children to the pleasures of g-forces and vertigo. The queue takes you past Hagrid's hut and then on board for a "training flight" above the grounds of Hogwarts Castle. On the brief journey, there are some nice little twists and dips that'll give them a pint-sized dose of adrenaline—just enough to please parents as well as the kids themselves. That said, this ride isn't appropriate for people with heart, back, or neck problems or who are prone to motion sickness. **For people with disabilities:** Guests using wheelchairs must transfer to a ride vehicle. **■ TIP→ Use Express Pass if the line is too long, which it often isn't.** ✉ *The Wizarding World of Harry Potter: Hogsmeade, Islands of Adventure* ☞ *Duration: 1 min. Crowds: Moderate. Audience: Small kids. Height requirement: 36 inches.*

★ Hagrid's Magical Creatures Motorbike Adventure
AMUSEMENT RIDE | FAMILY | A roller coaster with a twist and plenty of turns, this ride offers a magical blend of speed with an interesting collection from Hagrid's unusual menagerie. It surpasses expectation despite the potentially hour-plus wait in line. Whether you've got a grip on the handlebars or are tucked into a sidecar, amid Hagrid's commentary and

Did You Know?

The level of detail in Hogsmeade, right up to the snowy roofs, is amazing. You can even buy an “interactive” wand and use it to cast “spells” while standing on special medallions in the pavement.

the sound of a motorcycle revving, you rocket into a series of low angle turns that snap around corners and into tight curves. You'll slow down long enough to meet one of Hagrid's friends (one with an unusual defense mechanism), and then it's back to the track with more speedy curves and more surreal creatures before you enter a fog bank and ... begin the experience backward! One more turn-around, and you're blazing full-speed to the exhilarating end. **For people with disabilities:** Guests must transfer from wheelchairs to the ride vehicle. **■TIP→ Lines can be incredibly long, and Express Pass isn't an option, so check the wait time before lining up. Parents can also take advantage of Child Swap.** ✉ *The Wizarding World of Harry Potter: Hogsmeade, Islands of Adventure* ☞ *Crowds: Huge. Audience: Everyone but young kids. Height Requirement: 48 inches.*

★ **Harry Potter and the Forbidden Journey**
AMUSEMENT RIDE | FAMILY | Of all of Universal's Harry Potter rides, this is the one that *really* puts you in the movies. In the queue, you enter the hallowed halls of Hogwarts, where you are introduced to the founders of the school, and you see the sights you know from the books and films: Headmaster Dumbledore's office, Defence Against the Dark Arts classroom, Gryffindor common room, Room of Requirement, and the greenhouse. You also encounter the Sorting Hat, the One-Eyed Witch statue, and several talking portraits. Keep in mind, all this is just the preshow. Eventually heroes Harry, Ron, and Hermione arrive, encouraging you to skip a lecture and follow them on a soaring journey—and so you go.

Thanks to a combination of live-action, robotic technology, and innovative filmmaking, your broomstick flight brings you face-to-face with a flying dragon and the Whomping Willow before being propelled into the heart of a Quidditch match. You also zip through a dozen scenes and encounter supporting characters Albus Dumbledore, Rubeus Hagrid, Draco Malfoy, and members of the Weasley family. It's a fantastic attraction—especially for fans of the series. Alas, this is another ride that's not suitable for those with neck, back, or heart problems, as well as those who are pregnant or suffer from motion sickness. **For people with disabilities:** Guests using wheelchairs must transfer to a ride vehicle. **■TIP→ Use Express Pass if the line is long, or simply relax and enjoy your tour of the school: the preshow here is a large part of the fun.** ✉ *The Wizarding World of Harry Potter, Islands of Adventure* ☞ *Duration: 5 mins. (after 45–55 mins. in the preshow/queue area). Crowds: Yes! Audience: All but small kids. Height requirement: 48 inches minimum; 75 inches maximum. Weight requirement: less than 250 pounds.*

Hogwart's Express—Hogsmeade Station
AMUSEMENT RIDE | FAMILY | A trip on the Hogwarts Express will enchant you—from departure at Hogsmeade Sation to arrival at King's Cross Station (on Platform 9¾ no less) in Universal Studios. Settle into the compartment, and gaze out your window at the village of Hogsmeade and towering Hogwarts Castle. As the train leaves the station on its four-minute journey, Hagrid waves good-bye, Centaurs gallop beside you, and the Weasley brothers fly by on their broomsticks. Hogwarts gradually recedes, and you move briskly through the rainy British countryside and to the streets of London. When the train stops, you're just steps from the magic of Diagon Alley. **■TIP→ This ride accepts Express Pass. Just remember that to travel between one area of the land known only to wizards and another, you need a two-park Universal ticket.** ✉ *The Wizarding World of Harry Potter: Hogsmeade Village, Islands of Adventure.*

Restaurants

Three Broomsticks

$$ | BRITISH | FAMILY | Rickety staircases and gaslit chandeliers set the tone for this counter-service restaurant, where families feast on ample portions of shepherd's pie, fish-and-chips, turkey legs, and Cornish pasties—accompanied, of course, by pumpkin juice (with hints of honey and vanilla) or butterbeer (sort of like a butterscotch cream soda). Some of the beverages have more of a kick in the adjacent Hog's Head pub, where a faux hog's head sneers at you every now and then. It was all personally approved by J.K. Rowling herself. **Known for:** full English breakfast daily; quirky Harry Potter atmosphere; quick and courteous service. *Average main: $16* ✉ *The Wizarding World of Harry Potter: Hogsmeade, Islands of Adventure* ☎ *407/224–4233* 🌐 *www.universalorlando.com/web/en/us/things-to-do/dining/three-broomsticks.*

Shopping

Both the Harry Potter parks conjure the spirit of the movies with atmospheric shops. Here you'll find the original Ollivanders (where the wand selects the wizard), though this location is smaller than the branch at The Wizarding World of Harry Potter: Diagon Alley. For magical supplies, check out Dervish and Bangs. Zonko's, which shares space with Honeydukes, sells a wide range of magical tricks, practical jokes, and gag gifts that annoy adults and delight adolescents.

Filch's Emporium of Confiscated Goods

SOUVENIRS | FAMILY | Swing by Filch's Emporium of Confiscated Goods for Hogwarts regalia plus authentic prop replicas like Death Eater masks. ✉ *The Wizarding World of Harry Potter: Hogsmeade, Islands of Adventure* 🌐 *www.universalorlando.com/web/en/us/things-to-do/shopping/filchs-emporium-of-confiscated-goods.*

Honeydukes

CANDY | FAMILY | Come here for chocolate frogs, every-flavor jelly beans, exploding bonbons, and many other as-seen-in-the-movies treats. ✉ *The Wizarding World of Harry Potter: Hogsmeade, Islands of Adventure* 🌐 *www.universalorlando.com/web/en/us/things-to-do/shopping/honeydukes.*

Lost Continent

Just beyond a wooden bridge, huge mythical birds guard the entrance to a land where trees are hung with weathered metal lanterns, and booming thunder mixes with chimes and vaguely Celtic melodies. Farther along the path, the scene looks similar to a Renaissance fair. Seers and fortune-tellers practice their trade in tents, and the land's lone ride—Poseidon's Fury—lets you bypass lines using Express Pass.

Sights

Poseidon's Fury

PERFORMANCE VENUE | FAMILY | This walk-through attraction begins only after a long walk through cool ruins guarded by the Colossus of Rhodes before a young archaeologist arrives to take you on a trek to find Poseidon's trident. Each chamber you enter looks interesting, and there's a story told in each one, but actually very little happens in most of them. Most of the time your group is simply walking through the ruins, though the attraction does attempt to ratchet up the entertainment value in the final scene.

After you walk through a water vortex, you enter the final hall where, on a 180-degree

Islands of Adventure Family Tour

As you go through IOA, it enhances the experience if you pretend that you're not so much a park guest as you are a fledgling explorer and amateur sociologist (sometimes just watching people having fun *is* the fun). Imagine that you're taking in an entirely new world, rather than merely visiting a theme park.

In **Marvel Super Hero Island,** most guests race into the Hulk roller coaster and Spider-Man attractions. Instead, spend some time on the bridge or along the waterfront, where you can watch the frequent launching of the Hulk coaster and perhaps meet some of Marvel's superheroes.

Toon Lagoon, the less intense alternative to Super Hero Island, provides plenty of places to explore, including a marked path that lets you follow the trail of Billy (of *Family Circus* comic fame), who's wandered off on his own. In **Jurassic Park**'s Camp Jurassic, paths loop through a prehistoric playground. Why not get lost for a while? Take time to explore the hallowed halls of Hogwarts and surrounding Hogsmeade village at **The Wizarding World of Harry Potter.**

Next, the **Lost Continent** is one of the most richly themed lands and, with its tents and crafters and colorful bangles, is yet another place to explore and take things in. Finally, **Seuss Landing** looks unusually surreal, but there are quiet places to sit and spend some time just watching children (and adults). For parents, spinning on a carousel, riding on a Seussian trolley, and meeting the fabled Cat in the Hat can take years off your actual age.

movie screen, actors playing Poseidon and his archenemy appear. As they shout at each other, a fire- and waterworks extravaganza erupts all around you, and massive waves crash and scorching fireballs fly. This finale is loud, powerful, and hyperactive. Is it worth the investment of time? Meh. Give this one a whirl only if you've done everything else. **For people with disabilities:** The theater is equipped for assisted-listening devices and is wheelchair accessible. **■ TIP→ Stay left against the wall as you enter, and position yourself opposite the central podium. In each succeeding section of the presentation, get into the very first row, particularly if you aren't tall. Express Pass is accepted here but might not save you any time if you arrive just as a show is starting.** *✉ Lost Continent, Islands of Adventure ☞ Duration: 20 mins. Crowds: Moderate. Audience: All but small kids.*

Restaurants

★ Mythos

$$$ | ECLECTIC | FAMILY | Built into a rock cliff, this enchanting table-service restaurant has an eclectic menu that includes pad Thai, pan-seared salmon with lemon-basil butter, seared lamb chops, and brick oven–roasted chicken. The building itself—which looks like a giant rock formation from the outside and a huge cave (albeit one with plush upholstered seating) from within—is enough to grab your attention, but so does the waterfront view of the big lagoon in the center of the theme park. **■ TIP→ Reserve online or with the Universal phone app for lunch or an early dinner. Known for:** lamb burgers and crab cake sandwiches; spectacular decor; one of the best theme-park restaurants. *$ Average main: $25 ✉ The Lost Continent, Islands of Adventure ☎ 407/224–4533*

🌐 *www.universalorlando.com/web/en/us/things-to-do/dining/mythos-restaurant.*

Seuss Landing

This 10-acre tribute to Dr. Seuss puts you in the midst of his classic children's books. This means spending quality time with the Cat, Things 1 and 2, Horton, the Lorax, and the Grinch. From topiary sculptures to lurching lampposts to curvy fences (there was never a straight line in any of the books) to buildings that glow in lavenders, pinks, peaches, and oranges, everything seems surreal. It's a wonderful place to wrap up a day. Even the Cat would approve.

At Seuss Landing, Thing 1 and Thing 2 T-shirts are always a hit with couples and siblings. Or how about a couple of red-and-white-striped Cat in the Hat mugs? Here, the Caro-Seuss-el and High in the Sky Seuss Trolley Train Ride accept Express Pass.

Sights

Caro-Seuss-el

AMUSEMENT RIDE | FAMILY | Ordinary horse-centric merry-go-rounds seem so passé compared with the menagerie on this one: the cowfish from *McElligot's Pool,* the elephant birds from *Horton Hatches the Egg,* and the Birthday Katroo from *Happy Birthday to You!* It's an entire ark of imaginary and interactive animals—indeed, the animals' eyes blink, and their tails wag. It might be a cliché, but there's a good chance you'll feel like a kid again when you hop aboard one of these fantastic creatures. You'll love it. **For people with disabilities:** Modified mounts let guests using wheelchairs ride without having to transfer to a ride vehicle. **■ TIP→ Use Express Pass, and/or make this a special end to your day. Lines move pretty well, so don't be intimidated.** ✉ *Seuss Landing, Islands of Adventure* ☞ *Duration: 2 mins. Crowds: Moderate. Audience: All ages. Height requirement: Under 48 inches must ride with an adult.*

The Cat in the Hat

AMUSEMENT RIDE | FAMILY | Here, you encounter a crazy cat ready to wreak havoc while your mom is out. As you sit on a couch that spins, whirls, and rocks its way through the house, you'll roll past 18 scenes, 30 characters, and 130 effects that will keep you on the edge of your seat. You're never alone. The mischievous cat appears balanced on a ball; hoists china on his umbrella; introduces Thing 1 and his wild sibling, Thing 2; and flies kites in the house while the voice of reason, the fish in the teapot, sounds the warning about the impending return of the family matriarch. As the tension builds, so does the fun—and kids love pointing out scenes from the classic book. This isn't the right ride for anyone who's pregnant; prone to motion sickness; or suffers from heart, neck, or back problems. **For people with disabilities:** The ride accommodates guests using wheelchairs and is equipped for assisted-listening devices. **■ TIP→ Come early or late.** ✉ *Seuss Landing, Islands of Adventure* ☞ *Duration: 4½ mins. Crowds: Heavy. Audience: All ages. Height requirement: Under 48 inches must be accompanied by an adult.*

The High in the Sky Seuss Trolley Train Ride!

AMUSEMENT RIDE | FAMILY | Colorful and quirky miniature Seussian trains on separate tracks embark on a slow and pleasing tour that provides an aerial view of the area, with Seusslike narration along the way. You'll roll right through the Circus McGurkus Café Stoo-pendous and along the shores of the lagoon, where you can see the Sneetches as they enjoy the beaches. Kids love trains, and with its cartoonish design, they'll love this one even more. A treat for kids (and grown-ups, too!). **For people with disabilities:** Guests using wheelchairs must transfer to a ride vehicle. **■ TIP→ Kids love trains,**

In Seuss Landing, the under-7 set and their families can grab a bite at Circus McKurkus Café Stoo-pendus and have encounters with The Cat in the Hat as well as fish both red and blue.

so plan to get in line, especially if you have young ones. Express Pass is available here. ✉ *Seuss Landing, Islands of Adventure* ☞ *Duration: 3 mins. Crowds: Heavy. Audience: Small kids. Height requirement: 34 to 48 inches must ride with an adult.*

If I Ran the Zoo

OTHER ATTRACTION | **FAMILY** | In this interactive Seussian maze, kids can leave the adults behind and have fun at their level. Exploring involves climbing, jumping, and crawling around several of Dr. Seuss's fantasy creatures, as well as pushing buttons to animate them. Park designers have learned that kids' basic needs include eating, sleeping, and getting splashed, so they've thoughtfully added some interactive fountains as well. **For people with disabilities:** The area is wheelchair accessible. ■ **TIP→ If you can talk your little ones into waiting, come at the end of your visit.** ✉ *Seuss Landing, Islands of Adventure* ☞ *Duration: Up to you. Crowds: Moderate. Audience: Small kids.*

One Fish, Two Fish, Red Fish, Blue Fish

AMUSEMENT RIDE | **FAMILY** | Dr. Seuss put elephants in trees and green eggs and ham on trains, so it doesn't seem far-fetched that his fish can circle "squirting posts" to a Jamaican beat. After a rather lengthy wait for what will seem like a very short experience, you climb into your fish, and, as it spins around a center pole, you (or your child) control its up-and-down motion. The key is to follow the lyrics of the special song—if you go down when the song tells you to go up, you might be drenched courtesy of the aforementioned squirting post. Then again, if the guests ahead of you miss their cue, the water's still spraying—and will likely splash you, too. Mighty silly, mighty fun. **For people with disabilities:** Modified mounts let guests using wheelchairs ride without having to transfer to a ride vehicle. ■ **TIP→ Come early or late. Consider skipping it on your first visit.** ✉ *Seuss Landing, Islands of Adventure* ☞ *Duration: 2+ mins. Crowds: Heavy. Audience: Small kids. Height requirement: Under 48 inches must ride with an adult.*

Coffee and Quick Bites

A very colorful big top is the setting for **Circus McKurkus Café Stoo-pendus,** with its quick-service menu of burgers and pizza. For dessert, head over to **Hop on Pop Ice Cream Shop** for a brownie sundae or a waffle cone—with or without sprinkles.

Volcano Bay

It might come as a surprise that when you're at Volcano Bay, you're not at a water park: you're at a 25-acre *water theme park.* The distinction is clear when you see the detailed South Pacific theme woven into every attraction, every cabana, every locker, every restaurant, and every white-sand beach. It doesn't take much imagination to feel as if you really are on a South Seas island, miles from civilization but somehow surrounded by more than 30 unique experiences.

Some guests drop by for a few hours after visiting Universal Studios or IOA, but with the park's multidirectional wave pool, sandy beaches, winding river, raft rides, body slides, and other aquatic attractions, you can definitely make a full day of it.

GETTING ORIENTED

Vibrant, lively Volcano Bay features innovative wet-and-wild designs and an incredibly detailed South Seas setting. You might experience moments of sensory overload from the visuals alone: the towering volcano—and the light and water shows within it—the multicolor slides and chutes, the torrents of whitewater, and the endless parade of people. But don't be overwhelmed. Just take your time, find a spot to settle down, and explore at your own pace.

If you anticipated a day when you can lose track of technology, this is not that day. Every guest is given a waterproof TapuTapu wristband that can be paired with an account they create online, so meals and merchandise can be charged with a wave of the hand. Even if you opt out of tying it into a personal account, the wristband is still needed to reserve a place in a "virtual line" on most rides. You go to the attraction, pass the wristband by a scanner, and you're shown the estimated waiting time; the wristband buzzes when it's time for you to return.

■ TIP→ Volcano Bay has one drawback: no on-site parking. Instead, you must park at the main Universal garages ($27) and wait for a shuttle to take you to the entrance.

PARK AMENITIES

Baby Care: A nursing station is available near the entrance, by First Aid.

Photo ops. Volcano Bay is nothing if not a visual wonder, which is one reason there are interactive photo kiosks throughout the park. Take souvenir pictures through your TapTu Snap/My Universal Photo Access feature, and those pictures, which automatically link to your account, can be viewed, shared, and purchased later at the Waturi Marketplace.

First Aid: If you require care, tell a host or lifeguard. For more serious issues, you'll find First Aid near the entrance.

Lockers: Three different sizes of lockers are available throughout the park and can be linked to as many as four TapuTapu wristbands so the entire family pay for and unlock them. You can also pay for lockers with cash or a credit card.

Lost People and Things: Missing someone? Missing something? The first place to look is Guest Services near the entrance.

Services for People with Disabilities: The park is wheelchair accessible, and a limited number of wheelchairs are available for rent on the third floor of the parking and transportation center. A refundable deposit is required. Note, though, that ECVs are not available for rent, and none of the attraction lines can accommodate them.

Stroller Rentals: There are no stroller rentals in the park, but you're welcome to bring your own.

Where to Snack: The range of dining options is impressive, with kiosks and sit-down restaurants flavored with South Pacific–inspired dishes, from mahi-mahi sandwiches to tropical salads to chocolate pineapple upside-down cake.

VISITING TIPS

Tap in. Volcano Bay prides itself on its TapuTapu wearable, waterproof wristband device, which can assist you in multiple ways, including saving your place in a virtual line at an attraction. The TapTu Play feature lets you try experiences throughout the park, say, shooting jets of water at guests floating down the Kopiko Wai Winding River, illuminating images in the volcano's hidden caves, or making whales spurt water at the Tot Tiki Reef.

With the TapTu Pay feature, you can sync the wristband to a credit card and use it to purchase meals and merchandise throughout the park. Link your whole party to your account, and everyone can pay with their own wristbands.

Book a cabana. On the sands of Waturi Beach, there are hundreds of free beach chairs along with dozens of "premium seats"—a pair of padded loungers with an adjustable shade canopy, a built-in storage lockbox, and the fee-services of an area attendant, who'll see to your food and drink orders.

The most luxurious offerings are private one- and two-story cabanas for between six and 16 guests. Each features padded lounge chairs, bottled water stored in a small refrigerator, complimentary fruit and snack baskets, towels and lockers, and concierge service that brings meals right to your door. There are cabanas throughout the park, with prices varying by season from around $160 to $300 a day.

Stick close. If you're a guest at the neighboring Cabana Bay Beach Resort, avoid the shuttle bus and parking fee by taking a walkway from the hotel to the Volcano Bay entrance. The Sapphire Falls resort is also within walking distance, though you need to walk to the Cabana Bay walkway (about 15 to 20 minutes) first. Shuttle buses run directly from premium resorts (Hard Rock, Royal Pacific, Portofino Bay) to Volcano Bay.

Buy park tickets in advance. Like you, every other guest is anxious to get inside, claim their spot, and start their day. So, as at the other theme parks, it's best to buy tickets in advance (online, at your Universal hotel, or when buying tickets for other Universal parks or activities).

Arrive early. In the morning, you have a better choice of beach locations and can get a lead on reaching the most popular rides. But if you're a little late, just head to the back of the park, where there's plenty more room. In fact, there are lockers, restaurants, and refreshment kiosks in every part of the park.

Devise a wait time strategy. After you've reserved your place in a virtual line, how do you spend that wait time? Well, you can drift along the Kopiko Wai Winding River, hang out on Waturi Beach, grab a bite, or simply lounge on a beach chair or in your cabana. You can also visit other attractions and watch for "Ride Now" signs, jumping into one attraction without losing your place in the virtual line at another.

Mind the lunch lines. Peak dining times are between noon and 2 pm. Plan to eat an hour earlier or later to avoid long lines.

Be ready for showers. Thunderstorms can roll in from the coast, especially in summer, but they don't usually last long. While others pack up their things and go, duck out of the rain and into a gift shop or restaurant until the sun comes out.

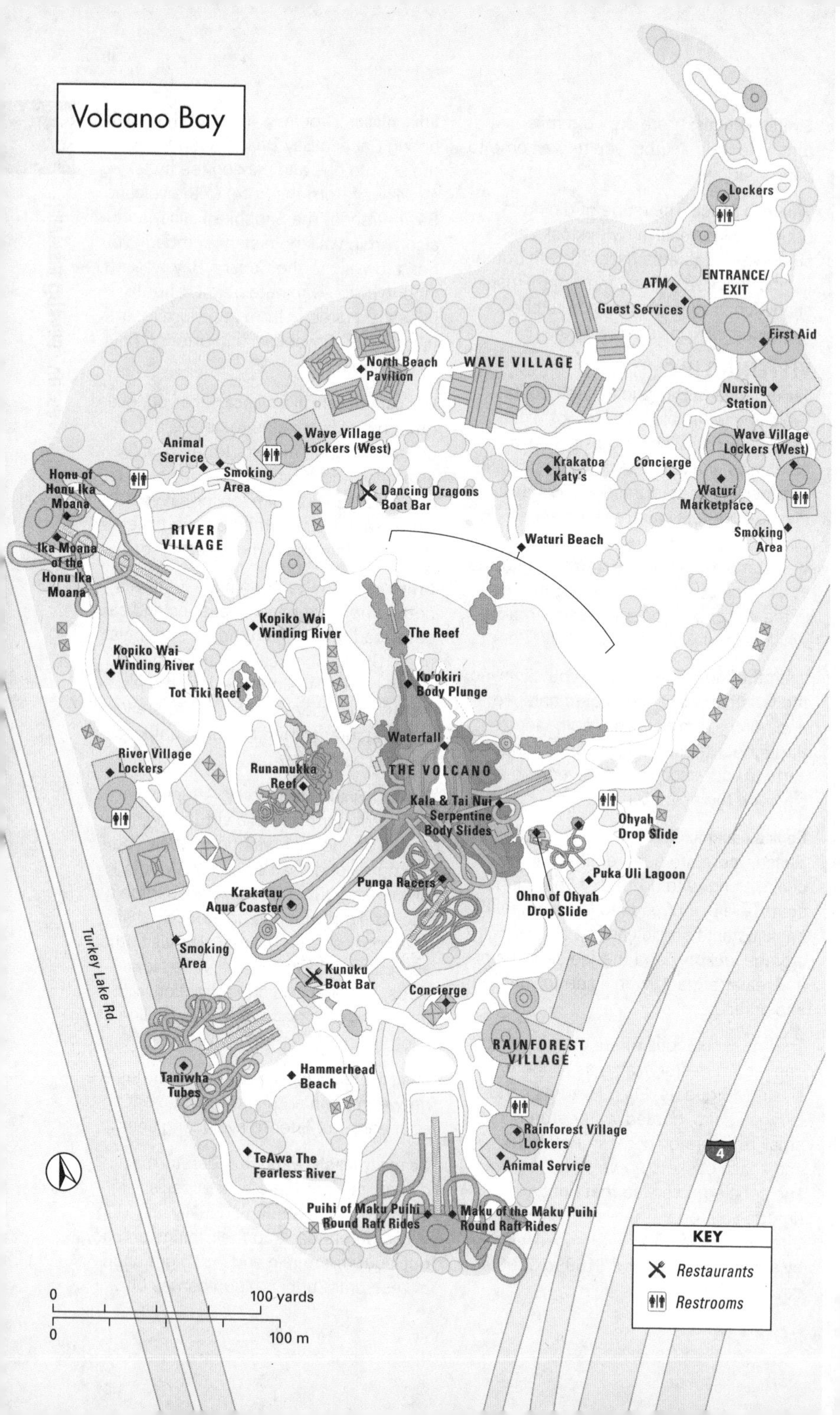

Volcano Bay
Lockers
ENTRANCE/ EXIT
ATM
Guest Services
First Aid
North Beach Pavilion
WAVE VILLAGE
Nursing Station
Wave Village Lockers (West)
Animal Service
Smoking Area
Wave Village Lockers (West)
Krakatoa Katy's
Concierge
Waturi Marketplace
Honu of Honu Ika Moana
Dancing Dragons Boat Bar
RIVER VILLAGE
Smoking Area
Ika Moana of the Honu Ika Moana
Waturi Beach
Kopiko Wai Winding River
The Reef
Kopiko Wai Winding River
Ko'okiri Body Plunge
Tot Tiki Reef
Waterfall
River Village Lockers
Runamukka Reef
THE VOLCANO
Kala & Tai Nui Serpentine Body Slides
Ohyah Drop Slide
Puka Uli Lagoon
Punga Racers
Krakatau Aqua Coaster
Ohno of Ohyah Drop Slide
Smoking Area
Turkey Lake Rd.
Kunuku Boat Bar
Concierge
RAINFOREST VILLAGE
Taniwha Tubes
Hammerhead Beach
Rainforest Village Lockers
TeAwa The Fearless River
Animal Service
4
Puihi of Maku Puihi Round Raft Rides
Maku of the Maku Puihi Round Raft Rides
KEY
Restaurants
Restrooms
0
100 yards
0
100 m

Top Attractions

Ages 7 and Up

Kala & Tai Nui Serpentine Body Slides. Packed with a lot of twists, these twin drops inside the volcano send you through winding, serpentine tubes before you make a splashdown.

Ko'okiri Body Plunge. When a trapdoor is sprung, so begins a 12-story plunge from the top of the volcano into the pool below.

Ohyah and Ohno Drop Slides. Riding either of these sloshing tubes is a thrill that reaches its peak when you come to the end of the line. From here, it's a 4- or 6-foot fall into a deep pool.

TeAwa the Fearless River. More lively than your old run-of-the-mill streams, this not-so-lazy river's swift current and circuitous course takes you past attractions and through the volcano, making it worth some tube time.

Ages 6 and Under

Runamukka Reef and Tot Tiki Reef. The side-by-side play areas are filled with activities and water toys specifically designed for children under 48 inches.

Pick a rendezvous point. The park is surrounded by winding walkways that branch off toward attractions. Before you get lost, agree on a meet-up point like the visually memorable Dancing Dragons or Kunuku Boat Bars or, even simpler, Guest Services near the entrance.

Sights

Hammerhead Beach

BEACH | FAMILY | If you arrive too late to find a prime spot on Waturi Beach, this smaller, secluded, less-crowded beach near the back of the park is the perfect alternative. It's between the Taniwha Tubes and TeAwa the Fearless River attractions. ✉ *Volcano Bay.*

Honu of Honu Ika Moana

AMUSEMENT RIDE | FAMILY | This attraction comes stamped with the postscript "Turtle and Whale," which simply means that when you reach the top you'll find two tubes (the other being the "Ika Moana" of Honu Ika Moana). It's similar to other rides where you slip into an inner tube and then ride through a slick channel, but the difference here is that you join three others in a four-person raft. Although the speed isn't as fast as single-rider attractions, the sensations are just as enjoyable as the raft sloshes and sweeps around huge walls and rounded corners, into tubes and then out again, before flopping into the final pool. **For people with disabilities:** Guests must be able to climb stairways and exit the splash pool without assistance or with help from members of their party. **■ TIP→ This ride accepts Universal Express Pass.** ✉ *Volcano Bay* ☞ *Height requirement: 48 inches.*

Ika Moana of the Honu Ika Moana

AMUSEMENT RIDE | FAMILY | The counterpart to the Honu four-passenger raft is a few feet away in this five-passenger raft. The ride is slow, sloshy, and easy to handle, even when the raft glides around turns and passes over geysers that erupt like whale spouts. **For people with disabilities:** Guests in wheelchairs must transfer to the ride raft unassisted or with help from members of their party. **■ TIP→ This ride accepts Universal Express Pass.** ✉ *Volcano Bay* ☞ *Height requirement: 42 inches; under 48 inches must ride with an adult.*

The centerpiece of Universal Orlando's Volcano Bay water park is, of course, a giant volcano.

Kala & Tai Nui Serpentine Body Slides

AMUSEMENT RIDE | FAMILY | A sign stating that this is a "freefall slide that starts when a trap door is removed" could be a warning to some, an invitation to others. If you're among the latter, then step into the volcano that's the centerpiece of the park, and begin your ascent. Scaling what seems like endless stairwells, you'll be sprinkled with water dripping from intertwined blue and green tubes twisting overhead. These are Kala and Tai Nui, which are soon to be your ride home. As you climb higher and higher, occasionally you'll catch a wonderful aerial view of the park (as well as neighboring I–4), a vista that reveals just how far you've come—and just how far you'll fall.

When you enter your tube, cross your arms, cross your feet, and then just wait for gravity to do its stuff. When the door drops, so do you, shooting down the slick, splashing tube as it sends you into high, banking corners and spinning around for nearly 25 seconds in a thrilling race (with the person in the opposite tube) to a splashdown finish. **For people with disabilities:** Guests must be able to climb stairways and exit the splash pool unassisted or with help from members of their party. **■ TIP→ This ride accepts Universal Express Pass Plus.** ✉ *Volcano Bay* ☞ *Height requirement: 48 inches.*

Ko'okiri Body Plunge

AMUSEMENT RIDE | FAMILY | The towering, steaming volcano commands attention from every part of the park. But even that doesn't compare to the experience waiting inside the volcano. The ride is based on the concept that a body remains at rest until acted upon by another force. You step onto a seemingly solid floor that supports your body weight; the "other force" is gravity, when the door disappears. That's when the reaction is your body falling through the void and into a 70-degree, 12-story drop—a dizzying descent that rockets you right into the splashdown pool. Rinse and repeat. **For people with disabilities:** Guests must be able to climb stairways and exit the splash pool unassisted or with help from members of their party. ■ **TIP→ This ride accepts Universal Express Pass Plus.** ✉ *Universal Orlando Resort* ☞ *Height requirement: 48 inches.*

Kopiko Wai Winding River

POOL | FAMILY | Encircling a substantial portion of the park and winding through the lush foliage, this lazy river lets you go with the flow. As you drift on an inner tube past tropical surroundings, you're occasionally sprayed by streams of water triggered by guests along the banks. When you enter Stargazer's Cavern inside the volcano, the scenery changes again—this time to a brilliant night sky. Along the way are several entrance and exit points, as well as lifeguards keeping an eye on things. **For people with disabilities:** some entrance points are sloped, making it easier for guests using wheelchairs to transfer to the pool. ✉ *Volcano Bay* ☞ *Height requirement: Under 48 inches must wear a life vest.*

Krakatau Aqua Coaster

AMUSEMENT RIDE | FAMILY | A sign that reads "Greater than any man-made thrill" greets you at this attraction. But is it really greater? You'll find out after you slip into a four-person canoe that speeds down a toboggan-style run, whips around corners, shoots you through dark tubes, and then drops you down steep falls again and again and over and over until you're alternately screaming and laughing. A quick 60 seconds later, you plunge toward the finish through a shimmering waterfall. So, yeah, it's pretty great. **For people with disabilities:** Guests in wheelchairs must transfer to the ride's canoe. ■ **TIP→ This ride accepts Universal Express Pass.** ✉ *Volcano Bay* ☞ *Height requirement: 42 inches; under 48 inches must ride with an adult.*

Maku of the Maku Puihi Round Raft Rides

AMUSEMENT RIDE | FAMILY | It will take several flights of stairs to reach the starting point of this ride, one that pairs you up with as many as five others on a rafting adventure. After settling in, a little push is all it takes for gravity to take over and water to wash you into a humongous enclosed tube for a short stretch before you are spat out into the daylight and into a massive basin where your forward motion sends you up toward the rim (but not over it). From here, you wash back down again and slide into another tube before the cycle repeats, taking you through another tube followed by a circular tour of another basin before finally flowing into a calm pool. **For people with disabilities:** There's a lift to the right of the main queue area; wheelchair users must be able to transfer to the raft unassisted or with help from a member of their party. ■ **TIP→ This ride accepts Universal Express Pass.** ✉ *Volcano Bay* ☞ *Height requirement: 42 inches; under 48 inches must ride with an adult.*

Ohno of Ohyah Drop Slide

AMUSEMENT RIDE | FAMILY | At some point, you'll realize that the most thrilling rides at Volcano Bay involve climbing several flights of stairs. Height is what makes such attractions work, and this is one of them. On your way to the top, you cross a deep chasm and walk across rope bridges before finding yourself at the entrance to the Ohno tube (Ohyah is right nearby). Like its counterpart, you'll slip and slide through a serpentine run until the tube runs out and you're flying out on a 6-foot drop into the waters at the base of Krakatau. **For people with disabilities:** Guests must be able to climb stairs, cross rope bridges, and exit the pool without assistance. ■ **TIP→ This ride accepts Universal Express Pass Plus.** ✉ *Volcano Bay* ☞ *Height requirement: 48 inches.*

Ohyah Drop Slide

AMUSEMENT RIDE | FAMILY | You don't need a mat; you don't need a raft; you just need *you* to enjoy the first of two side-by-side body slides that snake around corners and shoot into straightaways on a fast-paced slide to the finish. On this side of the ride (next to the Ohno portion), the finish comes with a 4-foot drop into a swirling pool. Oh yeah! **For people with disabilities:** Guests must be able to climb stairs and exit the splash pool without assistance. ■**TIP→ This ride accepts Universal Express Pass Plus.** ✉ *Volcano Bay* ☞ *Height requirement: 48 inches.*

Puihi of Maku Puihi Round Raft Rides

AMUSEMENT RIDE | **FAMILY** | This multiperson rafting ride follows a journey similar to that of its neighbor, Maku. But this one includes a few different twists and turns—primarily one with a moment of zero-gravity hang time as you spring out of an immense funnel. The twists keep coming as you cling to the raft handles and rock and roll to a spectacular splash finish. **For people with disabilities:** There's a lift next to the main queue area; guests must be able to transfer to the ride raft unassisted or with help from a member of their party. ■**TIP→ This ride accepts Universal Express Pass.** ✉ *Volcano Bay* ☞ *Height requirement: 42 inches; under 48 inches must ride with an adult.*

Puka Uli Lagoon

AMUSEMENT RIDE | **FAMILY** | A relaxing place for families, this small leisure pool is relatively secluded from the park's most active areas (albeit beside the splashdown pool of the Ohyah and Ohno slides) and includes elements that kids will appreciate—namely jets of water they can spray and tropical bongo drums they can beat. **For people with disabilities:** A pool lift makes it easier for guests in wheelchairs to transfer into pool, but they must do so unassisted or with help from a member of their party. ✉ *Volcano Bay* ☞ *Height requirement: Under 48 inches must wear a life vest.*

Punga Racers

AMUSEMENT RIDE | **FAMILY** | For some friendly family competition, grab a mat and pick a lane. There are four tracks on this attraction, and once you have your mat, you'll launch yourself into a tube that twists and turns and then changes to an open-air slide just to keep things interesting. The first person to cross the finish line of this race receives a celebratory spray of water. **For people with disabilities:** Guests must be able to climb stairs and exit the finish area unassisted. ■**TIP→ This ride accepts Universal Express Pass.** ✉ *Volcano Bay* ☞ *Height requirement: 42 inches; under 48 inches must ride with an adult.*

The Reef

POOL | **FAMILY** | This intimate leisure pool has one of the best views in the park, at the base of Krakatau and beside the clear acrylic tube that carries those who've braved the Ko'okiri Body Plunge. You'll often see people lined up along the tube, watching as guests drop out of sight at the top of the mountain and reappear seconds later en route to the splashy finish. With its own waterfall, this is a nice spot to find a little peace and quiet that's still close to many of the park's main attractions. **For people with disabilities:** Guests must transfer from a wheelchair onto the pool lift without assistance or with help from a member of their party. ✉ *Volcano Bay* ☞ *Height requirement: Under 48 inches must wear a life vest.*

Runamukka Reef

OTHER ATTRACTION | **FAMILY** | This colorful, creative aquatic playground gives kids plenty to discover through a wide range of toys and activities that'll keep them busy and entertained. There are shallow wading areas, low-pitched slides (that probably seem stupendously huge from their perspective), spray guns, bubbling geysers, and dump cups. **For people with disabilities:** Guests in wheelchairs can transfer into the wading areas. ✉ *Volcano Bay* ☞ *Height requirement: Under 48 inches must wear a life vest.*

Taniwha Tubes

AMUSEMENT RIDE | **FAMILY** | Two slides are better than one, but this attraction doubles that with four slides that mimic the snaking trunks and twisting roots of puka trees. The tubes alternate in color (green and blue), and they alternate in experiences from channels that are completely enclosed for the entire run to tracks that are enclosed until they suddenly reveal the open air and use your speed to send you up on a high-banked turn. So take it for a spin. Or two. Or four. **For people with disabilities:** Guests must be able to climb stairways and exit the splash pool unassisted. **■TIP→ This ride accepts Universal Express Pass.** ✉ *Volcano Bay* ☞ *Height requirement: 42 inches; under 48 inches must ride with an adult.*

TeAwa the Fearless River

AMUSEMENT RIDE | **FAMILY** | This is definitely not your typical gentle river. The water's fairly shallow, but a strong current means life vests are required (and that's on top of the inner tube you're riding). There are several things to like about this attraction, and one of those is its duration: Other rides are as short as 10 seconds; this one lasts a good six minutes. In addition, the river flows through various areas of the park, traveling beneath bridges and passing rides and restaurants, from Hammerhead Beach to the volcano and Rainforest Village. **For people with disabilities:** A pool lift and a sloped entry make it easier for guests in wheelchairs to transfer into the water. ✉ *Volcano Bay* ☞ *Height requirement: 42 inches; under 48 inches must ride with an adult.*

Tot Tiki Reef

OTHER ATTRACTION | **FAMILY** | Directly across from Runamukka Reef is this shallow-water play area with kid-size slides, spraying fountains, singing whales, and a miniature water volcano. **For people with disabilities:** Guests must be able to climb stairways unassisted or with help from someone in their party. ✉ *Volcano Bay.*

Waturi Beach

BEACH | **FAMILY** | In the shadow of Krakatau, the volcano that looms over the park, is this wide beach with chairs by the hundreds. Arrive early to claim the best spot, or upgrade by renting a premium seat that includes a sun canopy. Park yourself in a chair and do absolutely nothing, or venture into the water, where, every so often, a set of waves washes across the bay. So the choice is yours: swim and splash, or rest and relax. Or maybe a little of both. **For people with disabilities:** A sloped entry makes it easier for guests using wheelchairs to enter the pool unassisted or with the help from someone in their party. ✉ *Volcano Bay* ☞ *Height requirement: Under 48 inches must wear a life vest.*

CityWalk

Restaurants, bars, clubs, shops, live entertainment, and movie theaters make Universal CityWalk an attraction on its own. The upbeat expanse serves as the entrance to both Universal Orlando theme parks—you can't reach the parks from the parking lot without walking through—and is an after-dark destination for tourists and locals alike.

Restaurants

Antojitos Authentic Mexican Food

$$ | **MEXICAN** | **FAMILY** | The massive and very noisy Antojitos brings the specialties of Mexican cantinas and food carts to CityWalk. The outside looks like it's been spray-painted with shocking pastels; inside, the grand two-story space is chic yet rustic, sparse but dotted with Mexican folk art. **Known for:** beer-braised goat stew; noisy atmosphere; table-side guacamole. Ⓢ *Average main: $17* ✉ *6000 Universal Blvd., CityWalk* ☎ *407/224–2807* 🌐 *www.universalorlando.com/web/en/us/things-to-do/dining/antojitos-authentic-mexican-food* ⏲ *No lunch.*

Bigfire

$$$ | **AMERICAN** | **FAMILY** | A flashback inspired by camping trips and cooking over an open flame, this restaurant features a menu that brings back memories. Among the entrées are fire-grilled steaks, Colorado lamb shanks, beer-glazed scallops, barbecue shrimp, skillet-roasted

Restaurants ▼

1 Antojitos Authentic Mexican Food......... **C4**

2 Bigfire....... **C3**

3 The Cowfish..... **C3**

4 Hard Rock Cafe Orlando..... **B2**

5 NBC Sports Grill & Brew...... **C2**

6 The Toothsome Chocolate Emporium and Savory Feast Kitchen...... **A3**

7 Vivo Italian Kitchen...... **C3**

Quick Bites ▼

1 Hot Dog Hall of Fame..... **C3**

2 Voodoo Doughnut... **C2**

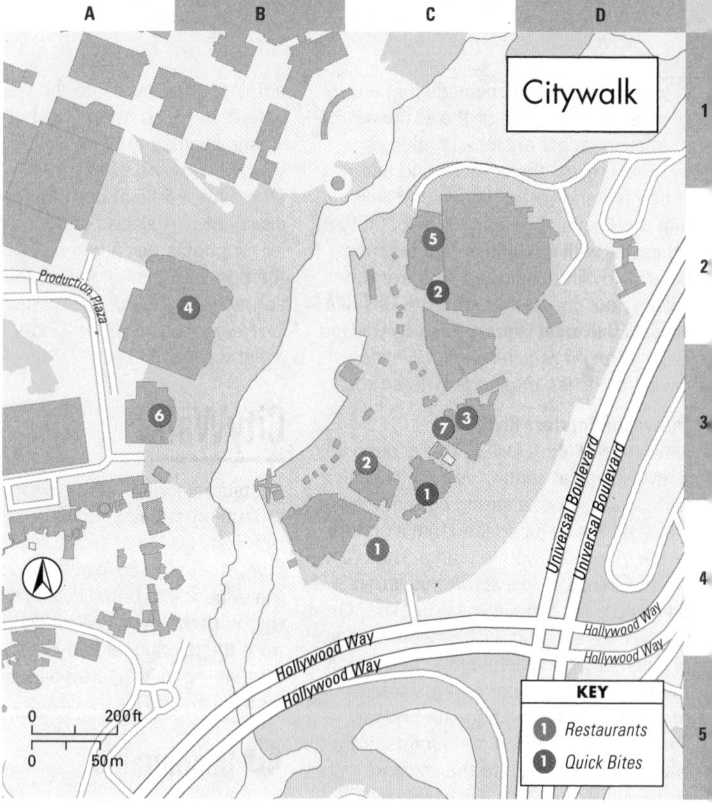

half-chicken, and the Heathstone Seafood Bake, which includes wood oven-baked northern whitefish, shrimp, cold water mussels, andouille sausage, fresh corn, red potatoes, and lemon butter. **Known for:** extensive menu; open-fire cooking; casual, nostalgic atmosphere. *$ Average main: $25 ✉ 6000 Universal Blvd., CityWalk ☎ 407/224–2074 🌐 www.universalorlando.com/web/en/us/things-to-do/dining/bigfire.*

The Cowfish

$$ | **BURGER** | **FAMILY** | Burgers, sushi, bento boxes, and a combo the founders call "burgushi" bring Universal goers to this contemporary second-story restaurant. The setting is flashy, with colorful booths and playful decor complementing video screens showing schools of fish swimming by, aquarium-style. **Known for:** large burger menu; unusual combinations of beef and fish sushi; signature "fusion" rolls. *$ Average main: $15 ✉ 6000 Universal Blvd., CityWalk ☎ 407/224–9255 🌐 www.thecowfish.com.*

Hard Rock Cafe Orlando

$$$ | **AMERICAN** | **FAMILY** | Although this restaurant is built to resemble Rome's Colosseum and contains 1,000 seats, there's often a wait at lunch or dinner. The music is always loud, the walls are covered with rock memorabilia, and the menu still features the burger that started it all: the steakburger with applewood bacon, cheddar cheese, a crispy onion ring, leaf lettuce, and vine-ripened tomato. **Known for:** cowboy rib-eye steak; largest Hard Rock in the world; on-site smoked barbecue. *$ Average main: $23 ✉ 6050 Universal Blvd., CityWalk ☎ 407/351–7625 🌐 www.hardrockcafe.com.*

NBC Sports Grill & Brew

$$ | AMERICAN | FAMILY | Though the giant beer tanks are just for show, this bar has plenty of brews to accompany everything from loaded nachos, fish tacos, giant pretzels, and sturdy sandwiches to ½-pound premium Black Angus beef burgers (the Grand Slam features a pound of beef), sirloin and strip steaks, cedar-plank salmon, and ribs. If you're looking to watch a game, this is the spot: it has more than 100 giant TV screens. **Known for:** more than 100 beers on tap and bottled; massive burgers; giant TV screens at every turn. *Average main: $20 ✉ 6000 Universal Blvd., CityWalk ☎ 407/224–3663 🌐 www.universalorlando.com/web/en/us/things-to-do/dining/nbc-sports-grill-brew.*

The Toothsome Chocolate Emporium and Savory Feast Kitchen

$$$ | AMERICAN | FAMILY | A steampunk decor of gizmos, gears, pulleys, belts, and smokestacks is the backdrop for this very popular restaurant, where chocolate and sweets rule. Desserts—ranging from artisanal milk shakes and sumptuous sundaes to chocolate brownie bark, bacon brittle, and salted caramel flan—are naturally big draws. **Known for:** lots of savory entrées in case dessert isn't enough; super-duper stupendous milk shakes; creative confections. *Average main: $25 ✉ 6000 Universal Blvd., CityWalk ☎ 407/224–3663 🌐 www.universalorlando.com/web/en/us/things-to-do/dining/toothsome-chocolate-emporium-and-savory-feast-kitchen.*

Vivo Italian Kitchen

$$$ | ITALIAN | House-made pasta and inventive cocktails are highlights at the ultrahip Vivo, which is styled after a trendy Roman nightclub. The waiters are attentive, the food—mussels marinara, lamb ragu, squid-ink seafood—is quietly impressive, and the blazing wood-fired oven makes almost instantaneous pizzas. **Known for:** Tuscan chicken and beef specialties; wood-fired pizza; fresh-made pasta. *Average main: $22 ✉ 6000 Universal Blvd., CityWalk ☎ 407/224–2691 🌐 www.universalorlando.com/web/en/us/things-to-do/dining/vivo-italian-kitchen.*

Coffee and Quick Bites

Voodoo Doughnut has developed a cult following, which explains why you'll spy guests carrying to-go boxes packed with some of the more than 50 types of confections they make each day. Selections like the Dirt Doughnut, Memphis Mafia, and Bacon Maple Bar are fuel for a day in the parks. For a less sugary snack, the **Hot Dog Hall of Fame** has specialty dogs from stadiums across America: Boston, New York, Washington, Chicago, Kansas City, and points farther west. CityWalk includes links in chains familiar to most, among them **Bubba Gump's, Burger King, Panda Express, Fat Tuesday,** and **Moe's Southwest.**

Nightlife

Bob Marley—A Tribute to Freedom

BARS | Modeled after the King of Reggae's home in Kingston, Jamaica (even down to the air-conditioning window units), this nightclub is also part museum, with more than 100 photographs and paintings showing pivotal moments in Marley's life. Though the place does serve Jamaican-influenced meals, most patrons are at the cozy bar or on the patio, where they can be jammin' to a (loud) live band that plays nightly. For a nice souvenir, pose by the Marley statue outside the club. Sunday is ladies' night from 10 pm to 2 am. *✉ 6000 Universal Blvd., CityWalk ☎ 407/224–2692 🌐 www.universalorlando.com/web/en/us/things-to-do/dining/bob-marley-a-tribute-to-freedom.*

CityWalk's Rising Star

BARS | Here you and other hopeful (and hopeless) singers can really let loose in front of a live audience. You'll croon to recorded tracks on Sunday and Monday,

CityWalk is Universal Orlando's dining, shopping, and nightlife area that's popular with both visitors and locals.

but between Tuesday and Saturday, you'll be accompanied by a live band complete with backup singers. A full bar is always on tap. Friday and Saturday are reserved for an over-21 crowd. ✉ *6000 Universal Blvd., CityWalk* ☎ *407/224–2961* 🌐 *www.universalorlando.com/web/en/us/things-to-do/entertainment/rising-star-karaoke.*

the groove

DANCE CLUBS | In this cavernous, multilevel hall, images flicker rapidly on several screens, and the lights, music, and mayhem appeal to a mostly under-30 crowd. Prepare for lots of fog, swirling lights, and sweaty bodies. The '70s-style Green Room is filled with beanbag chairs and everything you threw out when Duran Duran hit the charts. The Blue Room is sci-fi Jetson-y, and the Red Room is hot and romantic in a bordello sort of way. The music is equally diverse: Top 40, hip-hop, R&B, techno, and the occasional live band. When you need a break, step out to the balcony for some fresh air and a view of the action on CityWalk. **■ TIP→ There's a $7 cover charge after 10 pm.** ✉ *6000 Universal Blvd., CityWalk* ☎ *407/224–2692* 🌐 *www.universalorlando.com/web/en/us/things-to-do/entertainment/the-groove.*

Hard Rock Cafe

LIVE MUSIC | The Hard Rock Cafe here is the largest on Earth, which means you can see plenty of memorabilia, including such Beatles rarities as John Lennon's famous New York City T-shirt, Paul's original lyrics for "Let It Be," and the doors from London's Abbey Road studios. The food's great, too. Next door, the Hard Rock Live concert hall (The Coliseum of Rock) hosts comedians, solo acts, and internationally recognized bands that make it one of the most popular venues at Universal. A few drawbacks: the seating's not the greatest, and if you arrive at the door carrying a large purse or bags, it won't be time to rock, it'll be time to walk—about a ¼-mile back to the parking garage to stow your stuff. ✉ *6000 Universal Blvd., CityWalk* ☎ *407/351–5483* 🌐 *www.hardrocklive.com.*

Jimmy Buffett's Margaritaville

BARS | Buffett tunes fill the air at the restaurant and at the Volcano, Land Shark, and 12 Volt bars. There's a miniature Pan Am Clipper suspended from the ceiling, music videos projected onto sails, limbo and hula-hoop contests, a huge margarita blender that erupts "when the volcano blows," and live music nightly—everything that Parrotheads need to roost. Across the promenade, another full-size seaplane (emblazoned with "Jimmy Buffett, Captain") is the setting for the Lone Palm Airport, a pleasing and surprisingly popular outdoor waterfront bar. ✉ *6000 Universal Studios Plaza, Suite 704, CityWalk* ☎ *407/224–2155* 🌐 *www.universalorlando.com/web/en/us/things-to-do/dining/jimmy-buffetts-margaritaville.*

Pat O'Brien's

BARS | An exact reproduction of the legendary New Orleans original comes complete with a flaming fountain and dueling pianists who are playing for highly entertained regulars and visitors—even on weekday afternoons. Outside, the cozy and welcoming Patio Bar has a wealth of tables and chairs, allowing you to do nothing but enjoy the outdoors and your potent, rum-based Hurricanes in Orlando's version of the Big Easy. ✉ *6000 Universal Blvd., CityWalk* ☎ *407/224–2692* 🌐 *www.universalorlando.com/web/en/us/things-to-do/dining/pat-o-briens.*

Red Coconut Club

BARS | Paying tribute to kitsch design of the 1950s, the interior here is part Vegas lounge, part Cuban club, and part Polynesian tiki bar. It's "where tropical meets trendy." There are three full bars on two levels, signature martinis, an extensive wine list, and VIP bottle service. Hang out in the lounge, on the balcony, or at the bar. On a budget? Take advantage of the daily happy hours and gourmet appetizer menu. Latin music takes over from 8 pm to midnight, then a DJ from midnight until 2 am. Thursday is ladies' night. ■ **TIP→ There's a $7 cover charge after 10 pm.** ✉ *6000 Universal Blvd., CityWalk* ☎ *407/224–2425* 🌐 *www.universalorlando.com/web/en/us/things-to-do/entertainment/red-coconut-club.*

Performing Arts

FILM

Universal Cinemark Movie Theater

FILM | **FAMILY** | Why spend your time watching a movie when you're on vacation? Who cares? It's your vacation. Here there are 20 screens and 5,000 seats in a bilevel venue that provides an escape from the crowds, and, in summer, the Florida heat. In addition to "meal deals" that include admission to a show, there are nightly midnight movies. ✉ *6000 Universal Blvd., CityWalk* ☎ *407/354–3374 box office* 🌐 *www.universalorlando.com/web/en/us/things-to-do/entertainment/universal-cinemark.*

Shopping

Most stand-alone shops in the 30-acre entertainment hub of promenades leading to Universal Studios and IOA have been replaced by restaurants, leaving primarily retail outlets affiliated with establishments like the Hard Rock Cafe, Jimmy Buffett's Margaritaville, and the Chocolate Emporium. You can still stop by the Huntington & Hart tattoo parlor, though, should you have an itch for ink during your visit.

Quiet Flight Surf Shop

MIXED CLOTHING | **FAMILY** | Granted, the closest beach is about 60 miles east, but you can still get outfitted like a surfer at this shop, where the inventory includes brands such as Billabong, Quicksilver, Hurley, and Oakley. In addition to shorts and shirts, look for sandals, watches, sunglasses (Ray-Ban, Prada, and D&G among the featured names)—and surfboards! ✉ *6000 Universal Blvd., CityWalk* ☎ *407/224–2125*

CityWalk's Hard Rock Café is not only the largest in the world, but its Hard Rock Live concert hall draws big-name acts to Orlando year-round.

🌐 *www.universalorlando.com/web/en/us/things-to-do/shopping/quiet-flight-surf-shop.*

Universal Orlando Resort Area

Universal Orlando's three original on-site hotels were built in a little luxury enclave that has everything you need so you never have to leave Universal property. In minutes, you can walk from any hotel to CityWalk, or take a ferry to the parks. Cabana Bay Beach Resort and Lowes Sapphire Falls are farther afield but are adjacent to the aquatic theme park, Volcano Bay.

In 2020, at the site of Universal's former water park, Wet 'n Wild, the second of two hotels opened at the Endless Summer Resort: the Dockside Inn and Suites joined the Surfside Inn and Suites as a "Value" option—the least expensive of four tiers of pricing (the others are Prime Value, Preferred, and Premier).

A burgeoning hotel district across Kirkman Road and down to Sand Lake Road offers convenient accommodations and some even less expensive rates. Although these off-property hotels don't have the perks of the on-site places, you'll probably be smiling when you see your hotel bill.

Restaurants

Bice Ristorante Orlando
$$$$ | ITALIAN | "Bice" (pronounced *beach-ay*) is an Italian nickname for Beatrice, as in Beatrice Ruggeri, who founded the original Milan location of this upscale Italian chain in 1926. At the Orlando branch, starched linens, frescoed ceilings, marble floors, and bay-view picture windows set the stage for sophisticated (and pricey) dishes such as pan-seared wild halibut with Swiss chard or veal scallopini with lemon-caper sauce. **Known for:** braised veal osso buco; upscale Italian cuisine;

house-made pasta. $ *Average main: $34* ✉ *Loews Portofino Bay Hotel, 5601 Universal Blvd., Universal Orlando Resort* ☎ *407/503–1415* 🌐 *www.universalorlando.com/web/en/us/things-to-do/dining/bice* ⏲ *No lunch.*

Islands Dining Room

$$$ | **ASIAN** | **FAMILY** | An airy room and tropical decor complement the menu's curries, pad Thai, coconut soup, and other Asian-inspired dishes. Islands, which serves breakfast and dinner, also has a play area to keeps tots entertained, and you can create your own stir-fry combos during the Wok Experience on Friday and Saturday evenings. **Known for:** sometimes has free character dining; breakfast buffet; extensive kids' menus. $ *Average main: $22* ✉ *Loews Royal Pacific Resort, 6300 Hollywood Way, Universal Orlando Resort* ☎ *407/503–3463* 🌐 *www.universalorlando.com/web/en/us/things-to-do/dining/islands-dining-room* ⏲ *No lunch.*

Jake's American Bar

$$$ | **AMERICAN** | With an adventurer's theme honoring its namesake aviator (Captain Jake McNally), this gastropub is a great place to grab a cold one as well as anything from a Caesar salad or flatbread sandwich to shrimp mac 'n' cheese or roasted chicken. Jake's also hosts seasonal beer dinners that feature regional and specialty brews. **Known for:** crawfish chowder; live entertainment some nights; beer festival events. $ *Average main: $27* ✉ *Loews Royal Pacific Resort, 6300 Hollywood Way, Universal Orlando Resort* ☎ *407/503–3463* 🌐 *www.universalorlando.com/web/en/us/things-to-do/dining/jakes-american-bar.*

The Kitchen

$$$$ | **AMERICAN** | **FAMILY** | This casual restaurant has omelet stations at breakfast; flatbreads, sandwiches, and salads at lunch; and grilled salmon, filet mignon, and roast chicken at dinner. The kids' menu is entertaining, with plates such as I Don't Want That (grilled cheese) or I'm Not Hungry (chicken tenders) that are served with a choice of fries, a salad, or fresh fruit. **Known for:** pricey at dinner; '50s diner styling; very kid friendly. $ *Average main: $31* ✉ *Hard Rock Hotel, 5800 Universal Blvd., Universal Orlando Resort* ☎ *407/503–3463* 🌐 *www.universalorlando.com/web/en/us/things-to-do/dining/the-kitchen.*

Mama Della's Ristorante

$$$ | **ITALIAN** | **FAMILY** | The premise here is that you're eating at a home-turned-restaurant—there's an actual "Mama Della," who appears nightly, and you'll be serenaded by an accordionist, guitar player, and vocalist. The menu features Italian classics like homemade gnocchi, chicken parmigiana, and lasagna alongside more ambitious dishes like *bistecca* (steak) with truffle mashed potatoes, roasted wild mushrooms, broccolini, onions, and carrots. **Known for:** outdoor seating; intimate New York/Neapolitan setting; better-than-usual Italian cuisine. $ *Average main: $30* ✉ *Loews Portofino Bay Hotel, 5601 Universal Blvd., Universal Orlando Resort* ☎ *407/503–3463* 🌐 *www.universalorlando.com/web/en/us/things-to-do/dining/mama-dellas* ⏲ *No lunch.*

The Palm Restaurant

$$$$ | **STEAKHOUSE** | With its dark-wood interior and hundreds of framed celebrity caricatures, this pricey restaurant resembles its famed New York City namesake. For most diners, steak steals the show (aged beef is a specialty), but the gargantuan Nova Scotia lobsters are nearly as popular. **Known for:** Italian dishes from old family recipes; steak, steak, and steak; superb seafood dishes. $ *Average main: $42* ✉ *Hard Rock Hotel, 5800 Universal Blvd., Universal Orlando Resort* ☎ *407/503–7256* 🌐 *www.universalorlando.com/web/en/us/things-to-do/dining/the-palm* ⏲ *No lunch.*

★ **Strong Water Tavern**

$$ | **CARIBBEAN** | Billed as a "hotel lounge," Strong Water breaks all the rules for hotel dining: the surroundings are comfortable, and the food is some of the most

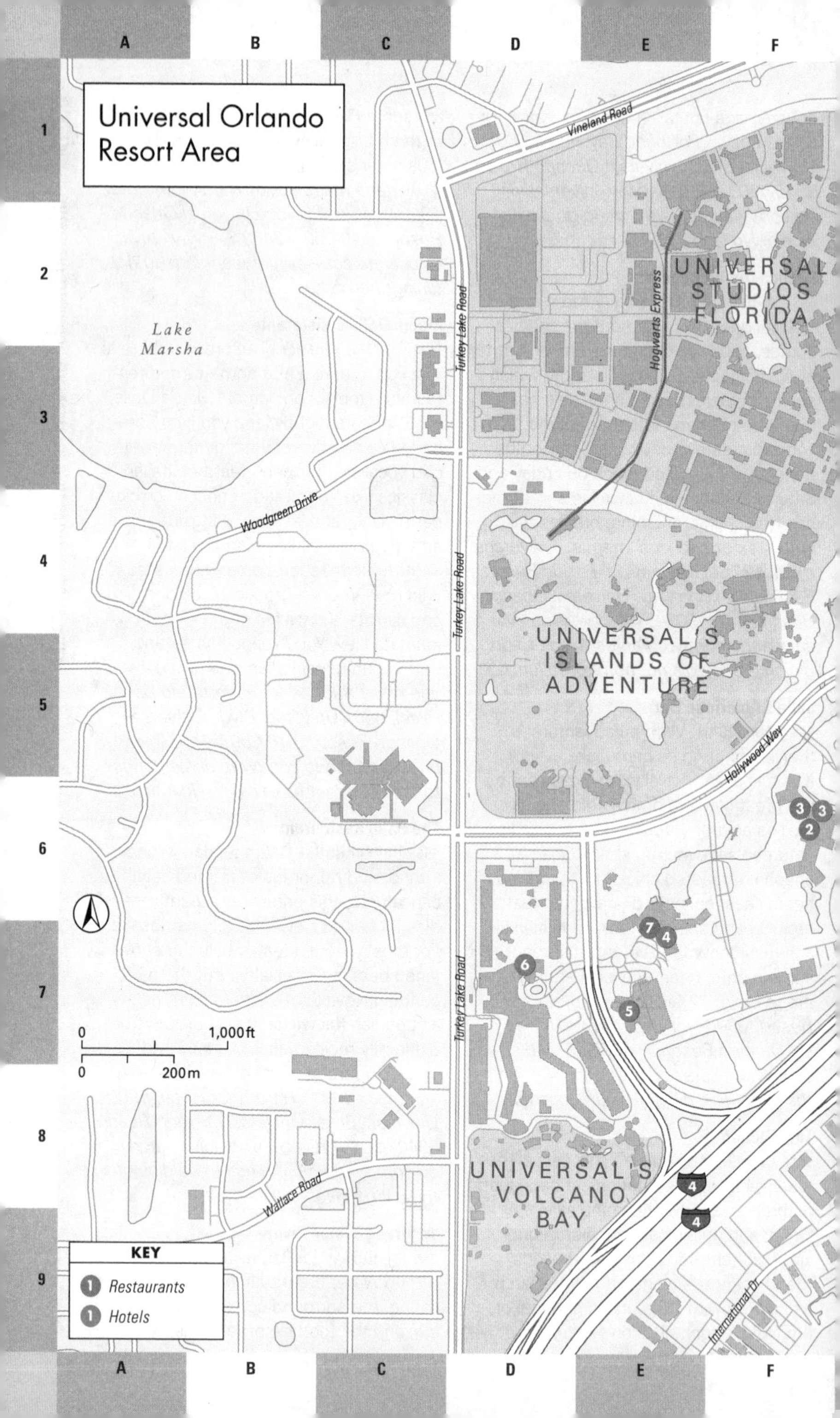

Universal Orlando Resort Area
A
B
C
D
E
F
1
2
3
4
5
6
7
8
9
Vineland Road
Hogwarts Express
UNIVERSAL STUDIOS FLORIDA
Lake Marsha
Turkey Lake Road
Woodgreen Drive
UNIVERSAL'S ISLANDS OF ADVENTURE
Hollywood Way
0
1,000 ft
0
200 m
UNIVERSAL'S VOLCANO BAY
Wallace Road
4
International Dr.
KEY
Restaurants
Hotels

Restaurants ▼

1 Bice Ristorante Orlando **H1**
2 Islands Dining Room **F6**
3 Jake's American Bar **F6**
4 The Kitchen **G3**
5 Mama Della's Ristorante **I1**
6 The Palm Restaurant **G3**
7 Strong Water Tavern **E7**
8 Trattoria del Porto **I1**

Hotels ▼

1 Hard Rock Hotel at Universal Orlando Resort **G2**
2 Loews Portofino Bay at Universal Orlando Resort **H1**
3 Loews Royal Pacific Resort at Universal Orlando Resort **F6**
4 Loews Sapphire Falls Resort at Universal Orlando Resort **E7**
5 Universal's Aventura Hotel **E7**
6 Universal's Cabana Bay Beach Resort **D7**
7 Universal's Endless Summer Resort–Dockside Inn and Suites **H9**
8 Universal's Endless Summer Resort–Surfside Inn and Suites **G9**

memorable in Orlando. Specializing in the cuisines of "the rum latitudes," the menu features dishes from Cuba, Jamaica, Puerto Rico, Haiti, Colombia, U.S. Virgin Islands, and Mexico. **Known for:** extensive rum menu; attentive staff; surprisingly popular curried goat. *$ Average main: $20 ✉ Loews Sapphire Falls Resort at Universal Orlando, 6601 Adventure Way, West Orlando ☎ 407/503–5000 🌐 www.universalorlando.com/web/en/us/things-to-do/dining/strong-water-tavern.*

Trattoria del Porto

$$$ | **ITALIAN** | **FAMILY** | Overlooking a tranquil harbor, this is a family-friendly option with a dash of Italiano. The breakfast buffet features both omelets and other hot dishes as well as baked goods and fruit; dinner starters like shrimp polenta and Caprese flatbread segue to entrées such as chicken marsala, grilled beef tenderloin, and shrimp Alfredo. **Known for:** outdoor dining; family meals; in-house pastry chef. *$ Average main: $30 ✉ Loews Portofino Bay Hotel, 5601 Universal Blvd., Universal Orlando Resort ☎ 407/503–3463 🌐 www.universalorlando.com/web/en/us/things-to-do/dining/trattoria-del-porto.*

Hotels

Hard Rock Hotel at Universal Orlando Resort

$$$$ | **HOTEL** | **FAMILY** | Music rules in this mission-style building, from public areas decorated with rock memorabilia—Elvis's pajamas, Lady Gaga's latex gown, and Elton John's boots—to stylishly modern rooms, with deluxe bed linens, an entertainment center with a flat-panel TV, and lots of accessible media-device plugs. **Pros:** charge privileges extend to the other on-property Universal hotels; shuttle, water taxi, or short walk to Universal Parks and CityWalk; Universal Express Unlimited pass included. **Cons:** loud rock music in public areas, even the pool; fee for parking; rooms and meals are pricey. *$ Rooms from: $390 ✉ 5800 Universal Blvd., CityWalk ☎ 407/503–7625, 800/232–7827 🌐 www.universalorlando.com/web/en/us/places-to-stay/hard-rock-hotel 650 rooms No Meals.*

★ **Loews Portofino Bay at Universal Orlando Resort**

$$$$ | **HOTEL** | The charm and romance of Portofino, Italy, are conjured up at this lovely luxury resort, where part of the fun is exploring the waterfront Italian "village" from end to end; the other part is relaxing in well-appointed rooms (decorated in aqua and cream, with deluxe beds and flat-screen TVs) and by one of the three pools that offer aquatic fun or peaceful sunning. **Pros:** Universal Express Unlimited Pass included; large spa; short walk or ferry ride to CityWalk, Universal. **Cons:** not convenient to Disney parks; daily fee for parking; rooms and meals are pricey. *$ Rooms from: $414 ✉ 5601 Universal Blvd., Universal Orlando Resort Hotels ☎ 407/503–1000, 800/232–7827 🌐 www.universalorlando.com/web/en/us/places-to-stay/loews-portofino-bay-hotel 795 rooms No Meals.*

Loews Royal Pacific Resort at Universal Orlando Resort

$$$ | **RESORT** | **FAMILY** | This Pacific Rim–theme hotel—amid 53 serene acres of lush shrubs, soaring bamboo, orchids, and palms—features lots of amenities, including a weekly Polynesian-style luau, a 12,000-square-foot lagoon-style pool bordered by a white sand beach, an interactive water-play area, and kid-friendly activities. **Pros:** shuttle to CityWalk and parks; Universal Express Unlimited pass included; character dining. **Cons:** can be busy with conventioneers; steep parking fee; rooms can feel smallish. *$ Rooms from: $339 ✉ 6300 Hollywood Way, Universal Orlando Resort Hotels ☎ 407/503–3000, 800/232–7827 🌐 www.universalorlando.com/web/en/us/places-to-stay/loews-royal-pacific-resort 1000 rooms No Meals.*

Loews Portofino Bay Hotel at Universal Orlando

Loews Sapphire Falls Resort at Universal Orlando Resort

$$ | **RESORT** | **FAMILY** | The romantic and sophisticated Sapphire Falls is connected by walkway and water taxi to Universal and CityWalk and has a beach vibe that carries through from its blue waterfalls to the distant sound of steel drums. **Pros:** outstanding on-property bar–restaurant; all the perks of staying at a Universal property except Express Pass; boat takes you to Universal and CityWalk. **Cons:** it's a long way to Disney; water taxis and shuttles can be crowded; few activities for kids. *Rooms from: $234* *6601 Adventure Way, Universal Orlando Resort Hotels* *888/430–4999* *www.universalorlando.com/web/en/us/places-to-stay/loews-sapphire-falls-resort* *1000 rooms* *No Meals.*

Universal's Aventura Hotel

$$ | **HOTEL** | **FAMILY** | Within view of all three Universal theme parks (best seen from the rooftop bar), this Miami Beach–style resort hotel has a casually elegant look and simple, modern rooms with free Wi-Fi, in-room safes, mini-refrigerators, flat-panel TVs, and on-demand movies. **Pros:** free transportation to Universal theme parks; within walking distance to Volcano Bay theme park; access to amenities at other Loews hotels. **Cons:** high-tech tablets for room controls can be confusing; limited storage space for families with a lot of luggage; no Universal Express Pass. *Rooms from: $184* *6725 Adventure Way, Universal Orlando Resort Hotels* *407/503–6000* *www.universalorlando.com/web/en/us/places-to-stay/universals-aventura-hotel* *611 rooms* *No Meals.*

★ **Universal's Cabana Bay Beach Resort**

$ | **RESORT** | **FAMILY** | Universal's nostalgic, mid-century-theme beach resort transports you to a 1950s Florida beach town with a modern twist; it also offers families a less-expensive but still benefit-rich alternative to on-site Universal properties. **Pros:** two swimming pools; early access to Universal; bowling alley. **Cons:** some rooms open onto outdoor passageways; Disney is not close by; very expensive parking fee. $ *Rooms from: $173 ✉ 6550 Adventure Way, Universal Orlando Resort Hotels ☎ 407/503–4000 🌐 www.universalorlando.com/web/en/us/places-to-stay/universals-cabana-bay-beach-resort* *1800 rooms* *No Meals.*

Universal's Endless Summer Resort–Dockside Inn and Suites

$ | **HOTEL** | **FAMILY** | The far larger half of a dual-resort created atop what was once the Wet 'n Wild water park, this property is massive even by Orlando standards, and about half the rooms are two-bedroom suites, making it a smart choice for families who need a little more space. **Pros:** well-suited for families; an affordable option close to Universal and International Drive; early admission to the parks and free transportation. **Cons:** not within walking distance to Universal theme parks; add $15 per night for parking; some might find the massive size off-putting. $ *Rooms from: $163 ✉ 7125 Universal Blvd., Universal Orlando Resort Hotels ☎ 888/273–3111 🌐 www.universalorlando.com/web/en/us/places-to-stay/universals-endless-summer-resort-dockside-inn-and-suites* *2050 rooms* *No Meals.*

Universal's Endless Summer Resort–Surfside Inn and Suites

$ | **RESORT** | **FAMILY** | Opened nearly in tandem with its larger sister property, the Dockside Inn and Suites, the family-friendly sun-and-surf-theme Surfside Inn and Suites is considered a value property. **Pros:** includes early admission to theme parks and free transportation; one of Universal's least expensive properties; surfboard-shape pool. **Cons:** check-in is an hour later than usual, at 4 pm; $15 per day to park; not directly on Universal Orlando property. $ *Rooms from: $139 ✉ 7000 Universal Blvd., Universal Orlando Resort Hotels ☎ 407/503–7000 🌐 www.universalorlando.com/web/en/us/places-to-stay/universals-endless-summer-resort-surfside-inn-and-suites* *750 rooms* *No Meals.*

Activities

SPAS

★ Mandara Spa at Loews Portofino Bay Hotel

SPAS | The doors to this 13,000-square-foot, Asian-theme sanctuary open to a tranquil world of bamboo screens, exotic statuary, and silk hangings. Warm blankets provide comfort while you wait in the relaxation lounge for one of the 14 treatment rooms. Try the Ritual of the Hands and Feet, an indulgence that scrubs, exfoliates, and massages your extremities, finishing with a mani-pedi. The lounge and hydropool are co-ed, with separate men's and women's steam rooms and saunas. Portofino's serene sand-bottomed pool is next door, as is the fitness center. Facials and peels are available, as are full makeup, hair, and other salon services. ✉ *Loew's Portofino Bay Resort, 5601 Universal Blvd., Universal Orlando Resort Hotels ☎ 407/503–1244 🌐 www.mandaraspa.com.*

Chapter 10

ORLANDO

Updated by
Jennifer Greenhill-Taylor
and Joseph Reed Hayes

Sights	Restaurants	Hotels	Shopping	Nightlife
★★★☆☆	★★★★☆	★★★★★	★★★★☆	★★★☆☆

WELCOME TO ORLANDO

TOP REASONS TO GO

★ **Cultivated Spaces:** The Harry P. Leu Gardens are known for their historical blooms, camellias, and striking Floral Clock. Lake Eola Park has a landscaped waterfront stroll and azaleas, roses, and swans.

★ **Liberal Arts:** Orlando's theaters host symphony orchestras, Broadway road shows, and local thespians of all types. Jazz, blues, world music, and rock are all part of the music scene. Area museums showcase folk art, Tiffany glass, and 14th- through 20th-century European and American paintings.

★ **The Sciences:** The Orlando Science Center has many worthwhile exhibits and hosts traveling exhibitions from around the world. At WonderWorks, simulators let you survive an earthquake or pilot a jet.

★ **Sports:** Orlando is home to the Orlando Magic, an NBA team housed at the Amway Center, in addition to Orlando City, a Major League Soccer team, which plays at Exploria Stadium.

1 **Central Orlando.** Orlando has a thriving downtown and bustling residential areas.

2 **International Drive.** Called "I-Drive," this conduit is lined with hotels, chain restaurants, and attractions.

3 **South Orlando.** South Orlando is the dynamic home of Lake Nona, one of the fastest-growing communities in Florida.

4 **Sand Lake Road.** The eastern side bisects I-Drive; the western end has been dubbed "Restaurant Row."

5 **Orlando International Airport.** Chain hotels and restaurants offer convenience for early-morning or late-night flights.

6 **Lake Nona.** A new high-tech community with hip eateries and a cutting-edge hotel.

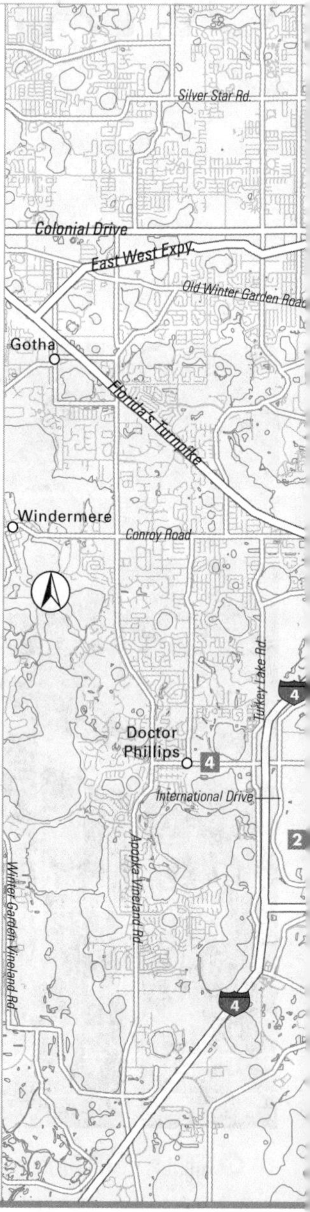

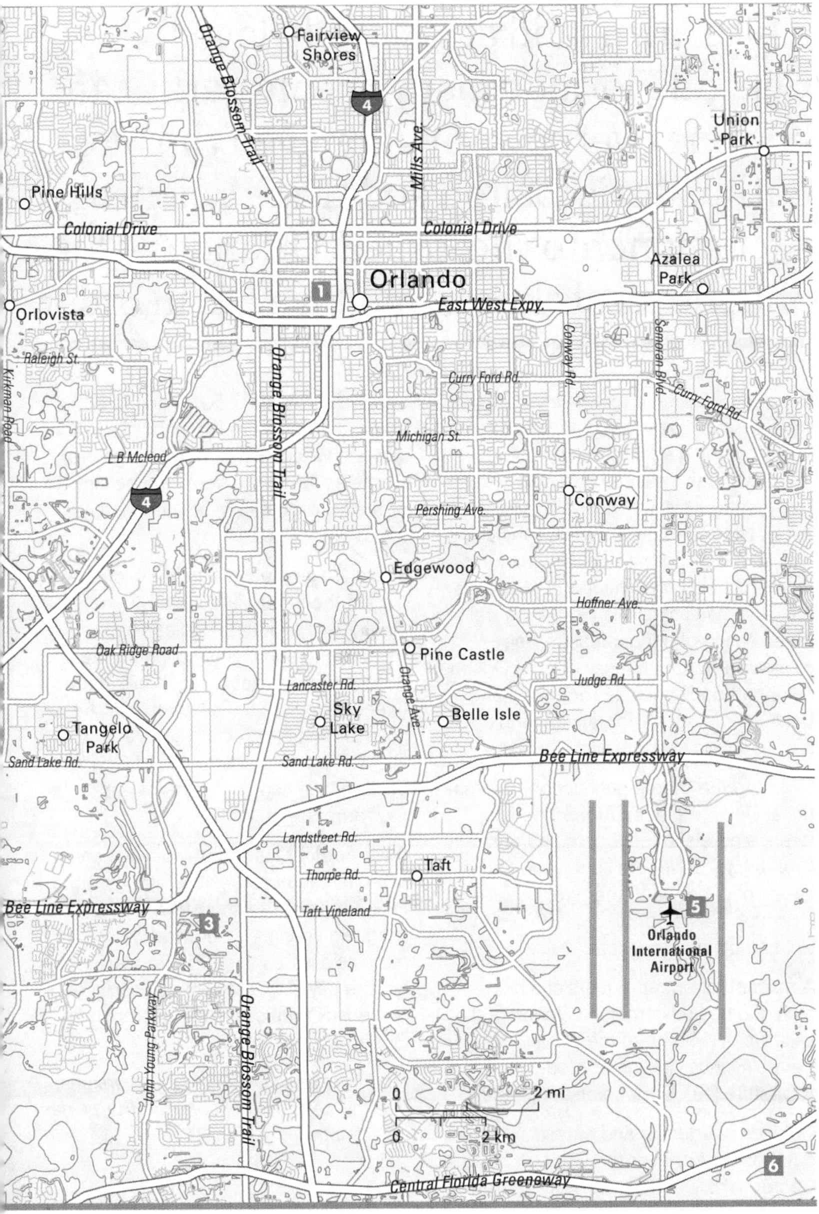
Fairview
Shores
4
Orange Blossom Trail
Mills Ave.
Union
Park
Pine Hills
Colonial Drive
Colonial Drive
Azalea
Park
Orlando
1
Orlovista
East West Expy.
Conway Rd.
Semoran Blvd.
Raleigh St.
Curry Ford Rd.
Curry Ford Rd.
Kirkman Road
Orange Blossom Trail
Michigan St.
L B Mcleod
4
Conway
Pershing Ave.
Edgewood
Hoffner Ave.
Oak Ridge Road
Pine Castle
Judge Rd.
Lancaster Rd.
Orange Ave.
Sky
Lake
Belle Isle
Tangelo
Park
Sand Lake Rd.
Sand Lake Rd.
Bee Line Expressway
Landstreet Rd.
Taft
Thorpe Rd.
Bee Line Expressway
Taft Vineland
5
3
Orlando
International
Airport
John Young Parkway
Orange Blossom Trail
0
2 mi
0
2 km
6
Central Florida Greeneway

Most Orlando locals look at the theme parks as they would unruly neighbors: they're big and loud, but they keep a nice lawn (and are secretly loved). Central Florida's many theme parks can become overpowering for even the most enthusiastic visitor, and that's when an excursion into the "other" Orlando—the one the locals know and love—is in order.

Orlando is a diverse town. Downtown, though small, is dynamic, thanks to an ever-expanding skyline of high-rises, sports venues, museums, restaurants, nightspots, a history museum, and several annual cultural events—including film festivals and the popular Orlando International Fringe Theater Festival. The area also has Lake Eola Park, a central green space offering a respite from otherwise frantic touring. Central Orlando neighborhoods such as Thornton Park, Baldwin Park (great for dining), and hipster Audubon Park are fun to wander.

Closer to the theme-park action, International Drive, the hub of resort and conference hotels, offers big restaurants and even bigger outlet-mall bargains. Sand Lake Road, between the two, is home to Orlando's Restaurant Row, with plenty of exciting dining prospects.

A magnet for entrepreneurs and high-tech, the up-and-coming neighborhood of Lake Nona is home to the University of Central Florida College of Medicine, Nona Adventure Park, restaurants, and hotels.

Got kids to educate and entertain? Check out WonderWorks or the Orlando Science Center, where you can view live gators and turtles, or visit ICON Park and its seaquarium, wax museum, and towering viewing wheel. Even more live gators (some as long as 14 feet) can be viewed or fed (or even eaten) at Gatorland, just south of Orlando.

There are ample opportunities for day trips in the immediate area. Mount Dora offers antiquers endless opportunities and surprisingly sophisticated dining; Sanford, easily reachable via the (weekday only) SunRail commuter train, is becoming a hip dining area; and LEGOLAND, an hour southwest of Orlando, offers a "we can do it" alternative to the Big Three theme parks.

If the outdoors is your thing, you can swim or canoe at Wekiwa Springs State Park or one of the area's many other sparkling springs, where the water remains a refreshing 72°F no matter how hot the day. Alternatively, you can hike, horseback ride, canoe, and camp in the Ocala National Forest.

For information on all these excursions, see the separate "Excursions from Orlando" chapter.

Planning

Getting Here and Around

Orlando is spread out and filled with lakes, making straight-line surface travel almost impossible. During rush hour, car traffic crawls along the often-crowded Interstate 4 (particularly now that the multibillion-dollar upgrade has relocated and closed key exits and entrances), which runs to both coasts. If you're heading east, you can also take Route 528 (aka the Beachline), a toll road that heads directly for Cape Canaveral and points along the Space Coast.

The Central Florida GreeneWay avoids major highway traffic between Sanford and Lake Mary to the north and Celebration to the south and is a pleasant, albeit expensive, way to approach Disney. Another toll road, Route 429, offers an easy journey from Disney to the north via the west side of Orlando.

Orlando International Airport is only 9 miles south of downtown, but it takes about 30 minutes via a circuitous network of highways (Interstate 4 west to Florida's Turnpike south to Route 528 east).

The SunRail commuter trains run weekdays and offer a traffic-free option on a south–north route from Kissimmee to Deltona, with stops that include downtown Orlando, downtown Winter Park, and Sanford.

LYNX Bus service runs from the main Downtown depot to theme parks, outlet shopping, and even the airport for a fraction of what a taxi would cost. And, like most urban areas, Uber and Lyft are ubiquitous (and much cheaper than regular cabs), even within the theme parks.

CONTACTS LYNX Bus. ✉ *455 N. Garland Ave., Downtown Orlando* ☎ *407/841–5969* 🌐 *www.golynx.com.*

Visitor Information

CONTACTS Orlando Visitors Bureau. ✉ *8102 International Dr., Orlando* ☎ *407/363–5872* 🌐 *www.visitorlando.com.*

Central Orlando

Central Orlando is a thriving metropolis of brick-streeted neighborhoods, urban sprawl, and quiet lakeside parks. It's also just minutes from the world's biggest theme parks. To get here, take Exit 83B off I–4 westbound or Exit 84 off I–4 eastbound.

Sights

CityArts Orlando

ART GALLERY | Housed in one of Downtown's oldest buildings, this charming, small gallery features mostly local and regional artists. ✉ *39 S. Magnolia Ave., Downtown Orlando* ☎ *407/648–7060* 🌐 *www.facebook.com/CityArtsFactory.*

Crayola Experience Orlando

CHILDREN'S MUSEUM | **FAMILY** | One of Crayola's five "experiences" in the country is a 70,000-square-foot haven of color at the Florida Mall. The two-floor center contains an overwhelming 27 interactive stations, including painting and modeling stations, where tykes can create animals out of clay and melted crayons. Don't miss the younger set's favorite: You Design, a virtual studio for coloring and digitally accessorizing a car or fashioning a wardrobe and then seeing the design projected on a large screen. Also be sure to check out the Crayon Factory, where live demonstrations show crayon creation—from wax to wrapper. ✉ *The Florida Mall, 8001 Orange Blossom Trail, South Orlando* ☎ *407/757–1700* 🌐 *www.crayolaexperience.com/orlando* 🎟 *$24.*

A
B
C
D
E
F
1
2
3
4
5
6
7
8
9
Edgewater Drive
Hazel St.
King St.
Clayton St.
Bryn Mawr St.
Rugby St.
Smith St.
Harvard St.
Yale St.
Stetson St.
Dartmouth St.
Winter Park Street
Amherst Ave.
Depauw Ave.
Musselwhite Ave.
Formosa Avenue
North Orange Avenue
Princeton Street
Yale St.
New Hampshire St.
Lake Ivanhoe
Lakeview Street
Lake Concord
West Colonial Drive
Mills Avenue
Rollins St.
Princeton St.
Alden Road
Ferris Ave.
Asher Ln.
Virginia Drive
Montana St.
Lake Highland Dr.
Oregon St.
Canton St.
Weber St.
Highland Avenue
Marks St.
Park Lake St.
East Colonial Drive
Lake Sue
Lake Rowena
Harry P. Leu Gardens
Nebraska Street
Virginia Drive
Fern Creek Avenue
Altaloma Ave.
Moris Ave.
Hampton Avenue
Garden Plaza
Meridale Ave.
Hillcrest St.
Concord St.
Amelia St.
Harwood St.
Summerlin Avenue
Hyer Ave.
Shine Ave.
Amelia St.
Paramore Avenue
Magnolia Avenue
Livingston Street
Livingston Street
Robinson Street
Robinson Street
Robinson Street
Washington Street
Lake Eola Park
Lake Eola
Washington St.
Central Boulevard
Central Boulevard
Central Boulevard
Mayor Carl T. Langford
Hughey Avenue
Garland Avenue
Pine St.
Church Street
Church St.
Mariposa St.
Jackson St.
South Street
South Street
East-West Expressway
Anderson Street
Anderson Street
Greenwood Urban Wetlands
Hampton Ave.
Summerlin Ave.
Delaney Ave.
Lake Davis Park
Gore Street
Gore Street
Gore Street
South Orange Ave.
Antilles Pl.
Bimini Dr.
Antigua Dr.
Columbia Street
Division Avenue
Briercliff Dr.
4

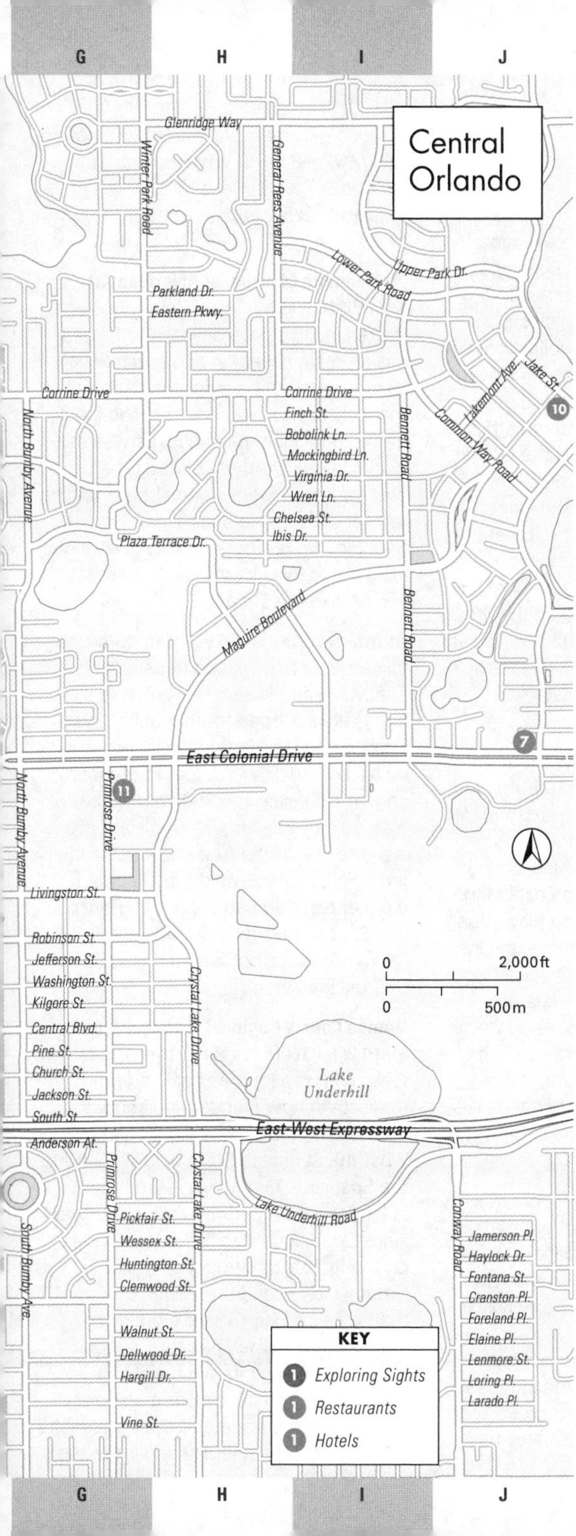

Sights

1 CityArts Orlando **C7**
2 Crayola Experience Orlando **A9**
3 Harry P. Leu Gardens............... **F3**
4 Lake Eola Park **C6**
5 Mennello Museum of American Art....................... **D2**
6 Orange County Regional History Center....................... **C7**
7 Orlando Museum of Art............ **E2**
8 Orlando Science Center **D2**
9 SNAP! Orlando.......................... **D7**

Restaurants

1 Armando's College Park **A2**
2 Black Rooster Taqueria **E3**
3 The Boheme Restaurant........... **C7**
4 DoveCote Restaurant **B6**
5 Graffiti Junktion Thornton Park...................... **D6**
6 Hawkers **E4**
7 Linda's La Cantina **J5**
8 Maxine's on Shine.................. **E6**
9 Reyes Mezcaleria **C4**
10 Seito Sushi and New Japanese...................... **J3**
11 Se7en Bites......................... **G5**
12 Soco................................... **D7**

Hotels

1 Aloft Orlando Downtown **C8**
2 Embassy Suites by Hilton Orlando Downtown................. **C7**
3 Grand Bohemian Hotel Orlando, Autograph Collection............... **C7**
4 Wellborn **C8**

★ Harry P. Leu Gardens

GARDEN | Just blocks from Downtown—on the former lakefront estate of a citrus entrepreneur—is this 50-acre garden. Among the highlights are a collection of historical blooms (many varieties of which were established before 1900), ancient oaks, a 50-foot floral clock, and one of the largest camellia collections in eastern North America (in bloom November–March). Mary Jane's Rose Garden, named after Leu's wife, is filled with more than 1,000 bushes; it's the largest formal rose garden south of Atlanta. The simple, 19th-century Leu House Museum, once the Leu home, preserves the furnishings and appointments of a well-to-do, turn-of-the-20th-century Florida family. Admission is free on the first Monday of the month. ✉ *1920 N. Forest Ave., Audubon Park* ☎ *407/246–2620* 🌐 *www.leugardens.org* 🎫 *$10.*

★ Lake Eola Park

CITY PARK | FAMILY | Ringed by modern high-rises, this peaceful, beautifully landscaped, 43-acre park is the verdant heart of Downtown. Its mile-long walking path attracts families, health enthusiasts out for a run, and culture mavens exploring area offerings; its well-lighted playground is alive with children; and ducks, swans, and native Florida birds call its lake home. A popular farmers' market takes up residence on Sunday; the lakeside Walt Disney Amphitheater is a dramatic site for concerts, festivals, and July 4 fireworks; and a landmark fountain features an LED-light-and-music show on summer evenings at 9:30.

Don't resist the park's biggest draw: a ride in a swan-shape paddleboat that can comfortably accommodate up to five people (children under 16 must be accompanied by an adult). The Relax Grill, by the swan-boat launch, is a great place for lunch, and the park is surrounded by a variety of restaurants and lounges in both Downtown and Thornton Park. ✉ *195 N. Rosalind Ave., Downtown Orlando* ✣ *Center of Downtown Orlando* ☎ *407/425–8440* 🌐 *www.orlando.gov/Parks-the-Environment/Directory/Lake-Eola-Park* 🎫 *Swan boat rental $15 per ½ hr.*

★ Mennello Museum of American Art

ART MUSEUM | One of the few museums in the United States devoted to folk art has intimate galleries, some with lovely lakefront views. Look for the nation's most extensive permanent collection of Earl Cunningham paintings, as well as works by many other self-taught artists. There's a wonderful video about Cunningham and his "curio shop" in St. Augustine, Florida. Temporary exhibitions have included the works of Wyeth, Cassatt, and Michael Eastman.

At the museum shop you can purchase folk-art books, toys, and unusual gifts. The Marilyn L. Mennello Sculpture Garden is always open to the public. Oversized outdoor sculptures include works by Alice Aycock and Barbara Sorensen, shown alongside the 350-year-old live oak tree called "The Mayor." The Mennello is also the site of the free annual Orlando Indie-Folk Festival, held the second weekend of February. ✉ *900 E. Princeton St., Lake Ivanhoe* ☎ *407/246–4278* 🌐 *www.mennellomuseum.org* 🎫 *$5* ⏲ *Closed Mon.*

Orange County Regional History Center

HISTORY MUSEUM | FAMILY | The center takes you on a journey back in time to discover how Florida's indigenous peoples hunted and fished the land, what the Sunshine State was like when the Spaniards first arrived, and how life in Florida was different when citrus was king. Exhibitions also include displays on the history of citrus-growing in Central Florida and the advancement of theme parks, samples of work by the famed Highwaymen painters, a diorama showing how an infamous sinkhole ate a city block, and documentation on the Pulse nightclub tragedy. Traveling exhibits bring modern technology and art to the

The 300-seat Dr. Phillips CineDome, a movie theater with an eight-story screen at the Orlando Science Center, offers large-format IMAX films.

museum. Free audio tours are available. ■ **TIP→ Ticket holders get two hours free parking.** ✉ *65 E. Central Blvd., Downtown Orlando* ☎ *407/836–8500, 800/965–2030* 🌐 *www.thehistorycenter.org* 🎟 *$8.*

Orlando Museum of Art

ART MUSEUM | FAMILY | Part of the City of Orlando's collection of arts venues, the Museum of Art sits in the Loch Haven Park complex. It exhibits contemporary art, mid-18th- and 19th-century American art, and an important collection of ancient artifacts of the Americas. In addition to American art created before 1945, and an extensive photography collection, exhibits of African textiles, and graphic art from such artists as Andy Warhol and Jasper Johns add to the diversity of its displays. The museum's collection of Chihuly glass, obtained during an exclusive exhibition in 2004, is among the finest in the country. A live music and art social mixer, called 1st Thursdays, runs 6 to 9 pm. ✉ *2416 N. Mills Ave., Lake Ivanhoe* ☎ *407/896–4231* 🌐 *omart.org* 🎟 *$20* 🕒 *Closed Mon.*

★ Orlando Science Center

SCIENCE MUSEUM | FAMILY | With exhibits about the human body, mechanics, computers, math, nature, the solar system, and optics, the science center has something for every child's inner geek. The 11,000-square-foot Kids Town is the center's most popular attraction, and traveling shows have included those on the astronaut experience and the science of human anatomy. There's also an annual interactive technology expo called Otronicon.

The four-story, internal atrium is home to live gators and turtles and is a great spot for simply gazing at what Old Florida once looked like. The 300-seat Dr. Phillips CineDome, a movie theater with a giant eight-story screen, offers films and planetarium programs. The Crosby Observatory and Florida's largest publicly accessible refractor telescope are here, as are several smaller telescopes. Late-evening weekend date nights make the observatory a fun draw for adults, who can enjoy events like the annual Science of Wine

Central Florida Art

Central Florida has several world-class art museums, including those that feature sublime stained-glass, American art, and folk art.

CityArts Orlando, Orlando. Housed in one of the oldest buildings in downtown, this small gallery features mostly local and regional artists.

Charles Hosmer Morse Museum of American Art, Winter Park. In what is known as the "Tiffany museum," the galleries contain the largest and most comprehensive collection of art by Louis Comfort Tiffany, including stained-glass windows and lamps, blown-glass vases, and gem-studded jewelry. For more information, see Winter Park in "Excursions from Orlando."

Mennello Museum of American Folk Art, Central Orlando. The Mennello holds the nation's most extensive permanent collection of Earl Cunningham paintings, as well as pieces by many other "outsider" artists. Works by Wyeth, Cassatt, Eastman, and others have made their Central Florida debuts here.

Modernism Museum, Mount Dora. A refined and dazzling private collection of American and international works from modernist artists features the work of George Nakashima and Wendell Castle, as well as that of the more radical Memphis group, including pieces collected by musician David Bowie. For more information, see Mount Dora in "Excursions from Orlando."

Orlando Museum of Art, Orlando. Here you'll find contemporary, mid-18th- and 19th-century American art and one of the largest collections of ancient artifacts of the Americas in the South. In addition, the museum's collection of Chihuly glass is among the finest in the country.

Snap! Orlando. Artistic, thoughtful, and at times challenging, the gallery operated by local photographer Patrick Kahn highlights the value of the still frame, with exhibits from internationally known artists and talented newcomers to the camera.

and the very popular monthly Science Night Live. *✉ 777 E. Princeton St., Lake Ivanhoe ☎ 407/514–2000 🌐 www.osc.org 🎫 $21; parking $5 ⏲ Closed Wed.*

SNAP! Orlando

ART GALLERY | Founded by international photographer Patrick Kahn, SNAP! is the leading repository of contemporary images in Orlando. The gallery in Colonialtown has shown cutting-edge photos from artists such as Shawn Theodore, Roger Ballen, and musician Moby, along with world premiere exhibitions, emerging graffiti artists, and even jewelry makers. *✉ 420 E Church St., Downtown Orlando ☎ 407/286–2185 🌐 snaporlando.com ⏲ Closed Sun.*

Restaurants

Central Orlando is quintessential urban Florida and offers much more than typical chain restaurants. Here you'll find a local, independent dining scene that's driven by award-winning and inventive chefs, creating a hot spot for creative cuisine.

Armando's College Park

$$$ | ITALIAN | FAMILY | Armando Martorelli has opened many local restaurants in his career since coming from Italy to Florida, but his namesake eatery is the epitome of his craft. It has a relaxed neighborhood vibe and serves what is perhaps the area's best Neapolitan-style pizza. **Known for:** extensive wine and cocktail list with a very popular bar area; wood-fired oven pizza and other Neapolitan specialties; superb seafood. *Average main: $22* *2305 Edgewater Dr., College Park* *407/930–0333* *armandosorlando.com.*

★ Black Rooster Taqueria

$ | **MEXICAN FUSION** | **FAMILY** | Nestled in the funky Mills 50 neighborhood, this small, casual, award-winning taco place serves corn tortillas and fresh guacamole with every dish. Tacos like the vegetarian (shiitake mushrooms, onions, zucchini, and crema fresca) or the smoked greens (kale, shiitake, plantain, onions, and ricotta) are unusual alternatives to the classic chicken tinga or carne asada options. **Known for:** made-to-order guacamole; inventive and flavorful tacos; chocolate chip spicy flan. *Average main: $12* *1323 N. Mills Ave., Central Orlando* *407/601–0994* *www.blackrooster-taqueria.com* *Closed Mon.*

★ The Boheme Restaurant

$$$$ | **ECLECTIC** | The Grand Bohemian, a boutique, luxury hotel, is the setting for this sleek city-center restaurant. Start with the calamari or porcini mushroom flatbread appetizers followed, perhaps, by a selection from the famed Angus beef menu, the Chilean sea bass, or the Hunter's Board of handcrafted charcuterie. **Known for:** elaborate Sunday jazz brunch; upscale, chef-driven dining in a fashionable hotel; pre- and postdinner cocktail lounge. *Average main: $38* *Grand Bohemian Hotel Orlando, Autograph Collection, 325 S. Orange Ave., Downtown Orlando* *407/313–9000* *kesslercollection.com/boheme-restaurant.*

DoveCote Restaurant

$$$ | **BRASSERIE** | Talented chefs bring big city sophistication to Downtown Orlando at this casual eatery with a French-American fusion menu and craft cocktails. Everything that can be made in-house—pickles, condiments, bread—is, and although the chicken, steak, and seafood entrées are fantastic, the frites (fries) alone are worth the trip. **Known for:** braised short ribs with trumpet mushrooms; handcrafted charcuterie and cocktails; raw bar with Florida oysters. *Average main: $24* *Bank of America Building, 390 N Orange Ave., Central Orlando* *407/930–1700* *dovecote-orlando.com* *No dinner Sun. Morning hours vary.*

Graffiti Junktion Thornton Park

$ | **BURGER** | **FAMILY** | Noisy and visually loud (commissioned graffiti makes up the decor), casual and astoundingly popular Graffiti Junktion holds the burger/wrap/sandwich crowd in thrall. Burgers run large and juicy, with hand-formed patties bursting from the bun in varieties like the Iron City (Angus beef, Canadian bacon, cheese, and a fried egg), and all three of the Orlando locations are open until 2 am. **Known for:** hand-cut french fries; late hours and noisy sports bar atmosphere; fresh-formed burgers with inventive toppings. *Average main: $12* *700 East Washington St., Thornton Park* *321/424–5800* *graffitijunktion.com* *Closed Mon.*

★ Hawkers

$ | **ASIAN FUSION** | **FAMILY** | Hipsters, families, and business groups dine side by side at this popular restaurant, a laid-back spot that specializes in Asian street food and has quickly become a Southern institution with 13 locations in 7 states. Travel the continent with scratch-made family recipes from across Southeast Asia. **Known for:** extensive and exotic beer selections; dishes like roti canai, sesame noodles, and stir-fried udon; hip and casual atmosphere. *Average main: $9* *1103 N. Mills Ave., Mills 50 District* *407/237–0606* *eathawkers.com.*

Linda's La Cantina

$$$ | **STEAKHOUSE** | **FAMILY** | A local favorite since 1947, this down-home steak house serves good cuts of meat, expertly cooked and reasonably priced. Butchery is done on premises, and there are no TVs over the bar to distract from a pleasant conversation over a great steak. **Known for:** seafood and pasta entrées; an Orlando classic; hand-cut, house-aged steaks. *Average main: $26* *4721 E. Colonial Dr., Downtown Orlando* *Near Orlando Executive Airport* *407/894–4491* *lindaslacantinasteakhouse.com* *Closed Sun. and Mon. No lunch.*

Maxine's on Shine

$$$ | **AMERICAN** | A holdover from when neighborhood restaurants were actually in a neighborhood, award-winning Maxine's is casual, hip, local, and friendly. The menu ranges from sophisticated seafood to brisket burgers and Black Angus filet mignon. **Known for:** seafood dishes from a veteran local chef; lively, neighborhood atmosphere; outdoor dining. *Average main: $25* *337 N. Shine, Downtown Orlando* *407/674–6841* *maxinesonshine.com* *Closed Mon. and Tues.*

★ Reyes Mezcaleria

$$$ | **MEXICAN** | **FAMILY** | Standing out in a town saturated with taco places, Reyes brings authentic (read: real Mexican) cuisine in the form of Michoacán-born chef Wendy Lopez, who honors the food of her homeland while adding inventive modern touches. Yucatán pork ribs, duck enchiladas, and a mixed grill of NY strip, chicken, and shrimp are just a taste. **Known for:** everything from casual tacos to sophisticated dinners; bar with more than 150 agave selections; crispy whole-fish platter for two. *Average main: $26* *821 N. Orange Ave., Central Orlando* *407/868–9007* *reyesmex.com* *Closed Mon.*

★ Seito Sushi and New Japanese

$$$ | **JAPANESE FUSION** | **FAMILY** | The epitome of modern Japanese cuisine, Seito offers crowd-pleasing traditional and contemporary ramen bowls as well as unique, handcrafted sushi combinations and Japanese "kitchen food." The sophisticated and fun bar specializes in Japanese cask whiskey and multiple exclusive sake brands. **Known for:** Wagyu steak tartare; hand-pulled ramen noodles; exclusively crafted sushi. *Average main: $22* *4898 New Broad St., Central Orlando* *407/898–8801* *seitosushibp.com* *Closed Mon.* *Baldwin Park.*

★ Se7en Bites

$$ | **AMERICAN** | **FAMILY** | Trina Gregory-Propst and her team of bakers and cooks make the biggest and most satisfying breakfasts, lunches, and sweet treats in town. Try a from-scratch chicken pot pie, which has the most glorious crust; the mile-high meat loaf sandwich; or the "7th Trimester" of buttermilk garlic biscuit, over-medium egg, and smoked bacon, smothered in five-cheese mac-and-cheese. **Known for:** featured on TV show *Diners, Drive-ins, and Dives*; over-the-top Southern breakfast specials; funky Downtown location. *Average main: $15* *617 Primrose Dr., Central Orlando* *407/302–0727* *www.se7enbites.com* *Closed Mon.–Wed. No dinner.*

★ Soco

$$$ | **AMERICAN** | In the talented hands of executive chef Greg Richie, Southern staples get mighty fancy at Soco, and both the menu and the decor mesh classic and creative in a suave way. Vegetarians get one of the best meatless entrées in town with the chicken-fried cauliflower steak, a massive dish finished with a rich tomato gravy; meat eaters enjoy playful touches like lobster-mashed potatoes served with the meat loaf. **TIP→ Start your meal with the handmade buttermilk biscuits, and end with one of the house special desserts like a "Moon Pie."** **Known for:** stellar vegetarian options; funky daily specials like TV Dinner Thursday; sophisticated bar. *Average main: $23* *629 E. Central Blvd., Thornton Park*

☎ *407/849–1800* ⊕ *socothorntonpark.com* ⏱ *Closed Mon. No lunch.*

Hotels

Central Orlando, north of Walt Disney World and the I-Drive area, is a thriving business district on weekdays and attracts a club and restaurant crowd on weekend nights.

Aloft Orlando Downtown

$$ | HOTEL | In the heart of Orlando, steps from the arts center, sports arena, and nightlife, this former utilities building has been transformed into a trendy urban hotel, with a busy bar, innovative rooms, and high-tech amenities. **Pros:** trendy urban vibe; just steps from Downtown nightlife, arts, and sporting events; easy access to highways. **Cons:** an urban vibe can be noisy; only parking choice is valet or street parking; Disney is a 45-minute drive away on I–4. *$ Rooms from: $209* ✉ *500 S. Orange Ave., Downtown Orlando* ☎ *407/380–3500* ⊕ *www.aloftorlandodowntown.com* *111 rooms* *No Meals.*

Embassy Suites by Hilton Orlando Downtown

$$ | HOTEL | FAMILY | A short walk from a half-dozen cafés and restaurants, the Orange County History Center, and the performing arts center and sports venue, this hotel has numerous suites with views of nearby Lake Eola and its centerpiece fountain, swan boats, and jogging path. **Pros:** free Wi-Fi; near Lake Eola and Downtown; free breakfast and evening reception (with snacks). **Cons:** Disney is at least 45 minutes away (an hour or more during rush hour); on-street parking is hard to find, and there's a fee for on-site parking; traffic can be heavy. *$ Rooms from: $211* ✉ *191 E. Pine St., Downtown Orlando* ☎ *407/841–1000, 800/609–3339* ⊕ *www.embassysuites.com* *167 suites* *Free Breakfast.*

Grand Bohemian Hotel Orlando, Autograph Collection

$$$ | HOTEL | Adjacent to the performing arts center and a block from the sports venue, this luxurious, European-style property affords city-center views and showcases hundreds of pieces of art, along with a rare Imperial Grand Bösendorfer piano, which is played by jazz pianists in the popular Bösendorfer Lounge. **Pros:** quiet, adult-friendly atmosphere; art gallery and sophisticated entertainment; critically acclaimed restaurant. **Cons:** fees for parking and far from Disney and Universal; meals are pricey; little to attract kids. *$ Rooms from: $299* ✉ *325 S. Orange Ave., Downtown Orlando* ☎ *407/313–9000* ⊕ *www.kesslercollection.com/bohemian-orlando* *212 rooms* *No Meals.*

Wellborn

$ | B&B/INN | Built more than a half century before Disney arrived, these three beautifully restored Victorian houses were rescued and moved to this palm-lined courtyard that's within blocks of the city's arts and sports venues. **Pros:** free parking and Wi-Fi; great Victorian architecture; short walk to Downtown restaurants, the Amway Center, and performing arts center. **Cons:** popular event venue, thus noise could be an issue; walking in some parts of Downtown at night can be dicey; far from theme parks and I-Drive. *$ Rooms from: $100* ✉ *211 N. Lucerne Circle E, Downtown Orlando* ☎ *321/837–9614* ⊕ *www.sonder.com* *20 rooms* *Free Breakfast.*

Nightlife

The heart of Orlando nightlife extends several blocks from the intersection of Orange Avenue and Church Street. Bars, cantinas, lounges, dance clubs, movie theaters, a sports arena, and the performing arts center are all within this core area, creating an energetic blend of bourgeoisie and bohemian.

BARS

AERO Rooftop Bar

BARS | On a starry, starry night it's nice to retreat from the crowded street-level drinking establishments to this spot atop The Social music club. Surrounded by some of Orlando's tallest buildings, it exudes hip, trendy vibes that are just right for those looking to dance to a DJ outdoors. Ladies' nights, theme events, and even yoga classes are offered. ✉ *60 N. Orange Ave., Downtown Orlando* ☎ *407/274–8452* 🌐 *www.facebook.com/aeroorl* ⏲ *Closed Mon.–Wed.*

Bull and Bush Pub

PUBS | Here since 1987, this pub just a few miles east of Downtown has become a neighborhood institution. It's an atmospheric place to get a hand-drawn pint, play a game of darts, and have a (still) smoky chat. The tap lineup covers 10 imported beers and ales and quadruples that number in bottled selections, while the kitchen prepares fish-and-chips, cottage pies, and Scotch eggs. Darts leagues, comedy nights, and weekly pub quizzes make it feel like a piece of old London. ✉ *2408 E. Robinson St., Downtown Orlando* ☎ *407/896–7546* 🌐 *www.bullandbushorlando.com* ⏲ *Closed Sun.*

Chillers-Cahoots-Latitude

BARS | Known as Orlando's original party bar (it's been here since 1992), Chillers is a Key West–themed nightspot that features a wall of frozen daiquiri machines. Upstairs, Chillers' sister club, Cahoots, offers more than 100 craft beers and 40 bourbon whiskeys. Latitudes is a large rooftop bar with a tropical theme and Top 40 music. ✉ *33 W. Church St., Downtown Orlando* ☎ *407/649–4270* 🌐 *www.churchstreetbars.com.*

Wall Street Plaza

BARS | Wall Street Plaza is a complex of seven distinct, themed venues. Choose the Wall Street Cantina for Mexican fare, the Hen House ("The World's Smallest Bar-dello") for craft beers, Hooch for an outdoor bar, the Shine dance club for its "moonshine warehouse" look, the Monkey Bar martini lounge, the outdoor WaiTiki Bar, or Sideshow for a party scene. With a calendar packed with events, this is considered Party Central for many in the Downtown crowd. ✉ *25 Wall St. Plaza, Downtown Orlando* ☎ *407/420–1515* 🌐 *www.wallstplaza.net.*

Wally's Bar & Liquors

BARS | One of the city's oldest bars (circa 1954), this longtime local favorite, in the middle of the funky Mills 50 neighborhood, is a hangout for a cross section of cultures and ages. Some would say it's a dive—even in its cleaned-up state—but that doesn't matter to the students, bikers, lawyers, and barflies who land here. Just grab a stool at the bar to take in the scene and down a cold one. ✉ *1001 N. Mills Ave., Downtown Orlando* ☎ *407/440–2800* 🌐 *www.wallysbarandliquors.com.*

MUSIC CLUBS

Bösendorfer Lounge

LIVE MUSIC | A rare Imperial Grand Bösendorfer piano takes center stage at what might be the city's classiest gathering spot. The highly civilized (but not stuffy) lounge attracts a cross section of trendy Orlandoans, especially the after-work crowd, among whom conversation and camaraderie flow as smoothly as the champagne, beer, wine, and cocktails. And, with its location across from the performing arts center, it's a draw pre- and postconcert. Call in advance for the schedule of jazz combos and solo pianists who perform in the lounge. Many are among the area's finest and most talented musicians. ✉ *Grand Bohemian Hotel Orlando, Autograph Collection, 325 S. Orange Ave., Downtown Orlando* ☎ *407/313–9000* 🌐 *www.kesslercollection.com/bohemian-orlando.*

★ The Social

LIVE MUSIC | Beloved by locals, The Social is a great place to see touring and area musicians. Up to seven nights a week, you can sip trademark martinis while listening to anything from indie rock to rockabilly to music mixed by DJs. Fans love the venue because the stage is low, the bands are close, and the enthusiasm is high. Hours vary, and there is usually a cover. ✉ *54 N. Orange Ave., Downtown Orlando* ☎ *407/710–1279* 🌐 *foundation-presents.com/the-social.*

Tanqueray's

LIVE MUSIC | Of all the entertainment possibilities in Downtown Orlando, the most interesting one might be the hardest to find. Housed in a former bank vault, Tanqueray's is a below-ground hideaway featuring live music and a full bar, including craft beers and drink specials. You can enjoy a variety of entertainment from one night to the next, including reggae, funk, and high-energy blues. No food is served here, though. ✉ *100 S. Orange Ave., Downtown Orlando* ☎ *407/649–8540.*

Performing Arts

THEATER

★ **Dr. Phillips Center for the Performing Arts**

ARTS CENTERS | FAMILY | When this stunning, state-of-the-art venue opened in the heart of Downtown, it elevated the arts for Orlando. Encompassing three unique stages, it's where major Broadway productions found a home; where musicians such as Bob Dylan, Brian Wilson, and Elvis Costello have performed; and where opera, symphonies, ballet, and comedy shows fill the calendar year-round. ✉ *445 S. Magnolia Ave., Downtown Orlando* ☎ *844/513–2014, 407/839–0119* 🌐 *www.drphillipscenter.org.*

Mad Cow Theatre

THEATER | FAMILY | Orlando's longest-standing professional theater company is where risks are taken. Regional premieres, new works, and thoughtful interpretations of classics make this a stage worth seeking. Local actors eager to show their talents line up to work here. ✉ *54 W. Church St., Downtown Orlando* ☎ *407/297–8788* 🌐 *www.madcowtheatre.com.*

★ **Orlando Shakes**

THEATER | FAMILY | The theater complex has four stages, where a typical season includes 11 plays covering classics (including Shakespeare, of course), contemporary, musicals, comedies, and family shows. The theater also hosts the very popular Orlando International Fringe Festival, the oldest in America. The season runs June through April, with the Fringe Festival in May. PlayFest! The Harriett Lake Festival of New Plays offers world-premiere and staged-reading opportunities for new playwrights. The theater is in Loch Haven Cultural Park, just a few minutes north of Downtown, where the Orlando Science Center and the Museum of Art also stand. ✉ *812 E. Rollins St., Lake Ivanhoe* ☎ *407/447–1700* 🌐 *www.orlandoshakes.org.*

International Drive

The sprawl of hotels, time-shares, restaurants, malls, and entertainment complexes known as International Drive (I-Drive to locals) makes a central base for visits to Walt Disney World, Universal, and other Orlando attractions. Parallel to I–4, this four-lane boulevard stretches from Universal in the north to near Kissimmee in the south.

Entertainment choices include roller coasters, go-carts, and miniature golf, as well as the attractions at ICON Park, including Madame Tussauds, the SEA LIFE Orlando aquarium, the 450-foot tall Starflyer swing ride, and The Wheel, which offers breathtaking views of the entire, glittering, neon-shiny area. I-Drive hotels, many attached to the convention center, range from high-end luxury to affordable family spots, and they contain some of Orlando's finest restaurants.

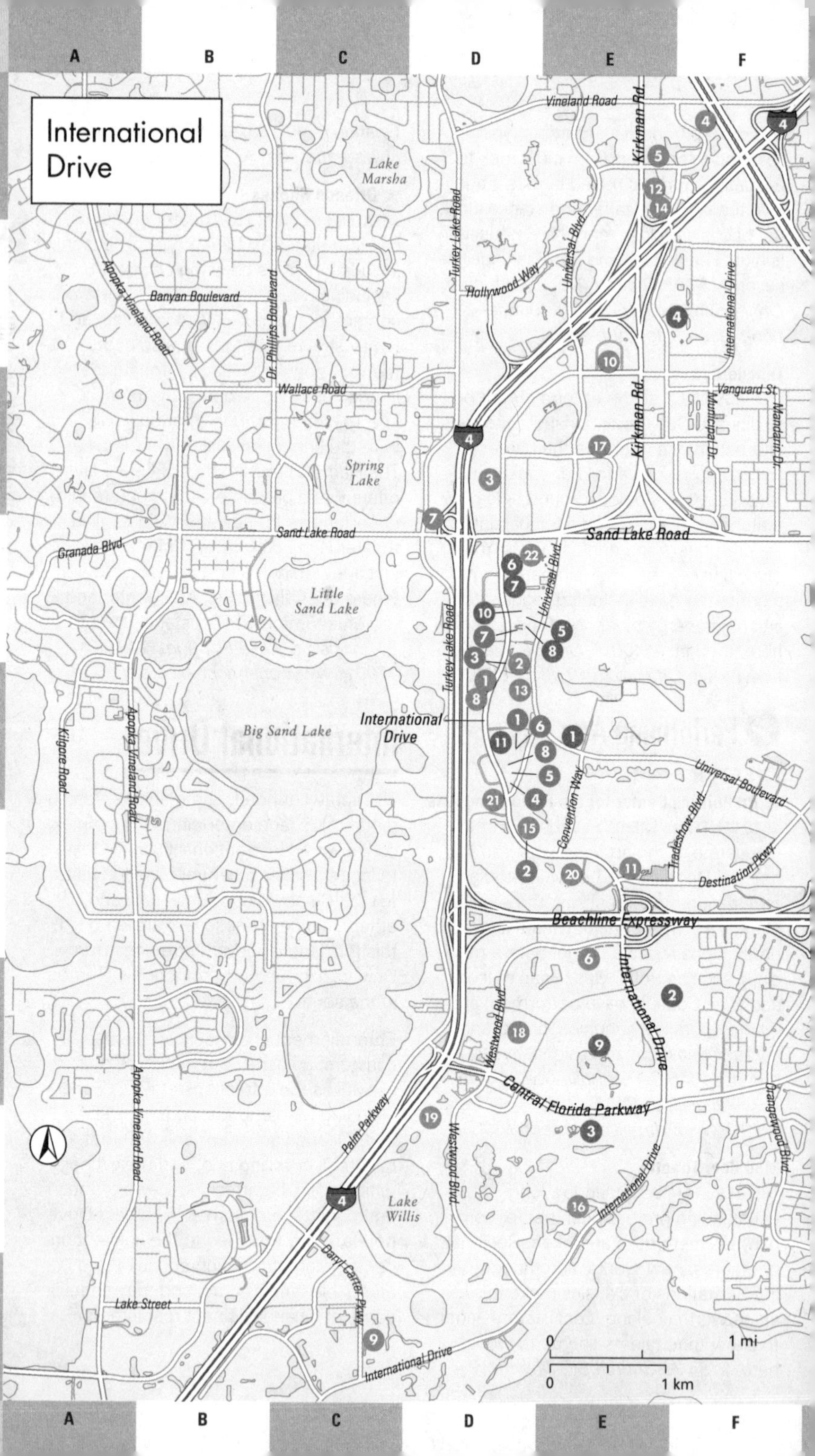
International Drive
A
B
C
D
E
F
1
2
3
4
5
6
7
8
9
Vineland Road
Kirkman Rd.
Lake Marsha
Turkey Lake Road
Universal Blvd.
Hollywood Way
Banyan Boulevard
Apopka-Vineland Road
Dr. Phillips Boulevard
International Drive
Wallace Road
Vanguard St.
Municipal Dr.
Mandarin Dr.
Spring Lake
Sand Lake Road
Granada Blvd.
Little Sand Lake
Big Sand Lake
Kilgore Road
Convention Way
Universal Boulevard
Tradeshow Blvd.
Destination Pkwy.
Beachline Expressway
Westwood Blvd.
Central Florida Parkway
Palm Parkway
Lake Willis
Orangewood Blvd.
Daryl Carter Pkwy.
Lake Street
0
1 mi
1 km

Sights

1 Andretti Indoor Karting and Games...... **E5**

2 Aquatica.................. **E7**

3 Discovery Cove **E8**

4 Fun Spot America........ **E2**

5 Madame Tussauds Orlando **D4**

6 Orlando Starflyer **D4**

7 Ripley's Orlando......... **D4**

8 SEA LIFE Orlando Aquarium **D4**

9 SeaWorld Orlando....... **E7**

10 The Wheel at ICON Park **D4**

11 WonderWorks Orlando **D5**

Restaurants

1 B.B. King's Blues Club **D5**

2 B-Line Diner............. **D6**

3 Café Tu Tu Tango........ **D4**

4 Cuba Libre Restaurant & Rum Bar............... **D5**

5 The Hampton Social.... **D5**

6 Oceanaire Seafood Room **D5**

7 Tapa Toro **D4**

8 Taverna Opa Orlando... **D5**

Hotels

1 Avanti Resort............ **D5**

2 Castle Hotel, Autograph Collection... **D4**

3 CoCo Key Hotel and Water Resort............ **D3**

4 Comfort Suites Near Universal Orlando Resort...................... **F1**

5 DoubleTree by Hilton at the Entrance to Universal Orlando **E1**

6 DoubleTree by Hilton Orlando at SeaWorld.................. **E6**

7 Drury Inn and Suites near Universal Orlando Resort.......... **D4**

8 Embassy Suites by Hilton Orlando International Drive Convention Center...... **D5**

9 Floridays Resort Orlando **C9**

10 Four Points by Sheraton Orlando International Drive....... **E2**

11 Hilton Orlando............ **E6**

12 Holiday Inn and Suites Across From Universal Orlando **E1**

13 Hyatt Place Orlando/ I-Drive/ Convention Center...... **D5**

14 Hyatt Place Orlando/ Universal.................. **E1**

15 Hyatt Regency Orlando **D6**

16 Parc Corniche Condominium Suite Hotel................ **E8**

17 The Point Hotel and Suites **E3**

18 Renaissance Orlando at SeaWorld............ **D7**

19 Residence Inn by Marriott Orlando at SeaWorld................ **D8**

20 Rosen Centre Hotel...... **E6**

21 Rosen Plaza Hotel **D5**

22 Wyndham Orlando Resort International Drive...... **D4**

Sights

Andretti Indoor Karting and Games

SPORTS VENUE | FAMILY | The racing legend lent his name to this entertainment facility that offers boutique bowling on black-lit lanes, a video game and pinball arcade, a sky-trail ropes course with curved ziplines, virtual reality attractions, a shoot-em-up 7-D dark ride, and, naturally, racing. Pro racing simulators add motion, vibrations, sound effects, and even add tension in the seatbelt so you feel as if you're on an actual racetrack. When you're ready to actually race, three indoor tracks let you whip around corners, change elevation, and zip into banked curves on small, high-torque karts. Add laser tag, a restaurant, and more than 100 screens tuned into the day's top sporting events, and you have a lot of entertainment packed into one exciting complex. ✉ *9299 Universal Blvd., International Drive* ☎ *407/374–0042* 🌐 *andrettikarting.com/orlando* 🎟 *Racing from $22; ropes course, laser tag, other games from $13.*

Aquatica

WATER PARK | FAMILY | In terms of water thrills, SeaWorld's 59-acre Aquatica holds its own against Disney's water parks and Universal's Volcano Bay. It offers more than 40 waterslides, from the gentle Kata's Kookaburra Cove to the freefall experience of Ihu's Breakaway Falls, as well as beaches and lagoons, fast and slow rivers, two massive wave pools, and an extensive kids' area.

Younger children are attracted to Walkabout Waters, a 60-foot-tall water-soaking jungle gym, where they can climb, slide, and get soaked. Teens and adults flock to the Dolphin Plunge, where two, side-by-side, transparent tubes allow riders to join a pod of black-and-white dolphins underwater. The Ray Rush family raft ride offers multiple high-speed paths through enclosed tubes and transparent spheres. There are height requirements of at least 42 inches for some rides, and all visitors need to know how to swim. ✉ *5800 Water Play Way, International Drive* ☎ *407/545–5550* 🌐 *aquatica.com* 🎟 *$55; parking is $25 per car (combo tickets for SeaWorld and Discovery Cove are also available)* ⏲ *Closed some days in Jan. and Feb.*

Discovery Cove

WATER PARK | FAMILY | The only theme park in Orlando that can be called "exclusive," Discovery Cove offers uncrowded, daylong encounters with dolphins, otters, sharks, and rays, as well as relaxing swims and resort-style amenities—all right next door to SeaWorld. Lockers, wet suits, parking, breakfast, lunch, drinks, and snacks are all included in the admission price. The park has tropical landscaping, white-sand beaches, waterfalls, and vast freshwater lagoons.

Regular park admission includes snorkeling with tropical fish and rays in the Grand Reef, hand-feeding exotic birds in the Explorer's Aviary, or just floating on the Wind Away lazy river. Add-ons—such as using a diving helmet in the Grand Reef, swimming with the sharks, or Atlantic bottlenose dolphin swim experiences—are available for an additional cost and often sell out, despite having been criticized by some animal-rights activists. Note that the Discovery Cove Plus ticket gets you into this park as well as SeaWorld and Aquatica. Ticket prices vary wildly depending on day, the season, and the package options (there are many). ✉ *6000 Discovery Cove Way, International Drive* ☎ *407/513–4600* 🌐 *discoverycove.com* 🎟 *From $199; package options can add several hundred dollars to the tab.*

Fun Spot America

AMUSEMENT PARK/CARNIVAL | FAMILY | You can see the neon-lit rides from miles away as you approach International Drive. Four go-kart tracks offer a variety of driving experiences. Though drivers must be at least 10 years old and meet height

The views from The Wheel at ICON Park can extend to more than 50 miles on a clear day.

requirements, parents can drive younger children in two-seater cars on several of the tracks, including the Conquest Track. Nineteen rides range from the dizzying Enterprise to an old-fashioned Ferris wheel to the twirling toddler Teacups.

Fun Spot features Central Florida's only wooden roller coaster as well as the Freedom Flyer steel suspension family coaster, a kiddie coaster, and SkyCoaster—part skydive, part hang-glide. There's also an arcade. Gator Spot, created in partnership with the iconic Gatorland and starring several live alligators and other Florida wildlife, is a throwback to the old days of Orlando roadside attractions. ✉ *5700 Fun Spot Way, International Drive* ✥ *From Exit 75A, turn south onto Grand National Dr., then east on Fun Spot Way* ☎ *407/363–3867* 🌐 *www.fun-spot.com* 🎟 *$49 for most rides (online discounts available); some rides extra; admission for nonriders free.*

Madame Tussauds Orlando

OTHER MUSEUM | FAMILY | Featuring wax copies of real and fictional characters, Madame Tussauds lets you grab a selfie with the faux superheroes, including Wonder Woman, Superman, Batman, and Aquaman, as well as celebrities both living and dead—from Taylor Swift and Pink to Pitbull and Michael Jackson—and the rich and famous from politics and sports. **■ TIP→ Combo tickets are available for this museum, The Wheel at ICON Park, and SEA LIFE Orlando Aquarium.** ✉ *ICON Park, 8387 International Dr., International Drive* ☎ *855/450–0581* 🌐 *www.madame-tussauds.com/orlando* 🎟 *$34 (combo tickets, coupons, and online discounts available).*

Orlando Starflyer

AMUSEMENT RIDE | FAMILY | You can travel at 45 mph on this 450-foot-tall swing, said to be the tallest in the world, which also rotates 360 degrees. It's as terrifying as it sounds, so this ride is not for either the faint of heart or small children.

The clear tunnel at Shark Encounter in SeaWorld takes you underwater and underneath the sharks.

■ **TIP→ Ticket packages for ICON Park attractions are available.** ✉ *ICON Park, 8265 International Dr., International Drive* ☎ *407/640–7009* 🌐 *starflyer.com* 🎫 *$13 (combo tickets, coupons, and online discounts available).*

Ripley's Orlando

OTHER MUSEUM | FAMILY | A 10-foot-square section of the Berlin Wall, a pain-and-torture chamber, two African fertility statues that women swear have helped them conceive—these and almost 200 other oddities (shrunken heads included) speak for themselves in this museum-cum-attraction in the heart of tourist territory on International Drive. The building itself is designed to appear as if it's sliding into one of Florida's notorious sinkholes. Give yourself an hour or two to soak up the weirdness, but remember: this is a looking, not touching, experience; it might drive antsy youngsters—and their parents—crazy. ■ **TIP→ Buy tickets online ahead of time, and you can get discounts.** ✉ *8201 International Dr., International Drive* ☎ *407/345–0501* 🌐 *www.ripleys.com* 🎫 *$30; parking free.*

★ **SEA LIFE Orlando Aquarium**

AQUARIUM | FAMILY | In the shadow of a 400-foot observation wheel and within the ICON Park entertainment complex stands a kaleidoscope of underwater colors, where you can see some 5,000 sea creatures and experience various habitats. Plan to spend the better part of an afternoon exploring, as all ages delight at the close encounters with the aquarium's sharks, green sea turtles, and jellyfish. With an emphasis on education and conservation, exhibits are playful and informative, with fun features that include a 360-degree ocean tunnel and a children's soft play area. ■ **TIP→ Combo tickets are available for the aquarium, The Wheel at ICON Park, and Madame Tussauds.** ✉ *ICON Park, 8449 International Dr., International Drive* ☎ *407/270–8610* 🌐 *visitsealife.com* 🎫 *$34 (combo tickets, coupons, and online discounts available).*

SeaWorld Orlando

THEME PARK | FAMILY | The oldest operating, biggest, and perhaps most controversial marine-mammal park in the country has been anchoring the Orlando Disney–alternative theme-park business since 1964. Much has been made of the company's handling of animals, and they've been in "rebuild and repair" mode for several years after attendance and stock prices plummeted.

SeaWorld still features dolphins and orcas, but thrill rides and literal spills are now the order of the day, with more swirling, looping, and splashing than just about anywhere. The Kraken Unleashed coaster soars to 150 feet while riders dangle their feet from the floorless track. The Manta and the Mako—which SeaWorld claims is Orlando's tallest, fastest, and longest coaster—skim tantalizingly close to the water. Other offerings include Infinity Falls River Rapids, with the world's tallest river-raft drop, and the 400-foot Sky Tower, with bird's-eye views of the park. The newest ride is Ice Breaker, a launch coaster that features a 93-foot tall spike with a 100-degree angle.

Animal attractions here now focus more on education than performance. Shark Encounter leads you through one of the world's largest underwater viewing tunnels, and Stingray Lagoon offers encounters with both stingrays and mantas. You can visit the ice-filled home of Puck the penguin in Antarctica: Empire of the Penguin and observe sea lions, walruses, and otters at Pacific Point Preserve, which doubles as a sea-lion rehabilitation facility. Helping injured marine animals is also the focus of the Manatee Rehabilitation Area and the Pelican Preserve, which offer up-close views of rescue operations. ✉ *7007 SeaWorld Dr., International Drive* ☎ *407/545–5550* 🌐 *seaworldorlando.com* 🎫 *$92, $25 parking (online discounts and combo tickets for Aquatica and Discovery Cove available).*

★ The Wheel at ICON Park

AMUSEMENT RIDE | FAMILY | The star ICON Park attraction is the 400-foot-tall observation wheel known simply as The Wheel, which offers an almost unobstructed view of all the distant theme parks, lush green landscape, and the soaring buildings of the City Beautiful. Visibility on clear days can be more than 50 miles, reaching all the way east to Cape Canaveral. The wheel's 30 high-tech capsules complete a rotation every 30 minutes, and riders can use onboard Apple iPad Air tablets to locate points of interest. Rent a private capsule for up to 15 people, with champagne, for a sky-high experience. **■ TIP→ Ticket packages for ICON Park attractions are available.** ✉ *ICON Park, 8401 International Dr., International Drive* ☎ *407/601–7907* 🌐 *iconparkorlando.com* 🎫 *$30.*

WonderWorks Orlando

OTHER MUSEUM | FAMILY | The building seems to be sinking into the ground—at a precarious angle and upside down. Many people stop to take pictures in front of the topsy-turvy facade, complete with upended palm trees and broken sidewalks. Inside, the upside-down theme continues only as far as the lobby. After that it's a playground of 100 interactive experiences—some incorporating virtual reality, others educational (similar to those at a science museum), and still others pure entertainment. You can experience an earthquake or a hurricane, land a space shuttle using simulator controls, make giant bubbles in the Bubble Lab, play laser tag in the enormous arena and arcade, design and ride your own roller coaster, lie on a bed of real nails, and play baseball with a virtual Major League batter. ✉ *9067 International Dr., International Drive* ☎ *407/351–8800* 🌐 *www.wonderworksonline.com/orlando* 🎫 *$35 (online discounts available); parking from $5.*

Manta is one of several thrilling roller coasters at SeaWorld Orlando.

Restaurants

Restaurants are in or scattered amid the hotels that line International Drive. Many are branches of chains, from fast-food spots to themed coffee shops and up, but the food here can be quite good. To get here, use Exit 72 or 74A off I–4. The travel time can be up to 30 minutes from the Kissimmee area or a WDW property.

B.B. King's Blues Club

$$ | **SOUTHERN** | **FAMILY** | This massive restaurant is dedicated to soul food, live blues, and the legacy of B.B. King. Look for a menu full of ribs, sandwiches, and hefty cocktails. **Known for:** messy and delicious burgers; live bands and dancing; barbecued ribs, brisket, and shrimp and grits. *Average main: $18* ✉ *Pointe Orlando, 9101 International Dr., International Drive* ☎ *407/370–4550* 🌐 *bbkings.com/orlando.*

B-Line Diner

$$ | **AMERICAN** | **FAMILY** | Open from early breakfast to late dinner in the Hyatt Regency, this slick modern diner is not exactly cheap, but the salads, sandwiches, and griddle foods are tops. The classic B Line Burger is done beautifully. **Known for:** large dessert menu; updated diner theme; breakfast and late-night specials. *Average main: $20* ✉ *Hyatt Regency Orlando, 9801 International Dr., International Drive* ☎ *407/284–1234* 🌐 *hyatt.com/en-US/hotel/florida/hyatt-regency-orlando/mcoro/dining.*

Café Tu Tu Tango

$$$ | **ECLECTIC** | **FAMILY** | The food here is served tapas-style, and although everything is appetizer-sized, it's plentiful and relatively inexpensive. The restaurant is designed to resemble an artist's loft: painters work at easels while diners take a culinary trip around the world with dishes such as black-bean soup with cilantro sour cream, guava-glazed barbecue pork ribs, hazelnut-lemongrass fish, or spiced alligator bites. **Known for:** "Bottomless Brunch" food and drink specials; small plates ideal for sharing; live entertainment and artists. *Average main: $23* ✉ *8625 International Dr., International Drive* ☎ *407/248–2222* 🌐 *www.cafetututango.com.*

Cuba Libre Restaurant & Rum Bar
$$$ | **CUBAN** | **FAMILY** | The dining rooms at this Cuban restaurant feel as if they're movie sets of Old Havana, with dramatic touches upstairs and down. Start your meal with a meat-filled arepa rellena corn cake or a platter of two to four empanadas filled with savory ground beef and olives, chicken, cheese, or pork; for the main course, consider the *churrasco a la Cubana* (grilled skirt steak) with a lemon-onion sauce plus a watercress-mushroom escabeche salad. **Known for:** Friday and Saturday late nights with salsa dancing; menu via celeb chef Guillermo Pernot; extensive rum bar. *Average main: $28* *Pointe Orlando, 9101 International Dr., International Drive* *407/226–1600* *www.cubalibrerestaurant.com* *No lunch. Closed Mon. and Tues.*

The Hampton Social
$$$ | **ECLECTIC** | **FAMILY** | Hampton Social covers many bases with its menu of "coastal inspired food." With options ranging from California-style pizzas and lobster rolls to steak or seafood tacos and crispy calamari, there's likely to be something for everyone in your party. Weekend brunch adds boozy and non-alcoholic bevs, as well as live music. **Known for:** weekend brunch with live music and kids' choices; free parking with $25 purchase; "Rosé all Day" lounge. *Average main: $25* *9101 International Dr., International Drive* *689/800–6760* *thehamptonsocial.com/orlando.*

Oceanaire Seafood Room
$$$$ | **SEAFOOD** | Don't let the 1930s-era ocean-liner interior fool you: as theme restaurants go, this place is a good one. The straightforward preparation—grilled or broiled, brushed with lemon butter—is welcome. **Known for:** "Grand Shellfish Tower" raw bar offering; exceptional fresh seafood; large wine menu. *Average main: $46* *Pointe Orlando, 9101 International Dr., International Drive* *407/363–4801* *theoceanaire.com/location/orlando-fl* *No lunch.*

Tapa Toro
$$$ | **SPANISH** | At this authentic Spanish restaurant, *Iron Chef* celeb Roberto Treviño uses unique grills to prepare inventive dishes, including seafood, chicken, lamb, or vegetarian paella. The tapas menu features a great gazpacho soup and fiery *patatas bravas* (home fries with a spicy tomato sauce). **Known for:** live entertainment; family-style tapas and entrées; several varieties of paella. *Average main: $22* *8441 International Dr., International Drive* *407/226–2929* *tapatoro.restaurant.*

Taverna Opa Orlando
$$$ | **GREEK** | **FAMILY** | In addition to excellent Greek staples and a nice selection of *meze* (small plates), this restaurant has a fun, high-energy ambience. The ouzo flows like a mountain stream, the Greek (and global) music almost reaches the volume level of a rock concert, and the roaming belly dancers actively encourage diners to join in. **Known for:** large selection of meze, with vegetarian options; traditional Greek taverna food; live (and lively) entertainment. *Average main: $28* *Pointe Orlando, 9101 International Dr., International Drive* *407/351–8660* *www.opaorlando.com.*

Hotels

The sprawl of hotels, time-shares, motels, condos, and other rentals offers visitors a varied choice in a central area that makes a great base for visits to Walt Disney World, Universal, and other Orlando attractions.

The I-Ride Trolley travels the length of I-Drive from Florida's Turnpike to the outlet center on Vineland Avenue, stopping at Universal Orlando, and SeaWorld. I-Ride is a more worthy transportation tool than you might think. Lots of hotels don't offer shuttle service to Disney, even for a fee, but you can take I-Ride to

Popular Chain Restaurants

When all you want is a quick bite, consider these chain restaurants. They seem to crop up everywhere, and all have tables where you can sit for a few moments before heading back out to the shops and attractions.

Anthony's Coal-Fired Pizza & Wings: Thin-crust pizzas with generous toppings like arugula and pepperoni are baked—charred, really—in a coal-fired oven at these bustling spaces on Sand Lake Road near Restaurant Row and in Altamonte Springs. The chicken wings are also popular. 🌐 *acfp.com.*

Bubbalou's Bodacious Bar-B-Que: This local smoker serves up mounds of Southern barbecue, from baby back ribs to pulled-pork sandwiches. The Kirkman Road branch is minutes from Universal Orlando; there's also a location in Altamonte Springs. 🌐 *bubbalous.com.*

Einstein Bros. Bagels: For a light breakfast or lunch, Einstein's satisfies with bagels, wraps, salads, and sandwiches. 🌐 *www.einsteinbros.com.*

First Watch: Breakfast classics like pancakes and waffles make First Watch a popular choice for locals, who line up on weekends for Key West "crepeggs" (a crepe filled with eggs that have been scrambled with turkey, avocado, bacon, tomatoes, and Monterey Jack cheese), and Floridian French toast with bananas, kiwi, and berries. 🌐 *www.firstwatch.com.*

Five Guys Burgers and Fries: This burger joint has a nearly cultlike following for its freshly ground beef. Fifteen toppings are available for no charge, and the fries are freshly cut. 🌐 *www.fiveguys.com.*

4 Rivers Smokehouse: The king of local barbecue slow-smokes Texas-style brisket, serves mountains of St. Louis ribs, and offers acres of towering desserts at seven Central Florida locations. 🌐 *www.4rsmokehouse.com.*

Hawker's: This local Asian street food restaurant has expanded from one location to 12—and from here to Maryland. 🌐 *eathawkers.com.*

Jimmy John's: Lunchtime lines are out the door at Orlando's many Jimmy John's, where the "world's greatest gourmet sandwiches" are essentially subs and clubs. 🌐 *www.jimmyjohns.com.*

Panera Bread: Fresh-baked pastries and bagels are the mainstays, although you can grab a hearty, inexpensive meal like smoked-turkey panino on three-cheese bread or a bowl of soup served in a hollowed-out sourdough loaf. 🌐 *www.panerabread.com.*

Pei Wei Asian Diner: Bold flavors from across Asia come together at these fast-casual restaurants, where a hearty noodle bowl, orange-peel beef, or sweet-and-sour tofu will come in at less than $10. 🌐 *www.peiwei.com.*

TooJay's Gourmet Deli: A New York deli it ain't, but the TooJay's chain offers a welcome pastrami fix for those with a yen for salty meat on crusty seeded rye. 🌐 *www.toojays.com.*

hotels that do offer a fee-based Disney shuttle, which, depending on the size of the family or group, can be cheaper than a ride share or cab.

Avanti Resort

$ | **RESORT** | **FAMILY** | In the middle of all the I-Drive activity, and a short walk from ICON Park, this resort offers families a home away from home with plenty of amenities at a reasonable price; rooms and public areas are decorated in mid-century chic, and the large pool has a children's play area, a sandy beach with volleyball court, a shuffleboard court, and a bar and grill. **Pros:** laundry facilities; scheduled shuttles to theme parks; complimentary cribs. **Cons:** theme-park shuttles can be slow and crowded; elevators can be sluggish for those on top floors; daily resort fee of $13.75 (for Wi-Fi, self-parking, shuttles). *Rooms from: $109 8738 International Dr., International Drive 407/313–0100 www.avantiresort.com 652 rooms No Meals.*

Castle Hotel, Autograph Collection

$$ | **HOTEL** | You can almost reach out and touch The Wheel at ICON Park from this hotel, which offers a slightly kitschy sophistication, combining Alpine castle with Mardi Gras glitz. **Pros:** close to Universal and SeaWorld; easy walk to I-Drive eateries and attractions; great views, sophisticated vibe. **Cons:** self-parking fee; not close to Disney parks; on a congested stretch of I-Drive. *Rooms from: $244 8602 Universal Blvd., International Drive 407/345–1511, 800/952–2785 www.castlehotelorlando.com 214 rooms No Meals.*

CoCo Key Hotel and Water Resort

$ | **HOTEL** | **FAMILY** | If swimming and sliding are among your family's top vacation desires, and your budget gets happy with value prices, this colorful resort with its on-property, 14-slide, three-pool water park could be the perfect destination. **Pros:** value price; on-site water park; shuttle to Universal. **Cons:** water park closed some days in winter; some rooms overlook noisy pools; $32.95 daily resort fee for Wi-Fi, parking, and shuttle. *Rooms from: $170 7400 International Dr., International Drive 407/351–2626 www.cocokeyorlando.com 391 rooms No Meals.*

Comfort Suites Near Universal Orlando Resort

$$ | **HOTEL** | **FAMILY** | If Universal's roller coasters and Harry Potter's Diagon Alley are your destinations, these homey accommodations just outside the park should fit the bill with budget-priced rooms that offer a kitchenette with microwave, refrigerator, and coffeemaker; some even have dining tables. **Pros:** free shuttle to Universal and SeaWorld; free hot breakfast; free Wi-Fi and free parking. **Cons:** no on-site full-service restaurant or room service; long way to Disney parks; a hike to shops, restaurants. *Rooms from: $188 5617 Major Blvd., International Drive 407/363–1967, 800/951–7829 www.choicehotels.com 150 suites Free Breakfast.*

DoubleTree by Hilton at the Entrance to Universal Orlando

$$ | **HOTEL** | **FAMILY** | The name is a mouthful, but it's an accurate description for this hotel, which caters to business-trippers and pleasure seekers alike; it's so close to Universal that some of the tower rooms offer roller-coaster and Hogwarts views. **Pros:** free shuttle to Universal; four on-site eateries; free Wi-Fi. **Cons:** need a car to reach Disney or Downtown; on a fast-lane tourist strip; $23 daily fee for self-parking. *Rooms from: $179 5780 Major Blvd., International Drive 407/351–1000 www.hilton.com/en/doubletree 742 rooms No Meals.*

DoubleTree by Hilton Orlando at SeaWorld

$ | **RESORT** | **FAMILY** | Combining low, bungalow-style buildings and a 17-story tower, this Bali-inspired hotel creates a warm welcome and a comforting escape—lush linens, tranquil guest rooms, three pools, and tropical landscaping—from hectic

I-Drive. **Pros:** carpet-free rooms available for those with allergies; on-site miniature golf; shuttles to Universal, SeaWorld, and Aquatica. **Cons:** $15 daily resort fee; few shops and restaurants within walking distance; $21 daily self-parking fee. *Rooms from: $115 10100 International Dr., International Drive 407/352–1100 www.hilton.com/en/doubletree 1020 rooms No Meals.*

★ Drury Inn and Suites near Universal Orlando Resort

$ | HOTEL | FAMILY | This reasonably priced hotel, refurbished in 2021, is less than a mile from Universal and offers free Wi-Fi, free parking, free shuttle to Universal, free hot breakfast, free long-distance and local phone calls, and free hot food and cold beverages in the late afternoon. **Pros:** reasonable price; freebies abound; central location. **Cons:** pool and gym are small; next to two busy roadways; if Disney is your destination, this might be a little far afield. *Rooms from: $129 7301 W. Sand Lake Rd., at I–4, International Drive 407/354–1101 www.druryhotels.com 238 rooms Free Breakfast.*

Embassy Suites by Hilton Orlando International Drive Convention Center

$$ | HOTEL | FAMILY | An airy, eight-story atrium with palm trees and fountains lends an air of luxury to this all-suites lodging, which offers free breakfast and late-afternoon drinks. **Pros:** free breakfast and afternoon cocktails; easy walk to shopping and dining; on-site restaurant, room service. **Cons:** no free shuttles to theme parks; daily Wi-Fi charge in rooms; on congested stretch of I-Drive, a half mile from convention center. *Rooms from: $237 8978 International Dr., International Drive 407/352–1400, 800/433–7275 www.hilton.com/en/embassy 244 suites Free Breakfast.*

Floridays Resort Orlando

$$ | RESORT | FAMILY | This pleasant, two- and three-bedroom condo resort with full kitchens, halfway between Universal Orlando and Disney World, has six six-story buildings, two pools, a game room, gym, business center, and café with room service. **Pros:** on the I-Ride trolley route; great, self-contained environment for a family vacation; shuttles to all theme parks. **Cons:** no full service restaurant; daily resort fee for Wi-Fi, parking, shuttles; a car would be helpful, as it's remote. *Rooms from: $249 12562 International Dr., International Drive 407/238–7700 www.floridaysresortorlando.com 432 units No Meals.*

Four Points by Sheraton Orlando International Drive

$$ | HOTEL | FAMILY | With a hard-to-miss giant ball perched atop its 20-story round tower, this hotel on the north end of I-Drive is visible for blocks and has a contemporary atmosphere, thanks to the clean, airy design of the lobby. **Pros:** free parking, basic Wi-Fi, no resort fee; convenient to Universal and SeaWorld; shuttle to Universal. **Cons:** restaurant is very basic; some noise issues between rooms; on a busy stretch of I-Drive. *Rooms from: $214 5905 International Dr., International Drive 407/351–2100, 800/327–1366 four-points.marriott.com 301 rooms No Meals.*

Hilton Orlando

$$$ | HOTEL | FAMILY | Families visiting this award-winning hotel get two pools, a palm-fringed lazy river to relax in, a kids' club, basketball court, tennis court, and a full-service spa; conventioneers appreciate the vast meeting space, direct connection to the convention center, substantial restaurants and bars, work desks with Herman Miller chairs, and an on-site steak house. **Pros:** on-site convenience store, full-service restaurants; multiple pools, including a lazy river; convenient to I-Ride Trolley stop. **Cons:** $35 daily resort fee and $27 daily parking fee; no free shuttle to Disney World or Universal; about 80% of guests are conventioneers. *Rooms from: $290 6001 Destination*

Pkwy., International Drive ☎ 407/313–4300 🌐 www.thehiltonorlando.com ⇨ 1417 rooms 🍽 No Meals.

Holiday Inn and Suites Across from Universal Orlando

$ | **HOTEL** | **FAMILY** | Staying at this hotel directly across the street from Universal could be a savvy budget move: the value price joins the perks on offer, from complimentary theme-park shuttles and Wi-Fi to free kids meals and more. **Pros:** you can walk to Universal and area shops (there's also a free shuttle); free Wi-Fi, parking, shuttles, and kids meals; no resort fee. **Cons:** busy traffic corridor; need a car to get to Disney or downtown Orlando; older hotel. $ *Rooms from: $99 ✉ 5916 Caravan Ct., International Drive ☎ 407/351–3333 🌐 hiuniversal.com ⇨ 390 rooms 🍽 No Meals.*

Hyatt Place Orlando/I-Drive/Convention Center

$$ | **HOTEL** | Youngish, high-tech-consuming business travelers and vacationing families find value here because of the location and amenities, such as 42-inch flat-panel HDTVs, work areas with computer access panel, wet bar with mini-refrigerator, and heated pool. **Pros:** 24/7 fitness center; free parking, free breakfast, free Wi-Fi; convenient to convention center, shopping, restaurants, and ICON Park. **Cons:** too far to walk to convention center; no theme-park shuttles; no kids' program or babysitting services. $ *Rooms from: $249 ✉ 8741 International Dr., International Drive ☎ 407/370–4720, 888/492–8847 🌐 www.hyatt.com ⇨ 149 rooms 🍽 Free Breakfast.*

Hyatt Place Orlando/Universal

$$ | **HOTEL** | Hyatt Place (not to be confused with neighboring Hyatt House) supports tech-savvy guests in what the company calls the 24/7 lifestyle, which means the hotel amenities available to guests at 3 in the afternoon are also on tap at 3 in the morning, and rooms have work spaces and computer-ready, flat-screen TVs. **Pros:** free high-speed Wi-Fi; walking distance to Universal as well as a free shuttle; free breakfast. **Cons:** noise from nearby highway; no shuttles to Disney; no kids' programs or babysitting service. $ *Rooms from: $249 ✉ 5976 Caravan Ct., International Drive ☎ 407/351–0627 🌐 www.hyatt.com ⇨ 151 rooms 🍽 Free Breakfast.*

Hyatt Regency Orlando

$$$ | **RESORT** | This deluxe, high-rise, conference hotel offers everything a resort guest could want, with richly appointed rooms, two pools with cabanas, a full-service spa and fitness center the size of your local Y, two large restaurants, and a 360-seat, glass-walled lounge overlooking the pool. **Pros:** on the I-Ride Trolley route; good spa, restaurants on site; walk to many shops and restaurants. **Cons:** $30 daily resort and $27 daily parking fees; long walk from end to end; check-in can take a while if a convention is arriving. $ *Rooms from: $299 ✉ 9801 International Dr., International Drive ☎ 407/284–1234 🌐 www.hyatt.com ⇨ 1641 rooms 🍽 No Meals.*

Parc Corniche Condominium Suite Hotel

$$$ | **HOTEL** | **FAMILY** | Set back from traffic on the south end of I-Drive, this condo hotel offers a good deal for a family, with suites that have separate bedrooms, flat-screen TVs, full kitchens with dishwasher, and bathrooms; the I-Ride Trolley passes the front door. **Pros:** free parking; on-site convenience store; well-equipped kitchens. **Cons:** parking can be crowded; $12 daily resort fee, $30 cleaning fee; not much within walking distance. $ *Rooms from: $267 ✉ 6300 Parc Corniche Dr., International Drive ☎ 407/239–7100, 800/446–2721 🌐 www.parccorniche.com ⇨ 210 suites 🍽 Free Breakfast.*

The Point Hotel and Suites

$ | **HOTEL** | **FAMILY** | In the center of the entertainment triangle bounded by I–4, Florida's Turnpike, and the Beachline Expressway, this all-suites resort is close to Universal, outlet shopping malls,

I-Drive attractions, and the convention center, making it a good option for family vacations, romantic getaways, and business travel. **Pros:** shuttle to Disney, SeaWorld, and Universal; central to I-Drive entertainment; Wi-Fi throughout the resort. **Cons:** no ergonomic chair for working; $11 daily resort fee; shuttles can be slow and crowded. *Rooms from: $139 ✉ 7389 Universal Blvd., International Drive ☎ 407/956–2000 🌐 www.thepointorlando.com 244 suites No Meals.*

Renaissance Orlando at SeaWorld
$$ | **HOTEL** | **FAMILY** | With a 10-story atrium full of ponds and palm trees, this SeaWorld neighbor, ironically, features a sushi bar in the lobby; rooms feature a king or two queen beds, sectional couches, flat-screen TVs, lush bedding, and ergonomic work areas. **Pros:** on-site water park for kids; across from SeaWorld; free shuttles to theme parks. **Cons:** $35 daily resort and $28 daily parking fees; many conventioneers; can be a long walk to rooms. *Rooms from: $180 ✉ 6677 Sea Harbor Dr., International Drive ☎ 407/351–5555, 800/468–3571 🌐 www.marriott.com 781 rooms No Meals.*

★ **Residence Inn by Marriott Orlando at SeaWorld**
$$ | **HOTEL** | **FAMILY** | From the welcoming lobby to the well-appointed suites (including dishwasher, microwave, pots, pans, dishes) and the parklike atmosphere around the pool, this hotel is a great choice if SeaWorld, Aquatica, I-Drive shopping, Universal, or the convention center are on your to-do list; a huge laundry is a boon for families. **Pros:** free breakfast and Wi-Fi; roomy suites with well-equipped kitchenettes; free shuttles to theme parks. **Cons:** nightly parking fee $15; right next to busy Interstate 4; not much within walking distance. *Rooms from: $185 ✉ 11000 Westwood Blvd., International Drive ☎ 407/313–3600, 800/889–9728 🌐 www.marriott.com 350 suites Free Breakfast.*

Rosen Centre Hotel
$$$ | **RESORT** | **FAMILY** | Connected by a covered sky-bridge to the Orange County Convention Center, this 24-story resort with a half-dozen on-site restaurants attracts business customers but doesn't ignore families. **Pros:** high-speed Wi-Fi in rooms; free shuttles to Universal, SeaWorld, and Aquatica; preferred tee times at sister resort Rosen Shingle Creek Golf Club. **Cons:** lots of convention guests; parking fee $25, need a car to get anywhere off I-Drive; no free shuttle to Disney. *Rooms from: $329 ✉ 9840 International Dr., International Drive ☎ 407/996–9840 🌐 www.rosencentre.com 1334 rooms No Meals.*

Rosen Plaza Hotel
$$$ | **HOTEL** | Close to the convention center, this 14-story hotel caters to its corporate clientele, but leisure travelers also like the prime location and long list of amenities, including a heated swimming pool, fitness center, babysitting services, and a vibrant nightclub that opens onto the pool. **Pros:** free shuttle to Universal; within walking distance of Pointe Orlando and other I-Drive restaurants and cinema; several on-site eateries. **Cons:** not geared toward families; $20 daily parking fee; convention center traffic can be heavy. *Rooms from: $293 ✉ 9700 International Dr., International Drive ☎ 407/996–9700, 800/366–9700 🌐 www.rosenplaza.com 800 rooms No Meals.*

Wyndham Orlando Resort International Drive
$ | **RESORT** | **FAMILY** | Located in the walkable neighborhood around Orlando's ICON Park entertainment complex, this leafy resort of two-story buildings offers a central location for family theme-park visits and also has high-tech amenities for business travelers. **Pros:** shuttle to Universal and SeaWorld; guests get a discount at the adjacent ICON Park complex; within

a short walk of I-Drive restaurants and entertainment. **Cons:** $22.50 daily resort fee; Disney (about 30 minutes away) shuttle is pricey; no elevators. *$ Rooms from: $136 ✉ 8001 International Dr., International Drive ☎ 407/351–2420, 800/996–3426 🌐 www.wyndhamhotels.com 613 rooms No Meals.*

Nightlife

BARS

ICEBAR

BARS | Thanks to the miracle of refrigeration, this is Orlando's coolest bar—literally and figuratively. Fifty tons of pure ice are kept at a constant 27°F and have been cut and sculpted by world-class carvers into a chilly sanctuary of tables, sofas, chairs, and a bar. The staff loans you a thermal cape and gloves (upgrade to a faux fur coat for an extra $10), and when you enter the frozen hall your drink is served in a glass made of crystal clear ice. There's no cover charge if you just want to hang out in the nonfrozen Fire Lounge or the outdoor Polar Patio, but you will pay a cover ($15 with upgrade packages available) to spend as much time as you can handle in the subfreezing ICEBAR. There's no beer or wine inside; it's simply too cold. ✉ *Pointe Orlando, 8967 International Dr., International Drive ☎ 407/426–7555 🌐 www.icebarorlando.com.*

Performing Arts

Dinner shows are an immensely popular form of nighttime entertainment around Orlando, particularly on I-Drive. For a single price, you get a theatrical production and a multicourse dinner. Performances run the gamut from jousting to jamboree tunes, and meals tend to be better than average. Unlimited beer, wine, and soda are usually included, but mixed drinks (and often *any* drinks before dinner) cost extra.

What the shows lack in substance and depth they make up for in grandeur and enthusiasm. The result is an evening of light entertainment, which youngsters in particular enjoy. Seatings are usually between 7 and 9:30, and there are usually one or two performances a night, with an extra show during peak periods. You might sit with strangers at tables for 10 or more, but that's part of the fun.

If you're in Orlando off-season, try to take in these dinner shows on a busy night—a show playing to a small audience can be uncomfortable. It's also good to make reservations, especially for weekend shows, and to verify show times in advance, as schedules can vary by season. Don't let the big prices fool you—there's a flood of coupons (sometimes half-off) offered online, in I-Drive restaurants and hotels, and at the Orlando/Orange County Convention & Visitors Bureau. If you don't have a coupon when booking, ask about discounts *and* whether or not the cost includes a gratuity—servers anxious to pocket more cash might hit you up for an extra handout.

The Outta Control Magic Comedy Dinner Show

THEATER | FAMILY | Held at the Wonderworks hands-on science and activity center, this dinner show is exactly as its name suggests: a magic show filled with jokes, gags, and tricks. The magicians' juvenile one-liners make this delightful for kids and pleasingly silly for adults, and audience participation plays a huge part in the experience. A pizza/salad/soft drink buffet is open prior to the show. ✉ *Wonderworks, 9067 International Dr., International Drive ☎ 407/351–8800 🌐 www.wonderworksonline.com/orlando $33.*

★ Sleuths Mystery Dinner Show

THEATER | FAMILY | If Sherlock Holmes has always intrigued you, head to this long-running show for a four-course meal served with a healthy dose of conspiracy. Sleuths is a hotbed of local acting talent,

Sleuths Mystery Dinner Show on International Drive is one of several popular dinner theater performances in Orlando.

with several totally different whodunit performances staged throughout the week. The comedy-mystery show begins during your appetizer. You'll discuss clues and question still-living characters over dinner and then solve the crime during dessert. Prizes go to top sleuths. ✉ *8267 International Dr., International Drive* ☎ *407/363–1985* 🌐 *www.sleuths.com* 🎟 *$53.*

Activities

SPAS

Eforea Spa at Hilton Orlando

SPAS | From the deeply cushioned chaise longues in the waiting room, where you can relax in fleecy robes and cozy blankets, to the complimentary infused water, juices, teas, and fruit, this large, tropical spa makes you feel pampered. Offerings include more than a dozen body treatments, massages, and facials, as well as hair, nail, and waxing services. Day passes are available, and self-parking is free for spa guests, who also receive access to the pool and fitness center before or after a treatment. Special services are available for youngsters and teens in the salon. ✉ *Hilton Orlando, 6001 Destination Pkwy., Orlando* ☎ *407/313–4300* 🌐 *www.thehiltonorlando.com/discover/spa-and-fitness.html* ☞ *20% service charge is added to the bill.*

The Spa at Hyatt Regency Orlando

SPAS | Reaching this 22,000-square-foot, full-service contemporary retreat, set at the heart of a huge convention resort, can be quite a hike, so by the time you arrive you'll be happy to shed your clothes and cares, don a fluffy robe and slippers, and settle in for some serious rejuvenation. Massages, a variety of facials, and complete salon services are all available, and a treatment also gets you access to a co-ed relaxation lounge and separate spa areas with whirlpools, steam room, and showers. ✉ *Hyatt Regency Orlando, 9801 International Dr., International Drive* ☎ *407/345–4431* 🌐 *www.hyatt.com/en-US/spas/The-Spa-Orlando/home* ⏲ *Closed Mon.–Wed.* ☞ *Gratuity is added to the bill.*

The Spa at Rosen Centre
SPAS | Set in a resort across from the convention center, this intimate spa caters to busy, stressed-out businesspeople—as well as bridal parties, girlfriends' getaways, and spa parties. After donning luxurious robes and comfy slippers, you move to the serene, candlelit, and aroma-enhanced relaxation rooms. If your muscles need a real workout, try a traditional Ashiatsu massage, where the masseuse, supported by a wooden frame, uses gravity and her bare feet to reach deep into knots. The Lavish Milk and Honey Ritual is 80 minutes of indulgence, complete with a skin-firming milk-and-honey treatment, exfoliation, and a warm honey-butter body masque. Day passes are available, and parking is validated for nonguests. ✉ *Rosen Centre Hotel, 9840 International Dr., International Drive* ☎ *407/996–1248* 🌐 *spaatrosencentre.com.*

South Orlando

South Orlando is home to expansive resort hotels, chain restaurants, the headwaters of the Everglades, and not much more.

Restaurants

★ A Land Remembered
$$$$ | **STEAKHOUSE** | The name of this award-winning steak house comes from the iconic novel about Florida by Patrick D. Smith. Notable menu choices include the 20-ounce chateaubriand for two carved tableside and the best seller, a 20-ounce Harris Ranch Prime bone-in rib eye, perhaps with a shared appetizer of collard greens braised in Gator Drool beer, or mac and cheese with big lobster chunks. **Known for:** Cataplana broiled seafood sampler; house-aged steaks; resort atmosphere. 💲 *Average main: $58* ✉ *Rosen Shingle Creek, 9939 Universal Blvd., South Orlando* ☎ *407/996–9939* 🌐 *www.landrememberedrestaurant.com* 🕓 *Close Mon.–Wed.* ☞ *Attached Clubhouse Grill open Thurs.–Sat. for lunch.*

★ Highball & Harvest
$$$ | **AMERICAN** | Modern spins on locally sourced Southern staples are the crux of this sprawling restaurant, where scratch cooking by Ritz chefs is the rule; produce is grown on the resort's own Whisper Creek private farm. Dinner entrées change regularly and might include Florida shrimp and grits, waffle fried quail or diver scallops with wild mushrooms. **Known for:** extensive bar bites menu; seasonal dishes made using produce from on-site farm; handcrafted cocktails. 💲 *Average main: $25* ✉ *Ritz-Carlton Orlando Grande Lakes, 4012 Central Florida Pkwy., South Orlando* ☎ *407/393–4422* 🌐 *ritzcarlton.com/en/hotels/florida/orlando/dining/highball-and-harvest.*

★ Knife & Spoon
$$$$ | **MODERN AMERICAN** | Two-time *Top Chef* contestant John Tesar (you know, the mean one) bravely opened Knife & Spoon in late 2020, and the critics responded. Focused on turf (prime, house-aged steaks) and surf (raw bar, local seafood), Tesar features interesting dishes like sushi-grade tuna and torched foie gras or 45-day, dry-aged, 32-ounce, bone-in rib eye (at $130). **Known for:** creative cocktails; pricey seafood and even pricier steaks; inventive preparations from a celebrity chef. 💲 *Average main: $50* ✉ *The Ritz-Carlton, 4012 Central Florida Pkwy., South Orlando* ☎ *407/206–2400* 🌐 *ritzcarlton.com/en/hotels/florida/orlando/dining/knife-spoon* 🕓 *Close Mon. and Tues.*

★ Primo
$$$$ | **ITALIAN** | Chef Melissa Kelly cloned her Italian-organic Maine restaurant in an upscale Orlando hotel and brought her farm-to-table sensibilities with her. Homemade pasta, Florida meats, and offerings from the pizza oven are essential; locally caught fish is served with Florida clams; and the chicken from nearby Lake Meadow Naturals is, yes, primo.

Restaurants

1 A Land Remembered... **B4**

2 Bosphorous Turkish Cuisine.......... **A3**

3 Boxi Park **E5**

4 Cask & Larder........... **D3**

5 Cedars Restaurant...... **A3**

6 Christini's Ristorante Italiano...... **A3**

7 Dragonfly Robata Grill & Sushi............. **A3**

8 The H Orlando........... **A3**

9 Highball & Harvest **B4**

10 Kabooki Sushi........... **B3**

11 Knife & Spoon........... **B4**

12 Melting Pot.............. **A3**

13 Morton's The Steakhouse......... **A3**

14 Nona Blue **E4**

15 Ocean Prime **A3**

16 Peperoncino............. **A3**

17 Primo...................... **B4**

18 Saffron Indian Cuisine........... **A3**

19 Seasons 52 .... **A3**

20 Susuru **A5**

21 Vines Grille & Wine Bar................. **A3**

Hotels

1 The Florida Hotel & Conference Center......**C3**

2 Hyatt Regency Orlando International Airport.................... **D4**

3 JW Marriott Orlando Grande Lakes **B4**

4 Lake Nona Wave Hotel............... **E5**

5 Ritz-Carlton Orlando, Grande Lakes **B4**

6 Rosen Shingle Creek... **B4**

Known for: homemade pastas; constantly changing menu using locally sourced ingredients; award-winning celebrity chef. *Average main: $45 ✉ JW Marriott Orlando Grande Lakes, 4040 Central Florida Pkwy., South Orlando ☎ 407/393–4444 ⊕ grandelakes.com/dining/primo ⊙ No lunch.*

Hotels

JW Marriott Orlando Grande Lakes
$$$$ | RESORT | FAMILY | This lush resort, amid 500 acres of natural beauty, offers amenities galore, including a European-style spa, a Greg Norman–designed golf course, a lazy river–style pool complex, and kids' programs. **Pros:** free shuttle to theme parks; pool is great for kids and adults; shares amenities with the Ritz Carlton, including huge spa. **Cons:** remote location requires a car to go shopping; the resort is huge and spread out; $40 daily resort fee, $30 daily parking fee. *Rooms from: $499 ✉ 4040 Central Florida Pkwy., South Orlando ☎ 407/206–2300, 800/576–5750 ⊕ www.grandelakes.com ⇒ 1000 rooms No Meals.*

★ **Ritz-Carlton Orlando, Grande Lakes**
$$$$ | RESORT | FAMILY | Orlando's only Ritz-Carlton is a particularly extravagant link in the luxury chain: it shares a lush, 500-acre campus with the JW Marriott and offers exemplary service, excellent restaurants, children's programs, a golf course, and a 40-room spa. **Pros:** transportation to theme parks; truly luxurious; impeccable service. **Cons:** daily resort fee is $40 and parking fee is $40; lots of convention and meeting traffic; distant from theme parks and other attractions. *Rooms from: $799 ✉ 4012 Central Florida Pkwy., South Orlando ☎ 407/206–2400, 800/576–5760 ⊕ www.ritzcarlton.com ⇒ 582 rooms No Meals.*

★ **Rosen Shingle Creek**
$$$ | RESORT | FAMILY | Sitting amid 255 acres of subtropical landscape, including a cypress-fringed creek and a championship golf course, this award-winning luxury resort offers a golf academy; fishing; nature trails; four swimming pools; tennis, basketball, and volleyball courts; and a huge spa to soothe those aching muscles. **Pros:** free shuttle to Universal, SeaWorld, Aquatica; many on-site dining choices; huge spa and fitness center. **Cons:** $18 daily parking fee; no free shuttle to I-Drive or Disney; expansive grounds mean long walks between on-site amenities. *Rooms from: $349 ✉ 9939 Universal Blvd., South Orlando ☎ 407/996–9939, 866/996–6338 reservations ⊕ www.rosenshinglecreek.com ⇒ 1501 rooms No Meals.*

Activities

SPAS

Ritz-Carlton Spa Orlando, Grande Lakes
SPAS | Prepare to be wowed as you enter this lavish spa, Orlando's largest with 40 treatment rooms, a fitness center, salon, private pool, and café—which means it can get busy. Get here in plenty of time to take a tour and get your bearings, shed your tourist togs, don a plush robe, and prepare to unwind. Unisex and co-ed waiting areas with couches and chairs are available, each on a different floor, with tea, water, fruits, and snacks. Treatments include massage, skin therapy, and deep-cleaning HydraFacials that gently extract impurities from the skin. Valet parking is discounted with a spa validation. *✉ Ritz-Carlton Orlando, 4024 Central Florida Pkwy., South Orlando ☎ 407/393–4200 ⊕ www.ritzcarlton.com/en/hotels/florida/orlando/spa ☞ 20% service charge is added to the bill.*

The Spa at Shingle Creek
SPAS | Most of the treatments here feature Florida products such as citrus and cedar oils, aloe, and Everglades sugar. The Everglades scrub and body wrap begins with a brown-sugar body scrub and oils infused with sweet almond, apricot kernel, and wheat germ, followed by a wrap

of nutrient-rich Everglades mud with hints of grapefruit, lime, jasmine, and lemongrass. Types of massage include Swedish, aromatherapy, warm stone, and Ashiatsu barefoot massage. A variety of facials and salon treatments is available. For supreme relaxation, you can even add on a 25-minute siesta where you're wrapped in hot packs after your treatment and awakened by gentle bells. Parking, either self or valet, is validated for day guests. ✉ *Rosen Shingle Creek, 9939 Universal Blvd., South Orlando* ☎ *407/996–9939* 🌐 *www.spaatshinglecreek.com* ☞ *Gratuity is included in the cost.*

Sand Lake Road

The eastern end of Sand Lake bisects tourist-heavy International Drive at one of the busiest intersections in town; the western end has been dubbed "Restaurant Row" for its abundance of eateries.

Restaurants

This area, known as Restaurant Row, is the only place in town where locals dine beside convention goers and adventuresome theme-park visitors. From I–4, take the Sand Lake Road exit, 74A.

Bosphorous Turkish Cuisine

$$$ | TURKISH | FAMILY | Exceptional Turkish cuisine served in a relaxing, indoor-outdoor setting is a welcome surprise among the big-budget chains on Sand Lake Road. Servers at this independently owned neighborhood favorite bring to the table piping-hot, oversize *lavas* (hollow bread) to dip in appetizers such as a hummus, *ezme* (a zesty, garlicky, chilled chopped salad), and baba ghanoush. **Known for:** chicken and lamb shish kebab; Turkish appetizer plates; grilled sea bass. [$] *Average main: $26* ✉ *Marketplace at Dr. Phillips, 7600 Dr. Phillips Blvd., Suite 108, Sand Lake Rd. Area* ☎ *407/352–6766* 🌐 *www.bosphorousrestaurant.com.*

Cedars Restaurant

$$$ | MIDDLE EASTERN | This family-owned Lebanese eatery, set in a major upscale strip shopping center that's become part of Restaurant Row, serves Middle Eastern standards like shish kebab, baba ghanoush (an ultrasmoky variety that is the very best in town), and hummus as well as tasty daily specials. One of the most notable regular entrées is the *samak harra* (sautéed red snapper fillet topped with onions, tomatoes, and cilantro). **Known for:** rack of lamb; authentic hummus and falafel; kafta kebab. [$] *Average main: $27* ✉ *Plaza Venezia, 7732 W. Sand Lake Rd., Sand Lake Rd. Area* ☎ *407/351–6000* 🌐 *www.cedarsorlando.com.*

Christini's Ristorante Italiano

$$$$ | ITALIAN | Business travelers love to spend money at Christini's, one of the city's fanciest places for northern Italian cuisine. A throwback to elegant dining in the 1950s, the menu is filled with high-end versions of familiar dishes like chicken marsala and veal with lemon-wine sauce. **Known for:** distinguished wine list; Chris Christini, the charming owner since 1984; upscale classic Italian cuisine. [$] *Average main: $50* ✉ *Marketplace at Dr. Phillips, 7600 Dr. Phillips Blvd., Sand Lake Rd. Area* ☎ *407/345–8770* 🌐 *www.christinis.com* ⏲ *No lunch.*

Dragonfly Robata Grill & Sushi

$$ | ASIAN | Sleek and stylish, Dragonfly is a bit of everything the young and beautiful people want: a pretty space featuring sushi, colorful martinis, and modern, *izakaya*-style small plates. Groups of dressed-up twenty- and thirtysomethings gather indoors and out to share plates of *robata*-cooked meats and vegetables, along with tempura, rolls, noodle dishes, and salads, all beautifully presented. **Known for:** daily happy hour specials; modern takes on traditional Japanese; robata charcoal-grilled specialties. [$] *Average main: $20* ✉ *Dellagio, 7972 Via Dellagio Way, Sand Lake Rd. Area*

☎ *407/370–3359* 🌐 *dragonflyrestaurants.com/orlando-florida* ⏲ *No lunch.*

★ The H Orlando

$$$$ | TURKISH | Sophisticated Turkish and other Mediterranean dishes are the focus here, where haloumi cheese and Spanish octopus are among the grilled starters, and flamboyant entrées to consider include strozzapreti pasta served with wild mushrooms, corned beef, and a cream sauce that's made at table with flambéed cheese. There's an entire glass-walled room full of aging beef (this is not a place for vegetarians). **Known for:** butter-aged tenderloin and traditional Turkish aged beef; unusual Turkish brunch menu; tableside prep of steaks and pasta. *$ Average main: $45* ✉ *7512 Dr. Phillips Blvd., Sand Lake Rd. Area* ☎ *407/930–3020* 🌐 *thehorlando.com* ☞ *Fri. and Sat. evenings are for adults (21 and over) only.*

Kabooki Sushi

$$$ | SUSHI | Sushi-ya Henry Moso makes hip, modern day variants of old school sushi, with everything from standard spicy tuna rolls to tempura-fried St. Louis sticky ribs. Of (very) special note are the 17-course omakase events, costing as much as $250 and featuring such rare delights as Japanese flying fish or live scallops—all prepared by chef Moso himself. **Known for:** favored by local chefs; rare varieties of seafood; fun, casual, and expensive. *$ Average main: $25* ✉ *7705 Turkey Lake Rd., Sand Lake Rd. Area* ☎ *407/776–2001* 🌐 *kabookisushi.com.*

Melting Pot

$$$ | AMERICAN | FAMILY | One word: fondue—the bubbling pots of bouillon, cheese, or chocolate offered here give fans of food-on-skewers a chance to share plates with friends. It may seem like an old idea, but Melting Pot continues to draw families and dating couples for a surprisingly fun meal. **Known for:** four-course meals from starters to desserts; cheese, wine, and chocolate fondue; flattop cooking for the fondue-averse. *$ Average main: $30* ✉ *7549 W Sand Lake Rd., Sand Lake Rd. Area* ☎ *407/903–1100* 🌐 *meltingpot.com.*

Morton's The Steakhouse

$$$$ | STEAKHOUSE | This fine choice among Orlando's many steak houses looks like a sophisticated private club, and youngsters with mouse caps are not common at the nationwide chain's local outpost. Center stage in the kitchen is a huge broiler, kept at 900°F to sear in the flavor of the porterhouses, sirloins, rib eyes, and other cuts of aged beef. **Known for:** mixed grill assortments with steak and lobster; house-aged steaks; seafood towers. *$ Average main: $46* ✉ *Marketplace at Dr. Phillips, 7600 Dr. Phillips Blvd., Sand Lake Rd. Area* ☎ *407/248–3485* 🌐 *www.mortons.com* ⏲ *No lunch.*

Ocean Prime

$$$$ | SEAFOOD | From the Berries & Bubbles martinis that start off the meal to the chocolate peanut butter dessert draped in bittersweet chocolate ganache, Ocean Prime wows. This local outpost of an upscale chain holds its own with consistently good food, if uneven service. **Known for:** gluten-free menu; great lakeside view; inventive seafood selections. *$ Average main: $34* ✉ *Rialto, 7339 W. Sand Lake Rd., Sand Lake Rd. Area* ☎ *407/781–4880* 🌐 *www.oceanprimeorlando.com* ⏲ *No lunch.*

★ Peperoncino

$$$ | ITALIAN | FAMILY | You'll be transported to Calabria at this comfortable Italian restaurant, which is divided into a trattoria and a pizzeria. Chef-owners Barbara Alfano and Danilo Martorano put out a fresh menu of Italian specialties every evening, and the finishing kitchen is in the dining room, so diners lucky enough to snag the few indoor seats (the outside patio has extras) can see Alfano and her team composing the dishes. **Known for:** classic pizzas; southern Italian cuisine; mushroom risotto. *$ Average main: $25* ✍ *Reservations Essential* ✉ *Dellagio, 7988 Via Dellagio Way, Suite 108, Sand*

Lake Rd. Area ☎ *407/440–2856* 🌐 *facebook.com/peperoncinoorlando.*

Saffron Indian Cuisine

$$ | **INDIAN** | **FAMILY** | Family recipes and beyond-standard Indian dishes makes Saffron a small gem in Orlando's subcontinental culinary scene. The classics—lamb korma, tandoori chicken, and tikka masala—are joined by specialties from Chettinad, Goa, and Kerala. **Known for:** Punjabi goat curry; favorite and exotic dishes; sampler of samosa, vegetable tiki, bhajiya, and pakora. *Average main: $20* ✉ *7724 West Sand Lake Rd., Sand Lake Rd. Area* ☎ *407/674–8899* 🌐 *saffronorlando.com.*

Seasons 52

$$$ | **AMERICAN** | **FAMILY** | It's hard to believe that a chain restaurant can offer healthful yet hearty and very flavorful food, but the innovative Seasons 52 does just that, with some of its menu changing weekly as well as seasonally. Nearly everyone orders the flatbread starters, and entrées might include wood-roasted, dry-rubbed pork chop with braised cabbage, or caramelized grilled sea scallops with butternut squash and leek risotto, broccolini, and lemon butter. **Known for:** flatbread starters that are big enough to share; waits for tables, even when you have a reservation; entrée salads using seasonal ingredients. *Average main: $24* ✉ *Plaza Venezia, 7700 Sand Lake Rd., Sand Lake Rd. Area* ✥ *I–4 Exit 75A* ☎ *407/354–5212* 🌐 *www.seasons52.com.*

★ **Susuru**

$ | **JAPANESE** | **FAMILY** | A retro-themed Japanese bar–suburban rec room, Susuru serves memorable charcoal-grilled skewers, ramen, chicken *karaage* (deep fried in oil), tempura, and tofu bowls. Bar bites, craft beer, and cocktails add casual flair to the almost unbelievably casual atmosphere. **Known for:** unusual cocktails; possibly the best ramen in Orlando; casual Japanese bar food. *Average main: $10* ✉ *8548 Palm Pkwy., Sand Lake Rd. Area* ☎ *407/778–4813* 🌐 *susuruorl.com* ⏲ *Closed Mon.*

Vines Grille & Wine Bar

$$$$ | **STEAKHOUSE** | In the evenings, live jazz and blues music fills the bar of this dramatically designed restaurant, but the food and drink in the snazzy main dining room are headliners in their own right. A perennial winner of the *Orlando* magazine Dining Awards for best wine bar (and a *Downbeat* magazine Top Jazz venue), this restaurant has an extensive wine list (its cocktails are serious business, too), and entrées that range from prime steaks or a 1-pound Wagyu burger with truffle fries to pork osso buco or pan-seared Chilean sea bass with lobster risotto and basil *beurre blanc*. **Known for:** live jazz (starts nightly at 7); extensive wine selection and cocktails; prime steaks cooked on a wood-fired grill. *Average main: $62* ✉ *The Fountains, 7533 W. Sand Lake Rd., Sand Lake Rd. Area* ☎ *407/351–1227* 🌐 *vinesgrille.com* ⏲ *No lunch.*

Orlando International Airport

The area around the airport isn't a convenient base for exploring the Orlando area, but it can make arrivals or departures more convenient owing to its reliable hotel brands, fast food chains, car rental agencies, and gas stations (albeit expensive ones).

Restaurants

★ **Cask & Larder**

$$ | **SOUTHERN** | **FAMILY** | People have been known to check their bags at the airport and then go back through security and change terminals just to eat at C&L. The draws at this locally owned restaurant are the gastropub-inspired menu and the microbrews. **Known for:** organic, locally sourced ingredients; farm-to-terminal dining; breakfast starts at 7 am. *Average*

main: $15 ✉ Orlando International Airport, 9202 Jeff Fuqua Blvd., Southwest Terminal, Airport Area ☎ 407/204–3296 🌐 www.caskandlarder.com.

Hotels

The area around the airport, especially the neighborhood just north of the Beachline Expressway, has a surfeit of hotels, mostly used by business travelers and airline staff. They're worth checking out if you have an early departure.

The Florida Hotel & Conference Center
$ | **HOTEL** | **FAMILY** | Five miles from Orlando International Airport, and midway between it and I-Drive, this hotel is connected to the upscale Florida Mall—with major department stores, an Apple Store, hundreds of specialty shops, the Crayola Experience, and currency exchange—so stays here are a treat if you like to shop. **Pros:** short drive to airport; in-room Wi-Fi, mini fridge, microwave; free parking. **Cons:** Disney is 18 miles away, but there are no free shuttles; daily service fee; neighborhood less than scenic. *$ Rooms from: $149 ✉ 1500 Sand Lake Rd., Airport Area ✥ At S. Orange Blossom Trail ☎ 407/859–1500, 800/588–4656 🌐 www.thefloridahotelorlando.com 511 rooms No Meals.*

Hyatt Regency Orlando International Airport
$$ | **HOTEL** | **FAMILY** | If you have to catch an early-morning flight or have a long layover, this hotel inside the main terminal complex is a very convenient option; counting the time you spend waiting for the elevator, your room is a five-minute walk from the nearest ticket counter. **Pros:** terminal has ample shopping and dining; despite being at the airport, rooms are quiet; people-watching from terminal-side balconies can be fun. **Cons:** daily fee for parking; downtown Orlando and theme parks at least 30 minutes away; nothing around but the airport. *$ Rooms from: $249 ✉ 9300 Jeff Fuqua Blvd., Airport Area ☎ 407/825–1234, 800/233–1234 🌐 www.hyatt.com 445 rooms No Meals.*

Lake Nona

The "new kid" in Orlando, Lake Nona was built as a high-tech community, centered around the Lake Nona Medical City and holdings from the Tavistock private investment group. Driverless shuttles provide local transit, bungalows and cottages dot areas around lakes and golf courses, and the Town Center has intriguing dining and lodging options.

Restaurants

Boxi Park
$$ | **ECLECTIC** | **FAMILY** | With nine permanent food and drink vendors, all housed in colorful repurposed shipping containers, Boxi Park is like a big, stationary, food-truck park, just with more alcohol. Three of the venues serve microbrew beers and margaritas or other mixed cocktails to go with the hand-rolled sushi, burgers, chicken sandwiches, tacos, lobster rolls, and more. **Known for:** casual, fun outdoor neighborhood setting; everything from lobster rolls to sushi; beer and cocktail stations. *$ Average main: $15 ✉ 6877 Tavistock Lakes Blvd., Lake Nona ☎ 407/536–9666 🌐 boxiparklakenona.com ⏲ Closed Mon.–Wed.*

Nona Blue
$$$ | **AMERICAN** | **FAMILY** | Part tavern, part bistro, and part sports bar, Nona Blue has a little something for everyone. Kettle chips smothered in blue cheese or Buffalo chicken wings, check; burgers and salads, check; filet mignon or a 16-ounce, $44 Delmonico rib eye, also (very much) check. **Known for:** bar with craft beers and single-malt whiskeys; casual atmosphere with high-end steaks; signature burgers. *$ Average main: $26 ✉ 9685 Lake Nona Village Pl., Lake Nona ☎ 407/313–0027 🌐 nonablue.com/locations/orlando.*

Hotels

★ **Lake Nona Wave Hotel**

$$$ | **HOTEL** | **FAMILY** | In the middle of the high-tech Lake Nona community and handy to the airport, the high-concept Wave bills itself as "the most technologically advanced hotel in the world," offering amenities like giant TVs, a "digital concierge," smart windows, and high-end Toto Neorest Smart toilets. **Pros:** state-of-the-art fitness center; high-tech amenities; Bacán open-kitchen restaurant and poolside cocktail bar. **Cons:** airport traffic can be noisy; no theme-park transportation; about 20 miles from Disney. *Rooms from: $303* *6772 Tavistock Lakes Blvd., Lake Nona* *833/462–9283* *lakenonawavehotel.com* *234 rooms* *No Meals.*

Chapter 11

EXCURSIONS FROM ORLANDO

11

Updated by
Jennifer Greenhill-Taylor
and Joseph Reed Hayes

Sights ★★★★☆ | Restaurants ★★★★★ | Hotels ★★★★★ | Shopping ★★★★★ | Nightlife ★★★☆☆

WELCOME TO EXCURSIONS FROM ORLANDO

TOP REASONS TO GO

★ **Historic areas.** Sanford's main street is lined with low brick buildings that date from the mid-19th century. Maitland has three diminutive but fascinating history museums.

★ **LEGOLAND.** The biggest collection of plastic-brick constructions in the world offers fun for kids. Right next door, a separate theme park devoted to Peppa Pig will also delight the little ones.

★ **Waterways.** Towns such as Sanford and Mount Dora have scenic lakefronts. Kayaks, canoes, and airboats are all available to cruise the region's waterways.

★ **Wild Florida.** Acres of untouched forests and crystal clear springs and rivers are just a few miles out of town. Maitland's Audubon Birds of Prey center houses and rehabilitates great raptors.

★ **Winter Park.** This charming town adjacent to Orlando offers brick-paved streets and a main thoroughfare that's perfect for strolling or sidewalk-café dining.

Most of these destinations are within minutes of Orlando and offer enough diversions to fill a day; some are a bit more distant. Combining a couple could make for a pleasant drive into the outlying countryside. Several of them are connected by the weekday SunRail commuter train line, a traffic-free alternative.

1 Winter Park. This upscale enclave just north of Orlando features two world-class art museums, brick streets, and a walkable downtown with a park and unique shops and eateries. A serene boat tour through lush landscapes offers glimpses of lakefront homes built a century ago by escapees from the North who named the town.

2 Maitland. North of Winter Park, one of the area's oldest incorporated municipalities has an Audubon sanctuary for birds of prey and small museums, including one in nearby Eatonville dedicated to author Zora Neale Hurston.

3 Wekiwa Springs State Park. A crystal-clear fast-flowing spring is at the heart of this park, a half-hour drive from Downtown Orlando. You can swim, canoe, and kayak along the river, enjoying Florida at its most natural.

4 Sanford. One of Central Florida's early towns sits on the south shore of Lake Monroe. It retains a rustic, turn-of-the-century charm, with brick buildings housing indie restaurants, art galleries, and shops. In the 19th century, this was a major entry port for adventurous Europeans arriving by steamboat on the St. Johns River.

5 Mount Dora. Another lakefront gem, this charming town 35 miles north of Orlando is known for its varied art galleries, its restaurants, and its antique boats.

6 LEGOLAND. Bricks of another sort line the streets of this collection of theme parks, where kids and adults can experience a whole world dedicated to colorful plastic LEGOs. Between driving little

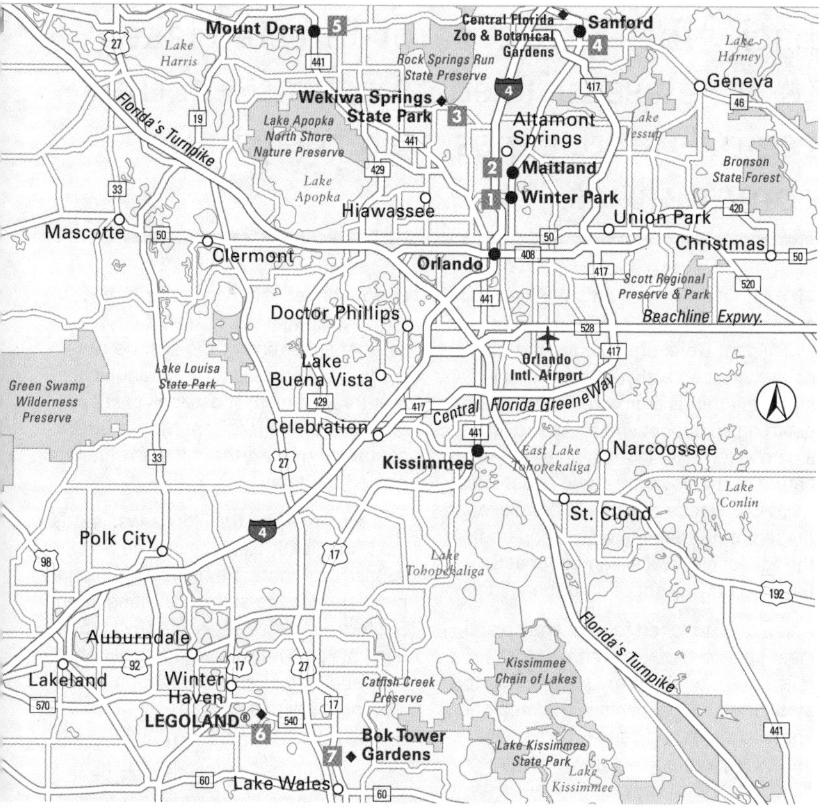

LEGO cars, hoisting themselves up tall LEGO poles, or floating in LEGO boats, kids leave happy and tired. With three on-site hotels, you don't have to make the nearly 90 mile round-trip from Orlando in one day.

7 Bok Tower Gardens. One of Florida's oldest attractions, this contemplative garden designed by Frederick Law Olmstead Jr.—whose father designed New York's Central Park—perches on one of the highest spots in the state, and its 205-foot-tall Singing Tower carillon has drawn millions of visitors since 1929.

Visitors to Orlando's theme parks who want a taste of authentic Central Florida can experience thrills and chills or laid-back vibes—from gator-infested lakes to art-glass-infused museums—in the region's landscapes, waterways, and communities.

Although they are not on the ocean, most communities, including Sanford and Mount Dora, are built around lakes, so water-based activities are a mainstay. Few things are more exciting than boarding an airboat and rocketing across a gator-filled lake. In addition to the edgy nature of the adventure, you experience what Old Florida must have been like for those first Europeans who stepped off the St. Johns River steamboats at Sanford and bravely set off into the wild.

Acres of untouched forests and crystal clear springs and rivers sit a scant few miles north or south of Orlando, and the state and national parks in the area offer spots to swim and canoe. Hikes here let you explore some true wilderness filled with Florida's flora, as well as its fauna (some of which is dangerous). A silent journey along a river into the subtropical jungle, where turtles bask on logs and snakes and alligators—yes, alligators—snooze on the banks, is an unforgettable trip. At the end of any exploration on a blistering summer day, a leap into the refreshing 70-degree water of a turquoise spring cools the body and the mind.

For a more serene experience, several charming towns to the north of Orlando offer oak-lined streets, sidewalk cafés, and great restaurants. Winter Park's main thoroughfare, Park Avenue, is perfect for strolling or enjoying a meal at a sidewalk café. At either end of the avenue sits a world-class art museum. A tranquil boat tour through lush landscapes gives you glimpses of the lakefront homes built a century ago by northern transplants who named the town.

This region of Central Florida was settled early, in the 1800s, because the St. Johns River formed a highway bringing pioneers into the state's daunting interior. Sanford's main street is lined with low brick buildings that date from that era. Maitland, site of a fort built during the Second Seminole War, has three diminutive but fascinating history museums.

For decades, Central Florida has been home to theme parks and other tourist attractions, some featuring the lush subtropical landscape. Today's visitors can still experience Bok Tower Gardens, a sanctuary of plants, flowers, trees, and wildlife surrounding the 200-foot Bok Tower carillon. Close by is Cypress Gardens, which is now part of LEGOLAND, so children and adults both have much to see and do in this theme park.

Winter Park

6 miles northeast of Orlando, 20 miles northeast of Walt Disney World.

This peaceful, upscale community might be just outside the hustle and bustle of Orlando, but it feels like a different country. The town's name reflects its early role as a warm-weather haven for those escaping the frigid Northeast winters. From the late 1880s until the early 1930s, wealthy industrialists and their families would travel to Florida by rail on vacation, and many stayed, establishing grand homes and cultural institutions.

The lovely town retains its charm (and upper crust), with brick-paved streets, historic buildings, and well-maintained lakes and parkland. Even the bucolic nine-hole golf course (open to the public) is on the National Register of Historic Places.

On Park Avenue, you can spend a few hours sightseeing, shopping, dining, or all three. The street has boutiques, fine restaurants, and two world-class museums: the Charles Hosmer Morse Museum of American Art, with the world's largest collection of artwork by Louis Comfort Tiffany, and the Rollins Museum of Art on the campus of Rollins College (the oldest college in Florida). In addition to Park Avenue, Winter Park has three other restaurant hubs: Orange Avenue, Hannibal Square, and Winter Park Village.

GETTING HERE AND AROUND

To reach Winter Park from Downtown Orlando, take I-4 for 4 miles to Exit 87, and head east on Fairbanks Avenue for 3 miles to Park Avenue. LYNX buses 102 and 443 run from the main depot to Winter Park. The commuter train, SunRail, links downtown Orlando and Winter Park, running every half hour on weekdays.

If you avoid rush-hour traffic (and I-4 construction work), traveling to points of interest shouldn't take too much time out of your vacation. Winter Park is no more than 20 minutes from Downtown; International Drive and the theme parks are about 30 minutes away.

TOURS

Scenic Boat Tour

BOAT TOURS | FAMILY | Head east from Park Avenue to the end of Morse Boulevard, where you'll find the launching point for this tour, a Winter Park tradition since 1938. The one-hour cruise takes in 12 miles of waterways, including three lakes and narrow, oak- and cypress-shaded canals built in the 1800s as a transportation system for the logging industry. A well-schooled skipper shares stories about the moguls who built their mansions along the shore and points out wildlife and other remnants of natural Florida that still surround the expensive houses. Drinks (no alcohol) and snacks are allowed. Payment is by cash or check only. ✉ *312 E. Morse Blvd., Winter Park* ☎ *407/644–4056* 🌐 *www.scenicboattours.com* 🎫 *$14.*

VISITOR INFORMATION

CONTACTS City of Winter Park. ✉ *151 W. Lyman Ave., Winter Park* ☎ *407/599–3399* 🌐 *cityofwinterpark.org.*

Sights

Albin Polasek Museum and Sculpture Gardens

ART MUSEUM | Stroll along on a guided tour through gardens showcasing the graceful sculptures created by internationally known Czech sculptor Albin Polasek (1879–1965). The late artist's home, studio, galleries, and private chapel are centered on 3 acres of exquisitely tended lawns, colorful flower beds, and tropical foliage at the edge of Lake Osceola. Paths and walkways lead past classical life-size figurative sculptures and whimsical mythological pieces. Inside the museum are works by Hawthorne, Chase, and Mucha. The Capen House, a historic 1885 building, has been moved

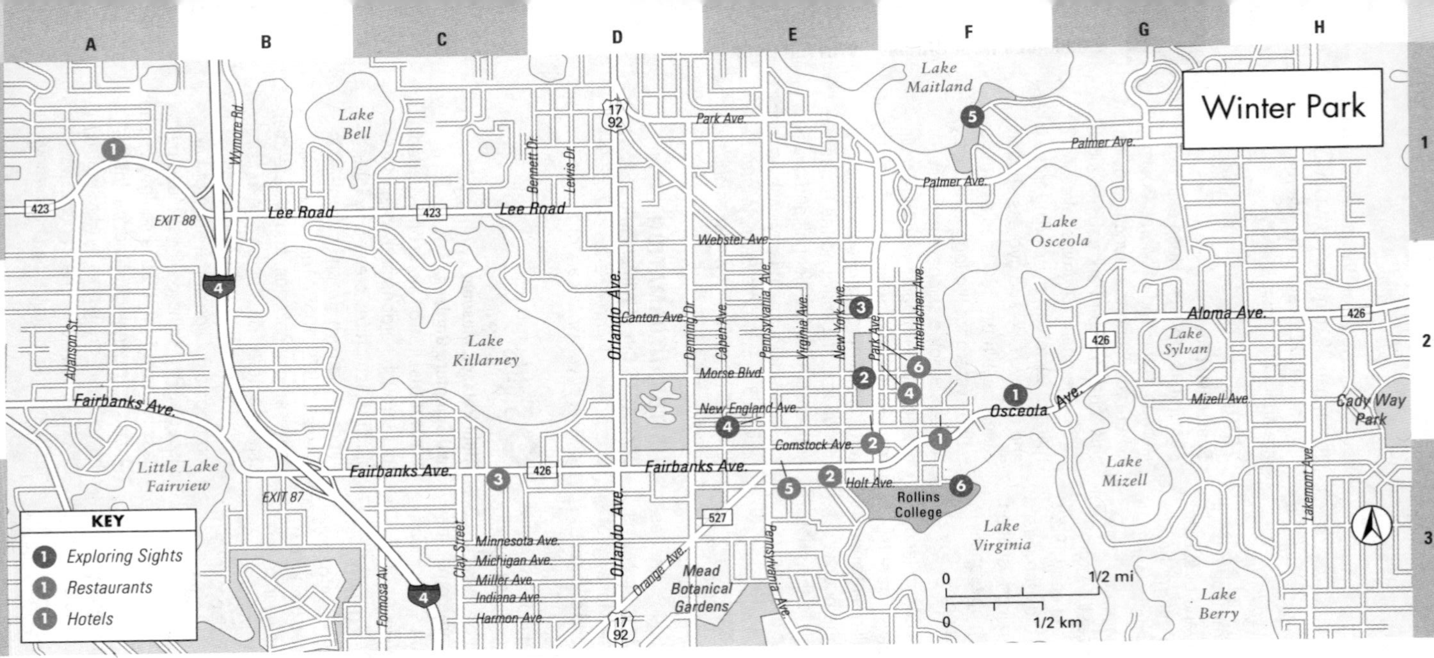

Sights ▼

1 Albin Polasek Museum and Sculpture Gardens **F2**

2 Central Park **E2**

3 Charles Hosmer Morse Museum of American Art.............. **E2**

4 Hannibal Square Heritage Center........... **E2**

5 Kraft Azalea Garden...... **F1**

6 Rollins Museum of Art (formerly Cornell Fine Arts Museum) **F3**

Restaurants ▼

1 Christner's Prime Steak & Lobster........... **A1**

2 Ethos Vegan Kitchen **E3**

3 4 Rivers Smokehouse **C3**

4 Prato **E2**

5 The Ravenous Pig **E3**

6 Tabla Indian Restaurant................. **E2**

Hotels ▼

1 The Alfond Inn **F2**

2 Park Plaza Hotel **E2**

to the grounds to be used for public events. ✉ *633 Osceola Ave., Winter Park* ☎ *407/647–6294* 🌐 *polasek.org* 🎫 *$10* 🕘 *Closed Mon.*

★ Central Park

CITY PARK | FAMILY | Given to the City of Winter Park by the Genius family (benefactors of the Morse Museum), this 11-acre green space has manicured lawns, specimen plantings, a beautiful rose garden available for private functions, a fountain, and a gazebo. If you take a seat and listen as the Amtrak passenger train rolls by, it's not hard to imagine how Winter Park looked and sounded in the late 19th century. The SunRail commuter and Amtrak trains stop right within the park, giving great car-free access, particularly during the packed art festivals, to and from Downtown Orlando, Kissimmee, and Sanford. The Winter Park Farmers' Market draws people to the southwest corner on Saturday between 8 am and 1 pm. If you don't want to browse in the shops across the street, a walk beneath the park's moss-covered trees is a delightful alternative. There's free Wi-Fi within the park, as well. ✉ *251 Park Ave. S, Winter Park* ☎ *470/599–3334* 🌐 *cityofwinterpark.org* 🎫 *Free* 🕘 *Closed 2 am–6 am* ☞ *No pets.*

★ Charles Hosmer Morse Museum of American Art

ART MUSEUM | FAMILY | The world's most comprehensive and important collection of works by Louis Comfort Tiffany—including immense stained-glass windows, lamps, watercolors, and desk sets—is in this museum, which also contains American decorative art and paintings from the mid-19th to the early 20th century. Among the draws is the 1,082-square-foot Tiffany Chapel, originally built for the 1893 World's Fair in Chicago. It took craftsmen 2½ years to painstakingly reassemble the chapel here. Many of the works were rescued from Tiffany's Long Island estate, Laurelton Hall, after a 1957 fire destroyed much of the property. The 12,000-square-foot Laurelton Hall wing allows for much more of the estate's collection to be displayed at one time, including architectural and decorative elements from the dining room, living room, and Fountain Court reception hall. There's also a re-creation of the striking Daffodil Terrace, so named for the glass daffodils that serve as the capitals for the terrace's marble columns. Admission is free on Friday after 4 pm from November through April. ✉ *445 N. Park Ave., Winter Park* ☎ *407/645–5311* 🌐 *www.morsemuseum.org* 🎫 *$6* 🕘 *Closed Mon.*

Hannibal Square Heritage Center

HISTORY MUSEUM | FAMILY | Almost crowded out by the glitz of new shops, restaurants, and art galleries is the original, once-thriving area of Hannibal Square, one of the oldest African-American communities in the country and home to Pullman porter families to this day. The Heritage Center has a permanent collection of photographs and oral histories of the significant West Winter Park area. It's a touching and important memorial to a neighborhood that influenced American history. ✉ *642 W. New England Ave., Winter Park* ☎ *407/539–2680* 🌐 *www.hannibalsquareheritagecenter.org* 🎫 *Free* 🕘 *Closed Sun. and Mon.*

Kraft Azalea Garden

CITY PARK | FAMILY | Enormous cypress trees shade this 5-acre public park on the shores of Lake Maitland. It's hidden within an upscale neighborhood and comes alive with heady color from January through March. The thousands of blooming azaleas (hence the name) make a perfect backdrop for romantic strolls, and sunset weddings are common at the park's Exedra monument overlooking the lake. ✉ *1365 Alabama Dr., Winter Park* ☎ *407/599–3334* 🌐 *cityofwinterpark.org* 🎫 *Free* 🕘 *Closed dusk–8 am.*

The Charles Hosmer Morse Museum of American Art is also known as the Tiffany Museum because of its extensive collection of works by Louis Comfort Tiffany.

★ Rollins Museum of Art (formerly Cornell Fine Arts Museum)

ART MUSEUM | **FAMILY** | On the Rollins College campus, this museum houses Florida's oldest art collection (its first paintings acquired in 1896)—one with more than 5,000 pieces, from Italian Renaissance works to 19th- and 20th-century American and European paintings. Special exhibitions feature everything from Native American artifacts to Soviet propaganda posters. Outside the museum, a small but charming garden overlooks Lake Virginia. Some of the museum's collection graces the walls of the nearby, Rollins-owned, Alfond Inn. The museum is free to visit; free guided tours are offered on weekends at 1 pm. A new downtown Winter Park home for the renamed Rollins Museum of Art will break ground in 2023. ✉ *Rollins College, 1000 Holt Ave., Winter Park* ☎ *407/646–2526* 🌐 *web.rollins.edu/rma* 🎫 *Free* 🕓 *Closed Mon.*

Restaurants

★ Christner's Prime Steak & Lobster

$$$$ | **STEAKHOUSE** | Locals like this legendary, uncomplicated, very large, family-run steak house, which delivers carefully prepared food and attentive service in a traditional setting of red leather and dark wood. When your steak arrives—still sizzling on a hot plate—the waiter asks you to cut into it and check that it was cooked as you ordered. **Known for:** extensive wine list; simple, perfectly executed steaks; house-made mandarin orange cake. $ *Average main: $45* ✉ *729 Lee Rd., Winter Park* ☎ *407/645–4443* 🌐 *christnersprimesteakandlobster.com* 🕓 *Closed Sun. No lunch.*

★ Ethos Vegan Kitchen

$$ | **VEGETARIAN** | **FAMILY** | Ethos has been vegan for so long (it opened in 2007) that if feels as if the rest of the culinary world has simply caught up with it. "Chickun" of the plant-based variety substitutes for meat, along with tofu, tempeh, and seitan. The black bean Samson Burger is one of the best veggie burgers in town. **Known for:** chickpea bay crab cake substitute; long dedicated to a meat-free menu; plant-based "meats." *Average main: $15 ✉ 601-B S. New York Ave., Winter Park ☎ 407/228–3898 🌐 ethosvegankitchen.com.*

★ 4 Rivers Smokehouse

$ | BARBECUE | FAMILY | What started as a tiny business in a former tire-repair shop has turned into a multilocation dynasty. The popular 4 Rivers turns out slow-cooked barbecue standards like pulled pork and Texas-style brisket, as well as more unusual items such as bacon-wrapped smoked jalapeños, the Six Shooter with cheese grits, and a sausage-filled pastry called *kolache*. **Known for:** addictive bacon-wrapped smoked jalapeños; slow-smoked ribs, brisket, and chicken; Sweet Shop bakeries. *Average main: $13 ✉ 1600 W. Fairbanks Ave., Winter Park ☎ 844/474–8377 🌐 www.4rsmokehouse.com ⏲ Closed Sun.*

★ Prato

$$$ | ITALIAN | Progressive Italian cuisine in a casual, bustling, wood-and-brick setting immediately made Prato a local favorite. Every item, from the pancetta to the amaretti, is crafted from scratch, and many are prepared in one of two imported Italian wood-burning ovens, dubbed Johnny Cash and June Cash because "they make music," the chefs say. **Known for:** Neapolitan pizzas and fresh pasta; the "Prato meatball"; outdoor curbside dining. *Average main: $23 Reservations Essential ✉ 124 N. Park Ave., Winter Park ☎ 407/262–0050 🌐 www.prato-wp.com ⏲ No lunch Mon. and Tues.*

★ The Ravenous Pig

$$$$ | AMERICAN | The Pig established the gastro-pub category in Orlando and then went on to spawn several offshoots. Run by James and Julie Petrakis, a husband-and-wife chef team with multiple James Beard Award nominations, its delicacies include pork porterhouse and the pub burger, though the daily-changing menu always includes less-expensive pub fare like rock shrimp tacos and homemade pretzels. **Known for:** adjacent Ravenous Pig Brewing Co. beer garden; popular foodie destination; homemade charcuterie. *Average main: $31 Reservations Essential ✉ 565 W. Fairbanks Ave., Winter Park ☎ 407/628–2333 🌐 www.theravenouspig.com ⏲ Closed Mon. No lunch Tues.–Sat.*

★ Tabla Indian Restaurant

$$$ | INDIAN | Tabla's reputation for great Indian food has lasted since 2008. Start with a selection from the enormous range of house-made breads before choosing from the menu of biryanis, curries, tandoor-fired meats, or vegetarian dishes like bhindi masala and sautéed paneer. **Known for:** wide range of vegetarian dishes; food from every territory of India; chicken, seafood, lamb, or goat curries. *Average main: $22 ✉ 216 N. Park Ave., Winter Park ☎ 407/422–0321 🌐 tablacuisine.com.*

Hotels

★ The Alfond Inn

$$$ | HOTEL | This serenely sophisticated property, in the heart of Winter Park and owned by neighboring Rollins College, combines an art gallery with an upscale hotel, where rooms are decorated in cool grays, with touches of the iconic Winter Park peacock blue, and have workstations and flat-screen TVs. **Pros:** free Wi-Fi; five-minute walk to Park Avenue for pleasant strolls and dining; first-rate on-site restaurant. **Cons:** does not cater to young children; day parking $12 (though free with restaurant visit), valet overnight $22; at least an hour's drive to the theme parks. *Rooms from: $332 ✉ 300 E. New England Ave., Winter Park ☎ 407/998–8090 🌐 thealfondinn.com 112 rooms No Meals.*

Park Plaza Hotel

$$ | HOTEL | Small and intimate, this beautifully updated, 1922 establishment charms with its fern-bedecked wrought-iron balconies and such offerings as free Wi-Fi and free breakfast in bed. **Pros:** view of Park Avenue shops and restaurants; valet parking; romantic atmosphere. **Cons:** far from theme parks; small rooms; railroad tracks are close, making for train noise at night. *Rooms from: $199 307 Park Ave. S, Winter Park 407/647–1072, 800/228–7220 parkplazahotel.com 28 rooms Free Breakfast.*

Shopping

Winter Park doesn't have just a few standout stores. It has dozens. By far the most alluring area is downtown's Park Avenue, a shopper's heaven that's akin to Worth Avenue in Palm Beach. Carve out an afternoon (or evening) to meander the inviting brick street lined with chic boutiques, sidewalk cafés, and hidden alleyways that lead to peaceful nooks and crannies with even more shops and eateries. Chain stores are scarce; instead, indy shops offer merchandise not readily found elsewhere. Even if you don't buy a thing, the beauty of the avenue is priceless. Note, too, that nearby Hannibal Square, at the intersection of New England and Pennsylvania avenues, offers still more upscale dining and shopping opportunities.

Winter Park Farmers' Market

MARKET | FAMILY | It's worth getting up early on a Saturday to amble through the local farmers' market (8 am to 1 pm), a favorite destination for food, flowers, and fellowship since 1979. Within and just outside a historical train station, some 85 vendors hawk everything from fresh vegetables and artisanal cheeses to locally produced honey and dried fruit. Eggs from Lake Meadow Naturals share space with Luna moth and swallowtail chrysalises from the "Butterfly Man" or chopped pineapple from Indian River fruit. A quick coffee and fresh croissant from the market is a great way to jump start a day of Park Avenue shopping. You can park on nearby streets and the public lots on New York Avenue and Morse Boulevard and Lyman and New England avenues. *200 W. New England Ave., Winter Park 407/599–3341 cityofwinterpark.org.*

SPECIALTY SHOPS

Charles Hosmer Morse Museum Gift Shop

MUSEUM SHOP | The museum contains the world's most comprehensive collection of Tiffany stained glass, drawings, paintings, jewelry, pottery, and other objets d'art—so naturally shoppers come here for the representations of Tiffany glass, silk scarves with stained-glass motifs, and fine-art glass that Louis Comfort himself would have treasured. There are also many objects from world museum gift collections and a wide assortment of books about the Arts and Crafts movement. *445 N. Park Ave., Winter Park 407/645–5316 shop.morsemuseum.org Closed Mon.*

Kathmandu

OTHER SPECIALTY STORE | You'll think you're on a trek in the Himalayas instead of a stroll on Park Avenue when you spy this unique store, noticeable for its colorful, flag-festooned exterior. Items come from exotic locales like India, Indonesia, Nepal, and Turkey. Hats, turquoise and crystal jewelry, wooden necklaces, clothing, and brass figures of Indian gods are among the merchandise. Follow your nose to the smell of patchouli and sandalwood. *352 N. Park Ave., Winter Park 407/647–7071 facebook.com/kathmanduorlando.*

Shoooz on Park Avenue

SHOES | While strolling along Park Avenue, your feet might tell you that you need a new pair of shoes from this cozy shoe-only shop, which carries reliable designer brands including Mephisto, Naot, Arcopedico, and Birkenstock. *303 N. Park Ave., Winter Park 407/647–0110 shooozonparkave.com.*

Ten Thousand Villages

OTHER SPECIALTY STORE | Selling products from more than 130 artisan groups in 38 countries, this fascinating little store offers fair-trade, artisan-crafted home decor, jewelry, paintings, and gifts of all kinds. ✉ *329 N. Park Ave., Winter Park* ☎ *407/644–8464* 🌐 *www.tenthousandvillages.com/winterpark.*

Activities

WinterClub Indoor Ski & Snowboard

SKIING & SNOWBOARDING | **FAMILY** | Heading south doesn't necessarily cancel out winter sports: here, you can opt for the truly unique experience of skiing and snowboarding in shorts and a T-shirt at this indoor ski slope. The region's first indoor ski center welcomes participants of all skill levels to practice and play on high-tech "endless slopes." WinterClub's interactive Ski Simulator fuses high-definition, large video wall ski runs with a unique chassis that allows skiers to experience the same g-force effects as they would in real life. ✉ *2950 Aloma Ave., Winter Park* ☎ *407/618–1123* 🌐 *www.winterclubski.com* 🎟 *From $69 per person; packages available.*

Maitland

10 miles northeast of Orlando, 30 miles northeast of Walt Disney World.

An Orlando suburb with an interesting mix, Maitland is home to the Florida Save the Manatee Society and one of Central Florida's larger office parks. A number of spectacular homes grace the shores of this town's various lakes, and there's a bird sanctuary and an art center.

GETTING HERE AND AROUND

Take I–4 (check construction alerts first) to Exit 90A, and then Maitland Boulevard east. Turn right (south) on Maitland Avenue.

Sights

Art and History Museums Maitland

ARTS CENTER | **FAMILY** | This group of museums, divided into two campuses a block apart, includes the Maitland Art Center, the Maitland Historical Museum, the Waterhouse Residence Museum, and the quirky Telephone Museum. Hidden down a tree-lined side street, the Maitland Art Center is a collection of 23 buildings in the Maya Revival style—with Mesoamerican motifs—that contain an art gallery and artists' studios. The restored Waterhouse museum reflects the life of a middle class Victorian family during the early days of the City of Maitland. Recognized by Florida as a historic site and on the National Register of Historic Places, the center was founded as an art colony in 1937 by American artist and architect André Smith (1880–1959). It continues his tradition of art instruction and houses a major collection of his works. ✉ *231 W. Packwood Ave., Maitland* ☎ *407/539–2181* 🌐 *www.artandhistory.org* 🎟 *$6* 🕐 *Closed Mon.–Wed.*

Audubon Center for Birds of Prey

NATURE PRESERVE | **FAMILY** | More than 20 bird species, including hawks, eagles, owls, falcons, and vultures, make their home at this wildlife rehabilitation center on Lake Sybelia. You can take a self-guided conservation tour with interactive exhibits and walkways through the wetlands, or you can call ahead for a private tour ($50 annual pass), which includes an up-close look at different birds in the center. There's an earnestness to this working facility, which takes in more than 800 injured wild birds of prey each year. Fewer than half can return to the wild; some permanently injured birds continue to live at the center and can be seen in aviaries along the pathways. To get here, take U.S. 17–92, and turn west on Lake Avenue and then north on East Street. ✉ *1101 Audubon Way, Maitland* ☎ *407/644–0190* 🌐 *cbop.audubon.org* 🎟 *$8* 🕐 *Closed Mon.*

Zora Neale Hurston National Museum of Fine Arts
ART MUSEUM | **FAMILY** | This museum, just a few minutes west of Maitland, is in Eatonville, the first African-American town to be incorporated after the Civil War. It showcases works by artists of African descent during five six-week-long exhibitions each year, with one reserved for up-and-comers. The museum is named after former resident Zora Neale Hurston (1891–1960), a writer, folklorist, and anthropologist best known for her novel *Their Eyes Were Watching God.* This is the home of Zora Fest, a street festival and cultural arts and music event celebrating Hurston's life, which is held each year in late January. ✉ *227 E. Kennedy Blvd., Eatonville* ☎ *407/647–3307, 800/704–1920* 🌐 *www.zoranealehurstonmuseum.com* 🎫 *Donations accepted* ⏲ *Closed Sun.*

Restaurants

★ Luke's Kitchen & Bar
$$$ | **AMERICAN** | At this restaurant, award-winning, James Beard–nominated chef Braden McGlamery emphasizes innovative American dishes. Sophisticated barbecue might find a place on the menu next to Florida redfish as well as some of the best burgers in the area. **Known for:** creative cocktails; seasonal menu; Sunday brunch. $ *Average main: $27* ✉ *640 South Orlando Ave., Maitland* ☎ *407/674–2400* 🌐 *eatatlukes.com* ⏲ *No lunch Mon. and Tues.*

Performing Arts

★ Enzian Theatre
FILM | **FAMILY** | This nonprofit arthouse is a cinematic treasure. First-run, quirky independent films are shown in this intimate theater, where locally sourced food is brought right to your table (yes, there are tables). Home to the acclaimed Florida Film Festival—as well as Jewish, South Asian, and Reel Short Teen film fests—the cinema also houses the very popular outdoor Eden Bar. ✉ *1300 S. Orlando Ave., Maitland* ☎ *407/629–0054* 🌐 *enzian.org* 🎫 *$12.*

Wekiwa Springs State Park

13 miles northwest of Orlando, 28 miles north of Walt Disney World.

GETTING HERE AND AROUND

Take I–4 (check construction alerts first) to Exit 94. Head west on State Road 434 and then north on Wekiwa Springs Road.

Sights

★ Wekiwa Springs State Park
NATURE PRESERVE | **FAMILY** | *Wekiva* is a Creek word meaning "flowing water"; *wekiwa* means "spring of water." The different spellings appearing on signs are both correct: each refers to either the river or the springs. Regardless, the surrounding 6,400-acre Wekiwa Springs State Park is well suited to camping, hiking, picnicking, swimming, canoeing, and fishing (license required). The area is also full of Florida wildlife: otters, raccoons, alligators, bobcats, deer, turtles, birds, and bears.

You can rent canoes or kayaks at the park for $27 for two hours. Canoe trips can range from a simple paddle around the lagoon to observe a colony of water turtles to a full-day excursion through the less-congested parts of the river, which haven't changed much since the area was inhabited by the Timucua people.

The park has 60 campsites: some are "canoe sites" that you can reach only via the river, and others are "trail sites," meaning you must hike a good bit of the park's 13½-mile trail to reach them. Most, however, are for the less hardy—you can drive right up to them. Sites have electric and water hookups. ✉ *1800*

Wildlife-rich Wekiwa Springs State Park is a great place to camp, hike, picnic, canoe, fish, swim, or snorkel.

Wekiva Cir., Apopka ✥ Take I–4 Exit 94 (Longwood) and turn left on Rte. 434. Go 1¼ miles to Wekiwa Springs Rd.; turn right and go 4½ miles to entrance, on right ☎ 407/553–4383 🌐 floridastateparks.org/index.php/parks-and-trails/wekiwa-springs-state-park 🎫 $2 per pedestrian or bicycle; $6 per vehicle ⏲ Closed dusk–dawn for day use.

Sanford

30 miles northeast of Orlando, 45 miles northeast of Walt Disney World.

At one time, Sanford was the heart of Central Florida—a vital vacation spot and transportation hub on the St. Johns River. But that was long before vacationers focused on Orlando and Walt Disney World. In recent years, Sanford has been focusing on its downtown area, increasing the size of its airport (Orlando–Sanford International) and gaining new trendy restaurants.

GETTING HERE AND AROUND

From Orlando International Airport or Downtown Orlando, take I–4 to Exit 104 and follow U.S. 17–92 to West First Street. The SunRail commuter train's Sanford stop has a regular trolley that takes visitors right into the heart of town, making the commuter train popular with day-trippers.

Sights

Central Florida Zoo and Botanical Gardens

ZOO | **FAMILY** | Sanford has had a zoo since 1923, and there's a certain charm about the place. In addition to 400-plus animals, including giraffes (you can feed them), cheetahs, monkeys, and crocodiles, there's the Seminole Aerial Adventures, with rope bridges and a zipline through the treetops, and the Wharton-Smith Tropical Splash Ground, a mini water playground. Evening events for grownups are as popular as summer camps for kids. The Florida black-bear habitat and Florida Trek are delightful, as is the steam-powered, 1/5-scale train that puffs around the grounds. Burgers, salads, and kids' meals are available ✉ *3755 N.W. U.S. 17–92, Sanford* ✢ *Take I–4 to Exit 104 and turn left on U.S. 17–92; zoo is on right* ☎ *407/323–4450* 🌐 *www.centralfloridazoo.org* 🎟 *$19.50 (online), $21.50 (on site).*

Restaurants

The Tennessee Truffle

$$$ | **SOUTHERN** | Using locally sourced ingredients, the chef at this small, independent redbrick eatery on Sanford's main drag creates Southern-fusion dishes. His house-made biscuits and gravy are renowned, the Saturday brunch menu includes a BLT with house-cured bacon and heirloom tomatoes, and dinner choices include pan-seared Florida trout with bacon from Tennessee and the ever-popular shrimp and grits with corn from Zellwood, Florida. **Known for:** shrimp and grits; Saturday brunch; great Southern-inspired food. $ *Average main: $28* ✉ *125 W. 1st St., Sanford* ☎ *407/942–3977* 🌐 *thetennesseetruffle.com* ⏲ *Closed Sun.–Wed.*

Mount Dora

35 miles northwest of Orlando, 50 miles north of WDW.

The unspoiled Lake Harris chain surrounds remote Mount Dora, an artsy community with a slow-and-easy pace, a rich history, New England–style charm, and excellent antiquing. Although the town's population is only about 16,000, there's plenty of excitement here, especially in fall and winter. The first weekend in February sees the Mount Dora Art Festival, which opens Central Florida's spring art-fair season. Attracting more than 250,000 people over three day's, it's one of the region's major outdoor events. The calendar here also includes the Storytelling Festival (January), Taste in Mount Dora event (March), a sailing regatta (March), a bicycle festival (October), a crafts fair (October), and many other happenings. In addition, Mount Dora draws large crowds during monthly antiques fairs (third weekend, except December) and thrice-yearly antiques "extravaganzas" (third weekends of January, February, and November) at popular Renninger's Twin Markets, an antiques center plus farmers' and flea markets. The Royal Palm Railroad Experience and Polar Express Christmas trains run between the cities of Mount Dora, Tavares, and Eustis.

GETTING HERE AND AROUND

Take U.S. 441 (Orange Blossom Trail in Orlando) north or take I–4 to Exit 92, then Route 436 west to U.S. 441, and follow the signs. From the Disney area, take SR 429 north (a toll road) to Exit 34 and then U.S. 441 north.

VISITOR INFORMATION

CONTACTS Mount Dora Chamber of Commerce. ✉ *341 Alexander St., at 3rd Ave., Mount Dora* ☎ *352/383–2165* 🌐 *www.mountdora.com.*

Sights

Lakeside Inn

HOTEL | Listed on the National Register of Historic Places, this country inn, built in 1883, overlooks 4,500-acre Lake Dora and is Florida's oldest continuously operating hotel. A stroll around the grounds, where seaplane passengers board or disembark, makes you feel as if you've stepped into the pages of *The Great Gatsby*. You, too, can book a seaplane tour or a cruise; both leave from the inn's large dock. Three restaurants offer indoor and outdoor dining. There are 90 guest rooms if you have time in your schedule for an overnight stay. ✉ *100 N. Alexander*

LEGOLAND Florida is a kid-friendly attraction a little more than an hour from Orlando.

St., Mount Dora ☎ *352/383–4101* 🌐 *www.lakeside-inn.com.*

★ Modernism Museum

ART MUSEUM | **FAMILY** | A refined and dazzling private collection of American and international pieces by mid-20th-century modernist artists features the work of George Nakashima, Wendell Castle, and the more radical Memphis Group, as well as pieces collected by musician David Bowie. The museum shares resources and a gift shop with the 1921 restaurant across the street, so special dining and exhibition events are held throughout the year. ✉ *145 E. 4th Ave., Mount Dora* ☎ *352/385–0034* 🌐 *www.modernismmuseum.org* 🎫 *$8* ⏲ *Closed Mon.–Thurs.*

Mount Dora Center for the Arts

ARTS CENTER | **FAMILY** | Local and national artists are highlighted in this lovely art center, which grew out of the annual arts festival. The center is a focal point for the community, serving as headquarters of the arts festival, a gallery, a gift shop, and a place to take art lessons. A new facility is in the works. ✉ *138 E. 5th Ave., Mount Dora* ☎ *352/383–0880* 🌐 *mountdoraart.com.*

Restaurants

★ 1921 Mount Dora

$$$$ | **SOUTHERN** | The gift shop of the Modernism Museum across the street is attached to this tearoom-turned-restaurant, which helps to explain its striking and sublime decor. The menu features dishes from Florida and elsewhere in the South that are made using local ingredients whenever possible; wood oven–fired oysters, slow-cooked octopus with Japanese eggplant, or barbecue lamb shank are just some of the possibilities. **Known for:** in-house pastry chef; new interpretations of Florida cuisine; locally sourced seafood and chicken. 💲 *Average main: $32* ✉ *142 E. 4th Ave., Mount Dora* ☎ *352/385–1921* 🌐 *1921mountdora.com* ⏲ *Closed Mon.*

LEGOLAND

50 miles southwest of Orlando.

From 1936 to 2009, the sleepy town of Winter Haven was home to the Sunshine State's first theme park, Cypress Gardens. Today, the lush gardens are still there, in addition to the world's largest LEGOLAND, 150 acres of buildings built using nearly 56 million LEGOs. Next door is the world's first Peppa Pig theme park, which opened in February 2022.

GETTING HERE AND AROUND

About an hour from Downtown Orlando, LEGOLAND is reached by I–4 West to Exit 55 and U.S. 27 to SR 540/Cypress Gardens Boulevard. If this is an important destination, save yourself the commute time by spending a night or two here. Three hotels—the 152-room LEGOLAND Hotel, the seaside-themed Beach Retreat, and the Pirate Island Hotel—offer building-block accented accommodations right by the parks.

Sights

★LEGOLAND Florida

THEME PARK | FAMILY | In addition to its 1:20-scale LEGO reproductions of U.S. cities and sights, the park has more than 50 rides, shows, and attractions throughout 10 different zones, as well as the marvelous botanical gardens from the original Cypress Gardens park.

The Danish toy company's philosophy is to help children "play well." And play they do, as LEGOLAND attractions are very hands-on. Kids can hoist themselves to the top of a tower, power a fire truck, or navigate a LEGO robot. Sights include huge LEGO dragons, wizards, knights, pirates, castles, roller coasters, racetracks, villages, and cities.

The cityscapes in Miniland USA fascinate children and adults, who delight in discovering what's possible when you have enough bricks. Miniland opens with Kennedy Space Center, where a 6-foot shuttle waits on the launch pad. Miami Beach features bikini-clad bathers and art deco hotels; St. Augustine and its historic fort play into LEGO's pirate theme; Key West's Mallory Square is accurate right down to the trained cats leaping through rings of fire. The rest of the country is not ignored: New York City, Las Vegas, San Francisco, and Washington, D.C., appear in intricate detail. Visitors spend hours looking for amusing details (like New York's purse snatcher) hidden in each city.

Among other highlights are Ninjago, where kids battle computer-generated bad guys; LEGO Kingdoms, whose castle towers over a jousting area and a roller coaster and where knights, damsels, dragons, and ogres are found; Land of Adventure, where you can explore hidden tombs and hunt for treasure; and the Imagination Zone, showcasing LEGO Mindstorms robots and where a giant head of Albert Einstein invites kids to explore and invent. Things get wild in LEGO Technic, the most active of the park's zones, where Test Track, Aquazone Wave Racers, and Technicycle let the family expend some energy.

During the live *Pirates' Cove* show, seafaring sailors wearing LEGO suits defend a huge ship from attacking pirates on water skis. LEGO Movie World features rides and attractions from the blockbuster, including Splash Battle, Masters of Flight, where guests soar above *The LEGO Movie* universe aboard a triple-decker flying couch, and Unikitty's Disco Drop, taking riders to the top of Cloud Cuckoo Land.

LEGOLAND Water Park features a wave pool; Build-a-Raft, where families construct a LEGO vessel and float down a lazy river; a 375-foot pair of intertwined

Bok Tower rises 200 feet in a garden in Lake Wales that was designed in 1929 by Frederick Law Olmstead, Jr., the son of the builder of New York City's Central Park.

waterslides that plunge riders into a pool; and a DUPLO toddler water play area. Not to be forgotten, Cypress Gardens, at the heart of the park, preserves one of Florida's treasures. Families can wander the lush, tropical foliage and gasp at one of the world's largest banyan trees. Three on-site hotels offer LEGO-theme accommodations and park packages. ✉ *1 LEGOLAND Way, Winter Haven* ☎ *855/753–8888* 🌐 *legoland.com/florida* 🎟 *$99; parking $23; water park $33 additional; discounts available online* 🕘 *Closed Tues. and Wed. in Jan. and Feb; opening hours vary the rest of the year.*

Peppa Pig Theme Park Florida

THEME PARK | FAMILY | Based on the popular and long-running British kids' show and built with accessibility and the little ones in mind, this park is also a Certified Autism Center. Explore playscapes such as Rebecca Rabbit's playground, Grandpa Pig's Greenhouse, and the Muddy Puddles Splash Pad, which has slides and water fountains. At the Fairgrounds, play games and ride on Peppa Pig's Balloon Ride and Mr. Bull's High Striker.

Other attractions include Grampy Pig's Dinosaur Adventure, Grandad Dog's Pirate Boat Ride, and the popular Daddy Pig's Roller Coaster—a great introduction to coasters for little ones. At The Cinema, relax indoors and watch episodes of Peppa Pig cartoons. Peppa tells interactive stories in live shows at Mr. Potato's Showtime Arena, Miss Rabbit's Diner offers kid-friendly meals, and Mr. Fox's Shop sells exclusive park merchandise. The park is just steps from LEGOLAND Florida but requires a separate ticket; combo tickets are available, though. ✉ *1 LEGOLAND Way, Winter Haven* ☎ *888/753–8888* 🌐 *www.peppapigthemepark.com* 🎟 *$30.99; parking $25.*

Bok Tower Gardens

57 miles southwest of Orlando, 42 miles southwest of Walt Disney World.

GETTING HERE AND AROUND

Take I–4 West to Exit 55, U.S. 27 South to Burns Avenue in Lake Wales, and then follow Tower Boulevard to Gardens.

Sights

★ Bok Tower Gardens

GARDEN | **FAMILY** | You'll see citrus groves as you ride south along U.S. 27 to the small town of Lake Wales and the Bok Tower Gardens. This appealing sanctuary of plants, flowers, trees, and wildlife has been something of a local secret for years. Shady paths meander through pine forests with silvery moats, mockingbirds and swans, blooming thickets, and hidden sundials. The majestic, 200-foot Bok Tower is constructed of coquina—from seashells—and pink, white, and gray marble. The tower houses a carillon with 60 bronze bells that ring out each day at 1 and 3 pm during 30-minute recitals that might include early American folk songs, Appalachian tunes, Irish ballads, or Latin hymns. The bells are also featured in recordings every half hour after 10 am; sometimes there are even moonlight recitals. The Blue Palmetto Cafe offers salads, soups, and sandwiches, as well as beer and wine. The landscape was designed in 1928 by Frederick Law Olmsted Jr., son of the planner of New York's Central Park. The grounds include the 20-room, Mediterranean-style Pinewood Estate, built in 1930 and open for self-guided touring. From January through April, guides lead 60-minute tours of the gardens (included in the admission price); tours of the inside of the tower are a benefit of membership. ✉ *1151 Tower Blvd., Lake Wales* ☎ *863/676–1408* 🌐 *boktowergardens.org* 🎫 *$16.*

Restaurants

Crazy Fish Bar and Grill

$ | **SEAFOOD** | **FAMILY** | You can enjoy outdoor patio dining at this popular seafood shack in Lake Wales, which was visited in 2016 by Emeril Lagasse for his show *Emeril's Florida.* Fresh shrimp, blue crab, and catfish sourced from Florida fishers are all on the menu in season. **Known for:** appearance on Emeril's Florida TV show; fresh Florida seafood; very casual atmosphere. $ *Average main: $12* ✉ *802 Henry St., Lake Wales* ☎ *863/676–6361* 🌐 *www.facebook.com/CrazyFishLakeWalesFL* ⏲ *Closed Sun. and Mon.*

Chapter 12

ACTIVITIES

Updated by
Gary McKechnie

With the sun shining virtually every day and moderate temperatures throughout the year, nearly anytime is a good time to be outdoors and active in Orlando. Surfing, horseback riding, and hang gliding just scratch the surface of what's available.

According to folks at the Orlando Convention and Visitors Bureau, there are more than 170 golf courses in the area (although another source, Golflink, pegs the number closer to 60 or so), with about 20 golf academies offering lessons. Even the city's recreation department gets in on the act with country club–like golf courses accessible at bargain prices. Meanwhile, inside and outside the theme parks are hundreds of tennis courts.

In and around Orlando and Central Florida, you can also navigate more than 2,000 lakes and waterways via canoe, kayak, paddleboard, or airboat. A fishing excursion is well worth considering, too, as this is one of the bass-fishing capitals of the world. In addition, unique to Central and North Florida are natural springs where crystal clear waters flow at a constant (and cool) 72 degrees. You can also rise above it all in a sailplane, hot-air balloon, or hang glider, or you can stay firmly planted on the ground by exploring forested hiking trails and modified rails-to-trails.

Orlando's sports arena and its pro hockey and basketball teams bring in the crowds. As they've done for more than a century, professional baseball teams venture down from the frozen North to warm up during spring training at stadiums across Central Florida.

If your vacation is based at Walt Disney World, you'll find many outdoor activities right outside your door. Anglers get hooked on fishing charters, and runners and bikers get their adrenaline rush on trails across the property. Spectators can take themselves out to the ESPN Wide World of Sports Complex where, during the COVID-19 outbreak, NBA teams played their season in the "bubble" of the complex. But it's not just basketball. Baseball, volleyball, cheerleading, softball, track, and weightlifting are just a few of the other events held here throughout the year in a wide world of competition. For Disney recreation information, call ☎ *407/939–7529.*

Ballooning

Central Florida's temperate weather is ideal for ballooning excursions, and it's not uncommon to rise early and see a colorful, puffy balloon—or even an entire flotilla of them—drifting above the countryside. Prices and flight durations are roughly the same among the tight-knit community of balloonists in the Orlando area, as is the ceremonial toast at the conclusion of your flight.

Often the gondola may be more tightly packed than you'd prefer (you'll pay a considerable premium for the romantic

Top 5 Recreational Experiences

Airboat Tours. Outside the parks, you can see the beauty and wildlife of lakes and swamps on airboat tours that skim across the waters and straight into the heart of natural Florida.

Golf. Set aside a few hours for a round of golf, which (depending on your skill level) could be 18 holes at Arnold Palmer's Bay Hill, an easy 9 holes at the historic and charming Winter Park Country Club, a family round of minigolf at a theme park, or a high-tech practice session at the TopGolf driving range.

iFly Orlando. Totally safe skydiving? That's right. In this indoor chamber, a massive turbine lets you fly like a bird without jumping out of an airplane (or even getting that far off the ground).

Seminole Lake Gliderport. There's hardly any experience simultaneously more thrilling and peaceful than being hauled to 2,000 feet in a sailplane, and then releasing the cord that secures you to the towplane in front of you. After that, it's a silent soaring adventure in the clear skies of Central Florida.

Fort Wilderness Resort. One of the original Disney resorts is a hub of activities for guests and nonguests alike. Options include archery, biking, boating, fishing, horseback riding, and Segway tours.

two-person flight of your imagination), but the experience, along with the views, is unforgettable.

★ Bob's Balloons

BALLOONING | **FAMILY** | Flying since 1980, Bob will meet you in the predawn hours at the ChampionsGate golf resort before heading to one of several popular launch sites, where you'll watch your balloon being prepared to go up, up, and away. Then you'll float between the treetop level and as high as 1,000 feet for about an hour, with views of farms and forest land; horses, deer, wild boar, and cattle; and birds flying *below* you.

In the distance, you'll likely see Disney landmarks like the Animal Kingdom's Expedition Everest and EPCOT's Spaceship Earth. Several balloons often launch at roughly the same time from nearby destinations, which provides an unparalleled sightline of these colorful sky ornaments. The memories will literally last a long time: Bob presents you with a flash drive of images from your flight. ✉ *Orlando* ☎ *407/466–6380, 877/824–4606* 🌐 *www.bobsballoons.com* 🎫 *From $175 per person.*

Maverick Hot Air Balloon Adventures

BALLOONING | **FAMILY** | Like other ballooning services, this one is ready to go seven days a week (weather permitting) although the exact launch site is dependent on the direction of the breeze. Pilots prefer to take to the skies near Walt Disney World, so you can take in an aerial view of the four theme parks. But wherever you travel—by Walt Disney World, above fragrant orange groves, or over undeveloped swampland—each flight is unique and memorable. If you're staying near the attractions area (Kissimmee, Celebration, I-Drive, etc.), the company can pick you up and return you to your hotel for an additional fee. ✉ *Orlando* ☎ *407/786–7473* 🌐 *maverickballoonadventures.com* 🎫 *From $245.*

Painted Horizons Balloons
BALLOONING | **FAMILY** | Like its local counterparts, Painted Horizons is ready to fly every day that the weather allows, and, like others, it offers specialties like private flights (for a premium, of course) or proposal flights (during which you're accompanied by a plane towing a "Will You Marry Me?" banner). Regardless of which option you choose, after flying wherever the wind carries you, the flight concludes with a toast of sparkling wine or cider and snacks of pastries, cheese, and crackers. ✉ *Orlando* ☎ *407/578–3031* 🌐 *www.paintedhorizons.com* 🎫 *From $210.*

Basketball

Orlando Magic
BASKETBALL | **FAMILY** | Since it became the city's NBA team in 1989, the popularity of the Orlando Magic has waxed and waned, perhaps reaching its peak in the early 1990s, when Shaquille O'Neal became the team's most recognized player and helped it become the second-fastest team to advance to the NBA Finals. Its venue is now downtown's multimillion-dollar, state-of-the art Amway Center.

The season runs October–June, and ticket prices vary greatly depending on where you sit and how well the season is going. Seats go for as little as $18, though courtside seats creep up toward $1,000 when the Magic is playing against a top team. ✉ *Amway Center, 400 W. Church St., Downtown Orlando* ☎ *407/896–2442* 🌐 *www.nba.com/magic* 🎫 *Tickets from $18; parking from $10; VIP parking from $50.*

Biking

Walt Disney World

Disney covers an area roughly the size of San Francisco, and within its boundaries are miles of paved trails that take you past forests, lakes, wooded campgrounds, and resort villas. If you're 18 or older, you can rent bikes at multiple locations, but you must ride them in the area where you rent them. Rental locations include several Disney resort hotels—Port Orleans, Old Key West, Caribbean Beach, Saratoga Springs, Coronado Springs, and the Fort Wilderness Campground among them. If renting a bike is important, ask about their availability when booking your reservation.

Most locations have children's bikes with training wheels, as well as those with toddler seats, and all guests are provided with helmets. Rates start at $10 an hour for regular beach cruiser–style bikes, but it's better to pay $20 for a full day. At Fort Wilderness, you can also rent surrey bikes, which look like old-fashioned four-wheel carriages and are very popular since the tops provide a rare commodity at Disney: shade. They cost between $20 and $25 per half hour depending on whether they have two, four, or six seats.

Orlando Area

Thanks to the Orlando community's commitment to the nationwide Rails to Trails program, the city now has several former railroad lines—in both rural and urban settings—that have been converted into biking, running, and in-line skating routes.

City of Orlando Trails
BIKING | **FAMILY** | Weaving around busy Orlando and into rural Orange County outposts are miles of trails modified from old railroad tracks. A few miles from Downtown, Winter Park's Cady Way

Trail passes some picturesque lakes and connects restaurants and retail centers along the way. The Lake Underhill Path connects to six city parks, while 20 miles east of Downtown, the 13-mile Orlando Southeast Trail is popular due to its distinctly rural landscapes and a generous 12-foot width.

The 3-mile Orlando Urban Trail near Downtown is considered the backbone of Orlando's trail network and connects several of the city's cultural highlights such as Lake Highland, Loch Haven Park, Mead Gardens, Orlando Cultural Park, and the Gaston Edwards Trail. The Shingle Creek Trail will eventually run through the city of Orlando and into the city of Kissimmee. For a comprehensive list of trails and where they lead, check the city's biking website. ✉ *Orlando* ☎ *407/246–2821* 🌐 *www.orlando.gov/Parking-Transportation/Bike-Trails-and-Paths.*

West Orange Trail

BIKING | FAMILY | With about 150,000 pedestrians, bicyclists, joggers, roller skaters, and skateboarders traveling some, or all, of its 22 miles every month, this is easily the most popular trail in the area thanks in large part to its pleasingly rural setting and a route that takes it through the charming community of Winter Garden. Spanning the Orange and Lake county lines, the 14-foot-wide path rolls through the towns of Killarney and Oakland and across U.S. 441 through downtown Apopka. Highlights include views of Lake Apopka and the butterfly garden at the Tildenville outpost.

Among the trail's most popular access points is Chapin Station (✉ *501 Crown Point Cross Rd., Winter Garden*), since it's just a few blocks from what is clearly the most popular place to rest and eat: Downtown Winter Garden. With sidewalk cafés, bicycle shops, gift shops, boutiques, candy stores, a community theater, history museum, and several other interesting sights, it's the perfect place to put down the kickstand and stay awhile. ✉ *501 Crown Point Cross Rd., Winter Garden* 🌐 *www.traillink.com/trail/west-orange-trail.*

West Orange Trail Bikes & Blades

BIKING | FAMILY | Bicycles—comfort style, hybrids, road bikes, kids' bikes, tandems—and in-line skates can be rented from a log cabin on the West Orange Trail at Chapin Station, just a few blocks east of downtown. The facility is perfectly placed right beside the trail and offers parking, changing areas, bike racks, and assistance getting the bike fitted for the ride. This center's sister shop is the Winter Garden Wheel Works, a full-service store a few blocks away in the heart of the shopping village. ✉ *17914 State Rd. 438, Winter Garden* ☎ *407/877–0600* 🌐 *www.orlandobikerental.com* 🎫 *From $9 per hr or $35 per day.*

Boating

Walt Disney World has one of the nation's largest fleets of rental pleasure craft, with marinas at the Caribbean Beach Resort, Contemporary Resort, Disney Springs, Fort Wilderness Resort, Grand Floridian Resort, Old Key West Resort, Polynesian Resort, Port Orleans French Quarter and Riverside resorts, and the Wilderness Lodge. You can rent 12-foot sailboats, catamarans, motor-powered pontoon boats, pedal boats, kayaks, canoes, and tiny two-passenger Sea Raycers—a hit with children—for use on Bay Lake and the adjoining Seven Seas Lagoon, at Crescent Lake by the EPCOT resorts, at Lake Buena Vista, or at the Buena Vista Lagoon.

You can also sail and water ski on Bay Lake and the Seven Seas Lagoon. You'll find sailboats at the Fort Wilderness, Contemporary, Polynesian, and Grand Floridian marinas. Call ☎ *407/939–7529* for more information.

But Disney certainly isn't the only place where you can take to the waters. Head to the outskirts of Orlando, and you can see Florida's lakes and backwaters via speedboats, motorboats, airboats, and even houseboats.

★ Boggy Creek Airboat Ride

BOATING | Just outside the attractions area, creeks, lakes, and swamps comprise the headwaters of the Florida Everglades. On an airboat tour, you'll explore these still-wild wetlands populated with exotic birds, turtles, and alligators. Boggy Creek, the best Orlando-based airboat tour company, offers four adventures, each of which will take you into the real Florida. When you're done, you can visit a recreation of a Native American village of the Jororo Tribe that lived along these same waterways hundreds of years ago. ✉ *2001 E. Southport Rd., Kissimmee* ☎ *407/344–9550* 🌐 *bcairboats.com* 🎟 *From $30.*

Marsh Landing Airboat Ride

BOATING | **FAMILY** | The thrill of an airboat really is something else. At this location, about 25 miles southeast of Disney, a fleet of 6-, 10-, and 14-passenger stadium-seating boats gives everyone an unobstructed view of the water speeding past. The airboat draws just a few inches of draft, so you skim through the reeds and near the shore to see alligators, cattle, egrets, anhingas, osprey, eagles, and deer, to name a few. Tours range in duration, distance, and cost, with the longest tour being a half-day venture into the marshlands of Osceola County. ✉ *2830A Neptune Rd., Kissimmee* ☎ *407/624–0973* 🌐 *orlandoairboattours.com* 🎟 *From $50.*

Spirit of the Swamp

BOAT TOURS | **FAMILY** | There's a common thread to airboat rides, and it's not just the wildlife. It's also the passion the captains have for explaining what you see. At this Kissimmee location, you'll head out onto Lake Toho where, since nothing is staged, you'll see what nature has in store—and often that includes an abundance of alligators, eagles, herons, ibis, kites, and osprey along with views of Florida that have remained unchanged for hundreds of years. The two-hour tour heads into Shingle Creek, the headwaters of the Everglades. ✉ *2830 Neptune Rd., Kissimmee* ☎ *321/689–6893* 🌐 *spiritoftheswamp.com* 🎟 *From $50.*

Wild Willy's Airboat Tours

BOAT TOURS | **FAMILY** | When you need to escape the concrete jungle, head to the Lake Toho Fish Camp on Lake Tohopekeliga and embark on an hour-long exploration of natural Florida. Instead of smiling mice and sailor-suited ducks, out here chances are you'll see alligators, blue herons, endangered snail kites, and bald eagles. If you'd like a closer look, following the tour get the camera ready for a photo with one of the resident gators. Call ahead; appointments are required. ✉ *4715 Kissimmee Park Rd., St. Cloud* ☎ *407/891–7955* 🌐 *www.wildwillysairboattours.com* 🎟 *From $42.*

Fishing

Central Florida freshwater lakes and rivers teem with all kinds of fish, especially largemouth black bass but also perch, catfish, sunfish, and pike, which makes this area a popular spot for fishing tournaments.

To fish in most Florida waters, anglers over 16 need a fishing license, which is available at bait-and-tackle shops, fishing camps, most sporting goods stores, and in the sporting goods section of Walmart and Bass Pro Shops. Some of these locations might not sell saltwater licenses, or they might serve non-Florida residents only, so call ahead.

For nonresidents of Florida, freshwater or saltwater licenses cost $17 for three consecutive days, $30 for seven consecutive days, and $47 for one year. For Florida residents under age 65, a freshwater or saltwater license is $17 per year for each or $32.50 for both. A five-year fishing license costs Florida residents $79 for both. Fishing on a private lake with the owner's permission—which is what anglers do at Disney World—does not require a Florida fishing license. For more information on proper licensing, contact Florida Fish and Wildlife (☎ *888/347–4356* ⊕ *gooutdoorsflorida.com).*

Walt Disney World

Disney Fishing Excursions

FISHING | **FAMILY** | Natural Bay Lake and the man-made Seven Seas Lagoon (whose excavation helped create the foundation of the Magic Kingdom) are connected by a channel, and each is heavily populated with fish. Two- and four-hour catch-and-release excursions—with additional hours upon request—depart in 21-foot, five-passenger Sun Tracker pontoon boats from the marinas at Fort Wilderness, Wilderness Lodge, Contemporary, Grand Floridian, and Polynesian resorts. Other waterfront resorts, including the Yacht and Beach Club, Saratoga Springs, Caribbean Beach, Port Orleans, and Old Key West, also have excursions from their marinas, with the trips including a boat, equipment, live bait, and a guide for up to five anglers. Your guide will get you to the best fishing spots, bait your hook, unhook your catches, and even snap pictures of you with your fish. Prices vary by time and number of guests, but generally the pontoon boat excursions range between $170 and $455. More-experienced anglers may prefer heading out on a Nitro tournament-style bass boat, which, in addition to the guide, accommodates two guests on two- to four-hour excursions ranging from $270 to $455 that include a voucher for membership into BASS (the Bass Anglers Sportsmen Society). Since these are private lakes on Disney property, a fishing license is not required. ✉ *Magic Kingdom Resort Area* ☎ *407/939–2277 fishing reservations* 🎫 *From $170 per person and $270 per group.*

Ol' Man Island Fishin' Hole

FISHING | **FAMILY** | An inexpensive alternative to a fishing charter is casting a line from a dock at Port Orleans–Riverside. At Ol' Man Island, a 3½-acre refuge that features a "swimmin' hole" themed like an abandoned sawmill, the Fishin' Hole offers cane poles and bait for $15 per half hour for a family of up to six. You must rent equipment here to use the dock. Fishing is also available from the Fort Wildernes docks on Bay Lake. Rental poles as well as bait can be picked up at the Bike Barn, and, like at any fishing spot at Disney, you're required to release any fish that you catch. Easy come, easy go. ✉ *Disney's Port Orleans, 1251 Riverside Dr., Disney Springs Resort Area* ⊕ *www.disneyworld.com* 🎫 *From $15.*

Orlando Area

Favorite Orlando fishing spots include Lake Kissimmee and the Butler and Conway chains of lakes. Kissimmee's massive Lake Tohopekaliga (aka Lake Toho) is held in high regard by the Bass Anglers Sportsman Society, as it's the source of the all-time-record Tournament Catch. Note that the lake's Native American name means "Sleeping Tiger," appropriate given that its generally placid waters become incredibly rough during thunderstorms and have sent more than a few fishermen to a watery grave. (Be careful in summer when you see storm clouds.)

The Butler area yields largemouth, some pickerel, and the occasional huge catfish. It's also very scenic, with lots of live oaks and cypresses, plus the occasional osprey or bald eagle. Toho and Kissimmee are good for largemouth bass and crappie; between November and April is the best period for catching trophy fish.

With their weatherbeaten docks, the fish camps around Lake Toho and other natural waterways offer an authentic glimpse of Old Florida. Most have general stores offering bait and tackle, boat rentals, snacks, beer, ice, and anything else you need for a day on the water. Lodging often consists of rustic campgrounds with cabins or trailers that have standard amenities and, occasionally, kitchenettes.

Unlike at Disney, on public lakes you need a license to fish, and you can keep what you catch. Fishing-operator services range from equipment and boat rental to full-day trips with guides and guarantees. Many guides operate out of the fishing camps, and you can usually make arrangements to hire them through the camp office. Rates vary, but for two people, a good price is around $300 for a half-day and $450 for a full day. Many area guides are part-timers, who fish on weekends or take a day off from their full-time job.

Like virtually all lakes in Florida, the big Orlando-area lakes teem with alligators, which are harmless unless you engage in the unwise practice of swimming at night. Small pets are more vulnerable than humans and should never be allowed to swim in Florida lakes or rivers.

Bass Challenger Guide Service

FISHING | Captain Eddie takes you wherever the fishing is best that day. It might be Lake Toho or the St. Johns River—Florida's longest and one of the few that runs north—which is a prime bass site. Indeed, bass is the only quarry. BCG also sells bait, arranges for transportation to and from your hotel, organizes multiday trips, and books area accommodations. Check in advance for advice on practical fishing apparel and accessories as well as license requirements. ✉ *Sanford* ☎ *321/878–4777* 🌐 *www.basschallenger.com* 🎫 *Half-day trips from $300.*

East Lake Toho RV Resort & Marina

FISHING | You can see what kept tourists entertained in pre-Disney days at this camp, which has a country store, sells live bait and propane, and offers airboat rides. It's hard to believe this much of Old Florida is just a few minutes (but several decades) away from Walt Disney World, but it is, and that's why you're here.

The camp has 256 RV sites and 24 simple, rustic cabins (which should be reserved at least two weeks in advance during peak winter and spring months). In 2021, new owners launched a multimillion-dollar improvement project which, among other things, will enhance the cabins and add a bar and grill. While boat rentals went away, the resort maintains a list of guides available for private fishing excursions. ✉ *3705 Big Bass Rd., Kissimmee* ☎ *407/348–2040* 🌐 *www.easttohorv.com* 🎫 *Cabins from $79 per night.*

Lake Charters

FISHING | This outfitter conducts trips from November to May on Lake Toho (January through April is high season, so reserve accordingly). Rods and reels are included in the cost, transportation is available, and you can also buy your licenses here. An informative website will fill you in on details regarding rates and what you'll catch (which might be a 14-pound bass). ✉ *1550 Scottys Rd., Kissimmee* ☎ *407/891–2275, 877/326–3575* 🌐 *www.lakecharter.com* 🎫 *Half-day trips from $275.*

Richardson's Fish Camp

FISHING | Rustic and remote, this camp on western Lake Toho is a place where time began standing still when it opened in the 1950s (hence the lack of a website). Relaxing by the water, setting up a cookout, watching the wildlife (deer, osprey, eagles, and company), and catching a glorious Florida sunset are just a few of the activities you'll enjoy in a place where the most pressing issue is whether to fish or not (you'll probably fish). The camp has 7 cabins with kitchenettes, 16 RV sites, and 6 tent sites, as well as boat slips and a bait shop. The camp is peaceful, quiet, and pet-friendly. ✉ *1550 Scottys Rd., Kissimmee* ☎ *407/846–6540* 🎫 *Cabins from $44.*

Golf

With dozens and dozens of courses and academies in and around Orlando, it's no wonder that the International Association of Golf Tour Operators has recognized Orlando as a top golf destination. Sunny weather almost year-round doesn't hurt, and though most of Florida is extremely flat, many of the courses feature hills that make them more challenging.

Note, too, that resort hotels often let nonguests use their golf facilities and that some country clubs are affiliated with hotels whose guests can play at preferred rates.

Greens fees fluctuate by the time of the day, the day of the week, and the season. Except for a few 9-hole walking courses, cart rental is generally mandatory, and even public courses have dress codes. To get current prices, check on attire requirements, and reserve tee times (essential for this very popular sport), call the course of interest or visit its website.

■ TIP→ Twilight discounts (usually half off the normal rates) often apply after 2 pm in busy seasons and after 3 pm the rest of the year.

GOLFPAC Travel

GOLF | GOLFPAC Travel packages golf vacations and arranges tee times at nearly all Orlando courses, as well as elsewhere in Florida and the U.S. Rates vary based on hotel and course, and 60 to 90 days' advance notice is recommended to set up a vacation. Its website has convenient searchable, clickable options that let you pick the time and place for a golf outing, adding them to a cart for checkout. ✉ *483 Montgomery Pl., Altamonte Springs* ☎ *407/260–2288, 888/848–8941* 🌐 *www.golfpactravel.com.*

Walt Disney World

Where else would you find a sand trap shaped like the head of a well-known mouse? Disney has 54 holes of golf on three championship courses—all on the PGA Tour route—plus a 9-hole walking course. And any guest at a WDW hotel who checks in specifically to play golf gets free transportation to the course.

The original Palm and Magnolia 18-hole courses are across the Seven Seas Lagoon near the Magic Kingdom by the Grand Floridian and Polynesian resorts, as is the 9-hole Oak Trail walking course. The 18-hole Lake Buena Vista course is near the Disney Springs retail/entertainment area. If you plan to play only once, leave the gear at home—you can rent shoes, range balls, and clubs at any of the courses.

GREENS FEES AND TEE TIMES

Rates at all 18-hole courses vary throughout the year, with prices hovering between $70 and $130. Disney resort guests get a price break and there are twilight discount rates as well. All fees include an electric cart, although the 9-hole Oak Trail is a walking course, where a pull cart for your bag costs $9.

If you've got the stamina and desire to play the same course twice in the same day, you can do so for half price the second time around, but you can't reserve that option in advance. This Re-Play Option, as Disney calls it, is subject to availability.

Golf shoes rent for $10 a pair, and range balls are available for $8 to $12 a bucket. If you'd rather not pay a baggage fee to haul your clubs onto your plane, you can rent the latest Sims woods, irons, and a putter for $49.

Tee times are available daily from dawn until dusk. You can book them up to 90 days in advance if you're staying at a WDW-owned hotel, 60 days ahead if you're staying elsewhere. You must cancel at least 24 hours out or be subject to a charge on the credit card you used to reserve your tee time.

GOLF INSTRUCTION

One-on-one instruction from PGA-accredited professionals is available at any Disney course. Prices for private lessons vary: 45 minutes costs $85 for adults and $60 for youngsters 17 and under. As with tee times, reservations (☎ *407/939–4653* 🌐 *www.golfwdw.com*) for private lessons are essential.

COURSES

Disney's Lake Buena Vista Golf Course

GOLF | This favorite among golfers, which has hosted the PGA Tour, LPGA Tour, and USGA events, winds among Disney Springs–area town houses and villas. Greens are narrow, and hitting straight is important because errant balls might end up in someone's bedroom. Be prepared for the famous island green on the 7th. This is a pleasant location surrounded by wonderful scenery. ✉ *2200 Golf Dr., Disney Springs Resort Area* ☎ *407/939–4653* 🌐 *www.golfwdw.com* 💵 *From $49* 🏌 *18 holes, 6745 yards, par 72.*

Disney's Magnolia Golf Course

GOLF | One of the originals when the park opened in 1971, the Magnolia has been lavished with four stars by *Golf Digest* and was certified by Audubon International as a Cooperative Wildlife Sanctuary. The long but forgiving classic course features extra-wide fairways, and its name stems from the more than 1,500 magnolia trees that line it.

While you're working to avoid the woods, try avoiding the water hazards at 11 of the 18 holes. But that's not all. There are 97 bunkers spread throughout the fairway. Play here, and you're playing the course that welcomed Nicklaus, Palmer, Player, and other legends. ✉ *Shades of Green, 1950 W. Magnolia Palm Dr., Magic Kingdom Resort Area* ☎ *407/939–4653* 🌐 *www.golfwdw.com* 💵 *From $39* 🏌 *18 holes, 7516 yards, par 72.*

Disney's Oak Trail Golf Course

GOLF | Located across from the Grand Floridian at the Shades of Green Resort (used primarily by military families), the 9-hole Oak Trail was designed by Ron Garl to be fun for the entire family. Certified by Audubon International as a Cooperative Wildlife Sanctuary, this tranquil walking course is noted for its small, undulating greens and particularly affordable fees. ✉ *Shades of Green, 1950 W. Magnolia Palm Dr., Magic Kingdom Resort Area* ☎ *407/939–4653* 🌐 *www.golfwdw.com* 🏌 *9 holes, 2913 yards, par 36.*

Disney's Palm Golf Course

GOLF | Although it's not as long as the Magnolia, nor as wide, the 6,870-yard Palm has been confounding the pros for years. The course, located across from the Grand Floridian Resort, has 9 water holes and 94 bunkers—including one in the iconic shape of Mickey Mouse's head. ✉ *Shades of Green, 1950 W. Magnolia Palm Dr., Magic Kingdom Resort Area* ☎ *407/939–4653* 🌐 *www.golfwdw.com* 🏌 *18 holes, 7011 yards, par 72.*

★ Tranquilo Golf Club at Four Seasons Resort

GOLF | Once known as Disney's Osprey Ridge, this Tom Fazio–designed course is on Disney property but part of the Four Seasons Resort Orlando, which means it's only available for resort guests or members. Sculpted from still-forested portions of the huge WDW acreage, some of the tees and greens sit as much as 20 feet above the fairways to keep competitive players from getting too comfortable.

Amenities include luxury golf carts with GPS, a Cuban-American clubhouse restaurant, driving range, and putting green. Greens fees drop significantly for "twilight" play starting at 2 pm. Have time for only 7 holes? There's a special for that, too. ✉ *10100 Dream Tree Blvd., Lake Buena Vista* ☎ *407/313–6881* 🌐 *www.fourseasons.com/orlando/golf* 🎫 *From $175* ⛳ *18 holes, 6968 yards, par 71.*

Orlando Area

Golf has no better hometown than Orlando. With temperate weather and dozens and dozens of public and private courses, the longtime residence of the late Arnold Palmer has enticed scores of other PGA professionals to make the city their home as well.

Palmer's landmark Bay Hill Invitational is held here each March, and the Daytona-based LPGA hosts several tournaments in Orlando every year. Appearing with great frequency (every single day) are the programs and tournaments aired on the Golf Channel, which broadcasts from Orlando. Note that the greens fees listed reveal a wide range of prices, which can change by season and time of day. Call pro shops or check websites for the most-current rates.

Arnold Palmer's Bay Hill Club & Lodge

GOLF | It was golf legend Arnold Palmer who helped put Orlando at the forefront of the sport, and this course was his pride and joy. Each March, at the Arnold Palmer Invitational, pros and amateurs anticipate the 18th hole here, which is considered one of the toughest on the PGA tour. Courses are open only to those who have been invited by a member or who book a stay at the club's 70-room lodge, where double-occupancy rates for rooms overlooking the course run as low as $200 per evening in summer. Keep in mind this rate does not include your greens fees, which are necessary: staying here in essence buys you a day of "membership" at the club, which also features a spa, fitness center, swimming pool, and tennis courts. ✉ *9000 Bay Hill Blvd.* ☎ *407/876–2429, 407/422–9445* 🌐 *www.bayhill.com* 🎫 *From $75* ⛳ *18 holes, 7207 yards, par 72; 9 holes, 3409 yards, par 36.*

Celebration Golf Club

GOLF | Talk about a great pedigree—the Celebration course was designed by Robert Trent Jones Jr. and Sr. Located just 10 minutes from Walt Disney World, the course is paired with the master-planned Disney community, just 1 mile off the U.S. 192 strip. Lovely and serene, the fairways are framed by natural woods and wetlands to create what the Joneses envisioned: "Every hole a hard par and an easy bogey." Rates drop after 1 pm and again around dusk. ✉ *701 Golf Park Dr., Celebration* ☎ *407/566–4653* 🌐 *www.celebrationgolf.com* 🎫 *From $79* ⛳ *18 holes, 6783 yards, par 72.*

ChampionsGate Golf Club

GOLF | Just about 10 minutes west of Disney, from the vantage point of I–4 you can see that there's some serious golfing inside the gates of ChampionsGate. The two courses here were designed by Australia's Greg Norman, and there's an on-site David Leadbetter Golf Academy. The 7,363-yard International has the "Down Under" style of Australia's coastal links, whereas the 7,128-yard National course is designed in the style of the better domestic courses, with a number of par-3 holes that have unusual bunkers.

The golf shop is ranked among the Top 100, and the Pipers Grille sports lounge is a great 19th hole. At sunset, step onto the veranda and watch a piper play as he walks the greens. Can't get enough? There's a four-star Omni hotel here. ✉ *1400 Masters Blvd., ChampionsGate* ☎ *407/787–4653 ChampionsGate, 407/787–3330 Leadbetter Academy, 888/633–5323 Leadbetter Academy* 🌐 *www.championsgategolf.com* 🎫 *From $49* ⛳ *International: 18 holes, 7363 yards, par 72. National: 18 holes, 7128 yards, par 72.*

Falcon's Fire Golf Club

GOLF | Designed by Rees Jones, Falcon's Fire has strategically placed fairway bunkers that demand accuracy off the tee. This club is just off Kissimmee's Irlo Bronson Memorial Highway and is convenient to the hotels in the so-called Maingate area. A round here includes complimentary valet parking, club cleaning, and golf carts equipped with GPS navigation. ✉ *3200 Seralago Blvd., Kissimmee* ☎ *407/239–5445* 🌐 *www.falconsfire.com* 🎫 *From $49* 🏌 *18 holes, 7015 yards, par 72.*

Hawk's Landing Golf Club at the Orlando World Center Marriott

GOLF | Near the entrance to Walt Disney World at the monumental World Center Marriott (the world's largest Marriott), the 220-acre Hawk's Landing course includes 15 water holes, lots of sand, and exotic landscaping. As you play, you'll see they've maintained the natural surroundings and enhanced the same with vibrantly colored azaleas. This is a good choice if you're here on business and want to get in a round.

No need to pack your clubs—Callaway rental equipment is available. Need some help? Lessons are offered by top-ranked PGA instructors at the Orlando Golf Academy. ✉ *Orlando World Center Marriott, 8701 World Center Dr.* ☎ *407/238–8660, 800/567–2623* 🌐 *www.golfhawkslanding.com* 🎫 *From $69* 🏌 *18 holes, 6602 yards, par 71.*

The Links Course at Evermore

GOLF | When it opened, the Grand Cypress resort elevated Orlando golf by transforming pasture and prairie into four elegant courses. The transformation continues as these greens become part of the new Evermore resort area. Currently open for play, The Links Course (formerly the New Course)—designed by Jack Nicklaus who was inspired by the Old Course at St. Andrews in Scotland—still features deep bunkers, double greens, and even an old stone bridge. ✉ *1 N. Jacaranda* ☎ *407/239–1909* 🌐 *evermoreresort.com/tee-time* 🎫 *From $79* 🏌 *The Links: 18 holes, 6773 yards, par 72.*

Marriott Golf Academy

GOLF | The Marriott Golf Academy is an extensive-curriculum golf school and 9-hole golf course on the grounds of the corporation's biggest time-share complex, Marriott's Grande Vista. Here you can do anything from taking a one-hour lesson with a certified instructor (all of whom are highly experienced PGA career pros) to immersing yourself in a three-day extravaganza during which you'll learn more about golf technique than you ever thought you could. The Swing Studio offers high-tech teaching methods, and the course, designed by Ron Garl, is geared to make you use every club in your bag—and perhaps a few you might elect to buy in the pro shop. ✉ *Marriott Grande Vista, 12001 Ave. Verde* ☎ *855/642–2369, 407/238–7677* 🌐 *www.marriottgolfacademy.com* 🎫 *Lessons from $99; 3-day courses from $949* 🏌 *9 holes, 2400 yards, par 32.*

Orange Lake Resort

GOLF | About five minutes from Walt Disney World's main entrance, Orange Lake has two 18-hole courses (the Legends and the Reserve), two 9-hole courses (Crane's Bend, Legends Walk), and pro instruction at the McCord Golf Academy where a one-hour session is $99. The Legends is a signature Arnold Palmer–designed championship course; the Reserve was designed by Mike Dasher and has unique land and water challenges. Crane's Bend is family-friendly. Legend's Walk is an executive walker's course open until 9 pm nightly, where children 15 and younger play free with complimentary clubs. The signature hole for the entire group of courses is the Island Oak, No. 13, a 432-yard, par-4 hole in the Pines section (the back 9) of the Legends Course. Rental clubs and range balls are available. ✉ *8505 W. Irlo*

Bronson Memorial Hwy., Kissimmee ☎ 407/239–1050 🌐 orangelakegolf.com 💵 From $35 for resort guests; from $60 for nonguests ⛳ The Legends: 18 holes, 7072 yards, par 72. The Reserve: 18 holes, 6670 yards, par 71. Crane's Bend: 9 holes, 1901 yards, par 30. Legend's Walk: 9 holes, 1581 yards, par 30.

Rosen's Shingle Creek Golf Club

GOLF | Rosen's Shingle Creek Golf Club, designed by David Harman, lies alongside a lovely creek that is a headwaters of the Everglades. The course is challenging yet playable, with dense stands of oak and pine trees and interconnected waterways. The golf carts even have GPS yardage systems. Since Universal Studios and the Orange County Convention Center are within a few minutes' drive, this is a favorite for conventioneers. *✉ 9939 Universal Blvd. ☎ 407/996–1559 🌐 www.shinglecreekgolf.com 💵 From $85 ⛳ 18 holes, 7069 yards, par 72.*

TopGolf

GOLF | Way back when, bowlers would mark their own scores on a strip of paper. Then, computers came along to track the ball's path, and scores would be tallied and automatically displayed on colorful screens. Now, picture that level of technology at a driving range. At this fantastic complex near the Orange County Convention Center, golf balls are embedded with a tracking chip so you and your friends can enter your names on a computer, choose from a few dozen clubs, wait for a ball to drop out by a tee, and start swinging. Within seconds of hitting the shot, the height, distance, and course of the ball will be shown on a screen.

Play for points by hitting the microchipped ball close to one of 11 targets that are spread out from 20 to 240 yards away. Multiple levels accommodate multiple golfers, and the pub and club atmosphere (there's a bar and restaurant here as well) makes this a popular meeting place for friends—even if they've never swung a club. *✉ 9925 International Dr., International Drive ☎ 407/218–7714 🌐 topgolf.com/us/orlando 💵 From $30 per hr, per group with discount specials available.*

Waldorf Astoria Golf Club

GOLF | The Rees Jones–designed course has maintained some of the original landscape's natural elements while enhancing its existing contours. Majestic stands of pine and cypress line the fairways, which wind through a scenic wetland preserve and are sprinkled with bunkers reminiscent of century-old hazards. It has a five-tee system for all playing levels. *✉ 14224 Bonnet Creek Resort La. ☎ 407/597–5500, 888/924–6531 🌐 www.waldorfastoriaorlando.com/golf/golf-club 💵 From $65 ⛳ 18 holes, 7113 yards, par 72.*

Winter Park Country Club

GOLF | Located in Winter Park, an upscale suburb of Orlando, this charmingly simple course is at the north end of Park Avenue, Central Florida's version of Worth Avenue in Palm Beach or Rodeo Drive in Beverly Hills. A point of pride for residents, this historic country club offers nonresidents access to its immaculate golf course. Opened in 1914, the 9-hole walking course was modeled after authentic Scottish links. Notably, residents were once given a choice to sell the golf course to developers or raise their own taxes to preserve it for the city. They chose to tax themselves and keep the course, which remains one of the region's most affordable and authentic recreational experiences. *✉ 761 Old England Ave., Winter Park ☎ 407/599–3419 🌐 www.winterparkcountryclub.com 💵 From $16 ⛳ 9 holes, 2480 yards, par 36.*

Orlando's Solar Bears professional hockey team plays in downtown Orlando's Amway Arena.

Hockey

Orlando Solar Bears

HOCKEY | FAMILY | Taking the ice at downtown's Amway Center, the Orlando Solar Bears play in the South Division of the Eastern Conference Hockey League, a mid-level league one tier below the American Hockey League (which is one tier below the National Hockey League). Still, it's affordable evening of exciting action on the ice during a season that runs from October to April. ✉ *Amway Center, 400 East Church St., Downtown Orlando* ☎ *407/951–8200* 🌐 *orlandosolarbearshockey.com* 🎟 *From $12.*

Horseback Riding

Fort Wilderness Resort

HORSEBACK RIDING | FAMILY | Backwoods horseback trail rides have been a popular activity since the earliest days of Disney World, and they depart from the Tri-Circle-D Ranch at 8:30 am and continue through mid- to late afternoon. Children must be at least 9 years old and 48 inches tall to ride, and adults must weigh less than 250 pounds. Trail rides start at 45 minutes; hours vary by season. You must check in 30 minutes prior to your ride, and reservations must be made at least one day ahead.

Both horseback riding and the campground are open to nonresort guests. Also available are wagon rides, carriage rides, and, for the kids, pony rides. ✉ *Tri-Circle D Ranch, 4510 Fort Wilderness Trail, Magic Kingdom Resort Area* ☎ *407/824–2832* 🎟 *From $55.*

Ice Skating

The Ice Factory

ICE SKATING | FAMILY | Ice-skating in Florida? Yup! This Olympic-class facility has two rinks and several theme evenings each week. Teens are drawn to Friday's DJ Night, there are family rates on Saturday night, and you can arrange birthday parties as well. Skate rentals are included with admission, and an upgraded pair (which costs a little extra) features extra padding (wearing thick socks is an option). Hours vary, and often the rink is being used for training, so visit its website to check the public-skating schedule.

New to the ice? No worries: you can also get private ice-skating and hockey lessons. And dress in layers—on the rink the temperature averages between 50 to 65 degrees year-round. Long pants and a sweater are usually fine since you're moving around. ✉ *2221 Partin Settlement Rd., Kissimmee* ☎ *407/933–4259* 🌐 *www.icefactory.com* 🎟 *From $9.50; skate rental $3.50.*

Miniature Golf

If minigolf is your game, Disney has two courses, but there are several others in Orlando.

Congo River

GOLF | FAMILY | In this clever creation, it's miniputt meets theme park as multilevel courses wander amid waterfalls, rocky summits, caves, and rain forests. Popular with families and, believe it or not, couples, it's clearly kids who are the prime audience since they love the live alligators (albeit not ones loose on the course). The arcade room and and the treasure hunt are bonuses. Congo River also has locations in Kissimmee and East Orlando. Hint: Check local coupon booklets for discounts. ✉ *5901 International Dr., International Drive* ☎ *407/248–9181* 🌐 *www.congoriver.com* 🎟 *From $15.*

Fantasia Gardens Miniature Golf

MINIATURE GOLF | FAMILY | Nearly every miniature golf course uses cartoon characters of some sort, but only Disney can use classic characters you'd recognize from Walt's bold experiment, *Fantasia*. Along the course are tutu-clad hippos, marching broomsticks, and pirouetting ostriches. Making things even more challenging are all the elements of a traditional golf course: sand traps, bunkers, water hazards, and sloping greens. ✉ *1205 EPCOT Resorts Blvd., EPCOT Resort Area* ☎ *407/824–4500* 🌐 *disneyworld.disney.go.com/recreation/fantasia-gardens-fairways-miniature-golf* 🎟 *From $14.*

★ Hollywood Drive-In Golf at Universal CityWalk

MINIATURE GOLF | FAMILY | With a science-fiction alien invasion course paired with a 1950s horror movie monster course, there's something for kids and fun-loving adults alike. Spectacular lighting and sound effects mean that the play is different day and night. A 36-hole Double Feature package is available, and the course is generally open until 2 am for after-theme-park romping. ✉ *6000 Universal Blvd., CityWalk* ☎ *407/802–4848* 🌐 *hollywooddriveingolf.com* 🎟 *From $19.*

Pirate's Cove Adventure Golf

MINIATURE GOLF | FAMILY | Two, 18-hole, miniature golf courses with a buccaneer theme wind around artificial mountains, through caves, beside waterfalls, and into foliage. For beginners, there's the Captain's Course with Blackbeard's Challenge being more demanding. In addition to this location, there's one in Lake Buena Vista (near Disney). ✉ *8501 International Dr.* ☎ *407/827–1242* 🌐 *www.piratescove.net* 🎟 *From $14.*

Winter Summerland Miniature Golf

MINIATURE GOLF | FAMILY | Not content to build just one themed miniature golf course, Disney built two very different courses beside the Blizzard Beach water park: one themed for the Florida summer sun, the other a perpetual winter wonderland. The Summer course mixes things up with surfboards, sand castles, peppermint-striped inner tubes, and palm trees decorated with Christmas ornaments. As you play your way toward the North Hole on the Winter Course, obstacles include giant peppermints, hockey sticks, and the drawbridge of a melting castle. ✉ *1548 Buena Vista Dr., Blizzard Beach* ☎ *407/824–4500* 🌐 *disneyworld.disney.go.com/recreation/winter-summerland-miniature-golf* 🎟 *From $14.*

Rodeos

Silver Spurs Rodeo
RODEO | FAMILY | You can still find a bit of Old Florida on Disney's doorstep, right in neighboring Kissimmee at the Silver Spurs Rodeo. Launched here by ranching families in 1944, the largest rodeo east of the Mississippi features bull riders and cowboys (many working nearby ranches) competing in bull and bronco riding, steer wrestling, barrel racing, and other high-energy, high-adrenaline events. If you'd like to hang out with some of the original ranchers whose families pre-date Disney by a century, this is the place to do it. The main rodeo is held each February, and the National Barrel Horse Association competition is held in June. ✉ *1875 Silver Spur La., Kissimmee* ✣ *From I–4 Exit 77, take Florida's Tpke. south to Exit 244 (Kissimmee–St. Cloud)* ☎ *321/697–3495* 🌐 *www.silverspursrodeo.com* 🎟 *From $15.*

Running

Disney features several scenic running trails in the Magic Kingdom area, near the Grand Floridian, Polynesian, and Contemporary resorts. At the EPCOT resort area, you can get your heart rate up along the promenade that circles Crescent Lake past the BoardWalk and Yacht and Beach Club resorts. You can also work up a sweat on trails near the Port Orleans; Coronado Springs guests run along the resort's 1-mile esplanade.

The roads that snake through Disney Springs resorts are pleasant, and early in the morning traffic isn't too bad. At the Caribbean Beach Resort, there's a 1½-mile running promenade around Barefoot Bay. Fort Wilderness Campground has a woodsy 2-mile course with numerous exercise stations along the way.

Walt Disney World sponsors many running events throughout the year, highlighted by its popular January marathon.

Skydiving and Hang Gliding

★ iFLY Orlando
SKYDIVING | FAMILY | Okay, so technically you aren't really skydiving, but you come pretty close as you float atop a cushion of air in this 12-foot-high, 1,000-horsepower wind tunnel. Letting you experience everything skydivers do but closer to the ground, the two-hour, two-flight session starts with instruction, warm-up, and stretching. You then suit up, and, with a certified instructor, enter the wind tunnel, where you soar like a bird (or try to).

It's all so realistic that skydiving clubs come to hone their skills. The attraction is safe for anyone under 250 pounds and older than age 3. You can purchase a video of your "jump" at the end. ✉ *8969 International Dr., International Drive* ☎ *407/337–4359* 🌐 *www.iflyworld.com/orlando* 🎟 *From $65.*

Seminole Lake Gliderport
HANG GLIDING & PARAGLIDING | From settling into the sleek sailplane to closing the clear bubbletop canopy to being able to take the controls, flying without an engine is the rare peaceful adventure. With a pilot in the seat behind you, the adventure begins as a towplane takes off and carries you aloft where, at around 3,000 feet, you'll detach from the plane. The engine noise will instantly be replaced by the sound of your pounding heart. Once you're accustomed to the sensation of flying without an engine, it's as pleasing as sailing a boat on a lake. The glideport is just outside Orlando in

the countryside of Clermont. There's a weight limit of 240 pounds. ✉ *4024 Soaring La., Clermont* ⊕ *Clermont is 25 miles west of Orlando, 22 miles northwest of Walt Disney World* ☎ *352/394–5450* 🌐 *www.soarfl.com* 🎫 *From $140 for a 20-min flight.*

Wilotree Park-Paradise Airsports
HANG GLIDING & PARAGLIDING | This grassy airfield has everything you need for assorted aerial adventures. For a hang gliding thrill, you and an instructor are towed as high as 5,280 feet (1 mile) before releasing the line from the towplane ahead of you. After that, you're free to experience what is best described as a motorcycle ride in the sky. The instructors will let you maneuver the glider so you can turn, bank, rise, and dip as you soak in incredible views of the Orlando countryside.

Note that the higher you soar, the more you pay; from $199 at 2,500 feet to $399 at 5,280 feet. Paradise also offers tandem flights with a pilot in an acrobatic ultralight called the Dragonfly (which is a kick for adrenaline junkies). ✉ *6548 Groveland Airport Rd., Groveland* ⊕ *Groveland is 30 miles west of Orlando, 31 miles northwest of Walt Disney World* ☎ *352/429–0210* 🌐 *www.wilotreepark.com.*

Surfing

Surfing? Here, in landlocked Central Florida? You bet. Early in the morning, before Typhoon Lagoon opens to waterpark visitors, you can hit some man-made waves with 11 other novices and a professional instructor. Run by local surf pros, the three-hour session begins with a half-hour beachside lesson on surfing moves and basics. Before you know it, you're in the heated wave pool and headed for your first ride. There will be about 100 waves, broken into sets of 25, so the chance of learning how to master the board is pretty good. Session costs $190 per person, and soft-sided boards are provided. You must be at least 8 years old and have transportation to Typhoon Lagoon (even if you're staying at Disney, buses don't run before the class begins at 6:45 am). Call ahead (☎ *407/939–7529*) to check on schedules and to snag one of the 12 slots.

Tennis

Walt Disney World

You can play tennis at several Disney hotels: Animal Kingdom (two hard courts), Bay Lake Tower at Disney's Contemporary Resort (two hard courts), BoardWalk (two hard courts), Fort Wilderness (two hard courts), Old Key West Resort (two hard courts), Saratoga Springs Resort & Spa (two Hydrogrid clay courts), and Yacht Club Resort (one hard court). Courts are available without charge on a first-come-first-serve basis for resort and nonresort guests. All have lights, and most have lockers and rackets available to rent or borrow.

At the Walt Disney World Swan and Dolphin hotels, you can get an hour-long private lesson on one of four courts for $90 from 7 am to 9 pm. For private lessons at the other resort hotels, check with Orlando Tennis (☎ *321/228–1146* 🌐 *www.orlandotennis.com*).

Orlando Area

Tennis is one of the most popular sports in Orlando, with hundreds of well-tended public tennis courts and resort hotels that offer a court or two (or more) for their guests. The city of Orlando operates more than 50 courts, some free and others reasonably priced.

César Villarroel Tennis Academy
TENNIS | **FAMILY** | Based at the Mission Inn Resort, 6th Sense is run by Davis Cup player, César Villarroel. It offers everything from two-hour lessons to five-day intensive programs for adults, and seasonal tennis camps for kids in both winter and summer. The resort is approximately 40 miles west of Orlando. ✉ *10400 County Rd. 48, Howie In The Hills* ☎ *352/455–6815* 🌐 *www.facebook.com/TheCVTA.*

Fort Gatlin Tennis Complex
TENNIS | **FAMILY** | Close to Downtown Orlando, Fort Gatlin has the finest city-run courts open to the public. Ten hard courts equipped for day or night play, a pro shop that's open daily, and lessons are among this beautiful facility's offerings. ✉ *2009 Lake Margaret Dr., Downtown Orlando* ☎ *407/254–9878* 🌐 *www.fortgatlin.com* 🎫 *From $4/hr.*

Orlando Tennis Centre
TENNIS | **FAMILY** | Run by the City of Orlando and located near Downtown, this fine facility offers adult tennis clinics (18 and up), private lessons, and youth tennis programs (six and up). The center features five hard courts, nine clay courts, two racquetball courts, and three hitting walls. ✉ *363 N. Parramore Ave., Downtown Orlando* ☎ *407/246–4469* 🌐 *www.orlando.gov/Parks-the-Environment/Directory/Orlando-Tennis-Centre* 🎫 *From $4/hr.*

Index

A

B

C

I

J

K

L

M

N

O

Photo Credits

Front Cover: Disney [Description: Disney Skyliner]. **Back cover, from left to right:** Disney, chensiyuan/Wikimedia Commons, legenda/Shutterstock. **Spine:** Jennifer Lynn/Flickr **Interior, from left to right:** Carrie Parker (1) Viavaltours/Dreamstime (2) Disneyland Paris/David Jafra (5) **Chapter 1: Experience Orlando and the Parks:** Greg Balfour Evans / Alamy Stock Photo (6) Tribune Content Agency LLC / Alamy Stock Photo (8) Rain0975/Flickr (9)Peanutroaster/Dreamstime (9) Theme Park Tourist/Flickr (10) Joni Hanebutt/Shutterstock (10) Howie Muzika/Flickr (11) Ingus Kruklitis / Shutterstock (12) 2012 Universal Orlando Resort (12) ALLAN HUGHES / Alamy Stock Photo (12) Donfink/Dreamstime (12) Larryfmscotland/Dreamstime (13) L. Sloan/Flickr (13) Quackersnaps/Dreamstime (13) Theme Park Tourist/Flickr (13) Songquan Deng/Shutterstock (14) Brian Hubbard/Flickr (14) msivyi/Dreamstime (14) Andrew Barker / Alamy Stock Photo (14) Szilkov/Dreamstime (15) Blaine Harrington III / Alamy Stock Photo (15) Rich Kane Photography / Alamy Stock Photo (16) 2012 Universal Orlando (16) Kphotos6411/Dreamstime (16) ecadphoto/Dreamstime (16) Blackghost600/Dreamstime (17) Visit Orlando (22) Solarisys/Shutterstock (22) M. Timothy O'Keefe / Alamy Stock Photo (22) World Travel Collection / Alamy Stock Photo (23) aphotostory/Shutterstock (23) 2014 Universal Orlando Resort (24) Courtesy SeaWorld Orlando (24) 2016 Universal Orlando Resort (24) Carrie Parker (24) Richard Green / Alamy Stock Photo (25) Cafe Tu Tu Tango (26) The Ravenous Pig (27) Courtesy Rosen Shingle Creek (28) Courtesy Walt Disney World Resort (28) 2020 Hilton (28) Courtesy Walt Disney World Resort (29) Courtesy Walt Disney World Resort (29) Disney (30) Universal Orlando Resort (30) Debi Harbin/Disney (30) Disney (30) Universal Orlando Resort (31) James Kilby/Disney (31) Disney (31) MontenegroStock/Shutterstock (31) Courtesy Walt Disney World Resort (32) Courtesy Walt Disney World Resort (33) Photos 12 / Alamy (38) Dashu Pagla (38) Courtesy Everett Collection (39) Courtesy Everett Collection (40) Dashu Pagla (40) Courtesy Everett Collection (40) WALT DISNEY PICTURES / Ronald Grant Archive / Mary Evans (40) Courtesy Everett Collection (41) Walt Disney Co./courtesy Everett / Everett Collection (41) Courtesy Everett Collection (41) Daryl Mithcell (41) Bob B. Brown/Flickr (42) Disneyland Paris/David Jafra (42) Buena Vista Pictures/Courtesy Everett Collection (42) Walt Disney Co./Courtesy Everett Collection (43) Walt Disney Co./Courtesy Everett Collection (43) Prosthetic Lips (43) Jeffrey Holcombe/Dreamstime (44) **Chapter 2: Travel Smart:** Frank Lervik/Shutterstock (76) SeaWorld Parks & Entertainment (77) 2009 SeaWorld (78) liangjinjian/Flickr (78) Sleuths Mystery Dinner Shows (79) 2007 Universal Orlando Resort (79) Danp68/Dreamstime (80) Kmiragaya/Dreamstime (80) **Chapter 3: The Magic Kingdom and Resort Area:** Massimo Gherardi/Dreamstime (81) Rebecca Siegel/Flickr (94) Bob B. Brown/Flickr (96) Josh McConnell/Flickr (98) SteamFan/WIkimedia Commons (100) Orlando CVB (103) Steven Miller/Flickr (105) Joni Hanebutt/Dreamstime (110) Scott R. Smith/Flickr (119) **Chapter 4: EPCOT and Resort Area:** Jeff Whyte/Dreamstime (121) Disney_photo06 (122) Viavaltours/Dreamstime (123) meshmar2/Flickr (123) Disney (136) Jhernan124 / Dreamstime (138) Viavaltours / Dreamstime (146) Theme Park Touris/Flickr (153) Viavaltours | Dreamstime.com (155) wbeem/Flickr (157) Craig Russell/Dreamstime (161) Tony Bosse/Dreamstime.com (162) **Chapter 5: Disney's Hollywood Studios:** Lori Barbely / Alamy Stock Photo (165) Disney (166) Sunshine / Alamy Stock Photo (167) daryl_mitchell/Flickr (180) Hemis / Alamy Stock Photo (189) **Chapter 6: Disney's Animal Kingdom and Resort Area:** Tangibleday/Dreamstime (195) Jason Pratt/Flickr (200) tom.arthur/Flickr (206) Brewie79/Dreamstime (210) marada/Flickr (214) Courtesy Walt Disney World Resort (216) coconut wireless/Flickr (219) **Chapter 7: Disney Springs and Resort Area:** VIAVAL/Shutterstock (221) Vkkarri/Dreamstime (233) Disney Magic / Alamy Stock Photo (241) **Chapter 8: Kissimmee, Lake Buena Vista, and Celebration:** MontenegroStock/Shutterstock (243) Orlando CVB (248) Orlando CVB (250) Experience Kissimmee/Flickr (252) Jerome LABOUYRIE/Shutterstock (260) **Chapter 9: Universal Orlando:** Mia2you/Shutterstock (263) Universal Orlando Resort (269) Universal Orlando Resort (278) Russell102/Dreamstime (281) Universal Orlando (286) Jessica Walsh (297) Universal Orlando Resort (300) Dreammediapeel/Dreamstime.com (305) Universal Orlando Resort (310) Solarisys13/Dreamstime (316) Solarisys13/Dreamstime (318) Universal Orlando Resort (323) **Chapter 10: Orlando:** Sean Pavone/Shutterstock.com (325) Orlando CVB (333) elisfkc/Flickr (343) SeaWorld (344) SeaWorld (346) Experience Kissimmee/Flickr (354) **Chapter 11: Excursions from Orlando:** Roberto Pascual Gomez/Shutterstock (363) Courtesy of The Charles Hosmer Morse Museum of American Art (370) spakattacks/Flickr (375) Ciolca/Dreamstime (377) Sean Pavone/Shutterstock (379) **Chapter 12: Activities:** Matthew Kaiser 7/Shutterstock (381) Sharife/wikimedia (394) **About Our Writers:** All photos are courtesy of the writers.

*Every effort has been made to trace the copyright holders, and we apologize in advance for any accidental errors. We would be happy to apply the corrections in the following edition of this publication.

Notes

Notes

Notes

Notes

Notes

Notes

Notes

Fodor's WALT DISNEY WORLD

Publisher: Stephen Horowitz, *General Manager*

Editorial: Douglas Stallings, *Editorial Director*, Jill Fergus, Amanda Sadlowski, Caroline Trefler, *Senior Editors*; Kayla Becker, Alexis Kelly, *Editors;* Angelique Kennedy-Chavannes, *Assistant Editor*

Design: Tina Malaney, *Director of Design and Production*; Jessica Gonzalez, *Graphic Designer*

Production: Jennifer DePrima, *Editorial Production Manager*, Elyse Rozelle, *Senior Production Editor;* Monica White, *Production Editor*

Maps: Rebecca Baer, *Senior Map Editor*, Mark Stroud (Moon Street Cartography), David Lindroth, *Cartographers*

Photography: Viviane Teles, *Senior Photo Editor;* Namrata Aggarwal, Payal Gupta, Ashok Kumar, *Photo Editors;* Eddie Aldrete, *Photo Production Intern*

Business and Operations: Chuck Hoover, *Chief Marketing Officer*, Robert Ames, *Group General Manager*, Devin Duckworth, *Director of Print Publishing*

Public Relations and Marketing: Joe Ewaskiw, *Senior Director of Communications and Public Relations*

Fodors.com: Jeremy Tarr, *Editorial Director;* Rachael Levitt, *Managing Editor*

Technology: Jon Atkinson, *Director of Technology;* Rudresh Teotia, *Lead Developer*, Jacob Ashpis, *Content Operations Manager*

Writers: Jennifer Greenhill-Taylor, Joseph Reed Hayes, Leigh Jenkins, Gary McKechnie, Carrie McLaren

Editor: Laura M. Kidder

Production Editor: Elyse Rozelle

11th Edition

ISBN 978-1-64097-498-2

ISSN 1531-443X

PRINTED IN CANADA

10 9 8 7 6 5 4 3 2 1

FSC www.fsc.org MIX Paper from responsible sources FSC® C016245

About Our Writers

Jennifer Greenhill-Taylor has been a journalist for more than two decades—working as a travel editor, theater and film critic, wire editor, and freelance writer/editor. She was born in Edinburgh, Scotland, has lived in four countries and a dozen states, and travels widely for pleasure and profit. She lives in Orlando with her partner, playwright and freelance writer Joseph Reed Hayes, and enjoys sharing her extensive research on the area's hospitality with friends and family. Jennifer and Joseph updated the Kissimmee, Lake Buena Vista and Celebration, the Orlando, and the Excursions from Orlando chapters.

Joseph Reed Hayes (🌐 *jrhays.net*) has informed the world about travel, food, and the arts in Central Florida for print and online publications since 1998. He won five Florida Magazine Association Charlie Awards for his work as the restaurant critic for *Orlando Magazine*. His other hat is worn in performance spaces, as an award-winning playwright produced in New York, California, Florida, and the United Kingdom; a jazz event producer; and an advocate for new, original creative work for in-house and online audiences. Born in Manhattan, Joseph worked in publishing in New York before moving to Central Florida to take up writing and traveling as a full-time career. He and Jennifer Greenhill-Taylor updated the Kissimmee, Lake Buena Vista, and Celebration, the Orlando, and the Excursions from Orlando chapters.

Leigh Jenkins has visited Walt Disney World more than 50 times since the age of 2. Her longest visit was for two years, when she was a Guest Relations cast member at the Magic Kingdom. She began writing about Disney at the age of 15, when she co-authored *Walt Disney World 4 Teens by Teens* and was featured in *Disney Magazine*. She also co-authored *Fodor's Walt Disney World with Kids* and has contributed to Fodors.com. She lives in Spartanburg, South Carolina, with her husband and two daughters, both Disney princess experts. Leigh updated all the Walt Disney World chapters.

Gary McKechnie, who updated the Experience, Travel Smart, Disney Springs, Universal, and Activities chapters, knows a lot about Florida—his native state. During his student days, he worked as a Walt Disney World ferryboat pilot, Jungle Cruise skipper, steam train conductor, double-decker bus driver, and was also an improv comedian at EPCOT. He wrote the award-winning *Great American Motorcycle Tours,* the nation's best-selling motorcycle guidebook, and, following years of travel and research, National Geographic's *USA 101,* which highlights 101 iconic American places, events, and festivals. Gary also speaks on America's cultural heritage aboard the Cunard Line ships *Queen Mary 2* and *Queen Victoria* and at business and tourism meetings across America.